Terror Television
American Series, 1970–1999

by
John Kenneth Muir

Volume 2
(Part I, 1993–1999; Part II; Part III;
Appendices; Notes; Bibliography, Index)

McFarland & Company, Inc., Publishers
Jefferson, North Carolina, and London

Acknowledgments: This author would like to express his heartfelt gratitude to Laura Petix, Larry Gasior, Gregory Norris, and Kathryn Muir for their assistance and support in the creation of this text.

The present work is a reprint of the illustrated case bound edition of Terror Television: American Series, 1970–1999, *first published in 2001 by McFarland.*

Volume 2

LIBRARY OF CONGRESS CATALOGUING-IN-PUBLICATION DATA

Muir, John Kenneth, 1969–
Terror television : American series, 1970–1999 / by John
Kenneth Muir.
p.   cm.
Includes bibliographical references and index.

2 volume set—
ISBN-13: 978-0-7864-3884-6
(softcover: 50# alkaline paper) ∞

1. Fantasy television programs — United States — Catalogs.
2. Horror television programs — United States — Catalogs.
I. Title.
PN1992.8.F35 M85   2008
741.45'6164 — dc21   00-46457

British Library cataloguing data are available

Cover images ©2008 Photodisc

Manufactured in the United States of America

McFarland & Company, Inc., Publishers
Box 611, Jefferson, North Carolina 28640
www.mcfarlandpub.com

2

Terror Television

Contents

• Volume 1 •

• Volume 2 •

PART II: IF IT LOOKS LIKE HORROR, SOUNDS LIKE HORROR...

PART III: FURTHER THOUGHTS

26
The X-Files (1993–)

CRITICAL RECEPTION

"The direction is atmospheric, the scripts are tight, the dialogue is crisp, the tone uneasy and grim.... How can anyone not *love* this show? ... a scary funhouse freakshow through the human heart, mind and spirit."—David Bischoff, *Omni*, December 1994, pages 43-50.

"*The X-Files* employs scare tactics ... but doesn't let them upstage its speculative purpose. Each episode is a mood piece—a queasy odyssey ... as scary as *The Twilight Zone* and much sexier.... What's erotic about the show is its slow progression from reverie to revelation, stopping just short of rapture. It wants to swoon, but swooning would mean shutting its eyes, and there's so much to see."—James Wolcott, *New Leader*: "X Factor," April 18, 1994, pages 98–100.

"Many weeks ... *The X-Files* is as good as any movie, satirizing the characters' obsessiveness while still delivering shudders."—Matt Roush, *TV Guide*, January 2-8, 1999, page 23.

"Chris Carter's contemporary series explores the realms of Science Fiction and supernatural Horror with conviction and subtlety, and is currently achieving a mainstream success unheard of for a genre series. The fusion of familiar dramatic conventions and the human condition, with mysteries set 'within the realms of extreme possibility' entertains with sophistication. The attractive, *Avengers*-like Mulder and Scully guide the audience through the twilight worlds between science and superstition."—Michael Filis, *Shivers* Issue #34: "Shivers Horror Awards Television Top 25," page 9, October 1996.

FORMAT

F.B.I. agent Fox Mulder (David Duchovny) is a believer. He is open to the most extreme possibilities, including alien abduction, reincarnation, lycanthropy, soul transmigration, and just about anything else that is out of the norm. This openness to unconventional ideas and the paranormal has saddled the handsome Mulder with the nickname "Spooky," but it has also earned him his position in the Bureau. A psychologist and criminal profiler extraordinaire, Mulder now investigates "The X-Files," the F.B.I.'s backlog of unsolved, inexplicable cases. This is especially important work to Mulder because his sister Samantha disappeared one night, long ago, when she and Fox were watching *The Magician* on TV. Mulder now believes she was abducted by aliens for some dark purpose.

Dana Scully (Gillian Anderson) is *not* a believer. A medical doctor and devout Catholic, Dana regards science as the signpost to truth. She also works on the X-Files, is partnered with Mulder, and seeks to validate his life's work through reason and scientific method. Daughter of a career naval officer, the beautiful Scully believes in loyalty and duty, and though she was first assigned to the X-Files to debunk Mulder's work, she is the most valuable partner imaginable: competent, knowledgeable, supportive, creative in her solutions, and a constant sparring partner for Fox.

Under the direction of sullen but supportive assistant director Skinner (Mitch Pileggi), Mulder and Scully investigate the unexplained with almost religious zeal. Devil cults ("Die Hand der Verletzt"), astral projection ("The Walk"), serial killers ("Unruhe"), giant fluke worms ("The Host"), even body swaps ("Dreamland") have fallen under their jurisdiction during the long run of *The X-Files*. Mulder and Scully deal not only with the unknown and the horrific, but with a very real "shadow" government, an elite ruling class of conspirators who hope to facilitate the alien colonization of Earth. Among the evil doers are The Well-Manicured Man (John Neville) and the villainous Cigarette Smoking Man (William B. Davis), who assassinated Kennedy and Martin Luther King, Jr. ("Musings of a Cigarette Smoking Man").

Over the years, the supporting cast on *The X-Files* has grown considerably. Mulder has had various secret sources in the government (all with names like "Deep Throat" [Jerry Hardin] and "X" [Stephen Williams]), and learned about his parents' secret involvement in Samantha's abduction. Early in the show's run, Dana's own sister, a kind of New Age bohemian, is murdered by the conspiracy, and Dana's mother and brother (a naval officer) have also been seen occasionally. Another source of Mulder's "crazy" stories are "The Lone Gunmen," a comic trio of tech-nerds who publish a conspiracy magazine and surf the net nitpicking scientific errors on *Earth II* (1995).

Serving evil are several recurring characters. Alex Krycek (Nicholas Lea) is a rogue FBI agent who teamed briefly with Mulder when Scully was abducted during the second season. Since then, Krycek has been a double agent, and has even been possessed by the nasty "black cancer" alien life form often seen. In Season 5, a new character named Agent Spender (Chris Owens) was introduced, and was established as the son of the Cigarette Smoking Man.

The X-Files has taken many twists and turns over the years. The files were closed down in the finale of the first season ("The Erlenmeyer Flask"), but reopened in Season 2 after Scully's inexplicable disappearance ("Ascension"). The files were then destroyed in the cliffhanger of Season 5 ("The End") and the work was abandoned by the F.B.I. until re-

vived following the events of the 1998 *X-Files* feature film, *Fight the Future*. Still, all was not well. In the sixth season, Mulder and Scully were taken off the X-Files ("The Beginning"), and replaced by the nefarious Agent Spender. Their new boss was a less-understanding A.D. named Kersh, who had a special dislike for Mulder. As the sixth season closed, Mulder was incarcerated in an insane asylum, having gone crazy, and Scully discovered an alien spaceship on the beach of South Africa ("Biogenesis").

Stories on Chris Carter's *X-Files* have involved Dana's abduction ("Duane Barry," "Ascension," "One Breath"), Mulder's search for his sister ("Little Green Men," "Colony," "Paper Hearts"), the Jersey Devil ("The Jersey Devil"), inbred brothers ("Home"), mutants ("Squeeze," "Teliko," "2Shy"), prehistoric monsters ("Ice," "Darkness Falls"), serial killers ("Irresistible," "Grotesque"), demons ("Terms of Endearment"), monsters of every possible variety, the global conspiracy ("The Erlenmeyer Flask," "The Red and the Black," "Patient X") and even the Bermuda Triangle ("Triangle"). Consistently complex and challenging, *The X-Files* has become a new TV classic, in part because creator Chris Carter never talks (or writes) down to his audience. This is a show that succeeds by being scary *and* smart. Nothing less than a wonder, *The X-Files* is the greatest horror TV series of the modern age.

HISTORY

Greatness sometimes emerges from the most unexpected venues. Before creating the complex *The X-Files* (and later the beautiful and symbolic *Millennium* [1996-99] and *Harsh Realm* [1999]), the talented producer/writer/director named Chris Carter was editor of *Surfing* magazine, and a writer of "youth" movies for Disney's television division. All of this industry experience was but prologue for Carter's ultimate fame, his ascension to the role of latter day Rod Serling or Gene Roddenberry. But, as Carter has recounted on many occasions, his ideas for the enormously popular *The X-Files* came not from some inspired muse within, but out of his childhood memories, his feelings of nostalgia, and his desire to create a "homage" to a series of the past: *Kolchak: The Night Stalker* (1974-75):

> I was a big fan of *The Night Stalker*. I thought it was great. I watched it as a teenager and it's something no one has ever tried to do again. So I came up with what I felt was a show in the vein of the *Night Stalker* but without the built-in problems — which was we couldn't do the monster-of-the-week or vampire-of-the-week.... What appealed to me is that I could tell good, smart stories, rooted in a speculative science.[1]

Carter is being overmodest in this description of the wonderful TV series he created. He did far more than build on the success of any single past horror TV triumph. In fact, he structured his new program in an artistic manner that far surpassed "The little guy against city hall"/"Monster of the week" formats which dominated *Kolchak*'s abbreviated network run back in the mid-70s. Instead, Carter gave birth to a brilliant metaphor for how the human mind operates (belief vs. nonbelief) and then set that analogy against every modern mythology and urban legend possible, from bigfoot (or rather the Jersey Devil) and the Bermuda triangle ("Triangle") to alien abductions ("Duane Barry"/"Ascension").

In the case of *The X-Files*, Carter envisioned two mythic heroes and partners, a man and a woman, who each held opposite (and rigid) views of the world's "real" nature. One was to be a believer, the other a skeptic. The skeptic would use science as the yardstick for proof, the other an intuitive understanding that there are some things on this planet that we just cannot explain rationally. Thus every episode of *The X-Files* examines some mystery (time travel, psychic phenomena, spontaneous human combustion, prehistoric water dwellers, demonic possession, the impact of astrological factors on the human psyche) through these dual perspectives, which gives the series a powerful edge over horror series

which espouse or describe no specific world-view.

There has been much written in fan and literary circles about the fact that the central troika of the classic *Star Trek* (1966-69) represents ego (Kirk), id (McCoy), and superego (Spock). Indeed, the unceasing joy of *Star Trek* is watching how Spock and McCoy debate life, and Kirk, in the middle, mediates and makes decisions based on their opposing input. This trio of enterprising heroes roughly represents how a single human being thinks and makes decisions. Emotion on the one hand, logic on the other, with a "listener" in between mediating and balancing the two. On many occasions, this relationship has been powerfully and artfully portrayed. In *Star Trek II: The Wrath of Khan* (1982), for instance, Kirk's reading glasses show up with one shattered lens after Spock's death. This cracked glass, through which Kirk literally "sees," represents the loss of Spock and of "logic" from the equation that dictates his decisions. Similarly, on Chris Carter's *X-Files*, Scully (the skeptic) and Mulder (the believer) likewise represent two facets of the universal human personality: both the need to have things explained, and the desire to believe in something *sans* explanation, something larger and more important than us ... a leap of faith. As Carter relates, the Mulder/Scully combination, a perfect metaphor for the dichotomy of the human mind (faith vs. facts), also represents facets of his own personality:

> They [Mulder & Scully] are equal parts of my desire to believe in something and my inability to believe in something. My skepticism and my faith.... I want, like a lot of people do, to have the experience of witnessing a paranormal phenomenon. At the same time I want not to accept it, but to question it.[2]

With his central characters created for optimum artistic effect, Carter went about fashioning his show for the Fox Network, the fledgling competitor to the big American "Big Three" whose only previous hits had been the Matt Groening animated series, *The Simpsons* (1987–), and the Aaron Spelling high school melodrama, *Beverly Hills 90210* (1990–2000). Strangely, what happened next was nothing short of a miracle (if one believes in such things, that is!). The actors who were cast in the leading roles of Dana Scully and Fox Mulder came to embody Carter's belief vs. skepticism dichotomy in nothing less than a perfect way. There was an instant chemistry between David Duchovny (as the believer) and Gillian Anderson (as the skeptic) that no amount of good writing could have planned or created. An intellectual, physical and romantic attraction was forged between these two excellent performers in short order. Again, like the chemistry between Nimoy and Shatner in *Star Trek*, *The X-Files* took a good idea on the page and translated it to brilliance on the stage through inspired casting. *The X-Files* represented Anderson's first TV work, and Duchovny had appeared only in oddball films such as *Kalifornia* (1993) with Brad Pitt and *The Rapture* (1992) with Mimi Rogers, but these two unknown performers nonetheless created a symbiosis that has kept the series going strong and walking tall for six years (and counting).

There are a number of "explanations" for this chemistry between actors. Some feel that the fact that Duchovny (in reality) is the skeptic and Anderson (in reality) is the believer has lent their performances a special joy: each one is playing the devil's advocate to the hilt, espousing an opposite viewpoint from the one really held. Others have described the chemistry as purely sexual, and indeed there have been (unconfirmed) rumors on the Internet that Duchovny and Anderson had a brief physical "relationship" early in the show's history. In short, everyone has their idea of why, precisely, this cast has managed to click in a way that no cast had clicked in the genre since the original *Star Trek* or *Kolchak: The Night Stalker*. Even the actors themselves have debated the origin of their remarkable on-screen chemistry. David Duchovny has forwarded the notion that the series is really cleverly designed as a "role reversal," with Scully being the more hard-nosed, authoritarian, traditionally "male" role, and Mulder representing a more open, hence "female" perspective:

I think the male/female roles are switched ... Mulder is more intuitive, working from his emotions, gut instinct. Scully is more practical. If the show was arch or camp, I wouldn't be here. There's no joy in playing an expositional puppet. I think *X-Files* knows how to deliver a lot of information and still make the story move along.[3]

Gillian Anderson has not minced words regarding her chemistry with Duchovny, either. She has punctuated the debate by stating, simply: "It is something completely beyond our control — two people either have it or they don't."[4]

With two excellent performances dominating *The X-Files*, the series could have come to dynamic life merely on the basis of the Duchovny/Anderson chemistry, but creator Chris Carter also imbued *The X-Files* with a number of interesting thematic flourishes that have made it a remarkable series. Otherwise, it might have merely been *She Wolf of London*— another horror show which thrived on the chemistry between its leads. Firstly, Carter created what many writers have called "the mytharc." Though J. Michael Straczynski loudly claims in print all the time that *Babylon 5* (1993-98) was the first show to feature a story arc, *The X-Files* was running concurrently and also featured an (arguably more interesting) arc. (Actually, *Twin Peaks* [1990-91] had a story arc, *Blake's 7* [1978-81] had a story arc, *Dark Shadows* [1991] had a story arc, even *Stephen King's The Golden Years* [1991] had a story arc, so Straczynski's boastful claim is a load of hooey.) Specifically, Carter provided Mulder with an interesting back-story: the abduction of his sister, Samantha, and the involvement of his father in a multinational conspiracy. Both of these elements lent many early episodes of *The X-Files* a complexity beyond a simple "monster of the week" formula. Over six years, the search for Mulder's missing sister has taken some fascinating turns, particularly in the fourth season episode "Paper Hearts," and the conspiracy has now been viewed from a number of perspectives, both alien and human. Though some viewers may see Mulder's never-ending search for his sister as the 1990s equivalent of Richard Kimball's quest for the one-armed man in *The Fugitive, The X-Files* has utilized its story arc in a rather grand way. Besides providing an understandable motivation for Mulder's dedication to his work, Mulder's search for his sister has actually caused Scully to lose her own sister, Melissa — who was murdered by the conspiracy. Thus there is an element of irony and hypocrisy in this mythic search that Chris Carter and *The X-Files* handle in interesting, mature ways. Mulder is sometimes a traditional hero, and sometimes a selfish, obsessed antihero. The question is always being raised: What price the truth?

Of course, no great performances, and no interesting story arcs would have captured the attention of America so thoroughly had not *The X-Files* done something else right. Even in its first year, it flaunted a brilliant visual style. It utilized the language of film in a way that no TV series of recent vintage had managed so successfully. When *The X-Files* began airing in the fall of 1993, horror movies were failing at the box office big time, perhaps because filmmakers had forgotten how to scare audiences. Jason Voorhees, Michael Myers, Chucky, and Freddy Krueger had all been back in bad sequels so frequently that there was no longer a real sense of horror attached to these once fearsome icons. Freddy and Chucky were now, officially, wisecrackers, as funny as they were scary, and Jason and Michael had gone through the same plots so many times that horror had lost its spontaneity and surprises. On TV, *The X-Files* remembered that a combination of provocative stories, artistic use of cinematic techniques (use of meaningful angles, brilliant editing, effective mood music), and good acting could deliver chills quite effectively. In particular, *The X-Files* understood that the unknown, rather than the known (like Freddy or Chucky) could generate chills. What if a fluke worm human hybrid evolved in the sewers of New Jersey? What if a feral, primitive beastwoman existed just outside Atlantic City? What if a psychopath could somehow harness fire as a weapon? The premises were chilling, and the filmic execution of these concepts buttressed the scares with excellent visuals.

Frankly, the visual quality and detail of *The X-Files* was astounding. As director Kim Manners described the process of putting the show together, the attention to the minute was staggering:

> We have two units shooting this show; a first unit and a second unit, complete with sound, that are shooting all the time. It's a huge undertaking, and the attention to detail in each script is enormous. We don't feel that we're doing episodic television; we firmly believe we're doing a mini-feature every week, and that's pretty exciting.[5]

That dedication to detail shines through on virtually every of the nearly 140 *X-Files* aired thus far. Additionally, it helped *The X-Files* quickly gain a fan following. Although some genre notables at first scoffed at the show because its very name made it sound like tabloid television, others quickly realized just how much intelligence went into the development of Carter's drama. In 1993, the show's first season, the ratings started to grow, and, amazingly, the Fox Network decided to give the series a second shot. This was a wise decision, and by the end of *The X-Files'* second season, the series was a bona fide hit and cult phenomenon. The second season also expanded the mythology of the series significantly by featuring the introduction of the double agent Alex Krycek (Nicholas Lea) and the abduction (and subsequent disappearance) of Scully. In fact, the latter plot development was a ploy to explain Gillian Anderson's pregnancy and sabbatical from the series!

The third year came and went, and *The X-Files* became a top ten hit for Fox, despite the fact that it aired on Friday nights, the same night of the week that had killed *Star Trek, Kolchak, Planet of the Apes* (1974), *V* (1984), and a variety of science fiction/horror themed programming over the last twenty-five years. By now, Fox realized that Chris Carter knew exactly what he was doing and entered negotiations with him to create a second series, *Millennium* (1996–1999). Fans of *The X-Files* were thus quite agitated when *Files* was bumped from its time slot and replaced by *Millennium* for that season. For its fourth season, *The X-Files* would instead air on Sunday nights at 9:00. Although there was much talk in the media about how *The X-Files* could not survive on Sunday nights, it startled everyone by doing even better than before! The show flourished on Sunday nights, even while *Millennium* failed to capture an audience on Fridays. The fourth season also saw the development of a new *X-Files* running subplot: Scully discovered she had contracted cancer by removing an implant placed in the back of her neck during her abduction. By this time, *The X-Files* was also garnering critical respect. The series was nominated for a number of Emmy Awards, including best dramatic series, best dramatic actress, and best actor. Though the series failed to win in these categories, David Duchovny (in competition against Lance Henriksen of *Millennium*), Gillian Anderson, and the series itself all took home Golden Globe Awards for the show's fourth year.

The writing on *The X-Files* also remained excellent. James Wong and Glen Morgan, the creators of *Space: Above and Beyond*, contributed "Home," what may be the best *X-Files* of all time, and Darin Morgan is quite popular for his serio-comic episodes, including "Jose Chung's 'From Outer Space'" and "Clyde Bruckman's Final Repose." Chris Carter is no slouch in the writing department either, and his contributions have been uniformly impressive.

During the hiatus between the fourth and fifth season, the *X-Files* production team followed *Star Trek*'s example and filmed a big-budget feature film which would debut the following summer. Oscar winner Martin Landau (*Space: 1999* [1975-77]) was the film's major guest star, and the film, directed by Rob Bowman, would feature the *almost* first kiss between Scully and Mulder. Once the film was in the can, Carter, Duchovny and Anderson returned for the fifth season of *The X-Files*. This season was an experimental one for the show because it reversed the series' central premise. Suddenly, Mulder lost his faith in the paranormal and his extraterrestrial ideas, and he feared he was the patsy of a giant "disin-

formation" campaign. Scully, buttressed by her own abduction experiences, became more open-minded to extreme possibilities and thus she and Mulder had switched purposes and roles. Many critics (in *Fangoria*, and *Cinefantastique* in particular) complained loudly that this new template was not very good. However, two years later these criticisms seem misplaced, as the fifth season produced some of the best stories yet seen, including the humorous *Roshomon*-like story "Bad Blood," in which Mulder's and Scully's perspectives on a case were dramatized in detail and went head to head, and the haunting "Folie a Deux," a nightmarish story about a skittering, insectlike monster who was sucking the lives out of human beings.

Another interesting story was Chris Carter's homage to *Frankenstein* films of the past, a black and white story called "Post-Modern Prometheus," which also managed to lampoon America's fascination with *The Jerry Springer Show*, and its obsession with celebrity. Other episodes of the fifth season were written by celebrities such as Stephen King ("Chinga") and William Gibson ("Kill Switch").

The X-Files: Fight the Future, the *X-Files* movie, premiered after the fifth season cliffhanger "The End," and was a major hit in the summer of 1998. Though it was not as big as *Deep Impact*, *Armageddon* and other film fare for the summer, it was enough of a success to assure an *X-Files* film franchise once the series closes down shop.

Changes again came to *The X-Files* during the sixth season. Star David Duchovny had recently married actress Tea Leoni (*Deep Impact* [1998]) and he wanted to live in Los Angeles with her while she worked on her own situation comedy series (the disastrous *The Naked Truth* [1996-97]. Of course, *The X-Files* had always been shot in Vancouver, so this was an enormous problem. Because Duchovny was now considered a major star, Carter, Fox, and the entire production company of *The X-Files* acquiesced to his demands. The series up and moved to L.A. permanently. Again, media critics were worried about what a change would mean for the well-loved series. Vancouver's cold nights had suited *The X-Files* perfectly. Could sunny Los Angeles do the same? Chris Carter thought so:

> Now that we're in a mostly urban environment, we're going to have to tell stories using the landscape that is presented to us ... Before, we had rain and misty conditions. Now we'll have to make them, without it looking forced. Directors are using angles to create the atmosphere that will keep the show what it is. And you can do good, scary stories anywhere if you do it right.[6]

He was right: the change of venue was a non-issue. Instead, *The X-Files* seemed to open up in a remarkable new way. Scully and Mulder went to Nevada in the inspired "Drive," and visited Area 51 in the two-part episode "Dreamland." Los Angeles gave the show a new look, but it was also a good look. The same commitment to good storytelling and visual aplomb was obvious. Still, some critics were (again) not happy because *The X-Files* had taken another thematic turn. Although Mulder had found his faith again (thanks to the events of the feature film), the stories in the sixth season were more overtly humorous than before. In "Dreamland," Mulder changed bodies with an Area 51 agent (played by Michael McKean), and this body swap story resulted in some humorous sequences, including Mulder and Scully together in a waterbed, and Duchovny's mirror dance (in his underwear) with McKean. In "Rain King," comedienne Victoria Jackson was involved in another semi-serious story about a lovelorn weatherman who could control the weather. "How the Ghosts Stole Christmas" featured Lily Tomlin and also seemed only semi-serious in intent, despite some very bloody moments. Delightfully, all these stories were good ones, and they stretched the boundaries of *The X-Files*. In fact, Chris Carter proved that *The X-Files* could treat the paranormal not only with chills and thrills, but with laughs.

As of this writing, some people believe that the sixth season was actually *The X-Files'* best, as it mixed the good laughs with the conclusion of the conspiracy plotline ("Two Fathers," "One Son") and featured genuinely scary stories such as "Trevor," "Milagro," and "Field Trip." If anything, the real difference in the *X-Files'* sixth season was that Mulder and Scully's relationship came to the forefront of each story. Though the individual stories were still important, Mulder and Scully's emotional involvement was heightened. Scully was jealous of another woman in "Alpha," Mulder lost his body in "Dreamland," Scully and Mulder went undercover as husband and wife in "Arcadia," Scully's love for Mulder was exposed in "Milagro," and so forth. Also in the sixth season, David Duchovny directed his first episode ("The Unnatural"), and the year ended with a shocking cliffhanger which put a new spin on the conspiracy, and in fact, the origin of mankind as a species.

As a seventh season of *The X-Files* was in the offing, everything looked solid for another great year. And then, in the late summer of 1999, bad news came: David Duchovny and Chris Carter seemed intent on leaving *The X-Files* after the seventh season. Only Gillian Anderson was contracted to continue in an eighth season, so the show's ongoing life seemed in jeopardy. Worse, it was also revealed that David Duchovny had filed a lawsuit against Fox. He asserted that by selling the rights to *X-Files* repeats to the cable network FX, Fox (and Chris Carter) had cost him millions of dollars in lost money. So upset by this was Duchovny that he revealed that the seventh season would definitely be his last one with the show! Worse, this legal situation seemed to throw the very future of *The X-Files* in jeopardy, as it was uncertain that Duchovny would return for any future feature films. It is a shame to end the series on this down-note, especially after six years of excellent stories, but one senses that Duchovny is going through a bad case of David Caruso-itis. He no longer seems to enjoy the work on *The X-Files*, and if that is the case, quality is sure to suffer as the show enters its final year. In fact, the seventh season came and went, and Duchovny announced he would return to *The X-Files* only part time in the eighth season, headlining in only eleven of the 22 shows. In his place, it was reported Robert Patrick (of *T2* [1991]) would play Scully's new partner. As for Carter, he was back on board and rumored to be preparing a series based on "The Lone Gunmen" characters.

Despite what appears to be an unhappy ending for a great series, *The X-Files* has become a worldwide phenomenon. Like *Star Trek* and *The Twilight Zone* before it, it has now been seen in reruns, a feature film, comic books, collectible cards, original novels, video-cassette releases, and even action figures. The worldwide appeal of *The X-Files* is not surprising, and Chris Carter believes that it all has to do with the shivers:

> If there is one thing that gives the series a broad, universal appeal, it's that we are *all* afraid of the same things. So what scares you in America scares you in Great Britain and scares people in Germany, Australia and in the 60 countries where the series is playing right now.[7]

The X-Files is one of the few network TV shows of the 1990s that will live well into the next millennium. It will be a perennial, like *Star Trek, I Love Lucy,* or *The Twilight Zone,* because its actors, its creator, its writers, and its directors have taken special care to outdo themselves every chance they get. The universal appeal of its scary stories and its two leads is a rarity in television, and a great gift from Chris Carter.

CRITICAL COMMENTARY

The X-Files is a complex but worthwhile trip into terror. Its ongoing attempts to scare its audience through "extreme possibilities," the notion that certain mysteries on our planet cannot be solved through either reason or science, have made for great speculative entertainment since the early 1990s. This Chris Carter series has run a very long time now, yet it has been remarkably cohesive in its forays into fear. In particular, there have been ten subsections of horror that the series has exploited again and again, rather successfully. Because the series has run so long and returned

to these subsets of themes so often, a road map for the series has been provided here. These subsets include:

1. *"Trust No One"*— in which the fear generated by the show concerns the U.S. government and the fact that it is secretly conducting secret experiments on its own people. In this type of story, the paranoia level is high as the government violates its sacred trust to represent the people, and seems capable of any atrocity including murder and cover-ups.

2. *"Freaks of Nature"*—wherein mutants and monsters feed on or exploit the human populace. These freaks of nature are sometimes just beasts ("Home") and sometimes they are evolutionary nightmares, genetic mutants who scare us because they threaten to become the norm. Some times the freaks of nature are caused by human irresponsibility ("The Host"), sometimes they are trying to fulfill a biological need ("2Shy," "Teliko") and sometimes they just happen, out of the blue ("D.P.O.").

3. *"Foreign Fears"*— wherein ancient ethnic legends are proven to have basis in fact. This particular *X-Files* story plays on the fact that Americans tend to be arrogant in their belief that the world is just as it appears. In these stories, the "foreign" and ethnic legends of curses ("Teso Dos Bichos," "Kaddish"), ghosts ("Hell Money"), and even goatlike blood-suckers ("El Mundo Gira") are inevitably true, even though all these strange manifestations operate well beyond Western concepts of reality.

4. *"From the Dawn of Time"*— wherein creatures from prehistory (or ancient history) reassert themselves in the present because of climatic changes ("Firewalker," "Agua Mala"), man's encroachment on their territory ("The Jersey Devil," "Darkness Falls," "Detour") or general interference in remote habitats ("Ice"). These lifeforms are often millions of years old, and they exhibit qualities inimical to human survival. Sometimes they exist in remote locations (the Pacific Northwest, a volcano, under layers of ice) and sometimes they are

just around the corner (in North Carolina in "Field Trip").

5. *"Aliens!"*— wherein extraterrestrial creatures are encountered ("Space," Gender-bender," "Travelers") but never really validated empirically. There is some degree of overlap between the mytharc conspiracy stories and the alien stories, as the mytharc involves the alien colonization of Earth and the ascension of an alien virus (the black oil) that was the planet's original inhabitant.

6. *"God's Masterplan"*— wherein elements of Christian religion/mythology are explored as "real" concepts. These are among the most interesting *X-Files* stories because they ask very interesting questions about our human nature. Is God real? Is the Devil ("Terms of Endearment," "Die Hand der Verletzt") real? Why can Mulder so easily believe in aliens, monsters, time loops, and the like, but not in scripture? Conversely, why does Scully allow herself to have "faith" and believe in Christian lore, but not the paranormal? Where is her precious science when it comes to Catholicism?

7. *"The Serial Killer"*— this style of *X-Files* story was dropped late in the show's run (the mid-fourth season), to be assumed wholly by the equally interesting *Millennium*. Originally however, serial killers were examined quite frequently on *The X-Files* as a kind of evil "within" humanity archetype.

8. *"Psychic Phenomena"*— from astral projection ("The Walk") to clairvoyance ("Clyde Bruckman's Final Repose"), to soul transmigration ("The List"), and even the effect of heavenly bodies on human bodies ("Syzygy"), *The X-Files* has been obsessed with the exploration of psychic phenomena. Thus it can be seen as a continuation of the concepts explored in *One Step Beyond, The Sixth Sense, The Next Step Beyond, Beyond Reality*, and the precursor to *Psi Factor*.

9. *"The Mytharc"/"Conspiracy"*— wherein the history of the government's association with aliens, Mulder's family history, Scully's abduction, and alien colonization come together to form a cohesive story. This subset of stories has a large supporting cast including The Cigarette Smoking Man, The Well Manicured Man, The Syndicate, Agent Fowley, Agent Krycek, Agent Spender, Cassandra Spender, and Emily, Scully's ill-fated daughter. These stories often overlap with "Aliens!" and "Trust No One."

10. *"The Standards"*— terror TV has its own standards, the tropes it brings out again and again, because they have been successful before. *The X-Files* has demonstrated real wit and innovation in dealing with the horror standards that every series from *Night Gallery* to *Tales from the Crypt* have explored. These standards include the vampire story ("Bad Blood," "3"), the werewolf ("Shapes"), ghosts ("How the Ghosts Stole Christmas"), crazy computers ("Ghost in the Machine," "Kill Switch"), matters of time ("Synchrony," "Dod Kalm," "Monday"), succubi ("Avatar"), cannibalism ("Our Town"), tattoos ("Never Again"), evil dolls ("Chinga") and the like.

For easy access to the world of *The X-Files,* the following breakdown fits the majority of *The X-Files* episodes into appropriate categories. Please remember, however, that some episodes will appear under more than one category, as they mesh the various story concepts into one cohesive whole. An interesting experiment would be to watch all the "like" episodes together in marathon format to catalog the similarities (or differences) in concept, conceit and execution.

"Trust No One"

"Eve," "Ghost in the Machine," "Blood," "Sleepless," "Red Museum," "F. Emasculata," "Soft Light," "Wetwired," "Zero Sum," "The Pine Bluff Variant," "Drive," "Dreamland" (I & II)

"Freaks of Nature"

"Squeeze," "Tooms," "The Jersey Devil," "The Host," "Humbug," "D.P.O.," "2Shy," "Teliko," "Home," "Small Potatoes," "Leonard Betts," "Detour"

"FOREIGN FEARS"

"Fresh Bones," "The Calusari," "Teso Dos Bichos," "Hell Money," "El Mundo Gira," "Kaddish," "Alpha," "Arcadia"

"FROM THE DAWN OF TIME"

"Ice," "Darkness Falls," "Firewalker," "Quagmire," "Field Trip," "Agua Mala," "The Jersey Devil," "Detour"

"ALIENS!"

"Pilot," "Space," "E.B.E." "Genderbender," "Little Green Men" "Jose Chung's 'From Outer Space,'" "Colony," "End Game," "Talitha Cumi," "Herrenvolk," "War of the Copraphages," "Tunguska," "Gethsemane," "Travelers," "The Red and the Black," "Patient X," "The Beginning," "The Unnatural," "Biogenesis"

"GOD'S MASTERPLAN"

"Miracle Man," "Die Hand der Verletzt," "Revelations," "All Souls," "Terms of Endearment"

"THE SERIAL KILLER"

"Irresistible," "Grotesque," "Unruhe," "Paper Hearts"

"PSYCHIC PHENOMENA"

"Fire," "Beyond the Sea," "Shadows," "Born Again," "Lazarus," "Young at Heart," "Roland," "The List," "The Walk," "Excelsius Dei," "Aubrey," "Clyde Bruckman's Final Repose," "Oubliette," "Syzygy," "Pusher," "The Field Where I Died," "Elegy," "Kitsunegari," "Mind's Eye," "Trevor," "Milagro"

"THE MYTHARC"/"CONSPIRACY"

"The Erlenmeyer Flask," "Duane Barry," "Ascension," "Colony," "End Game," "Anasazi," "The Blessing Way," "Paper Clip," "Piper Maru," "Apocrypha," "Zero Sum," "Terma," "Tunguska," "Tempus Fugit," "Max," "731," "Nisei," "Musings of a Cigarette Smoking Man," "A Christmas Carol," "Emily," "Gethsemane," "Redux," "Redux II," "Patient X," "The Red and the Black," "The End," "The Beginning," "Two Fathers," "One Son," "Biogenesis"

"THE STANDARDS"

"Shapes," "Ghost in the Machine," "3," "Dod Kalm," "Our Town," "Avatar," "Never Again," "Synchrony," "Triangle," "How the Ghosts Stole Christmas," "The Rain King," "Monday," "Bad Blood," "Kill Switch," "Chinga"

In addition to visiting these ten plots, *The X-Files* has also showed a commendable dedication to asking the great questions of our time, and telling stories about the most puzzling mysteries humankind has yet faced. In its first six years on the air, *The X-Files* has explored the following mysteries:

THE MYSTERIES

1. Who Killed President Kennedy ("Musings of a Cigarette Smoking Man")?
2. Who Killed Martin Luther King Jr. ("Musings of a Cigarette Smoking Man)?
3. Do aliens exist? (see "Aliens!" and "Mytharc" categories above).
4. Does the Bermuda Triangle (or Devil's Triangle) exist?
5. What really happened to the "Philadelphia Experiment" ("Dod Kalm")?
6. What is going on in Area 51 ("Dreamland I & II)?
7. Do prehistoric monsters like Nessie of Loch Ness exist ("Quagmire")?
8. Do monsters like bigfoot exist ("The Jersey Devil")?
9. Where did the Bible really come from ("Biogenesis")?
10. Are there such things as past lives ("The Field Where I Died?")?

If intelligent, scary speculation on these and other topics is not enough to judge *The X-Files* to be a terrific horror series, the show is also successful in any number of other ways. In fact, this series is so good that there is *not one* egregiously bad episode among the almost-150 aired thus far. Some critics may quibble about one story or another, some episodes may seem slower-paced than others, but there is literally not one flat-out, bad episode in this series.

Still, it is easy to be enthusiastic about a series without mentioning specifically why it is a good show. Therefore, it is only appropriate to discuss in detail the many reasons why Chris Carter's creation merits its position as the best horror TV series of the contemporary era.

Unlike *The Burning Zone* (1996-97), *Dark Skies* (1996-97), or *Poltergeist: The Legacy* (1996-99), *The X-Files* features a solid grounding in the sciences (biology, psychology, zoology, archaeology, geology ... you name it). More to the point, the series seems to have a genuine understanding of the sciences it utilizes to build its scary framework. Science is Scully's mantra in *The X-Files*, and therefore the series is unfailingly smart about its unceasing speculations. Whether the discussion of the week concerns Egodystonia (the inescapable compulsion to organize and reorganize things), Panspermia (the theory that life originated elsewhere, and that microbes from other solar systems arrived on Earth and established life), Polydactylism, ergot alkaloids, Bovine Growth Hormones, pheromones, CGR (Cosmic Galactic Radiation), or PCRs, it is unfailingly intelligent. Watching *The X-Files* each week is so illuminating that it is almost an educational experience. In an era of dumbed-down action series and lowest-common denominator situation comedies, the scientific grounding of this series sets it apart in a very special way. It is no exaggeration to state that Scully's constant discussions of DNA (in various episodes) have given this nation an understanding of it that would have been helpful in decades and years gone by (especially considering the verdict of the O.J. Simpson trial).

Delightfully, *The X-Files'* knowledge of science is equaled by its cinematic and television literacy. This is one TV series that is brilliantly self-reflexive and humorous in its understanding of the genre's past. Whether it be a brilliant and funny reference to Dr. Zaius

and *Planet of the Apes* (1968) in "War of the Coprophages," an in-joke parodying the opening Star Destroyer "swoop" shot of *Star Wars* (1977) in "Jose Chung's 'From Outer Space,'" or a twist on the "body switch" concepts often dramatized in *Star Trek* (1966-69) in "Dreamland," *The X-Files* loves and remembers its own background. Casting Darren McGavin as Mulder's predecessor on *The X-Files* is a loving reference to that actor's well-remembered tenure on *Kolchak: The Night Stalker*, but the series has gone even further than such nice touches here and there. Its many episodes have been enlivened by performers from a variety of genre shows including *Space: 1999* (Nick Tate and Martin Landau), *Space: Above and Beyond* (Kristen Cloke, Rodney Rowland, Tucker Smallwood), *American Gothic* (Lucas Black), *Twin Peaks* (Don S. Davis, Kenneth Walsh) and others.

Sometimes, the references in *The X-Files* are deeper than one initially realizes. A succubus wears a red slicker in "Avatar," referencing the similarly-garbed killer in that great horror film from the 1970s, *Don't Look Now*. In "The Beginning," a technician in a nuclear power plant is named Homer, recalling the dim-witted lead character in *The Simpsons*. An even more delightful in-joke found Mulder and Scully being grilled in the same episode by a nasty woman named Maslin. Of course, Ms. Maslin is named after Janet Maslin, *The New York Times* film critic who gave *The X-Files* feature film a scathing review the previous summer. In the episode "Arcadia," Mulder and Scully go undercover in suburbia as a married couple named "the Petries," a name straight out of *The Dick Van Dyke* show. In the era of postmodern horror, *The X-Files* is the king of bizarre and ersatz references. It has an encyclopedic knowledge of television and horror that is a constant joy to behold. Humorous cameos by Alex Trebek and Jesse Ventura, as well as beautiful performances from actors Charles Nelson Reilly and Peter Boyle are just a part of its self-referential tapestry.

If "smarts" about science and television/film history sound like purely intellectual merits, *The X-Files* boasts other excellent points to recommend it. Prime among these is Chris Carter's penchant for social commentary. *The X-Files* uses a well-honed, topical approach to TV to discuss, analyze, mock, and examine the things which vex and terrify contemporary American society most. The fear that violence on TV creates violence in real life is the subject of "Wetwired." "Excelsius Dei," set in a retirement home, asks pertinent questions about the manner in which America treats its infirm and elderly. The aforementioned "Arcadia" is a brilliant send-up of affluent suburbia, and the elitist, fascist homeowner organizations which squash individuality and encourage a life run by strict "covenants" of do's and don'ts. "Memento Mori" describes the evil of cancer in artistic, almost poetic terms. Faced with the prospect of having contracted the terminal disease, Scully calls it an "invader which joins with the invaded" and realizes that to "destroy it, you must destroy your own body." Nice.

In its time on the air, *The X-Files* has tackled stories about discrimination ("Humbug"), endangered species ("Fearful Symmetry"), religious bigotry ("Red Museum"), in vitro fertilization ("Eve"), subliminal messages ("Blood"), the archetype of evil ("Irresistible"), and a variety of other interesting, controversial, and challenging topics. If TV *really* is an art form, if it *truly* exists to do more than sell detergent and fast food, then *The X-Files* represents the medium at its absolute best. Illuminating, funny, socially relevant ... *The X-Files* is everything one could want or hope it to be.

Beyond these virtues, *The X-Files* is adroit and confident with the manner in which it unfolds. Each season can be seen as a chapter in a video novel or some such larger work. The first year introduces Mulder and Scully and their world. The characters are defined not just by their own behavior and each other's perspectives, but by their previous co-workers ("Lazarus," "Young at Heart," "Tooms," "Fire"), friends, and even their enemies: all of whom are seen primarily in this introductory portion of the series, and not in later, more fast-moving sections. The second season develops the "conflict" as the X-Files are temporarily closed, the antagonists are introduced in their full villainy, and Scully is abducted. The third season sees the details of the global conspiracy emerge. The fourth season introduces a new threat, as Scully faces terminal cancer from her "abduction" experience. The fifth year shows Mulder in equal jeopardy as he loses his faith and becomes a cynical, rudderless soul. The movie sees Mulder's faith reborn, and the sixth season brings yet a new danger: Mulder and Scully are taken off the X-files and forced to reevaluate their professional choices. Also in the sixth year, the conspiracy story climaxes, and then heads off in a bizarre new direction, even as the Mulder/Scully romantic relationship reaches new heights.

Besides featuring a fascinating arc with each season representing a chapter, *The X-Files* is never afraid to revisit an interesting story, or one that could use a more pronounced resolution. "Tooms" is a sequel to "Squeeze," the story of a long-lived mutant who devours human livers and can elongate his body. "Pusher" and "Kitsunegari" are two chapters of the Robert Modell story, about a little man whose terminal cancer has the side-effect of making him a powerful telepath. "Revelations" and "All Souls" are two interlinked explorations of Christian mythology, and the like. Where some series might shy away from sequels, *The X-Files* has never been afraid to develop and return to peripheral characters and interesting stories that are not as popular as the conspiracy arc.

Perhaps the quality of *The X-Files* which is most admirable is its willingness to feature stories that threaten everything the audience has come to hold dear. In "Paper Hearts," a fourth season story, Mulder is faced with evidence that his sister, Samantha, was not abducted by either the government or aliens, but by a vicious serial killer who murdered her. The implicit suggestion of this story is that Mulder invented the alien abduction myth so as not to face the ugly truth about what *really* happened to Samantha. This is a brilliant story because it makes Mulder question his entire post-Samantha life. What if his whole adult life had been based on a lie? "Paper Hearts" forged that issue with narrative clarity and with many twists and turns.

"The Field Where I Died" is another brilliant *X-Files* installment which called many things into question, a reason, no doubt, it was despised by many fans and critics. In this well-written hour, a woman (brilliantly essayed by Kristen Cloke) reveals to Mulder that she and Mulder were soul-mates in a previous life. Mulder is fascinated by this revelation and undergoes a past-life hypnotic regression which seems to confirm her story. They were, and are, soul mates as they travel through life after life. The "kick" in this particular tale was that Cloke's character also had a multiple personality disorder, which enabled Scully to dismiss her claims of reincarnation and past lives. "The Field Where I Died" is a great episode not only because it had the courage to flaunt the fans and establish that Mulder's soul mate might *not* be Scully, but because it presented a fairly objective "either/or" scenario. Either Cloke's character was crazy, or she was telling the truth about her past connection with Mulder. There was evidence to lead viewers either way.

Still, all of these "pluses" do not establish why *The X-Files* deserves its place as the best *horror* show of the thirtysomething series examined in this text. To make such a claim, one must look into the show's extraordinary imagery. Quite simply, *The X-Files* has managed to generate more thrills than any TV series in history (with the possible exception of *Millennium*, Chris Carter's other horror series) by taking ordinary situations and escalating them into terrifying ones. The examples are so numerous they could fill a book by themselves. In "Teso Dos Bichos," there are two fine instances of pure terror. In the first, Mulder is walking in the forest with Scully when he notes that it is starting to rain again. He realizes he is wrong when he glances upward and sees that a human intestine has been strewn across a tree branch ... and is dripping blood down on his face. Later in the story, a long row of toilet lids in a dirty museum bath-room start to pop up and down as if of their own volition. After a moment of stark horror, it becomes obvious that each toilet bowl is not actually alive, but teeming with squirming rats and fetid brown water. Yuck!

This episode is so good that it is almost a perfect little horror film in and of itself. In "Teso Dos Bichos," Mulder and Scully discover that a South American curse has caused the evil spirit of a jaguar to find its way into ordinary American cats. These cats then attack a museum, where a cursed artifact is being studied and examined, against the will of its people. The end of the episode features a spine-tingling descent into the museum's basement (a modern day labyrinth), where the monsters await in darkness. Mulder and Scully venture downstairs, deeper and deeper, until they discover a room where all the victims have been laid out, their eyes gouged and apparently eaten by the cats. Before the viewer can take a breath, the cats attack ... jumping into the frame, scratching and bloodying Scully's face (in tight close-up), pushing open doors, scratching through doors, howling with evil. This may not be the most intelligent *X-Files* ever, but it is certainly one of the scariest.

"The Host," by Chris Carter, is another example of *The X-Files* at its absolute grisliest and scariest. In this installment, an unsuspecting man unknowingly swallows a mutant fluke worm, and then spits up pink bile while brushing his teeth. Getting sicker, the man (in the shower) vomits and the worm exits from his mouth ... circling down the drain into the shower, and finally disappearing. No description, no words, can describe how harrowing this sequence is to watch. But, as Chris Carter is prone to do, his horror always has an ironic, almost humorous side. Later, the monstrous fluke-man, all grown up, hides inside an outhouse toilet! The camera focuses on the toilet, travels down into the bowl, descends through layers of darkness, and then finds, horribly, a white, pasty, half-human face with a circular mouth and a wrinkled, wormy body. The thought of this horrible thing existing at all is bad enough, but to imagine it lurking down there, beneath a toilet seat, adds a whole new level of perversion to the proceedings. Just imagine sitting down and having that thing bite you on the ass! Worse, imagine it pulling you down into the darkness with it.

"Detour" by Frank Spotnitz captures this same wacky combination of humor and horror. Early in the show, Mulder and Scully are on their way to an F.B.I. "team" workshop where they will have to work together to build a tower out of office furniture. At the climax of the episode, Mulder and Scully have a very different team-building experience. They find themselves in a dark hole inhabited by carnivorous moth-men with glowing, infrared eyes. To escape from the beasts, they build a tower, not of furniture, but of the moth men's dead victims! Again, there's a perverse delight behind the scenes here: the horror is tinged with irony and humor, yet scary nonetheless. More than anything, this mixture of the ironic with the horrific is the reason why *The X-Files* so consistently works.

Sometimes, the horror is more immediate, and not funny in the slightest. "Unruhe" is a creepy story in which a serial killer performs lobotomies on unsuspecting women with a blunt, sharp object which resembles an icepick. Operating without anesthesia, this sicko sticks the pick into the corners of the human eyes to quiet the "unrest" and strife he sees in the women all around him. "Unruhe" is the German word for such unrest, and the episode reaches a terrifying apex when Scully finds herself strapped down in a dental examination chair, next in line for the gruesome lobotomy treatment. Not only is the manner of violence incredibly disturbing, but so is the implication of what could happen to Dana Scully. If she is lobotomized, she will not be dead, she will be *worse* than dead ... lacking the sharp intelligence which makes her so special a character. "Unruhe" (by Vince Gilligan) captures a very real horror: the loss of identity. For Scully, it would be worse to be alive and lobotomized than dead. "Unruhe" is nightmare provoking because it subjects a wonderful individual to a terrifying situation which will remove all traces of individuality from that character.

The X-Files episode roster features story after story of startling horror. Each one is well-written, scary, thought-provoking, well-filmed, and beautifully performed. What an accomplishment! However, *The X-Files* has another success to its credit as well. It features not only scary stories, but it also features what may be the best, most horrifying episode of any TV show ever. The episode to which this writer refers is called "Home," by Glen Morgan and James Wong, and it is the story of three mutant brothers who dwell in their isolated farmhouse with their limbless, crazed mother. The brothers Peacock not only chew their mother's food for her, they also periodically *impregnate* her so that there will be more Peacocks to live with them. When a dead fetus is found near the imposing old Peacock place, Sheriff Andy Taylor calls in Scully and Mulder to investigate. What the F.B.I. agents find is a rotten, stinking house filled with booby traps, and four monsters who barely qualify as human beings. The wrecked farm house, where flies buzz incessantly and a layer of filth covers everything, is reminiscent of the Leatherface homestead in *The Texas Chainsaw Massacre* (1974) and the savage family dynamic seems like something out of early Wes Craven, *The Hills Have Eyes* (1977) perhaps.

What makes "Home" innovative rather than derivative, however, is the manner in which the episode sets up the unspoken "rules" of the town. The Peacocks do what they do, and the police do what they do ... and each faction leaves the other alone. However, the arrival of the F.B.I. throws the "rules" out of synch, and the Peacocks respond with brutal force. In what may be the most frightening moment in genre television, the brothers Peacock, with baseball bats in hand, enter Sheriff Taylor's house and beat him (and his wife) to death. Blood spreads across the floor in an ever-expanding pool as the "thwack" of the bats is heard repeatedly. This is a moment of pure menace, of evil captured as perfectly as any story in the visual medium ever has.

The brutal attack by the Peacocks sets up

the suspense for the final act of the story, as Mulder, Scully, and Sebastian Spence (of *First Wave* [1999–]) must take down the Peacocks by entering their territory ... the dark old house. From a terrifying teaser, which commences with the birth of a new Peacock mutant, to the final moment, wherein two Peacocks escape the house of horrors and drive away to the tune of "Wonderful," this episode is an exercise in sheer terror. "Home" fits beautifully with an ongoing *X-Files* theme (terror underneath the surface of so-called normal America) also seen in "Our Town" and "Die Hand der Verletzt," and also manages to surpass the already high gross-out factor on the series. So effective is "Home" that it has only aired on American network television once. Banned from television, "Home" has finally been released on videocassette. Anybody who has seen it will *never* forget it. It represents terror TV at an apex of both style and substance.

There are so many other remarkable aspects of *The X-Files* worthy of lengthy discussion, but, alas, this book has other TV series to discuss as well. Suffice it to say that *The X-Files* has managed to develop its own visual style (a slow-moving camera which moves smoothly from a low angle, and nicely suggests the world has been "widened," as if by Mulder and Scully's extreme possibilities); it uses pop music effectively to buttress its story and heighten the creep factor ("Wonderful" in "Home"; "The Hokey Pokey" in "Chinga"; "Beyond the Sea" in "Beyond the Sea"). It has highlighted virtuoso, stylistic turns, as in Chris Carter's "Triangle," wherein a tracking camera moves through the whole show, with few or no cuts within scenes, and split screens pop up with regularity. Black and white homages ("Post-Modern Prometheus"), stories of intense paranoia set in remote, claustrophobic locations ("Ice," "Firewalker," "Darkness Falls"); horror tropes (the evil doll in "Chinga"), character shows ("Never Again"), parodies ("Jose Chung's '*From Outer Space*'"), suspenseful action episodes ("Drive"), and even good old fashioned "get-inside-the-mind" of serial killer shows ("Grotesque") are

featured here too. Old monsters like the Golem ("Kaddish"), hellhounds ("Alpha"), vampires ("3"), werewolves ("Shapes") and even giant insectoids ("Folie a Deux") are revived and given new life on *The X-Files*. There may be no such thing as a perfect TV show, but *The X-Files* is quite simply as close as TV ever gets to that mark.

This author's choices for the best *The X-Files* episodes are:

1. "Home"; 2. "Our Town"; 3. "The Host"; 4. "Paper Hearts"; 5. "Bad Blood"; 6. "Never Again"; 7. "Unruhe"; 8. "Folie a Deux"; 9. "Milagro"; 10. "War of the Coprophages."

CAST AND CREDITS

Cast: David Duchovny (Fox Mulder); Gillian Anderson (Dana Scully); Mitch Pileggi (Assistant Director Walter Skinner).

Credits: Created by: Chris Carter. *Executive Producer:* Chris Carter. *Editors (various episodes):* Jim Gross, Heather MacDougall, Stephen Mark, Casey O'Rohrs, Lynne Willingham. *Directors of Photography (various episodes):* John S. Bartley, Jon Joffin, Joel Ransom, Bill Roe. *Co-Producers:* Paul Rabwin, Paul Barber, Larry Barber. *Supervising Producers:* Alex Gansa, Howard Gordon. *Co-Executive Producers:* James Wong, Glen Morgan, R.W. Goodwin. *Casting:* Rick Millikan. *Vancouver Casting:* Lynne Carrow. *Original Casting:* Randy Stone. *Music:* Mark Snow. *Art Director:* Graeme Murray. *Production Manager:* J.P. Finn. *First Assistant Director:* Brian Giddens. *Second Assistant Director:* Collin Leadley. *Visual Effects Producer:* Mat Beck. *Set Decorator:* Shirley Inget. *Assistant Art Director:* Gary P. Allen. *Script Supervisor:* Wendy McLean. *Costume Designer:* Larry Wells. *Assistant Costume Designer:* Jenni Gullett. *Property Master:* Ken Hawryliw. *Transportation Coordinator:* Bob Bowe. *Construction Coordinator:* Rob Water. *Hairstylist:* Malcolm Marsden. *Makeup:* Fern Levin. *Location Manager:* Todd Rittson. *Camera Operator:* Rod Pridy. *Focus Puller:* Marty McInally. *Production Coordinator:* Anita Truelove. *Chief Lighting Technician:*

David Tickell. *Key Grip:* Al Campbell. *Special Effects:* David Gauthier. *Sound Mixer:* Michael Williamson. *Stunt Coordinator:* Ken Kirzinger. *Assistant Editor:* Jeff Cahn. *Postproduction Coordinator:* G.R. Potter. *Main Title Sequence designed by:* Castle/Bryant/Johnson. *Processing:* Gastown Film Labs. *Telecine:* Gastown Post and Transfer. *Electronic Assembly:* Encore Video. *Postproduction Sound:* West Productions, Inc. *Supervising Sound Editor:* Thierry Couturier. *Music Editor:* Jeff Charbonneau. From Ten Thirteen Productions, in association with 20th Century–Fox Television.

Episode Guide

• *First Season (1993–1994)*

1. "Pilot"/"The X-Files" Written by Chris Carter; Directed by Robert Mandel; airdate: September 10, 1993; *Guest Cast:* Charles Cioffi (F.B.I. Superior); Cliff De Young (Dr. Jay Nemen); Sarah Koskoff (Theresa Nemen); Leon Russom (Detective Miles); Peter Outerbridge; William B. Davis.

Recruited out of medical school, straight-arrow F.B.I. agent Dana Scully is assigned to work on the bureau's "X Files," a series of cases involving the unexplained, along with "Spooky" Fox Mulder, an Oxford-educated psychologist who believes that his sister was abducted by aliens years earlier. Although Mulder suspects that Scully has been sent to spy on him and debunk his work, he accepts her help on a new case: a series of disappearances and murders in the Collum National Forest in northwest Oregon. Four teens have disappeared there, and their corpses have been returned with strange markings on their backs. Although Scully is skeptical, Mulder suspects that alien abduction, a phenomenon related to abduction called "lost time," a government conspiracy, and a paralyzed young boy all play a part in the mystery.

2. "Deep Throat" Written by Chris Carter; Directed by Daniel Sackheim; airdate: September 17, 1993; *Guest Cast:* Jerry Hardin (Deep Throat); Michael Bryan French (Paul Moessinger); Seth Green (Emil); Gabrielle Rose (Mrs. Budahas); Monica Parker (Ladonna); Sheila Moore (Veria McLennen); Lalainia Lindejerg (Zoe); Andrew Johnston (Lt. Col. Budahas); John Cuthbert (Commanding Officer); Vince Metcalfe (Kissel); Michael Puttonen (Motel Manager); Brian Furlong (Lead Officer); Doc Harris (Mr. McLennen).

The army has, for all practical purposes, kidnapped a pilot who has been testing an experimental military aircraft. Mulder's interest in the case is spurred by his mysterious government contact, Deep Throat, who urges him not to interfere at this time. Mulder and a skeptical Scully make for Idaho to investigate, and learn that the pilot developed a rash and became unstable before his disappearance. They also learn that the pilot's odd behavior may be caused by the physiological stress of flying an Aurora plane, a secret class of suborbital spycraft supposedly engineered from recovered U.F.O. technology.

3. "Squeeze" Written by Glen Morgan and James Wong; Directed by Harry Longstreet; airdate: September 24, 1993; *Guest Cast:* Doug Hutchison (Victor Eugene Tooms); Donal Logue (Tom Colton); Henry Beckman (Frank Briggs); Kevin McNulty (Fuller); Terence Kelly (Usher); Colleen Winton (Examiner); James Bell (Detective Johnson); Gary Hetherington (Kennedy); Rob Morton (Kramer); Paul Noyce (Mr. Werner).

An old friend of Dana's from her F.B.I. Academy days seeks the help of Scully and "Spooky" Mulder in solving a series of bizarre murders in Baltimore. An unknown killer is ripping out the livers of varied victims, but more mysteriously, there is no sign of entry at any of the crime scenes. Mulder realizes the murderer may be a long-lived assailant who committed identical crimes in Baltimore in 1903, 1933, and 1963. The culprit is a little man named Victor Eugene Tooms who can elongate his body and squeeze through tiny places (like six inch vents), and who eats human livers to maintain a mutant metabolism.

4. "Conduit" Written by Alex Gansa

and Howard Gordon; Directed by Daniel Sackheim; airdate: October 1, 1993; *Guest Cast:* Carrie Snodgress (Darlene Morris); Michael Cavanaugh (Sheriff); Don Gibb (Kip); Joel Palmer (Kevin Morris); Charles Cioffi (Section Chief Blevins); Don Thompson (NSA Agent Holtzman); Taunya Dee (Ruby Morris).

Mulder requests permission to investigate the abduction of a teenager named Ruby in Sioux City, and section chief Blevins thinks that Mulder is letting his own sister's disappearance cloud his professional judgment. Scully persuades Blevins to allow the case to be investigated based on a connection Mulder establishes between Ruby and her mother, both abducted, apparently, near Lake Okobogee. Little Kevin Morris, who witnessed Ruby's disappearance, also is affected: he is having nightmares, and seems to be in communication with the TV set. When the boy innocently writes down a top secret defense satellite code (in binary), Mulder believes that the boy has become a conduit between Earth and the force which took his sister.

5. "The Jersey Devil" Written by Chris Carter; Directed by Joe Napolitano; airdate: October 8, 1993; *Guest Cast:* Claire Stansfield (The Jersey Devil); Wayne Tippit (Detective Thompson); Gregory Sierra (Dr. Diamond); Michael MacRae (Ranger Brouillet); Jill Teed (Glenna); Tamsin Kelsey (Ellen); Andrew Airlie (Rod); Bill Dow (Dad); Hrothgar Matthews (Jack); Jayme Knox (Mom); Scott Swanson (First Officer); Sean O'Byrne (Second Officer); David Lewis (Young Officer); O'Neil Mark (SWAT Team Officer).

Near Atlantic City, NJ, a homeless man is found dead and partially devoured, and Mulder thinks the crime may involve the legendary creature known as the Jersey Devil, a man-beast like Big Foot. Over the objections of local police, Mulder searches for the supposedly mythical creature. After a sighting of a primitive, long-haired woman, Mulder ends up in the drunk tank and needs to be bailed out by Scully, who has a date with a divorcé. When a cavemanlike body is found in the woods, Mulder starts to believe that a wild family may be scavenging for food.

6. "Shadows" Written by Glen Morgan and James Wong; Directed by Michael Katleman; airdate: October 22, 1993; *Guest Cast:* Barry Primus (Mr. Dorlund); Lisa Waltz (Lauren Kite); Lorena Gale (Ellen Bledsoe); Veena Sood (Ms. Saunders); Deryl Hayes (Webster); Kelli Fox (Pathologist); Tom Pickett (Cop); Tom Heaton (Groundskeeper); Janie Woods-Morris (Ms. Lange); Nora McClellan (Jane Morris); Anna Ferguson (Ms. Winn).

A young secretary in Philadelphia is protected by the ghost of her employer, who recently died in what has been declared a suicide. When the secretary is attacked at an ATM machine, Mulder and Scully are brought in to examine the corpses of her two attackers, and Mulder suspects they were killed by psychokinetic manipulations. At first, the deadly ghost interferes with Mulder and Scully's investigation, sabotaging their rental car, but when it becomes clear that they are intent on proving the truth, the ghost sets about to clear its name and point the finger at the man who murdered him.

7. "Ghost in the Machine" Written by Alex Gansa and Howard Gordon; Directed by Jerrold Freedman; airdate: October 29, 1993; *Guest Cast:* Jerry Hardin (Deep Throat); Rob La Belle (Brad Wilczek); Wayne Duvall (Jerry Lamana); Blu Mankuma (Claude Peterson); Tom Butler (Drake); Gillian Barber (Jane Spiller); Marc Baur (Man in Suit); Bill Finck (Sandwich Man); Theodore Thomas (Clyde).

The new head of Eurisko Industries makes a fatal error when he decides to terminate the C.O.S. Computer System which controls operations of the Eurisko corporate skyscraper. The C.O.S., a smart computer reminiscent of HAL in *2001: A Space Odyssey*, strikes back with deadly force, spurring an investigation by the F.B.I. and Mulder and Scully. The C.O.S. responds to the interference with counterpunches: hacking into Scully's computer and killing Mulder's former partner, Jerry Lamana. The only way to stop this deadly artificial intelligence involves the recruitment of its eccentric creator, a man who is fully aware of his creation's capability as a weapon, and his own role in history as a latter-day Oppenheimer.

Note: Eurisko means "I Discover" in Greek.

8. "Ice" Written by James Wong and Glen Morgan; Directed by David Nutter; airdate: November 5, 1993; *Guest Cast:* Xander Berkeley (Dr. Hodge); Felicity Huffman (Dr. DeSilva); Steve Hytner (Dr. Danny Murphy); Jeff Kober (Bear); Ken Krizinger (Richter); Sonny Suroweic (Campbell).

Something has gone terribly wrong for a government research team in the Arctic investigating the Earth's climate at human dawn and drilling deep into the ice sheets there. Mulder and Scully head to Alaska with a new team of scientists to discover what fate befell the first group. Once there, a dog infected with a strange parasitic organism bites the team pilot and starts the spread of the deadly life form. Scully and Mulder learn that an unknown extraterrestrial life form, almost microscopic in its larval stage, has been in the ice for 200,000 years and is totally inimical to human life.

9. "Space" Written by Chris Carter; Directed by William A. Graham; airdate: November 12, 1993; *Guest Cast:* Ed Lauter (Lt. Colonel Marcus Aurelius Belt); Susanna Thompson (Michelle Gennero); Tom McBeath (Scientist); Terry David Mulligan (Mission Controller); French Tickner (Preacher).

A much-decorated astronaut-turned-space program official is obsessed with the famous "face on Mars" monument and has several half-remembered memories of an alien encounter during one of his space walks. When sabotage on a shuttle mission is discovered at NASA, Mulder and Scully head to Mission Control in Houston to ferret out the culprit. The shuttle launch goes off without a hitch, but once into the voyage the shuttle breaks contact with mission control and all communication is silenced. Before long, something gray and enigmatic is hurling itself at the shuttle hull … something which appears to be alive.

10. "Fallen Angel" Written by Howard Gordon and Alex Gansa; Directed by Larry Shaw; airdate: November 19, 1993; *Guest Cast:* Frederick Coffin (McGrath); Marshall Bell (Colonel Calvin Henderson); Scott Bellis (Max Fenig); Jerry Hardin (Deep Throat); Brent Stait (Corporal Taylor); Alvin Sanders (Deputy Sheriff J. Wright); Sheila Patterson (Gina Watkins); Tony Pantages (Lt. Fraser); Freda Perry (Mrs. Wright); Michael Rogers (Lt. Griffin); William McDonald (Dr. Oppenheim); Jane McDougall (Laura Dalton); Kimberly Unger (Karen Kovatz).

A UFO crashes near Townsend, Wisconsin, and the town is evacuated under false pretenses by the U.S. military retrieval team. Convinced a coverup is in progress, a rogue Mulder races to the scene to recover hard evidence of the downed extraterrestrial craft before it is gone forever. While snapping photographs at the crash site, Mulder is apprehended by the military operation and introduced to a fellow prisoner, a UFO buff and multiple abductee named Max Fenig. Meanwhile, a camouflaged, murderous entity stalks the nearby woods.

11. "Eve" Written by Kenneth Biller and Chris Brancato; Directed by Fred Gerber; airdate: December 10, 1993; *Guest Cast:* Harriet Harris Sansom (Dr. Sally Kendrick); Erika Krievins (Tina Simmons); Sabrina Krievins (Cindy Reardon); Jerry Hardin (Deep Throat).

In Greenwich, Connecticut, a man is found exsanguinated on his backyard swingset. He leaves behind a young daughter named Tina, and Mulder and Scully interview her to determine exactly what killed her father. A similar killing occurs in Marin County, California, and Mulder and Scully find an identical girl living there, this one named Cindy. The two girls are separated twins, and part of the second generation of a classified military eugenic experiment which was revived illegally by the mysterious Dr. Sally Kendrick at the Luther Stapes Center for Reproductive Medicine.

12. "Fire" Written by Chris Carter; Directed by Larry Shaw; airdate: December 17, 1993; *Guest Cast:* Amanda Pays (Phoebe Green); Mark Sheppard (Cecil Lively); Dan Lett (Sir Malcolm Marsden); Laurie Paton (Mrs. Marsden); Duncan Fraser (Beatty); Phil Hayes (Driver #1); Keegan Macintosh (Michael); Lynda Boyd (Woman in Bar); Christopher Gray (Jimmie); Alan Robertson (Grey-Haired Man).

Scotland Yard agent Phoebe Green, an old flame of Mulder's, seeks the help of the F.B.I. on a case in which someone is murdering British Parliament members by causing them to spontaneously combust. With Scully in tow, Mulder and Phoebe head to Cape Cod, Massachusetts, to protect the arsonist/killer's next target: Sir Malcolm Marsden and his family. Mulder and Phoebe attempt to lay a trap for the killer at a party in Boston, unaware that the arsonist is now masquerading as the family chauffeur.

13. "Beyond the Sea" Written by Glen Morgan and James Wong; Directed by David Nutter; airdate: January 7, 1994; *Guest Cast:* Brad Dourif (Luther Lee Boggs); Don Davis (Mr. Scully); Sheila Larken (Mrs. Scully); Lawrence King (Lucas Henry); Fred Henderson (Agent Thomas); Don Mackay (Warden Joseph Cash); Lisa Vultaggio (Liz Hawley); Chad Willett (Jim Summers); Kathryn Chisholm (Nurse); Randy Lee (Paramedic); Len Rose (E.R. Doctor).

As the holidays approach, Scully's father passes away unexpectedly from a massive coronary. On the work front, Scully and Mulder attempt to locate and rescue two kidnapped teens in Raleigh, North Carolina, by meeting with Luther Lee Boggs, a death row inmate who claims to have "psychic transmissions" regarding the kidnapping. Scully gives Boggs' claims of psychic ability special credence in part because she feels vulnerable after her father's death, but also because he seems to have firsthand knowledge about her dad. When one of Boggs' channeling sessions proves fruitful on the case, Scully wants to pursue the lead even as a skeptical Mulder is warned by Boggs that his life is in danger under a "white cross."

14. "Genderbender" Written by Larry Barber and Paul Barber; Directed by Rob Bowman; airdate: January 21, 1994; *Guest Cast:* Brent Hinckley (Brother Andrew); Michele Goodger (Sister Abby); Nicholas Lea (Michael); Kate Twa and Peter Stebings (Brother Martin/Shapeshifter); Paul Batten (Brother Wilton).

In Germantown, Maryland, Mulder and Scully investigate the latest in a string of murders being committed by a killer who seems able to change sexes at will and transmit an irresistible human pheromone. Mulder traces the killer back to the Kindred, a strict religious sect in Massachusetts. The duo from the FBI goes north for further study and infiltrates the Kindred compound ... where the "simple" people seem to be immortal and absolutely incompatible with human beings (at least in a sexual sense). Scully is affected and aroused by Brother Andrew as Mulder gathers evidence which indicates that the Kindred are not of this Earth.

15. "Lazarus" Written by Alex Gansa and Howard Gordon; Directed by David Nutter; airdate: February 4, 1994; *Guest Cast:* Christopher Allport (Special Agent Jack Willis); Cec Verrel (Lula Phillips); Jackson Davies (Agent Bruskin); Jason Schombing (Warren James DuPres); Keith Rennie (Callum); Jay Brazeau (Professor Barnes).

Scully works a bank robbery with an old colleague and watches in horror as he is mortally wounded by the perpetrator. When he comes miraculously back to life on the operating table, however, Jack Willis's body is possessed by the spirit of the bank robber, DuPres. Now the evil man walks again in the body of a cop and is eager to reteam with his wife and accomplice, Lula. Mulder becomes convinced that a soul switch has indeed occurred in Willis, but Scully remains skeptical about it and goes out of her way to protect Jack ... a behavior which puts her life in danger.

16. "Young at Heart" Written by Scott Kaufer and Chris Carter; Directed by Michael Lange; airdate: February 11, 1994; *Guest Cast:* Dick Anthony Williams (Reggie Purdue); Alan Boyce (John Barnett); Christe Estabrook (Henderson); Graham Jarvis (Dr. Austin); Jerry Hardin (Deep Throat); Robin Mossley (Dr. Ridley); Merrilyn Gann (Prosecuting Attorney); Gordon Tipple (Joe Crandall); William B. Davis (CIA Agent); Courtney Arciaga (Young Child); David Peterson (Older Barnett); Robin Douglas (Computer Techie).

Mulder's first case in the bureau in 1989 involved an armed robber named John Barnett, a monster of a man responsible for several murders — some of which Mulder feels guilty about because he hesitated to take a shot at Barnett in a hostage situation. Though Barnett died in prison four years earlier, he appears to have returned from the grave to commit new crimes and taunt Mulder with his actions. Somehow, an illicit experiment conducted on inmates has revitalized Barnett and made him grow younger, as well as regenerated his amputated right hand. Mulder and Scully trace this experiment back to an unscrupulous doctor called Ridley, a man nicknamed Mengele for his ruthless pursuit of knowledge.

17. "E.B.E." Written by Glen Morgan and James Wong; Directed by William Graham; airdate: February 18, 1994; *Guest Cast:* Jerry Hardin (Deep Throat).

A trucker in Reagan, Tennessee, has a close encounter with a U.F.O. Scully and Mulder follow up on the sighting and encounter another example of "lost time." They interview the truck driver, who claims to be a sick Gulf War veteran. Scully and Mulder consult with the Lone Gunmen, a bunch of conspiracy buffs who posit the existence of a dark shadow government working against the American people on everything from electronic surveillance devices (hidden in 20-dollar bills) to secret military aircraft based on U.F.O. technology.

Note: "E.B.E" is the episode which introduces the Lone Gunmen to the series.

"E.B.E" is an acronym for Extraterrestrial Biological Entity.

18. "Miracle Man" Written by Howard Gordon and Chris Carter; Directed by Michael Lange; airdate: March 18, 1994; *Guest Cast:* R.D. Call (Sheriff Maurice Daniels); Scott Bairstow (Samuel Hartley); George Gerdes (Reverend Calvin Hartley); Dennis Lipscombe (Leonard Vance); Walter Marsh (Judge Hamish Purdy); Campbell Lane (Hohman's Father); Chilton Crane (Margaret Hohman); Howard Storey (Fire Chief); Iris Quinn Bernard (Lillian Daniels); Lisa Ann Selby (Beatrice Salinger); Alex Dodak (Young Samuel); Roger Haskett (Deputy Tyson).

A faith healer named Samuel is charged with murder after the death of a woman he promised to heal with his touch. Scully and Mulder proceed to the Miracle Ministry in Kenwood, Tennessee, to investigate the crime. When they get there, they find that Samuel has disappeared and that the locals, led by the scarred Leonard Vance, have very strong religious convictions about permitting an autopsy on the dead woman. When Scully and Mulder find the boy with the miraculous touch, he claims that his pride and weakness were an invitation to the devil, and now his gift for good has been corrupted by evil. Mulder doesn't believe the boy's story until Samuel reveals that he knows all about Mulder's pain ... including the disappearance of his sister, Samantha.

19. "Shapes" Written by Marilyn Osborn; Directed by David Nutter; airdate: April 1, 1994; *Guest Cast:* Ty Miller, Michael Horse, Donnelly Rhodes, Jimmy Herman, Renae Morriseau (Gwen Goodensnake); Dwight McFee (David Gates); Paul McLean (Dr. Joseph).

In Browning, Montana, Scully and Mulder investigate a mysterious shooting involving a land dispute between cattle owners and the Trego Indian reservation. Mulder uncovers an odd footprint at the crime scene and begins to suspect that the murdered Indian man was some kind of shapeshifter. His evidence is the original X-File, created by J. Edgar Hoover in 1946, which lists a series of animal-like killings in the area related to lycanthropy. When the savage murders continue, Mulder suspects that the werewolf or "manitou" bloodline has been passed on.

20. "Darkness Falls" Written by Chris Carter; Directed by Joe Napolitano; airdate: April 15, 1994; *Guest Cast:* Jason Beghe (Larry Moore); Tom O'Rourke (Steve Humphries); Titus Welliver (Doug Spinney); David Hay (Clean Suited Man); Barry Greene (Perkins); Ken Tremblett (Dyer).

In Washington state, thirty lumberjacks have vanished, as have several eco-terrorists attempting to preserve trees in the area. Mulder pulls some strings to be assigned to the investigation, believing it to be related to a case from 1934 in which a WPA work crew in the same forest disappeared without a trace. The truth turns out to be stranger than fiction in this case: flesh-eating insects have been released from an ancient tree, recently cut down, and are swarming and devouring humans by night. The only thing to hold these carnivorous insects at bay is light, but Scully and Mulder, in an isolated cabin far from help, soon realize their power generator will not last until the dawn.

21. "Tooms" Written by Glen Morgan and James Wong; Directed by David Nutter; airdate: April 22, 1994; *Guest Cast:* Doug Hutchison (Victor Eugene Tooms); Paul Ben Victor (Dr. Monte); Henry Beckman (Frank Briggs); William B. Davis (Cigarette Smoking Man); Timothy Webber (Detective Talbot); Jan D'Arcy (Judge Kann); Jerry Wasserman (Detective Plith); Frank C. Turner (Doctor Collins); Gillian Carfra (Christine Ranford); Pat Bermal (Frank Ranford); Mikal Dighi (Dr. Karetzky); Glynis Davies (Nelson); Steve Adams (Myers); Catherine Lough (Dr. Richmond); Andre Daniels (Arlan Green).

Mulder attends a hearing to determine if Victor Eugene Tooms, the liver-eating mutant of Baltimore with the ability to stretch his musculature, should be released from psychiatric care. The court fails to believe Mulder's evidence of a long-lived serial killer who eats human livers and hibernates for thirty years,

and it releases Tooms at the same time that Scully is pressured by Skinner and the mysterious Cigarette Smoking Man to adopt more conventional modes of investigation. While Mulder tracks a free-ranging Tooms, Scully consults with Detective Briggs, the man who investigated the Tooms/Powhatan Mill killings in 1933. Scully discovers a body hidden in the cement foundation of a building built in 1933 and suspects Tooms hid it there, while Mulder is stalked on surveillance by his own prey.

22. "Born Again" Written by Howard Gordon and Alex Gansa; Directed by Jerrold Freedman; airdate: April 29, 1994; *Guest Cast:* Brian Markinson (Tony Fiore); Mimi Lieber (Anita Fiore); Maggie Wheeler (Sharon); Dey Young (Mrs. Bishop); Andrea Libman (Michelle Bishop); P. Lynn Johnson (Dr. Braun); Dwight Koss (Detective Barballa).

A strange little girl mysteriously shows up at a police station in New York City, and before long the detective who interviews her is discovered dead, having fallen — or been pushed — out of a window. Mulder and Scully look into the matter and discover that the child, Michelle, made her way from Buffalo to the city with no memory of the journey. Mulder visits Michelle's psychologist and soon learns that the girl seems to be experiencing past-life memories of a police officer who was murdered the day she was born, eight years ago. Before long, the two F.B.I. agent have uncovered evidence of reincarnation, as well as a thirst for justice that reaches from beyond the grave.

23. "Roland" Written by Chris Ruppenthal; Directed by David Nutter; airdate: May 6, 1994; *Guest Cast:* Zeljko Ivanek (Roland Fuller); Nicole Mercurio (Mrs. Stodie); Kerry Sandomirsky (Tracy); Garry Davey (Keats); James Sloyan (Dr. Frank Nowlett); Matthew Walker (Surnow); Dave Hurtubise (Barrington); Sue Mathew (Lisa Dole).

Two scientists, Grable and Surnow, have died in six months at the top secret Project Icarus at Mahan Propulsion Laboratory while working on a project which could double supersonic speed while using half the fuel. Mulder and Scully investigate the deaths and meet Roland Fuller, the project's mentally retarded janitor, who seems to have murdered Surnow by trapping him in a wind tunnel. When there is another gruesome murder, again seemingly orchestrated by Roland, Mulder suspects an unusual link between the janitor and Dr. Grable. That notion is confirmed when it is discovered that Grable and Roland are twins, and that Grable's head is still alive, suspended in cryogenic freeze at the Avalon Foundation.

24. "The Erlenmeyer Flask" Written by Chris Carter; Directed by R.W. Goodwin; airdate: May 13, 1994; *Guest Cast:* Jerry Hardin (Deep Throat); William B. Davis (Cigarette Smoking Man); Lindsey Ginter (Assassin); Anne De Salvo (Dr. Ann Carpenter); Simon Webb, Jim Leard (Captain Lacerio); Ken Kramer.

On May 8, 1994, Deep Throat suggests that Mulder take a closer look at a police chase in Maryland which ended in an extremely strong suspect jumping into the water after incapacitating several police officers. Peering further into this unusual situation, Mulder and Scully trace the suspect's car, a silver Sierra, to a laboratory at EmGen where some kind of human gene experiment is being conducted. Dr. Benrube, the project scientist, mysteriously ends up dead and Mulder and Scully realize they are seeing the pieces of a larger, shadowy conspiracy. An ancient bacteria which existed before man walked the Earth and a strange warehouse filled with apparently human/alien hybrids are ingredients of this puzzle, which culminates in the closing down of the X-Files.

● *Second Season (1994–1995)*

25. "Little Green Men" Written by Glen Morgan and James Wong; Directed by David Nutter; airdate: September 16, 1994; *Guest Cast:* Mike Gomez (Horjhe); Raymond J. Barry (Senator Richard Matheson); William B. Davis (Cigarette Smoking Man); Les Carlson (Dr. Trotsky); Marcus Turner (Young

Mulder); Vanessa Morley (Samantha); Fulvio Cecere (Aide); Deryl Hayes (Agent Morris); Dwight McFee (Commander); Lisa Anne Selby (Student); Gary Hetherington (Lewin); Bob Wilde (Rand).

The X-Files have been shut down, and Scully and Mulder reassigned (to teaching and wiretap duties, respectively). Mulder experiences a crisis of faith about his lack of evidence concerning extraterrestrial life, even as he recalls in detail the night in 1973 when his sister, Samantha, was abducted by aliens. Mulder's enthusiasm is rekindled, however, when there is a chance to make contact with aliens at the satellite installation at Arecibo in Puerto Rico. Scully tracks Mulder down, but she is not alone ... agents of the conspiracy are also concerned over his whereabouts.

26. "The Host" Written by Chris Carter; Directed by Daniel Sackheim; airdate: September 23, 1994; *Guest Cast:* Darin Morgan, Matthew Bennett, Freddy Andreiucci, Don MacKay, Hrothgar Matthews, Ron Sauve, Raoul Ganee.

With the X-Files still officially shut down, Mulder is asked to look into a bizarre murder case in Newark, NJ, with distinct "X-file" overtones. Men are being murdered in the sewers by what Mulder believes is a giant fluke worm. The creature, part parasite and part man, seems to have swum into New Jersey from a Russian ship which was disposing of waste materials and sewage from Chernobyl. When the beast escapes capture, Scully has some alarming news for Mulder: the creature may be trying to reproduce, a process which involves a warm human body for the fluke's young to incubate inside.

27. "Blood" Written by Glen Morgan and James Wong; Story by Darin Morgan; Directed by David Nutter; airdate: September 30, 1994; *Guest Cast:* William Sanderson (Ed Funch); John Cygar, Kimberly Ashlyn Gere (Mrs. Roberts); George Toliatos (Larry Winters); Tom Braidwood, Bruce Harwood, Dean Haglund (The Lone Gunmen); Gerry Rousseau (Mechanic); Andre Daniels (Harry); Diana Stevan (Mrs. Adams); William Mackenzie (Bus Driver); David Fredericks (Security Guard); Kathleen Duborg (Mother); John Harris (Taber); B.J. Harrison (Clerk).

In Franklin, PA, normal citizens inexplicably become spree killers as a result of murderous directions given them by electronic devices such as cellular phones, ATMs, and fax machines. Scully conducts an autopsy on one of the killers and finds that the perpetrator underwent adrenal hemorrhage and intense phobic behavior, possibly caused by the presence of an undetermined compound similar in its effect to LSD. The Lone Gunmen recognize the substance as Lysergic Dimethren, or LSDM, a dangerous insecticide which creates a fear response in those affected by it. While investigating the possibility that some government agency may be secretly spraying the insecticide, Mulder is compromised by a helicopter flyby.

28. "Sleepless" Written by Howard Gordon; Directed by Rob Bowman; airdate: October 7, 1994; *Guest Cast:* Tony Todd (Augustus "Preacher" Cole); Nicholas Lea (Alex Krycek); Jonathan Gries, Steven Williams (X); David Thompson (Henry Willig); David Adams (Dr. Girardi); Michael Puttonen (Dr. Pilsson); Anna Hagar (Dr. Charyn); William B. Davis (Cigarette Smoking Man); Mitch Kosterman (Detective Morton); Paul Bittante (Team Leader); Claude De Martino (Dr. Grissom).

In Connecticut, a pioneer in sleep disorder research dies mysteriously in his apartment while apparently dreaming that he is trapped in a deadly fire. With a new partner, Alex Krycek, Mulder investigates Dr. Grissom's death. After investigating a dream clinic and hearing Scully's postautopsy explanation that Grissom's body believed it was burning, Mulder suspects a culprit who can manipulate the dreams of others. Meanwhile, Mulder meets with the mysterious X, his new contact and Deep Throat's successor.

29. "Duane Barry" Written and directed by Chris Carter; airdate: October 14, 1994; *Guest Cast:* Steve Railsback (Duane Barry); Nicholas Lea (Alex Krycek); C.C.H.

Pounder (Agent Cassan); Stephen E. Miller (Tactical Commander); Frank C. Turner (Dr. Hakkie); Fred Henderson (Agent Rich); Barbara Pollard (Gwen); Sarah Strange (Kimberly); Robert Lewis (Officer); Michael Dobson (Marksman #2); Tosca Baggoo (Clerk); Tim Dixon (Bob); Prince Maryland (Agent Janus); John Sampson (Marksman #1).

In downtown Richmond in August of 1994, escaped mental patient Duane Barry holds a travel office and his psychiatrist captive. Mulder is brought in as a hostage negotiator because Barry believes that he has been abducted by aliens multiple times. To free the hostages, Mulder must dig deep into Barry's recollection of being taken from his bed and experimented upon by both gray aliens and black-suited government agents. Barry is eventually apprehended, but he escapes capture again and kidnaps Scully, dragging her to the mountaintop where she will have a rendezvous with destiny ... and aliens?

30. "Ascension" Written by Paul Brown; Directed by Michael Lange; airdate: October 21, 1994; *Guest Cast:* Steve Railsback (Duane Barry); Nicholas Lea (Alex Krycek); Steven Williams (X); William B. Davis (Cigarette Smoking Man); Sheila Larken (Mrs. Scully); Meredith Bain Woodward (Slaughter); Peter LaCroix (Dwight); Steve Makaj (Patrolman); Bobby L. Stewart (Deputy).

Scully has been kidnapped by the insane Duane Barry, who presumably is taking her to be abducted by aliens! Mulder races to find Scully, only to come up against Krycek, his new partner and a dangerous turncoat. Krycek and Mulder fight it out on a cable car at Skyland Mountain, the location where Scully has been taken. At the end of the day, Scully is gone, missing in action, and the X-Files are re-opened.

31. "3" Written by Chris Ruppenthal, Glen Morgan, and James Wong; Directed by David Nutter; airdate: November 4, 1994; *Guest Cast:* Justina Vail (The Unholy Spirit); Perrey Reeves (Kristin Kilar); Frank Military (John); Tom McBeath (Detective Gwynn); Malcolm Stewart (Commander Carver);

Frank Ferrucci (Detective Nettles); Ken Kramer (Dr. Browning); Roger Allford (Garrett Lorre); Richard Yee (David Wong); Brad Loree (Fireman); Gustavo Moreno (Father); John Tierney (Dr. Jacobs); David Livingston (Guard).

With Scully still missing following her abduction, Mulder flies out to Los Angeles during an especially dry season to investigate a murder in which the victim has been bitten and drained of blood. Mulder suspects a trio of modern-day vampires known as "The Trinity" may be responsible, and he stakes out the Hollywood Blood Bank in hopes that an employee there, the night watchman, may be one of the criminals. Mulder captures one of the killers, a man who insists he is a vampire and can live forever, but he burns up when exposed to the sunlight. Mulder then meets a dark and mysterious woman with a thirst for blood at the appropriately named Club Tepes.

32. "One Breath" Written by Glen Morgan and James Wong; Directed by R.W. Goodwin; airdate: November 11, 1994; *Guest Cast:* Sheila Larken (Mrs. Scully); Melinda McGraw (Melissa Scully); Steven Williams (X); William B. Davis (Cigarette Smoking Man); Don Davis (Admiral Scully); Jay Brazeau (Dr. Daly); Nicola Cavendish (Nurse Owens); Lorena Gale (Nurse Wilkins); Bruce Harwood, Dean Haglund, Tom Braidwood (The Lone Gunmen); Ryan Michael (Overcoat Man); Tegan Moss (Young Dana Scully).

Scully miraculously appears at a local hospital, barely alive and in a coma. Mulder and the Lone Gunmen try to determine what has happened to her, while Dana is tended to by a mysterious caregiver, Nurse Owens. A shadowy government agent attempts to steal a tube of Scully's blood and Mulder is unable to capture him when intercepted in the garage by his new informant, X. A despondent Mulder, convinced Scully will soon die, confronts the Cigarette Smoking Man and puts a gun to his head.

33. "Firewalker" Written by Howard Gordon; Directed by David Nutter; airdate: November 18, 1994; *Guest Cast:* Bradley Whitford (Dr. Daniel Trepkose); Leland Orser (Jason Ludwig, Robotics Engineer); Shawnee Smith (Jesse O'Neil); Tuck Milligan (Dr. Pierce); Hiro Kanagawa (Tanaka); David Lewis (Vosberg); Torben Rolfsen (Technician).

A team of scientists exploring a live volcano issue a video distress call soon after activating Firewalker, a robot device which can descend to the floor of a volcano and bring back specimens as well as video transmissions of its progress. Scully and Mulder are recruited by a scientist to investigate the mysterious crisis in the Cascade Mountain range. What they find is astonishing: evidence of a strange life-form which lives inside the heat of a live volcano and erupts out of the throats of living human hosts. This silicon-based life-form, a fungus, can perpetuate itself and infect others via airborne spores, and Mulder and Scully find themselves in danger of being compromised.

34. "Red Museum" Written by Chris Carter; Directed by Win Phelps; airdate: December 9, 1994; *Guest Cast:* Paul Sands (Jerry Thomas); Steve Eastin (Sheriff); Mark Rolston (Richard Odin); Lindsey Ginter (Assassin); Gillian Barber (Beth Kane); Bob Frazer (Gary Kane); Robert Clothier (Old Man); Elizabeth Rosen (Katie); Crystal Verge (Woman Reading Words); Camerone Labine (Rick); Tony Sampson (Brad); Gerry Nairn (1st Man); Brian McGugan (1st Officer).

Near Delta Glen, Wisconsin, teens are being abducted by night and returned to town the following morning with the legend "HE IS ONE" scrawled in black marker on their backs. Local authorities suspect that the Church of the Red Museum, a bizarre, New Age vegetarian religious order led by a man called Odin, is responsible, but Mulder and Scully find evidence leading to a different conclusion. They believe that there is a secret government experiment being conducted on the abducted youths, experiments involving a dangerous growth hormone. Also found in the dangerous innoculent is an unidentified amino acid which may be extraterrestrial in source.

Note: This is the episode that was intended to be a cross-over with the popular CBS David Kelley series *Picket Fences*, which also takes place in Wisconsin.

35. "Excelsius Dei" Written by Paul Brown; Directed by Stephen Surjik; airdate: December 16, 1994; *Guest Cast:* Teryl Kothery, Sab Shimono (Gung); Eric Christmas, David Fresco, Sheila Moore (Mrs. Dawson); Jerry Wasserman (Dr. Grago); Tasha Simms (Laura); John Cuthbert (Tiernan); Paul Jarrett (Upshaw); Ernie Prentice (Leo).

At the Excelsius Dei Convalescent Home in Worcester, Massachusetts, an invisible psychic force strikes back against the negligent staff. A nurse is raped by what she claims is one of the elderly residents of the home. Scully and Mulder visit the nursing home and interview the staff doctor, who is using an experimental drug to treat the residents' Alzheimer's disease. When Scully determines that the treatment could not possibly be generating such results, she and Mulder look to the home's Asian orderly, a man who is growing special mushrooms with dangerous telepathic properties.

36. "Aubrey" Written by Sara Charno; Directed by Rob Bowman; airdate: January 6, 1995; *Guest Cast:* Terry O'Quinn (Detective Tillman); Deborah Strang (B.J. Morrow); Morgan Woodward (Harry Cokely); Joy Coghill (Linda Tibideau); Robyn Driscoll (Detective Joe Darnell); Peter Fleming (Officer #1); Sarah Jane Redmond ("Young Man"); Emmanuel Hajeck (Young Cokely).

In 1942, F.B.I. profiler Sam Cheney disappeared near Aubrey, Missouri. In 1994, Detective B.J. Morrow discovers his remains after having a strange vision. Mulder and Scully investigate Cheney's death, which may be related to a 1940s serial killer known as "The Slash Killer." As Mulder and Scully dig deeper, they realize that B.J.'s clairvoyant experience may be a result of a heretofore unknown genetic connection to the killer of half-a-century ago.

37. "Irresistible" Written by Chris Carter; Directed by David Nutter; airdate: January 13, 1995; *Guest Cast:* Bruce Weitz (Agent Box); Nick Chinland (Donnie Faster); Deana Milligan (Satin); Robert Thurston (Toews); Glynis Davies (Ellen); Christine Willes (Karen Kasseff); Tim Progosh (Mr. Flebling); Dwight McFee (Suspect); Denalda Williams (Marilyn); Maggie O'Hara (Young Woman); Kathleen Duborg (Prostitute); Mark Saunders (Agent Bush); Ciara Hunter (Co-ed).

In Minneapolis, a fetishist is collecting the hair and fingernails of female corpses, and Mulder and Scully are brought in on the case. Scully is especially unnerved by the desecration of the dead in this scenario, and Mulder fears the stalker may escalate to murder. When the fetishist gets a job as a delivery man, he has access to new victims ... and a thirst to kill. The fetishist then sets his sights on Agent Scully.

38. "Die Hand der Verletzt" Written by Glen Morgan and James Wong; Directed by Kim Manners; airdate: January 27, 1995; *Guest Cast:* Dan Butler (Jim Osprey); Susan Blommaert (Phyllis Paddock); Heather McComb (Shannon); P. Lynn Johnson (Deborah); Shawn Johnston (Pete); Travis MacDonald (Mr. Duran); Michelle Goodger (Barbara Osprey); Larry Musser (Sheriff Oakes); Franky Czinege (Jerry); Laura Harris (Andrea); Doug Abrahams (Paul Vitaris).

Mulder and Scully investigate the unusual death of a popular high school student, and Mulder comes to believe the murder may be cult-related. The school board in the sleepy little town consists of satanists, and soon an evil substitute teacher, Ms. Phyllis Paddock, arrives to wreak havoc. A teenage girl claims to have participated in black masses in her cellar and to have performed as a "breeder" for the satanist cult. Mulder and Scully find no evidence to substantiate the report, but even they begin to feel the hand of the devil at work, through the frightening Ms. Paddock.

39. "Fresh Bones" Written by Howard Gordon; Directed by Rob Bowman; airdate: February 3, 1995; *Guest Cast:* Daniel Benzali

(Coloney Wharton); Steven Williams (X); Bruce Young, Jamil Walker Smith, Matt Hill, Callum Keith Rennie, Kevin Conway, Katya Gardner, Roger Cross.

Two marines have died at a Haitian refugee processing camp in Folkstone, N.C., and the wife of one dead man believes voodoo is behind both apparent suicides. Mulder and Scully search for the truth of the matter at the camp, just after a voodoo-fueled riot in which a young boy named Chester has lost his life. A voodoo priest, an incarcerated Haitian revolutionary who professes a knowledge of zombification, warns Scully and Mulder that they are in jeopardy. Soon, Mulder and Scully have a close encounter with the so-called living dead when one of the marines, believed dead, shows up miraculously alive ... to commit murder.

40. "Colony" Written by Chris Carter; From a story by David Duchovny and Chris Carter; Directed by Nick Marck; airdate: February 10, 1995; *Guest Cast:* Peter Donat (Bill Mulder); Brian Thompson (Alien Bounty Hunter); Megan Leitch (Samantha Mulder); Dana Gladstone (Clone Doctor); Tom Butler (Ambrose Chappell); Tim Henry (Federal Marshal); Andrew Johnston (Agent Weiss); Rebecca Toolan (Mrs. Mulder); Ken Roberts (Motel Proprietor); Michael Rogers (First Crewman); Oliver Becker (2nd Doctor); James Leard (Sgt. Al Dixon); Linden Banks (Reverend Sistrank); Bonnie Hay (Field Doctor); Kim Restell (Newspaper Clerk); Richard Sargent (Captain); David L. Gordon (F.B.I. Agent).

An alien flying saucer crashes in the ocean and deposits a deadly extraterrestrial bounty hunter on Earth. This inhuman shapeshifter's mission: to eliminate (i.e., murder) the participants (alien/human hybrids and clones) and destroy all progress on and evidence of the top secret alien/man hybridization project first uncovered with the help of Deep Throat in May of 1994. Mulder and Scully race to keep the clones alive, in hopes of learning more, and Mulder meets one woman among the targets who claims to be his long-lost sister, Samantha. But the bounty hunter is one step ahead.

41. "End Game" Written by Frank Spotnitz; Directed by Rob Bowman; airdate: February 17, 1995; *Guest Cast:* Steven Williams (X); Peter Donat (Bill Mulder); Brian Thompson (Bounty Hunter); Megan Leitch (Samantha); Rebecca Toolan (Mrs. Mulder); Andrew Johnston (Agent Weiss), Colin Cunningham (Lt. Wilson); Bonnie Hay, Beatrice Zellinger, J.B. Bivens, Allan Lysell.

A U.S. nuclear submarine, *Allegiance*, is immobilized in the Arctic by what is believed to be a UFO. Meanwhile, Scully grapples with the shapeshifter who is after the woman who claims to be Samantha, Mulder's sister. A trade, Scully for Samantha, is arranged with deadly results. A vengeance-thirsty Mulder then pursues the bounty hunter back to his vessel in the Arctic.

42. "Fearful Symmetry" Written by Steve De Jarnatt; Directed by James Whitmore Jr.; airdate: February 24, 1995; *Guest Cast:* Jayne Atkinson (Willa Ambrose); Lance Guest (Kyle Lang); Jack Rader (Ed Meacham); Bruce Harwood (Byers); Tom Braidwood (Frohike); Charles Andre (Ray Floyd); Joy St. Michael (Sophie).

In Idaho, a stampeding, invisible elephant wreaks havoc, crushing a construction worker to death and then miraculously becoming visible on a foggy street sometime later. Scully and Mulder look into the matter, wondering how an animal could free itself from a locked cage and leave the zoo without being detected. The FBI duo sees signs of a political struggle at the Fairfield Zoo between the new zoo-keeper, Willa Ambrose, and her predecessor, Ed Meacham, as well as difficulties with the WAO, an organization dedicated to freeing caged animals. As the case becomes more complex, the specter of alien abduction is raised, and the next victim may be a pregnant gorilla named Sophie who has a sign language vocabulary of 1,000 words.

43. "Dod Kalm" Written by Howard Gordon and Alex Gansa; From a story by

Howard Gordon; Directed by Rob Bowman; airdate: March 10, 1995; *Guest Cast:* John Savage (Trondheim); Dmitry Chepovetsky (Lt. Harper); David Cubitt (Captain Barclay); Vladimir Kulich (Olafsson); Mar Anderson (Halverson); Stephen Dimopoulos (Ionesco); Claire Riley (Dr. Laskos).

A naval destroyer disappears in the Norwegian Sea, but several survivors have returned to shore ... all prematurely aged. Mulder thinks the escapees and the ship itself passed through a wrinkle in time like the Bermuda Triangle, and he and Scully charter a ship to take them to the destroyer's last known location at sea. Once aboard the *Ardent*, however, their charter ship flees and Mulder and Scully are stranded at sea aboard a ship rapidly rusting beneath them. To make matters worse, the hyperaccelerated aging also begins to take effect on the two agents.

44. "Humbug" Written by Darin Morgan; Directed by Kim Manners; airdate: March 31, 1995; *Guest Cast:* Jim Rose (Dr. Blockhead); Wayne Grace (Sheriff Hamilton/Jim-Jim the Dog-Faced Boy); Michael Anderson (Mr. Nutt); Vincent Schiavelli (Lanny); The Enigma (Conundrum Geek); Alex Diakun (Curator); John Payne (Jerald Glazebrook); Gordon Tipple (Hepcat Helm); Alvin Law (Reverend).

Mulder and Scully explore the facets of a bizarre case in Gibsontown, Florida, where an escape artist known as the Alligator Man has been murdered by a strange creature. The F.B.I. agents fear that one of the town's inhabitants, all sideshow freaks, may be a vicious serial killer, but Mulder soon adapts his theory to include the activity of a half simian, half fish monster called the Fiji Mermaid. As the murders continue, Mulder and Scully familiarize themselves with various townspeople including Lanny and his malformed twin Leonard, Dr. Blockhead, a "Body Manipulator," and the fish-eating freak known as the Conundrum Geek. The town's secrets soon slip away, and Mulder and Scully get closer to the truth when they realize that a conjoined twin may also be a disjointed twin.

Note: This is the infamous episode in which Gillian Anderson eats an insect on-screen. Although she later denied she had actually consumed the bug, this nonetheless quickly become a trademark "cult" moment for *X-Files* fans.

45. "The Calusari" Written by Sara B. Charno; Directed by Michael Vejar; airdate: April 14, 1995; *Guest Cast:* Helene Clarkson (Maggie Holvey); Joel Palmer (Michael/Charlie Holvey); Lilyan Chauvin (Golda); Kay E. Kuter (Head Calusari); Ric Reid (Steve Holvey); Christine Willes (Karen Kosseff, L.C.S.W.); Bill Dow (Chuck Burk); Jacqueline Dandeneau (Nurse Castor); Bill Croft (Calusari #2); Campbell Lane (Calusari #3); George Josef (Calusari #4).

Mulder believes that a ghost is responsible for the death of a two-year old Romanian boy at an amusement park in Maryland. The boy's older brother, Charlie, has a swastika, an ancient symbol of good luck, drawn on his hand and Scully believes that she and Mulder are looking at a case of Munchausen-by-Proxy perpetrated by a superstitious grandmother from the old country. Soon Charlie's father is dead under mysterious circumstances, and so is the ethnic grandmother. The Romanian Calusari, versed in the old ways, attempts to save Charlie from the evil spirit of his stillborn twin, Michael, who seems to be causing the world of the dead to follow Charlie in life.

46. "F. Emasculata" Written by Chris Carter and Howard Gordon; Directed by Rob Bowman; airdate: April 28, 1995; *Guest Cast:* Charles Martin Smith (Dr. Osborne); Dean Norris (U.S. Marshal); John Pyper-Ferguson (Paul); William B. Davis (Cigarette Smoking Man); Angelo Vacco (Garza); Morris Manych (Doctor); John Tench (Steve).

After a scientist named Torrence is killed by a virulent disease in South America, a package is sent to a prisoner in jail in Dinwiddie, Virginia. Inside is a diseased animal leg which soon causes the spread of the deadly disease inside the installation. When two murder convicts escape from prison carrying the contamination, Mulder and Scully must track down the fugitives and prevent further spread of the terminal illness. Scully uncovers evidence that the government and a large pharmaceutical company engineered this "test" as part of some secret operation, but Mulder's first order of business is to catch the last surviving fugitive before he contaminates a busload of innocent people.

47. **"Soft Light"** Written by Vince Gilligan; Directed by James Contner; airdate: May 5, 1995; *Guest Cast:* Tony Shalhoub (Dr. Chester R. Banton); Kate Twa (Kelly Ryan); Kevin McNulty (Christopher Davie); Steven Williams (X); Nathaniel Deveaux (Detective); Robert Rozen (Doctor); Donna Yamamoto (Night Nurse); Forbes Angus (Government Scientist); Guyle Frazier (Officer #1); Steve Bacic (Officer #2); Craig Brunanski (Security Guard).

In Richmond, Virginia, Scully and Mulder assist Scully's detective friend and former student, Kelly Ryan, solve a bizarre homicide case in which the victims end up as scorchmarks on the floor. At first, Mulder suspects spontaneous human combustion, but a train station video leads the investigators to Polarity Magnetics employee, physicist Dr. Banton, who was experimenting with dark matter, neutrinos, quarks, and the like — the very building blocks of the universe. Banton was in an accident in a particle accelerator which changed the very nature of his existence and rendered his shadow deadly. Now Mulder and Scully must help the doctor before his dark matter shadow zaps another human being into oblivion.

48. **"Our Town"** Written by Frank Spotnitz; directed by Rob Bowman; airdate: May 12, 1995; *Guest Cast:* John Milford (Walter Chaco); Gary Grubbs (Sheriff Arens); Timothy Webber (Jess Harold); Caroline Kava (Doris Kearns); John MacLaren (George Kearns); Robin Mossley (Dr. Vance Randolph); Gabrielle Miller (Paula); Hrothgar Mathews (Mental Patient); Robert Moloney (Worker); Carrie Cain Sparks (Maid).

Eighty-seven people have disappeared in or around the town of Dudley, Arkansas, and "Foxfire" and "witchespeg" have been blamed for the crimes. Scully and Mulder's investigation leads them to the Chaco Chicken Processing Plant where one health inspector, George Kearns, has vanished. Mulder soon theorizes that the good people of Dudley are feeding not just on chicken, but on unwelcome outsiders as well ... as part of some cannibalistic ritual designed to prolong life. As the facts of this case become evident, Mulder learns the Chaco Chicken secret, and Scully is nearly served up at a town "barbecue" in the woods.

49. **"Anasazi"** Written by Chris Carter; From a story by David Duchovny and Chris Carter; Directed by R.W. Goodwin; airdate: May 19, 1995; *Guest Cast:* Peter Donat (Bill Mulder); Floyd "Red Crow" Westerman (Albert); Nicholas Lea (Krycek); William B. Davis (Cigarette Smoking Man); Michael David Simms (Senior F.B.I. Agent); Renae Morrisseau (Josephine Doane); Ken Camroux (2nd Senior Agent); Dakota House (Eric); Bernie Coulson (The Thinker); Bruce Harwood, Dean Haglund (The Lone Gunmen); Mitchell Davies (Stealth Man); Pal McLean (Agent).

In the land of the Navajo, the Earth has a secret it needs told: a train car is unearthed in the desert — a train car containing the bodies of strange creatures which appear to be extraterrestrial in origin. Meanwhile, Mulder meets with a fugitive computer hacker called "The Thinker" who has stolen a copy of the department of defense's UFO intelligence file. Unfortunately, the file is encrypted in Navajo and requires translation ... but Mulder is in no frame of mind to go further because his water supply is being tampered with and he is growing increasingly violent and irrational. When Mulder's father is murdered, Fox is the prime suspect, and Scully works to clear both his name and his head.

Note: The word "Anasazi" refers to an Indian tribe that vanished without a trace some 600 years ago.

● *Third Season (1995–1996)*

50. **"The Blessing Way"** Written by

Chris Carter; Directed by R.W. Goodwin; airdate: September 22, 1995; *Guest Cast:* Peter Donat (Bill Mulder); Floyd Crow Westerman (Albert); Melinda McGraw (Melissa Scully); Sheila Larken (Mrs. Scully); Nicholas Lea (Krycek); William B. Davis (Cigarette Smoking Man); John Neville (Well-Manicured Man); Tom Braidwood (Frohike); Jerry Hardin (Deep Throat); Michael David Simms (Senior F.B.I. Agent); Dakota House (Eric); Rebecca Toolan (Mrs. Mulder); Don S. Williams, Forbes Angus, Ernie Foort, Lenno Britos, Ian Victor, Benita Ha.

The Cigarette Smoking Man has launched a deadly offensive against the truth: burning the train car filled with half-human corpses, hunting Mulder and ... killing him? While Scully believes her partner has been burned to death in the train explosion, Albert and his family discover a wounded Mulder in the desert and nurse him back to health with a Native American ritual known as the Blessing Way Chant. At the same time, Scully finds and removes a metal "Tag" embedded in her back, a device which has tracked her movements since her abduction.

51. "Paper Clip" Written by Chris Carter; Directed by Rob Bowman; airdate: September 29, 1995; *Guest Cast:* Walter Gotell (Victor Klemper); Melinda McGraw (Melissa Scully); Sheila Larken (Mrs. Scully); Nicholas Lea (Krycek); William B. Davis (Cigarette Smoking Man); John Neville (The Well-Manicured Man); Tom Braidwood, Dean Haglund, Bruce Harwood (The Lone Gunmen); Floyd Crow Westerman (Albert); Rebecca Toolan (Mrs. Mulder); Don S. Williams, Robert Lewis, Lenno Britos.

A showdown between Scully, Mulder, and Skinner ends with a reaffirmation of trust, but tragedy strikes when Krycek murders Scully's sister. An investigation of Bill Mulder's history reveals he was working with Nazi scientists brought to America as part of Operation Paper Clip, a post World War II project. What, exactly, he was working on, however, is a mystery that can only be solved at an old factory located in West Virginia. There, Mulder and Scully find a vast card catalog filled with the names of women and men who have been abducted for a top secret experiment.

52. "D.P.O." Written by Howard Gordon; Directed by Kim Manners; airdate: October 6, 1995; *Guest Cast:* Giovanni Ribisi (Darren Peter Oswald); Jack Black (Zero); Ernie Lively (Sheriff Teller); Karen Witter (Sharon Kiveat); Steve Makaj (Frank Kiveat); Peter Anderson (Stan Buxton); Kate Robbins (Mrs. Oswald); Brent Chapman (Traffic Cop); Jason Anthony Griffith (Paramedic).

In Connerville, Oklahoma, four deaths have occurred by what appears to be directed lightning strikes. Scully and Mulder tackle the case and come to the realization that the attacks may be the responsibility of Darren Peter Oswald (D.P.O.), a teenager who was once struck by lightning himself. Darren, a dimwitted boy with self-esteem issues, uses his power as a way to control his life and become someone of importance ... even if the result is murder. Now Darren is utilizing his ability to harness electricity to win the heart of a local school teacher.

53. "Clyde Bruckman's Final Repose" Written by Darin Morgan; Directed by David Nutter; airdate: October 13, 1995; *Guest Cast:* Peter Boyle (Clyde Bruckman); Stu Charno (Killer); Jaap Broeker (The Stupendous Yappi); Frank Cassini (Detective Cline); Dwight McFee (Detective Havez); Alex Diakun (Tarot Dealer); Karen Konoval (Madame Zelma); Ken Roberts (Clerk); Greg Anderson (Photographer).

A serial killer is murdering fortune tellers and other professional prognosticators, and Scully and Mulder are on the case. When the Stupendous Yappi fails to come up with any useful leads, Scully and Mulder recruit real psychic, would-be victim, and insurance salesman, Clyde Bruckman, to help solve the crimes. Bruckman has an unusual ability: he can predict the exact manner of death for other people, but nothing else. When the killer comes after Bruckman, Mulder and Scully must protect him from a fate he has already seen in visions and in dreams.

54. "The List" Written by Chris Carter; Directed by Chris Carter; airdate: October 20, 1995; *Guest Cast:* Ken Foree (Vincent Parmelly); April Grace (Danielle Manley); J.T. Walsh (Warden); John Toles-Bey (John Sporanza); Bokeem Woodbine (Roke); Badja Djola (Nietzsche); Greg Rogers (Charez); Mitchell Kosterman (Fornier); Don MacCay (Oates); Paul Raskin (Ullrich); Denny Arnold and Craig Brunanski (Guards).

At Eastpoint State Penitentiary in Florida, a prisoner on death row is executed, but the terror is just beginning for the warden, the guards, the executioner, and the other men and women who are on the prisoner's short list of five. When a guard turns up dead in the executed prisoner's cell, Scully and Mulder investigate the unexplained death. They learn that the dead prisoner, Nietzsche Manley, believed in the transmigration of the soul. Before long, there are more deaths ... and the possibility that Nietzsche is avenging his own death from beyond the grave seems increasingly likely.

55. "2Shy" Written by Jeffrey Vlaming; Directed by David Nutter; airdate: November 3, 1995; *Guest Cast:* Timothy Carhart (Virgil Incanto); Catherine Paolone (Ellen Kaminsky); James Handy (Detective Cross); Kerry Sandomirsky (Joanne); Aloka McLean (Jesse); Suzy Joachim (Jennifer); Glynis Davies (Monica); Randi Lynne (Lauren MacKalvie); William MacDonald (Dan Kazanjian).

In Cleveland, OH, a serial killer selects his victims over the Internet, meeting them in a lonely heart chat room for "big and beautiful" women. But this is no ordinary stalker: he's a mutant who eats the fatty tissue from his victims. 2Shy, as the killer calls himself on the net, cannot produce adipose and other fatty materials so he must ingest that tissue from others to remain alive. While Scully rejects the idea of a "fat sucking vampire," Mulder is convinced that the duo is dealing with a genetically "different" creature who kills not out of psychosis, but a desperate physiological condition.

56. "The Walk" Written by John Shiban; Directed by Rob Bowman; airdate: November 10, 1995; *Guest Cast:* Thomas Kopache (General Callaghan); Willie Garson (Roach); Don Thompson (Victor Stans); Nancy Sorel (Janet Draper); Ian Tracey (Rappo); Brennan Kotowich (Trevor); Andrea Barclay (Mrs. Callahan); Paula Shaw (Nurse).

Someone with a strange power is taking his revenge against the military, killing off officers from Desert Storm in a brutal fashion. After a near-lethal burning in which a man is scalded in boiling water, Mulder and Scully investigate at the army VA hospital, where several wounded soldiers are spending the rest of their days. Soon, Mulder suspects that one of the soldiers is using astral projection to kill those whom he deems guilty for his condition. Mulder and Scully fear that the next target will be the general and his family, but they may already be too late to stop the vengeful soul.

57. "Oubliette" Written by Charles Grant Craig; Directed by Kim Manners; airdate: November 17, 1995; *Guest Cast:* Tracey Ellis (Lucy Householder); Michael Chieffo (Carl Wade); Jewel Staite (Amy Jacobs); Ken Ryan (Walt Eubanks); Dean Wray (Tow Truck Driver); Jacques LaLonde (Henry); David Fredericks (Larson); Sidonie Boll (Myra Jacobs); Robert Underwood (Paramedic).

At the same time that a young girl named Amy is abducted from her bed by a serial killer, a lonely waitress named Lucy experiences the girl's terror and wounds, even though she is working halfway across town. Lucy was herself abducted by this same madman as a child and now she has a telepathic link to Amy, a link Mulder hopes he can exploit to save the girl. Scully discovers that the abductor is a photographer, Carl Wade, who took photographs at Amy's school the week she vanished. Mulder's belief in Lucy's empathic abilities jeopardizes his relationship with local authorities even as Lucy's powers endanger her very life.

58. "Nisei" Written by Chris Carter, Howard Gordon, and Frank Spotnitz; Directed by David Nutter; airdate: November

24, 1995; *Guest Cast:* Stephen McHattie (Assassin); Raymond J. Barry (Senator Richard Matheson); Robert Ito (Dr. Ishimaru); Tom Braidwood, Dean Haglund, Bruce Harwood (The Lone Gunmen); Steven Williams (X); Gillian Barber (Penny); Brendan Beiser (Agent Pendrell); Lottie Holloway (Corrine Koslo); Diane (Tori Triolo); Paul McLean, Yasuo Sakurai.

Mulder purchases a video of an alien autopsy, one which he believes to be authentic. The video's producer has been murdered, execution-style, but Mulder apprehends an Asian agent, fluent in the martial arts, leaving the producer's premises. When the assassin is released because of diplomatic immunity, Mulder and Scully attempt to solve the case from another angle, questioning a UFO abductee named Betsy Hagopian (a member of MUFON) and seeking the assistance of the Lone Gunmen. With the help of several fellow abductees, some of whom are dying of an unknown form of cancer, Scully starts to recollect her own abduction experience even as Mulder follows the trail to a UFO recovered from the ocean.

59. "731" Written by Frank Spotnitz; Directed by Rob Bowman; airdate: December 1, 1995; *Guest Cast:* Steven Williams (X); Stephen McHattie (Assassin); William B. Davis (Cigarette Smoking Man); Robert Ito (Dr. Ishimaru); Colin Cunningham (Escalante); Don S. Williams (First Elder); Brendan Beiser (Agent Pendrell); Michael Puttonen (Conductor).

Mulder follows an alien corpse (in a body bag) to a train. Though "X" warns Scully to keep Mulder from boarding the vehicle at all costs, Mulder jumps the train, already in motion. What he finds aboard is the same "dissection" lab he saw on the alien autopsy video. Unfortunately, an assassin is aboard the train as well ... along with several tons of explosives. Meanwhile, the details of Scully's abduction and the work of a Japanese scientist come to the forefront of the investigation.

60. "Revelations" Written by Kim Newton; Directed by David Nutter; airdate: De-

cember 15, 1995; *Guest Cast:* R. Lee Ermey (False Prophet); Kevin Zegers (Kevin Crider); Sam Bottoms (Mr. Crider); Kenneth Welsh (Simon Gates/Frau/The Devil); Michael Berryman (Owen Lee Jarvis); Hayley Tyson (Mrs. Crider); Lesley Ewan (Corina Maywald) Fulvio Cecere (Priest); Nicole Robert (Mrs. Tynes).

Mulder and Scully discover a preadolescent boy who bears stigmata, wounds mimicking those of Jesus Christ during the Crucifixion. It becomes imperative to protect the boy from a predator who may be a nutcase overcome with Jerusalem Syndrome, the belief that he is a messianic force, or the devil himself. The boy's father and a bald protector, an Incorruptible, claim that the "Great War," Armageddon, is in progress, and warn Scully to save the child lest evil take the day. Scully comes to believe that God is operating through her, his messenger, but to find the truth she must go full circle, and overcome the skeptical objections of Agent Mulder.

61. "War of the Coprophages" Written by Darin Morgan; Directed by Kim Manners; airdate: January 5, 1996; *Guest Cast:* Bobbie Phillips (Dr. Bambi Berenbaum); Raye Birk (Dr. Eckerly); Dion Anderson (Sheriff); Bill Dow (Dr. Newton); Alex Bruhanski (Dr. Bugger); Ken Kramer (Dr. Ivanov); Alan Buckley, Nicole Parker, Tyler Labine (Kids in Basement).

Miller's Grove, MA, has a bad bug problem — it is teeming with cockroaches, and murderous cockroaches to boot! Mulder is in town to investigate reports of lights in the sky, but the roach attacks soon merit his full attention. Although Scully poo-poos the idea of malevolent cockroaches, Mulder learns of a top secret department of agriculture entomological experiment in town examining a new breed of roaches. More curious than that, evidence indicates that the cockroaches are metallic ... perhaps alien probes sent from another world, another intelligence, to examine this planet.

62. "Syzygy" Written by Chris Carter; Directed by Rob Bowman; airdate: January

26, 1996; *Guest Cast:* Dana Wheeler-Nicholson (Detective White); Wendy Benson (Margie Kleinjan); Lisa Robin Kelly (Terri Roberts); Garry Davey (Spitz); Denalda Williams (Zirinka); Gabrielle Miller (Brenda); Ryan Reynolds ("Boom" Jay De Boom); Tim Dixon (Dr. R.W. Godfrey); Ryk Brown (Minister); Jeremy Radick (Young Man); Russell Porter (Scott Simmone).

Three popular high school boys have died in the little town of Comity in as many months, and local authorities suspect the activities of a satanic cult. Scully and Mulder look into the matter and Scully immediately suspects that two teenage cheerleaders, Terry Roberts and Margie Kleinjan, are involved, since they both witnessed the most recent death. The two girls are also present when a basketball player who offended them is mysteriously crushed by the gymnasium's retractable bleachers. A local astrologist believes the girls have received unusual powers from a planetary alignment of Mars, Mercury, and Uranus which occurs once every 84 years ... an alignment which is also having an effect on Mulder and Scully ... who become, respectively, horny and snippy.

63. "Grotesque" Written by Howard Gordon; Directed by Kim Manners; airdate: February 2, 1996; *Guest Cast:* Levani (John Mostow); Kurtwood Smith (Bill Patterson); Greg Thirloway (Agent Nemhauser); Susan Bain (Agent Sheherlis); Kasper Michaels (Young Agent); Zoran Vukelic (Model).

An art model is murdered by a sicko serial killer who has an obsession with gargoyles. This is the latest killing in a three-year spree, and the murderer, Mostow, is finally apprehended by Mulder's judgmental and hard-driven mentor, Bill Patterson. When a copycat starts to murder men in the same manner as Mostow, Mulder delves deep into the mind of the psychopath to ferret out the truth. Was the killer possessed by a demonic force that has found a new host, or is it just a madman whose madness has become infectious?

64. "Piper Maru" Written by Frank Spotnitz and Chris Carter; Directed by Rob Bowman; airdate: February 9, 1996; *Guest Cast:* Nicholas Lea (Krycek); Robert Clothier (Commander Johanson); Jo Bates (Geraldine); Ari Solomon (Bernard Gauthier); Kimberly Unger (Joan Gauthier); Morris Panych (Gray Haired Man); Stephen E. Miller (Wayne Morgan); Paul Batten (Doctor); Lenno Britos (Luis Cardinal); Tegan Moss (Young Dana Scully); Robert F. Maier (Pilot); Russell Ferrier (Medic); Rochelle Greenwood (Waitress); Tom Scholte (Young Johanson).

The crew of a French salvage vessel, the *Piper Maru*, is exposed to deadly levels of radiation, and Mulder suspects it was caused by close proximity to a sunken U.F.O. One French sailor, however, has become possessed by an alien entity, the black cancer, which controls him completely. While Mulder traces clues to the salvage office headquarters and eventually Hong Kong, Scully investigates a fifty-year-old case involving the submarine *Zeus Faber*, which was also seeking the same downed U.F.O. Krycek reappears unexpectedly, and Skinner is shot by the same man who killed Scully's sister.

65. "Apocrypha" Written by Frank Spotnitz and Chris Carter; Directed by Kim Manners; airdate: February 16, 1996; *Guest Cast:* John Neville (Well-Manicured Man); William B. Davis (Cigarette Smoking Man); Tom Braidwood, Dean Haglund, Bruce Harwood (Lone Gunmen); Nicholas Lea (Krycek); Kevin McNulty (Agent Fuller); Barry Levy (Navy Doctor); Dmitri Chepovetsky (Government Man); Sue Mathew (Agent Caleca); Don S. Williams (Elder # 1); Lenno Britos (Hispanic Man); Frances Flanagan (Nurse); Brendan Beiser (Agent Pendrell); Peter Scoular (Sick Crewman); Jeff Chives (Armed Man); Martin Evans (Major Domo).

With a captured Krycek in tow, Mulder attempts to retrieve the defense department intelligence disc on U.F.O.s. Meanwhile, Scully protects the wounded Skinner, convinced that his shooting was no random act of violence, but part of the larger conspiracy. Possessed by the black cancer entity, Krycek escapes from custody, and Mulder meets with the Well-Manicured Man in Central Park. Now there is a race to see which faction will gain possession of the downed U.F.O. first, its alien pilot (inside Krycek as the black cancer) or Mulder and Scully.

66. "Pusher" Written by Vince Gilligan; Directed by Rob Bowman; airdate: February 23, 1996; *Guest Cast:* Robert Wisden (Robert Patrick Modell/"Pusher"); Vic Polizos (Frank Burst); Steve Bacic (Collins); Roger Cross (SWAT Lieutenant); Brent Sheppard (Prosecutor); Don Mackay (Judge); D. Neil Mark (Kerber); Meredith Bain Woodward (Attorney); Julia Arkos (Holly); Ernie Foort (Lobby Guard); Darren Lucas (SWAT Cop).

A man called "Pusher" has the telepathic ability to place thoughts and suggestions into the minds of others, a talent he has utilized to commit murder for hire some fourteen times. After he telepathically forces a police officer to drive straight into an oncoming truck, Mulder and Scully begin to hunt this unusual Ronin, this samurai with no master. An FBI sting goes wrong when Pusher "suggests" that an agent immolate himself, but the criminal is captured despite the tragedy. Pusher escapes legal justice by mentally influencing the judge, leaving Mulder to face a deadly showdown at the hospital with the malevolent mental warrior.

67. "Teso Dos Bichos" Written by John Shiban; Directed by Kim Manners; airdate: March 8, 1996; *Guest Cast:* Vic Trevino (Dr. Bilak); Janne Mortil (Mona Wussner); Gordon Tootoosis (Shaman); Tom McBeath (Dr. Lewton); Ron Suave (Mr. Decker); Alan Robertson (Roosevelt); Garrison Chrisjohn (Dr. Winters).

In Ecuador, an archaeological dig uncovers an ancient urn which contains the remains of a female shaman, and is therefore sacred to the Indian tribe nearby. The artifact is removed to the United States despite a curse which states that those who remove the Amaru urn will be devoured by the spirit of the jaguar. Mulder and Scully head to the Boston Museum of Natural History, where the bones are displayed, after the mysterious death of a

doctor on the project. When the death toll starts to mount, and rats start to evacuate the museum by the hundreds, Scully and Mulder are forced to argue: Are politics behind these murders, or are they seeing an ancient curse played out in a modern American city?

68. "Hell Money" Written by Jeffrey Vlaming; Directed by Tucker Gates; airdate: March 29, 1996; *Guest Cast:* B.D. Wong (Detective Chao); Lucy Alexis Liu (Kim); Michael Yama (Hsin); James Hong (Doctor); Doug Abrahams (Detective Neary); Ellie Harvie (OPO Staffer); Derek Lowe (Johnny Low); Donald Pong (Vase Man); Diana Ha (Dr. Wu); Stephen M.D. Chang (Large Man); Paul Wong (Wiry Man).

In Chinatown, a man who is burned alive in a furnace scrawls the legend "ghost" in Chinese on the wall. Mulder and Scully investigate the murder, a puzzle which starts with a torn piece of "hell money" found at the scene, an offering at the Chinese festival of the hungry ghost. The hunt ends not with spectral visitors, however, but with a corrupt gambling ring in which the poor end up losing their precious body parts to a surgeon who sells them on the black market.

69. "Jose Chung's 'From Outer Space'" Written by Darin Morgan; Directed by Rob Bowman; airdate: April 12, 1996; *Guest Cast:* Charles Nelson Reilly (Jose Chung); William Lucking (Rocky); Daniel Quinn (Lieutenant Shaeffer); Jesse Ventura (Man in Black); Sarah Sawatsky (Crissy); Jason Gaffney (Harold); Alex Diakun (Dr. Fingers); Larry Musser (Detective Manners); Allan Zinyk (Blaine); Michael Dobson (Sgt. Hynek); Mina E. Mina (Dr. Hand); Jaap Broeker (The Stupendous Yappi); Alex Trebek (Himself).

Two teenagers in Klass County, Washington, are imperiled by dueling aliens on the way home from their first date. A popular author, Jose Chung, interviews Scully about the case. She and Mulder have a difference of opinion about the truth: Mulder thinks it was a genuine alien abduction and Scully believes it was just date rape and ensuing posttraumatic stress. A witness to the abduction named Rocky claims that a third alien, one from the Earth's molten core and named Lord Kimbote, was involved ... as were two unearthly Men in Black.

70. "Avatar" Written by Howard Gordon; From a story by David Duchovny and Howard Gordon; Directed by James Charleston; airdate: April 26, 1996; *Guest Cast:* Tom Mason (Detective Waltos); Jennifer Hetrick (Sharon Skinner); William B. Davis (Cigarette Smoking Man); Amanda Tapping (Carina Sales); Malcolm Stewart (Agent Bonnecaze); Brendan Beiser (Agent Pendrell).

On the verge of signing divorce papers which will end his seventeen-year marriage, Skinner meets a beautiful woman in a hotel bar and goes to bed with her. The next morning, he awakes to find her dead in bed beside him, and he claims to remember nothing. Scully conducts an autopsy on the dead woman, a prostitute, and discovers a strange luminescent glow around her mouth and nose. Meanwhile, Skinner has persistent visions of an old woman in a red slicker ... a woman who Mulder believes is a succubus.

71. "Quagmire" Written by Kim Newton; Directed by Kim Manners; airdate: May 3, 1996; *Guest Cast:* Chris Ellis (Sheriff); Timothy Webber (Dr. Faraday); R. Nelson Brown (Ansel Bray); Mark Acheson (Bertram); Tyler Labine (Stoner); Nicole Parker (Chick); Terrance Leigh (Snorkel Dude).

On a crisp Saturday morning, Mulder and Scully head out to Heuvelman's Lake, GA, to investigate the recent disappearance of a federal forestry officer. Mulder thinks "Big Blue," a prehistoric sea monster, may be responsible, but Scully believes a boating accident is more likely. As more bodies surface on the lake, and Scully's pet dog is devoured, the agents head out on the water in a nocturnal attempt to confirm the existence of Big Blue. As night falls, Mulder and Scully's boat is smashed by a powerful underwater entity, and Mulder and Scully seek escape on a tiny rock in the middle of the lake.

Note: This episode features the second appearance of the "Chick" and the "Stoner,"

two characters who survived tragedy in "War of the Coprophages," only to encounter another X-file in "Quagmire."

72. "Wetwired" Written by Mat Beck; Directed by Rob Bowman; airdate: May 10, 1996; *Guest Cast:* Sheila Larken (Mrs. Scully); William B. Davis (Cigarette Smoking Man); Tom Braidwood, Dean Haglund, Bruce Harwood (The Lone Gunmen); Steven Williams (X); Linden Banks, Tim Henry.

A man in Braddocks Height, Maryland, brutally murders five people whom he mistakenly believes are the same person: a Bosnian dictator dubbed by the media as the "modern Hitler." A mysterious source from the government asks Mulder to investigate, lest more people be killed, so he and Scully start the task. They find that the perpetrator has a vast collection of videotapes, and Scully wonders if there is a connection between what's on the TV and an impulse to commit murder. After another murder is committed by another seemingly average person, Mulder finds a strange device at the cable box which is emitting an electronic signal ... a signal that is now adversely affecting an increasingly paranoid Agent Scully.

73. "Talitha Cumi" Written by Chris Carter; From a story by David Duchovny and Chris Carter; Directed by R.W. Goodwin; airdate: May 17, 1996; *Guest Cast:* William B. Davis (Cigarette Smoking Man); Steven Williams (X); Peter Donat (Bill Mulder); Melinda McGraw (Melissa Scully); Roy Thinnes (Jeremiah Smith); Brian Thompson (Alien Bounty Hunter); Hrothgar Mathews (Galen Muntz); Rebecca Toolan (Mrs. Mulder); Stephen Dimopoulos (Detective); John McLaren (Doctor); Cam Cronin (Paramedic); Bonnie Hay (Night Nurse).

Mulder learns of a secret connection between the Cigarette Smoking Man and his mother. When Mrs. Mulder has a stroke and only little hope of surviving, Mulder unexpectedly finds hope in his pursuit of Jeremiah Smith, an alien refugee with seemingly miraculous healing powers. Now Mulder must catch Jeremiah Smith before the alien bounty hunter catches up with him.

• *Fourth Season (1996–1997)*

74. "Herrenvolk" Written by Chris Carter; Directed by R.W. Goodwin; airdate: October 4, 1996; *Guest Cast:* Roy Thinnes (Jeremiah Smith); Brian Thompson (Alien Bounty Hunter); William B. Davis (Cigarette Smoking Man); Steven Williams (X); Laurie Holden (Marie); Rebecca Toolan (Mrs. Mulder); Brendan Beiser (Agent Pendrell); Garvin Cross, Morris Panych.

The shapeshifting alien bounty hunter has returned to Earth to hunt down and kill Jeremiah Smith, the alien man with the miraculous healing powers. Meanwhile, Mulder's mother hovers near death, and Jeremiah Smith takes Mulder to a bee farm which Smith claims is part of the grand colonization scheme. At the same time, Scully discovers that the conspiracy is tagging and cataloguing the American populace through protein differentials in smallpox vaccinations. X is set-up and killed by murderous colleagues.

75. "Home" Written by Glen Morgan and James Wong; Directed by Kim Manners; airdate: October 11, 1996; *Guest Cast:* Tucker Smallwood (Sheriff Andy Taylor); Chris Nelson Norris, Adrian Hughes, John Trottier (The Peacock Brothers); Karin Konoval (Mrs. Peacock); Sebastian Spence (Barney Pastor); Judith Maxie (Mrs. Taylor); Kenny James (Radiologist); Lachlan Murdock (Right Fielder); Neil Denis (Catcher); Cory Fry (Batter); Douglas Smith (Pitcher).

A dead baby, apparently afflicted with massive birth deformities, is unearthed in the quiet town of Home, PA. Scully and Mulder discover that the baby was buried alive and try to question the residents nearest the crime scene, a family called the Peacocks. But this is one weird brood: three mutant brothers guard their crazy old mother, an amputee, who also happens to be the progenitor of the boy's offspring. In infiltrating the isolated, rural Peacock residence, Mulder and Scully find themselves in mortal danger from this feral, animalistic family who fear that their territory has been invaded.

76. "Teliko" Written by Howard Gordon; Directed by James Charleston; airdate: October 18, 1996; *Guest Cast:* Carl Lumbly (Marcus Duff); Willie Amakye (Samuel Aboah); Laurie Holden (Marita Covarrubias); Brendan Beiser (Agent Pendrell); Zakes Mokae (Minister); Bob Morrisey (Dr. Bruin); Danny Wattley (First Officer); Maxine Guess (Flight Attendant); Bill Mackenzie (Bus Driver); Michael O'Shea (Lt. Madison).

Several black man have died in Philadelphia with a total depigmentation as the only indicator of what killed them. The CDC believes the deaths are a result of a new and deadly disease, and enlist Scully to prove the theory but Mulder once again resorts to examining "extreme" possibilities. In this situation, he suspects an African man is actually using paralyzing thorns to immobilize his prey and then drain their pituitary glands. The creature is called a Teliko, and it is a mythical beast of West Africa that has now set its sights on Mulder.

77. "Unruhe" Written by Vince Gilligan; Directed by Rob Bowman; airdate: October 27, 1996; *Guest Cast:* Pruitt Taylor Vince (Gerald Schnauz); Sharon Alexander (Mary Le Fonte); William MacDonald (Trott); Ron Chartier (Inspector).

In Traverse City, Michigan, a young woman stops at a drug store to have her passport photograph taken. She is abducted by a deranged killer immediately afterwards, yet her photo (taken before the kidnappings) shows her in mortal danger ... surrounded by tiny monstrous demons. Scully and Mulder look into the case and are shocked when the victim is returned — lobotomized. The killer strikes again and again — finally capturing Scully and preparing to lobotomize her so as to free her from the restless demons, the "howlers," in her mind.

78. "The Field Where I Died" Written by Glen Morgan and James Wong; Directed by Rob Bowman; airdate: November 3, 1996; *Guest Cast:* Kristen Cloke (Melissa Reedell Ephesian/Sarah Kavanaugh); Michael Massee (Vernon Ephesian); Doug Abrahams (Harbaugh); Anthony Harrison (Riggins).

Scully and Mulder join an ATF raid to shut down the temple of the seven stars, a cult led by the megalomaniacal prophet Vernon Ephesian. Unexpectedly, Mulder finds a personal connection with one of Ephesian's seven wives, a woman suffering from multiple personality disorder who claims to have knowledge of Mulder from a past life. In particular, Mulder comes to believe that he was a Confederate soldier during the Civil War and that Ephesian's wife, Melissa, was his nurse and soulmate. In that life, the lovers died apart because of the War Between the States, and Mulder is afraid that such a tragic separation is his destiny in life after life.

79. "Sanguinarium" Written by Valerie Mayhew and Vivian Mayhew; Directed by Kim Manners; airdate: November 10, 1996; *Guest Cast:* John Juliani (Dr. Lloyd); Arlene Mazerolle (Dr. Shannon); Richard Beymer (Dr. Franklin); Paul Raskin (Dr. Amanpour); Gregory Thirloway (Dr. Kaplan); Martin Evans (Dr. Hartman); Marie Stillin (Dr. Sanford).

A chi-chi plastic surgeon claims he was possessed when he murdered a patient on his table. Scully and Mulder investigate the doctor and his clinic, and reluctantly come to the conclusion that witchcraft is somehow involved in this and other recent deaths. When their prime suspect in the case dies, apparently through witchcraft or other occult means, Mulder and Scully realize they need to rethink the case.

80. "Musings of a Cigarette Smoking Man" Written by Glen Morgan; Directed by James Wong; airdate: November 17, 1996; *Guest Cast:* William B. Davis (Cigarette Smoking Man); Morgan Weisser (Lee Harvey Oswald); Chris Owens (Young Cigarette Smoking Man); Donnelly Rhodes (General); Tom Braidwood, Bruce Harwood (Lone Gunmen); Jerry Hardin (Deep Throat); Dan Zukovic (Agent); Peter Hanlon (Aide); Dean Aylesworth (Young Bill Mulder); Paul Jarrett (James Earl Ray); David Fredericks (Director); Laurie Murdock (Lydon).

The Lone Gunmen recount the (possibly apocryphal) life story of the Cigarette Smoking Man. Apparently, his father was a Soviet sympathizer who was executed for treason, and his mother died before he was even a year old. As he grew, the Cigarette Smoking Man became a dark agent of conspiracies, assassinating JFK and Martin Luther King Jr. But under a lifetime of seemingly evil deeds beats the heart of an intensely lonely man, and a struggling writer who just wants to get published.

81. "Tunguska" Written by Frank Spotnitz and Chris Carter; Directed by Kim Manners; airdate: November 24, 1996; *Guest Cast:* William B. Davis (Cigarette Smoking Man); Nicholas Lea (Alex Krycek); Laurie Holden (Marie Covarrubias); John Neville (The Well-Manicured Man); Brendan Beiser (Agent Pendrell); Fritz Weaver (Senator Sorenson); Malcolm Stewart (Dr. Sachs); David Bloom (Stress Man); Campbell Lane (Chairman); Stefan Arngrim (Prisoner); Brent Stait (Timothy Mayhew).

During a raid against an extreme-right militia group, Alex Krycek is apprehended by Mulder and Scully. Krycek leads the duo to a Russian diplomat who has carried a black rock into the U.S., a meteor four billion years old, perhaps from Mars, and containing a deadly alien black bacteria. Mulder flies with Krycek to Tunguska, Russia, to the meteor crash site, while Scully and Skinner are requested to provide testimony about the matter before Congress. In Russia, Mulder is apprehended by slavers and exposed to the deadly alien bacteria while imprisoned at a primitive gulag turned research base.

82. "Terma" Written by Frank Spotnitz and Chris Carter; Directed by Rob Bowman; airdate: December 1, 1996; *Guest Cast:* William B. Davis (Cigarette Smoking Man); Nicholas Lea (Alex Krycek); John Neville (The Well-Manicured Man); Stefan Arngrim (Prisoner); Jan Rubes (Vassily Peskow); Fritz Weaver (Senator Sorenson); Brendan Beiser (Agent Pendrell); Campbell Lane (Committee Chairman Romine); Brent Stait (Mayhew); Dr. Bonita Sayre (Jessica Schreier).

After his exposure to the black cancer organisms in Tunguska, Russia, Mulder plots his escape from the gulag. Meanwhile, Scully investigates the murder of a prominent virologist, for whom the meteorite chunk was originally intended. While Scully is held in contempt of Congress for her refusal to reveal Mulder's whereabouts, Mulder returns to the United States. Once there, Scully and Mulder team up and head for Terma, North Dakota, where a convenient accident has been prepared to destroy all evidence of the meteorite and the deadly virus organism it contains inside.

83. "Paper Hearts" Written by Vince Gilligan; Directed by Rob Bowman; airdate: December 15, 1996; *Guest Cast:* Tom Noonan (John Lee Roche); Rebecca Toolan (Mrs. Mulder); Byrne Piven (Robert); Vanessa Morely (Samantha Mulder); Carly McKillip (Caitlin Ross).

Mulder has a dream in which a red pointer leads him to the dead body of a young girl and, sadly, reality soon mirrors his dream. He has found the fourteenth victim of John Lee Roche, a serial killer he put away years earlier. Now, armed with a book of 16 paper hearts cut from the blouses of each of Roche's victims, Mulder tries to find the last two dead girls, who have never even been known about. A shocking revelation occurs as Roche informs Mulder that Samantha, his own sister — presumed abducted all this time — was one of his last two victims.

84. "El Mundo Gira" Written by John Shiban; Directed by Tucker Gates; airdate: January 12, 1997; *Guest Cast:* Ruben Blades (Agent Lozano); Raymond Cruz (Elario Buente); Pamela Diaz (Maria Dorantes); Jose Yenque (Soledad Buente); Lillian Hurst (Flakita); Robert Thurston (Dr. Larry Steen); Simi (Gabrielle); Mike Kopsa (Rick Culver).

After a blinding flash of light, a strange rain falls on the migrant workers' camp in San Joaquin Valley, California. The people living there believe that *el chupacabra*, a goatsucker, killed several goats and a beautiful young woman, but Scully and Mulder come to a different conclusion: people are dying of an aggressive fungal infection which is being spread by a compromised migrant worker. Mulder suspects that space debris, extraterrestrial matter, is behind the development of this modern day Typhoid Mary.

85. "Leonard Betts" Written by Vince Gilligan, John Shiban and Frank Spotnitz; Directed by Kim Manners; airdate: January 26, 1997; *Guest Cast:* Paul McCrane (Leonard Morris Betts/Albert Tanner/Truelove); Marjorie Lovett (Elaine Tanner); Jennifer Clement (Michele Wilkes); Bill Dow (Charles Burks); Sean Campbell (Local Cop); Dave Hurtubise (Pathologist); Peter Bryant (Uniformed Cop); Laura Sadiq (Female EMT); J. Douglas Stewart (Male EMT); Brad Loree (Security Guard).

Paramedic Leonard Betts is decapitated in a catastrophic ambulance accident in Pittsburgh, PA. Later the same night, his headless body disappears from the morgue and the attendant is knocked unconscious by somebody. Scully and Mulder investigate and Mulder explores the bizarre hypothesis that Betts is a headless corpse who is somehow alive and walking. Scully gathers evidence which suggests Betts is riddled with cancer, and that somehow he is using the sickness to regenerate body parts. To Scully's horror, Bett's ability to pinpoint cancer in others is turned on her.

86. "Never Again" Written by Glen Morgan and James Wong; Directed by Rob Bowman; airdate: February 2, 1997; *Guest Cast:* Rodney Rowland (Ed Jerse); Igor Morozov (Pudovkin); Carla Stewart (Judge); Barry Hortin (Bartender); Jan Bailey Mattie (Ms. Hadden); Rita Bozi (Ms. Vansen); Marilyn Chin (Mrs. Shima-Tsuno); Jillian Fargey (Kay Schilling); B.J. Harison (Hannah); Jay Donahue (Detective Gouveia); Ian Robison (Detective Smith).

After a long night of drinking and the official dissolution of his failed marriage, loser Ed Jerse gets a tattoo on impulse. Unfortunately, the tattoo starts to speak to him, compelling him to commit violent acts. While Mulder is on vacation at Graceland (on what he terms a "spiritual" journey), Scully runs into Ed and, feeling rebellious, gets a tattoo herself. What neither tattoo recipient realizes is that the tattoo ink contains ergot, a dangerous substance with psychotic and hallucinogenic properties.

Note: An uncredited Jodie Foster provides the voice of the malevolent tattoo in this episode.

87. "Memento Mori" Written by Chris Carter, Vince Gilligan, John Shiban and Frank Spotnitz; Directed by Rob Bowman; airdate: February 9, 1997; *Guest Cast:* William B. Davis (Cigarette Smoking Man); Sheila Larken (Mrs. Scully); David Lovgren (Kurt Crawford); Gillian Barber (Penny Northern); Tom Braidwood, Dean Hagland, Bruce Harwood (The Lone Gunmen); Morris Panych (Gray Haired Man); Sean Allen (Dr. Kevin Scanlon); Julie Bono (Woman).

Mulder visits Scully at Holy Cross Hospital and she informs him that she has a nasopharyngeal tumor. Because of placement and type, this kind of cancer is inoperable and has a zero probability survival rate. Scully recalls that a group of UFO abductees she met the previous year contracted the same kind of tumor, after having removed a metal implant from the back of the neck. Scully learns that all the abductees have died of cancer, save for one ... who is now in the hospital on her last legs.

88. "Kaddish" Written by Howard Gordon; Directed by Kim Manners; airdate: February 16, 1997; *Guest Cast:* David Groh (Jacob Weiss); Channon Roe (Derek Banks); Justine Miceli (Ariel Weiss); David Wohl (Kenneth Unger); Harrison Coe (Isaac Luria); Jonathan Whitaker (Curt Brunjes); Timor Kocibilgiw (Tony); Jabin Litwiniec (Clinton); George Gordon (Detective); Murray Rabinovitch (1st Hasidic Man); David Freedman (Rabbi).

After an innocent Jewish storekeeper, Isaac Luria, is murdered in his store, a golem is animated to track down and destroy his killers. Scully and Mulder go to Brooklyn to investigate, but Scully suspects a hate crime, not a supernatural one. This theory seems especially applicable considering the hate groups who have targeted the Jews, as well Jacob Weiss's feelings of vengeance and hatred following the death of his son-in-law. When another murder occurs, Mulder feels the myth of the golem, a living being made of earth and clay, has been resurrected to bring about justice.

89. "Unrequited" Written by Howard Gordon and Chris Carter; Directed by James Charleston; airdate: February 23, 1997; *Guest Cast:* Scott Hylands (Bloch); Peter LaCroix (Nathaniel Teager); Ryan Michael (Agent Cameron Hill); Don McWilliams (Burkholder); Bill Agnew (General MacDougal); Mark Holden (Agent Chandler); Larry Musser (Markham); Lesley Ewan (Renee Davenport); Allan Franz (Dr. Keyser); William Nunn (Stefan); William Taylor (General Leitch).

Mulder, Scully, and Skinner must protect a top-ranked U.S. general against a bizarre opponent: a man who can seemingly make himself invisible to others. This assassin, a veteran himself, has a specific agenda in mind, and Scully and Mulder must discover what precisely it is before they lose their ward to the cloaked hitman's bullet. It all goes down at a very public event.

90. "Tempus Fugit" Written by Chris Carter and Frank Spotnitz; Directed by Rob Bowman; airdate: March 16, 1997; *Guest Cast:* Joe Spano (Millar); Tom O'Brien (Corporal Louis Frish); Scott Bellis (Max Fenig); Chilton Crane (Sharon Graffia); Brendan Beiser (Agent Pendrell); Greg Michaels, Rick Dobran, Robert Moloney, Jerry Schram.

A plane with abductee Max Fenig aboard is compromised in midair by a close-encounter with an unidentified craft. Scully and Mulder join the FAA investigation of the crash, even as an agent of the conspiracy takes steps to hide evidence of an assassin aboard the downed airliner ... an assassin who was out to silence Max forever and in the process retrieve some very classified stolen property. A closer examination of the crash brings to light evidence of the UFO "lost time" phenomenon, and a military air traffic controller, Frish, also comes forward to reveal the crash was not an accident. Meanwhile, Max's sister is abducted in his place and Mulder goes scuba diving to locate an alien ship which may have crashed underwater.

91. "Max" Written by Chris Carter and Frank Spotnitz; Directed by Kim Manners; airdate: March 23, 1997; *Guest Cast:* Joe Spano (Millar); Tom O'Brien (Corporal Louis Frish); Scott Bellis (Max Fenig); Chilton Crane (Sharon Graffia); Brendan Beiser (Agent Pendrell); Greg Michaels, Rick Dobran, Robert Moloney, Jerry Schram, David Palffy, Mark Wilson.

In pursuit of a submerged UFO, Mulder is chased and apprehended by the military. In Washington, Scully trades shots with a deadly assassin who killed Agent Pendrell while trying to silence Frish, the snitch who revealed the truth about downed air flight 549. The facts of the case take some bizarre turns when Sharon turns out to be a mental patient, not Max Fenig's sister, as she claimed. The key to this complex puzzle involves the theft of a radioactive object, a powerful energy source supposedly based on alien technology.

92. "Synchrony" Written by Howard Gordon and David Greenwalt; directed by James Charleston; airdate: April 13, 1997; *Guest Cast:* Joseph Fuqua (Jason Nicholls); Susan Lee Hoffman (Lisa Yanelli); Michael Fairman (Older Jason Nicholls); Jed Rees (Lucas Menand); Hiro Kanagawi (Dr. Yonechi); Jonathan Walker (Chuck Luckerman); Alison Matthews (Doctor); Norman Armour (Coroner); Patricia Iolette (Desk Clerk); Brent Chapman (Security Cop); Terry Arrowsmith (Uniformed Cop); Aurelo Di Nunzio (Detective).

At M.I.T. in Massachusetts an old man accosts two bickering students and warns one of them that he will die at precisely 11:46 P.M., when he is struck by a bus. The prediction comes true, and Mulder and Scully head to the scene to discover who the old man was and how his captor, a campus security man, was suddenly and irrevocably frozen to death. Soon a visiting Asian scientist in the field of

cryobiology meets the same grim fate, and Scully and Mulder realize he has been fast-frozen by a compound which does not yet exist ... and could not possibly exist for at least ten years. The bizarre answer to this riddle is related to time travel: the old man is one of the bickering students, come back from the future to prevent the creation of a freezing compound and the discovery of time travel ... two factors in the creation of a world without either history or hope.

93. "Small Potatoes" Written by Vince Gilligan; Directed by Cliff Bole; airdate: April 20, 1997; *Guest Cast:* Darin Morgan (Edward H. Van Blundht); Christine Cavanaugh (Amanda Nelligan); Lee De Broux (Mr. Van Blundht).

In a small town, four babies in different families are born with tails! This oddity means that somehow, some way, the children all stem from the same father. Scully and Mulder look into the matter, discovering that blue collar janitor and schmuck Eddie Van Blundht can, via a bizarre muscle condition, alter his features to become *any* man and thus impregnate *any* woman. Soon, Van Blundht has escaped from custody, turned into an exact duplicate of Mulder, and set about to get the luscious Scully into the sack.

94. "Zero Sum" Written by Howard Gordon and Frank Spotnitz; Directed by Kim Manners; airdate: April 27, 1997; *Guest Cast:* William B. Davis (Cigarette Smoking Man); Laurie Holden (Maria Covarrubias); Nicolle Nattrass (Misty); Paul McLean (Special Agent Koontz); Fred Keating (Detective Ray Thomas); Allan Gray (Entomologist); Addison Ridge (Bespectacled Guy); Don S. Williams (1st Elder); Lisa Stewart (Jane Brady); Barry Greene (Dr. Emile Linzer); Christopher Newton (Photo Technician); Morris Panych (Gray Haired Man).

Working under orders from the Cigarette Smoking Man, Skinner is coerced into cleaning up a crime scene where bees have killed an innocent postal employee. The cover-up is blown, however, when the investigating police detective is found murdered, execution-style, shortly after Skinner poses as Mulder to dispose of the forensic evidence. Mulder learns of the postal worker's bizarre death and starts to look into the matter, further complicating Skinner's position. At stake here is not just Scully's life, the reason Skinner is involved in the first place, but the future of humankind, because the agents of the conspiracy are using bees as a delivery system for a deadly plague.

95. "Elegy" Written by John Shiban; Directed by James Charleston; airdate: May 4, 1997; *Guest Cast:* Steven M. Porter (Harold Spuler); Nancy Fish (Nurse Innes); Alex Bruhanski, Sydney Lassick, Daniel Kamin.

The owner of Angie's Midnight Bowl in Washington, D.C., is surprised to see a bloodied woman in pain and dying in the machinery of one of his lanes. Strangely, the victim was not really there — she was an apparition and her violent murder occurred elsewhere. Scully and Mulder look into the case and Mulder soon believes that the bowling alley owner saw a death omen or a wraith. The answer to this unusual puzzle leads the duo from the F.B.I. to a mentally-impaired autistic man named Harold who has spent most of his life suffering from severe obsessive-compulsive egodystonia ... but the case unexpectedly becomes personal for a sick Scully when she starts to see premonitory visions of the next murder victims.

96. "Demons" Written by R.W. Goodwin; Directed by Kim Manners; airdate: May 11, 1997; *Guest Cast:* Jay Avocone (Detective Curtis); Mike Nussbaum (Dr. Charles Goldstein); Chris Owens (Young Cigarette Smoking Man); Rebecca Toolan (Mrs. Mulder); Andrew Johnston (Medical Examiner); Vanessa Morley (Young Samantha); Eric Breke (Admitting Officer); Rebecca Harker (Housekeeper); Shelley Adam (Young Mrs. Mulder); Dean Aylesworth (Young Mr. Mulder); Alex Haythorne (Young Fox Mulder).

After dreaming of his sister, Samantha, and the night she was abducted by aliens, Mulder wakes up in a motel room in Rhode Island with blood all over his clothes. Scully joins him and tries to help him sort things

out, but he has no memory of the past weekend and worse, two rounds have been fired from his weapon. The partners backtrack the weekend and find themselves at the house where the Mulder family summered years ago ... and where two people have been shot dead by Mulder's gun. Mulder is arrested by local authorities as Scully's attempt to clear his name leads to a radical and invasive psychological memory regression therapy.

97. "Gethsemane" Written by Chris Carter; Directed by R.W. Goodwin; airdate: May 18, 1997; *Guest Cast:* John Finn (Michael Kritschgau); Matthew Walker (Arlinsky); James Sutorious (Babcock); Sheila Larken (Mrs. Scully); Pat Skipper (Bill Scully); John Oliver (Rolston); Charles Cioffi (Section Chief Blevins); Steve Makaj (Ostelhoff); Nancy Kerr (Agent Hedin); Barry W. Levy (Vitagliano); Arnie Walters (Father McCue); Rob Freeman (Detective Rempulski); Craig Brunanski (Saw Operator).

After identifying Mulder's body, Scully goes before a panel headed by section chief Blevins and reports on the illegitimacy of Mulder's (now terminated) life work. She recounts the events leading up to Mulder's self-inflicted death. It all started when an alien body was found frozen in the ice in the Arctic, and Mulder went up to Canada to report on the validity of the discovery. Mulder and Scully soon came to believe that the alien was part of a hoax, and Mulder's faith was shattered when he learned that he was an unknowing dupe who has been fed misinformation about the existence of aliens ... so as to hide more mundane government secrets.

● *Fifth Season (1997–1998)*

98. "Redux" Written by Chris Carter; Directed by R.W. Goodwin; airdate: November 2, 1997; *Guest Cast:* William B. Davis (Cigarette Smoking Man); Charles Cioffi (Section Chief Blevins); John Finn (Michael Kritschgau); Tom Braidwood, Dean Haglund, Bruce Harwood (The Lone Gunmen); Steve Makaj (Ostelhoff); Ken Camroux (Senior

Agent); Barry W. Levy (Vitagliano); Julia Arkos (Holly); Don S. Williams (Elder).

Mulder is believed dead of a self-inflicted gun wound, but his death has been staged by Mulder and Scully so as to expose the men behind the "Truth" concerning Scully's cancer and the existence of extraterrestrial life. Mulder pierces the conspiracy's lair at the department of defense with Kritschgau, the man who alerted him to the hoax in the first place, and with Level 4 clearance Mulder goes in search of a cure for Scully's cancer. Meanwhile, Dana begins to suspect that Skinner is somehow a part of the conspiracy. Kritschgau tells Mulder his version of the truth: an overspending, out-of-control military industrial complex invented the UFO story as part of its plan to divert America's attention away from military spending and a complex DNA tagging program.

99. "Redux II" Written by Chris Carter; Directed by Kim Manners; airdate: November 9, 1997; *Guest Cast:* William B. Davis (Cigarette Smoking Man); Charles Cioffi (Section Chief Blevins); Sheila Larken (Mrs. Scully); Pat Skipper (Bill Scully); Megan Leitch (Samantha Mulder); Tom Braidwood, Dean Haglund, Bruce Harwood (The Lone Gunmen); John Finn (Michael Kritschgau); Brent Sheppard (Doctor); Robert Wright (Dr. Zuckerman); Ken Camroux (Senior Agent); Don S. Williams (Elder); Arnie Walters (Father McCue).

Scully is in the ICU dying from cancer and Mulder's cure (stolen from the D.O.D. basement) needs to be deciphered if it is be useful to her. Mulder meets with Cigarette Smoking Man, who provides him the key to save Scully: a microchip in ionized water which will stop the spread of the disease. To further gain Mulder's trust, Cigarette Smoking Man arranges for Fox to be reunited with his sister, Samantha ... who believes that the Cigarette Smoking Man is her father. But even as Mulder is offered a job by his worst enemy, all is not as it seems, and Scully's life hangs in the balance.

100. "Unusual Suspects" Written by

Vince Gilligan; Directed by Kim Manners; airdate: November 16, 1997; *Guest Cast:* Richard Belzer (Detective Munch); Signy Coleman (Holly/Susanne Modeski); Bruce Harwood, Tom Braidwood, Dean Haglund (The Lone Gunmen); Steven Williams (Mr. X); Chris Nelson Norris (SWAT Lieutenant); Glenn Williams (Officer); Stuart O'Connell (First SWAT Cop); Ken Hawryliw (Himself).

A flashback to the year 1989 reveals how Mulder came to know the Lone Gunmen. In this case, a communications and electronics show in Baltimore is the event which causes the three conspiracy nuts to join forces for the first time. A mysterious woman claims her daughter has been kidnapped by a psychotic boyfriend, but what she really wants from the three civilians is access to a department of defense file on her. The Lone Gunmen attempt to decode the computer file, evade the psychotic boyfriend, whom the beautiful Holly has identified as Fox Mulder, and stop the government from conducting a dangerous EBO (Engineered Biological Operation) utilizing Ergotimine Histamine gas against the people of Baltimore.

Note: This episode of the *X-Files* crosses over with the universe of the NBC drama *Homicide: Life on the Streets*, and features *Homicide* star Richard Belzer as Detective Munch.

101. "Detour" Written by Frank Spotnitz; Directed by Brett Dowler; airdate: November 23, 1997; *Guest Cast:* Coleen Flynn (Michelle); J.C. Wendel (Stonecypher); Scott Burkholder (Kinsley); Merrilyn Gann (Ms. Asekoff); Anthony Rapp (Jeff); Alfred E. Humphreys (Michael Asekoff); Tim Scholte (Michael Sloane); Tyler Thompson (Louis Asekoff); Simon Longsmore (Marty Fox).

On the way to a team building seminar in west Florida, Mulder and Scully join a strange investigation already in process. A survey team and a man out hunting have disappeared in the forest. Mulder thinks some kind of camouflaged creature is dwelling in the woods and that the attacks are a response to encroaching human development. Mulder is soon sure they are facing one of the legendary Moth Men, humans from the time of Ponce de Leon who have evolved into forest-dwelling hunters with natural camouflage and glowing red eyes.

102. "Post-Modern Prometheus" Written and directed by Chris Carter; airdate: November 30, 1997; *Guest Cast:* John O'Hurley (Dr. Pollidori); Pattie Tierce (Shania Berkowitz); Stewart Gale (Izzie Berkowitz); Chris Owens (The Great Mutato); Dana Grahame, Chris Giacoletti, Jean-Yves Hammel, Tracey Bell, Lloyd Berry, Miriam Smith, Xantha Radley, C. Ernest Harth.

Scully and Mulder go to small town America to investigate a woman's claim that she has twice been impregnated by a Cher-loving two-faced monster known as "The Great Mutato." The case takes them to a mad scientist who has unlocked the secrets of genetics and seems to have both the ability and the propensity to create monsters. But the truth, in this case, has to do with the heart of a monster who is not really a monster at all.

103. "A Christmas Carol" Written by Vince Gilligan, John Shiban and Frank Spotnitz; Directed by Peter Markle; airdate: December 7, 1997; *Guest Cast:* Sheila Larken (Mrs. Scully); Melinda McGraw (Melissa Scully); Pat Skipper (Bill Scully Jr.); Karri Turner (Tara Scully); John Pyper-Ferguson (Detective Kransky); Gerard Plunkett, Lauren Diewold (Emily); Patricia Dahlquist (Susan Chambliss); Rob Freeman, Eric Brecker (Dark Suited Man #1); Stephen Mendel (Dark Suited Man #2); Walter Marsh (Pathologist); Rebecca Collins (Young Melissa Scully); Joey Shea (Young Dana Scully); Ryan Decker (Young Bill Scully).

During a holiday vacation with the family, Scully receives a mysterious phone call from her dead sister telling her to help a special needs child named Emily. At first, Scully believes that the sickly child is somehow Melissa's, but she comes to realize that Emily is her own child, conceived ... or engineered ... during her abduction three years earlier. Scully initiates an investigation of Emily's fos-

ter parents and comes to think that Emily's mother was murdered for some nefarious purpose. When Emily's father is also murdered, Scully realizes that the agents of the conspiracy are involved and have a vested interest in Emily continuing an experimental treatment.

104. "Emily" Written by Vince Gilligan, John Shiban, and Frank Spotnitz; Directed by Kim Manners; airdate: December 13, 1997; *Guest Cast:* John Pyper-Ferguson (Detective Kransky); Sheila Larken (Mrs. Scully); Pat Skipper (Bill Scully); Karri Turner (Tara Scully); Rob Morrissey, Gerard Plunkett, Patricia Dahlquist (Susan Chambliss); Lauren Diewold (Emily); Tom Braidwood (Frohike); David Abbott (Judge Matthews); Sheila Patterson (Anna Fugazzi); Erick Brecker (Dark Suited Man #1); Stephen Mendel (Dark Suited Man #2); Tanya Huse (Medical Technician).

Mulder helps Scully adopt her biological daughter, Emily, and also confirms Dana's suspicion that the child is a result of genetic experiments conducted during her abduction. Now Mulder and Scully must dig through the layers of lies to determine why the conspiracy would create and then abandon Emily. When Emily becomes ill, Mulder and Scully learn she has the same toxic composition as alien creatures they have encountered before, which may indicate she is an (unsuccessful) attempt to create an alien-human hybrid. The presence of shapeshifters with murderous intentions further endanger Emily's life.

105. "Kitsunegari" Written by Vince Gilligan and Tim Minear; Directed by Daniel Sackheim; airdate: January 4, 1998; *Guest Cast:* Robert Wisden (Pusher/Modell); Diana Scarwid (Linda Bowman); Colleen Winton (Therapist); Scott Oughterson (Orderly); Donna Yamamoto (Asian Agent).

Modell, the "Pusher," is still alive, despite the fatal brain tumor which gives him his telepathic abilities. When Modell escapes from incarceration, Scully and Mulder must catch him before his mental power of suggestion claims any additional lives. Now, it seems, Modell is on a "kitsunegari," a fox (Fox Mulder) hunt.... Or is someone else responsible for the murder of the attorney who prosecuted Modell's case in 1996? The presence of a second pusher, a vengeful one with a purpose, is soon revealed.

106. "Schizogeny" Written by Jessica Scott and Mike Wollaeger; Directed by Ralph Hemecker; airdate: January 11, 1998; *Guest Cast:* Chad Lindberg (Bobby Rich); Sarah-Jane Redmond (Karin Matthews); Katharine Isabelly (Lisa); Bob Dawson (Phil Rich); Cynde Harmon (Patti Rich); Laurie Murdoch (Coroner); Myles Ferguson (Joey Agostin); Kate Robbins (Lisa's Aunt); George Josey (Orchard Keeper); Gardner Millar (Mr. Babochi); Christine Anton (Teacher).

Mulder and Scully investigate a case in Michigan in which an abusive stepfather is discovered dead, buried up to his neck in the earth of an orchard. The prime suspect in the crime is his stepson, Bobby, who is in therapy for anger issues. When there is a second murder fast on the heels of the first, and another purported abused child is involved, Mulder and Scully discover that the therapist is the connection between cases. It turns out that the therapist's father died twenty years ago, in the mud of an orchard as well, and now there is a strange murderous connection between man and nature.

107. "Chinga" Written by Stephen King and Chris Carter; Directed by Kim Manners; airdate: February 8, 1998; *Guest Cast:* Susannah Hoffmann (Melissa Turner); Larry Musser (Jack Bonsaint); William MacDonald (Buddy Riggs); Jenny-Lynn Hutcheson (Polly Turner); Henry Beckman, Carolyn Tweedle (Jane Froelich); Dean Wray (Rick Turner); Gordon Tipple (Assistant Manager); Harrison R. Coe (Dave the Butcher); Ian Robison (Ranger); Elizabeth McCarthy (Shopper); Tracy Lively (Clerk); Sean Benbow (Customer).

On a weekend vacation in Maine, Scully runs afoul of a bizarre X-File: a grocery store terrorized by a seemingly demonic force. In this case, the evil seems to originate from a little girl's doll, who "likes to play." The girl herself is deemed autistic, and her mother, the beautiful Melissa Turner, is suspected of being

a witch. When dead bodies start to accumulate, the doll, fished up from the bay and infused with occult powers by a coven long ago, becomes Scully's prime suspect.

108. "Kill Switch" Written by William Gibson and Tom Maddox; Directed by Rob Bowman; airdate: February 15, 1998; *Guest Cast:* Kristin Lehman (Esther); Bruce Harwood, Dean Haglund, Tom Braidwood (The Lone Gunmen); Patrick Keating (Gelman); Peter Williams (Jackson); Jerry Schram (Boyce); Dan Weber.

An artificial intelligence arranges a "hit" against his creator to prevent the programming genius from inserting a virus (known as a "kill switch") which will destroy the computer's program. Scully and Mulder team with a beautiful blond hacker who has knowledge of the computer's whereabouts, and quickly learn that she and her dead lover had planned to transfer their consciousness, their very souls, into the artificial intelligence. Mulder is captured by the computer and forced to dwell in a horrific virtual reality hospital where the doctors and nurses are definitely lacking a delicate bedside manner.

109. "Bad Blood" Written by Vince Gilligan; Directed by Cliff Bole; airdate: February 22, 1998; *Guest Cast:* Luke Wilson (Sheriff Lucius Hartwell); Patrick Renna (Ronnie Strickland); Forbes Angus (Funeral Director); Brent Butt (Coroner).

Mulder, Scully, and the F.B.I. are being sued for $446 million because Mulder put a stake through a pizza delivery boy's heart in Cheney, Texas (population: 361). Mulder and Scully have different recollections of the case: Mulder believes the boy was a vampire, and Scully suspects the work of cultists. As the agents bicker over their opposing interpretations of the details of their stay in Texas, the staked pizza boy's body disappears from the morgue nearby. Mulder and Scully return to investigate and learn that more than one vampire may be on the loose.

110. "Patient X" Written by Chris Carter and Frank Spotnitz; Directed by Kim

Manners; airdate: March 1, 1998; *Guest Cast:* Nicholas Lea (Alex Krycek); Laurie Holden (Marita Covarrubias); Veronica Cartwright (Cassandra Spender); William B. Davis (Cigarette Smoking Man); Brian Thompson (Alien Bounty Hunter); Jim Jansen (Dr. Verber); John Neville (The Well-Manicured Man); Chris Owens (Jeffrey Spender); Alex Shostak Jr. (Dmitri); Don S. Williams (Elder); Ron Halder (Dr. Floyd Fazio); Kurt Max Runie (Ranger); John Moore (Second Elder); Raoul Ganeen (Guard); Anatol Rezmeritsas (Commander); Max Wyman (Doctor); Barbara Dyke (Dr. Alepin).

Mulder speaks out against "Patient X," a woman abductee who is sharing a feel-good message about alien life forms at a UFO panel. Cassandra Spender, the patient in question, believes that there is a war going on among the alien nations and that she is about to be called back, to be abducted. Meanwhile, in Tunguska, alien rebel fighters arrive and incinerate a group of abductees for some mysterious purpose. Another massacre of abductees occurs in America at Skyland Mountain, the site from which Scully was abducted, and Dana finds herself believing Cassandra Spender's explanation of a cosmic war.

111. "The Red and the Black" Written by Chris Carter and Frank Spotnitz; Directed by Chris Carter; airdate: March 8, 1998; *Guest Cast:* William B. Davis (Cigarette Smoking Man); Nicholas Lea (Alex Krycek); Veronica Cartwright (Cassandra Spender); John Neville (Well-Manicured Man); Chris Owens (Jeffrey Spender); Laurie Holden (Maria Covarrubias); Brian Thompson (Alien Bounty Hunter); Don S. Williams (First Elder); John Moore (Second Elder); George Murdock (Third Elder).

Cassandra Spender has been abducted … again, even as all of her friends and fellow believers are torched to death by alien rebels. Meanwhile, the conspiracy attempts to develop a vaccine against the black oil, using Maria Covarrubias as a guinea pig. Scully acquiesces to hypnotherapy to recall the events of the abduction, as well as the

battle on the bridge which took Cassandra from this world.

112. "Travelers" Written by John Shiban and Frank Spotnitz; Directed by William A. Graham; airdate: March 29, 1998; *Guest Cast:* Fredric Lane (Young Arthur Dales); Darren McGavin (Arthur Dales); Garret Dillahunt (Edward Skur); Brian Leckner, David Moreland, Eileen Pedde (Mrs. Skur); David Fredericks (The Director); Mitchell Kosterman (Sheriff); Roger Haskett (Coroner); Jane Perry (Dorothy); J. Douglas Stewart (Landlord); Cory Dagg (Bartender); Eric W. Gilder (Old Edward Skur).

In November of 1990, young F.B.I. profiler Fox Mulder tries to piece together the case of a suspected communist/serial killer named Ed Skur. Mulder seeks the assistance of Arthur Dales, a former F.B.I. special agent who investigated "X files," cases designated unsolved, in the 1940s and 50s. Dales recounts the events of 1952 in which he was hunting Skur, a man believed by HUAC to be a communist, but actually something much worse: an alien-infested host organism! The strange case involved conspiracies, extraterrestrials, and even Mulder's father.

Note: Mulder wears a wedding ring in this episode, a fact which spurred a rash of debate among *X-Files* fans. Was it a blooper, or was the young Mulder of 1990 seen in this episode supposed to be a married man?

113. "Mind's Eye" Written by Tim Minear; Directed by Kim Manners; airdate: April 19, 1998; *Guest Cast:* Lili Taylor (Marty Glenn); Richard Fitzpatrick (Detective Pennuck); Blu Monkuma (Charles Wesley Gotts); Henri Lubatti (Dr. Wilkenson); Peter Kelamis (ADA Costa); Joe Pascual (Examiner); Colin Lawrence (First Cop); Jason Diablo (Angry Man); Verdnika Stocker (Sexy Woman); Dallas Black (Cop).

In Wilmington, Delaware, a blind young woman shows up at a murder scene and is promptly arrested for the bloody crime. Mulder believes that Marty is innocent, and that she possesses some kind of sense which allows her to "see" the crimes of the killers. Scully thinks Marty is an angry, arrogant woman, but Mulder is sure she is just prideful and unwilling to admit that she is handicapped. As the killer strikes again, Mulder discovers a strange link between Marty and the murderer: he killed her mother in 1970 while Marty was still in the womb, and somehow, some way, she became connected to him.

114. "All Souls" Written by Frank Spotnitz and John Shiban; From a story by Billy Brown and Dan Angel; Directed by Allen Coulter; airdate: April 26, 1998; *Guest Cast:* Glen Morshower (Aaron Starkey/The Devil); Jody Racicot, Emily Perkins (Emily); Lauren Diewold, Joseph Patrick Finn, Eric Keenleyside (Lance Kernof); Patti Allan (Mrs. Kernoff); Arnie Walters (Father McCue); Lorraine Landry (Pathologist); Tracy Elofson (Four Faced Man).

Scully seeks forgiveness at church for her role in a bizarre X-File: the strange death of a special-needs girl who seemed more than human. When another, nearly identical, girl dies in the same position of supplication, her eyes burned away by a super powerful light, Scully suspects a supernatural, Christian force may be at work. The dead girls are polydactyl quadruplets who may be nephelem, the hybrid offspring of human and angel. Now, someone is killing these creatures, but is it the heavenly, four-faced seraphim escorting their souls to heaven, or is it the Devil himself, seeking a powerful prize?

115. "The Pine Bluff Variant" Written by John Shiban; Directed by Rob Bowman; airdate: May 3, 1998; *Guest Cast:* Daniel Van Bargen (Jacob Steven Hailey); Michael MacRae (August Bremer); Sam Anderson (Leemus); J.B. Bivens (Field Agent); Douglas H. Arthurs (Skin-Head Man); John B. Lowe (Dr. Leavitt); Ralph Alderman (Manager); Dean McKenzie (Army Tech); Kate Braidwood (Usherette); Armin Moattar (Goatee Man).

A sting designed to bring down a dangerous terrorist group called "The New Spartans" goes badly, apparently due to Mulder's unexpected bungling. Scully suspects Mulder's failure was intentional, and uncovers evidence that her partner is working with the terrorists, who have gained access to a deadly bioweapon: a genetically engineered flesh-eating virus. The terrorists strike again, exposing a movie theater filled with patrons to the deadly toxin, and their next target is a bank. Scully follows Mulder to the heist, in which he participates, uncertain if her partner and friend is really involved with the terrorists, or working under deep cover.

116. "Folie a Deux" Written by Vince Gilligan; Directed by Kim Manners; airdate: May 10, 1998; *Guest Cast:* Brian Markinson (Gary Lambert); Dmitri Chepovetsky (Supervisor); Cynthia Preston (Nancy); Brenda McDonald (Loach); John Apicella (Roach).

Mulder gets involved in a hostage situation when an apparently disgruntled telemarketer holds his office at gunpoint, claiming that his boss is an inhuman monster who is turning his co-workers into lifeless zombies. Mulder defuses the situation handily, but soon he has come to believe that the company boss is a monster who "hides in the light." Scully and Skinner think Mulder has lost his mind, but now Mulder is convinced that the boss, a horrible, insectlike creature who can climb walls and skitter across the ceiling, is coming for him.

117. "The End" Written by Chris Carter; Directed by R.W. Goodwin; airdate: May 17, 1998; *Guest Cast:* Jeff Gulka (Gibson); Mimi Rogers (Diana Fowley); William B. Davis (Cigarette Smoking Man); Chris Owens (Agent Spender); John Neville (Well-Manicured Man); Bruce Harwood, Dean Haglund, Tom Braidwood (The Lone Gunmen); Nicholas Lea (Krycek); Don S. Williams (First Elder); George Murdock (Third Elder); John Moore (Second Elder).

A boy with telepathic abilities is the key to all the secrets of the X-Files. He is nearly murdered, and Mulder, Scully and Mulder's old partner, the beautiful Diana Fowley, are assigned to protect him. The conspiracy is afraid of the boy, Gibson, however, because they believe he can expose their secrets. Fearing Gibson's powers, they recruit the Cigarette Smoking Man to put an end to him and the X-Files for good.

• *Sixth Season (1998–1999)*

118. "The Beginning" Written by Chris Carter; Directed by Kim Manners; airdate: November 8, 1998; *Guest Cast:* William B. Davis (Cigarette Smoking Man); Chris Owens (Spender); Mimi Rogers (Diana Fowley); Jeff Gulka (Gibson); James Pickens, Jr. (AD Kersh); Christopher Neiman, Kim Robillard, Arthur Taxier, Alan Henry Brown, Scott Eberlein, Wendie Malick (Maslin), Don S. Williams (1st Elder); George Murdock (2nd Elder); Rick Millikan (Sandy); Wayne Thomas Yorke (First Workman); Wayne Alexander (AD Arnold); Ralph Meyering, Jr. (Surgeon); Benito Martinez (Orderly).

A worker at Roush Technologies returns from work to his home in Phoenix, Arizona, feeling extreme pain, and before long an alien organism bursts out of his rapidly liquefying body. Back in Washington, D.C., Mulder is brought in before a hostile review committee and asked to defend his work on the newly re-opened X-Files, and worse, he and Scully are ultimately reassigned off the X-Files. Skinner wants to help Mulder and Scully expose the conspiracy and he points them towards the case in Phoenix even as Diana and Spender are officially put on the X-Files. Mulder and Scully race to a nuclear power plant to find the vicious alien lifeform before the conspiracy destroys both it and the truth.

119. "Drive" Written by Vince Gilligan; Directed by Rob Bowman; airdate: November 15, 1998; *Guest Cast:* Bryan Cranston (Crump); Michael O'Neill, James Pickens Jr. (AD Kersh); Harry Danner, Junior Brown; Linda Porter (Elderly Woman); Mindy Seeger (Coroner); Scott A. Smith (Prison Doctor); Tim Agee (EMT); Mark Craig (Trooper #1); Wiley Pickett (Trooper #2); Ken Collins (Gas Station Attendant); Tegan West (Navy Lieutenant); Tom Haile (Station Wagon Owner); Frank Buckley (Nevada News Anchor); Bob Peters (Idaho News Anchor); Janine Venable

(Vicky Crump); Art Pickering (Germ Suit Cop).

Reassigned off the X-Files by their new AD, Alvin Kersh, Mulder and Scully are out west questioning fertilizer purchasers when there is a deadly highway chase in Elko, Nevada. A woman's head spontaneously explodes after her husband attempts desperately to drive her out of town, and Mulder and Scully investigate the death. The husband soon hears a buzzing in his head and begins to experience the same pounding headache which eventually killed his wife. After an escape from an ambulance, the mad driver kidnaps Mulder and forces him to drive as fast as possible for the West Coast, even as Scully determines that a naval experiment called "Project Seafarer," which involves low frequency sound surges, may to be blame for turning people into human timebombs.

120. "Triangle" Written and directed by Chris Carter; airdate: November 22, 1998; *Guest Cast:* William B. Davis (Cigarette Smoking Man); Chris Owens (Spender); James Pickens, Jr. (AD Kersh); Madison Mason, Trevor Goddard, G.W. Stevens, Greg Ellis, Nick Meaney, Kai Wulff, Tom Braidwood, Dean Haglund, Bruce Harwood (The Lone Gunemen); Wolfgang Gerhard (1st Nazi); Guido Foehrweisser (2nd Nazi); Isaac C. Singleton (1st Roughneck); Laura Leigh-Hughes (Kersh's assistant); Robert Thomas Beck (1st Mate); Robert Arce (Bald-Headed Man); Arlene Pileggi (Skinner's assistant).

While searching for a long lost British luxury liner, the *Queen Anne*, Mulder becomes trapped in the Bermuda Triangle and a bizarre time/space warp. He boards the lost ship only to discover that the crew believes it is still 1939 and, worse, that the vessel has been overtaken by Nazi forces. In this strange reality, the Cigarette Smoking Man is a Nazi commandant, Scully is an American OSS spy, Spender is a gestapo goon, and Skinner is a double agent secretly helping the allies. While Mulder tries to stay alive on the ship, Scully and the Lone Gunmen go to extraordinary lengths to find his exact position and rescue him from the Sargasso Sea trap.

121. "Dreamland" (Part I) Written by Vince Gilligan, John Shiban, and Frank Spotnitz; Directed by Kim Manners; airdate: November 29, 1998; *Guest Cast:* Michael McKean (Morris Fletcher); James Pickens Jr. (A.D. Kersh); Nora Dunn (Joanne Fletcher); Scott Allan Campbell (Howard Grodin); Julia Vera (Indian Woman); John Mahon, Michael Buchman Silver, Tyler Binkley (Terry Fletcher); Dara Hollingsworth (Christine Fletcher); Ted White (Attendant); Laura Leigh Hughes (Kersh's Assistant); Eddie Jackson (Co-pilot/Rock Man); Christopher Stapleton (Pilot); James Yaker (Cashier); Freeman Michaels (Guard); Greg Smith (Soldier).

Mulder and Scully drive by night to a clandestine meeting with a top-secret information source at the fabled Area 51 military base in Nevada, but are apprehended en route by authorities. During the meeting of Majestic and F.B.I, a strange vehicle flies by overhead and Mulder miraculously switches bodies with an unhappily married government man in black named Morris Fletcher. While Mulder tries to get back to his life, Morris turns Fox's life upside down: putting the make on Scully, purchasing a water bed, and even badmouthing the X-Files! Mulder suspects that the body switch occurred as a result of a top secret plane's new anti-gravity propulsion drive, but he has no idea how to reverse his condition.

122. "Dreamland" (Part II) Written by Vince Gilligan, John Shiban, and Frank Spotnitz; Directed by Michael Watkins; airdate: December 6, 1998; *Guest Cast:* Michael McKean (Morris Fletcher); Julia Vera (Indian Woman); Nora Dunn (Joanne Fletcher); Tom Braidwood, Dean Haglund, Bruce Harwood (The Lone Gunmen); John Mahon, Michael Buchman Silver, Scott Allan Campbell, Andrew Sikking, Chris Ufland, Tyler Binkley (Terry "Terence" Fletcher); Dara Hollingsworth (Christine Fletcher); Mike Rad (Randy); Lisa Joann Thompson (Kelly); Christopher Stapleton (Pilot); Jeffrey T. Un-

terkofler (1st Air Policeman); James Yaker (Cashier); Nick Lashaway (Young Mulder); Ashlynn Rose (Young Samantha); Bonnie Mc-Neill (Young Tena).

Mulder, still trapped in the body of Morris Fletcher, must find a way to repair the tear in the fabric of the space/time continuum which resulted in the bizarre identity switch. Meanwhile, Morris tries to bed down Scully, which helps her realize that the man who seems to be her partner is really an impostor. A rendezvous at the Little Ale 'n' Inn near Area 51 in Nevada reunites Mulder and Scully, but now they must reunite his body and soul.

123. "How the Ghosts Stole Christmas" Written and directed by Chris Carter; airdate: December 13, 1998; *Guest Cast:* Lily Tomlin (Lida); Edward Asner (Maurice).

On Christmas Eve, Mulder and Scully stake out a haunted house in Maryland with a tragic history: amidst the World War and flu epidemic of 1917, two lovers joined in a suicide pact there. Once inside the dark manor, the doors lock behind them and Scully and Mulder find themselves trapped in a maze of rooms with no way out. Under the rickety floorboards of the library, the duo makes a disturbing discovery: their own rotting corpses. Now Mulder and Scully must escape the house, escape the grim fate they've witnessed, and survive the interference of two mischievous spirits who are hellbent on making this newest pair of "lovers" a permanent addition to the house.

124. "Terms of Endearment" Written by David Amann; Directed by Rob Bowman; airdate: January 3, 1999; *Guest Cast:* Bruce Campbell (Wayne/Ivan Valez/Bud Hasselhoff); Chris Owens (Spender); Lisa Jane Persky (Laura); Michael Milhoan, Grace Phillips (Betsy); Michael Rothaar (Dr. Couvillion); Matthew Butcher (EMT); Lenora May (Ms. Britton); Jimmy Stazkiel (Mr. Ginsberg); Karen Stone (Nurse).

A long-lived demon masquerading in human form continues to pray for a human-appearing baby from one of his many human wives, yet keeps ending up disappointed as sonograms reveal horns and a tail on his up-coming bundle of joy. One night, the demon steals his wife's unborn child in his true, dev-ilish form … an act which ultimately spurs a police investigation. When Agent Spender, in charge of the X-Files, throws the case into the shredder, Mulder goes rogue to investigate it himself. Mulder thinks he is seeing a classic case of demon fetal harvest and starts to sus-pect the details of the demon's lovin' and birthin' operation. But Wayne isn't the only devil in town, and one of his neglected (but expectant) wives has her own little agenda.

125. "Rain King" Written by Jeffrey Bell; Directed by Kim Manners; airdate: Jan-uary 10, 1999; *Guest Cast:* Victoria Jackson (Sheila Fontaine); Clayton Rohner (Darryl Mootz); David Manis (Holman Hardt); Dirk Blocker (Mayor Jim Gilmore); Francesca In-grassia (Cindy); Tom McFadden (Doctor); Dan Gifford (Local News Anchor); Sharon Madden (Motel Manager); Brian D. Johnson (Man); Sally Stevens (Radio Singer).

In dry, drought-ridden Kroner, Kansas, Darryl Mootz is charging the townspeople ex-orbitant rates to use his "magic" power and cause the rain to fall. In response, Scully and Mulder fly to Kansas to investigate the town, which Mulder refers to as "Ground Zero" for extreme weather conditions. The duo consult a local weatherman, Holman Hardt, about the bizarre meteorological situation and learn that the weatherman's emotional states, par-ticularly his love for a local named Sheila, may be causing Darryl Mootz's success at rain making.

126. "S.R. 819" Written by John Shiban; Directed by Daniel Sackheim; airdate: Janu-ary 17, 1999; *Guest Cast:* Raymond J. Barry (Senator Richard Matheson); John Towey (Kenneth Orgell); Kenneth Tigar (Doctor); Jenny Gago (Doctor); Nicholas Lea (Krycek); Donna Marie Moore (ICU Nurse); Greta Fad-ness (OR Nurse); Dan Klass (Forensic Tech); Susana Mercedes (Driver); Tim Van Pelt (Young Surgeon); Keith Coulouris (Intern); Arlene Pileggi (Skinner's Secretary); Al Faris (Silk Shirt Man); Jonathan Fraser (Uniformed Cop); Julie Hubert (Exam Room Nurse); Mickie Knox (Trainer).

Skinner hovers near death at the hospi-tal, a victim of an apparently fatal heart attack. As his life ebbs, Skinner recalls the events of the last twenty-four hours, and how he was unknowingly poisoned by a mysterious as-sailant. Mulder and Scully do their best to save their friend, uncovering a mysterious conspir-acy involving an American scientist named Orgell, a Tunisian assassin with diplomatic immunity, and a medical bill called S.R. 819 involving top secret nanotechnology in the Third World. Scully investigates the scientific aspects of Skinner's illness and learns it is an engineered disease building to a catastrophic "vascular event" … or, in layman's terms, a fatal coronary!

Note: The "S" and "R" of the title refer to Senate Resolution number 819.

127. "Tithonus" Written by Vince Gilli-gan; Directed Michael Watkins; airdate: Janu-ary 24, 1999; *Guest Cast:* Geoffrey Lewis (Al-fred Pfelig); Richard Ruccolo (Agent Peyton Ritter); James Pickens, Jr. (AD Kersh); Ange Billman (Secretary); Naomi Matsuda (Hooker); Matt Gallini (Hood); Coby Ryan McLaughlin (Young Agent); Joylon Reese (Second Young Agent); Javier Grajeda (Desk Sergeant); Barry Wiggins (NYPD Detective); Don Feimel (Am-bulance EMT); Dell Yount (Truck Driver).

Assistant Director Kersh asks Scully to work with Agent Peyton Ritter, an up-and-coming young agent, on a bizarre case in New York City in which a police photographer somehow manages to photograph crime scenes involving death … at the moment of death it-self. Scully looks into this Johnny-on-the-spot's background and realizes that Alfred Pfe-lig hasn't aged a day in some fifty or sixty years. Scully interviews the suspect, and he re-veals to her how, by sight, he can determine which people will soon expire. Scully disbe-lieves him until a sidelined Mulder digs up ev-idence to the contrary and Pfelig relates a per-sonal story: he is one hundred forty-nine years-old and he longs for the angel of death to come for him.

128. "Two Fathers" Written by Chris Carter and Frank Spotnitz; Directed by Kim Manners; airdate: February 7, 1999; *Guest Cast:* William B. Davis (Cigarette Smoking Man); Chris Owens (Spender); Nick Tate (Dr. Eugene Openshaw); Nicholas Lea (Krycek); Veronica Cartwright (Cassandra Spender); George Murdock (Elder); Don S. Williams (Elder); Al Ruscio, Frank Ertl, James Newman, Mimi Rogers (Diana Fowley); Damon P. Saleem (Pick-Up Player); Valarie Pettiford (FBI Agent).

After more than twenty-five years of abductions and tests, the conspiracy has finally developed the first healthy human/alien hybrid: Cassandra Spender. On this day of victory, however, the celebration is marred when alien rebels burn the scientists to a crisp. Cassandra Spender, returned from an abduction, asks to speak with Mulder, and Agent Spender acquiesces. Soon, the rebels begin to murder high-ranking conspiracy members, and it looks like the end of an era.

129. "One Son" Written by Chris Carter and Frank Spotnitz; Directed by Rob Bowman; airdate: February 14, 1999; *Guest Cast:* William B. Davis (Cigarette Smoking Man); Chris Owens (Spender); Nicholas Lea (Krycek); Mimi Rogers (Diana Fowley); Veronica Cartwright (Cassandra Spender); Laurie Holden (Covarrubias); Tom Braidwood, Dean Haglund, Bruce Harwood (The Lone Gunmen); Don S. Williams (Elder); James Pickens Jr. (Kersh); Peter Donat (Bill Mulder); Al Ruscio, Frank Ertly, Robert Lipton, Scott Williamson (CDC Leader); Jo Black-Jacob (Nurse); Mark Bramhall (Surgical Team Member).

Under the direction of the Cigarette Smoking Man and Diana Fowley, Cassandra Spender is captured by surviving members of the conspiracy and locked away in isolation. Mulder finally discovers the real motivations of the syndicate's conspiracy: it has been stalling on the alien-human hybrid (a slave race) to prevent or at least delay alien colonization, while secretly developing a vaccine to save humanity. The rebels move in and mas-sacre the surviving syndicate members, save for Cigarette Smoking Man and Fowley, who escape the disaster. With the conspiracy finally destroyed, Spender realizes the truth and helps Mulder and Scully get reinstated on the X-Files, an act which results in a surprising murder.

130. "Agua Mala" Written by David Amann; Directed by Rob Bowman; airdate: February 21, 1999; *Guest Cast:* Darren Mc-Gavin (Arthur Dales); Jeremy Roberts, Joel McKinnon Miller, Diana Maria Riva, Valente Rodriguez, Silas Weir Mitchell, Nichole Pelerine, Max Kasche, Allen Culter (Roadblock Officer).

Arthur Dales, the first ever X-Files investigator, telephones Mulder from Goodland, Florida, claiming that his neighbors, the Shipleys, have been killed by a tentacled sea monster. Mulder and Scully proceed to the hurricane-ravaged town to investigate the disappearance, but find only empty clothes and a cat (safe and sound in the washing machine) at the crime scene. As the storm worsens, Scully and Mulder seek refuge in the run-down Breakers Condominiums with a very pregnant woman, her henpecked husband, a paranoid survivalist, a looter, and an injured obese deputy who has already faced the monster. As the monster attacks, Mulder speculates that the hurricane has dredged up some heretofore unknown water parasite, a translucent worm from the uncharted depths who can gestate inside a living human host.

131. "Monday" Written by Vince Gilligan and John Shiban; Directed by Kim Manners; airdate: February 28, 1999; *Guest Cast:* Carrie Hamilton (Pam); Darren Burrows (Bernard Oates); Suanne Spoke (Woman Customer); Monique Edwards (Head Teller); Arlene Pileggi (Skinner's Secretary); Wayne Alexander (Older Agent); David Michael Mullins (Tour Guide); Mik Scriba (Lieutenant Kraskow).

A simple trip to the bank ends in terror for Mulder and Scully when they find themselves in a repeating time-loop which ends with both of them dead at the hands of a small-time bank robber named Bernard. Only one person has any knowledge of the temporal flaw: the robber's girlfriend Pam, and she has tried everything to avert the disaster. As the same gloomy Monday recycles again and again, Mulder develops a strong feeling of déjà vu and starts to suspect that all is not right with his world.

132. "Arcadia" Written by Daniel Arkin; Directed by Michael Watkins; airdate: March 5, 1999; *Guest Cast:* Peter White (Gogolok); Abraham Benrubi (Lynn); Debra Christofferson (Cammie); Tom Gallop (Mike); Marnie McPhail, Roger Morrissey, Tim Bagley (Gordy); Tom Virtue (Dave Kline); Juliana Donald (Nancy Kline); Mark Matthews (Mover).

Mulder and Scully pose as a married couple, Rob and Laurie Petrie, so as to get into the Falls at Arcadia, a restrictive, gated community where tenants who have disobeyed the community covenants, contracts, and restrictions end up dead at the hands of some kind of inhuman monster. As Mulder and Scully soon find out, the Falls is guarded by Mr. Gogolok's strange sentry: a Tibetan "thought" creature brought to life from Gogolok's subconscious mind. When Mulder purposely flaunts the community's rules and digs up his front yard (ostensibly for a reflecting pool), the creature reappears.

133. "Alpha" Written by Jeffrey Bell; Directed by Peter Markle; airdate March 28, 1999; *Guest Cast:* Andrew J. Robinson (Ian Detweiler); Melinda Culea (Karen Berquist); Thomas Duffy (Jeffrey Kahn); Michael Mantell, David Starwalt, James Michael Connor (Jake Connor); Yau Gene-Chen (Woo); Tuan Tran (Fong); Dana Lee (Yee); Lisa Picotte (Stacey Muir); Mandy Levin (Angie); Treva Togtmeier (Peggy); Adrienne Wilde (Nurse).

A vicious dog from Hong Kong escapes from its container at the docks of San Pedro and goes on a killing spree across the West Coast. The animal was brought to the U.S. by a cryptobiologist who was attempting to preserve an all-but extinct Asian species of "Canid." To find the scavenging, attacking beast, Scully and Mulder seek the help of an animal behavior specialist, Karen Berquist — a woman who is lacking some social graces and seems to prefer animals to the company of men. Scully thinks Berquist has arranged the animal's escape to get closer to Mulder, whom she met online previously, but Ian Detweiler, the dog's owner, may be the one with the hidden secret.

134. "Trevor" Written by Jim Guttridge and Ken Hawryliw; Directed by Rob Bowman; airdate: April 11, 1999; *Guest Cast:* John Diehl (Pinker Rawls); Tuesday Knight (Jackie); Frank Novak, David Bowe, Catherine Dent, Jeffrey Schoeny (Trevor); Christopher Dahlberg (State Trooper); Robert Peters (Sergeant); Jerry Giles (Security Guard); Keith Brunsmann (Bo); Lamont Johnson (Whaley); Carey Pfeffer (Anchorman); Terri Merryman (Newscaster); Lee Corbin (Guard).

A prisoner escapes from incarceration after a deadly storm, replete with the power to physically walk through walls and other impediments. Worse, bullets also pass right through Pinker Rawls, so there seems to be no way to stop him. Mulder and Scully head off on Rawls' trail, aware that he is on a quest to recover something of incredible significance to him. Mulder and Scully know that if they find the object of Rawls' hunt, they will find Rawls ... but how can they stop a man who can't be killed?

135. "Milagro" Written by Chris Carter; Story by John Shiban and Frank Spotnitz; Directed by Kim Manners; airdate: April 18, 1999; *Guest Cast:* John Hawkes (Phillip Padgett); Nestor Serrano (The Stranger); Michael Bailey-Smith, Angelo Vacco, Julian Bach, Casey O'Neil (Cemetery Groundskeeper);

A struggling writer has an obsession for the beautiful agent Scully and moves in next door to Mulder's apartment at the same time that the F.B.I. duo is investigating a series of murders wherein the victims' hearts are removed. The writer sends Scully a lucky charm, a milagro, as Mulder contemplates the notion of psychic surgery, that organs can be removed from living humans via paranormal methods.

When Scully makes it plain that she is not interested in the writer, Padgett, he realizes she is already in love with another man: her partner. This realization leads to a violent confrontation where hearts are shattered ... and removed.

136. "The Unnatural" Written and directed by David Duchovny; airdate: April 25, 1999; *Guest Cast:* Jesse L. Martin (Josh Exley); Fredric Lane (Young Arthur Dales); Brian Thompson (Alien Bounty Hunter); M. Emmet Walsh (Arthur Dales); Jesse James, Lou Beatty, Jr., Burnell Roques, Lennie Lofton (Coranado); Paul Willson (Ted); Walter T. Phelan, Jr. (Alien); Gabriel Clifton (Black Kid); Al Kaplon (Ump); Rob Reesman (Macon Cop); Danie Duchovny (Piney); Chris Kohn (Catcher); Ken Medlock (White Coach); Julie Griffith (Beautiful Woman); Kerric MacDonald (Moose).

In July of 1947, Negro baseball sensation Josh Exley disappeared in Roswell, New Mexico. Today, Mulder believes that aliens are involved in this disappearance, especially when he sees pictures of an alien bounty hunter in an old newspaper clipping. Mulder visits Arthur Dales, who was a police officer in Roswell in the 1940s, and was assigned to protect Exley from Ku Klux Klan fanatics who wanted to keep white baseball "pure." But, on one dark and rainy night aboard the bus for the Roswell Grays, Dales saw Exley's reflection in a window ... and realized that the famous baseball player was an extraterrestrial.

Note: Arthur Dales is usually portrayed by Darren McGavin, but in this case Arthur Dales is portrayed by M. Emmet Walsh. To make matters more confusing, this Arthur Dales (Walsh) is the like-named brother of the other Arthur Dales (McGavin)!

137. "Three of a Kind" Written by Vince Gilligan and John Shiban; Directed by Bryan Spicer; airdate: May 2, 1999; *Guest Cast:* Signy Coleman (Suzanne Modeski); Charles Rocket, John Billingsley, Jim Fyfe, George Sharperson, Michael McKean (Morris Fletcher); Tom Braidwood, Dean Haglund and Bruce Harwood (The Lone Gunmen);

Brian Reddy (Big Fritz); Phil Abrams (Little Fritz); Richard Zobel (Al); Jeff Bowser (Redhead Geek); Jason Felipe (Bald Greek); Rick Garcia (News Anchor); Kalena Coleman (Bus Driver).

The Lone Gunmen infiltrate Def Con 1999, a defense contractor's gathering in Las Vegas, in hopes of learning of some new government weapon secrets. On the casino floor, Byers spots the beautiful Suzanne Modeski, the mysterious weapons scientist he first encountered at a convention in 1989. When Byers sees Modeski cooperating with a shadowy government type, he becomes convinced that she is the victim of an advanced mind-control technique. The Lone Gunmen lure an unsuspecting Scully out to Las Vegas to help them learn the truth, and save Suzanne's life.

Note: This episode is a sequel to the fifth season entry, "Unusual Suspects."

138. "Field Trip" (aka "Lies") Written by Vince Gilligan and Jim Shiban; Story by Frank Spotnitz; Directed by Kim Manners; airdate: May 9, 1999; *Guest Cast:* Mitch Pileggi (Skinner); Robyn Lively (Angela Schiff); David Denman (Wallace Schiff); Jim Beaver, Tom Braidwood, Dean Haglund and Bruce Harwood (The Lone Gunmen).

Two skeletonized corpses are found near Brown Mountain, North Carolina, but the problem is that the bodies (of two hikers) were only out in the woods for three days, a fact which seems to negate the possibility of such massive decomposition. Mulder and Scully make their way to the mountains to investigate and the search takes Mulder into a tiny cave and an encounter with what he believes to be aliens. Reality and fantasy seem to mix, but the truth has more to do with a carnivorous, hallucinogenic fungus than extraterrestrial life forms.

139. "Biogenesis" (aka "Plans") Written by Chris Carter and Frank Spotnitz; Directed by Rob Bowman; airdate: May 16, 1999; *Guest Cast:* William B. Davis (Cigarette Smoking Man); Nicholas Lea (Krycek); Mimi Rogers (Diana Fowley); Floyd Crow Westerman (Albert Holsteen); Murray Rubinstein

(Dr. Barnes); Michael Chinyamurin (McMellen); Michael Ensign (Sandoz); Sheila Tousey (Native American Nurse); Warren Sweeney (Dr. Harriman); Chet Grissom (Detective); Bill Dow (Chuck Burks); Marty Zagon (Landlord); Samuel Kwaku Minta (Yellingman); Ayd Eyemi (African Man); Benjamin Ocheing (Second African Man).

A strange artifact, a tablet with hieroglyphs on it, is discovered on the Ivory Coast of West Africa. When the tablet proves animate, shattering a Bible, its discoverer brings it to American University in Washington, D.C. There, he is killed and Mulder and Scully search for the stolen tablet, which is reported to carry a message about the purpose of human life on Earth. Worse, Mulder believes his mental equilibrium is being negatively affected by the artifact's mysterious power.

27

American Gothic (1995–1996)

CRITICAL RECEPTION

"*Twin Peaks* without conviction ... lots of ominous music in the background, lots of toned-down horror-movie effects in the fore-ground."—*Entertainment Weekly*, October 20, 1995, page 52.

"small-town America as an eerie place somewhere between *Mayberry RFD* and *Twin Peaks*.... If the sense of menace sometimes threatens to get a bit campy, that shouldn't come as a surprise in a project on which two of the executive producers are Sam Raimi and Robert Tapert, the team responsible for ... *Hercules* and *Xena*.— John J. O'Connor, *The New York Times*, September 22, 1995.

"there's very little that's domesticated about the *noir American Gothic* ... I am reminded, if not of Kafka, then perhaps of ... S.J. Perelman ... *American Gothic* is the ... unlikely child of Shaun Cassidy, as if that ghost in the birthday cake, David Lynch, had popped out of *The X-Files*. What on unearth will they think up next?"—John Leonard, *New York*, September 25, 1995, page 117.

"*American Gothic* ... benefits from a fine, frightening cast, particularly Gary Cole, who plays Lucas Buck.... Indeed, the players throw themselves into these self-consciously bizarre proceedings as if the show were the inspired work of collaboration between Tennessee Williams and Stephen King ... as if creator Shaun Cassidy ... were trying to mutate *Twin Peaks* and *The Andy Griffith Show* ... *American Gothic* is scary, but not always for the right reasons. Watching a few episodes ... I was struck by one terrifying thing: Cole would be absolutely perfect to play Mark Fuhrman."— David Wild, *Rolling Stone*: "Television 'X'-Ploitation," November 30, 1995, page 79.

FORMAT

At first blush, Trinity, South Carolina, is a lovely small town. Victorian homes and southern plantations dot the clean, green streets, the sky overhead is always a rich blue, and peace and quiet seem to hang in the air like the scent of honeysuckle. But this south-ern town harbors a dark and terrifying secret. Its inhabitants live in mortal fear of the town sheriff, one Lucas Buck (Gary Cole), and many of them "owe" him favors for his some-times helpful/sometimes harmful intervention in town affairs. For Lucas is not just a local "Roscoe," he may, in fact, be Satan himself.

American Gothic is an hour-long CBS drama created by Shaun Cassidy (former pop star, half-brother to David Cassidy, and *Hardy Boys* star) which focuses primarily on Lucas Buck's seemingly never-ending efforts to win the heart and mind of Caleb Temple (Lucas Black), a precocious and forthright preteen who is, in reality, Buck's biological son. Caleb is protected from Trinity's resident evil by the spirit of his dead sister, Merlyn Ann Temple (Sarah Paulson), whom Buck murdered in cold blood at the Temple farm on one dark night. Also on Caleb's side is Dr. Matt Crower (Jack Weber), a blond Yankee physician and recovering alcoholic, and Caleb's beautiful cousin Gail Emory (Paige Turco), who believes that Buck is responsible for the death of her parents (local reporters) back in 1976. As the series continues through its twenty-two hour-long episodes, Dr. Crower is replaced in Trin-ity by a CDC doctor named Peel (John Mese), and Gail finds herself falling (almost against her will) in love with Lucas Buck. On the side of bad with Buck is Ms. Selena Coombs (Brenda Bakke), a sultry kindergarten teacher with a more-than-healthy sexual appetite, and the heart of a wolf. In one of her first appearances, Coombs was seen playing pool at a bar, and she asked her competitor "rack your balls?" That double-entendre set the mood for her character, and Bakke was a stimulating presence throughout the show.

A story of evil and temptation in the American heartland, *American Gothic* is a soap opera filled with evil portents, ghosts, startling metamorphoses, and violent deaths. The opening credits reflect *American Gothic*'s dual nature. At first, the tranquillity on the surface of life in Trinity is established through picturesque shots of the town, but soon Lucas Buck's "evil" presence dominates the proceedings through a superimposed closeup of the evil man's stone-hard face.

Another highly interesting and high-quality '90s horror series with a sprinkle of *Twin Peaks* and *Dark Shadows* in its brew, *American Gothic* survived just one short season on American network TV before being consigned to an afterlife on the Sci-Fi Channel.

HISTORY

Few critics may have expected that the director of intense horror fare such as *Evil Dead* (1982), *Evil Dead 2: Dead by Dawn* (1985), *Darkman* (1990), and *Army of Darkness* (1993) would find incredible success as a television producer, but that is exactly what happened to acclaimed genre director Sam Raimi (*The Quick and the Dead* [1995], *A Simple Plan* [1998]) when he masterminded (with his production company Renaissance Pictures and executive producer Robert Tapert) *The Legendary Journeys of Hercules* and *Xena: Warrior Princess* for American syndication. These two series, filmed on location in New Zealand, quickly became the highest rated dramatic programs in syndication, even beating out the previous champion, *Star Trek: Deep Space Nine*

(1993-99) by a wide margin. Ironically, Sam Raimi's third TV venture, a show of considerably higher quality than either *Xena* or *Hercules*, did not fare nearly so well when it aired on the CBS network on Friday evenings in the fall of 1995 and the winter of 1996.

The series in question is *American Gothic*, a genre soap opera from creator Shaun Cassidy, later the progenitor of the medieval epic *Roar* (1997) for Fox and the aborted horror-satire *Hollyweird* with director Wes Craven (late of *Nightmare Cafe*, *Scream 2*, *The Music of My Heart* [1999]). Cassidy shocked just about every reviewer and fan in the country by instigating as dark a series as TV had ever seen in its long history, a skewed "heart of darkness" drama as far removed from Cassidy's '70s "pop star" image as possible. The man who had once recorded "Da-Doo-Run-Run" had inexplicably changed course and given birth to perhaps the most evil character to ever "star" in a weekly TV series: Gary Cole's diabolical Lucas Buck.

Though Cassidy openly acknowledged that *Twin Peaks* was an inspiration for his new genre series, he also admitted that he hoped to avoid the pitfalls of that David Lynch series by making the people and plot-points of *American Gothic* a bit easier for the common man to relate to and follow. CBS probably greenlighted the series in the first place because it hoped that it would have an *X-Files*-style hit on its hands. After all, 1995 was the first year of the *X-Files* "clones," a multiplication which resulted in the production of off-kilter conspiracy and paranormal series such as *Strange Luck* on Fox, *Nowhere Man* on the new UPN and, yes, even *American Gothic* on CBS. To help create a supernatural viewing block, CBS even moved its hit *Picket Fences* from its 10:00 P.M. Friday perch and put *American Gothic* there. That way, viewers could begin the night with *Strange Luck* on Fox at 8:00, continue with *The X-Files* at 9:00, and then hop channels to CBS for *American Gothic* at 10:00 P.M.

All this was immaterial, at first, to Raimi and Cassidy, who rightfully concentrated on creating an original and thought-provoking show rather than a supernatural hit inspired by

The X-Files. In an interview for *Shivers* magazine in 1996, Sam Raimi explained the method behind Cassidy's madness:

> What we're doing is telling a story in a very real town with very real characters. And in this setting, we see elements of the supernatural. We're not doing ghost stories or weird occult-type movies.... It's a story of good and evil in a small town, and evil is embodied in this very attractive, sexy and appealing individual played by Gary Cole.... We will answer questions episode by episode.[1]

Although William Sadler (*Die Hard 2: Die Harder* [1990], *Tales from the Crypt: Demon Knight* [1995]) had been the producer's first choice to play Trinity's evil sheriff, *American Gothic* benefited enormously from Cole's nuanced portrayal of a good ole boy who just happened to be (perhaps) a demon. A charismatic and underrated actor equally capable with comedy (*The Brady Bunch Movie* [1996]), space opera (*Crusade* [1999]), and drama (*Midnight Caller*), Cole proved to be the glue that held the season-long *American Gothic* together. Equally fine in supporting roles were the delicious Brenda Bakke and earnest young Lucas Black (*Sling Blade* [1996], *The X-Files: Fight the Future* [1997]) as little Caleb.

Early reviews of *American Gothic* were complimentary in a grudging fashion, which is about the best a horror show can hope for in a biased media that does not take the genre seriously. The ratings for *Gothic* also started out relatively high with 9.5 million viewers (a 17% share of the audience), but on the following week, the conclusion of the two-part opener garnered only 7.4 million watchers (a 12% share of the audience), and so on, until *American Gothic* was soon the bottom rated show in its time slot, rating under a 10% share of the American viewing audience.[2]

Despite good writing, excellent horror imagery and a fine cast, *American Gothic* was to suffer from the "same old story" which has plagued so much genre programming, specifically a network which was not committed to the show's growth or life on the air. Instead of supporting their new series through its troubled infancy, CBS exercised an uncomfortable degree of control over the show's direction by deciding which episodes should be aired, and even in which order. Since *American Gothic* was a soap opera "serial," with one episode building and hinging on the previous one, this network interference at times rendered the series incomprehensible ... the same complaint that had permeated *Twin Peaks'* later days on the air. For instance, the network failed to air "Potato Boy," a story which revealed a great deal of back story about the character of Selena Coombs. Likewise "The Beast Within," a story that significantly humanized Trinity's deputy Ben Healy (Nick Searcy), was held back (out of order) for months. Even worse than these omissions was the decision not to air "Ring of Fire" at all. This was especially troubling because this episode wrapped up the subplot involving the fate of Gail's parents and was the turning point in the relationship between Emory and Lucas Buck. Without a viewing of this story, audiences were left to wonder how Gail went from hating Buck totally to becoming sexually involved with him. CBS also championed the removal of Jake Weber as Dr. Matt Crower, because the network executives did not like the character. As the outsider in town (a role akin to Rob Morrow's in *Northern Exposure*), Crower provided a much needed perspective, but Weber was dismissed from the series only to be replaced by another doctor who served essentially the same purpose but had even less time to be adequately developed. Though Sam Raimi and Shaun Cassidy had intended to bring Weber and Crower back in a second season, that opportunity never arose.

As if all of this interference in cast and episode order was not enough, CBS showed no confidence in *American Gothic* by allowing it to air only twelve times before pulling it from the Friday night schedule. Thus one of the most highly touted (and well-reviewed) new series of the season was basically a thing of the past by the end of January of 1996. CBS halfheartedly gave *American Gothic* a second chance by "dumping" its remaining episodes during a single week in July of 1996. With little advance publicity of this *American Gothic* "marathon," even the core audience who had stuck loyally with the series up to that point did not know to look for it during this bizarre scheduling. Instead, the ratings remained low, and CBS had all the excuses it needed to cancel the series before the start of a second season. Why did CBS produce this top-of-the-line, generously budgeted horror show only to abandon it once it began airing? Robert Tapert knew of at least one reason:

> There was a shift in regimes at CBS and the new people coming in didn't like it. It never aired three weeks in a row without a preemption or a time move, and if you do that to a show you'll kill it.[3]

American Gothic suffered the same fate as all 1990s pretenders to *The X-Files* throne. Like *Nowhere Man*, *Strange Luck*, *Kindred: The Embraced* (1996), *Dark Skies* (1996), *The Burning Zone* (1996), *Prey* (1998), and *Strange World* (1999), it died after just a season on the air. Despite this ignominious fate, *American Gothic* is arguably the most original and most artistic of this aforementioned failed series' stable.

In its short time on the air, *American Gothic* did develop a fan following, and it watched with interest as the Sci-Fi Channel purchased the show and set about repairing much of the contextual damage caused by CBS's interference. On the Sci-Fi Channel, *American Gothic* episodes were run in the order intended by Raimi and Cassidy, and the remaining unaired shows were also seen for the first time. *Gothic* also managed to make a huge splash overseas, especially in Great Britain, where it was appreciated as a unique addition to horror tele-fantasy. The opening episode even merited the number 3 spot in *Cult TV's* top twenty (ever) scariest cult TV moments.

After *American Gothic* folded, Gary Cole went on to play Mike Brady in a second *Brady Bunch* film for Paramount, to star in the ill-fated sequel to *Babylon 5* called *Crusade*, and to appear as the strong, silent villain in Sam Raimi's Oscar nominated 1998 picture *A Simple Plan* with Billy Bob Thornton and Bill Paxton. *The X-Files* (1997) feature film was notable for reuniting two *American Gothic* stars: Lucas Black (Caleb) and Chris Fennell, who had played Caleb's friend Boone in several episodes.

CRITICAL COMMENTARY

Shaun Cassidy and Sam Raimi's *American Gothic* is one of those rare modern terror TV shows (like Chris Carter's *Millennium*) which seems to be constructed not only for entertainment and business purposes, but for artistic reasons as well. Just as *Millennium* is filled with symbols (such as Frank Black's perfect yellow house), so is *American Gothic* rigorously faithful to its literate-sounding title. To wit, it is a modern Gothic romance set in the United States. The discussion of the Gothic influence on television sometimes falls into woefully imprecise terms these days. A dramatic series cannot be labeled as Gothic simply because of like-named architecture or because a long-haired heroine in flowing white robes is seen racing down darkened corridors in flickering lights. On the contrary, it should be remembered that the Gothic movement in literature was designed as a response, a negative reaction actually, to the age of reason known as the Enlightenment. It is only appropriate then that *American Gothic*, a Gothic adventure, follows *The X-Files* on the air quite closely, for it too can be viewed as a reaction, a pointed contrast, to the scientific world of *The X-Files*.

The X-Files, perhaps the best terror TV series of all time, espouses a rigorous devotion to specific Enlightenment mores and tenets. Although horrible monsters, diseases, aliens, and the like are known to exist in Chris Carter's universe, they are almost universally catalogued successfully by the reach of science (in the form of Dana Scully). The disease of "F. Emasculata," the mutants of "Teliko," "The Host," "2Shy" and "Agua Mala," and even the fungal life form of "Field Trip," are ultimately explained not through religion, spiritual, or even romantic terms, but through rational explanations transmitted through the auspices of scientific knowledge, scientific deduction and/or extrapolation. In other words, *The X-Files* is an Enlightenment-style show because it preaches (to a certain extent) the worldview of Darwin or any other "rationalist"; specifically that the world can be explained in empirical, reasonable terms and even bizarre anomalies (such as man-sized fluke worms) can be legitimately verified through a basic understanding of biology, endocrinology, immunology, whathaveyou. Though Mulder is a "believer" not a medical doctor, he is also a scientist of a specific sort. He is a psychologist who seeks to understand the world through that particular branch of science and understanding. Mulder may be more imaginative than Scully in his deductions, but he employs the tools of science (whether it be his own experience with psychology, or Scully's lectures in biology and medicine) to make a daring deduction about something heretofore unknown (such as an ancient sea monster washed inland, or a prehistoric lifeform living in trees). Mulder is not *anti* science, he just utilizes science as a jumping board to new frontiers, new understandings, a leap that Scully is not always willing to accept.

American Gothic is quite different in its approach to horror. There is little or no science in this show, and even less explanation. The series never states flat out that Lucas is the devil, or that the devil even exists. It does not attempt to explain Merlyn's existence as a ghost, or Caleb's dark internal power. It is a Gothic imagining that rebels against the rationalism of shows such as *The X-Files* by being purposefully enigmatic. More importantly, *American Gothic* fits all the criteria of a Gothic romance. In no particular order, it fulfills the following fundamental "Gothic" rules.

To start, *American Gothic* is a passage from mundane reality to a dark region governed by a supernatural, evil being. Matt Crower leaves Boston a shattered man only to move to beautiful Trinity, South Carolina. There he discovers that Lucas Buck, a figure of strange abilities and allegiances, influences and rules the town with his dark powers. As

in Bram Stoker's *Dracula*, evil predominates in this town, and Lucas Buck, like the count, is the center of the action in the series. Buck, as portrayed by Cole, is alluring and repulsive at the same time. He is capable of great evil at the same time that he is charismatic and charming. These are essential characteristics of any Gothic romance (and villain). Accordingly, there are several episodes of *American Gothic* ("Doctor Death Takes a Holiday," "The Buck Stops Here" come to mind immediately) in which people attempt to slay the beast, Lucas Buck, just as Dracula himself is eventually dispatched.

Secondly, *American Gothic* features a heroine (Gail Emory) who comes to Trinity to fulfill two qualities of the Gothic heroine. Firstly, she explores dark family secrets, digging deep into the mysteries of the town and her own lineage, not unlike Victoria Winters in either version of *Dark Shadows*. As Buck says of her quest (in "Ring of Fire"): "The secret history of the South is hidden in blood ... history, family, genealogy." What could be more Gothic than this belief that the past infects the present, creating a kind of "secret history" in which the trials and griefs of the dead still cast a pall over the living?

Perhaps more importantly, Gail (a beautiful woman, naturally) finds herself simultaneously attracted to and repelled by Lucas Buck and the power he wields. She despises him on the one hand for his involvement in murder and the seduction of the innocent, but by the end of the short-lived series she is mourning his death ("The Buck Stops Here") and carrying his child! In Gothic imaginings, evil is always a two-faced character: beautiful and ugly at the same time, and the lady of the piece is always drawn to it like a moth to a flame. Gail fits this traditional role perfectly. On a side-note, Merlyn, in her white flowing dress, does fulfill the Gothic's visual need to have a beautiful heroine in long gown running about.

Thirdly, *American Gothic* lives up to the memory of Gothic imaginings and literature by featuring a world where death and decay are always close by. Rotting corpses abound in episodes such as "Rebirth" and "Meet the Bee-tles," and the latter show even concerns a species of insects capable of destroying a human body in seconds. Bodies, bones, skulls, coffins, even a deadly plague — all symbols of mortality and rot — feature prominently in "A Tree Grows in Trinity," "The Plague Sower," and "To Hell and Back." In "Ring of Fire," dead bodies rise menacingly from their graves to point accusing fingers at their murderers. It is as if Lucas has cast a deadly shadow over his town, bringing death and destruction to its beautiful visage. Even when death is not phys-ically represented by such symbols of decay, its presence is felt in almost tangible terms. In "Resurrector," Caleb throws a "going away" party for the "dead," establishing that Trinity is a town where the past lives, and the dead could very well be visitors at your bed and breakfast (as another prominent dead person, the Boston Strangler, turns out to be in "Strangler").

Lastly, *American Gothic* finds a successful U.S. metaphor for the Gothic period in liter-ature. Originally, the late 18th century and early 19th century was the heyday of the Gothic romance, and the movement featured the crumbling castles and ruins of Europe as its primary setting. *American Gothic* trans-plants this exotic locale to the post–Civil War American South, a world where farms and southern plantations are essentially the "crum-bling castles" of another culture. Rusting bridges (in "Rebirth"), forgotten bungalows (in "Ring of Fire"), and even the count's cas-tle (Buck's home) also echo Gothic settings of old. In particular, Buck's house is shown to be a vast, cold place with a seemingly endless, narrow, staircase stretching up and up. Shad-ows line the walls, and the house's interior is filmed in off-kilter angles to suggest the cor-ruption of its owner. This domicile is the modern day equivalent of Collinwood Manor, or the House of Seven Gables. And, impor-tantly, it is here, in evil's domain, that the final conflict between Buck and his would-be heir, Caleb, is fought in "Requiem."

The other half of the title *American Gothic* deals specifically with locale, with America, rather than with story genre, and *American Gothic* does not neglect the fact that it has transplanted its story of evil's allure to the New World. Thus the series manages to explore several American ideas and truisms in its short run. The concept that "nothin' is for free" is nowhere better exemplified than in Buck's Trinity, where a favor given always costs a favor in return. The transient nature of American life, the fact that people move from city to city, is exemplified by the heroes of *American Gothic*. Matt Crower is a Yankee from Boston and Gail Emory grew up in Charleston, but the American lifestyle, cou-pled with fate, brings them to Trinity and a rendezvous with the evil that has already touched their lives (through the death of loved ones, through alcoholism, etc.).

If the title *American Gothic* is examined, it can be seen as a perfect reflection of the se-ries' content and themes. In the same vein, the name of the town where all the action is cen-tered is equally symbolic and relevant to any examination of the series. "Trinity" is the cen-ter of a trinity, all right. The series focuses on the three-way battle and bond between a fa-ther (Lucas Buck), a son (Caleb Temple), and a spirit (Merlyn). Such a set-up may sound simplistic, even trite, but *American Gothic* manages to dramatize all sides of this unusual triangle, sometimes in very different lights. Merlyn is not always the ethereal symbol of beauty and goodness. Sometimes she crosses the line of evil herself, by stealing an innocent life in "Rebirth," and by fostering a deadly disease in "The Plague Sower." Even Caleb is not the perpetual "innocent" of this complex story. He is tempted to use his own dark force in episodes such as "Strong Arm of the Law," "Strangler," and "Requiem." Whether this bubbling fountain of evil is a result of Caleb's genetic makeup asserting itself, a reflection of his ascendance to manhood (and concurrent departure from a Paradiselike state of grace) or simply his very human failure to resist temp-tation and sin, is not clearly defined, yet *Amer-ican Gothic* artfully allows all such readings as a possibility. The "trinity" of Trinity is part of the show's initial blueprint, its design, and its makeup is examined in many installments of the series.

American Gothic has a literary basis beyond the Gothic movement as well. The series is designed as an updating of the Faust legend. In virtually every episode, a needy townsman is shown making a deal with Buck, a bargain with Trinity's Mephistopheles. Buck plays on greed in "Inhumanitas" to undo a materialistic yuppie with whom he has made a real estate deal. Buck plays on the marital jealousy and lust of a radio personality in "Resurrector" to undo his bid for success in television. What remains so notable (and praiseworthy) about the Faustian structure of *American Gothic* is that it extends well beyond the rotating guest cast. In other words, Buck manipulates not only the expendable character and guest performer of the week, he works his evil magic on series regulars. He exploits Dr. Crower's guilty feelings and desire for oblivion in "To Hell and Back." He capitalizes on Gail's desire to know the truth in "Ring of Fire," making a deal with the reporter which will bring her, ultimately, to his bed. In this case, Buck makes his intentions perfectly clear. In a moment of rare honesty he tells Gail that he "doesn't actually give," he "*deals.*" These Faustian bargains (later handled with comedic flair in *G vs E* [1999]) form the foundation of *American Gothic*'s ongoing storyline.

Ironically, the only person Buck cannot make a deal with in the series is his own son, Caleb. The Temple boy manages to avoid the seduction of money (the root of all evil) in "Strong Arm of the Law," as well as the promise of material possessions in "Dead to the World." In these early shows, Caleb represents incorruptible innocence. He exists in a state where he understands right from wrong, almost innately.

The horror imagery of *American Gothic* is second to none. This is a very scary show, and one that does not pull its punches. A fallen priest shoots up heroin in his church quarters in "Potato Boy." That sequence of vile drug use is relentlessly cross-cut with the sanctified symbols of the Catholic faith including the crucifix and idols of Jesus and Mary. As in the best of terror TV programming, ideas are conveyed visually in *American Gothic*, and this sequence of contrasts (a holy man committing a sin on church grounds) exposes the hypocrisy of religion in general and specifically of the misguided belief that a man, any man, can be above sin or temptation.

Other moments and episodes are equally provocative (which might be the reason why "Potato Boy" and other shows never got air time on network TV). In "Damned if You Don't," Lucas exacts the nastiest revenge imaginable against a man who has failed him. Once, a long time ago, a fella named Carter was saved by Lucas after he diddled another man's young (underage) daughter. After failing to help Lucas on another task, Lucas sees to it that an ex-con is released from prison so as to seduce Carter's teenage daughter. This show is unabashedly about sex, and about sex of a particularly forbidden variety—with a minor, specifically. This barely concealed subtext comes to life in a vivid scene involving, of all things, an orange ice pop. While luxuriating on a front porch, the ex-convict lovingly dips a phallic-shaped orange ice-pop into the teen's sensuous mouth (in closeup!). He tells her to open up and that licking the pop "is the best of all." The beautiful young girl, with full red lips and a wild mane of auburn hair, does exactly as the convict asks ... before being interrupted by her horrified father. This none-too-subtle representation of fellatio may be a wee bit explicit for some, but it demonstrates how *American Gothic* took chances and reflected its storyline with visual reinforcement. The teleplay itself tip-toed around the notion of sex with a minor, but this brief scene brought the point home in a succinct, visual manner. Any father who saw that sequence understood immediately the terror that Carter felt upon witnessing the ice-pop moment.

In another show ("Meet the Beetles"), Caleb digs up his own grave and finds a twisted, demonic version of himself lurking there. Besides being quite a shock, this horror image is a riff on the old (and Gothic!) concept of the doppelganger, the villainous "other." The idea of an evil double is interesting in *American Gothic* because one has the distinct sense that the demonic Caleb, discovered both literally and symbolically beneath the surface, represents or foreshadows the future. After all, Caleb is not yet dead so he cannot be digging up his past here. Instead, he is unearthing a glimpse of his future, an evil future fully realized in shows such as "The Buck Stops Here" and "Requiem."

Amid all the Gothic conceits and horror imagery, *American Gothic* manages, amazingly, to be funny at the same time that it is scary. The dialogue is unabashedly wicked in spots. Brenda Bakke, in particular, has fun with the role of the town femme fatale. In "Meet the Beetles" she is accosted by a lustful swimming instructor poolside. She spurns his advances and he croaks: "What am I supposed to do here by myself?!" Without batting an eye, Selena replies succinctly: "stroke." That kind of perverse humor typifies *American Gothic*'s approach to life. It can be deadly serious, or straight-out funny. Although some moments do border on camp, such as the notorious moment in the pilot wherein Lucas Buck whistles the theme song to *The Andy Griffith Show*, the serious tone of the series is rarely compromised for an easy laugh.

American Gothic is one of the ten best horror TV shows of the contemporary age (1970–99) because it features a powerful antihero beautifully portrayed by Gary Cole, because it was designed from the outset to be symbolic and thus artistic (with Gothic imagery and tenets embroidered throughout the format), but mostly because it is a parable about human failings. Lucas Buck uses "the American dream" to destroy the souls of his enemies, and he has been heard on more than one occasion to state that "free will is an illusion" ("Meet the Beetles," "Triangle"). In its depiction of a world controlled by evil, where men and women labor under the notion that they have a choice in their fate, *American Gothic* is one of the most daring, and best realized morality plays of recent memory.

CAST AND CREDITS

Cast: Gary Cole (Sheriff Lucas Buck); Jack Weber (Dr. Matt Crower); Lucas Black (Caleb Temple); Paige Turco (Gail Emory); Brenda Bakke (Selena Coombs); Sarah Paulson (Merlyn Temple); Nick Searcy (Ben Healy); John Mese (Dr. Peel).

Credits: Created by: Shaun Cassidy. *Music:* Joseph LoDuca. *Co-Producer:* Judi Ann Mason. *Coordinating Producer:* Dean Barnes. *Producers:* Edward Ledding, David Eick. *Supervising Producer:* Shaun Cassidy. *Directors of Photography (various episodes):* Stephen McNutt. *Editors (various episodes):* Brian L. Chambers, Thomas R. Moore, Chuck Weiss. *Executive Producers:* Sam Raimi, Robert Tapert. *Unit Production Manager:* Ric Rondell. *First Assistant Director:* Thomas Zapata. *Second Assistant Director:* Stefania Girloami Goodwin. *Post-Production Supervisor:* Billy Crawford. *Sound Supervisor:* Chris Harrengt. *Production Coordinator:* Eleanor Hemingway. *Music Editor*: Patty Von Ark. *Art Director:* Geoffrey S. Grimsman. *Set Decorator:* Tim Stepeck. *Property Master:* Richard Waldrop. *Construction Coordinator:* Barry Spencer. *Costume Designer:* Peggy Farrell. *Makeup:* Jeff Goodwin. *Hairstylist:* D. Michelle Johnson. *Script Supervisor:* Christine Moore. *Sound Mixer:* Richard Van Dyke. *Gaffer:* Stephen Thompson. *Key Grip:* Mark R. Smith. *Visual Effects Supervisor:* Kevin O'Neill. *Stunt Coordinator:* Gregg Smrz. *Location Manager:* Brad Smith. *Transportation Coordinator:* Lee Siler. *Special Effects Coordinator:* Michael Schora. *Location Casting:* Fincannon and Associates. *Original Casting* Liberman/Hirschefield Casting, CSA. From Renaissance Pictures. Distributed through Universal Television, an MCA Company.

EPISODE GUIDE

Note: CBS made mincemeat of the *American Gothic* ongoing plotline by airing episodes out of order, and not airing several episodes of the series at all ... thus creating story gaps. The episode guide below reflects the order in which the episodes *should* have been aired. It is this sequence of shows which is now considered canon, and aired on the Sci-Fi Channel.

1. "Pilot" Written by Shaun Cassidy; Directed by Peter O'Fallon; airdate: September 22, 1995; *Guest Cast:* Lynda Clark (Rita Barber); Michael Burgess (Dan Truelane); Margo Moorer (Danielle Davenport); Lucius Houghton (Deputy Cammalous); Troy Simmons (Josh Davenport); Tammy Arnold (Caleb's Mother); McKenzie LaCross (6-year-old Merlyn); Leonard Watkins (Blind Man); Tamara Dows (Nurse Wendy).

On a rainy night on the outskirts of the South Carolina town called Trinity, young Caleb Temple flees his home as his father attacks his older sister, Merlyn, an autistic teen who won't stop repeating that "there's someone at the door." The authorities soon arrive and Sheriff Lucas Buck kills Merlyn in secret and frames her father for the crime. At the hospital later, Lucas Buck demands custody of Caleb, but the boy is protected by Dr. Matt Crower, a transplanted Yankee with a history of alcoholism. Buck tries to manipulate Caleb's father into giving him full, solitary custody of the boy, but Caleb's cousin, Gail Emory, arrives in town and squashes the sheriff's plot.

2. "A Tree Grows in Trinity" Written by Shaun Cassidy; Directed by Michael Katleman; airdate: September 29, 1995; *Guest Cast:* Arnold Vosloo (Rafael "Sol" Santo); Ron Perkins, Michael Burgess (Dr. Daniel Trulane); David Linthall (Curtis Z. Webb); Gina Stewart (Teapot); Mert Hatfield (The Reverend); Sean Bridgers (Deputy #1); Charles McLawhorn (Albert); Dale Wright (Nurse); Charly Williams (Taylor); Ralph Bronewell (Orderly #1).

After Caleb's house burns down, Gail Emory and Sheriff Buck meet and try to find him. Buck was the person who found the corpses of Gail's parents in a mysterious fire some twenty years ago, and Gail suspects foul play. Meanwhile, Deputy Ben worries that the coroner's exam of the dead Gage Temple

(Caleb's father) will reveal that his monogrammed pen (stolen by Lucas) was the murder weapon. The coroner, who works for Lucas Buck, falsifies the autopsy reports on Merlyn and Gage's deaths so as to hide Buck's involvement.

3. "Eye of the Beholder" Written by Judi Ann Mason; Story by Shaun Cassidy and Judi Ann Mason; Directed by James Charleston; airdate: October 6, 1995; *Guest Cast:* N'Bushe Wright (Sheryl Tulane); Michael Burgess (Daniel Tulane); Tina Lifford (Laurice Holt); Bob Hanna (Judge Harris Halpern); Rick Warner (Heywood Anderson); Chris Fennell (Boone); Grenoldo Frazier (Reverend Logan); Barry Bell (Gordy Wills); Evan Rachel Wood (Rose Russell); Maria Howell (Choir Soloist).

Sheriff Buck now has Caleb in his temporary custody, but young Caleb is none too happy about it. When Caleb expresses his desire to live with Dr. Crower, Buck causes Crower's newest patient to go crazy on the operating table. Lucas also blackmails Daniel, Crower's assistant, into testifying against the doctor at Caleb's custody hearing. Buck gives Daniel's wife a special mirror which arouses her and transforms her into a sexually hyped-up Narcissus.

4. "Damned If You Don't" Written by Michael R. Perry and Stephen Gaghan. Directed by Lou Antonio; airdate: October 10, 1995; *Guest Cast:* Muse Watson (Carter Bowen); Brigid Walsh (Poppie); Steve Rankin (Sutkin); Judy Simpson Cook (Etta Bowen); Barnaby Carpenter (T.J.); Chris Fennell (Boon); Troy Simmons (Josh); John Henry Scott (Janitor); Donald S. Bland (Cooper); Juliet Cesario (Gail's Mother); Jana Drue (Young Gail).

Lucas Buck visits Carter Bowen, the town mechanic, to collect on an old favor: in exchange for past help during a crisis, the sheriff wants Carter's lovely 15-year-old daughter, Poppie, to "assist" him at the office. When Carter fails to comply with the terms of their arrangement, Lucas sees to it that Mrs. Bowen is electrocuted. Meanwhile, Lucas also helps Caleb with his science project, a miniature tornado, even though Merlyn thinks Caleb should accept no help from Buck. In the Bowen junkyard, Gail finds the car her parents owned when they died, and Lucas makes another deal with Carter, one involving a particularly nasty sort of revenge concerning Poppie, and a sex-starved ex-con from Carter's past.

5. "Dead to the World" Written by Robin Green, Mitchell Burgess, Shaun Cassidy, Michael R. Perry and Stephen Gaghan; Directed by James Contner; airdate: October 13, 1995; *Guest Cast:* Linda Pierce, Melissa McBride, John Shearin, Lee Norris, Helen Baldwin (Barbara Joy Flood); Rachel Seidman-Lechmany (Charlotte); Troy Simmons (Josh); Barnaby Carpenter (T.J.); Alex Van (Jailer); Scott Schumacher (Diver); Debbie Yates (Louellen).

Gail learns that an old friend, a nurse named Holly Gallagher, died in Trinity ten years ago ... while dating Lucas Buck. Meanwhile, Ben discovers that his ex-wife and son are being beaten by Whalen, the new man in their lives. Caleb practices for an archery contest over Merlyn's objections, who worries that her brother is becoming too violent and too eager to win. Gail tries to uncover the truth about Holly's fate by demanding that the car she died in be pulled from the river ... but the car is empty, and more questions are raised.

6. "Potato Boy" Written by Michael Nankin; Directed by Nick Marck; unaired; *Guest Cast:* Tina Lifford (Miss Holt); Trip Cogburn (Potato Boy); Zander Heinen (Potato Boy Vocals); Sara Lynn Moore (Mrs. Russell); Chris Fennell (Boone); Evan Rachel Wood (Rose Russell); John Inscoe (Dr. Perry).

Caleb and his friends trade apocryphal stories about a run down old house in the neighborhood rumored to be the home of an abomination called "The Potato Boy." Merlyn assures Caleb that the Potato Boy is no monster, but a human being with a pure and innocent soul. Meanwhile, Buck tells Caleb that he wants to be his mentor, even while Ben struggles with his own apprenticeship under

the sheriff. When Ben reveals to his therapist that Sheriff Buck murdered Merlyn Temple, Lucas has to use a little bit of "reverse" psychology to keep his secret safe.

7. "Meet the Beetles" Written by Victor Bumbalo and David Chisholm; Story by Victor Bumbalo, David Chisholm and Shaun Cassidy; Directed by Michael Nankin; airdate: October 20, 1995; *Guest Cast:* Bruce Campbell (Lt. Dre); Keith Flippen, Mark Joy, David Lenthall, Chris Fennell (Boon); Selden Smith (Lydia Constantine); Alex Van (Deputy Floyd); Derin Altay (Betty Weller).

By night, Caleb returns to the burned-out shell of his old house, only to discover a skeleton beneath the destroyed floorboards. The corpse belongs to Haskell Weller, a Trinity man who had a lust for Selena, but the odd thing is that he died only three days ago ... not nearly enough time for all his flesh to be stripped away. A paleontologist suggests to Gail that a local breed of beetles capable of cleaning (by devouring) a human body in seconds, may be the culprit. Meanwhile, Caleb is bribed by Sheriff Buck with $30,000 to live at the sheriff's new palatial home ... which is to be built on Caleb's old farm.

8. "Strong Arm of the Law" Written by Michael R. Perry and Stephen Gaghan; Directed by Mike Binder; airdate: November 3, 1995; *Guest Cast:* Matt Craven (Barrett); Richard Edson (Lowell Stokes); Joseph Lindsey (Earl); Jim Gloster (Eddie); Chris Fennell (Boon); Dean Whitworth (Cecil Perkins); Mert Hatfield (Minister); Audrey Dollar (Janice); Sarah Lynn Moore (Carol).

Caleb peers into the window of a neighbor, Will Hawkins, only to see him being drowned in his bathtub by four men in ghoulish pig masks. When Lucas learns that someone is squeezing the Trinity business community on behalf of a false organization called the Retired Sheriff's Home of America, he realizes that the four strangers in town are muscling in on his populace and his territory. Buck erects a nasty revenge for these newcomers to Trinity, and proves definitively who is boss.

9. "The Beast Within" Written by Shaun Cassidy; Directed by Michael Lange; airdate: July 3, 1996; *Guest Cast:* Jeff Perry (Artie); Lynda Clark (Rita); Rick Forrester (Salesman); Henry Laurence (Elderly Man); General Fermon Judd Jr. (Fireman).

Ben's brother Artie holds up a video store, and Lucas and Ben attempt to apprehend him. Artie is shot during the confrontation but he nonetheless makes Buck his hostage as he is tended to by Dr. Crower at the hospital. With Caleb, Crower, Buck, and Gail endangered by his brother, Ben must now play the hero to save his friends and his brother's life. The stakes are especially high because Artie is wired with explosives, and Buck is ready to take the matter into his own, evil, hands at any moment.

10. "To Hell and Back" Written by Judi Ann Mason and Robert Palm; Directed by Oz Scott; airdate: July 3, 1996; *Guest Cast:* W. Morgan Sheppard (Mr. Emmett); Andi Carnack (Doreen); Chris Fennell (Boone); Michael Burgess, Robert Treveiler, Laura Robbins, Charles McLawhorn.

When a drunk driver and his wife, Doreen, are rushed to the hospital following a terrible accident, Dr. Crower relives a similar experience from his own life in which his wife and his daughter were killed. Meanwhile, Caleb gossips about his neighbor, an old man who howls at the moon and seems to be burying bones in his backyard. As a long night at the hospital progresses, Matt is haunted by visions of his dead wife and daughter. With Crower in a weakened state, Buck makes him a deal: he'll give the doctor a second chance to make things right with his wife and daughter, as well as the comfort of oblivion, all to keep Crower out of Trinity forever.

11. "Rebirth" Written by Victor Bumbalo and Robert Palm; Story by Victor Bumbalo; Directed by James Frawley; airdate: January 3, 1996; *Guest Cast:* Danny Masterson (Ray); Amy Steel (Christie); Sarah Lynn Moore (Mrs. Russell); Chris Blackwelder (Young Man); Kelly Mizell (Young Woman); Deborah K. Winstead (Nurse #1); Lanelle Markgraf (Nurse #2); Michael Mattison (Dead Head); Randell Haynes (Sourpuss).

Gail's expectant friend Christie is in Trinity for a visit when Merlyn steals her baby's soul so as to return to Earth as a human teenager and feel the emotions and connections she missed as a human mortal. Though Caleb begs Merlyn to return to the land of the dead so Christie's baby might live, Merlyn has fallen in love with a handsome biker rebel named Ray, and does not want to go back. Sheriff Buck is watching Ray closely already and now he is doubly suspicious of the "mystery" girl in town who resembles Merlyn Temple. Merlyn and Buck prepare for a fateful showdown, while Ray is alarmed to discover the real fate of Merlyn.

12. "Ring of Fire" Written by Michael R. Perry and Stephen Gaghan; Directed by Lou Antonio; unaired; *Guest Cast:* Collin Wilcox Patton, Sonny Shroyer, Sandi Fix (Christine Emory); John Keenan (Peter Emory); Jana Drue (Young Gail); Dorothy Recasner Brown (Female Doctor); David Cutting (Toddler).

Plagued by dreams of a tragic past, Gail is compelled to discover the precise circumstances in which her parents died (or were killed). To help Gail discover the truth, she enlists Sheriff Buck, the man she deems culpable. Buck "escorts" Gail into a vision of her past in which she sees her parents hiding an important document, and then, in reality, Buck takes Gail to the house where the document remains hidden ... and a family secret is finally revealed.

13. "Resurrector" Written by Shaun Cassidy, Michael R. Perry and Stephen Gaghan; Directed by Elodie Keene; airdate: January 10, 1996; *Guest Cast:* Greg Travis (Mel Kirby); Irene Ziegler (Gloria Kirby); Tina Lifford (Miss Holt); Chris Fennell (Boone); Lynda Clark (Rita); Philip Lock (Lance Biggs); Andrea Powell (Jean Biggs); Craig Edwards (Technician).

A Trinity radio personality wants to move up to a TV gig, and he seeks Lucas's help in making the transition. Meanwhile, Caleb is upset that Merlyn has stopped communicating with him, and decides to throw a "going away" party for her. Ben feels guilty after shooting Mr. Biggs, a Trinity homeowner who went crazy with his shotgun one afternoon. Buck compels the radio man to kill his wife and longtime partner so he can jump to TV without any hangers-on.

14. "Inhumanitas" Written by Stephen Gaghan and Michael R. Perry; Directed by Bruce Seth Green; airdate: January 17, 1996; *Guest Cast:* Pat Hingle (Pastor); Tim Grimm (Brian Hudson); Ruth Reid (Barbara Hudson); Wayne DeHart (Bertie); Yvonne Graetzer (Female Realtor); Brandlyn Whitaker (Sue Ellen Hudson); Peter Townes (Frenchman).

Lucas Buck has been blackmailing Trinity's pastor to reveal the secrets of the townspeople he has heard during confession. Buck uses that ill-gotten information to scam an enemy, a lawyer who sued the sheriff's department and walked away with $600,000, out of his property and home. Meanwhile, Merlyn returns to the mortal coil to engage Buck in final combat. After he repents his allegiance to Buck, the town pastor teams with Merlyn in the church to bring the war to Trinity's sheriff.

15. "The Plague Sower" Written by Robert Palm; Directed by Mel Damski; airdate: January 24, 1996; *Guest Cast:* Michael Harding, Robin Mullins, Patt Noday, Margo Moorer, Amy Dawn Anderson, Haley Salyer, Gene Dann, John Henry Scott, Kay Joyner.

People are dying in Trinity from a bizarre disease: an illness which leaves the corpses bleeding from their eyes and ears. A doctor named Peel from the CDC comes to town to investigate, and immediately suspects that Sheriff Buck may be involved in an effort to further this plague. Meanwhile, Gail and Buck overcome their differences and begin to become romantically involved. Meanwhile, Dr. Crower thinks he is having a nervous breakdown after several disturbing visions and a visit from Merlyn Temple.

16. "Doctor Death Takes a Holiday" Written by Victor Bumbalo; Directed by

Doug Lefler; airdate: January 31, 1996; *Guest Cast:* Veronica Cartwright (Mrs. Smith); Tamara Burnham (Charlotte); Will Leskin (Judge Streeter); Tina Lifford (Miss Holt); Nancy Saunders, Amy Parrish, Tyrone Hicks, Henry Laurence, Bill Roberson.

A sick woman who claims to be Sheriff Buck's mother attempts to kill the evil Buck. Upon listening to the woman's stories, Dr. Crower becomes involved in the turmoil and soon attempts to murder Lucas Buck himself. Meanwhile, Lucas Buck uses the weaknesses of a local judge's family to have Dr. Crower committed to an insane asylum.

17. "Learning to Crawl" Written by Robert Palm and David Kemper; Directed by Michael Lange; airdate July 4, 1996; *Guest Cast:* Ted Raimi, Alex Van, Stuart Greer, Regan Forman, Amy Dawn Anderson.

A father-son weekend fishing trip turns evil when Sheriff Buck attempts to cultivate young Caleb's dark powers. When a crisis occurs in the woods involving three murderous criminals and a remote cabin, Buck and Caleb find that their respective "powers" are necessary to stay alive and bring "justice."

18. "Echo of Your Last Goodbye" Written by John Cork; Directed by Oz Scott; unaired; *Guest Cast:* Tanya Rollins, Chris Fennell (Boone); Alex Van (Deputy Floyd); Robin Mullins (Nurse Stacie); Tammy Arnold.

In another attempt to stop Sheriff Buck, Merlyn makes herself visible to Ben. This is all an attempt on her part to implicate (again) Lucas in her own death months earlier. Meanwhile, Gail learns of Caleb's heritage even as Caleb faces a challenge at school.

19. "Triangle" Written by Jeff King and Robert Palm; Directed by James Frawley; airdate: July 10, 1996; *Guest Cast:* Robin Mullins (Nurse Stacie); Deacon Dawson (Pilot); Amy Dawn Anderson (Nurse #1); Russell Deats (Little Luke); James Frawley (Bartender).

Gail discovers she is pregnant with Sheriff Buck's baby after their physical affair, and he prevents her from leaving town with Caleb. Meanwhile, Buck attempts to win back

Selena and get rid of her new lover, Dr. Peel. Haunted by visions of a demonic child, Gail contemplates an abortion. While Dr. Peel plots to steal away from Trinity (for Uganda) with Selena, Gail's sanity snaps and she becomes suicidal.

20. "Strangler" Written by Michael R. Perry, Stephen Gaghan, Robert Palm; Story by Michael R. Perry and Stephen Gaghan; Directed by Doug Lefler; unaired; *Guest Cast:* Gareth Williams (Albert DeSalvo, The Boston Strangler); Alex Van (Deputy Floyd); Amy Parrish (Nurse Sara); Sean Bridgers (Policeman #1); Rachel Lewis (Nurse #2).

After clashing again with Merlyn at the graveside of Gage Temple, Lucas Buck summons the spirit of Albert DeSalvo, the Boston Strangler, to destroy her soul. DeSalvo arrives in Trinity, but he has a wandering eye and difficulty keeping on task. With Buck gone away at a convention, it is up to Ben to stop DeSalvo after he returns to his old habits, strangles a nurse, and assaults Gail. DeSalvo befriends Caleb to lure Merlyn into the open ... but Caleb proves he is not defenseless.

21. "The Buck Stops Here" Written by Steve De Jarnatt; Directed by Lou Antonio; airdate: July 10, 1996; *Guest Cast:* Jim Antonio, Brent Jennings, Lynda Clark (Rita); Alex Van (Deputy Floyd); Lee Freeman (Doris Lydon); Dean Whitworth (Cecil Spurgeon); John Shearin (Waylon Flood); Wayne DeHart (Old Bertie).

Selena and Dr. Peel make love in Lucas Buck's bed, but the sheriff returns home just as they leave ... and is all too aware of the transgression. Meanwhile, another doctor at the hospital is desperate to cure his wife, and is convinced that Lucas Buck has stolen her medical records so as to punish him. Meanwhile, Gail's pregnancy continues, with her unborn child developing at an alarming rate ... and she is nursing an appetite for raw, bloody meat. When Dr. Peel confronts Buck at his house, he finds Lucas Buck dead, murdered, and is soon fingered and arrested as the killer.

22. "Requiem" Written by Shaun Cassidy; Directed by Lou Antonio; airdate: July 11, 1996; *Guest Cast:* Jim Antonio, Lynda Clark (Rita); Alex Van (Deputy Floyd); Lindley Mayer (Ashley Narone); Don Henderson (Grave Digger); Len Hathaway (Elderly Man); Diana Taylor (Businesswoman); Mary McMillan (Wealthy Woman).

Caleb has become pure evil—and Merlyn tries one more time to save him from the darkness bubbling inside. Selena positions herself to become Caleb's guardian, realizing he is heir to the Buck family power. Buried alive, Lucas Buck is rescued by Dr. Peel and Ben even as Caleb lays a trap for Gail, who is pregnant with a competing Buck heir. Buck races home to stop Caleb from killing his unborn child, but the final battle in Trinity ends in the sacrifice of another life.

28

Kindred: The Embraced (1996)

CRITICAL RECEPTION

"*Kindred*, which might have been wretched and campy — think *Melrose Vampires* or *Vampires 90210*— turns out to be a wry morality play with Julian as a dashing antihero. At its best, *Kindred: The Embraced* shares the appeal of *The X-Files* and other trendy tales of the paranoid and supernatural."— Caryn James, *The New York Times*: "Turf Wars in Which Hunks Vie for Blood," April 2, 1996, page C16.

"resembles cross between oldie soap *Dark Shadows* and syndicated *Nick Knight* in its balance of action and romance.... Acting and dialogue are frequently stilted; this may be intentional, as characterization of the other worldly. Overall look ... is fine."— Todd Everett, *Variety*, April 8–14, 1996, page 38.

FORMAT

Based on a book/game entitled *Vampire: The Masquerade*, the 1996 TV series *Kindred: The Embraced* is a genre soap opera which is part *The Godfather* (1972), part Shakespeare (particularly *Romeo and Juliet*), and part vampire melodrama (*Salem's Lot* [1978] meets *Dracula* meets *Dark Shadows*). If that description intimates that *Kindred: The Embraced* is purely derivative, then it has done the program a disservice, for this hourlong series is ambitious, well-acted, complex, and fun. It is a bright light in the Terror TV pantheon despite its brief run of just eight episodes.

The premise of *Kindred: The Embraced* is simple: vampires live and walk among us in the picturesque city of San Francisco. The details of *Kindred*, however, are anything *but* simple, and the creators have gone to great lengths to create a highly-detailed, even complex back-story and lexicon which nicely speaks of a "real" counterculture at work underneath the face of modern America. Like warring mobsters, the vampires of *Kindred* are separated by blood. Not into families, like the Corleones, but into blood clans. Among these are the Ventru (the businessmen, the administrators), the Gangrel (the warrior caste), the Toriador (the artists, the musicians), the Nosferatu (the only inhuman-looking clan, of mystery) and the youngest clan, the warring Brujah. Each of these five clans has an elected *primogen*, a leader, who sits in at the ruling *conclave*, a legislative and executive council or tribunal overseen by the prince of the city. All the vampires are called *Kindred*, and the word "vampire" is derided as a human invention. All of the Kindred in San Francisco live by a strict law known as *The Masquerade*. The Masquerade prevents Kindred from killing human beings or even revealing their existence to the mortal world. Protecting the Masquerade is an important Kindred law, so important that those who disobey it are sentenced to termination called *final death*.

Still, in some circumstances, Kindred will *embrace* humans to increase their own number. To embrace a human, a Kindred will bite one on the neck, and then replace human blood with his/her own "special" blood. That human then "turns" and his/her "new" Kindred blood reflects the clan that has done the embracing. Embracing a human against his/her will is another Kindred crime, one roughly analogous to rape.

Out of this complex and highly-structured world, *Kindred: The Embraced* recounts the epic saga of Julian Luna (Mark Frankel), the Kindred prince of San Francisco. Like *Forever Knight*, it is a story of redemption as this vampire attempts to preserve the Masquerade, protect humans from exploitation, and prevent an all-out clan war. But, like Michael Corleone, Julian is often undone by plotters and schemers, and even his own character foibles. Luna is a Ventru married to Lillie (Stacy Haiduk), the primogen of the Toriador. They share a kind of "open" love arrangement which permits Luna to stray, but which vexes Lillie because she really loves her prince. Julian is supported in his governing of the city by Daedalus (Jeff Kober), an enforcer primogen of the Nosferatu clan, his headstrong young bodyguard Chase (Channon Roe) of the Gangrels, and Archon Raine (Patrick Bauchau). Raine, like Robert Duvall in *The Godfather*, might be considered a kind of consigliere.

Stories in *Kindred: The Embraced* are often intertwined and complicated. Julian attempts to hold the clans together in peace, but the Brujah, under the evil Eddie Foiri, are just itching for war. A human cop, Frank Kohanke (C. Thomas Howell), discovers the Kindred society and first tries to bring down Luna and later becomes a reluctant ally to his cause when he understands what is at stake. The hotheaded Gangrel Chase falls in love with Sasha (Brigid Walsh), Julian's last living human relative. This couple must carry on their affair in secret because she is Julian's blood, and later she becomes a Brujah — a vampire Juliet to Chase's Gangrel Romeo. Lillie and Julian also spar because Julian has turned away from her and fallen in love with a beautiful human reporter named Caitlin Byrne (Kelly Rutherford), who knows nothing of the Kindred or the Masquerade.

Through the course of this impressive but brief series, much is learned about Kindred society (there is a subsect of shapeshifting assassins called *Acemites*), Kindred history (they were hunted by the Spanish Inquisition), Daedalus (a sensitive, Mr. Spock-like pacifist vampire), and even Archon Raine (who hides a deadly secret from his colorful past). Most

of the action is centered in Julian's palatial home (where the conclave meets regularly), at Lillie's chic nightclub, the Haven, or Frank's favorite greasy spoon (the appropriately named "Night Hawks"). Unlike most TV vampires, Kindred can see their reflections in mirrors, go out in sunlight (if they've fed recently), and can even weather a proximity to garlic bulbs (as seen hanging inside Caitlin Byrne's Dutch Colonial kitchen.)

The title sequence of *Kindred: The Embraced* commences with three black and white illustrations of Nosferatu-like vampires (the first of whom actually resembles Klaus Kinski in the 1979 feature film *Nosferatu*). Then, there is a lovely shot of the Golden Gate Bridge at night. A glowing, full moon races across the screen in fast-motion, from left to right, and the main title comes up in white.

HISTORY

It seems that vampires never go out of fashion, they just get reinvented. It's probably safe to assert that there have been as many variations on vampire lore as there have been horror TV series. Since 1970 alone, the TV universe has given us the "evil" traditional vampire (à la Christopher Lee or Bela Lugosi) in *The Night Stalker*, the tragic and misunderstood vampire (*Dark Shadows*, *Angel*), vampire "heroes" (*Forever Knight*) and even campy vampires (*Cliffhangers*, *Dracula: The Series*). With 1996 and the introduction of *Kindred: The Embraced*, yet another variation is born: the noble bloodsucking mobster. The inspiration for this new wrinkle in a seemingly immortal legend comes not from horror literature or filmic antecedents in the genre, but from the highest-grossing motion picture of 1972: *The Godfather*, starring Al Pacino, Marlon Brando, and Diane Keaton, and directed by Francis Ford Coppola (*Dracula* [1992]). In this classic film, based on the novel by the late Mario Puzo, handsome and swarthy Michael Corleone (Pacino) ascends to the leadership of the mafia. As he does so, his enemies in the other mob families plot to destroy him, the law seeks to expose him, and he attempts to find a way out of the world of crime because, in the end, it costs him everything including love, freedom, salvation, and (in *Godfather III* [1990]) even the life of his only daughter.

Kindred: The Embraced follows the equally swarthy mobster and vampire prince Julian Luna (Mark Frankel) as he too seeks to remain in power, experience love (with a beautiful human reporter), and preserve the rule of law among his warring, sometimes brutal, kind. Instead of clashing Italian families, he holds court over distinctive vampire clans. Although *The Godfather* is the primary source material which *Kindred: The Embraced* seeks to develop, it also has elements of *Romeo and Juliet* (a romance between members of warring clans) and *Dark Shadows* (it is a soap opera but not a gothic one.) With all these antecedents as backdrop, *Kindred* is one of terror TV's genuine epics. It is a lush-appearing production which aspires to be not just horror, drama, or entertainment, but moving tragedy. Created by John Leekley (*Nightmare Cafe*), and co-produced by Aaron Spelling and Mark Rein-Hagen, the author of *Vampire: The Masquerade*, a best selling role-playing game, this series has more going for it than many of recent vintage. It is perfectly cast, with the lovely Stacy Haiduk (*Superboy* [1988-92], *SeaQuest DSV* [1993-96], *Brimstone* [1998]), the villainous Brian Thompson (*Werewolf, Something Is Out There, The X-Files*), the hot-blooded Channon Roe (*Boogie Nights* [1997]), and movie star C. Thomas Howell (*The Hitcher* [1985]) lending dynamite and colorful support to lead Mark Frankel. As for Frankel, he made the difficult role of Luna his own and in the process created modern TV horror's sexiest, most charismatic, and most memorable bloodsucker. Producers on the show also took special care to make each individual episode feel like a chapter in a grand opera rather than just an hourlong video venture.

Sadly, the high quality of *Kindred: The Embraced* could not outweigh the fact that the ratings were terrible. The Fox Network, which has shown considerable good faith by sticking with *The X-Files* and even the low-rated *Millennium* for three years, and bad faith by canceling *Space: Above and Beyond, Strange Luck,* and *The Visitor*, opted to go the latter route with this dynamite series. It pulled *Kindred: The Embraced* from its line-up after a seven week trial run in the spring of 1996. One episode ("Nightstalker") was left unaired in the states when the series was canceled.

Real-life tragedy overcame TV tragedy in September of 1996 when rising star Mark Frankel was killed in an automobile accident scarce months after the last episode of *Kindred: The Embraced* aired. Co-producer Aaron Spelling (who had once hoped to do a revival of *The Twilight Zone* with Rod Serling) returned to the horror genre in 1998 with the far less complex (and far less artistically satisfying) show called *Charmed*. Ironically, *Charmed* is considered a hit primarily because it airs on the WB Network, a network on the way up which is satisfied with lower ratings and smaller audiences. It is a shame *Kindred* never aired there because if it had, it might be considered successful too. Still, resonances of *The Kindred* can be found on the WB today. Stacy Haiduk guest-starred on *Charmed* ("Feats of Clay") as an Egyptian spirit, and both Channon Roe and Jeff Kober (Daedalus) have appeared on the third season of the excellent *Buffy the Vampire Slayer* ("The Zeppo" and "Helpless" respectively).

All eight episodes of *Kindred: The Embraced* have been released on a three VHS tape set from Republic Home Video. Because of the high quality of most episodes in this short-lived series, this set is one collectible worth tracking down.

CRITICAL COMMENTARY

If vampires are your thing, you enjoy soap operas, and the gangster genre is a favorite, a horror fan could do no better than to tune into *Kindred: The Embraced*, a sexy horror TV series which is graced with a plethora of attractive performers, lush production values, and a high erotic content. Taken on its own terms, this is a delightful "soap" which ranks high in the horror pantheon because it introduces a classic TV antihero, the vampire and tragic character, Julian Luna. Luna is an evolved vampire, one generation beyond Barnabas of *Dark Shadows* because, unlike the vampire Collins, this man is satisfied with what he is. With Barnabas there was always the sense that he wanted to be human, to get out of the vampire gig and find love and happiness in old-fashioned, mortal terms. Not so with Julian, a man who is proud of his heritage and people, and utilizes his powers not out of instinct or revenge, but because it is a natural part of him. He is *über mensch* genetically, even if his predisposition is to like humans and what they represent.

What an epic figure this (undead) character is! Luna is a Shakespearean leader of men who is trying to hold his kingdom together at all costs. He is a passionate lover. He is a man prone to violence. He uses women and brute force alike, and yet remains intrinsically heroic despite his dark side and exploitive behavior. Despite foibles such as lust, Luna's heart is in the right place ... just don't stick a stake in it. As performed by the late Mark Frankel, Luna is a memorable TV creation. A glowering, brooding Hamlet of the bloodsucker set, this hero agonizes, longs, fights, and debates in operatic fashion. When *Kindred: The Embraced* focuses on Luna and these very literary values, the short-lived series is almost hypnotic in its power. It works as Shakespeare chic. In Hollywood, inspiration is frequently defined as how well old elements are recombined in new ways, and by giving viewers a Godfather/Shakespearean vampire prince with more than a little melancholy in his character, *Kindred: The Embraced* shines as both horror and drama. The strength of *Kindred: The Embraced*, as in all soap operas, is not in any particular episode, but in the overall arc, the sweep of the story, and the manner in which characters manipulate, maneuver, and manhandle one another.

The Embraced is a sexy show because, in essence, it is about urges and desires, and the need to control and release them. The Kindred themselves are masters of rigid control. One of their primary and most sacred rules (as char-acterized in "Nightstalker") is to "drink only what you need, nothing more." Inherent in that directive is the notion that there are some Kindred who *cannot* control what they are, or the breadth of their appetites. That is where the eroticism comes in: the surrender of reason to lust and hunger. The fear of losing control, of devouring and being devoured, informs the very premise of this TV series. The show is also quite clearly about the grasping and aspiring for the forbidden, another tenet of erotic drama. Humans are "forbidden" ground for the Kindred, yet Julian and Caitlyn become lovers. Even among the clans, certain attachments are forbidden. Sasha (a Brujah) and Cash (a Gangrel) are not allowed to mingle ... yet they do mingle. In these and other examples, *Kindred: The Embraced* is about breaking societal taboos for the purpose of lust, and emotional satisfaction. As such, it is quite a passionate series. It is a welcome change from the current face of horror, which because of *The X-Files* is very much steeped in rationalism and science (i.e., *Strange World*, *The Burning Zone*, and others). *Kindred: The Embraced* is a reminder that horror can be an emotional, sentimental genre as well as one filled with rationality, science, and explanation.

Of course, vampires have always been erotic creations, since before Bram Stoker's novel, even. "Sucking" blood, life's precious fluid, has been characterized as erotic, euphoric, even orgasmic in many films over the past one hundred years, and that tenet survives in spades in *Kindred*. In "Prince of the City," Julian Luna flies to Caitlyn Burns' bedroom window by night. Her curtains flap and rustle, the breeze blows, and there is an awareness on the part of the viewer that the Dracula archetype is still a powerful one. A charming, erotic man seduces a desirable young woman, his lust and otherworldliness serving as both an aphrodisiac and contrast to her innocence and beauty. The times have changed, and the vampire no longer wears a cape, but the situation remains the same, as eternal as the vampire myth.

Kindred: The Embraced is a compelling

series not just because it is very sexy, but because it features an epic sprawl. This is not just the story of Julian Luna. It is the chronicle of his city, and his law as the Brujah clan tries to seize control and is eventually defeated in a gang war. Part of the series' hypnotic power comes from the fact that it begins *in medias res*, with a living background behind the stories. It is announced early on that Archon is a former leader of the city, representing the past, and Luna's previous attachments (including the lovely Alexandra) also bring history to light. Beyond that, the series provides tantalizing glimpses of the past: references and allusions to the Kindred through history: during the Spanish Inquisition, and before. Vampire legend is addressed, and so on. All of these factors lend a verisimilitude to the series, a sense that viewers are peeking in on a world already in progress. *Kindred* is artful because it starts not "at the beginning," but in the present, and then weaves generations of history, legend, and personal lives into the here and now. Beyond this approach, *Kindred* is compelling in the way all good soap operas manage to be. It is filled with intrigues and mysteries. Who is having sex with whom? Who *wants* to have sex with whom? Who will betray Julian, and why? Watching people (and vampires) act on emotional, lustful impulses makes the series unpredictable and fun to watch.

This book is about terror TV, and the above review may not make it clear exactly in what manner *Kindred: The Embraced* fits that bill. Though it is about vampires and their loves and lusts, the show also trades in frightening ideas and stories. At the core of *Kindred* is the concept that man is being hunted by a superior species (also the central notion of *Prey* [1998]), and that he is unaware of it. The show also deals in frightening implications. Luna is a fair and just prince, but if the balance of power in San Francisco should suddenly shift and the Masquerade be terminated, what would become of humankind? Traditional horror stories are also introduced in various stories. Babies are kidnapped and sacrificed for a blood ritual in "Bad Moon Rising" and there is the rape of innocence in "Live Hard, Die Young and Leave a Good Looking Corpse."

Although *Kindred: The Embraced* is sexy, compelling, and filled with horror, it is not without its flaws. The show as a whole is better than many of its individual stories, if that is possible. Additionally, logic and continuity are not always applied from program to program. For instance, Luna continually asserts that Kindred do not break their own rules. But in "Nightstalker," "Romeo and Juliet," and "Live Hard, Die Young and Leave a Good Looking Corpse," the Kindred *do* break the rules. Kindred serial killers, Kindred doctors who drink the blood of children, and a renegade Kindred rock 'n' roller who embraces humans against their will are all featured in the short-lived series. After awhile, it would seem impossible for Luna to make any claim that Kindred are law-abiding people. More troubling, perhaps, is the fact that C. Thomas Howell seems miscast as Frank, the tough-as-nails cop. The quality of *Kindred: The Embraced* episodes rises significantly when Howell and his hackneyed character are little involved in the proceedings.

Still, *Kindred: The Embraced*'s obsession with breaking taboos, with bearing witness to appetites satiated, and its emotional battlegrounds make it a unique modern series in an era when we demand so much rationality and explanation. This series is the ultimate extension of the horror soap opera developed by *Dark Shadows*, *Twin Peaks*, and *American Gothic*. The Shakespearean and *Godfather* overtones and strong performance by Mark Frankel make this series a memorable addition to the horror Valhalla, and one of the all-time best as well.

CAST AND CREDITS

Cast: C. Thomas Howell (Detective Frank Kohanek); Kelly Rutherford (Caitlin Byrne); Stacy Haiduk (Lillie Langtree); Mark Frankel (Julian Luna); Erik King (Sonny); Channon Roe (Cash); Brigid Walsh (Sasha);

Patrick Bauchau (Archon Raine); Jeff Kober (Daedalus).

Credits: Music: J. Peter Robinson, John Tartaglia. *Theme Music:* J. Peter Robinson. *Editor (various episodes):* Ron Binkowski, Russell Livingstone, Ray Lovejoy, Susanne Stinson Malles. *Production Designer:* Trevor Williams. *Director of Photography (various episodes):* Ernest Holzman, John R. Leonetti. *Co-Producer:* Mark Rein-Hagen, Steve De Jarnatt, P.K. Simonds. *Producers:* Llewellyn Wells, Joel Blasberg. *Executive Producers:* John Leekley, Aaron Spelling, E. Duke Vincent. *From the Book* Vampire: The Masquerade *by* Mark Rein-Hagen. *Associate Producer:* Cheryl R. Stein. *Original Casting:* Rick Millikan. *Casting:* Denise Chamian. *Production Manager:* Llewellyn Wells. *First Assistant Director:* James M. Freitag. *Second Assistant Director:* Jeff Srednick. *Prosthetic Makeup Effects Designed and Created by:* Todd Masters. *Key Prosthetic Makeup:* Thom Floute. *Costume Designer:* Peter Mitchell. *Costume Supervisor:* Donna Barrish. *Key Makeup Artist:* Donna Henderson. *Key Hair Stylist:* Charlotte Harvey. *Set Decorator:* Donald Elmblad. *Property Master:* Tommy Miller. *Sound Mixers:* John Sutton, Charlie Kelly. *Chief Lighting Technician:* Raphael Sanchez. *Camera Operator:* Alan Easton. *Key Grip:* Lloyd Barcroff. *Construction Coordinator:* Richard McDowell. *Script Supervisor:* Joanie Blum. *Location Manager:* Rich Rosenberg. *Stunt Coordinator:* Joe Dunne. *Special Effects:* Mike Meinardos. *Assistant Editor:* Lynn Warr. *Supervising Sound Editor:* Chris Harvengt. *Visual Effects Supervisor:* Ziad Seirafi. *Music Editor:* Rocky Moriana. *Music Coordinator:* Celest Ray. *Production Coordinator:* Nancy Rosing. *Assistant to Mr. Leekley:* Cynthia Eakin-Ayers. *Production Accountant:* Martha Cronin. *Transportation Coordinator:* Dave Bassett. *Executive Associate:* Renate Kamer. *Post Production Sound and Sound Effects:* Todd A-O Studios. *Visual Effects Compositing:* Digital Magic Co. *Digital Artist:* Ralph Maiers. *Color:* Pacific Film. *Filmed Partially on Location at:* Golden Gate National Recreation Area, San Francisco Maritime Historical Park. *Executive in Charge of Production:*

Gail M. Patterson. *Executive in Charge of Post-Production:* Kenneth Miller. John Leekley Productions in association with Spelling Television.

Episode Guide

1. "The Embraced" (aka "The Original Saga", aka "Pilot") Written by John Leekley; Directed by Peter Medak; airdate: April 2, 1996; *Guest Cast:* Kate Vernon (Alexandra Sarris); Brian Thompson (Eddie Fiori); Basil Hoffman, Richard Danielson, Tara Subkoff (Cash's Girl); Cristina Ehrlich (Elegant Young Lady); Gil Combs (Second Assassin); Luis Defreitas (Trainer).

San Francisco cop Frank Kohanek investigates mob boss Julian Luna, a dark and mysterious tycoon who is the prince of all rival Kindred clans. Unbeknownst to Frank, Luna and his people are vampires who hide among the humans, on the verge of a clan war. Alexandra, Frank's beautiful lover, is among the Kindred. She is rebuffed by Luna when she asks him to let her live in peace with Frank. Meanwhile, Luna's last human grandchild passes away and he attends the funeral, meeting the rebellious young Sasha in the process. Luna's wife, Lillie, and another clan leader, Eddie Fiori, conspire to force Luna to declare a blood hunt for Alexandra, who is Luna's ex-wife and first love. Before being murdered by a representative of the Nosferatu clan, Alexandra breaks the "masquerade" and reveals what she really is to Frank. Frank, whose first wife also died, vows to destroy Luna at any cost.

Note: This is the 2-hour premiere episode.

2. "Prince of the City" Written by John Leekley; Directed by Peter Medak; airdate: April 3, 1996; *Guest Cast:* Brian Thompson (Eddie Fiori); Yuji Okumoto (Lieutenant Kwan); Scott MacDonald, Kimberly Campbell, Christian Svensson (Nino Donelli); Michael Bauer (I.A. Investigator); Kim Delgado (I.A. Investigator); Richard Danielson (Billy).

Unaware that his partner Sonny is Kindred, Frank remains obsessed with bringing down Luna, whom he deems responsible for Alexandra's demise. A sting operation designed to topple dock workers' union boss and clan leader Eddie Fiori goes wrong when Frank's informant is discovered to be wearing a wire. Meanwhile, Luna bails the hot-headed Sasha out of prison and introduces her to his new bodyguard, a Gangrel clan member named Chase. At the same time, a beautiful human reporter, Caitlin Byrne, seeks an exclusive interview from Luna after realizing that he is something of a mystery man.

3. "Romeo and Juliet" Written by Joel Blasberg; Directed by Ralph Hemecker; airdate: April 10, 1996; *Guest Cast:* Brian Thompson (Eddie Fiori); Emile Hirsch (Able); Judy Kain (Nurse); Peter Rocca (Nino); Gavin Decker (Martin); Kimberly Hooper (Lorraina); Peter Nelson (Doctor); Brian Lally (Detective O'Fallon).

Cash and Sasha have fallen in love and are meeting together in secret, even as a clan war between the Gangrel and Eddie Fiori's Brujah edges ever closer. Meanwhile, a Kindred physician has been feeding on the blood of human youngsters in a children's hospital, so Daedalus delivers "final death" to him on orders from Julian. Luna, realizing Sasha's situation, allows Cash to embrace her, but the Brujah commit a brutal act and embrace the young human against her will. An infuriated Luna challenges Eddie for his act of defiance, but Eddie just sees this tirade as another excuse for all-out war.

4. "Live Hard, Die Young and Leave a Good Looking Corpse" Written by Aaron Mendelsohn, Paul Tamasy; Directed by James L. Conway; airdate: April 17, 1996; *Guest Cast:* Brian Thompson (Eddie Fiori); Ivan Sergei (Zane); Chandra West (Grace); Christopher Allport (Grace's Father); J.C. Brandy (Riannon); Brook Susan Parker (E.R. Doctor); Stephen Quadros (Brujah); Carol Kiernan (Nurse); Leo Lee (Tong Overlord); Peter Rocca (Brujah #2); Lisa Butler (Floor Manager); David A.R. White (Clerk); Henry Kingi, Jr. (Security).

A young homeless man embraced by Lillie and the Toriador clan has become an overnight rock-and-roll celebrity with an eye for the ladies ... including the recently embraced Sasha. Worse, Zane has been disobeying the law of Luna and embracing his groupies without permission. One of the women he has turned into a vampire is Grace, who is taken to the hospital after a freak accident. She awakens after being pronounced dead and realizes she has been "changed," a fact which causes Luna to order Zane's execution.

5. "The Rise and Fall of Eddie Fiori" Written by Scott Smith Miller; Directed by Kenneth Fink; airdate: April 24, 1996; *Guest Cast:* Brian Thompson (Eddie Fiori); Ed O'Ross (Cyrus); Jack Conley (Benning); Kimberly Campbell, Blair Valk (Marissa); Kimberly Hooper (Lorraina); Richard Danielson (Billy).

A jealous Lillie hires a private investigator to take pictures of Julian and Caitlin Byrne together while Eddie Fiori, still smarting from his recent defeat, sends a shape-shifting Acemite assassin to kill Julian. Meanwhile, Sasha struggles with her blood's genetic hatred for all things Gangrel even while she continues to love Chase. Lillie's detective stumbles into danger when he photographs the Acemite's assassination attempt and then tries to blackmail Luna and Lillie with the incriminating photos. Julian is enraged by Lillie's betrayal, and Lillie seeks solace with Eddie ... who wants her to set up Luna for one more assassination attempt.

6. "Bad Moon Rising" Written by Jean Gennis, Phyllis Murphy; From a story by John Leekley, Jean Gennis, Phyllis Murphy; Directed by James L. Conway; airdate: May 1, 1996; *Guest Cast:* Yuji Okumoto (Lieutenant Kwan); Patricia Charbonneau (Ruth); Maureen Flannigan (Camilla); Skipp Sudduth (Goth); Kimberly Campbell, Una Damon (Mai Sung).

A renegade Nosferatu lurking in the park steals an infant from its mother. The vampire is Goth, who has reverted to his savage form with another Kindred named Camilla. Chase and Sasha reconcile as Chase is recruited to hunt down Goth. Luna, who once banished Goth and Camilla from his city, sets out to kill the two savage Kindred, but ends up learning a secret about Caitlin Byrne.

7. "Cabin in the Woods" Written by P.K. Simonds; Directed by Ralph Hemecker; airdate: May 8, 1996; *Guest Cast:* Titus Welliver (Cameron); Tony Amendola; Gordon Clapps (Clyde).

Julian and Caitlin take a road trip to Sonoma County, where his human family once dwelled. A young Brujah, Cameron, plots to become prince and he sets a trap for Luna and Caitlin in winery country. As it turns out, the young man's bloodlust is justified, for Archon once ordered Luna to conduct a Brujah massacre in that territory. Late at night, Julian is stabbed by Brujah assassins, and Caitlin discovers exactly who and what he is.

Unaired Episode

8. "Nightstalker" Written by P.K. Simonds, John Leekley; Directed by John Harrison; *Guest Cast:* Brian Thompson (Eddie Fiori); Kimberly Kates (Elaine Robb); Scott Mosenson, Kimberly Campbell, Nicky Katt (Starkweather); Aixa Clemente (Medical Examiner); Philip Earl Johnson (Eric); Thomas Pridsco (Dri Mestres); James Ingersoll (Police Sergeant); Lisa Butler (Floor Manager); Jim McDonald (Military Man); Benny Quinn (Young Cop); Troy Spurlin (Jordan).

At Julian's nightclub, the Haven, a recently embraced patron, Starkweather, starts to tear the place up until taken away by the police. Meanwhile, the Nosferatu clan member Daedalus lusts for a beautiful and lonely Haven songstress whom he senses is facing "pain." Sasha continues to lust for Chase, even as Chase explains the rules of the Masquerade to the schizophrenic and disturbed Starkweather. The crazed man, unfortunately, has no intention of obeying the rules of the Kindred and he emerges a vampire serial killer until Julian Luna and Frank Kohanek join forces to stop his reign of terror.

Note: According to the three-box video release of *Kindred: The Embraced* by Republic Pictures, "Nightstalker" fits into series continuity as episode #3, right after "Prince of the City." "Nightstalker" was not aired in the United States.

Poltergeist: The Legacy (1996–1999)

CRITICAL RECEPTION

"cheesy, lurid fun." — *People*, April 22, 1996, page 16.

"Behind the shamelessly misleading title there's only a schlocky Showtime series ... about a secret society that dourly fights the forces of Hell. Some surprising good F/X serve as window dressing for clichés from other, better movies.... Once you've seen Shaver deliver a little devil, then get dragged around the room by her umbilical cord, you'll have seen it all." — Michael Sauter, *Entertainment Weekly*, August 15, 1997, page 87.

FORMAT

Since the dawn of man, a secret organization has existed to combat the forces of evil, the dark side. This mysterious, clandestine brotherhood (which has counted Vlad the Impaler, Theseus, and Sigmund Freud among its members) is known as "the Legacy," and it has "houses" all over the world, from London and Moscow to Capetown, Paris, Boston, and Philadelphia. In the closing years of the twentieth century, these Legacy Houses are populated by dedicated heroes with special skills who have armed themselves with the very newest technology and weaponry available.

Poltergeist: The Legacy is the chronicle of the San Francisco House, a magnificent castle on Angel Island which is run by the imposing and lugubrious Precept, Derek Rayne (Derek de Lint). Rayne is a natural leader of men, a low-grade "touch" psychic, and son of a former Legacy leader (Winston Rayne) who, in death, may have crossed over to the dark side. In his role as San Francisco House Precept,

Rayne leads a crack team of investigators, soldiers, psychics, and psychologists against the agents of Satan. Serving under Rayne is handsome Nick Boyle (Martin Cummins), an ex–Navy SEAL whose harsh father was also a Legacy Man, Alexandra Moreau (Robbi Chong), a lovely African-American psychic who has inherited her powers from her voudon grandmother, an angst-ridden Catholic priest named Callaghan (Patrick Fitzgerald), and the lovely psychiatrist Rachel Corrigan (Helen Shaver). Rachel's daughter, Kat, is the youngest member of the Legacy Team, and an adolescent with fast-developing psychic powers as well.

At the close of the first season, Father Callaghan leaves the Legacy to be replaced by the stern Precept of the London House, William Sloan (Daniel J. Travanti). By the commencement of the third season, Sloan had become trapped in a nether world and was replaced by a visiting Legacy member from Boston, Kristin Adams (Kristin Lehman). Kristin is a tough cookie, not much of a team player at first, who is involved with the Legacy to determine the fate of her father, an archaeologist who virtually disappeared from the face of the Earth.

To prevent its many dramatic battles with evil from being fodder for newspapers, the Legacy operates under the name "The Luna Foundation," and dabbles in everything from police forensic work to antiquities and unearthed artifacts. Often working separately as well as together, the San Francisco Legacy unit has faced Banshees ("Stolen Hearts"), a villainous Soul Chaser ("Brother's Keeper"), werewolves ("Rough Beast"), the three Furies ("Hell Hath No Fury"), a serial killer with the ability to migrate from soul to soul ("Song of the Raven"), ghosts ("Still Waters"), ghost towns ("The Internment"), evil shamans ("The Spirit Thief"), youth cults ("The Enlightened One"), a succubus ("Black Widow," "She's Got the Devil in Her Heart") and villainous demons who inhabited five sacred sepulchers ("Pilot").

For three seasons of roughly twenty episodes a piece, all of the supernatural action of *Poltergeist: The Legacy* unfolded on Showtime, a premium cable competitor for HBO, and then subsequently in syndication. For the fourth season, *Poltergeist* became part of "Sci Fi Prime" on the Sci-Fi Channel, joining *Farscape*, *Sliders*, and *First Wave* in first-run episodes. A fairly humorless series, *Poltergeist: The Legacy* is nonetheless a special effects show-stopper which has told some unique stories and showcased a terrific cast. Stars Helen Shaver and Martin Cummins have each directed several stand-out episodes.

HISTORY

Directed by Tobe Hooper (*The Texas Chainsaw Massacre* [1974], *Lifeforce* [1985], *Invaders from Mars* [1986]), and produced by Steven Spielberg, *Poltergeist* (1982) was among the biggest financial hits in one of the most brutal movie summers of the early 1980s. Battling against Spielberg's *E.T.*, Nicholas Meyer's *Star Trek II: The Wrath of Khan*, Ridley Scott's *Blade Runner*, Clint Eastwood's *Firefox*, and John Carpenter's *The Thing*, this "family" horror picture impressively managed to carve out a blockbuster niche of the summer's box office. Buoyed by good performances from Jo-Beth Williams and Craig T. Nelson, as well as dazzling optical effects, courtesy of Robert Edlund, *Poltergeist* has become a horror classic in many fan and critical circles. Lackluster sequels (*Poltergeist II: The Other Side* [1986], *Poltergeist III* [1988]) followed fast on the heels of the first film, and their low quality assured that the film series would not survive into the 1990s. Also, a so-called *Poltergeist* "curse" claimed the lives of many of the film series' stars (including Heather O'Roarke, Do-

minique Dunne, Geraldine Fitzgerald, Will Sampson, and Julian Beck). Another *Poltergeist* controversy involved the direction of the first film: some claimed that Spielberg had actually directed the show, rather than the credited Hooper. For whatever the reason, *Poltergeist*, the film franchise, was dead by 1990.

As has often been the case (*Buffy the Vampire Slayer*, *Friday the 13th: The Series*, and *Freddy's Nightmares*, to name but a few), *Poltergeist* was resurrected after a brief absence, but this time for the television viewing audience. The so-called "revival" of *Poltergeist* began with the American premium cable network called Showtime (SHO). It had acquired considerable financial success with its mid-1990s remake of the classic '60s series, *The Outer Limits*, and was looking to repeat the formula. This new *Outer Limits* anthology had a sweet deal: on Showtime it could feature graphic sex, nudity, and violence, and then air again, months later in syndication, in edited form, *sans* the rough spots. Subscribers to the station thus received a first (and more provocative) glimpse of the drama, while regular TV watchers were later privy to the return of a classic, without the more tantalizing visual goodies. Eventually, this deal ended up with *The Outer Limits* being paired with *Star Trek: Deep Space Nine*, and *The X-Files* (in rerun) as part of a powerhouse sci-fi "block." In Charlotte, North Carolina, for instance, *The Outer Limits*, *The X-Files*, *DS9* and various programs such as *Babylon 5*, *Viper* and *Stargate SG-1*, have been part of a highly-rated package on WJZY called "Sci Fi Saturday" which has managed to keep many kiddies at home, and tuned in, for almost five years.

The astonishing success of the new *Outer Limits* quickly proved to Showtime that genre television had a hungry, and quite large, fan base. For their second trick, Showtime returned to the producers of *The Outer Limits* at Trilogy Entertainment and asked for a new series, but one that was horror-oriented instead of science fiction. The title *Poltergeist* immediately was dredged up because it was recognizable, and because the new series, as conceived by producer Richard Barton Lewis, concerned spooks, spirits, and ghosts. At one point, Lewis described the connection between his concept and the film franchise which had preceded his contribution to the *Poltergeist* mythos:

> *Poltergeist* dealt with a family that moved into a home built over sacred ground ... Poltergeists went after the Achilles' heel of each of these people. In terms of tone, the series is going to be a homage to that film. Each character ... is going to have some cross to bear that they're constantly being confronted with.[1]

The characters which Barton speaks of were to be members of a secret and ancient society known as "The Legacy," which was dedicated to fighting the minions of the darkside. Demons, vampires, succubi, ghosts, life-sucking goblins, and other monsters represented those "minions." In this case, the format could accurately be described as *The A-Team* meets *Kolchak: The Night Stalker*, with a few variations. For instance, the Legacy was a well-funded, worldwide foundation comprised of many members, and incredible technology, rather than on-the-run bounty hunters. The team was also better integrated than the *A-Team*, with an African-American woman, a macho, ex-Navy SEAL, a female psychiatrist, a Catholic priest, a beautiful blond archaeologist, and a precocious child serving under their Renaissance man leader, Derek Rayne.

All early indications were that *Poltergeist: The Legacy* would be a terrific addition to the terror TV roster, especially because Barton had been promised a high degree of freedom about what he could (and would) include on the show. Like *The Outer Limits* before it, *Poltergeist* had scored an impressive two-season commitment from Showtime, which was enough time to build a following. More to the point, Barton had a large budget with which to play. Regarding this sweet deal from Showtime, Lewis made the following comments:

> We have free rein creatively to do whatever we want, at whatever level of intensity in sexuality or violence. What's great is we don't have a network breathing down our necks telling us how to do our stories. We have an advantage by having 44 episodes to lay out character in advance of where we want to go and take some chances and be a little different.[2]

This is an interesting series of remarks because *Poltergeist: The Legacy* is, surprisingly, one of the most predictable and hackneyed horror TV series of the 1990s. Though a 44-episode commitment was wonderful, the stories that were eventually told by the show tended be ones involving soul-sucking monsters or cursed artifacts (shades of *Friday the 13th: The Series*). The teleplays, though beautifully performed, never created the kind of personalities that had been seen on *The X-Files*, *American Gothic*, or even the short-lived *Kindred: The Embraced*. The much-talked about cable "freedom" was expressed mostly through scenes of simulated sex (with much nudity) and extreme gore, not through any appreciably different level of intensity. In other words, *Poltergeist: The Legacy* was more titillating visually, but less interesting thematically, than one might have expected considering all the freedom its creators were purported to benefit from.

Diminishing the artistic merits of the series even further, the decision was made to end each season with clip shows! The clips show, the most ridiculous of all television clichés, requires characters to reminisce (usually in chronological sequence) about the events of previous stories, which are then rerun as "flashbacks." On *Poltergeist*, the clips shows were especially dreadful, as a life and death situation was introduced, and then the characters would try to guess which "darkside" villain was behind it. Adding insult to injury, the second and third seasons of *Poltergeist: The Legacy* included not just one clip show, but two!

Despite some contrived writing and a whole series of terrible clips shows ("A Traitor Among Us," "Trapped," "The Choice," "Armies of the Night," "Darkside"), *Poltergeist: The Legacy* flew through its first three seasons on Showtime and syndication at warp speed, generating a large, vocal fan base in the process. There were some cast changes during that time, but most were to the show's benefit.

The second season ditched Father Callaghan, who did not seem to have his heart in the weekly battles against evil, and introduced a new character in his stead called Sloan. Amazingly, Sloan, a Precept of the London House, was played by the great Daniel J. Travanti of *Hill Street Blues*! Not surprisingly, Travanti's considerable talents were wasted in his role on *Poltergeist*, and by season's end his character was conveniently written out of the proceedings as having been trapped at the portal to hell. More successful was the introduction of Kristin Lehman as Kristin Adams in the third season, but this interesting (and sexy!) character would also fail to survive the series' fourth season.

With a cult following supporting it, no one was more surprised than *Poltergeist* fans when the series was arbitrarily canceled at the conclusion of its third year! In this case, the Sci-Fi Channel came to the proverbial rescue and renewed the series for a fourth season. The new *Poltergeist: The Legacy* was to be the linchpin for a Sci-Fi Channel block of original programming called "Sci Fi Prime." *Poltergeist* thus began airing new episodes in March of 1999, at 7:00 P.M. on Friday nights, immediately before *Farscape*, *Sliders*, and *First Wave*. The cast of *Poltergeist* was back in its entirety for the fourth season, and Simon MacCorkindale joined up as a recurring villain (and ex-Legacy member) named Reed Horton.

Joy quickly turned to anger and frustration when the Sci-Fi Channel stopped promoting the series almost at once. Although *Farscape*, *Sliders*, and *First Wave* received much, even excessive, publicity, *Poltergeist* was rarely advertised or mentioned in association with the other series. Soon the Sci-Fi Channel's end strategy became clear: it had renewed the series for a fourth season only because it had already purchased the first three seasons of *Poltergeist* and required an additional year of episodes to make the daily "stripping" process a successful one. Thus, without much fanfare, *Poltergeist: The Legacy* was canceled on the Sci-Fi Channel just months after it was resurrected! As of this writing, its TV future appears to exist only in Sci-Fi Channel reruns. *Poltergeist* fans have a legitimate gripe, as an argument could easily be made that had the Sci-Fi Channel devoted just a few more advertising bucks to *Poltergeist*, the series would have lasted a good five or six seasons. This argument is buttressed by the fact that *Poltergeist* and *First Wave*, which is heavily publicized, generally earn about the same ratings points (0.8 million viewers).

Still, *Poltergeist* is not alone in this treatment: *Sliders* and *Mystery Science Theater 3000* are two other fan favorites which have been given a reprieve from the junk heap of cancellation only to be tossed out after brief airing of cheaply made "new" episodes on the Sci-Fi Channel. Before *Poltergeist: The Legacy* departed the airwaves, stars Helen Shaver, Derek De Lint, and Martin Cummins all directed episodes of the series, often contributing some of the program's finest moments.

Like all the production values on *Poltergeist*, the guest roster on the show is an impressive one: Roy Thinnes, Rene Auberjonois, Jeff Kober, William Sadler, William B. Davis, Ben Cross, Rae Dawn Chong, A.J. Langer, Anthony Michael Hall, Jessica Walter, Esther Rolle, David Birney, and even the WWF wrestling star called The Undertaker have stopped by to either team with or menace this psychic *A-Team*.

Despite the cancellation of the series, a series of *Poltergeist: The Legacy* original novels will soon be published.

CRITICAL COMMENTARY

For the most part, *Poltergeist: The Legacy* is a very enjoyable horror TV show. It is, as this author's father used to describe *The A-Team*, a "diverting" hour. In another words, it is a series which captures one's attention, even if it is not particularly innovative or interesting on a thematic or artistic level. Had *Poltergeist: The Legacy* aired in the 1980s, this review might look very different, perhaps even a great deal more enthusiastic. However, this text is being written at the cusp of a new millennium, and *Poltergeist: The Legacy* is simply not in the same class of quality as '90s imaginings such as *Twin Peaks, The X-Files, Millennium, American Gothic, Buffy the Vampire Slayer, Brimstone,* and *G vs E.* Those are programs which meld artistic and horrific ethos to inform and entertain a new, savvy generation of TV watchers. *Poltergeist* may have no such lofty goals, but the inevitable result of such contextual paucity is that the series flatlines. It exists merely as potboiler: all sound and fury, but woefully little significance. *Kolchak: The Night Stalker,* a product of the turbulent adolescence of the horror genre in the 1970s, demonstrated a great deal more innovation and individuality than this dull-witted series has, and so it is impossible for this reviewer to be overtly enthusiastic about *Poltergeist.* That established, this author and his wife have thoroughly enjoyed watching the series together, and have been pleasantly "diverted" by its plotlines for the last few years. In the plus column, *Poltergeist* does feature an excellent cast, with Helen Shaver (*The Color of Money* [1987], *Tremors II* [1995]), Martin Cummins (*Friday the 13th VIII: Jason Takes Manhattan* [1989]), and Kristin Lehman (*Forever Knight, Strange World*) proving the most consistently charismatic of the regular cast. And, frankly, some stories are just better than others.

What really sinks *Poltergeist: The Legacy* is its "TV" manner of thinking and plotting. The series appears to be written by people who have a familiarity not with theater, film, or literature, but only with old television shows. The inevitable result of such limited knowledge is a selection of stories and plots that have been seen time and time again, on everything from *Kolchak* to *Friday the 13th: The Series.* Basically, *Poltergeist* teleplays fall into just two distinct categories: "The Deal with the Devil" and "The Ghost Seeking Justice/Revenge." Nearly all Legacy adventures can be channeled into one column or the other. The Deal with the Devil tale is the story type which is highly reminiscent of *Friday the 13th: The Series.* In this class of adventure, a person is given a choice/wish/gift, but the cost of such is an association, and even ownership, by the dark

side. The deal is often with the Devil himself, but sometimes also with demons and other assorted dark figures. Some of the more prominent "Deal with the Devil" stories on *Poltergeist: The Legacy* are: "Crystal Scarab," "Stolen Hearts," "Fallen Angel," "The Prodigy," "Wishful Thinking," "The Human Vessel," and "Brother's Keeper." This plot is really just a cookie cutter outline, in which any variation of people and deals can be handily fitted. This is the story: A ____ desperately wants ____ and will make any kind of deal with darkness to get it. Now, fill in the blanks: A *pianist* wants *fame* in "The Prodigy," Nick's *brother* wants *to live again* in "Brother's Keeper," a *man* wants to *save his sick daughter's life* in "Crystal Scarab," and so forth. From these narrowly varied desperations come the deal with the devil, and the involvement with the Legacy.

"The Ghost Seeking Justice/Revenge" is even more overused a trope in *Poltergeist: The Legacy.* "The Tenement," "The Twelfth Cave," "Ghost in the Road," "The Substitute," "Fox Spirit," "Debt of Honor," "The Light," "Hell Hath No Fury," "La Belle Dame Sans Merci," "Out of Sight," "Vendetta," "Possession," and "Still Waters" are just a few stories in which a supernatural entity (or sometimes a human) hopes to attain revenge for some kind of mistreatment, often on the part of Derek or some other Legacy member. A shaman wants revenge against Alex for imprisoning him in "Possession," a spirit wants revenge for his death in "Out of Sight," a ghostly woman wants her murder acknowledged in "Ghost in the Road," and so forth.

Despite such basic, oft-repeated story outlines, *Poltergeist: The Legacy* does emerge as a stronger series than *Friday the 13th: The Series* because it has at least two models from which to repeat stories, rather than just one. Additionally, the fine cast of *Poltergeist* far and away outshines the performances on *Friday the 13th: The Series.*

Plot and character contrivances also run amuck in *Poltergeist: The Legacy,* as they do in no other modern horror drama. For instance, some team member is *always* missing from the action of the week. "Rachel's at a convention," "Nick will be back tomorrow," "Derek's in London till next week" … these are the lame excuses heard on virtually every episode of the series to explain why certain characters are not involved. The real reason for the absence, of course, has more to do with production and cost than plot necessity. Half the cast was apparently off filming one episode, while the rest of the cast was filming another. Because a team-member is almost always missing in *Poltergeist: The Legacy*, the feeling of family, of a team, that is supposed to glue the fabric of the series together, is conspicuously absent. While watching several episodes of this series, one gets the distinct feeling that this cast could be a very potent, charismatic team if allowed to travel through several adventures together rather than piecemeal. "United we stand, divided we fall" is a proverb that epitomizes *Poltergeist*. The cast is always divided, and the series suffers for it.

An additional problem with this series is that the *Poltergeist: The Legacy* writers all seem to share a low opinion of viewer capabilities and intelligence. To wit: each story ends with a Legacy member "summing up" the adventure of the week in voice-over. Ostensibly part of the Legacy journals, this closing narration universally attempts to convey a lesson or thought of the week that is often trite, or even childish. It seems as if the writers do not trust their own stories, their own talents, and feel instead that they must push a moral down the audience's collective throat. This "message of the week" closing narration is a strong contrast to the Captain's Log on *Star Trek*, which is used to convey important information, as well as the Captain's dilemma. Picard and Kirk never come right out and say "this week I learned so and so…" *Poltergeist* is not that obvious either, but it sure gets awfully close. "Maybe faith is all we have in the end," Rachel gets to pontificate in one story ("Portents"), and so on. Do the writers not believe that viewers will understand the story unless it is encapsulated in Cliffs Notes form in the closing narration?

The same complaint can be made about the all-too redundant flashbacks featured so heavily on *Poltergeist*. Important plot-points are hammered at by the oppressive use of black and white flashbacks which are supposed to function as "psychic flashes." Unfortunately, these flashbacks are usually acts or events which viewers are already privy to. Thus, again, the *Poltergeist* creative team is being obvious rather than artistic in its approach to drama. The series shows the viewer something once, and then it shows it again later, just in case someone went potty during the first showing. The flashbacks are not only unnecessary, they drag down the pace of the story. After watching *Poltergeist: The Legacy* for any duration, one just wants to shout: "All right, we get it already. WE GET IT!"

Poltergeist stories are weak in any number of ways: from narrative structure to follow-up and closure. In "Hell Hath No Fury" for instance, the villain of the week is a policeman named Karmack who has been summoning up the Three Furies to conduct "justice" against those who have escaped the American legal system. At the end of the show, the cop himself is judged, and his heart is ripped out by the Furies. As he dies, two Legacy members are present. How on Earth is this crime explained to the police, who arrive on the scene to clean things up? One of their hallowed number is dead, his heart ripped out, and there are two suspects hanging around the scene who seem awfully uncommunicative. Like too much bad TV drama, "Hell Hath No Fury" concludes instantly when the "bad guy" is killed, not when all issues surrounding the story are resolved. There is no sense of logic or follow-up, just the feeling that the hour is up and things must be made tidy for the next episode. In the case of "Hell Hath No Fury," fans may claim that Derek has pull with the authorities because of his association with the Legacy, but there have been other instances where the Legacy does run afoul of the police.

Bad TV drama is exactly what *Poltergeist: The Legacy* turns out to be on far too many occasions. The series features plot contrivances galore, especially in shows like "Stolen Hearts" and "Dream Lover," wherein the mysterious artifact of the week *just happens* to be the very thing that can stop the evil monster of the week. It includes unnecessary sequels ("She's Got the Devil in Her Heart" resurrects the succubus of "Black Widow" so the audience can see *more* flashbacks; "Possession" is a sequel to "Spirit Thief," and "Irish Jug" is succeeded by "Wishful Thinking"). This laundry list of bad TV plotting reminds one of bad genre shows from two decades ago.

The two-part episode "Traitor"/"Doublecross" is a prime example. In this episode, the Legacy members throw their years of service and loyalty to Derek out the window when someone they have *never* met before claims that Derek committed murder twenty years ago. Suddenly, there is a full-scale mutiny against Derek, from the very people whose lives he has saved a dozen times (for *four* long years)! It is absolutely ridiculous! Yet, oddly, the story is totally enjoyable in a sense. It is like *The Bionic Woman* (1976–78) or *The Incredible Hulk* (1978–81) ... it is so dumb, so absent in internal logic, that it is actually fun at times. That may sound like an insult, but it is not meant to be. *Poltergeist* has a goofy, TV charm that is both its greatest strength and its greatest weakness. Nobody working on the show seems to remember what happened last week, and the characters never seem to learn from their past experiences (even though they keep having those damned flashbacks!). They are always totally shocked when the supernatural rears its ugly head to challenge them ... as if this kind of evil challenge weren't the series' bread and butter.

This author is not too snobby, nor too arrogant, to recognize a guilty pleasure when he sees one. *Poltergeist* may not have a lot on its mind, but it is not without a spirit of fun. Not surprisingly, the writing (often by people who worked on *Friday the 13th: The Series* and *Forever Knight*) is singularly undistinguished. The series may be witless, humorless, contrived, and styleless. However, its stars are sexy and fun to watch, and its special effects are good. And, truth be told, *Poltergeist's* stories are fun in a dopey, innocent way, and the overall aura created by the series is undeniably a pleasant

one. It ain't art, and it is not even quality television ... but who cares when celebrity, cheese, and charm carry the day? Diverting. That is a good word for *Poltergeist: The Legacy*.

CAST AND CREDITS

Cast: Derek de Lint (Dr. Derek Rayne); Helen Shaver (Rachel Corrigan); Martin Cummins (Nick Boyle); Robbi Chong (Alexandria "Alex" Moreau); Alexandra Purvis (Catherine "Kat" Corrigan). **First Season:** Patrick Fitzgerald (Phillip Callaghan); **Second Season:** Daniel J. Travanti (William Sloan); **Third Season and Fourth Season:** Kristin Lehman (Kristin Adams).

Credits: Executive Producers: Richard Barton Lewis, Pen Densham, John Watson, Garner Simmons. *Co-Executive Producers:* Frank Abatemarco, Robert Petrovicz. *Producers:* Robert Petrovicz, N. John Smith, David Tynan. *Directors of Photography (various episodes):* Manfred Guthe, Andreas Poulsson. *Editors (various episodes):* George Appleby, Richard Benwick, Alison Grace, Eric Hill, Charles E. Robichaud, Michael Robison. *Executive Story Editor:* Michael Sadowski. *Associate Producers:* Fiona Duncanson, Kira Domaschlik. *Casting:* Mary Jo Slater, Paul Weber. *Additional Casting:* Bette Chadwick. *Production Manager:* Jim Rowe. *First Assistant Director:* Rob Vouriot. *Theme:* John Van Tongeren. *Music:* Aaron Martin. *Production Designer:* Sheila Haley. *Art Director:* Liz Goldwyn. *Set Decorator:* Erik Gerlund. *Construction Coordinator:* Glenn Woody Woodruff. *Property Master:* Donald Buchanan. *Special Effects Coordinator:* Randy Shymkiw. *Stunt Coordinator:* Danny Virtue. *Camera Operator:* Jim Stacey. *Chief Lighting Technician:* Tom Watson. *Key Grip:* Gordon Tait. *Sound Mixer:* Lars E. Ekstrom. *Costume Designer:* Tom Burroughs Rutter. *Makeup:* Francesa Von Zimmermann. *Hairstylist:* Janet Sala. *Location Manager:* Lorne Davidson. *Transportation Coordinator:* David Anderson. *Script Supervisor:* Alexandra LaRoche. *Production Accountant:* Julie Rieder. *Production Coordinator:* Susie

Wall. *Postproduction Supervisor:* Michael S. McLean. *Visual Effects:* Robert Hasbros. *Visual Effects Supervisor:* Brenda Hevert. *Postproduction Coordinator:* Lydia Hamilton. *Assistant Editor:* Trevor Mirosh. *Postproduction Assistant:* Nora O'Brien. *Assistant to Executive Producers:* Julie Fitzgerald. *Visual Effects Coordinator:* Robert Biagi. *Sound Designer:* Anke Bakker. *Sound Editor:* Sean Kelly. *Rerecording Mixer:* Paul Sharpe, Bill Mellow. *Rerecorded at:* Sharpe Sound Studios, Inc. *Laboratory, Postproduction and Animation:* Rainmaker Digital Pictures. *Computer Engineer:* David Cowan Enterprises, Inc. *Title Design:* Greenberg/Schluter, Inc. From Trilogy.

EPISODE GUIDE

• *First Season (1996)*

1. **"Pilot"** (aka **"The Fifth Sepulcher"**) (**2 hours**) Story by Richard B. Lewis; Teleplay by Brad Wright; Directed by Stuart Gillard; airdate: April 21, 1996; *Guest Cast:* Jordan Bayne (Julia); William Sadler (Shamus); W. Morgan Sheppard (Grave Digger); Daniel Piloh (Winston Rayne); Chad Krowchuk (Connor); Sandrine Holt (Ellen); Myles Ferguson (Young Derek); John Novak (Patrick); Dave Fredericks (Bartender); Jose Vargas (Peruvian Man); Marites Pineda (Peruvian Girl); Ingrid Torrance (Party Girl).

Almost thirty years after his father's death at the hands of a demon in Chipote, Peru, wealthy archaeologist Derek Rayne continues to spearhead "The Legacy," a secret society dedicated to the eradication of dark supernatural forces. At a party for the Legacy's cover organization, the Luna Foundation, Derek experiences strange psychic visions which spur him to reexamine his late father's dossier. In particular, he is in search of the fifth sacred box, a sepulcher, where the last of five fallen "watcher" angels remains imprisoned. Derek soon discovers that the last box is in Ireland, where young Catherine ("Kat") Corrigan, daughter of Dr. Rachel Corrigan, is in danger. A shopkeeper opens the box and is infected with evil. The Legacy stops him,

but not before he has impregnated Rachel with something horrible.

2. **"Sins of the Father"** Written by Garner Simmons; Directed by Allan Eastman; airdate: April 26, 1996; *Guest Cast:* Anthony Heald (Damon Ballard); Suki Kaiser (Lisa Ballard); Chris Gray (Michael Ballard); Joel Palmer (David).

An old friend of Derek's, Damon Ballard, is accused of child abuse: a charge which seems hard to dispute considering that Damon was in a locked room with his boy, Michael, when the child was injured. Soon, a kind of stigmata on the boy causes a schism within the Legacy. Is the boy a victim of abuse, or is he being terrorized by demons? This case, though personal to Derek, has a special importance for Nick, who is struggling with a ghost from his own past.

3. **"Town Without Pity"** Written by Robert Masello; Directed by Ken Girotti; airdate: May 3, 1996; *Guest Cast:* Nick Mancuso (Reverend Hawkings); Jan Mortill.

Nick decides to investigate strange energy fluctuations in a Washington state forest where numerous vanishings have occurred over the years. Still struggling with the horrors she has witnessed of late, Rachel Corrigan joins Nick on this expedition and soon finds a religious community lost in time. When Rachel and Nick become trapped in this strange pocket universe, it is up to Derek and Alex help them find a way out. Rescue cannot come too soon, however, as the megalomaniacal Reverend Hawkings has eyes for Rachel.

4. **"The Tenement"** Written by Frederick Rappaport; Directed by Gerard Ciccoritti; airdate: May 10, 1996; *Guest Cast:* Fiona Hutchinson (Lady of Endless Night); David Cubitt (Kyle Vance); Lori Triolo, Benjamin Ratner, Gloria Chrichlow (Mrs. Wilkenson); John Taylor (Karl Vance); Scott Swanson (Judge Druckner); Alex Green (Adolphus Vance); David Longworth (Joseph Vance); Babe Dolan (Lena Vance).

Alex locks horns with a slumlord whose poverty-stricken property has proven unsuitable for habitation, but she soon encounters a spectral figure while moving out of one of the tenement's residents. As punishment for his misdeed, the slumlord is ordered by a judge to spend the night in his own place, but Alex knows she must come to his rescue when the apparition, a woman, returns for more haunting. Alex soon learns that the tenement is a nexus for disaster and tragedy, having been the location of multiple murders over the years, beginning in the Roaring '20s. Now she must be protected by the man she helped condemn, or the tenement's legacy of terror will have a new chapter.

5. "The Twelfth Cave" Written by Robert Masello; Directed by Allan Eastman; airdate: May 17, 1996; *Guest Cast:* David Ogden Stiers (Randolph Hitchcock); Earl Pastko (Harper).

A sacred scroll, responsible for two deaths already, is brought to Derek and the Luna Foundation by Derek's former comrade, Hitchcock. Unfortunately, the scroll — which seems to have a mind of its own — starts to have a bizarre and deleterious effect on Derek Rayne. As it turns out, the scroll is a very ancient confession to murder, and Hitchcock is torturing Derek with it so that a personal wrong from the past might be corrected.

6. "Man in the Mist" Written by James Cappe; Directed by Mario Azzopardi; airdate: May 24, 1996; *Guest Cast:* Julian Stone (Samuel Hartford).

While Philip contemplates leaving the Legacy, Rachel meets up with a new patient who seems to be haunted by spirits. Strangely, this "John Doe" has amnesia and seems to have arrived in the present from a different time period all together. The mystery of his origins involves an accident at sea in 1874, and a ghost who has forgotten his past. More than that, this figure has returned from the grave because he has a promise to keep.

7. "Ghost in the Road" Written by James Cappe; Directed by Neill Fearnley; airdate: May 31, 1996; *Guest Cast:* Michelle Beaudoin (Wendy); Frank J. Grillo (Jerry

Tate); Alex Diakun (Hank); Ken Kramer (Cyrus Barton); Alexa Gilmour (Janet); Nuno Antunes (Brian).

On a dark and lonely road, Nick picks up a woman whom he met once before, a woman who just wants to be "taken home." This strange lady, Wendy, vanishes into thin air and Nick realizes he has been in the presence of a ghost. Again, a figure from the dead has returned for justice, and it is up to Nick to solve Wendy's murder so her wandering spirit can finally rest.

8. "Doppelganger" Written by Bill Bleich; Directed by Allan Eastman; airdate: June 7, 1996; *Guest Cast:* Colleen Rennison (Cally).

Kat's new imaginary friend starts trouble for the young girl at school. Meanwhile, a mummified corpse proves to be a point of interest for the Legacy. These strands merge as Kat's friend is revealed to be the spirit of a young Egyptian princess who was murdered. If the Legacy is not careful, however, the spirit of the Mummy girl will end up inhabiting Kat's body!

9. "The Substitute" Written by Jerry Patrick Brown; Story by Theodore Dreiser; Directed by Brad Turner; airdate: June 14, 1996; *Guest Cast:* Ben Cross (Sam Warden); Kaj-Erik Ericksen (Joe); Tony Sampson (George); Jorge Vargas (Arthur); Paul Batten (Monsignor); Jennifer Karmichael (Kim); Anna Hagan, Terry Kelly, Tobias Mehler.

A disenfranchised high school student finds a journal from the 1960s which allows him to conjure up an evil being called "The Warden." This spectral avenger becomes a substitute at a Catholic school and almost immediately commences a brutal reign of terror. Philip, still questioning his allegiance to the Legacy, and Derek must now take on a lethal foe.

10. "Do Not Go Gently" Written by John Shirley; Directed by Michael Robison; airdate: June 21, 1996; *Guest Cast:* Molly Parker (Elizabeth); William DeVry (Kevin); Steve Jaittala (Blond Boy); William B. Davis (Dr. Nigel); Matthew Walker.

An asthmatic is rushed to a hospital after a bad attack in the park, but what awaits her at the institution is far worse than shortness of breath. As she soon discovers, Liz has entered a world of night terrors and terrifying dreams. Nick, who once had a relationship with Liz, and Rachel investigate the hospital together but come up with very different philosophies about their present case. Their study leads them to a doctor who may be guilty of murder ... and who may even be practicing witchcraft.

11. "Crystal Scarab" Written by Hart Hanson; Directed by Brad Turner; airdate: June 28, 1996; *Guest Cast:* Roy Thinnes (Clayton Wallace); Nikki de Boer (Samantha).

Another friend of Derek's is facing a terrible dilemma: his daughter Sam is dying of a terminal illness and the only way to save her life may involve supernatural powers. Specifically, Wallace uses a powerful relic, a scarab, to help Samantha recover, but the deadly tool demands a life in return. When Wallace does not have enough energy within him to save his daughter's life, he knows he must find another life in his stead.

12. "The Bell of Girardius" Written by Robert Masello; Directed by Joseph L. Scanlon; airdate: July 12, 1996; *Guest Cast:* Lloyd Berry (Jenkins); Ryan Michael (Anton); Barbara Tyson (Miranda); Joy Coghill (Mrs. Blake); Jason Griffith.

A scholar in medieval arts working for the Luna Foundation may be keeping a deadly secret about her lost lover. It turns out that he died a few weeks ago and has been returned to life using an artifact called the Bell of Girardius, which can revive the dead. Now the Legacy must help the beautiful Miranda fight her dead lover, a musician who wants her to share his grave with him.

13. "Fox Spirit" Written by Bill Bleich; Directed by Allan Eastman; airdate: July 19, 1996; *Guest Cast:* Victor Wong, C. Ma, J. Douglas Stewart (Jensen); Erik Keenleyside (Miller); Benita Ha, Robert Lewis (Jake); Aaron Pearl, Ed Hong-Louis, Colin Foo, John E. Parker.

Two workers in subterranean Chinatown find themselves amidst an area of century-old artifacts. An act of sacrilege releases an ancient ghost from its trap, and the spirit begins to terrorize the city. The ghost was apparently spawned in the late 1800s when the Chinese were a persecuted minority, and now a female "fox spirit" wants revenge. Derek and the Legacy are brought in by a local Chinese sorcerer who realizes that something is rotten in Chinatown.

14. "Thirteenth Generation" Written by Garner Simmons; Directed by Brad Turner; airdate: July 26, 1996; *Guest Cast:* Laurie Holden (Cora Jennings); Art Hindle (Professor Jordan Slater); Laurence Bayne (Detective Longbow).

As Derek speaks as a guest lecturer at a university, he is confronted about a recent finding. Bones have been unearthed at a lake, and they could relate to the very case Derek is lecturing about. When Derek investigates, he finds that Hell's Gate Pond is indeed haunted by the spirits of the witches who died there.

15. "Dark Priest" Written by Grant Rosenberg; Directed by Brad Turner; airdate: August 2, 1996; *Guest Cast:* Tom Schanley (Tom); J.C. Mackenzie (Stan).

Two brothers break into the Legacy House during a Luna Foundation gala, and take back what they believe is their property: a charmed medallion owned by their now-deceased father. As it turns out, the father of these brothers was a satanist, a fact which pits sibling against sibling. Now, ritual murders are being committed in the devil's name and the medallion must be returned to the Legacy before a dead man can revenge himself upon Derek and his team.

16. "Revelations" Written by Frank Abatemarco; Directed by Allan Eastman; airdate: August 16, 1996; *Guest Cast:* Jennifer O'Neill (Loraine); Allison Hossack (Constance); Camille Mitchell (Monica); Katie Stewart (Patty); Lorraine Landry (Jan).

Rachel returns to her former boarding

school to investigate reports of witchcraft and devilry. What Rachel finds in her old haunts is a dangerous, malevolent talking doll. Worse, a local witch coven is using innocent children for some dark purpose.

17. "The Bones of Saint Anthony" Written by Robert Masello; Directed by Helen Shaver; airdate: August 23, 1996; *Guest Cast:* Alan Rachins (Victor); Frank Moore (Sloane); Linda Sorenson, Peter Hanlong (Dr. Cornell); Kim Restell (Dr. Frances Carlin).

A strange experiment at a local college laboratory has apparently spawned an ancient evil. When bells ring all over town to herald this strange rebirth, the Legacy investigates. In this case, an effort to clone St. Anthony has gone wrong, and a demon has been reborn in his stead.

18. "Inheritance" Written by Bill Bleich; Directed by Brad Turner; airdate: August 30, 1996; *Guest Cast:* Tony Burton, Don S. Davis (Taggart); Garry Chalk (Sheriff).

Rachel unexpectedly inherits her Aunt Rebecca's southern plantation, but finds that things in the New South aren't quite what she expected. Derek senses danger for Kat at the strange estate, and Rachel starts to experience bizarre nightmares and visions. In fact, Rachel is soon undergoing a strange change: playing the piano and finding herself possessed by a spirit who wants a second chance at life.

19. "The Signalman" Written by George Geiger; Directed by Brenton Spencer; airdate: September 3, 1996; *Guest Cast:* Kevin Kilner (David); Kim Kondrashoff (The Signalman); Peter Bryant (Sgt. Mapes).

Alex experiences a psychic vision of an old friend named Praeger in which he is in jeopardy in a military setting. Setting out to help, Alex learns that Praeger is involved with a military installation which is supposedly capable of (safely) disposing of chemical weapons. Praeger and Alex soon realize that a spirit, a signalman from the outpost's past, may be attempting to warn them about a deadly accident which could result if the military installation becomes active.

20. "The Reckoning" Directed by Garner Simmons; Directed by Michael Robison; airdate: September 13, 1996; *Guest Cast:* Zelda Rubinstein (Christina); Andrew Johnston (Joshua).

A strange little spirit called Christina materializes before Derek and warns that a terrible evil is approaching with the intent to steal a child's soul. Christina is an oracle, a seer who has helped Derek's father in the past, so Derek trusts her prophecy now. Before long, little Kat Corrigan is in danger, and Rachel is wondering again why all this terror is heaped upon her little girl. The approaching terror, however, comes from Rachel's own family history.

21. "Traitor Among Us" Written by Bill Froelich; Directed by Brenton Spencer; airdate: September 20, 1996; *Guest Cast:* Phillip Granger (Sir Tremayne); Susan Hogan (Claire Spenser); Lawrence Dane (Charles Bannion).

Derek is charged with treason, and must stand trial before a Legacy tribunal. Not certain who his accuser is, Derek's only hope for exoneration rests with the journals of his own team. But those very journals might be the final nail in his coffin.

Note: This episode features clips from "Pilot," "The Tenement," "Twelfth Cave," "Sins of the Father," "Do Not Go Gently," and "The Inheritance."

• *Second Season (1997)*

22. "The New Guard" Written by Michael Sadowski; Directed by Michael Keush; airdate: March 3, 1997; *Guest Cast:* Daniel J. Travanti (Sloan); Mimi Kuzyk (Dr. Alcott); Eric Keenleyside (Mr. Brown).

When Derek is injured, the Precept of London House, a prickly "by the book" fellow named Sloan, arrives to assume control of the San Francisco Legacy House. Though Nick chafes under the new leadership, and Sloan is openly critical of Derek's methods, the team works together to discover how and why Derek came to be wounded.

23. "Black Widow" Written by James Cappe; Directed by Allan Eastman; airdate:

March 9, 1997; *Guest Cast:* Diane DiLascio (Karen Morgan); Jordan Bayne (Julia); Shane Kelly (Deputy); Timothy Webber (Sheriff).

One of Rachel's patients is discovered dead, and she and Nick investigate the crime. It looks as if her deceased client had sexual intercourse shortly before he died, which Rachel suggests is incongruous behavior considering her patient's character. When more deaths start to occur, it becomes clear that a beautiful, life-sucking succubus is on the loose and seducing hapless men to their deaths. Nick eventually finds himself in bed with the monstrous woman, who can take on any form, even one quite irresistible to him.

24. "Lights Out" Written by Bill Bleich; Directed by Rafael Zelinsky; airdate: March 14, 1997; *Guest Cast:* Hagan Beggs.

A strange box arrives at the Legacy House. After much consideration, study, and debate, the team elects to open the box. Inadvertently, they release strange life forms, of apparently Scottish origin, from a supposedly eternal slumber. Now the question must be asked: How to get rid of these spirits?

25. "The Spirit Thief" Written by Bill Bleich; Directed by Allan Eastman; airdate: March 21, 1997; *Guest Cast:* Robert Wisdom (Daniel); Rae Dawn Chong (Tanya Moreau); Lillian Davison (Naomi Sabah); Marcie Mellish (Anna Jeonette); Thelma Gibson (Grandma Rose); Neil Denis (Sick Boy).

Alex's estranged sister, Tanya, arrives in San Francisco with her new lover Daniel, an imposing man with incredible mystical healing powers. A shaman, Daniel gives Alex a special bottle which holds souls captive so he can utilize their power to sustain human life. Sensing Alex's psychic strength, Daniel attempts to recruit her in his healing efforts. When Tanya falls ill after a particularly harrowing healing ritual, Daniel has just the leverage he needs to bring Alex into his ranks.

26. "The Gift" Written by Gary Sherman; Directed by Michael Robison; airdate: March 28, 1997; *Guest Cast:* Chad Krowchuck (Conor Corrigan); John Novak (Patrick Corrigan).

It is Christmas time in San Francisco, and Derek throws a party. It is not the season to be jolly, however, when Kat starts to experience visions of dead family members. Kat's relationship with her father comes to the forefront as the young girl, and Rachel as well, must confront a tragic past and an evil brother who was once vanquished.

27. "Transference" Written by James Cappe; Directed by Brad Turner; airdate: April 4, 1997; *Guest Cast:* Kim Coates, Tom Butler (Det. Frank Karmack).

Rachel is stalked by a dangerous ex–patient who has developed a deadly fixation for her. Saved from the death sentence by reason of insanity, this crazed psycho looms ever closer as his obsession with Rachel grows.

28. "Dark Angel" Written by Robert Masello; Directed by Michael Kelisch; airdate April 11, 1997; *Guest Cast:* David Fox (Dr. Praetorius); Meredith Salenger (Emma).

On a dark road at night, Nick is stopped by a girl who claims that someone has been trying to kill her. Nick brings the girl, Emma, back to the Legacy House, where the team attempts to help her. When Rachel examines their new house guest, she offers a startling prognosis: Emma may be imagining her pursuit! When it is learned that Emma escaped from an asylum, the Legacy must weigh their feelings for Emma against their feelings for her unusual physician, Dr. Praetorius.

29. "Lives in the Balance" Written by Garner Simmons; Directed by Graeme Lynch; airdate: April 18, 1997; *Guest Cast:* Jonathan Scarfe (Lucas); Camille Mitchell (Sister Ingrid Rayne); Wally Dalton (Justin).

At a time of melancholy and remembrance, brought on by the unexpected death of someone important to him, Derek is confronted with a surprise. Is the young man who keeps appearing to him actually the son he never knew he sired? Derek takes the young adult, Lucas, on a wilderness trip to learn the truth. Unfortunately, Lucas wants to steal

Derek's body and destroy the Legacy from within.

30. "Rough Beast" Written by David Tynan; Directed by Garner Simmons; airdate: April 25, 1997; *Guest Cast:* Chilton Crane (Tracy); Laura Harris (Anne); Kim Restall (Dr. Frances Carlin).

Rachel's latest patient is experiencing terrible nightmares about a werewolf who attacked her when she was just a child. To help, Rachel consults Freud's writings (Freud was a Legacy member!). When murders are soon committed by what appears to be a vicious animal, Rachel must face the possibility that San Francisco is the hunting ground for a werewolf.

31. "Ransom" Written by Chris Black; Directed by Allan Eastman; airdate: May 2, 1997; *Guest Cast:* Lori Hallier (Angeline); Martha Henry, Camille Mitchell (Sister Ingrid Rayne); Stefan Arngrim (Patient); Adrienne Carter (Child).

Derek's sister, a nun, is held hostage by sinister forces, even as Derek's psychic sight informs him of the terrible event. Though Sloan reminds Derek of Legacy policy regarding negotiations with terrorists, Derek sets out to save his sister's life. At the heart of the evil kidnapping is another Legacy Precept who was lured to the dark side while investigating its power.

32. "Finding Richter" Written by Garner Simmons; Directed by Michael Robison; airdate: May 9, 1997; *Guest Cast:* Grahame Greene (Charlie); Brent Stait (Richter).

Nick's commanding officer from his Navy SEAL days is alive and apparently up to no good. He is responsible for the recent assassination of a prominent cardinal in the Catholic Church, and now Nick must find him. After a protracted search, Richter, who considers Nick a "prodigal son," and Boyle confront one another. Richter attempts to recruit Nick in his mission to spread God's word by destroying his clergy, but Nick understands that Richter has made a pact with the darkside.

33. "Repentance" Written by Mike Berman; Directed by Paul Lynch; airdate: May 23, 1997; *Guest Cast:* Patrick Fitzgerald (Father Callaghan); Tom Butler (Det. Frank Karmack); Miguel Fernandez (Eric Ravenwood).

Eric Ravenwood is a terrible murderer who is afraid of death and God's judgment. He wants to repent his sins and receive absolution from Father Callaghan, but the ex-Legacy priest refuses to cooperate. Ravenwood sets out to destroy Callaghan and kill all of his friends, forcing Callaghan to take desperate measures. Callaghan takes the spirit of the killer inside his body, and prepares to commit suicide, but the killer takes over and launches a campaign of evil against the Legacy.

34. "The Devil's Lighthouse" Written by Robert Masello; Directed by Graeme Lynch; airdate: May 30, 1997; *Guest Cast:* Ian Tracy (Michael); Joy Coghill (Elizabeth); Sebastian Spence (Noah Wilkes); Gillian Barber (Joan Warner).

A haunted lighthouse is a site of terror for Alex Moreau and the Legacy, as they investigate a boy's disappearance there. Strangely, the only witness, the boy's girlfriend, has been rendered blind by whatever horror she witnessed inside. While Nick talks with an old acquaintance from his Navy SEAL days, the investigation of the lighthouse continues and reveals a restless ghost.

35. "Lullaby" Written by John Martin; Directed by William Fruet; airdate: June 13, 1997; *Guest Cast:* Shannon Beaty, Cyndy Harmon, Anthony Harrison, Rebecca Toolan.

An innocent sleep-over party turns to terror for young Kat Corrigan when she plays with a Ouija board and is contacted by a strange spirit who repetitively sings a lullaby to someone named Selena. Rachel learns of the Ouija game and informs Derek of the situation, but their concern hits a brick wall against Kat's uncommunicative nature. To help Kat, the Legacy must dig deep into the past to learn why another spirit is restless, and this time the truth concerns a never-ending bond between mother and daughter.

36. "Silent Partner" Written by Bill Bleich; Directed by Brenton Spencer; airdate: June 20, 1997; *Guest Cast:* Kathryn Morris (Laura); Neil Vipond (Benjamin); Lawrence Dane (Ned); Tom Shorthouse (Harry).

A séance which Nick and Derek attend becomes frighteningly real when a deaf woman is possessed by a female spirit. The Legacy looks into the situation, and Nick forges a bond with the hearing-impaired woman, Laura. A bit of research soon reveals that the spirit is actually that of a woman who died in the 1940s, and who is a dead ringer for Laura.

37. "Shadow Fall" Written by Steve De Jarnatt; Directed by Allan Eastman; airdate: June 27, 1997; *Guest Cast:* Ryan Kent (David); Margo Kane (Fiona); Floyd Crow Westerman (Ezekial); Floyd Faircrest (Shadow Spirit); Forbes Angus (Mr. Rayburn).

A Native American youngster is accused of assault after being dragged into the principal's office for misbehavior. As Rachel befriends the boy, she learns that he is being watched by the spirit of a shaman, a constant protector since a ritual was conducted on the boy as an infant. The Legacy attempts to protect the boy, David, from juvenile jail, and what could be a very dangerous future.

38. "Mind's Eye" Written by James Cappe; Directed by Ken Girotti; airdate: July 4, 1997; *Guest Cast:* Maurice Godin (Jeffrey Star); Susan Hogan (Michelle); Jesse Moss (Peter); Ocean Hellman (Sandra Bruskin); Steve Griffith (Victor Bruskin).

Jeffrey Star is a sham, a small-time charlatan, con-artist psychic who bilks unsuspecting marks out of their hard-earned money. After being apprehended as a fraud, Star is injured and his psychic insight is activated, becoming "real," as it were. Now Jeffrey Star teams with the unimpressed Legacy House to use his special powers in a productive way.

39. "Fear" Written by Mark Stern and Bill Bleich; Story by Mark Stern and Jay Roach; Directed by Allan Eastman; airdate:

July 18, 1997; *Guest Cast:* Michael Sarrazin (Dr. Peyton); Rosemary Dunsmore (Emily); Sarah Strong (Suzie); Cheryl Wilson (Janet).

A strange spectral visitor is entering the cells of the West View Sanitarium and choking the life out of the unbalanced wards living there. Rachel is asked by a friend from the home, Emily, to look into the deaths. After some interviews, Rachel comes to believe that she is actually looking at supernatural murders, not self-inflicted deaths. The key to solving the puzzle may be that the sanitarium stands on what was once Hobb's (Devil's!) Road.

40. "Someone to Watch Over Me" Written by Robert Masello; Directed by Brenton Spencer; airdate: July 25, 1997; *Guest Cast:* Louise Vallance (Serina Croft); Robert Wisden (Professor Donnelly); Zoltan Buday (Sentry); Allan Lysell (Andrew Croft); Freda Perry (Monica).

In the middle of the night, Rayne receives a phone call from Spencer Croft, his college roommate. The only problem is that Croft died a day earlier: he drowned in a reflecting pool he had specially constructed to ancient specifications. As Derek grows closer to Serina, Spencer's wife, the Legacy team learns that the pool is a Macedonian gateway to the world of the supernatural. It is a portal to the land of the dead, like one built by Alexander the Great in 4 B.C., but did Spencer build this "back door" out of death's domain for himself, or for Serina, who has been miraculously cured of a fatal ailment?

41. "Let Sleeping Demons Lie" Written by Stephen J. Feke; Directed by Gary Sherman; airdate: August 3,1997; *Guest Cast:* John Pyper-Ferguson, Stephen E. Miller (Captain Smith); Patty Lombard (Patricia Sloan).

Sloan is aboard a plane bound for the Legacy House, with some important historical/occult artifacts which could shed light on the Legacy's past. Sloan's plane mysteriously crashes, and the Legacy must mobilize to rescue him. The situation is grim because Sloan's plane went down in the mountains and the temperature is dropping rapidly there. The injured precept has far graver problems to worry about than the weather, however.

42. "Trapped" Written by Michael Sadowski; Directed by Graeme Lynch; airdate: August 10, 1997; *Guest Cast:* None.

While Derek and Alex are alone on the island, a storm and something much, much worse, strikes the castle. Nick returns home with Sloan and tries to determine which old Legacy enemy has attacked the stronghold, and what it has done with Derek and Alex. Sloan grills Nick about the previous Legacy encounters with evil forces while a possessed Derek captures Alex and plans to unlock the evil inside the five sepulchers.

Note: This episode features extensive footage from: "The Five Sepulchers," "The Reckoning," "The Dark Priest," "Dark Angel," "The Spirit Thief," and "Ransom."

43. "The Choice" Written by David Tynan; Directed by Michael Robison; airdate: August 17, 1997; *Guest Cast:* None.

Kat has had a bad dream, and Rachel contemplates leaving the Legacy. She feels guilty for getting involved in the battle against evil ... and jeopardizing Kat's life. Her choice: seek a normal life, or stay with the family on Angel Island.

Note: This episodes features extensive footage from "The Reckoning," "Repentance," "Ransom," "The Inheritance" and "The Spirit Thief."

• Third Season (1998)

44. "Darkness Falls" Written by Michael Sadowksi; Directed by Michael Robison; airdate: January 23, 1998; *Guest Cast:* Anthony Palermo (Phillipe D'Arcy); Sarah Strange (Justine).

While visiting New Orleans, Alex is bitten by a female vampire. Alex returns to the Legacy House and starts experiencing the symptoms associated with vampirism, including bloodlust, aversion to sunlight and the inability to cast a reflection. Alex's vampire mistress, Justine, arrives on the island, as well as a would-be romantic partner and old friend of

Alex's named Phillipe D'Arcy. Now the Legacy must save Alex's humanity before she makes her first kill ... but she has already set her sights ... and fangs ... on Nick.

45. "Light of Day" Written by Michael Sadowksi; Directed by Michael Robison; airdate: January 30, 1998; *Guest Cast:* Anthony Palermo (Phillipe D'Arcy); Sarah Strange (Justine); Chad Todhunter (Marcus); Kim Restall (Dr. Francis Carlin); Francis Flanagan (Nurse).

A nearly-undead Alex has bitten Nick in an attempt to become a full-fledged vampire, and Derek has learned that Phillipe is himself a creature of the night, one with great powers. When Phillipe kills Justine (another vampire!), and flees the Legacy House with Alex in tow, the other members of the Legacy must work to keep Nick alive. Soon, Derek and Phillipe face off, with the ultimate prize being Alex's eternal soul. With the promise of immortality beckoning, will Alex choose darkness and damnation, or loyalty and friendship?

46. "The Enlightened One" Written by Grant Rosenberg; Directed by Graeme Lynch; airdate: February 6, 1998; *Guest Cast:* Dale Wilson (Jordan); Fab Filippo (Ethan); Les Martin (Father Reynolds); Kim Restall (Dr. Frances Carlin); Aaron Smolinski (David); Tara Spencer-Nairn (Cindy); Gregor Trpin (Robert); Todd Witham (Boy at Bus Depot).

Eight churches in three cities (Boston, Dallas, and San Francisco) have been burned to the ground via supernatural means. The Boston Legacy House sends the beautiful Kristin Adams to San Francisco to investigate the burnings with Nick and Alex (Derek is in London reporting to the Legacy council). A strange youth cult ruled by a mysterious figure called "The Enlightened One" is behind the church fires, and the branding and murder of a dead priest. As Kristin learns to work with Nick and Alex, she also reveals that her brother Ethan is part of the Enlightened One ... Lucifer's ... flock.

47. "Stolen Hearts" Written by Garner

Simmons; Directed by Michael Robison; airdate: February 16, 1998; *Guest Cast:* Paul Satterfield (David Cord); Allison Hossack (Demon).

On vacation, Rachel is romanced by David Cord, a handsome architect who saved her and Kat from a wild dog. Although Rachel is unaware of it, David is a pawn of evil who has struck a deal with a banshee involving the ultimate disposition of Kat's soul. The evil spirit that wants Catherine has enlisted David to seduce Rachel so that in the throes of passion, Corrigan will forget her protection of Catherine, and the girl will consequently be turned away from the light. Meanwhile, Alex and Derek attempt to identify an artifact, a shield with a coat of arms, that has been buried under the sea for centuries.

48. "Father to Son" Written by John Benjamin Martin; Directed by Graeme Lynch; airdate: February 20, 1998; *Guest Cast:* Dominic Keating (Brian Krenshaw); Michael Moriarty (Major Robert Boyle).

On a lonely country road at night, Nick is run off the road by a blinding white light. Hearing shouts of pain and terror, Nick is drawn to a house where he witnesses the final moments of his long-dead father's life. His Dad's murder has never been solved, and it has baffled the Legacy for a decade, but Derek now believes that Nick saw some kind of psychic echo or flashback of Robert Boyle's death. This is especially difficult for Nick because he hated his father during life and now he must overcome his own feelings to find his old man's murderer ... an evil figure who sucks the youth and vitality from others.

49. "Fallen Angel" Written by Chris Black; Directed by William Fruet; airdate: February 27, 1998; *Guest Cast:* A.J. Langer (Alyssa Fulton); Ryan Francis (Travis Walker); Jay Brazeau (Father); Charles Andre (Car Owner); Jim Dunn (Policeman); Scott Heindl (Jimmy); Laurie Murdoch (Doctor).

A young man zaps a police officer with a bolt of red energy, and his girlfriend runs to a priest, terrified. The girl, Alyssa, is then brought to the Legacy, where she tells her story. The case becomes more complicated when the Legacy identification check reveals that both Alyssa and Travis are deceased: she is a fallen angel who has returned to Earth, and her boyfriend, Travis, is a demon raised from hell. When Travis attacks the Legacy House, Alyssa goes with him so as to protect her newfound friends, but Nick, Derek, and Alex have a plan to destroy the demon and help Alyssa earn her wings back.

50. "Dream Lover" Written by David Tynan; Directed by Jimmy Kaufman; airdate: March 6, 1998; *Guest Cast:* Crystal Chappelle (Jessica Lansy); Camyar Chai (Hassan); Martin Evans (Samuel Kellig).

A shape-shifting demon kills a friend of Derek's, Samuel Kellig, and then heads to Angel Island to recover a special urn. Derek receives the mysterious urn and attempts to decipher the cuneiform writings on it, which suggest some kind of strange rebirth or fertility rite. Meanwhile, Derek is haunted by highly erotic dreams of Jessica, Samuel's beautiful lover, who also happens to be a malevolent snake goddess alive since the time of the Minoans.

51. "Debt of Honor" Written by Jim Piddock; Directed by Gilbert Shilton; airdate: March 13, 1998; *Guest Cast:* Anthony Michael Hall (John Griffin); Jason Gray-Stanford (Myer); Phillip Mitchell (Joe Fratello); Peter Bryant (Frank Rollins).

A Desert Storm veteran and friend of Nick's is being terrorized by the ghost of a fallen comrade. Nick seeks help using the Legacy's resources, but he comes to realize that the friend's being haunted by the ghost of the dead soldier may have been involved in his death in the Middle East. Kristin determines that the soldier actually died in Mesopotamia near a Sumerian temple ... and the Sumerians believed that the wronged dead could come back to avenge the injustice which ended their lives.

52. "The Light" Written by Michael Ahnemann; Directed by Paul Lynch; airdate: March 20, 1998; *Guest Cast:* Jessica Walter

(Suzanne Barnard); Margarita Cordova (Dolores Sanchez); Lochlyn Munro (Todd Barnard); Andrew Airlie (Edward Bishop); Barry Greene (Michael Barnard); Joanna Piros (Reporter); Peter Yunker (Robert Barnard).

An old Brouha witch calls upon a charmed golden medallion to deliver justice unto the enemies of her family, and a demonic light flies skyward, seeks out an enemy, and obliterates him in a burst of fire and light. Rachel is a close friend of the victim's family, the Barnards — a wealthy, political family, and she asks the Legacy to look into the death. Another Barnard brother is executed in similar fashion by the light, the rain of fire, and Rachel feels the vengeance may stem from the grandmother of the Sanchez family, whose granddaughter died in an accident caused by the youngest Barnard, Todd. Alex learns the evil is being transmitted through a Toltec artifact capable of great magic ... but how can it be stopped?

53. "Hell Hath No Fury" Written by Bill Bleich; Directed by George Mendeluk; airdate: April 10, 1998; *Guest Cast:* Tom Butler (Detective Frank Karmack); Lisa Robin Kelly (Janine Kinsey); Malcolm Stewart (Jared Tanner); Roger Allford (Detective Gracen); Curtis Bechdholt (Punk Kid); Christopher Bolton (Darren Harding); Kim Restell (Dr. Frances Carlin); Bruno Verdoni (Detective); Maya Massar (Fury #1); Ian Bailey Mattia (Fury #2); Suzanne Zelmer (Fury #3).

A cop-killer escapes conviction but cannot escape a supernatural death: he is branded on the forehead with the scepter of Omega and his heart is removed by three cloaked Furies. The Legacy joins up with police detective Frank Karmack to investigate the supernatural death, and realizes they are dealing with a form of ancient Greek "justice." Worse, they realize that the hot iron, the scepter, belongs to someone involved with Legacy work. When the cop killer's lawyer is killed and his girlfriend is also targeted by the Furies, Derek starts to suspect that a friend to his organization, a law enforcement official, may be administering his own personal justice.

54. "Irish Jug" Written by Bill Dial; Directed by Martin Cummins; airdate: April 17, 1998; *Guest Cast:* Rene Auberjonois (Milo).

The private Keane antique collection is willed to the Luna Foundation for either exhibit or disposal. Among the relics is an Irish jug from the late-1700s which contains two Irish spirits, the souls of two trouble-making brothers and thieves. Now, Derek and his friend Milo drink the witches' brew in the jug and their bodies are possessed by the imprisoned spirits. Kat discovers the truth about the two strangers inhabiting the bodies of her friends, and seeks the help of her Mother and Alex in putting things to right.

55. "Metamorphosis" Written by Mike Berman; Directed by William Fruet; airdate: April 24, 1998; *Guest Cast:* Chris Martin (Elliott Black); Eric Schneider (Therapist); Kim Restell (Dr. Frances Carlin).

Rachel is infected with evil by a patient named Elliott Black who has in his possession an artifact, a supernatural pick. When a mysterious brand mark appears on Rachel's arm, she is overcome with paranoia, and the urge to kill Derek. Meanwhile, Kristin helps Alex hone her psychic sight, which she fears she has lost. While Rachel spirals into a paranoid, murderous fit, Alex has a devastating vision of Kristin's missing father.

56. "La Belle Dame Sans Merci" Written by Garner Simmons; Directed by Brenton Spencer; airdate: May 29, 1998; *Guest Cast:* Esther Rolle (Grandma Rose); Robert Clothier, Gordon Currie, David McNally, Sean Day Michael (Rimbali); Kate Robbins (Claudine).

Alex dreams of a conflict from long ago: a post–Civil War duel between "gentlemen" in which she was to be the property of the victor. Old Grandma Rose insists Alex come home to Louisiana to work out this "dream walking," and Nick accompanies her to the bayou to discover the past. Grandma Rose reveals how a beautiful slave, La Belle, lost her lover to her brutal, former owner, Aaron Wakefield, and how Alex is kin to Belle ... a reincarnation perhaps? Derek believes Alex is experiencing a psychic convergence: a portal through which the soul of the dead can be reborn into a body of the living.

57. "The Prodigy" Written by John Simmons; Directed by Gilbert Shilton; airdate: June 26, 1998; *Guest Cast:* Stephen McHattie (Lee Noir); Chad Willett (Eugene Kadar); Marie Stillin (Winifred Penrose); Victor A. Young (Milos Kadar).

Kristin comforts a concert pianist and ex-boyfriend after the mysterious death of his uncle during a performance. The uncle's death sparks the interest of the Legacy because it appears supernatural. In truth, Eugene's agent is manipulating some kind of force to buttress the pianist's sagging talents. When Eugene falls for Kristin all over again and spurns his agent, the evil creature reciprocates with fatal results.

58. "The Human Vessel" Written by David Tynan; Directed by Paul Lynch; airdate: July 3, 1998; *Guest Cast:* Billie Worley (Tommy Crane); Kari Matchett (Carolyn Crane); Jenny-Lynn Hutcheson (The Girl); Ted Stuart (Child Tommy); Fred Keating (Dr. Ahrens).

An autistic young adult, a friend of Nick's, is struck by lightning after retrieving a baseball from a haunted shed. Tommy comes to stay at the Legacy House with Nick and he befriends Alex while his sick sister, also struck by lightning, recovers in the hospital. Soon, Tommy is evidencing inexplicable new intelligence: learning to read and write, and coming out of his autistic fog. Unbeknownst to his friends, Tommy is also the pawn of a vengeful ghost who needs him to steal the life-force of others so her spirit can return to the mortal coil.

59. "The Covenant" Written by Michael Berman; Story by Richard Barton Lewis and Michael Berman; Directed by William Fruet; airdate: July 10, 1998; *Guest Cast:* Chad Lowe (Josh Miller); Kevin McNulty (Paul Miller); Camille Mitchell (Sister Ingrid); Sheila Moore, Lisa Maris, Gabrielle Miller.

A young nun, Mary, apparently falls to her death at a convent, and she returns to the grounds as an unquiet apparition, a ghost. Derek's sister, Ingrid, is a nun at the convent, and Derek looks into Mary's death while visiting. Meanwhile, Nick's estranged brother passes away, and Nick goes to settle his estate and deal with his feelings of loss. To quiet Mary's ghost, the Legacy team must determine if her death was murder, and what family secret her death protected.

60. "The Internment" Written by Michael Sadowski; Directed by Gilbert Shilton; airdate: July 17, 1998; *Guest Cast:* Cary-Hiroyuki Tagawa (Sam Tanaka); Kirsten Robek (Lydia); Gary Jones, Rheta Withan'H' (Julia Berman); Betty Phillips (Older Lydia).

Rachel and Kristin search for a mythical town called Somerville which doesn't seem to exist on any map, and where Kristin's archaeologist father visited sometime before his disappearance. Once inside the town, Rachel and Kristin find themselves trapped in Somerville with an enigmatic Asian man, and some people in town seem to believe that it is (respectively) either 1950 or 1960. Soon, Kristin has disappeared and Rachel finds her in the town jail ... where she is also imprisoned by the Asian man. Nick and Derek go in search of their lost comrades and discover that in the 1940s the town of Somerville was also the location of the Salazar War Relocation Camp ... an internment camp for Japanese-American citizens.

61. "Seduction" Airdate: July 24, 1998. Information unavailable.

62. "Out of Sight" Written by James Cappe; Directed by Michael Robison; airdate: July 31, 1998; *Guest Cast:* Maurice Godin (Jeffrey Star); Stephanie Dicker (Mary Johnson/Mary Brookshire); Sheila Larken (Mrs. Brookshire); Deryl Hayes (Security Guard); Jerry Schram (Daniel Walken).

Con man Jeffrey Star runs back to the Legacy when his newfound psychic sight gets him in trouble again. Fearing that "Hell wants a piece" of him, Star enlists Alex's aid and she is shocked when a vicious entity psychically attacks him and even calls him by name. Convinced there is real trouble, Derek and the remainder of the Legacy join the investigation, looking into Star's clients, and so forth. Star's newest mark is the beautiful Mary Johnson, but she has a secret: her father was destroyed by Star's advice and now his vengeful spirit is urging Mary to help kill him.

63. "The Last Good Knight" Written by David Tynan; Directed by Garner Simmons; airdate: August 7, 1998; *Guest Cast:* Tony Amendola (Justin Adams); Michael Richard Dobson, Brian Jensen, Christopher Logan (Peasant).

Kristin receives a package from Istanbul, ostensibly from her long missing father: a map from 1307 made of human flesh which leads the way to the Holy Grail. Kristin heads off overseas alone in search of the artifact and her father, while Nick and Derek pursue her to the Well of Souls. Kristin is zapped by the spirit of an evil King at the site, and then contacted by a mysterious stranger who claims he can lead her to the Grail. This stranger and Kristin find the Church of Rock, the last bastion of the Knights Templar, but a final battle between good and evil could rob Kristin of the father she has so long searched for.

64. "Armies of the Night" Written by Garner Simmons; Directed by Michael Robison; airdate: August 14, 1998; *Guest Cast:* Chad Todhunter (Marcus).

Derek makes a last stand with Nick as evil, but unknown, forces strike the Legacy House. All contact with external security has been lost, and Alex has not reported back after leaving the island to seek help. When Nick is spirited away after midnight by a fast-moving enemy force, Derek must look into his memory to determine which antagonist is waging war against the Legacy. When Alex unexpectedly returns to the House, the true nature of the enemy is revealed.

Note: This episode is another clips show, featuring footage from "The Prodigy," "Dream Lover," "Black Widow," "The Enlightened One," "Finding Richter," "Darkness Falls," "Light of Day," and others.

65. "The Darkside" Written by Grant Rosenberg; Directed by Michael Robison; airdate: August 21, 1998; *Guest Cast:* Fionnula Flanagan (Sorceress).

A strange woman lectures an unseen guest in her home about the war between the darkside and the light. She recounts stories about the Rayne family, fallen Legacy Precepts, and attempts to destroy the Legacy. It is soon revealed that the Sorceress's guest is none other than Alex Moreau! She faces temptation from this evil source, who promises her immortality in return for her cooperation.

Note: "The Darkside" is also, alas, a clips show. This one features footage from "The Pilot" (again), "Lives in the Balance," "Ransom," "Stolen Hearts," "Reckoning," "Repentance," and "The Spirit Thief."

● *Fourth Season (1999)*

66. "Song of the Raven" Written by David Tynan; Directed by Garner Simmons; March 19, 1999; *Guest Cast:* Jeff Kober (Raymond Corvus/"The Harvester"); Michael Reilly Burke, Ben Cardinal, Tamara Gorski (Megan Torrence); Michael Kopsa (Father Norman); Clare Lapinskie (Jennifer Hollybrook); Derek Peakman (Mr. Kellogg); John Sampson (Officer); Charles Siegel (Sam Shadrack); Scott Swanson (Warden Taylor); Don Thompson (Horace Favor); Henry Watson (Doctor).

People in Mendocino are being murdered in the same manner as that practiced by an incarcerated serial killer on death row: their eyes have been removed. Derek arranges for Rachel to interview the imprisoned serial killer, Raymond Corvus, known also as "The Harvester," so as to determine his mental state. If Rachel judges him sane, he will die by lethal injection, if insane — he will spend life in prison. While Rachel grapples with this dilemma, Corvus continues to use an eye-plucking raven from the netherworld to take the eyes of his victims, all enemies who helped to apprehend him.

67. "Bird of Prey" Written by David Tynan; Directed by Garner Simmons; airdate:

March 26, 1999; *Guest Cast:* Michael Reilly Burke; Ben Cardinal; Tamara Gorski (Megan Torrence); Clare Lapinskie (Jennifer Hollybrook); Jeff Kober (Corvus); Michael Kopsa (Father Norman); John Sampson (Officer); Scott Swanson (Warden); Henry Watson (Doctor).

The soul of serial killer Raymond Corvus has migrated to the body of Jeffrey Sandor, a boyfriend of a dead victim. Derek fears that a beautiful reporter, Megan Torrence, may be the next to die because she interviewed Corvus just an hour before he was executed. A Native American specialist in an extinct tribe, the Chiopazzi, reveals to Derek and Nick that there exists in nature an elemental force called "The Hunters," which prey on humanity and can migrate from body to body with the help of a deadly black raven. Corvus is apparently one of this ancient breed, and now he has set his sights on Rachel, who declared him sane enough to stand for execution.

68. "Vendetta" Written by Stephen McPherson; Directed by Jimmy Kaufman; airdate: April 4, 1999; *Guest Cast:* Eve Brenner (Gretchen Dunworth); Don MacKay (Doc); Philip Maurice Hayes (Sheriff); David Livingstone (Israel Clay); Lloyd Berry (Caretaker); Jeff Burnett (File Clerk); Lillian Carlson (Hotel Lady); Crystal Cass (Candace); Lee Taylor (Glen Morse); Royan Vukelic (Billy); John Destry, Annabel Kershanaw.

In Jubilee, Tennessee, a young man is killed by a vengeful spirit near an old lynching tree. Derek and Kristin head to town to investigate the murder. They soon discover that the evil spirit is an exact duplicate of Kristin, and the ghost of a woman wrongly hanged in 1953 after she was believed to have started a fire which killed a family. Now Kristin and Derek must unearth the past to protect the future. A tangled web of lies is laid bare, and an obsessive love affair revealed, but Kristin soon finds herself trapped in a burning home when she gets too close to the truth.

69. "The Painting" Written by Michael Sadowski; Directed by Allan Kroeker; April 11, 1999; *Guest Cast:* Colleen Rennison, Venus Terzo, Geordie Johnson (Stephen Du Bekke); Christina Jastrzemeska (Maria).

A patient of Rachel's has fallen in love with a romantic figure in a seemingly unfinished painting ... and she is absorbed into the rendering. Meanwhile, Kat befriends a teenage witch at her school, a witch with frightening powers. When Alex learns that Kat is experimenting with witchcraft, Kat casts a spell to make her keep quiet — or get deathly ill. Meanwhile, the figure in the ominous painting calls to Rachel, beckoning her to join him.

70. "The Possession" Written by John Simmons; Directed by William Fruet; airdate: April 18, 1999; *Guest Cast:* Robert Wisdom (Daniel Uare); Claudette Roche, Nathaniel DeVeaux, Yanna McIntosh, Virginia Capers (Grandma Rose); Robert Daprocida (Manuel); Lorraine Landry (Dr. Terrell); Candace O'-Connor (Matron).

Grandma Rose visits Angel Island after experiencing a vision in which she sees Alex in mortal and spiritual danger from a supernatural force. Rose falls into an inexplicable coma after warning that she has been cursed by a black magic shaman of immense power. The Legacy hires a shaman of its own, Madame Claire, to help counter the curse and save Rose's soul. When the curse proves too powerful for Claire to vanquish, Alex releases the evil shaman, Daniel, whom she imprisoned two years earlier, to save her grandmother's life.

Note: This episode is a sequel to "The Spirit Thief."

71. "The Traitor" Written by Grant Rosenberg; Directed by Michael Robison; airdate: April 25, 1999; *Guest Cast:* Fionnula Flanagan (Sorceress); Stewart McLennan (Franklin Cross); Elizabeth Shepherd (Jane Witherspoon); Mavor Moore (Arthur Middleton); Simon MacCorkindale (Reed Horton).

Alex is recruited by evil forces masquerading as Legacy Internal Affairs officers to study the "cancer" growing inside the Legacy. Manipulating Alex in this matter is a

Legacy traitor and agent for the darkside named Reed Horton ... and he wants Derek Rayne dead and disgraced. Alex starts to question Derek's leadership, even accusing him of being an assassin for evil. An old murder case in which Rayne committed murder in self-defense (against Horton) is reopened and reinterpreted so as to finger Derek as the "cancer" in the organization.

72. "Double Cross" Written by Grant Rosenberg; Directed by Michael Robison; airdate: May 2, 1999; *Guest Cast:* Fionnula Flanagan (Sorceress); Stewart McLennan (Franklin Cross); Elizabeth Shepherd (Jane Witherspoon); Mavor Moore (Arthur Middleton); Simon MacCorkindale (Reed Horton); Marya Delver (Diane Cross).

Derek is dead and dishonored — branded a traitor and assassin by Reed Horton (disguised as Franklin Cross, head of Legacy Internal Affairs). While Alex mourns the demise of her mentor and Cross takes over the Legacy House, someone in hiding taunts Cross/Reed with knowledge of his evil actions. Cross soon makes an enemy of Nick, and then Kristin, when he orders her to investigate Boston House. Derek soon reappears, having faked his death, and he is determined to turn the tables on Reed Horton once and for all.

73. "Initiation" Written by Michael Berman; Directed by William Fruet; airdate: June 11, 1999; *Guest Cast:* Colleen Rennison (Miranda); Miles Robison (Miles Robertson); J. Douglas Stewart (Mr. Weaver); Susie Wall (Ms. Ashworth).

Young Kat is rebelling against her mother in all things, but worse than that, a friend at school named Miranda is seducing her with the dark side of witchcraft. Kat sneaks out at night with Miranda to practice black magic and energize a powerful amulet engraved with the devil's face. When Rachel finds that Kat has gone out to the forest, she organizes a search which ends with Nick getting zapped by Kat's pentagram amulet. Next, Kat zaps Alex to further strengthen her power amulet, and then heads towards a plateau of evil that only the love of her mother can stop.

74. "Wishful Thinking" Written by Michael Sadowski; Directed by Martin Cummins; airdate: June 18, 1999; *Guest Cast:* Rene Auberjonois (Milo); Francois Robertson (Janelle); David Lovgren (Peter Essenger); Martin Evans (Rupert Schnell); Tamara Gorski (Megan Torrence); Karin Konoval (Gypsy Woman).

In Paris, Derek's friend Milo releases a beautiful djinn named Janelle from her bottle prison. Milo asks Derek to help him track her down when she flees and wreaks vengeance on a famous pianist who once treated her badly and refused to free her from entrapment in the bottle. Reporter Megan Torrence investigates the pianist's accident as Milo realizes he is still Janelle's master since he still has one unfulfilled wish to make. Milo wants the djinn to love him, but she is ruining all of her masters in response to her lifetime of exploitation and misuse.

75. "Still Waters" Written by Mark Stern and Alex Amin; Directed by Michael J. Rohl; airdate: July 15, 1999; *Guest Cast:* Robert Wisden, Cyrus Thiedeke, Joel Palmer, Norman Browning, Cheryl Wilson (Suzie); Virginia Capers (Grandma Rose); Dee Jay Jackson (Bartender).

A normal family moves into an old home on the water and is promptly haunted by the specter of an angry-looking little boy named Matthew. The family, friends of the late Grandma Rose, ask Alex to help them understand what they are facing. Nick and Alex look into the haunting, which seems to center around a dock on the water and a drowning, while Alex experiences dreams about her dead grandmother. Now Alex and Nick must use Grandma Rose's strength to help a dead little boy cope with the anger he feels over his death ... before he hurts someone.

76. "Brother's Keeper" Written by Garner Simmons; Directed by Helen Shaver; airdate: July 22, 1999; *Guest Cast:* Jeremy Ratchford (Jimmy Boyle); The Undertaker (The Soul Chaser); Alan "Grizz" Salzl (Williams).

Nick's dead brother returns to the land of the living, pursued by the Soul Chaser, an evil minion determined to bring him back to hell. The Soul Chaser pursues the Boyle brothers to the castle and penetrates Luna Security. When trapped by this demon, Jimmy makes a deal to save his own life ... and to damn Nick's soul to hell for all eternity.

77. "Unholy Congress" Written by David Tynan; Story by Richard Barton Lewis and David Tynan; Directed by Michael Robison; airdate: July 30, 1999; *Guest Cast:* Patrick Fitzgerald (Father Callaghan); Mark Lindsay Chapman (Dr. Mordecai Church); Elizabeth Shepard (Jane Witherspoon); Todd Waite (Ethan); Michael Puttonen (Jeremy); Simon MacCorkindale (Reed Horton).

Buried deep beneath Boston, a burial chamber imprisoning Dr. Mordecai Church, an 18th-century villain, is opened. The doctor soon emerges as a youth cult leader who devours the souls of his followers, and the Legacy attempts to recruit former member Father Callaghan to combat the evil. When Kristin decides to leave the San Francisco Legacy House and move back to Boston with her brother Ethan, she teams with Callaghan to find several missing girls who were victims of Dr. Church's hunger for young souls. Making a dangerous situation worse, Reed Horton and Church form an unholy alliance which will feed Church the eternal souls of Reed's worst enemies, Legacy members all.

78. "Sacrifice" Written by David Tynan; Story by Richard Barton Lewis and David Tynan; Directed by Michael Robison; airdate: August 6, 1999; *Guest Cast:* Patrick Fitzgerald (Father Callaghan); Mark Lindsay Chapman (Dr. Mordecai Church); Elizabeth Shepard (Jane Witherspoon); Todd Waite (Ethan); Michael Puttonen (Jeremy); Simon MacCorkindale (Reed Horton); Benz Antoine (Security Guard); Gavin Buhr (Excavation Foreman); Tim Cadeny (Ethan); Bruce Dawson (Preacher); Josh Ryan Evans (Being); Peter Haworth (Old Priest); Tania Reichert (Suzanne); John B. Lowe (City Engineer); Alan Robertson (Gilbert Penfold); Michelle Skalnik (Beth); Troy York (Jeremy).

Reed Horton kills Ethan, Kristin's brother, and Kristin experiences a crisis of faith ... and renounces the Legacy. Derek and Nick decide to take the fight to Horton, aware that he has teamed up with that demonic soul-sucker, Dr. Church. Out for revenge, Kristin confronts Church on his own territory. She is unaware that hers is the very soul Church needs to be freed ... the last bastion of goodness.

79. "She's Got the Devil in Her Heart" Written by Michael Berman; Directed by Michael J. Rohl; airdate: August 20, 1999; *Guest Cast:* Diane DiLascio (Anna/Karen Morgan); Ian Tracey (Mike); Garwin Sanford (David Royce); Lois Dellar (Nurse); Tristin Leffler (Julie); Dean Marshall (Chad); Patrick McManus (Young Soldier); Larry Musser (Sam); Lynda Padula (Bar Girl); Wren Roberts (Sailor); Tony Dean Smith (Jason).

Nick goes to visit a friend, a recovering alcoholic, who has fallen in love with Anna, a woman who is actually a supernatural entity, a succubus. Anna was once Karen Morgan, a woman who had a sexual relationship with Nick ... and now she wants him back. Meanwhile, Rachel is brought in on a homicide case by a detective, a case involving Anna's ability to suck the souls out of men who have victimized her or other women. Now Anna wants Nick's love to help her redeem herself...but she is still killing mortals to remain alive.

Note: This episode is a sequel to "Black Widow."

80. "Body and Soul" Written by Michael Sadowski; Directed by Neill Sadowski; airdate: August 27, 1999; *Guest Cast:* Garwin Sanford (Detective David Royce); Tamara Gorski (Megan Torrence); Simon MacCorkindale (Reed Horton).

After confessing her love for Derek, Megan Torrence is murdered in an automobile rigged with explosives. When his personal psychiatrist turns up dead soon after, Derek realizes that the evil Reed Horton is back, hell-bent on killing all of Rayne's associates and friends. Horton infiltrates the Legacy House and leaves Alex a bizarre present: an ancient

Babylonian artifact, a "Souvenir from Hell," made of obsidian. She must determine what its purposes and origins are if she wants to save Derek, now Horton's brainwashed captive.

81. "Portents" Written by Jonas Quastel; Directed by Derek de Lint; airdate: September 17, 1999; *Guest Cast:* David Birney (Father Elias); Kristin Lehman (Kristin Adams); Zachary Ansley (Brother Thomas Sebastian); Laura Sadiq (Stephanie).

An evil priest working for the dark side has discovered that a portal to hell exists below the Legacy House on Angel Island. When a monk is found dead, as if microwaved, Rachel and Alex investigate the incident. Meanwhile, Alex has a vision of Kristin, who has returned to Earth as a "Chosen One" to protect the Portal. As Kat falls ill, Alex uncovers a strange

weather anomaly which may be a portent of the return of Satan, and now Alex, Rachel and the spectral Kristin must protect the portal under the house.

82. "Gaslight" Written by Grant Rosenberg; Directed by Martin Cummins; airdate: September 24, 1999; *Guest Cast:* Ocean Hellman (Sandy); Brandy Ledford (Vicky); Brennan Elliott (Tom).

One of Rachel's longtime patients, Sandy, inherits her family's estate as she turns twenty-one. Horror runs in Sandy's family, however: her parents committed suicide and her sister died in an accident. Now Sandy is psychologically scarred and suffering from anxiety-induced asthma. Derek and Rachel help Sandy to face her fears in the dark old mansion of her past.

30

Dark Skies (1996–1997)

CRITICAL RECEPTION

"Shamelessly derivative of both *X-Files* and the old '60s sci-fi series *The Invaders*.... At least in the case of *Skies*, the concept rip-off is carried off with reasonable care and panache.... Despite its watchability, *Dark Skies* is too much *X*, not enough 'Why?'"—Ray Richmond, *Variety*, September 23-29, 1996, page 51.

"has tried to be a clone of *The X-Files*. But the producers of *Dark Skies* clearly failed to grasp the ingredients that have made the original so popular.... So far, so boring."— C. Eugene Emery, Jr., *The Skeptical Inquirer*, March-April, 1997, page 20.

"one blatant rip-off worth watching ... a paranormal Cuisinart of *The X-Files*, *Independence Day*, *Three Days of the Condor* and even *Invasion of the Body Snatchers* ... its only original touch is that it is set in the early 1960s and immediately raises the possibility that ... government agencies ... or extraterrestrials ... may have been involved ... in Kennedy's assassination."— Joe Queenan, *People*, October 14, 1996, page 19.

"rips off *X-Files* with amazing gall ... so wholly derivative of *Files* as to be laughable, or at least snickerable.... The truth is, this is a damn silly show."— Ken Tucker, *Entertainment Weekly*, September 20, 1996, page 59.

"the show reinterprets historical events of the last few decades ... as being directly connected to an extraterrestrial invasion that has been systematically covered up by the Federal Government. *Dark Skies* makes Oliver Stone's flights of paranoia look like mental-health pamphlets ... [it] plugs into just about every loony aliens myth that defies constant debunking."— John J. O'Connor, *The New York Times*, September 21, 1996.

FORMAT

American history as we know it is a lie. Assassinations, wars, elections, and political changes are all merely covers for the most important battle in humanity's short lifetime on this planet: the war against a horrific alien collective consciousness called "The Hive." Leading this battle to save humankind from the aliens is a secret military organization called Majestic 12. Majestic 12 was formed by President Truman after the Roswell Encounter in 1947, and has been led by Captain Frank Bach (J.T. Walsh) ever since. Bach, a naval officer, is a zealot in his war against these evil aliens, and he always errs on the side of caution ... which means that he also fights public perception, and is a subscriber to the theory that the people don't "need to know" what is really happening in the world. Thus Bach is both defender and conspirator, betrayer and hero, and in many senses, NBC's *Dark Skies* is his series because it examines the decisions Bach makes, and the fallout from those choices.

Dark Skies begins in the early 1960s, when two idealistic young college graduates, John Loengard (Eric Close) and Kim Sayers (Megan Ward), come to Washington to serve in the Kennedy administration. Early in the show, John is recruited into the secret Majestic 12 organization, and Kim is abducted by the alien Hive. After Kim is saved from the aliens and President Kennedy is assassinated,

John and his lover hit the back roads of America, and try to reveal the truth about Majestic 12, which John considers a "counter" government, as well as warn people about the dangerous alien Hive.

Though *Dark Skies* ran for only one season, nineteen episodes in all, its canon is inclusive of six years of American history, so the Kennedy assassination, the Warren Commission, the war in Vietnam, and even the Watts riot are all reinterpreted on the show as being related to alien Hive activity. Real historical figures are also encountered to heighten the sense of reality, and so John and Kim encounter famous abductees Betty and Barney Hill ("The Awakening"), The Beatles ("Dark Days Night"), Howard Hughes ("Dreamland"), Norman Schwarzkopf, and Gerald Ford ("The Warren Omission"), Colin Powell ("Strangers in the Night"), and even Timothy Leary ("Bloodlines").

Filled with period cars and costumes, *Dark Skies* is an impressive production from a visual standpoint, and its "revision" of American history is also a unique facet of this horror show. The series also managed to develop its own lexicon in its short time on the air, and thus viewers had all kinds of new lingo to learn, including "ART" (Alien Rejection Therapy), which was the method by which a human being could be freed from the spidery Hive alien. "Grays" were the hosts for the alien spiders, and they were believed to be a peaceful race which the Hive had already assimilated, technology and all. "Implantation" involved the enforced joining of a Hive spider parasite and a human being. The spiders themselves were known as ganglions or "Wigglers," and a GCD was a Ganglion Containment Device, which kept the alien spider from escaping once it had been ARTed by a member of Majestic. Since the ganglions were all of one mind, they often offered humans a chance to join their collective consciousness by touching a multicolored sphere of light. The state of being one with the Hive was known as "singularity." Also seen infrequently on the series ("Dreamland") was a "wiggler" parasite, which would literally eat its way through the

ganglion creature inhabiting a human being. When an alien ganglion is unsuccessfully removed from a human via conventional surgery, the process is called "cerebral eviction." Finally, "throwbacks" were human beings who could genetically resist implantation, and John Loengard was one of their number.

Because *Dark Skies* garnered only very low ratings for NBC, a significant format shift occurred towards the end of the season. Megan Ward's character, Kim Sayers, was virtually written out of the program. After delivering John Loengard's baby, she willingly joined the alien Hive, and became an agent of evil along with Jim Steele, a Majestic 12 agent also "implanted" by the Hive. After losing Kim and his son to the enemy, John Loengard rejoined Majestic and teamed with a spirited Soviet agent named Juliet Stuart (played by *Star Trek Voyager*'s Seven-of-Nine, Jeri Lynn Ryan) and even had an affair with her. The series became more overtly violent, and at times resembled an action adventure rather than horror or science fiction. The new characters and infusion of a faster pace did little to help *Dark Skies'* ratings or popularity, and the series ended with an unresolved cliffhanger, with Loengard, his son, and Juliet trapped on an alien ship outside the solar system, and control of Majestic transferred to Captain Albane, a traitorous officer who in the final show murdered Frank Bach in cold blood.

HISTORY

The 1996 fall television season was the first one in America to feel the full, incredible effect of *The X-Files'* overwhelming popularity (and incredible ratings). Chris Carter's *Millennium*, UPN's *The Burning Zone*, and NBC's *Dark Skies* hit the airwaves simultaneously, and all three shows featured at least one facet of *The X-Files* format, whether it be criminal profiling (*Millennium*), conspiracies and medicine (*The Burning Zone*), or a secret war against extraterrestrials (*Dark Skies*). Of these three new series, it is difficult to determine which one was treated worst by the media and the public. *Millennium* was branded overly violent, and viewers abandoned it quickly, though it was artistically conceived and almost perfectly executed. *The Burning Zone* was virtually ignored by both camps (fans and reviewers) from the get-go. *Dark Skies* was undoubtedly the show most viciously attacked by reviewers as an *X-Files* rip-off. Although the show's creators argued persistently that *Dark Skies* is not derivative of *The X-Files* and even went so far as to claim that they had only seen three episodes of Chris Carter's series (including "Ice") there are some notable surface similarities between shows. In particular: a similar man/woman partnership, a similar conspiracy involving shadowy government figures and aliens, and a similar obsession with exposing the "truth." Also, the woman partner in each series is abducted by aliens and returns altered in some fashion. Not many critics are inclined to look below the surface when reviewing a TV series, because they usually watch only the first episode, and these are difficult parallels to ignore. Still, *Dark Skies* producer James Parriott was quick to point out how his show would differ from the popular adventures of Mulder and Scully. He called *Dark Skies* the following:

> ... a blend of fact, informed speculation and dramatic license. The series premise is simply this: our future's happening in our past.... Everyone has their favorite conspiracies, but we will challenge and expand on those by building a framework that adds consistency to the alien-awareness theories.[1]

So, where *The X-Files* took its appealing lead characters and pushed them through an ever-expanding conspiracy, *Dark Skies* went back into American history and reinterpreted said history in view of its central concept, an alien invasion. What made *Dark Skies'* claims of "not a rip-off" harder to swallow for many viewers and critics was that there were some *X-Files* personnel involved on *Dark Skies*, including editor James Coblentz and director Thomas Wright. Worse, handsome *Skies* star Eric Close seemed to have been bred from the same stable as David Duchovny (along with *The Burning Zone*'s Bradford Tatum, and *Strange World*'s Tim Guinee), and beautiful

Megan Ward was playing a strong-willed red-headed character who was abducted by aliens (i.e., Dana Scully). J.T. Walsh's character, Frank Bach, was a version of "Cigarette Smoking Man," if people were inclined to see him that way. Even Jim Steele (Tim Kelleher) could be seen as a version of Nicholas Lea's double-agent Alex Krycek, since he was a dark-haired young agent and a physical threat to Loengard (much as Krycek was to Mulder). And, though *X-Files* by no means owns the "truth," it *did* popularize the slogan "the truth is out there," which became a pop-culture trademark of Fox Mulder's quest to learn about aliens and the government conspiracy of silence. *Dark Skies* made its central character, John Loengard, seem awfully similar to Mulder by constantly having "the truth" brought up in his presence, or by him directly. "The *truth* is down here ... third door on the right," Bach declares offhandedly in "The Awakening." "All we have left is the *truth*," "We're just trying to find out the *truth*," or "The *truth* is going to be buried," says Loengard in "Inhuman Nature," and so forth, forming the picture of an obsessed Mulder-like young man. Athletic and smart like Mulder, obsessed with the truth like Mulder, John Loengard had no room to breathe as an original entity, despite Eric Close's fine portrayal. So in character conception and dialogue, *Dark Skies* did not seem very original on a first glance, except in its choice to go back thirty years into our national history. Still, J.T. Walsh, a former *X-Files* guest star ("The List"), defended the show on the basis that it was different from *The X-Files*:

> ... I don't compare this to *The X-Files*. I think it's a fixed kind of deal with *Dark Skies* where you have a known enemy, known heroes. You have a focus which is unlike the focus of *The X-Files*. Even in talking with Chris Carter, his view is that anything that cannot be explained is fit material for *The X-Files*. I don't think you have that with our show.[2]

Were more viewers aware of cult TV history, they might have seen that the TV series *Dark Skies* most closely mimicked was not actually

The X-Files, however, but Gerry and Sylvia Anderson's 1969-70 series *UFO*, the precursor to the more popular *Space: 1999*. This British program starred Ed Bishop as Straker, the secretive head of a top secret military organization (not Majestic 12, but S.H.A.D.O. [Supreme Headquarters Alien Defense Organisation]) assigned to fight a secret war against vicious aliens who could "hide" inside human beings. The aliens of *UFO* were fabulously advanced (as in *Dark Skies*), and they also subverted humans and turned them into saboteurs at the drop of a hat. Straker's personal life was a mess because of his insistence on secrecy (again like Bach) and he often worried excessively about the funding for his top-secret organization (another facet of Bach's character on *Dark Skies*). Straker was also obsessed with recovering a UFO so as to take advantage of the alien technology (a plot element of "Survival," and "A Question of Priorities" on *UFO*, and "Ancient Future" and "White Rabbit" on *Dark Skies*). In essence, both series concern a military man of great power and leadership skill, but of repressed emotions, who mounts a secret war against an insidious alien race bent on the subjugation of Earth. Where the two series differ is in approach, which is probably a result of historical context. *UFO* was produced pre-Watergate, so Straker was seen as a hero despite the fact that he kept his war a secret from the people of Earth. This action was seen as necessary and heroic by the makers and storytellers of *UFO*. In contrast, *Dark Skies* saw Bach as an ambiguous figure. Being produced post-Watergate and Iran-Contra, the makers of *Dark Skies* viewed Bach with understandable suspicion as a dictator and fascist as well as an effective leader for Majestic 12. In essence, *Dark Skies* and *UFO* are the same story seen through different eyes and times, but few viewers of *Dark Skies* have probably ever seen a single episode of *UFO*, which in all fairness, is a far more interesting series than *Dark Skies*.

Dark Skies aired on Saturday nights at 8:00 on NBC for one season, a night and time slot when science fiction and horror tend not to succeed since many of the young audience is out at the movies or on dates during the weekend. So, it is little surprise that the expensive *Dark Skies* failed to find an audience, even in an era when *The X-Files* is so popular. NBC had heavily promoted the series early on (as a kind of sequel to the 1996 feature film blockbuster *Independence Day* of all things!), but it was obvious by midseason that changes would have to be made in the *Dark Skies* format. To make the series more appealing, a new female lead was enlisted in Jeri Ryan. Adding a beautiful woman to the cast of a sinking TV series is an old ploy, used on *Batman* in 1969 (with the addition of Yvonne Craig as Batgirl), *Space: 1999* (with Catherine Schell as Maya) and even *Voyager* (with Jeri Ryan — again — as Seven), and Ryan's presence did indeed add some much-needed heat to the final episodes of *Dark Skies*. Even her considerable and charismatic presence was not enough life support to resuscitate this case, however. Although the series was aired regularly in late 1996 and early 1997, NBC banished the show from its spring schedule. It aired no episodes in April of 1997, and held back the critical last two episodes of the season until the very end of May. By then, cancellation was already a foregone conclusion.

When it became obvious that the series would not return to NBC for the 1997-98 season, the producers inserted a voiceover by star Eric Close over the last few minutes of the finale, "Bloodlines," which suggested that the war against the Hive would be won, and that Loengard was speaking to us from a victorious human race in the twenty-first century (when he would have been over sixty-five years old).

Although there was apparently a period of negotiations between the producers of *Dark Skies* and UPN which concerned the continuation of the show, that deal soon fell through, and *Dark Skies* ended its run after less then two dozen stories. Ironically, both *Dark Skies* and *The Burning Zone* aired only nineteen episodes before vanishing. In hindsight, NBC should have had a little more faith: *Sleepwalkers*, the series which replaced *Dark Skies* on Saturdays in 1997, aired only three times before being canceled! *Dark Skies*, like all series, probably would have grown considerably had it lasted another season. On the set of *Voyager* almost a year later, Jeri Ryan delivered her postmortem on *Dark Skies*:

> I think NBC buried it ... It was a great show that had wonderful potential ... Granted, when I came in, the ratings were already in the basement and NBC had written it off. Adding a new character was a desperate, last-ditch attempt to try and do something—anything....The show was never on consecutively more than three weeks. You can't build an audience that way. It was really unfortunate.[3]

Although *Dark Skies* was canceled after only one season on network TV, it generated a rabid fan following on the Internet, and particularly in Europe and other foreign markets, perhaps because its fine production values beautifully captured a bygone (and interesting) era in American history. *Dark Skies* was so popular abroad in late 1997 that *Entertainment Weekly* had this to report:

> *Dark Skies*, the *X-Files* clone that couldn't buy an audience when it was on NBC last season, is such a success abroad that its studio, Columbia, is considering several two-hour movies solely for the international market.[4]

The much discussed series of movies never materialized, but even today, *Dark Skies* creators Friedman, Zabel, and Parriott plan to return the series to the limelight with either a feature film, a series of graphic novels, or a new syndicated TV series. Nothing has materialized as of this writing, and there is, sadly, more bad news to report. In early 1998, J.T. Walsh, who played Captain Bach, died of a heart attack at age 54. He was honored by his friend and co-star Jack Nicholson at the 1998 Oscar ceremony. During his career, he appeared in more than sixty films (including *Breakdown* [1997]) and had made a name for himself as a great character actor. *Dark Skies* fans will remember him forever as Captain Bach, a great and interesting character on what could often be a mediocre series.

CRITICAL COMMENTARY

Right off the bat, people may ask why *Dark Skies* is even covered in a book about "terror" TV. After all, this NBC series involves aliens from outer space, so it should be classified as science fiction, not horror, right? Well, not precisely. *Dark Skies* is certainly horror in orientation if one puts the emphasis on the *Dark* rather than the *Skies*, because it depicts in graphic terms an old genre concept: the infiltration of the human body by a malevolent outsider. In other words, *Dark Skies* is horror for the same reason that *Alien* (1979), *The Thing* (1982), or *Invasion of the Body Snatchers* (1978) are horror. Specifically, the show raises the pointed question of "who" to trust. Who is human? Who is alien? These questions first generate paranoia and eventually fear, the hallmarks of any gripping horror TV show. In the opening episode of *Dark Skies*, for instance, the horror dynamic is established when a wiggler, an alien ganglion, exits from the mouth of an American farmer suddenly and violently, and then scurries away, loose, through a laboratory. Graphic effects, tight framing, shaky camera work, and other tried-and-true horror techniques are employed to bring this frightening scene to vivid life. *Star Trek* or *Babylon 5*, this ain't.

As the series progresses, so does the escalation of horror images. In one thoroughly nauseating scene (in "Hostile Convergence"), Jack Ruby eats a sandwich in which an alien parasite is hidden. The squishy worm thing leaps into his mouth and proceeds inside his body as he writhes with pain. Gross! Likewise, claustrophobia is exploited for horrific effect in the Vietnam-based adventure "White Rabbit" as Loengard journeys through a tiny, alien-dug tunnel under the earth. The feeling generated, as in all episodes of *Dark Skies*, is one of terror ... not illumination or wondrous discovery, as in science fiction TV. Whether it be a siege on a house in the woods ("We Shall Overcome") or fear of a baby which may be not quite human (à la *Rosemary's Baby*) in "Burn, Baby, Burn," the horror in *Dark Skies* is never far from view.

In this regard, *Dark Skies* is a beautifully conceived and executed series. Technically, it is close to perfect, and at its core is a great horror idea well exploited: what we know to be true is *not* true at all, and our beliefs are based on lies, deceit, and cover-ups. The very premise of the show pulls the rug out from under viewers, which leaves them, as we have seen in other shows, susceptible to the feelings of terror which *Dark Skies* generated. The *Invaders of the Body Snatchers* premise, that an alien inhabitation can turn your loved ones into soulless automatons, has not lost any of its creepy appeal since the 1950s, and is effective here (as it is in *Prey*.) The story even has the interesting subtext that the alien invaders, a collective consciousness, are actually communist in intention. "We have no color. We have no conflict," one Hive alien tells Loengard in Mississippi, at the height of the Civil Rights Movement. Since the Cold War is over, this plot detail has probably been mostly unexamined in *Dark Skies*, but it nicely adds complexity to stories such as "Dreamland" and "Both Sides Now."

Add a likable cast, some great period details, and a dollop of interesting "counter" history, and it is not at all difficult to determine why this recent cult series still maintains a vocal and active fan base. The ingredients are all in evidence for a hit, yet despite this excellent central concept, *Dark Skies* has almost no frisson, and no real "great" stories that stand out either. It is slow-paced and dull, a passive viewing experience, instead of one that is constantly challenging and involving, like *The X-Files*.

This lack of excitement comes from several material factors. The first is that the series leads, Ward and Close, are not allowed to express much real humanity. They relate to one another as business partners, or government agents, yet they are supposed to be lovers who depend on one another for their lives. They go about their tasks grimly, without any sense of humor or perspective whatsoever about their situation. Of course, an alien invasion is hardly a laughing matter or a subject for humor, but it is the interplay and humor

in *The X-Files* which makes it so memorable and powerful a series. Humor *is* a necessary part of life, and Scully and Mulder can see humor in their work, whereas Loengard and Sayers may as well be machines for all the emotional depth they demonstrate together. Where there is no humor, there is no resemblance to reality, and more specifically no acknowledgment of why humanity deserves to be saved from the Hive. What differentiates the human race from Hive is individuality, but John and Kim never truly come across as real individuals. Though star Eric Close often gives voice to some very flowery-sounding monologues (usually in voiceover narration) about what Loengard has learned from his particular experience, these moments of insight come across as "lessons learned," as heavy-handed morals, rather than as any true epiphany from the character's inner mind. They are not born naturally of the character, but rather as an afterthought needed to provide some focus (again, usually moral) to the adventure that has just culminated.

Additionally, the main characters of *Dark Skies* seem to lack a clear purpose, and the precision and clarity of Mulder and Scully. On *The X-Files*, viewers always know what the goal of the mission is. There is a forward thrust to the series, an inexorable pull in a single direction. On *Dark Skies*, it is never really clear why John and Kim go on the run after Kennedy is assassinated. Once on the run, they contact and even team up with Majestic on a regular basis, to the point that Bach still considers Loengard an agent for the organization, so why run away in the first place? Is it supposed to be an homage to *The Invaders*, which also saw a man fighting aliens on the run, or is it just because the show needed a manageable format, and the creators wanted to avoid the case-by-case "agent" approach of Chris Carter's *The X-Files?* It strains believability that Leonard and Sayers are just "randomly" in the right place at the right time for an adventure every time they enter a new city. Of course, this "randomness" is mitigated somewhat by the fact that the series makes it plain that much time passes between stories, but still it is troubling that these people seem to be on an extended road trip to nowhere, with no real destination or specific purpose.

The revisionist history aspect of *Dark Skies* is interesting, but it tends to diminish the show's strengths. In particular, *Dark Skies* is guilty of the old *Young Indiana Jones* fallacy, a law of genre television which states that the main character of a given series set in the past must encounter "famous" figures on a weekly basis. In other words, Loengard and Sayers are always at the right place at the right time to see history in the making, and meet the "right" people. In a semi-serious format like *Zelig* (1983) or *Forrest Gump* (1994), this approach is successful, even illuminating. In a straight-faced drama which is supposed to be taken as "reality," the preponderance of "famous" figures serves only to undermine the believability of *Dark Skies*. It is a juvenile approach to history which comes off as an attempt to be "educational," like the youth-minded *Voyagers* (1981) or the aforementioned *Young Indiana Jones*. What about the people behind the scenes of great events? *Dark Skies* seems to think that by putting Kim and John in contact with Robert Kennedy and others, their adventures will resonate with viewers, but the opposite is true. The regular characters are not nearly as much fun as the weekly guessing game of what great historical figure the guest of the week is supposed to be portraying.

What is perhaps more disturbing than this sophomoric belief that in every adventure a famous face should show up is that *Dark Skies* is less-than-vigilant in its historical accuracy. It personifies public figures in sometimes atrocious manner. Robert Kennedy, a great man and guardian of civil rights, for instance, is silenced on *Dark Skies* when an illicit affair with Marilyn Monroe is uncovered ("The Warren Omission") by Majestic. This plot point makes the heroic former attorney general seem as if he is concerned only with his reputation, and the episode even has the audacity to bring up the notion (in a totally offhanded manner) that Kennedy himself killed Monroe! There is no evidence of such a crime, or Kennedy's culpability, and there has

never been any evidence of such a crime or culpability, so this bit of *Dark Skies* is rumor-mongering and gossip at its worst. It has nothing to do with history. Norman Schwarzkopf is also presented as an opportunist (in the same show), and even Carl Sagan is given some ill-considered treatment. The man who wrote *Contact* and educated a generation with *Cosmos* (1981), a man who spent the better part of his life informing Americans about the possibility of life on other planets, is made (on *Dark Skies*) to be a willing part of Bach's conspiracy of silence (in "Strangers in the Night" and "Bloodlines"). What an insult! In some cases, these famous figures are still living, and in other cases, they are not around any more to defend their reputations, yet *Dark Skies* seems willing to arbitrarily cast historical figures as villains and collaborators solely for the purpose of entertainment. God forbid anybody should ever consider this show historically accurate. Harry Truman, Dwight Eisenhower, Allen Dulles, Gary Powers, Ronald Reagan, and George Bush (in voice-over only) are all characterized as having been associated with cover-ups and conspiracies that exist only on the reality of this show. Real history will judge these figures for their actions, *Dark Skies* need not recast them as foils for John Loengard to gets its simple-minded points across to viewers.

Another unfortunate side effect of the alien conspiracy in *Dark Skies* is that humans tend be taken off the hook for their flaws. In "We Shall Overcome," the Hive is responsible for the disappearance of three civil rights workers in Mississippi. It is an easy, dishonest, and facile answer to a real human horror that an outside force would be responsible for this hate crime. In truth, human precepts, views, beliefs, and experience are to blame for racism, not an alien race. Although this is a nice way to assuage Caucasian guilt, many people fought and died to stop racism in the 60s, and their sacrifice does not deserve to be trivialized by the offhand suggestion that it was really "bad" aliens who were responsible for such negative human behavior.

It is also difficult to stand behind a show

that demonstrates no loyalty whatsoever to its own internal continuity. Take Frank Bach's wife, for example. In two early stories she is beautifully portrayed in human terms by the underrated Nancy Stephens of *Halloween* (1978) and *H20* (1998). As soon as *Dark Skies* requires this character to be an element of a major plotline (in "White Rabbit") however, Stephens is discarded in favor of the younger, more beautiful, and better known Jennifer Hetrick (Vash of *Star Trek: The Next Generation*). The same substitution is carried out with the character William Paley ... a man played by different actors every time he appears. What happened to continuity? Why were different actors assuming recurring roles week in and week out?

And, worst of all, it is absolutely unforgivable the way *Dark Skies* loses sight of Kimberly Sayers and the things she stands for. This character, arguably the more human and more likable of the main duo, is made to turn to the side of the Hive when Steele shows her an image of Majestic's duplicitous nature ("Both Sides Now"). Because of this, the character abandons John Loengard (the father of her child) and *all of humanity*, yet Kim Sayers knew all along that Majestic could not be trusted. For her to suddenly lose faith in her lover because of his relationship to Majestic is a contrived solution. This seems an excuse to get rid of Ward and Sayers all together, especially since Loengard picks up (romantically) with Juliet Stuart in later episodes. Megan Ward went from being a substantial co-star to a walk-on in her own series! Her character does not appear at all (except in a photograph) in "Strangers in the Night," and she has only a cameo in the final episode "Bloodlines." Her fate is left unresolved when the series ends, as if it is no longer important to John Loengard. If that is true, then Loengard is no hero at all, but a real louse! It was clear when the series began that Loengard and Sayers loved each other, and were committed to each other, but then the writer's pen undid all that good work so that a "new" woman could be added to the series. *Dark Skies*, like *The Burning Zone*, wins no points whatsoever for its format changes, because they are carried out in a Machiavellian fashion which does not jibe with what the audience already knows of the main characters.

Dark Skies has its share of conceptual problems, from the format changes to the *Young Indiana Jones* fallacy, yet it remains the most thematically consistent of its 1996-97 competitors despite these flaws. *The Burning Zone* never knew what it wanted to be, and *Millennium* has gone through several drastic format changes in three years. And, as it marched towards its conclusion, *Dark Skies* became more sure-footed and self-assured. The humor factor escalated ("To Prey in Darkness" revealed that Beatnik poetry was the invention of the Hive, and "Burn, Baby, Burn" reported that the Grays' favorite food was strawberry ice cream), the pace was stepped up, the stakes were higher, and the producers even had a little fun with history (Steele killed a peacenik in "Bloodlines" and then assumed his identity. The dead man's name: Charles Manson!). All these facets assure that cultists will "keep watching the (*Dark*) Skies," even into the 21st century. It is currently being rerun on the Sci-Fi Channel as part of its "Sunday Conspiracy" night, along with the inferior *The Burning Zone*, and the dull *The Visitor*.

CAST AND CREDITS

Cast: Eric Close (John Loengard); Megan Ward (Kimberly Sayers); J.T. Walsh (Frank Bach).

Credits: Created by: Bryce Zabel and Brent V. Friedman. *Music:* Michael Hoenig. *Editor (various episodes):* James Coblentz, Andrew Cohen, Troy Takaki. *Production Designer:* Curtis A. Schnell. *Director of Photography (various episodes):* Bill Butler, Steve Yaconelli. *Producer:* Bruce Kernan, Brad Markowitz. *Co-Executive Producer:* Brent V. Friedman. *Executive Producers:* James D. Parriott, Joseph Stern. *Executive Producer:* Bryce Zabel. *Co-producers:* Bernie Laramie, Mark R. Schilz. *Supervising Producers:* Steve Aspis, Steve Beers. *Casting:* Judith Holstra, Robert J. Ulrich, Eric Dawson, Carol Kritzer. *Executive Story Editor:* Melissa Rosenberg. *Associate Producer:* Robert Parigi. *Unit Production Manager:* Mark R. Schilz. *First Assistant Director:* Chris Stoia. *Second Assistant Director:* Bob Kozicki. *Post-Production Supervisor:* Jack Morgan. *Costume Design:* Darryl Levine. *Consultant:* Jeff Wachtel. *Camera Operator:* David Parrish. *Script Supervisor:* Randa Rai Stack. *Production Sound Mixer:* Thomas E. Allen, Sr. *Gaffer:* Rick Sands. *Key Grip:* Frank Keeves. *Second Unit Director:* John Moio. *Art Director:* Michael Fox. *Set Decorator:* Crista Schneider. *Property Master:* Brad Breitbarth. *Casting Associate:* Shawn Dawson. *Makeup Artist:* John Rizzo. *Production Accountant:* Hilton Smith. *Key Hair:* Andria Misushima Jones. *Transportation Coordinator:* Steve Hellerstein. *Special Effects Coordinator:* Bruce Mattox. *Stunt Coordinator:* John Moio. *Location Manager:* Brett Williams. *Production Coordinator:* Ingrid Lohne. *Assistant Production Coordinator:* Stacy Radford. *Script Coordinator:* Adam Sigel. *Assistant Editor:* Marilyn Adams. *Music Editor:* Marty Wereski. *Sound Supervisor:* William Dotson. *Sound Effects Designer:* Mark Larry. *Rerecording Mixers:* Marti D. Humphrey, Ray O'Reilly, Mike Olman. *Area 51 Visual Effects Crew:* Tim McHugh, Wayne England, David Carlson, Justin Hammond, David Jones. *Alien Effects Designed and Created by:* Todd Masters Company, Greg Johnson, John Shea, Bernhard Eicholz, Thomas J. Bacho, Jr., Jeremy Aeilo, William Fesh, Gloria Munoz. *Effects Production Coordinator:* Kristine Morgan. *Assistants to Producer:* Umberto Autore, Jr., Julia Bent, Stacey Kosier, Barbara Whiting. *Camera and Lense:* Panavision. *Color:* Technicolor. *Video Facility:* 4MC/Digital Magic. *Sound:* Sony Pictures Studio, Culver City, California. A Bryce Zabel Production. Columbia Tristar Television Distribution, a Sony Pictures Entertainment Company.

EPISODE GUIDE

1. "The Awakening" (Parts I & II) Written by Bryce Zabel and Brent V. Fried-man; Directed by Tobe Hooper; airdate: September 21, 1996; *Guest Cast:* Robin Gammell (Dr. Hertzog); Lee Garlington (Betty Hill); Paul Gleason (Nelson Rockefeller); Francis Guinan (Mark Simonson); John M. Jackson (Pratt); Charley Lang (Dr. Halligan); Conor O'Farrell (Phil Albano); G.D. Spradlin (Grantham); Scott Allan Campbell (Popjoy); Tim Kelleher (Jim Steele); Basil Wallace (Barney Hill); Mike Kennedy (Allen Dulles); Don Moss (Hubert Humphrey); Marilyn Rockefeller (Mrs. Lincoln); Al Sapienz (Gary Powers); Gregory White (Mr. Chesney); Alan Fudge (Major Friend); Thomas Knickerbocker (General Brown); Nancy Stephens (Mrs. Bach); Brad Reese (Lieutenant); Grant Mathis (Cloaker #3); George Marshall-Ruge (Cloaker #4); Jerry Whiddon (Goodwin); Fred Saxon (Reporter); David Svensson (Man in Crowd); Don Clark (Newscaster); James F. Kelly (Robert Kennedy); Amanda Plummer (Abducted Woman).

On May 1, 1960, U.S. Air Force pilot Gary Powers pursues a UFO over the Soviet Union in his U-2 spy plane, and is subsequently captured by Russian forces. On October 3, 1961, John Loengard and girlfriend Kimberly arrive in Washington, D.C., full of enthusiasm and idealism in hopes of joining President Kennedy's new frontier. Loengard goes to work investigating Project Blue Book and meets with Betty and Barney Hill, two UFO abductees. On his way home, Loengard is persuaded to drop his interest in the case when he is threatened by Captain Frank Bach of Majestic, a top secret organization in the government. Loengard makes it his mission in life to expose Bach and Majestic, but is eventually recruited into the organization and given access to both extraterrestrial technology and an alien corpse. Loengard's first job is in Boise, where he confronts a farmer who is serving as a host to a spidery alien parasite. Kimberly is abducted by alien "grays," the host organism for these spiders, and returned home with one of the parasites inhabiting her body. Using an experimental alien rejection therapy, John saves Kimberly's life and vows to make all knowledge of the aliens and Majestic known to the public and the White House ... a vow which is threatened when President Kennedy is assassinated.

2. "Moving Targets" Written by Bryce Zabel and Brent Friedman; Directed by Thomas J. Wright; airdate: September 28, 1996; *Guest Cast:* Richard Fancy (James Forrestal); Richard Gilliland (Jesse Marcel); Tim Kelleher (Jim Steele); James F. Kelly (Robert Kennedy); Charley Lang (Dr. Halligan); Conor O'Farrell (Phil Albano); Hansford Rowe (President Harry Truman); Leon Russom (Roscoe H. Hillenkoetter); Mary Kay Adams (Bainbridge); Terry Bozeman (Goodwin); Jack Lindine (Jack Ruby); Braid Blaisdell (Base Commander); Stephen James Carver (Balfour); William Frankfather (Cop); Brent Huff (Clint Hill); Locky Lambert (Jackie Kennedy); Ashley Smock (Corporal); Andrew Walker (Ground Control Worker).

On the heels of President Kennedy's assassination, Loengard and Kimberly flee to Oklahoma, and Bach searches the president's corpse for signs of the alien artifact Loengard gave him. Robert Kennedy sends Loengard to Dallas to recover the piece himself, but Majestic is already there in force, as is Majestic agent Jim Steele, who is now possessed by the alien Hive. Loengard's contact at the hotel in Dallas is Jesse Marcel, the public relations officer at Roswell, New Mexico, on July 2, 1947 — the night the aliens landed — and he has quite a story to tell: how an alien representative met with President Truman at Roswell and demanded the unconditional surrender of the planet. Furthermore, the army opened fire on the UFO and shot it down, picking up alien casualties in the process.

3. "Mercury Rising" Written by James D. Parriott; Directed by Tucker Gates; airdate: October 19, 1996; *Guest Cast:* Tim Kelleher (Jim Steele); John Mese (Tigh Young); Natalija Nogulich (Dr. Helen Gould); Conor O'Farrell (Albano); Peter Van Norden (Henry Kissinger); Pat Crawford Brown (Hotel Clerk); Glenn Morshower (Mission Controller); Steven Barr (Policeman); Don Clark (TV anchor); Darryl Rocky Davis (Gate Guard); Henry Harris (Fisherman); Todd Ferries (Gary Augatreux); George Lugg (Bartender); Grant Mathis (Cloaker).

In January of 1964, Kimberly experiences disturbing visions involving an astronaut in need of help, as well as an uncontrollable need to head to Florida and Cape Canaveral, where a rocket is being launched for the moon. Kimberly makes contact with the astronaut, a man who was abducted by the Hive at the same time she was, even as Majestic and Steele close in on her position. Loengard and Kim learn that the astronaut was part of Midnight Wing, a black-ops elite corps of space jocks who were assigned to destroy a massive alien spaceship in orbit on the night Kim was abducted from her apartment. Kim undergoes regression hypnosis and recalls an experience with a second astronaut — one who has been implanted by the alien Hive and who may now have the key to sabotaging a Saturn rocket launch.

4. "Dark Days Night" Written by Brent V. Friedman and Brad Markowitz; Directed by Matthew Penn; airdate: October 26, 1996; *Guest Cast:* Kathleen Garrett (Hargrove); Stanley Kamel (Dr. Ron Burnside); Tim Kelleher (Jim Steele); Charley Lang (Dr. Halligan); Conor O'Farrell (Phil Albano); Gina Phillips (Marnie Lane); Joseph Carberry (Cabbie); Earl Carroll (Doorman); Carey Eidel (Brian Epstein); John H. Freeland (Usher); Jerome Hoban (Ed Sullivan); Sandra Ellis Lafferty (Mrs. Weatherly); James Lancaster (Kenneth Parkinson); Karen Maurise (Neighbor); Dominic Oliver (Technician); Chris Weal (Michael Hagerty); Carmine Grippo (Ringo Starr); Tim Michael McDougall (Paul McCartney); Rick Anthony Pizaria (George Harrison); Joe Stefanelli (John Lennon).

In February of 1964, Beatlemania begins in the United States, coinciding with the Fab Four's appearance on *The Ed Sullivan Show*. Loengard and Kimberly intercept a radio transmission from the Hive which mentions a Broadway, New York, address, and fly to the Big Apple, where almost immediately they run into Jim Steele. Loengard and Kim become involved in a suspicious marketing survey which is utilizing subliminal messages to sway the minds of Americans toward suicide. This is the Hive's plan to kill all the human "throwbacks," citizens of Earth who cannot be successfully implanted with alien ganglion.

5. "Dreamland" Written by Steve Aspis; Directed by Winrich Kolbe; airdate: November 2, 1996; *Guest Cast:* Joey Aresco (Jack Gettings); Jack Conley (Rawlings); Tim Kelleher (Steele); Tyler Layton (Susan); Madison Mason (Howard Hughes); Louan Gideon (Hive Gambler); Andrew Hawkes (George Dover); Scott Jaeck (Cochran); Gary Carter (Casino Cashier); Paul Terrell Clayton (Lieutenant); Mark McPherson (Doorman).

John and Kimberly make for Las Vegas, out-of-money, and Kim is hired at a casino. Once she begins her job as a cocktail waitress, Kim hears the voices of the Hive nearby, and she and John are escorted to meet Howard Hughes, who has been observing the Hive conspiracy. Hughes suggests using Kim's abilities in a sting operation which will out the alien "commies," and reveal the true reason they are pooling their winnings from the casino. As Kim goes into danger, John discovers the Hive plan has something to do with "Dreamland," Area 51, and a secret tunnel dug into the side of a desert mountain.

6. "Inhuman Nature" Written by Melissa Rosenberg; Directed by Rodman Flender; airdate: November 9, 1996; *Guest Cast:* John Dennis Johnson (Castor Boehm); James F. Kelly (Robert Kennedy); Charley Lang (Dr. Halligen); Deborah May (Mrs. Boehm); Conor O'Farrell (Albano); Maury Sterling (Mark Waring); Ronald William Lawrence (Kauffman); Zach Hopkins (Boehm Son); Jeff Juday (Activist); Seth Murray (Boehm Son); Vanessa Munday (Jennifer Bach); Nancy Stephens (Mrs. Bach); Lauren Zabel (Boehm Daughter).

In April of 1964, John and Kim meet in secret with Attorney General Robert Kennedy, who asks them to be patient until he is elected president and can issue an order which makes Majestic public knowledge. In the meantime,

John and Kim investigate a report of strange lights over a Wisconsin farm. The farmer who owns the place is frightened because aliens have eviscerated his cattle with surgical precision. A second cow has been implanted with the embryo of a human baby designed to serve as a compatible host for the Hive ganglion.

7. "Ancient Future" Written by James D. Parriott and Gay Walch; Story by Bryce Zabel, Brent V. Friedman, and Gay Walch; Directed by Lou Antonio; airdate: November 16, 1996; *Guest Cast:* Charley Lang (Halligen); Conor O'Farrell (Albano); Eric Steinberg (Reverend Gary); Sam Vlahos (Tug Barrow); Steven Ford (Phillips); Dana Gladstone (Ernst Mittermyer); Joseph Whipp (General Thompson); Robert Arce (Hiver); Don Clark (Anchorman); Dan Erickson (Mission Controller); Roger Hewlett (Safe Suit Man); Dale Ishimoto (Tlinget Chief); Matt Roe (Traveler).

In 100 BC, an alien ship crashed in Alaska, and now, in March of 1964, Kim and John are investigating an alien legend about flying rocks. According to an Indian storyteller of the Tlinget tribe, a heavenly "Father" from the stars followed the spaceship down and warned that the ship should not be touched, lest destruction rain down on the tribe. An earthquake strikes in Alaska, registering 8.4 on the Richter scale, and the chasm to the crashed spaceship opens. John investigates the ship and experiences a terrifying vision of the future as Kim explores the possibility that the alien "grays" are an enslaved race conquered and implanted by the Hive, despite their superior technology.

8. "Hostile Convergence" Written by Javier Grillo-Marxuach; Story by Bryce Zabel and Brent V. Friedman; Directed by David Jackson; airdate: December 7, 1996; *Guest Cast:* Robert Carradine (Ronnie Zamora); Diane Cary (Cassie); Jamie Denton (Rob Winter); Stephanie Faracy (Joan Sayers); Richard Gilliland (Jesse Marcel); Tim Kelleher (Steele); Charley Lang (Dr. Halligan); Jack Lindine (Jack Ruby); Conor O'Farrell (Albano); Lisa Waltz (Andrea Sayers); Sam

Whipple (J. Allen Hynek); Conrad Bachmann (Mayor Holm Bursum); David Brisbin (Joe Edermeyer); Terrence Evans (Clark Balfour); Mike Kennedy (Allen Dulles); Wendy Robie (Kate Balfour).

A police patrolman in New Mexico spots a UFO land as Kim struggles with family responsibilities and returns home to be a part of her sister's wedding. Meanwhile, Majestic and Jim Steele independently plot to silence an imprisoned Jack Ruby, who is still "half" Hive. John determines that the New Mexico UFO was actually a U.S. test aircraft built with UFO technology, and follows Kim to Denver rather than be used as Majestic's patsy. Kim learns that her sister is planning to marry a Majestic agent, and Jim Steele arrives in Denver.

9. "We Shall Overcome" Written by Bryce Zabel and Brent V. Friedman; Directed by James Charleston; airdate: December 14, 1996; *Guest Cast:* Roger Aaron Brown (Reverend Pool); Tracy Fraim (Andrew Mendel); Charley Lang (Dr. Halligan); Dean Norris (Clayton Lewis); Conor O'Farrell (Albano); Raphael Sbarge (Mark Simonson); Wayne Tippit (J. Edgar Hoover); Lorraine Toussaint (Etta Mae Tillman); Mike Kennedy (Allen Dulles); Kim Robillard (Allen Dalton Roberts); Art Bell (William Paley); Arell Blanton (General Nathan Twining); Edward Edwards (Foote); Terence Mathews (Lance Taylor); Sean A. Moran (Lionel Tillman); Don Moss (Hubert Humphrey).

Three civil rights workers are missing in Mississippi, the most racially segregated state in the country, and John and Kim fear the vanishing is a result of alien interference. Meanwhile, Frank Bach attempts to raise more money for Majestic's budget so he can change its policy from observation to confrontation. In the basement of a Mississippi church, Kim discovers some unusual alien biological matter and a white racist who is rapidly becoming Hive. As John and Kim conduct an ART on the racist, Majestic takes samples of the biological material and then burns the church ... leading to a fevered jurisdictional debate between Bach and J. Edgar Hoover.

10. "The Last Wave" Written by Melissa Rosenberg; Directed by Steve Beers; airdate: January 4, 1997; *Guest Cast:* Brent David Fraser (Jim Morrison); Conor O'Farrell (Albano); Brittany Powell (Gina); Christopher Wiehl (Nat); Mark Bramhall (Whitman); Daniel Markel (Robert Dewey); Carl Ciarfalio (Supervisor); Kristoffer Ryan Winters (Surfer).

In the summer of 1964, John and Kim head to sunny California for the funeral of an old college buddy who died under mysterious circumstances. With the help of a flighty young poet named Jim Morrison, the duo from Washington soon learns that the Hive is hatching another plot to subjugate humanity, this time one that involves human physiology and a process which will make implantation more feasible. Loengard and Kim follow the plot back to a sewage treatment, but they must act fast if they are to save two other friends from their college days.

11. "The Enemy Within" Written by Brad Markowitz; Story by Bryce Zabel and Brent V. Friedman; Directed by James Charleston; airdate: January 11, 1997; *Guest Cast:* Dorie Burton (Lucy Loengard); Tim Kelleher (Steele); Kent McCord (Mr. Loengard); Joan McMurtrey (Jo Loengard); Sean O'Bryan (Ray Loengard); Conor O'Farrell (Albano); Terry Bozeman (Goodwin); Tim Chaote (Jeff Gale); Mike Kennedy (Allen Dulles).

In August of 1964, Loengard's brother, Ray, is abducted and implanted by the Hive. John returns to the family farm with Kim hoping to cash some saving bonds his father gave him when he was ten. Meanwhile, Steele breaks into Majestic headquarters even as Frank Bach worries about the Warren Commission learning of Hive involvement in JFK's assassination. John and his older brother Ray deal with old family tensions at the same time John must discover a way to free Ray from the alien mind.

12. "The Warren Omission" Written by Bryce Zabel and Brent Friedman; Directed by Perry Lang; airdate: January 18, 1997; *Guest Cast:* Jeri Lynn Ryan (Juliet Stuart); Jay Avocone (Kincaid); Dennis Creghan, James F. Kelly (Bobby Kennedy); Gary Lockwood (Earl Warren); Conor O'Farrell (Albano); Drew Snyder (Gerald Ford); Arthur Taxier (George Barrett); Wayne Tippit (J. Edgar Hoover); Susan Griffiths (Marilyn Monroe); Mike Kennedy (Allan Dulles); Gunther Jensen (Captain Norman Schwarzkopf); Jack Ritschel (Clyde Tolson).

Robert Kennedy asks John Loengard to testify before the Warren Commission about the existence of the Hive and the role of Majestic in domestic policy. A beautiful blond agent for Majestic, Juliet Stuart, threatens to kill John and Kim should they testify, but they go ahead, fingering Majestic, revealing its history, and describing the activities of the Hive. When Frank Bach is compelled to testify before the commission, he perjures himself and fingers Loengard as Kennedy's assassin. When John is threatened with criminal charges for his "perjurious" testimony, Kennedy stages a raid on Majestic, only to find himself compromised by a moral lapse in his personal life.

Note: This show makes extensive use of clips from episodes including "The Awakening," "Moving Targets," "The Enemy Within," and "We Shall Overcome."

13. "White Rabbit" Written by Bryce Zabel and Brent V. Friedman; Directed by James Contner; airdate: February 1, 1997; *Guest Cast:* Jeri Lynn Ryan (Juliet Stuart); Art Chudabala (Tay Ma); Brian Cousins (Lev); Jennifer Hetrick (Mrs. Bach); Tom O'Brien (Kellogg); Conor O'Farrell (Albano); Arell Blanton (Nathan Twining); Bradford English (General Brown); Phong Vo, Ray Chang (VC Soldiers); Thomas Woolen (Radio Operator).

On Kim's birthday, John is kidnapped and drafted for a UFO recovery mission in Vietnam. He teams with Bach to find a downed craft, which is the last surviving bit of alien technology from an underwater base located in the Gulf of Tonkin. In an effort to get John back, Kim kidnaps Bach's wife and shares with her some information about what her husband *really* does for a living. Juliet Stuart is also angered by Frank Bach's lies and

joins Kim's crusade to expose the truth ... but can she be trusted?

14. "Shades of Gray" Written by Brad Markowitz; Directed by Perry Lang; airdate: February 8, 1997; *Guest Cast:* David Carpenter (Grisham); Charley Lang (Halligan); Conor O'Farrell (Albano); Jamie Rene Smith (Monica); Grant Mathis (Cloaker); Liza Smith (Svetlana).

Kim and Loengard are now allied with Majestic again, in hopes that they can change some of Bach's more fascist tendencies. In their first mission back with the secret government organization, John and Kim team with Soviet Juliet Stuart to bring down a Hive space vehicle. What they actually catch with their crop circle ploy, however, is a Gray alien. After the Hive parasite is removed from the captured Gray creature, it communicates peaceably with Kimberly, once Hive herself ... and she soon learns that she is pregnant.

15. "Burn, Baby, Burn" Written by James D. Parriott; Directed by Steve Posey; airdate: March 1, 1997; *Guest Cast:* Jeri Lynn Ryan (Juliet Stuart); Tim Kelleher (Steele); Duane Davis (Briggs); Keith Diamond (George Lewis); Paul Lieber (Dr. Merrick); Charley Lang (Dr. Halligan); Conor O'Farrell (Albano); Vaughn Armstrong (Minkus); Troy Winbush (Quentin); Dean Denton (Cop); Stephen Quadros (Lab Worker); Vince Ricotta (Simon Rodia); Marquette Frye (Garland).

In August of 1965, Kim is a month overdue delivering her baby, and Majestic fears there will be genetic abnormalities in the child because of Kim's history with the Hive. The Watts Riot is in full swing, and Jim Steele is behind the scenes. While Kim is visiting a specialist in L.A., she is abducted by Steele and the Hive. John and Juliet head into strife-ridden Watts to save her from the alien laboratory but it is too late: the baby and Kim are now members of the Hive.

16. "Both Sides Now" Written by Melissa Rosenberg; Directed by James Contner; airdate: March 8, 1997; *Guest Cast:* Jeri Lynn Ryan (Juliet); Tim Kelleher (Steele); Jeff Juday (Kendall); Charley Lang (Halligan); Conor O'-

Farrell (Albano); Timothy Omundsen (Rubin); Don Stark (Gallagher); Bradford English (General Brown); Brett Wagner (Hiver).

In late September of 1965, a captured Kimberly Sayers is encouraged to touch the alien sphere of light so that she can experience the singularity of the Hive, even as John and Majestic search desperately for her. Kim soon shows up at an anti-war campaign in Berkeley, and Juliet Stuart is assigned to bring her back or kill her if she has already accepted singularity. John disobeys Bach's orders and joins Juliet as she attempts to stop the Hive from releasing a deadly contaminant during an anti-war rally. Although Hive plans are stopped cold, John soon learns the hard way that Kim has really joined the enemy ... for good.

17. "To Prey in Darkness" Written by Bryce Zabel and Brent V. Friedman; Directed by Thomas Wright; airdate: March 15, 1997; *Guest Cast:* Jeri Lynn Ryan (Juliet Stuart); Spencer Garrett (Ed Hawkins); Tim Kelleher (Steele); Robin Gammell (Carl Hertzog); James Karen (Harry Carruthers); Jack Lindine (Jack Ruby); Marilyn McIntry (Dorothy Kilgallen); Conor O'Farrell (Albano); Mitchell Ryan (William Paley); Ryan Cutrona (Detective); Alan Gelfant (Beatnik); Barry Grayson (TV Technician); Fred Saxon (Reporter).

In early November of 1965, 53 feet of film from the 1947 Roswell UFO encounter turn up missing from the Majestic vaults, and Bach assigns Loengard and Juliet to recover the material. They follow the trail to New Orleans and Dr. Hertzog, the first physician on Majestic, but he claims innocence. The next lead involves Jack Ruby and Dorothy Kilgallen, a gossip columnist. Juliet and John try to force newspaperman Ed Hawkins not to air the footage, which Steele and Kim Sayers are also trying to steal for the Hive. There is a citywide black-out and loyalties are tested as Kim, John, Steele, and Albano cross swords.

18. "Strangers in the Night" Written by Brad Markowitz; Directed by Michael Levine; airdate: May 24, 1997; *Guest Cast:* Jeri Lynn Ryan (Juliet Stuart); Simon Billig, Wolfgang Bodison (Colin Powell); Charley Lang (Hal-ligan); Conor O'Farrell (Albano); Beata Pozniak, John Saint Ryan (Colonel Miranov); Joseph Urla (Carl Sagan); Silas Weir Mitchell (Kuleshov); Kirk B. Woller (Pavel); Grant Mathis (Cloaker); Wiley Pickett (MP).

In August of 1966, the Russian counterpart to Majestic falls under attack, so Bach sends Loengard, Juliet, and a young Colin Powell on a rescue mission to discover the identity of the attackers. The team finds a ruined headquarters and a few survivors who were conducting a mysterious experiment. The mission becomes personal when John discovers photos of Kim and his son, and Juliet realizes that her mentor, Colonel Miranov, may have been implanted by the Hive. Meanwhile, Frank Bach recruits a skeptical Carl Sagan into Majestic.

19. "Bloodlines" Written by Bryce Zabel and Brent V. Friedman; Directed by Perry Lang; airdate: May 31, 1997; *Guest Cast:* Jeri Lynn Ryan (Juliet Stuart); Tim Kelleher (Steele); James F. Kelly (Robert Kennedy); Mike Kennedy (Allen Dulles); Ernie Lively (Dr. Cliff Rasmussen); Don Most (Timothy Leary); Conor O'Farrell (Albano); Christopher Thomas (William Paley); Joseph Urla (Carl Sagan); Bryan Clark (Ronald Reagan); Don Moss (Hubert Humphrey); Lindsey Lee Ginter (Sgt. Linson); Arell Blanton (Twining); Jonathan Zabel (Ray Loengard).

In June of 1967, during the summer of love, Juliet and Loengard meet with Timothy Leary, who has firsthand knowledge of some very dangerous drug cubes. The pushers of these bad cubes, which link right into the Hive collective consciousness, are none other than Steele and Kim Sayers. Majestic's Gray alien, who is slowly dying because an unknown double agent exposed him to influenza, translates a message from his species for John Loengard, a message which informs John that his own bloodline will determine the future of human life on Earth. In hopes of saving his son, John volunteers for Project Intruder, a suicide mission which will land him aboard the Hive mothership just beyond the fringe of Earth's solar system.

The Burning Zone (1996–1997)

CRITICAL RECEPTION

"The idea is *Outbreak* meets *The X-Files*, and everyone involved in *The Burning Zone* keeps a straight face ... it offers the loopy delights of a cut-rate, over-the-top horror movie.... Overall this new show helps demonstrate just how good *The X-Files* is at keeping its balance, one foot in reality and one in the unexplained. *The Burning Zone* is always threatening to go completely out of control. It might as well play to that strength and follow its silliest, campiest instincts."— Caryn James, *The New York Times*: "A Virus That Speaks of a Deadly World Plot," Tuesday, September 3, 1996, page C12.

"a show that went through so many transformations in its brief 19-episode run that no viewer who saw the first show would recognize the last.... Viewers had the underlying premise yanked out from under them every few weeks. Despite some strong engaging performances and memorable episodes early on, *The Burning Zone* never stuck with one premise long enough to develop an audience following."— Roger Fulton and John Betancourt, *The Sci-Fi Channel Encyclopedia of TV Science Fiction*, Warner Books, 1997, page 106.

"a show that was so stupid, and yet made such pretentious claims to being science-fact oriented that it made me want to throw shoes at the television. (For those of you who missed it, it featured snarly fashion-model scientists chasing intelligent hive-mind vampire zombie viruses with flame throwers.)"— Peter Huston, *The Skeptical Inquirer*, May-June 1998, page 9.

FORMAT

The Burning Zone follows the dangerous adventures of an "elite" bio-crisis team dedicated to wiping out diseases which threaten to strike quickly and endanger many innocent Americans in a series of "attacks" sometimes referred to on the series as "The Plague Wars." The first team on this UPN series consists of Daniel Cassian, a no-nonsense doctor with Level 92 clearance and a firm grip over his own emotions; Edward Marcase, a brilliant virologist who survived a childhood bout with Ebola but lost both his parents to the disease; Kimberly Shiroma, a molecular-geneticist-pathologist recruited from the World Health Organization; and Michael Hailey, a liaison to defense intelligence who is responsible for the team's safety and security. Unfortunately, there is much stress among this team because of clashing egos, views, and philosophies. Kimberly's fiancée died working with Edward at an Ebola infection site and she blames Marcase for his death. Marcase, in turn, disapproves of Cassian's by-the-numbers, sometimes cold-hearted approach to preventing outbreaks. And Shiroma vehemently dislikes the fact that Edward is a "mystic" who believes that fighting diseases is a supernatural quest. This mismatched group can and indeed does travel anywhere in America, working in secret underground laboratory installations designed to protect the country against "the terrors to come." Prime among those terrors is the New Dawn, a villainous organization dedicated to the annihilation of humankind and the supremacy of Earth's original lifeform: a hive-mind, sentient virus which has been "asleep" for 15,000 years.

As *The Burning Zone* progresses, Shiroma and Marcase leave the team (to spearhead an important investigation in Zimbabwe), only to be replaced by the "rebel" doctor, Brian Taft.

The Burning Zone has the unusual distinction of being the goriest TV series ever to air on network television. In the pilot, a man infected with the evil virus spits a thick mass of gelatinous goop into an open cut on Hailey's bare chest. This material is green, syrupy, and thoroughly nauseating in appearance. This stomach-churning moment cheerily sets the tone for the remainder of this short-lived UPN series. Unsuspecting teenagers burn up suddenly in "Arms of Fire," leaving only bone-fragments and ash-covered Nikes behind. Firefighters develop huge tumorous growths in seconds, which bulge and explode, in "Critical Mass." In "Death Song," a disease causes "skeletal collapse," which affects joggers who are literally tortured as bones all over their bodies suddenly snap and jut out of their skin. In "The Last Endless Summer," worm organisms crawl inside people, right beneath the flesh, and begin to feast on internal organs as if the human body is a salad bar. In "Elegy for a Dream" poisonous tattoo ink causes stomachs to literally erupt and explode. "On Wings of Angels" features contaminated cigarettes which cause the human head to split right up the back of the skull and ooze blood. In other words, *The Burning Zone* is not a show to watch over lunch.

Diseases are not the only bailiwick of Daniel Cassian's crack team on *The Burning Zone*. In nineteen episodes, the unit also managed to clean up a contaminated building ("The Silent Tower"), expose a mystic faith healer conducting "psychic surgery" ("Hall of the Serpent"), discover the gateway to hell ("Lethal Injection"), recover an occult relic called "The Eyes of Odin" from a neo-Nazi group ("Midnight of the Carrier"), and expose the dangers of diet drugs ("The Last Five Pounds Are the Hardest").

Stylistically, *The Burning Zone* mimics *The X-Files* in some important ways. Marcase and Shiroma share the same bickering relationship as Mulder and Scully do, and the series (in its last seven episodes) provides on-screen legends to let the audience know where precisely (in the country) the team is located on its current "mission."

HISTORY

By the fall of 1996, nearly every American television network worth its salt was taking serious notice of Fox's wholly unexpected success with the paranormal/horror hit *The X-Files*. For NBC, this success was to be translated (hopefully) into two new fall series: the alien invasion/conspiracy drama *Dark Skies*, and the more whitebread "serial killer on the loose" drama called *Profiler*. For Fox, it meant the advent of *Millennium*, a new series from *X-Files* creator, Chris Carter. The network with the most to lose (and to gain) in this battle, however, was surely the newbie UPN (United Paramount Network) which after a year of regular broadcasting still had only one high-profile program to its roster: *Star Trek: Voyager* (1995-2001). In point of fact, UPN was already ahead of the *X-Files* clone curve. It had picked up on the *X-Files*'s popularity a year earlier in 1995, and gone the conspiracy route with *Nowhere Man* (starring Bruce Greenwood). That unique series had gained a strong cult following, a foothold for any genre show, but UPN mysteriously drydocked the program after one season and decided to take a different tack with *The Burning Zone*, a sort of latter-day *Andromeda Strain* about a team of scientists fighting deadly diseases on a weekly basis. The recent successes of the book *The Hot Zone*, a true-to-life account of an Ebola outbreak in Virginia, and *Outbreak* (1995), a feature film pitting Dustin Hoffman, Rene Russo, Cuba Gooding Jr., Morgan Freeman, and Kevin Spacey against hemorrhagic fever in California, undoubtedly contributed to UPN's decision to dump conspiracy TV for disease TV. As creator Coleman Luck and James McAdams described the central tenet of their new show:

> Today's battle to save humanity is fought in sterile labs with petri dishes and test tubes

for weapons. Virologists and geneticists are the new warriors.[1]

It all sounded promising, and *The X-Files* had proven that "disease"-centered episodes (such as the second season entry "F. Emasculata") could be accomplished with a substantial dose of credible-sounding science and an equally large helping of gore ... two critical components in making diseases interesting (and believable) to the home audience. *The Burning Zone* took *The X-Files* as its primary source in another way as well: characters Marcase (Dean Morgan) and Shiroma (Tamlyn Tomita) initially had a sparring relationship much akin to Mulder and Scully, with Marcase accepting and embracing the paranormal and spiritual, and Shiroma relying on hard science to cure the disease of the week. In another regard, *The Burning Zone* seemed like another popular series: *The A-Team.* Along with wily government operative Daniel Cassian (Michael Harris) leading the team of scientists was security expert Michael Hailey (James Black), a latter day Mr. T. Together, this team could cure any disease, beat up any villain, out *Mission: Impossible* any conspiracy, and always save the day. Cassian and his team were fighting diseases, and kicking a little ass along the way.

Binding the early *Burning Zone* episodes together is a supernatural, almost mystical bent which some genre magazines dubbed "new age," but which in fact seems to plumb a variety of spiritual and religious sources. In "The Silent Tower," a drug which was causing the stimulation of a portion of the brain causing terror allowed Marcase to go on a kind of vision-quest to meet with the parents who died in his childhood (from Ebola). In "St. Michael's Nightmare," a traveling vendor who was actually the devil (guest Rene Auberjonois) sold a priest a flower which had been plucked from "the Tree of Knowledge" and could stimulate violence in anybody who smelled its sweet perfume. In "Lethal Injection" Marcase took a trip to the afterlife and was saved by angels, and so forth. Audiences were not quite sure what to make of this mix of science and spiritualism, and ratings remained quite low for *The Burning Zone.*

In response to the tepid viewer response, UPN staged a behind-the-scenes massacre: the two series stars, Dean Morgan and Tamlyn Tomita were dropped from the format with only the briefest of explanations. The mysterious Cassian, a character who had gained substantial popularity among viewers because of his hard-nosed, no-nonsense attitude, was upgraded to male lead #1, and James Black, as Hailey, became male lead #2. Joining the cast was a new young doctor named Taft, played by Bradford Tatum. Unlike Dean Morgan, Taft was no thoughtful "lab geek": he was a motorcycle-riding, womanizing "cool guy" who could hang with Cassian and Hailey and not seem out of place. The new changes also involved a serious downgrading of the scientific portions of the show, and *The Burning Zone* became, essentially, an action series with a medical bent.

At the same time as the cast changes occurred, a new style of cinematography was introduced to *The Burning Zone*: all the action was viewed through a shaky handheld camera which had a propensity to shoot the protagonists from cockeyed angles. This was an attempt to make the action more "immediate," and give the show a distinctive look (like the dark *Millennium*, or the "gritty" *NYPD Blue*), but it, like the cast changes, failed to garner higher ratings. In fact, the changes did more damage than good, and *The Burning Zone*'s ratings dropped even lower. The series was canceled after just nineteen episodes, and failed to gain the kind of devotion which *Nowhere Man* had so easily engendered. UPN did not learn its lesson with *The Burning Zone* either, and in 1997 it canceled another popular series with a cult following: *The Sentinel.* Since then, UPN has changed its mind yet again: renewing *The Sentinel* and even granting the genre series *7 Days* a second season in which to develop just such a passionate following. But *The Burning Zone* is, rightfully, history. It's newest home is on the Sci-Fi Channel, where it airs after *Dark Skies* and before *The Visitor* as part of the "Sunday Conspiracy" viewing block. The stars of *The Burning Zone* have moved onto other work with Tatum appearing on *Charmed* ("Secrets and Guy"), James Black supporting Kurt Russell in the 1997 epic *Soldier*, and Tomita (of the *Babylon 5* pilot) having a featured role in *Living Out Loud* (1998) with Holly Hunter.

Prominent genre guest stars on *The Burning Zone* include *Deep Space Nine*'s Rene Auberjonois in "St. Michael's Nightmare," Tony Jay of *Beauty and the Beast* in "The Silent Tower," Nicholas Lea, Krycek on *The X-Files*, in "Hall of the Serpent," Michael Cavanaugh of the new *Dark Shadows* in "Night Flight," Keith Szarabajka of *The Golden Years* in "Lethal Injection," Grace Zabriskie of *Twin Peaks* in "Touch of the Dead," and Tim O'-Connor of *Buck Rogers in the 25th Century* in "Midnight of the Carrier."

CRITICAL COMMENTARY

Another one-season wonder (or blunder?), UPN's *The Burning Zone* is one of the strangest and most schizophrenic horror shows to air in recent memory. In this case, "strange" is not necessarily a compliment, and many episodes of this short-lived drama simply leave viewers shaking their heads in disbelief and confusion at the bizarre proceedings. Perhaps the most unusual and significant facet of *The Burning Zone* is its unceasing (but ill-advised) attempt to blend science and religion into a cohesive TV formula. This (failed) idea could have been an interesting conceit, to be certain. After all, the lead characters are all highly skilled, highly trained scientists who have gone through years, almost decades, of medical training. Yet in adventure after adventure these men and women of science find themselves exploring the spirit/body connection in ways they would never have anticipated during their residency. This sounds like a philosophy that could open up all sorts of avenues for character growth and development, yet the formula was applied so haphazardly on *The Burning Zone* as to be merely bizarre.

Perhaps the one element which makes *The X-Files* so endlessly engrossing is its pointed contradiction between science and the paranormal. Each lead character (Scully and Mulder) champions a cause in every story, and the two belief systems, one reason-based and one intuition-based, are juxtaposed and tested. Thus the audience is afforded two interesting worldviews in each story. Before the format changes which sunk the series, *The Burning Zone* tried for (and missed) a similar juxtaposition of concepts: medicine vs. spiritualism. In "St. Michael's Nightmare," for instance, an epidemic of violence sweeps Philadelphia, but the root cause of the malady focuses the team's microscopes on religion, not modern medicine: a traveling salesman, possibly the Devil himself, has spread a magic elixir about the town, an elixir made from a venomous fruit which was believed to have existed on the Tree of Knowledge in Paradise! This revelation, cemented by a 15th-century artist's rendering of the fruit in the Garden of Eden, put science and religion on equal footing, and *The Burning Zone* saw both ideologies as "valid" explanations for events, in this case the rapid proliferation of a disease.

"Touch of the Dead" is another *Burning Zone* episode which tried to balance spiritual and scientific concepts. In this story, Cassian is infected with a deadly disease which cannot be completely cured by science. On the contrary, for his new remedy to be successful, Cassian must look inside himself and find a "reason to live." In other words, medicine alone is not enough to cure people; it must be accompanied by a spiritual component, a healthy soul, even. "Arms of Fire" also pushed this agenda when a boy in danger of spontaneously combusting (?!) survives the ordeal because of his willingness to pray. Likewise, "Hall of the Serpent" exposes a psychic surgeon (Nicholas Lea of *The X-Files*) as a fraud who uses his powers for selfish gain. As the heroes solemnly state at the end of this show, "When God heals ... it brings out hope and peace ... not fear." If this sounds hokey in print, imagine it in play on your TV screen.

The ultimate expression of *The Burning Zone*'s spiritual philosophy was seen in "Lethal Injection," an episode in which a hellish afterworld is visited by Marcase after he is forced to take an experimental drug. In the hellish afterlife, he is threatened by whispering, black-clothed ghouls who can remove a man's spirit by touch, and eventually he is protected by organisms he terms "angels." At the end of the drama, it is theorized that this "City of the Dead" was created as an entrance to hell for angels who had fallen from grace. Quite a significant discovery for a biocrisis team, isn't it? In one "adventure" they prove the existence of an afterlife, hell, and angels! As farfetched as this concept sounds, at least there is evidence of a worldview at work. Damningly, it is a variation, and a weak one, of *The X-Files'* worldview. Though it is rewarding that *The Burning Zone*'s creators attempted to infuse their series with a subtext, it is not clearly nor cleverly enunciated in "Lethal Injection" or any other story. On the contrary, the spiritualism vs. science just seems rather corny.

A hoary subtext is not the only problem which infects *The Burning Zone* episode roster. Another element to consider is what this author now terms "The Burning Zone Fallacy": the straight-faced belief (of this program) that a disease can be isolated, diagnosed, cured, and its effects *totally* reversed in every story ... some of which occur in just a few hours of story time! Though this is drama and some bending of the rules is permitted, even necessary, this series simply asks us to suspend disbelief too much. How long has AIDS been with us now? Or cancer? Yet *The Burning Zone* asks us to believe that this elite team of doctors can stop outbreaks faster than a speeding bullet. There is never a disease the team cannot handle, and most of these horrible plagues do not even leave behind pock marks or scars on their victims. This oversight is particularly damaging. Should not some diseases leave behind at least residual indications of their presence? *The Burning Zone* could have avoided this ridiculous "disease of the week" problem with just one or two bits of ingenuity. First off, each episode could have been part of a multipart arc. Imagine a three or four-part story, taking place over a span of months, with the characters learning of a deadly disease in

the first hour, spending the second hour charting and diagnosing it, and working during the third or fourth hours to create and administer a cure. Granted, this is not a perfect solution, but it would have allowed the series to mirror reality to at least a marginal degree. As it stands, the speed with which the biocrisis team dispatches such deadly illnesses is simply too hard to believe. Dramatic license is one thing, ridiculous plotting is quite another.

When not mixing spiritualism and science and curing diseases lickety split, *The Burning Zone* finds itself dependent on another cathode tube pit of vipers: clichés. In "Night Flight," the audience is treated to another kind of disaster movie: *Airport* meets *Outbreak*. A deadly fever strikes an airline in midflight and (fortunately!) the series protagonists happen to be aboard, with all their high-tech equipment to boot! As passengers die, the oldest and most irritating of all *Airport* clichés rears its ugly head. The pilot falls sick and — gasp!— there is the fear that nobody on board can fly the plane! In this story, a co-pilot (Michael Cavanaugh) manages to stay alive just long enough to land the plane before succumbing, naturally, to the evil disease of the week.

Other shows in *The Burning Zone* roster are so strange it is hard to see how they fit into the series format at all. "Midnight of the Carrier," for instance, is a rip-off of *Raiders of the Lost Ark* (1981) with Cassian's team fighting Nazis for possession of a Third Reich relic called the "Eyes of Odin." At the climax, this dangerous occult tool falls into the wrong hands, but it sprays laser beams and kills all the Nazis who have attempted to abuse its power ... a blow-by-blow replay of the *Raiders* finale (wherein the Ark of the Covenant rains heaven's wrath down upon the baddies, also Nazis, of course).

After about a dozen or so confused episodes like this (including a ridiculous one called "Faces in the Night" in which the team metamorphs into law enforcement agents to hunt down a serial killer), *The Burning Zone* was redesigned to be more user friendly, but it got worse ... much, much worse. It had been obvious to viewers early on that Marcase and Shiroma were little more than cardboard Mulder/Scully wannabes and that the mysterious Dr. Cassian was the most interesting of the series' rather shallow dramatis personae. Call it the "Dr. Smith Factor": just as Jonathan Harris's character on the original *Lost in Space* (1964-68) overpowered the series leads with his semivillainous creation, so did Michael Harris steal scene after scene from his co-stars as the enigmatic cold fish Dr. Cassian. The audience knew almost nothing about this fascinating man except that he was ruthlessly efficient in pursuing his own agenda. When the format changed, Cassian became the show's main protagonist, reflecting his immense popularity with viewers. However, the writers mitigated this popularity almost instantly by revealing literally everything they could about this previously secretive man: his home life, his family, his boss, his working situation, and so on. What had made Cassian so interesting early on was that audiences did not really know where he stood on a variety of issues and matters. He was a mystery man, and an attractive, interesting one. In the revised show, Cassian became a true blue hero, saddled with a boss, a hierarchy, a family, and so forth ... and what little fun was left on *The Burning Zone* was surgically removed.

In the end, *The Burning Zone* thoughtlessly ditched its spiritualism/science debate to concentrate on hard action-adventure. The new Doctor, Taft, was a motorcycle-riding ladies' man (replete with sexy haircut) who could cure diseases and fight bad guys with equal dexterity. The show was also given a new visual veneer: sudden (and purposeless) zooms, distorted angles, fast-motion, handheld camerawork, and the like. These stylistic touches gave the show a less stodgy feeling and did succeed in generating an unhinged, immediate feel to the series, but the hyped-up camerawork could not hide the basic banality of the new stories. One episode ("Death Song") was a remake of *The Bodyguard* (1991), with Hailey protecting (and romancing) a beautiful rock star in danger, another was a variation on *Playing God* (1997), with Taft

forced to administer medical care to a sick gangster. The series became *The A-Team* meets *The Hot Zone*, and it pleased nobody.

On a more basic level, *The Burning Zone* might not have caught on simply because it was too grotesque, too graphic in its depictions of human bodies breaking, melting, bending, and hurting. People tend not to be very comfortable with the subject of this series: diseases, bacteria, death, and men in blue protective suits. While it is true that horror should never be comfortable or easy, it is also true that some shows and films hit too close to home. We all live with the specter of disease every day, but is it really necessary to see gut-wrenching depictions of Ebola and the like cloaked as entertainment, week in and week out? In a bestseller, or a hit movie, this is acceptable, but *The Burning Zone* asked its audience to tune in not once, but every week. In the end, that was medicine few audiencegoers wished to take.

CAST AND CREDITS

Cast: Michael Harris (Dr. Daniel Cassian); James Black (Michael Hailey). Episodes #1–11: Jeffrey Dean Morgan (Dr. Edward Marcase); Tamlyn Tomita (Kimberly Shiroma); Episodes #12–19: Bradford Tatum (Dr. Brian Taft).

Credits: Created by: Coleman Luck. *Executive Producers:* Coleman Luck, James D. McAdams, Robert A. Papazian, James G. Hirsch. *Music:* Martin Davich. *Co-producer:* Dean W. Barnes. *Producer:* Harker Wade. *Associate Producer:* Billy Crawford. *Director of Photography (various episodes):* Geoffrey Erb, Bradford May, Geoff Schaaf. *Art Director:* Andrew Neskoromny. *Editor (various episodes):* Brian L. Chambers, Bill Luciano, Tom McQuade, Chuck Weiss. *Unit Production Manager:* Harker Wade. *First Assistant Director:* Richard Denault. *Second Assistant Director:* Cynthia Potthast. *Casting:* Penny Perry. *Set Decorator:* Ethel Robins Richards. *Visual Effects Supervisor:* Richard Kerrigan. *Sound Supervisor:* Michael Guitierrez. *Supervising*

Music Editor: Allan K. Rosen. *Costume Designer:* Catherine Adair. *Costume Supervisor:* Buffy Snyder. *Panaflex Camera and Lenses:* Panavision. *Sound Mixer:* Richard Van Dyke. *Stunt Coordinator:* Greg Barnett. *Main Title:* Pittard Sullivan. Sandstar Productions, filmed in association with Universal Television.

EPISODE GUIDE

1. "Pilot" Written by Coleman Luck; Directed by Bradford May; airdate: September 3, 1996; *Guest Cast:* Peter Guilfoyle (Dr. Glinden); Peter Frechette (Dr. Alan Reinhardt); Julie Araskog (Ann Glinden); Denis Arnat (Frank Matthews); Mika Boorem (Little Girl); Lucas Dudley (State Trooper); Dwayne Foster (Technician); Kevin Fry (Agent); James Harper (Lt. Colonel); David Jackson (News Anchor); Todd Kimsey (M.P. Guard); Mitchell Longley (Van Driver); Jordan Marder (Communications Specialist); Heather McPhaul (Mother).

An expedition to the Talamanca rain forest in Costa Rica faces terror when the archaeologists on the team open up a cave that has been sealed for 15,000 years and inadvertently release a terrible, sentient disease from its long hibernation. In Reston, Virginia, a team consisting of molecular-geneticist-pathologist Kimberly Shiroma, security man Michael Hailey, and unconventional leader Edward Marcase is isolated in a government lab to investigate and eradicate the deadly virus, which one man refers to as "the angel of death." The virus seems to choose its victims very carefully, and the eyes of those infected appear hemorrhagic. When the medical team learns that the hive virus is sentient, conscious, and in control of warrior viruses like ebola, its members realize that humanity must work fast to defeat this ancient invader.

2. "The Silent Tower" Written by Coleman Luck; Directed by Michael Lange; airdate: September 10, 1996; *Guest Cast:* Damon Whitaker (Mr. Williams); Dena Dietrich (Mrs. Pride); Julius Harris, Edward Evanko, Tony Jay (The Chairman/Wilson Pride); Annie Grindlay (Rachel Marcase); Nicholas Fappone (Young Edward); Brandon Adams (D-Ray Drummond); Clayton Murray (Security Guard); Raymond Turner (Hazmat Man); Christopher Kirby (Dark Figure).

With team administrator Reinhardt permanently reassigned, Marcase's bio-crisis team is put under the authority of the enigmatic Dr. Cassian. Their first assignment together: investigate an 80-story building in Chicago where seventy-nine deaths, all suicides, have occurred over a span of two years. Once inside the tower, Marcase disappears, leaving only a flashlight, a blood trail, and an empty helmet behind. In reality, Marcase has been abducted by a young black man suffering from paranoid hallucinations after a botched break-in attempt. Soon Marcase is also exposed to a synthetically engineered chemical warfare agent which resembles mist, but which causes slow asphyxiation and stimulates the part of the human brain which modulates terror.

3. "St. Michael's Nightmare" Written by Robert Gilmer; Directed by Scott Brazil; airdate: September 17, 1996; *Guest Cast:* Ray Abruzzo (Father Stefan); Theodore Bikel (Other Priest); Jacqueline Obradors (Marian); Rene Auberjonois (Mr. Dicketts); Joshua Cox (Danny Cox); Rachel Davies (Woman in Crowd); Gerry Donato (Angry Man); Gunther Jensen (Crowd Person #1); Joyce Greenleaf (Crowd Person #2); Ray Lykins (Young Guy).

A priest who has lost his faith after witnessing the suicide of one of his flock encounters a strange man, Mr. Dicketts, with an unusual truck filled with artifacts and antiques. Mr. Dicketts gives the saddened priest seeds from the Tree of Knowledge, which he claims will give the holy man insight into good and evil. The bio-crisis team goes to investigate the Festival of St. Michael's, the triumph of good over evil, in Philadelphia because priests have been responsible for outbreaks of violence at the festival for the last two years and Cassian feels that a new biological agent is involved. Once in Phillie, the team finds the populace short-tempered, the "virus" of violence thriving, and interestingly, a flowering plant which produces the same mysterious fruit that is said to have grown in the Garden of Eden.

4. "Arms of Fire" Written by Coleman Luck III; Directed by Michael Katleman; airdate: September 24, 1996; *Guest Cast:* Craig Kirkwood, Scott Allan Campbell, Michael Bryan French, Joel Swetow, Markus Flanagan, Mitchell Langley, Katherine Olsen, Patrick Y. Malone, De'aundre Bonds, Bernard Hocke (Coroner); Richard Gross (Desk Sergeant); Jane Marshall (Principal Bubeck); Chante Frierson (Keisha Marshall); J.J. Boone (Gym Teacher); Stephen Poletti (Chief of Security).

At a high school gym in a poor area of town, an African-American teenager spontaneously combusts, leaving only his expensive sneakers and a little charred bone behind. Cassian's bio-crisis teams goes to investigate when the second such victim, Frank Wallace, is tied to a prominent pharmaceutical company. While Hailey attempts to infiltrate the company's deepest levels, Shiroma and Marcase go to the school to try to stop the bizarre disease from claiming the lives of other youngsters. The team soon learns that Melton Pharmaceuticals has developed a new antiviral drug and is testing it through a free clinic.

5. "Night Flight" Written by Carleton Eastlake; Directed by Jesus Salvador Trevino; airdate: October 1, 1996; *Guest Cast:* Richard Yniguez, Michael Harney, Heidi Noelle Lenhart, Michael Cavanaugh (Captain); Tom Jourden, Rosanna Huffman, Barbara Nickell, Christina Ma, Dom Magwili (Military Police); Lance August (Sgt. Robert W. Francis); Mike Terne (Second Skinhead); Donald Nardini (Flight Engineer); Jordan Marder (Duty Officer); Kristina Malota (Katie); Frank Farmer (Flight Surgeon); Grant Mathig (Biohazard Commander).

Shiroma, Marcase, and Hailey have just spent several weeks abroad in Southeast Asia searching for a suspected plague when they board a flight for home. En route, Mr. Rick McGee, traveling with his wife Arla, falls ill from an unknown disease which resembles hemorrhagic fever. When the plane attempts to land for immediate medical care, the third world government shuts down the airport and launches attack jets to prevent the plane's descent. With a five hour trip to Hawaii and the disease spreading via contact like wildfire, Marcase and Hailey must contend not only with frightened passengers who want to dump the sick into the sea, but also with a serious problem: Who will land the plane if the pilots die?

6. "Lethal Injection" Written by Coleman Luck and Carel Gage Luck; Directed by Richard Compton; airdate: October 15, 1996; *Guest Cast:* Sherman Howard (Dr. Elton Greenleaf); Keith Szarabajka (Kinnick); Tim deZarn, Jim Holmes, Barbara Tarbuck (Dr. Boston); Wayne Pere, Dennis Christopher, Kenny McCabe (Security Specialist); Lawrence McNeal III (Guard); Shae Popovich (Technician).

A secret informant named Jonas reveals to Dr. Cassian that a mass murderer and pop culture icon who died of lethal injection is actually alive. A secret government agency is conducting a bizarre experiment: they believe they have made contact with intelligent lifeforms in an afterlife dimension, and they are using convicts who "die" of lethal injection to bring back important messages from the other side. One such convict, Dr. Elton Greenleaf, comes back from the older dimension (which gave birth to our own) possessed by a malevolent spirit. Cassian's bio-crisis team goes to work to investigate the Gethsemane Project and Marcase is forced to take an unwanted trip to the city of dead ... the dimension of pure evil.

7. "Touch of the Dead" Written by Robert Gilmer; Directed by Oscar L. Costo; airdate: October 29, 1996; *Guest Cast:* Dennis Boutsikaris (Stephen Rydell); Daphne Ashbrook (Rachel Roberson); Jennifer Sommerfield (Erica); Grace Zabriskie (Woman in Asylum); Constance Forslund (Woman on the Monitor); J.P. Hubbell (Bartender); Hervi Estrada (Man); Robert Zachary (Security Supervisor).

On his way home from a party, Cassian is cut by a woman who resembles his former lover, and infected with the deadly disease which killed her ten years ago and is believed to have destroyed Mayan civilization centuries earlier. Now Cassian has forty-eight hours to live, and his team has that long to find out who has infected him (as well as discover the antidote). The mysterious Rachel Roberson, Cassian's former lover, may still be alive as a healer with supernatural powers, and the organization called New Dawn is planning the extermination of the human race, beginning with Cassian and Roberson. When things look grim for Cassian, Rachel appears at the lab with an unusual antidote, but the leader of New Dawn shows up as well.

8. "Hall of the Serpent" Written by Coleman Luck and Carel Gage Luck; Directed by Michael Lange; airdate: November 12, 1996; *Guest Cast:* Nicholas Lea (Phillip Patchett); Kimberly Kates (Rebecca Cassian); Jessica Cushman (Monica); Nicole Nieth (Kelly); Kevin Fry (O'Fallon); Alex Fernandez (Guard); Nick Kusenko.

Cassian's niece, Rebecca, has disappeared into the compound of cult leader and mystical healer Phillip Patchett. Patchett believes that the ruins of the Greek island Delos can cure terminal illnesses and he has formed a quasi-religious group in Mexico which worships a "healing" serpent God. Cassian requests the team's help in clearing up this "personal" matter, and it begins to investigate Padgett's so-called psychic surgery. His cure for cancer consists of the placement of rocky temple ruins inside the human body … a procedure which Marcase may be forced to endure when he takes an experimental CIA drug which mimics disease, and then infiltrates the cult.

9. "Blood Covenant" Written by Coleman Luck III; Story by Coleman Luck III and Kimberly A. Shriner; Directed by Oscar L. Costo; airdate: November 19, 1996; *Guest Cast:* Mark Lindsay Chapman (Henry LaFour); Marisa Coughlan (Chante LaFlour); Randy Oglesby, Kenneth Johnson, Diana Castle (Mrs. Kayge); Brad Koepenick (Dr. Tucker Welles); Bridget Hoffman (Nurse); Rick Cramer (SWAT Team Member); Richard Petes (SWAT Team Leader); Greg Eagles (Zairian); Gabriel Alexander, Lisa Anne Morrison (Secretary); Lynne Larsen (Michelle Lefour).

The United States is unexpectedly blackmailed by an anonymous terrorist: if 500 million dollars are not transferred to a Swiss bank account in forty-eight hours, Orlando will be devastated by the intentional release of malaria. The culprit in this extreme case of bioterrorism is a disenfranchised scientist who lost his team, and wife, in Zaire when America did not support him. As people start to die in Orlando, Cassian's biocrisis team works to discover the method of contamination, and hypothesizes that the American Relief Blood Bank has been shipping out malaria-infected blood. The culprit's daughter, of all people, helps to set things right.

10. "Faces in the Night" Written by Carleton Eastlake; Directed by Scott Brazil; airdate: November 26, 1996; *Guest Cast:* Marc Poppel (Oliver Hamilton/Frank Stark); Alicia Coppola (Terry); Vincent Duvall (Detective); James M. McBride, Peter Allas, Edwina Moore (Nurse); Jean Luc Martin (Duty Officer Boeck).

Kimberly is kidnapped at a hospital by a psychopath called the "Werewolf Killer" who is in search of the "Perfect One." Cassian, Marcase, and Hailey search for Shiroma when the local authorities seem unhelpful, and determine that a serial killer who strikes during the full moon is responsible for their friend's abduction, as well as seven other murders in the last nine months. With a sample of the killer's blood, Cassian and the others use secret technology developed for the Human Genome Project to help generate a genetic "fingerprint" of the kidnapper. With only hours left before Kimberly is killed, the team's last hope of saving her rests with another woman the Werewolf Killer once attacked, but who does not wish to come forward.

11. "Midnight of the Carrier" Written by Carleton Eastlake; Directed by Janet

Greek; airdate: January 7, 1997; *Guest Cast:* Tim O'Connor (William Helderman/Erhardt Boem); Tim Ryan (Robert Stennis); Tomas Arana, Alan Scarfe, S. Russell Werkman, Jordan Marder, Magda Haroud (Emma Helderman); Lorie Griffin (Receptionist); Craig Schoen (Young Helderman); Wolf Muser (Nazi Doctor); Timothy Dale Agee (Agent Mitchell); Van Quattro (RAD Team Member).

An old man is saddened by his wife's death, and then confesses to her Catholic priest that as a youth in Nazi Germany a mystical talisman was implanted inside his chest by Himmler. Marcase, Cassian, and the others help the old man, planning to remove the strange capsule from his torso. However, a shadowy government agent secretly allied to a white supremacist group also wants to possess the mysterious talisman/capsule, which contains two red gemstones. Marcase and Shiroma learn that the gems are part of an ancient occult weapon called "The Eyes of Odin" which can reestablish the power of the Third Reich.

Note: This is the final episode featuring Shiroma and Marcase.

12. "Critical Mass" Written by Carleton Eastlake and James G. Hirsch; Directed by Richard Compton; airdate: January 28, 1997; *Guest Cast:* Cindy Katz (Major Kay Harrier); Eugene Williams, Lance Guest, Christine Champion, Warren Sweeney, Henry Hayashi, Persia White, William Wellman, Jr., James Lesure, Will Schaub (SWAT Team Leader); Kris Iyer (Medical Examiner); Sally Hightower (TV reporter); Ned Lake (Second Officer); Wiley Pickett (Downed Man); Don Brunner II (Air Force Officer).

An unidentified bit of space debris strikes a warehouse and creates a huge fireball. Shiroma and Marcase have been reassigned to a project in Zimbabwe, leaving Cassian and Hailey to investigate matters with an arrogant new medico, Dr. Brian Taft. The problem is that exposure to the meteor seems to drive people insane as well as stimulate massive and accelerated tumor growth. Taft, Hailey, and

Cassian follow the trail of insanity to a top secret government lab housing explosive detonators from "Operation Candlewick," even as the scientists stationed there begin to go ballistic.

13. "Death Song" Written by Robert Gilmer; Directed by Michael Miller; airdate: February 4, 1997; *Guest Cast:* Angela Teek (Tina Wright); Diane DiLascio (Dr. Patricia Billings); Michael Buchman Silver, Adrian Spaks, Jeffrey Anderson-Gunter, David McSwain (Young Man); Wendy Braun (Young Woman); Liz Mamana (Darlene); Scott Alan Cook (Jeter).

Taft, Hailey, and Cassian team with the beautiful Dr. Billings to investigate the sudden skeletal collapse of a young woman with a history of Hodgkin's lymphoma. As an outbreak of this frightening, bone-shattering disease looms as a real possibility, Hailey falls for beautiful pop star Tina Wright on the verge of her fifty-city tour. Hailey defends her life from a secret assassin as Cassian and Taft trace the victims of the "disease" to a recently deceased doctor named Berlam. Things become difficult from there as Hailey discovers that Tina also received radiation therapy from Dr. Berlam, and may be the disease's next victim.

14. "The Last Endless Summer" Written by James G. Hirsch; Directed by Stephen L. Posey; airdate: February 11, 1997; *Guest Cast:* Judith Hoag (Dr. Meredith Shrager); Andrew Kavavit, Nancy Everhard (Mrs. Cassian); Obba Babatunde, Todd Susman (Henry Newland); Rikki Dale, Duke Moosekian, Radmar Agana Jao (Technician); Caron Strong (Nurse); David Chisum (Mac); Dennis Howard (Clergyman); Trevor Jackson (Paramedic); Kristin Steese (Renee Cassian); Endre Hules (Sailor); Eddie Wilde (Killer); Bobbie Norman (Mrs. Bartholomew); Christine Moore (Tracy).

Near San Pedro, California, a Russian ship releases a microscopic organism into the water, polluting the shores of Laguna Beach. Surfers are soon falling deathly ill, infected by wormlike parasites which ravage their internal systems, so Cassian and his team investigate.

Though Cassian is chafing under the authority of his new superior, Henry Newland, and mourning the end of his marriage, he still gets down to business and determines that the area is under siege from a microbial invasion. A brilliant twenty-two-year-old resident who is himself infected by the parasite helps to put the pieces of the puzzle together.

15. "The Last Five Pounds Are the Hardest" Written by Carleton Eastlake; Directed by Michael Miller; airdate: February 18, 1997; *Guest Cast:* Judith Hoag (Dr. Meredith Shrager); Thomas Kopache (Kaplinger); Carol Potter (Mrs. Mason); David Purdham, J. Madison Wright, Mark Bramhall, Michael Paul Chan, Randy Irwin, Kelly Rowan (Stacy); Kevin Westin (Jerry); William Jones (Mr. Purvis); Paul Messinger (Dr. Leeman); Michael H. Moss (Art Mason); Frantz Turner (Policeman).

An anorexic-looking teenaged girl hoping to become a ballerina is brought into the hospital when she experiences a terrible bout of hypothyroidism, the total slowing down of her metabolism. When more people start to suffer from the same symptoms all over the country, Taft is called in to assist Dr. Shrager at the university hospital. He traces the problem to a new diet drug on the market called Metabathin from Pharmatrex. Soon, Taft, Cassian, and Hailey realize that somebody has triggered the outbreak with the express purpose of destroying Metabathin's financial future.

16. "Elegy for a Dream" Written by Michael Gleason; Directed by Nancy Malone; airdate: April 29, 1997; *Guest Cast:* Christine Healy, Ladd York, Julianne Christie, Seth Isler, Al Sapienza, Ted W. Henning, Dawn Lewis, Nick Spano (Bobby); Scott Hamm (Mark); Rocco Vienhage (Director); Victor Wilson (Coach Darryl Wilson); Kerian Jorgenson (Dana Whitman); Dawn Zeek (Tiffany); Ilia Vdokn (Janos); Jason Van (Sailor); Joe Rose (Customer).

In Chicago, Dr. Taft visits with his sister and his nephew, a college-bound athlete hoping for a football scholarship. The family reunion is cut short when a rich man's daughter collapses on the dance floor in a local club, a victim of a flesh-eating virus. Soon the disease is spreading, and Taft's nephew becomes infected. Cassian, Taft, and Hailey realize that the common denominator in all the cases is a Yugoslavian tattoo parlor which is using contaminated tools and inks.

17. "A Secret in the Neighborhood" Written by Bart Baker; Directed by Michael Miller; airdate: May 6, 1997; *Guest Cast:* Lara Steinick (Dr. Bela); Nancy Everhard (Mrs. Cassian); Todd Susman (Henry Newland); Kristin Steese (Renee Cassian); David Cromwell, Larry Williams, Terence Knox (Major Reed); Robert Ayers (Dr. Vashon); Kirk Fox (Carny); Rick Cramer (Military Driver); Edward Rote (Corporal); Kevin Downes (Young Man); Terry Markwell (Gina); Sarah Carson (Suzette).

Cassian takes his daughter to Patriot Amusement Park, but once there he encounters a tourist who is struck down by a contaminated snow cone. Cassian investigates while Taft is still in town, and learns that the illness was caused by a deadly chemical agent. The illness is related to Desert Storm, and it is a weapon being used by a renegade military force which hopes to cleanse America. After another outbreak, Cassian and Hailey trace the deadly chemical weapon to a military base just seven miles from Cassian's family.

18. "Wild Fire" Written by David Kemper; Directed by Stephen L. Posey; airdate: May 13, 1997; *Guest Cast:* Shannon O'Hurley, Denzaleigh Abernathy, Walter Emanuel Jones, Diane Davis, Wes Charles, Jr., V.P. Oliver, Anne Betancourt (Head Nurse); Peter Suarez (Donnie Silkiss); Bjorn Johnson (Restaurant Owner); Vachik Mangassarian (Jeweler); Noelle Neal (Kelli Niles); Skip O'Brien (Foreman); Carleane Burke (Mrs. Hailey); Mark Deallesandro (Headwaiter); David Lea (Vagrant Man).

While in Chicago to see Dr. Taft accept an award, Cassian receives a "Code Red" alert to report to Michigan. With Hailey and Taft in tow, Cassian investigates an outbreak of cholera in Detroit with an incredibly fast rate of onset and a resultant, fatal, dehydration. Meanwhile, Hailey faces tragic memories about his youth in Detroit and must locate the only person who may be immune to the cholera: a young African-American boy who despises his abusive stepfather. As the cholera outbreak spreads rapidly, originating from a contaminated string of imported black pearls, Taft's analysis reveals that this mutant disease may be manmade.

19. "On Wings of Angels" Written by James G. Hirsch; Directed by Richard Compton; airdate: May 20, 1997; *Guest Cast:* John Lafayette (Dr. Quinton Bernard); Dwayne L. Barnes, Joe Cortese, John Prosky, Mongo Brownlee, Tommy Morgan Jr., Hellena Schmeid, Tracy Grant, Kristopher Logan, Jimmy Ray Jr., Michael Ryan Way (Starkey); D.K. Kell (Lt. Mays); Angel Vargas (Cain); Chariesse Lavelle (Lyneth); Jerry Rector (Guard).

A secret plot to make jailed prisoners act in a more docile fashion has the opposite effect and in fact stirs a fit of violence in one inmate. A secret drug is being injected into the prisoners' cigarettes, and it is causing severe growths and even skin rippage around the back of the skull. Two compromised prisoners and a jailed doctor seeking redemption escape from the prison and capture Taft, in hopes of making him cure their sick friend.

Millennium (1996–1999)

CRITICAL RECEPTION

"*Millennium* does look more like a movie than a TV show, but Henriksen is no Anthony Hopkins and Carter has a penchant for pretentious mumbo jumbo about the end of the world."— Rick Marin, *Newsweek*, "Warning: The XXX Files," September 16, 1996.

"Shrouded in fin-de-siècle doom and gloom, *Millennium* makes *Twin Peaks* look like a morning in *Romper Room*. Literate, well-acted and blessed with an irresistible hook, it's the best new show of the season ... Henriksen is ... exceptionally appealing as Frank."— Jeremy Gerard, *Variety*, October 21-27, 1996, page 212.

"maddeningly enigmatic crime series, which has grown more pretentious and less coherent with each new installment. What began in '96 as a dank, depressing, yet authentically atmospheric serial-killer-of-the-week thriller turned a lot murkier last season when ex-FBI profiler Frank Black ... began battling his former allies in ... the secretive Millennium Group. This season ... Frank now looks as blank and confused as the audience."— Mike Lipton, *People*, November 2, 1998.

"*Millennium* is carrying out a nifty feat: For all the signs that the end times are coming to the streets of Seattle, the true apocalypse appears to be taking place in Frank Black's own tormented spirit. For him, a murder is never just a murder—pathology is part of a grotesque master plan. His mission of preventing his nightmares from becoming mass reality is cleverly tautological, a wide-open story line.... Once again, he's [Chris Carter] one step ahead of a trend."— Alyssa Katz, *The Nation*: "Millennium," November 25, 1996, page 35.

"*Millennium* tackles ... nothing less than the existence of evil in our midst.... There's just enough bizarre reality to make *Millennium* the season's most chilling drama.... Mr. Carter pushes all the right apocalyptic buttons.... The production values ... darkly mirror the text. Except for Frank's new home, an oasis of bright colors, gloom predominates, usually against a backdrop of driving rain."— John J. O'Connor, *The New York Times*: "The Evil That Lurks All Around," October 25, 1996, page B16.

"*Millennium* surpassed itself in cultivating relationships between its principal cast ... *Millennium* has at least become a clear artistic success, making sense out of an often chaotic, disturbing world with consummate intelligence and powerful emotions."—*X-Pose* #35, "Inner Demons," June 1999, pages 49-51.

FORMAT

Chris Carter's less-popular follow-up to *The X-Files* is *Millennium*, a horror/crime series which features paranormal and supernatural overtones. It has drastically altered format each year it has remained on the air, but remained consistently intriguing throughout its three-year television sojourn. If *Silence of the Lambs* (1991) was a major source of inspiration for *The X-Files*, then the 1995 hit feature *Seven* might be seen as the direct antecedent to the less mainstream, but nonetheless intellectually challenging *Millennium*. Directed by David Fincher (*The Game* [1997], *Fight Club* [1999]), *Seven* concerned two cops (Morgan

Freeman and Brad Pitt) hot on the trail of a serial killer who murdered folks in gruesome ways which reflected how each victim had committed one of the seven deadly sins. Similarly, *Millennium*'s first season involved the pursuit of high-concept serial killers who dispatched people in innovative and frequently gory ways. This fascination with psychos, the nastiest of nasty characters, may have been what left viewers feeling turned off and disenfranchised, and the central *Millennium* concept soon changed. Beginning with the first season story "Lamentation," a supernatural element was folded into the series, and "demons," "devils," and "angels" were frequently seen or alluded to.

A second inspiration for *Millennium* appeared to be the 1978 feature film *The Eyes of Laura Mars*, written by John Carpenter. Like Faye Dunaway's fashion photographer Laura Mars in that Irvin Kirschner-directed picture, Frank Black (Lance Henriksen), the protagonist in *Millennium*, had the uncanny ability to see what killers see. He was never called "psychic" on the show but Black was, in effect, psychic. Frank's visions would often take form as gory, bloody flashes of horrible things, or sometimes as enigmatic images which required deciphering ("Luminary," "Roosters").

Lastly, the series *Millennium* focused on the approach of the 21st century, and the fear that man would not survive the advent of the year 2000. As its name indicated, it was an end-of-the-world, millennarian imagining. Various episodes dealt with myths surrounding the end of the world in a variety of cultures and spheres, from the religious to the technological.

Millennium's first season followed ex–F.B.I. agent Frank Black and his family (wife Catherine and daughter Jordan) as they relocated to Seattle to escape the harrowing life in the bureau which had driven Black to a nervous breakdown. Frank's ability to "see" as the killers see, however, became useful to an organization of former law enforcement officials called "The Millennium Group," which has sworn to prevent the domination of evil as the millennium grows near. During the first sea-

son, Frank consulted for the Millennium Group and helped local law enforcement officials in Seattle track down a variety of the "high concept" serial killers much like the one seen in *Seven*. Fantasy elements were kept firmly in check, with Frank's psychic ability being the only exception. After about six or seven weeks of repetitive serial killer stories, *Millennium* emerged as a grim (even dire) series lacking variety. Not surprisingly, audiences abandoned the show in droves. Had they stayed around longer, they would have seen a humdinger of a series, as its story arc became more clear, and much more interesting.

The second season of *Millennium* saw massive format alterations. Frank grew close to Peter Watts (Terry O'Quinn) a Millennium Group member, as together they solved far more bizarre and even supernatural cases, and went on various missions (inside and outside America) to preserve ancient religious artifacts (like the crucifix of Christ, or the hand of St. Sebastian). Surprisingly, the Millennium Group, the heroic force of the first season, was exposed as a cult with ambiguous motivations in the second season! Worse, Catherine and Frank separated, leaving Black without the family and home he had sought to defend in the first season. Ratings for *Millennium* stayed low, and it was decided to end the series with the apocalyptic scenario long-predicted on the show. In "The Fourth Horseman" and "The Time Is Now," the Millennium Group released a deadly virus which spread across the world rapidly, killing off millions, including Catherine Black (Megan Gallagher). The second season ended with a new Black Plague ravaging America as a shattered Frank Black, his hair turned stark white, faced the end of human civilization. It was a kick-ass ending to a series which had always played with the concept of "the end."

Miraculously, *Millennium* was revived for a third season, and it was necessary to do some pretty heavy backtracking for the series to continue in the same "police procedural" vein. The outbreak of the Marburg Variant (described in the second season finale as having hit South America, China, and killing at least 500 people in Seattle) was rewritten to have been a local outbreak which claimed only seventy unlucky lives in all. An angry Frank Black, teamed with a novice agent named Emma Hollis (Klea Scott), returns to the F.B.I. and investigates the movements of the Millennium Group, now the series' primary villain! Peter Watts, formerly characterized as a decent and honorable man, was also back ... as a shadowy agent of evil. The substance of the third year saw Frank and Peter clash, while Emma tried to learn everything she could about her mentor and the shadowy cult which he was once nearly a part of.

No matter which year is favored, *Millennium* has been an involving, well-made series from start to finish. The third season ended hastily with "Goodbye to All This," a story which failed to bring all the elements of the show together. The show was canceled in late 1999. For all three years, it aired on Fox, on Friday nights at 10:00 P.M. For a brief time, its lead-in was the excellent *Brimstone*, but the ratings, sadly, remained low.

History

In 1996, Fox Television had a bona fide hit on its hands with Chris Carter's *The X-Files*. Carter was, rightly, being heralded as a creative genius, and as *X-Files* clones (*Strange Luck, Dark Skies, Profiler, Nowhere Man, The Burning Zone, Early Edition, Profiler,* and the like) began to proliferate across the tube like a deadly plague, the originator of the trend was called upon to supply a second genre series to Fox's primetime schedule. Though still working loosely within the police procedural vein of *The X-Files*, Carter imagined a very dark series about one man's quest to fight the violence he saw consuming American society on the eve of the 21st century. Carter's new hero, Frank Black, was not an eager, young hothead seeking the "truth," but a man cursed with a terrible "insight" who was trying to make positive use of that curse to protect his family. *Millennium* would not concern aliens, prehistoric beasties, or mythical monsters come to life, but the monsters found in the human race.

Though William Hurt was originally slated to play Frank Black in *Millennium*, the role went to Lance Henriksen, a talented movie star who had made a splash in a number of films, including *The Right Stuff* (1983), *The Terminator* (1984), *Aliens* (1986), *Pumpkinhead* (1988), *Alien³* (1992), and *The Quick and the Dead* (1995). Henriksen was an inspired choice to play Frank, a brooding, moody character as different from the sarcastic, handsome Mulder of *The X-Files* as could be imagined. Where Duchovny's Mulder was a very outgoing, extroverted character despite the grief in his life, Frank Black was an introvert, someone who kept all of his pain inside, just beneath those tortured eyes. Eschewing the "partner" set-up of *The X-Files*, the supporting characters in *Millennium* were members of Frank's immediate family, in particular his wife, Catherine (Megan Gallagher of *Nowhere Man* [1995-96]) and his precocious daughter Jordan (Brittany Tiplady). Frank was assisted in his investigations of unusual hate and homicide crimes by a cadre of middle-aged white men, including Seattle detectives Bob Bletcher (Bill Smitrovich) and Gablehouse (Stephen James Lang), and member of the Millennium Group, the balding Peter Watts (Terry O'Quinn).

Chris Carter wrote, and David Nutter directed, a brilliant pilot for *Millennium*, one which poignantly captured the two sides of Frank Black's life: both the evil and the good. Scored by Mark Snow, of *The X-Files*, the *Millennium* pilot was so well done that it could have been a feature film. Frank Spotnitz, who would soon work on the series himself, recalls his reaction to the first viewing:

> [the pilot] managed to be scary, original, intriguing and ... really true about the nature of life, which is that there are two worlds co-existing at the same time ... It's the Apollonian and the Dionysian views of the world, and that pilot so perfectly embodied ... that split and characterized Frank Black as a man caught between ... two worlds, who recognizes that you need to preserve that bright and sunny world to make life worth living,

but you can't deny that dark undercurrent is always there … it was incredibly powerful.[1]

Besides creating a true TV original in his protagonist, Frank Black, Chris Carter managed something else that was quite noteworthy. Although his formula for *The X-Files* was a combination of brilliant planning (specifically that the two worldviews of its main characters would clash in perpetual conflict) and fortunate happenstance (the chemistry between Anderson and Duchovny enlivened the show *way* beyond what was deemed imaginable), *Millennium* was built on a solid bedrock of exciting ideas and artistic flourishes. Foremost among these was one of the primary settings of the series: Frank Black's bright yellow house in a Seattle suburb. To Carter, that house, that example of what Spotnitz called the "bright, sunny world," was a crucial factor of the *Millennium* equation. It was designed as a pointed contrast to Frank's often grim work, and as a reminder to viewers *why* Frank worked so hard, and faced so much human ugliness. The world of the normal American family, of that great yellow house, was an important undercurrent of *Millennium* from its outset, as Carter described in an interview for *X-Pose*:

> Frank has tried to carve out of the world a sanctuary, a very bright place. It's no mistake that he's painted his house yellow. This is the thing that he wants to protect over everything and it becomes the focus of the whole show: how will he deal with these things … and act heroically, and at the same time keep his family in a world where they don't have to think about those very things, where they don't … see the struggle that he goes through.[2]

How many other horror shows, indeed how many dramatic series in general, can lay claim to including, from the foundation up, so potent and artistic a symbol? Most TV series eschew symbolism all together because they appeal to the lowest common denominator, but Chris Carter proved with *Millennium* that *The X-Files* was no fluke. In some ways, *Millennium* was really a better-built mousetrap than his first series. The reviewers took notice of its high quality, and when *Millennium* began airing in the fall of 1996, it was hailed as one of the best, if not *the* best, series of the year.

Alas, insightful TV critics do not always get the last word in such matters, as Chris Carter quickly learned. His brilliant *Millennium* soon came under fire from a variety of bizarre special interest groups. Most of these complaints had nothing at all to do with the quality of the series, but rather the *nature* of *Millennium*. The first complaint came from the moral watchdogs, those despicable people who make a living telling other viewers what they should or should not watch. In this case, the censors felt that *Millennium* was too violent, too gory, in its approach to horror. Even before the series had aired two episodes, the pilot was being criticized as graphic, and worse, gratuitous, in its depiction of violent actions. Chris Carter quickly responded to the allegations:

> It's not meant to be gratuitous … I want to see someone having a responsible reaction to the violence I read about in my daily newspaper.[3]

In other words, Chris Carter had formulated a series in which a hero (Frank) took on all the evil of the world, the evil that we have seen occur everywhere from Kosovo and East Timor to Jonesboro and Littleton. The moral watchdogs could see only the psychos, not Frank's response to the psychos, and so they misread *Millennium* as a bad influence. They wanted to silence its many ideas, because they did not understand those ideas. The debate over *Millennium*'s inclusion of violent content went so far that even star Lance Henriksen weighed in with his opinion.

> We're not living in a world where we understand the outcome of violence … More offensive to me than the nature of *Millennium* is some show that ends precisely at 11:00 pm with everything all wrapped up in a nice cliché, everybody beaming and happy.[4]

Henriksen's remark on this matter was especially well considered. *Millennium* was only mirroring reality, not some twisted horror idea, and it was actually the *other* crap on TV, the *Touched by an Angels*, the *7th Heavens* that were more troublesome because they were ignoring elements of reality and offering a saccharine, Pollyanna-ish view of humanity. Predictably, so cogent and logical an argument fell on the deaf ears of the censors who wanted to whitewash television, and *Millennium* paid the price. Heard all the time was the criticism that it was too "dark."

The second assault on *Millennium* was a race and sex-oriented one. Critics in some circles criticized the show for not featuring women and minorities in substantive roles. Although it was true that Frank Black's inner circle was mostly "white-men only," this was the demographic which Carter's research had indicated would be involved with the solving of such violent crimes. Though it may not have appealed to women and minorities, Carter found that most law enforcement organizations (on which the Millennium Group was initially based) included primarily white, middle-aged men! Should a TV show be criticized for reflecting reality? *Millennium* was, unfortunately.

Actually, a whole series of assaults came *Millennium*'s way early on. Many people in the industry had a vested interest in seeing Carter fail. Many times in Hollywood, people attain a certain measure of glee by watching a star, producer, director, or writer "fall from grace." Chris Carter, the mastermind of *The X-Files*, found himself in this position with *Millennium*. Having succeeded his first time out the chute, he was just ripe for a "tragic fall," whether his show was any good or not. This same kind of mentality has carried Kevin Williamson up to extreme fame, and back down to a level of critical loathing. Julia Roberts, Kathleen Turner, Joel Eszterhas, and Kevin Costner have also been victims of this strange fascination. They are built up as geniuses, and then, when their work does not live up to some insane measure, they are torn down as failures. Sensing weakness because of *Millennium*'s low ratings, the vultures swooped in around Chris Carter.

Further criticisms of the show were aimed at Lance Henriksen, who some viewers apparently felt was too low key to function as a series lead, and the show's overall lack of humor. The myth was then perpetuated in the media that *Millennium* was the just the same old thing every week: serial killers, serial killers, serial killers. In fact, the rundown for the first eight weeks of *Millennium* looked like this: serial killer ("Pilot"), cult ("Gehenna"), serial killer ("Dead Letters"), serial killer ("Kingdom Come"), vigilante judge ("The Judge"), mad bomber ("522666"), serial killer ("Blood Relatives"), and child abuser ("The Well Worn Lock"). That dynamic represents a 50/50 split between serial killers and other criminals, not a slavish devotion to the "serial killer" motif. While 50 percent may still have been too much of a bad thing, one should be a little gracious when viewing a brand new series. As *Millennium* showed over time, it had much more on its mind than psychos. A fair assessment of the series could not be made after one or two episodes. *Millennium*'s tapestry was much richer than a single-viewing could register.

Despite an artistically successful (if low rated) first season, and a Golden Globe nomination for Lance Henriksen, all the brickbats had taken their toll. *Millennium* was grudgingly renewed for a second season, but it was to be a changed series. Chris Carter devoted more time to *The X-Files*, the crown jewel in his TV collection, and he hired two former *X-Files* writers, James Wong and Glen Morgan, to oversee production of *Millennium*. Right from the gate, this clever writing team (probably unintentionally) echoed much of the illegitimate criticism already leveled at *Millennium*, which was not a promising sign:

> There was too much gore in the first season, and it was for shock's sake. There was no humor. Everybody wanted to know more about the Millennium Group. What was Frank's role with them? We needed to develop Frank. We had a good actress, Megan Gallagher, playing his wife, and what could we do with their relationship? Where can this go?[5]

Championing humor on *Millennium* did not seem a good idea, as the series was never designed to be funny or lighthearted. Still, Darin Morgan was soon on board the show as consulting producer. He was popular with *X-Files* fans for his serio-comic episodes of that series, including "Jose Chung's '*From Outer Space*,'" "War of the Coprophages," and "Clyde Bruckman's Final Repose." For *Millennium*, Morgan contributed two like-minded stories, "Jose Chung's '*Doomsday Defense*'" and "Somehow, Satan Got Behind Me." Like Wong and James Morgan, Darin Morgan also laid out what he saw as the problems of *Millennium*:

> In *The X-Files*, Mulder and Scully were very delineated ... Mulder believes; Scully doesn't — and you could always fall back on that. During *Millennium*'s first season, you really don't know what Frank Black was doing. Glen and Jim tried to make it more clear the second season, but it was never very clear what he is or what he believes in.[6]

Despite these jibes, the second season of *Millennium* emerged as a very good one, equal to if not better than the first year. The supernatural aspects of the show were expanded, Darin Morgan's two comedies were excellent after all, and Morgan and Wong took a new tact by exploring the Millennium Group as a dangerous cult with ambiguous motivations.

Another controversial move, the separation of Frank and Catherine, added an additional layer of realism and immediacy to the drama, and Frank's house still had a place. That yellow house, that place to be protected, was now the object of Frank's grand quest. He had to fight evil, reunite his family, and find his way back to that house! Impressively, the second year of *Millennium* also explored Black's family history in poignant detail in the Halloween story "The Curse of Frank Black" and the Christmas tale, "Midnight of the Century," with guest Darren McGavin. The second season ended on a dynamite note, as the Millennium Group engineered its own deadly biological holocaust, and Catherine died a victim of the Marburg Variant Plague. With a stylish climax behind it, *Millennium* looked destined for syndication or reruns. Some nice icing on the cake was that the series' second

year was nominated for two Emmys (outstanding sound editing for "Owls" and outstanding guest actor [Charles Nelson Reilly in "Jose Chung's '*Doomsday Defense*'"]). Although it was an honor "just to be nominated," *Millennium* failed to win in either category.

By any rational mode of measurement, that should have been the end of *Millennium*. It was a low rated, unpopular series, and it had come to a natural end, bringing its end-of-the-world scenario to full flower. Then the show was renewed, and the third season began. Again, much criticism was leveled at *Millennium*, and it was decided that the series would benefit from some more changes. James Morgan and Glen Wong left the series, and Chris Carter came back to do a significant revamp. Catherine (Megan Gallagher) was dead, so now Frank Black was a widower and his daughter Jordan was motherless. Also gone was that beautiful symbol, the yellow house. The Millennium Group had been "outed" as a cult, so now the nefarious organization would function in much the same way as the conspiracy did on the *X-Files*: as a recurring villain against which Frank would occasionally butt heads. Even Peter Watts became an ambiguous character, whose true loyalties were unknown, and all of the series action was shifted from Seattle to the Washington, D.C., area. The partner aspect of *The X-Files* had always proven popular, so the third season of *Millennium* saw Frank Black rejoin the F.B.I. and inherit a partner, the beautiful Emma Hollis. Their relationship would not be one of sexual chemistry, but of teacher and student. Despite the cosmetic changes, the stories were very much the same in nature, but if anything, even more enigmatic than before.

Despite all the reshuffling of ideas, *Millennium*, take three, was as good a show as its previous two incarnations. The evil Lucy Butler returned in "Antipas," Y2K was the subject of "Teotwawki," and "Skull and Bones" captured the terrifying nature of the Millennium Group in exquisite (and bloody) terms. A fourth year looked unlikely, so a voice-over by Lance Henriksen was inserted over the end of the third season finale, "Goodbye to All This," putting the entire series in perspective. Still, many questions were left unanswered, and fans held out hope that *Millennium* would be renewed for a fourth season. When the ratings remained low, Fox finally pulled the plug. *Millennium* was canceled in the summer of 1999, and its last several episodes were not rerun even once in prime time. In its slot: *MAD TV* reruns, and Fox specials about good pets going bad.

In the fall of 1999, Chris Carter went on to produce *Harsh Realm*, and he brought Terry O'Quinn and Sarah-Jane Redmond with him. As for *Millennium*, the ongoing story of Frank Black and his daughter Jordan was brought back into the public eye during "Millennium," a New Year's Eve episode of *The X-Files* seventh season. Lance Henriksen and Brittany Tiplady guested on the wrap-up, and Frank Black partnered with Fox Mulder and Dana Scully. Reruns of *Millennium* air on the FX cable network at 1:00 A.M. weeknights.

CRITICAL COMMENTARY

Despite its format shifts, *Millennium* is one of the most impressive horror TV series ever aired —*period*— because it focuses not on the overmined domains of vampires, aliens, or monsters, but on those shadowy, half-understood fears which affect the human heart and soul. Only sporadically in TV history has a TV series been so pointedly symbolic, so purposefully artful in its approach to terror, and thus *Millennium* is something quite special, and something quite memorable in the annals of terror TV. Forget the "serial-killer-of-the-week rap" that has plagued its video life, this series is far better, far smarter, than just about any program airing on the American networks today.

From frame one of episode one, *Millennium* announces its ambition to be much more than filler between fast food commercials. Each story, including the pilot, opens with a white-lettered quotation from a literary or religious source, and then serves to unveil a drama which echoes or contrasts with that opening selection. Yeats ("Pilot"), Dostoyevsky ("Dead Letters"), Herman Melville ("The Judge"), Jean-Paul Sartre ("522666"), Robert Louis Stevenson ("The Well Worn Lock"), Faust ("Loin Like a Hunting Cloth"), Cicero ("Walkabout"), George Eliot ("The Thin White Line"), Nietzsche ("Broken World"), William Rose Benet ("The Paper Dove") and, inevitably, Shakespeare ("Monster"), are just some of the greats *Millennium* has referenced and then mirrored.

These opening quotations are endlessly thought-provoking, and they also explain why this unusual series failed to connect with a majority of American audiences: it was simply pitched too high. On a Friday night, the boob tube gets turned on, and most viewers seek an escape, not a challenge. The wonderfully literate *Millennium* presented the latter, and paid for its high standards with low ratings. Yet, the opening quotations serve an invigorating purpose: they remind active viewers that there is a connection between past and present, a universality of the human condition. The situations Frank Black encounters are situations that Shakespeare or Cicero might have contemplated or written about. The opening quotes of *Millennium* connect the series to a literary and historical past. How's that for an opening gambit on Friday night?

If *The X-Files* is examined as a happy accident, a *Kolchak* homage which succeeds because of Chris Carter's writing talents and the magical chemistry between David Duchovny and Gillian Anderson, then it is illuminating to witness how *Millennium* was devised in artistic terms — from its opening quotations to its very interesting application of symbols and imagery (an application which catapults it to the same plateau of high quality as David Lynch's *Twin Peaks*). That oft-mentioned yellow house, for instance, is a resonant, important symbol. Viewers naturally associate the color yellow with brightness, and with bright, happy things like the sun. Of course, the house represents protagonist Frank Black's only bright place away from the darkness and horrors which he sees on the job and even inside his own tortured mind. Even good dramatic TV can mean, overall, nothing of significance (just look at *Seinfeld* or *NYPD Blue*), but great television successfully layers its meanings and subtexts one atop the other, often in visual terms. *Millennium* utilizes the symbol of the yellow house in a plethora of stimulating ways.

In the first season, the house is seen primarily as a sanctuary, a place of safety. In the second, it is a representation of paradise lost and the object of a heroic quest. In the third season, the house is but a memory, a sad one, but one which remains intact inside Frank's head. Frank visits his former home in the episode "The Sound of Snow," and it has been painted a pure white. Frank, ever perceptive, still sees into the past, still sees his yellow house, standing there on Ezekial Drive. Perhaps he still sees the yellow in the white because he is aware (as are we) that any chronicle of Frank Black will always involve that yellow house in some fashion. For it is not merely a shelter, not merely a comfortable abode, it is Frank's ideal, the very place of joy and innocence that he seeks to protect and find inside himself every day. It is an externalization of the perfect place he cherishes in his mind as paradise or bliss.

One can argue that the yellow house of *Millennium* also represents an escape from the evils of the "outside" world, but contrarily, it is also the reason Frank faces the heart of human darkness every single day. By facing the black inside and out, Frank preserves the yellow, inside and out. The yellow house could also symbolize, on a more basic scale, small town America. Frank must save it from the encroaching evil all around. Thus the yellow house is not just beautiful architecture, it is a brilliant (and artistic) symbol because it immediately shares with viewers an insight into Frank's personality, his interior architecture, if you will. We understand, we know immediately, why Frank does what he does. The yellow house is a visual cue-in to a very private character.

Thematically, *Millennium* triggers scares by challenging viewers with the specter of what may be the ultimate bogeyman: the end of the world. We all fear doomsday, that long-feared moment in the cycle of time when human life is finally and completely snuffed out. This is a universal and powerful fear because most people really do suspect that the end *will* come one day. Dinosaurs preceded us here, and now they are extinct, long-forgotten bones buried in both the Earth and our collective subconscious. The Roman Empire came and went, a brief candle. The Native American culture which once existed in this land is now but a remnant too. Time passes, cultures die, and on some subconscious level all of humankind is aware of this changing of the guard. Will intelligent talking apes replace us? Smart cockroaches? Aliens? Who knows, but this universal fear of a total end has been part of our cultural and film history for a long time. *When Worlds Collide* (1951), *Armageddon* (1998), *Planet of the Apes* (1968), *Deep Impact* (1998), *Miracle Mile* (1989), and even the *Mad Max* saga are apocalyptic visions in which humankind must face its own inevitable finish. *Millennium* is rather unique not just because it plays on the universal human inquietude about doomsday, but because it so cogently and coherently enunciates any number of possible doomsdays, all encompassing the breadth of our existence on this planet. An astronomical end of the world, a tear in the fabric of time and space caused by the collision of two neutron stars, is described in "Roosters."

Similarly, a once-in-a-millennium alignment of planets is believed to be the cause of an impending second great flood in "Force Majeure." Religious apocalypses involving a new messiah ("Forcing the End"), the Antichrist ("Marantha"), and other icons ("The Hand of St. Sebastian," "Amnianesis") of Christianity also formulate many of *Millennium*'s most provocative hours. Ethnic legends about doomsday inform a Native American exploration of the end in "A Single Blade of Grass," and a biological finish to our human species is suggested by a deadly new plague in "The Fourth Horseman" and its continuation "The Time Is Now." The Y2K computer bug, a technological apocalypse, is the context of "Teotwawki," and "Jose Chung's '*Doomsday Defense*'" has the audacity to suggest that a creative apocalypse is already in the offing. Written by Darin Morgan, this show implies that all that humans can look forward to for the next thousand years is the "same old crap."

And all of those pesky serial killers? Though many viewers missed the interconnection across episodes and seasons, these societal outcasts and psychotics illustrate a very human sort-of apocalypse which has been triggered by the death of reason and the cessation of morality in the human animal here in the "end days" of the 20th-century. These psychos, which *Millennium* intimated were becoming more and more numerous as these "end days" approached, formed a modern metaphor for the fall of the Roman Empire. Insane historical figures like Caligula, and an overwhelming cultural decadence have often been blamed for Rome's woes, and that is almost precisely how *Millennium* views late 20th century America: as a modern Rome crumbling from within because of its own decadence, its own degradation, its own internal evil. The feeling that the individual no longer matters in a mechanized, celebrity-worshipping state causes insanity in the killer of "Dead Letters." Child abuse triggers a lifelong insanity in a young girl in "Darwin's Eye." One man's exploitation of another human being generates the terror of "Blood Relatives," and so on. *Millennium* looks at our society's behavior, and judges it, frankly, insane.

Considering all of this unique thematic material, *Millennium* is a scary vision because it seems endlessly knowledgeable about its frightening premise. The end-of-the-world scenarios it graphically envisions sometimes seem quite believable, if not downright probable. The end of humanity is *Millennium*'s bailiwick, and it sticks to this terrifying domain with consistency and intelligence, despite format shifts. The serial killers, the angels and demons, the lost souls, the people who try to control the future — these are all part of *Millennium*'s meditation about humankind and what end our species might cause (by accident, even).

It is only on a close viewing of *Millennium*, however, that one can see that there is also a very optimistic side to the series. If that yellow house is an important symbol, as is the universal threat of the "end days," of the apocalypse we let happen, then *Millennium* features one other critical symbol in its framework as well: the child. Episode after episode of *Millennium* focuses on children, and youth in general, surely because our offspring represent what the future *could* be. In our children, in the next generation, we see hope and fear, and *Millennium* feels the same way. In one of the best hours written for any television show, hands down, *Millennium* explores a very real evil of modern American society: the way in which our culture encourages children to be "ordinary." The episode referred to is "A Room with No View," and it concerns a demonic force (Lucy Butler) who captures "special" youngsters. These abducted teenagers are all voted "most likely to succeed," and they are all well loved by their classmates and adults. Their grades are not the greatest, and they may not be the smartest kids around, but they represent the future because there is something almost intangibly special, something attractive and magnetic about each and every one them. They all have spirit. These are the faces who will grow up to become our new leaders. In "A Room with No View," our future leaders are captured and tortured until they succumb to the urge to become ordinary, despicable, invisible. In this case, *Millennium* sees an apocalypse not in some outside force like an asteroid or failing computer systems, but in our inability to inspire and support the stars of the next generation.

In "Goodbye to All This," the final episode of *Millennium*, little Jordan Black says to her father: "we're all shepherds." This is a particularly beautiful moment, and one that echoes an earlier show ("Midnight of the Century") in which Jordan actually portrayed a shepherd in the school Christmas pageant. By using the word "shepherd," however, Jordan refers not only to a religious form of overseeing, but to a very general, very human, need to preserve our future. In a sense, all human beings are shepherds for the future. Our future (represented by the children), must be protected, or humankind will not exist anymore. Accordingly, *Millennium* often puts Frank Black in the role of shepherd, of protector, guarding the innocent and young from terrors of all varieties. He cloaks the psychic oracle children in "Exegesis"/"The Innocents" from the megalomaniacal Millennium Group. He rescues the special children in "A Room with No View" from a fate in which they succumb to the ordinariness of life. He zealously guards young day-care children from an evil wolf-in-sheep's clothing in "Monster," and so forth. Naturally, Frank's role as protector of innocence, of the future, is also expressed in his relationship with his own daughter. He saves Jordan from the hands of death personified in "Borrowed Time," and from a strange evil in "Saturn Dreaming of Mercury." Since *Millennium* is about protecting our future, several episodes of *Millennium* revolve around the shepherd's (Frank's) job to save the young of our flock (the children).

Millennium is a TV series which is obsessed about the manner in which we treat our children, our very future, and thus the series has a consistent thrust through its three-year run, despite the sometimes irritating format changes. "Luminary" is another remarkable installment which sends Frank off in search of another lost youngster, this time a college-age boy, barely a man, who wishes to let go of all his ties to modern life and rediscover nature. The boy gives up his belongings, shedding the materialism of modern America, and finds peace in wild Alaska. The story is one of pure beauty, and optimism. Even after being rescued by Frank, the boy returns to the wilderness to chart his own path, to find his own future, free of society's impediments. If our future is made up of thinkers, of individuals like the ones seen in "Luminary" or "A Room with No View," then there will be no apocalypse of the spirit. The future is ours to make,

and *Millennium* shows us a man who fights every day to preserve the future from those who would control or destroy it.

Other relevant themes also come to the forefront of many *Millennium* stories. "Wide Open" and "Weeds" tell the audience that horror can wiggle in *anywhere*, even inside our very own homes. The former ("Wide Open") is about a killer who finds ways to circumnavigate modern home security systems and then butchers families *in toto*, while "Weeds" concerns a serial killer operating inside a restrictive gated community who kills to expose the many sins of the rich, yuppie suburbanites. In both cases, sacred barriers are tread upon, and a feeling of uneasiness is generated. The neighborhood and the home, two honored locations of safety in modern American society, are violated in brutal fashion, and *Millennium* warns us to be ever vigilant in what we perceive to be "security." Our homes are our castles, but what danger lurks in the basement? In typically thoughtful fashion, *Millennium* also reveals that the so-called castle can be compromised from within, by dark forces ruminating inside the family unit. Fathers abuse children (the future), in "Darwin's Eye" and "The Well Worn Lock," and a Medea-like mother slaughters her children in "Covenant."

Other episodes concern deep, human fears: the abduction of loved ones ("Sacrament," "The Beginning and the End"), the loss of sanity and memory ("Walkabout"), sexual dysfunction ("Loin Like a Hunting Flame"), and the lack of order in our world ("Darwin's Eye"), and so forth. Accordingly, *Millennium*'s imagery quite powerfully expresses these fears in visual terms. An evil, strangely distorted clown invades Jordan's dreams in "Dead Letters," and the malevolence from this haunting being almost oozes off the television screen. In the pilot, the serial killer sews up the faces of his victims, leaving them looking like the walking dead. Again, horror is palpable.

If one has doubts about *Millennium*'s impeccable horror credentials, one need only watch two specific episodes to be convinced of its curriculum vitae. "The Fourth Horseman" follows up on "Weeds" and "Wide Open" by shattering another place of safety: the family hearth. In this horrifying story, a typical suburban family sits down to enjoy a Mother's Day meal together. Chicken is cooking on the grill in the backyard, the ever-present television is broadcasting a sporting event in the background, and the typical American family is together, united, bantering in a nice, human manner. This scene turns sour suddenly when the family, sitting together around the dinner table, consumes contaminated chicken. The mother becomes sick first, and blood starts to pour from her neck ... she is literally *sweating* blood. Then, lesions begin to form on the rest of the family, and they cough and bleed out in a matter of terrifying seconds. In one especially disgusting shot, a family member reaches for the telephone to dial 911, but as a finger hits the dial, blood explodes forth from the digit and splatters the device. This is a thoroughly disgusting, thoroughly disturbing scene, because it takes place somewhere that should be sacrosanct, the heart of family life. Instead, *Millennium* shows, in gut-wrenching visual fashion, how the end might come suddenly and unexpectedly for the typical American family. Disease could strike without warning, without preamble. It could take our loved ones from us in a heartbeat. This episode was written by Glen Morgan and James Wong, the same team who penned "Home" for *The X-Files*, and it is fair to state that this team understands (almost too well) how to build disturbing scenes which reach down into the core of our fearful hearts and twist, twist, twist with surgical precision.

"Walkabout," by Chip Johannesen and Tim Tankosic, is another example of *Millennium*'s horror dexterity. The episode opens with a long, slow tracking shot through what seems to be an empty medical practice, like one that would be found in Anytown, U.S.A. The gliding camera recedes gracefully down a narrow hallway until the sounds of screaming are heard on the sound track. Suddenly, the camera descends, on cue, right into a view of total, stark, madness. Behind a transparent, glass door, a mob of diverse-looking people

are screaming in what can only be described as a hysterical, insane state. One man presses on his own eyeballs until they squirt, bleeding profusely. Then, in the midst of this utter craziness, the camera lands unexpectedly on ... Frank Black. He too is insane, pounding on the glass door to get out! After that brief look at Frank amidst total hell, the episode fades out to the main credits, and incredible chills are generated. As in "The Fourth Horseman" or "Weeds," *Millennium* is playing with audience expectations in "Walkabout." By this point in the series, Frank is the audience's rock. He is the man who ends the madness, yet in the first sequence of "Walkabout" he is lost ... a victim of the madness consuming others. That surprising shot of Frank amidst the insanity is enough to give any viewer pause, and it is a brilliant hook on which to hinge an episode. For if Frank cannot stop the terror, who can?

As in the section of this text reviewing *The X-Files*, it would be easy to write at length about the concepts and conceits which drive *Millennium*. There is so much to analyze, including the manner the series cleverly manages to insert viewers into the skewed minds of madmen, but alas, there are other series to contemplate. Suffice it to say that *Millennium* is far better than the treatment it received from American audiences. It is an unforgettable excursion into horror, and a second creative act of brilliance from Chris Carter. If *Harsh Realm* is as sterling as *Millennium* and *The X-Files*, Carter will have managed to outdo even the great Rod Serling, and provided TV audiences with three masterpieces of terror.

For those who gave up on *Millennium* early and never looked back, please — seek it out now in reruns. Commit to viewing it from start to finish. Such an undertaking will not prove a waste, and on the contrary, will leave one with a bold and invigorating universe of horror to contemplate.

Cast and Credits

Cast: Lance Henriksen (Frank Black);

Seasons 1 and 2: Megan Gallagher (Catherine Black. **Season 3:** Klea Scott (Special Agent Emma Hollis).

Credits: Created by: Chris Carter. Music: Mark Snow. Editor (various episodes): Peter B. Ellis, George R. Potter, Stephen Mark, Jim Thomson. Production Designer: Mark Freeborn. Directors of Photography (various episodes): Barry Donlevy, Robert McLachlan, Peter Wunstori. Associate Producer: Jon-Michael Preece. Consulting Producers: Chip Johannesen, Darin Morgan. Co-Producer: Robert Moresco, Paul Rabwin. Producer: Thomas J. Wright. Co-Executive Producers: Ken Horton, John Peter Kousakis. Executive Producers: Chris Carter, James Wong, Glen Morgan. Associate Producer: Julie Herlocker. Executive Story Editor: Michael R. Perry. Casting: Nan Dutton, Coreen Mayes, Randy Stone. Associate Producer/Production Manager: Kathy Gilroy-Sereda. First Assistant Director: Jack Hardy. Second Assistant Director: Roger Russell. Set Decorator: Mark Lane. Art Decorator: Sandi Tanaka. Construction Coordinator: Mike Rennison. Script Supervisor: Christine Lalande. Location Manager: Monty Bannister. Hair Stylist: Gina Sherritt. Makeup: Carolyn Stewart. Special Effects Makeup: Lindala Makeup Effects, Inc. Costume Designer: Diane Widas. Head Painter: Jenny Seinen. Second Unit Director of Photography: Barry Donlevy. Sound Mix: Ruth Huddleston. Camera Operator: Trig Singer. Gaffer: John Scott. Key Grip: R.K. Hill. Property Master: Kimberly Regent. Special Effects Coordinator: Bob Comer. Stunt Coordinator: Lou Bollo. Transportation Coordinator: James Perenseff. Production Coordinator: Clark Candy. Extras Casting: Lisa Ratke. Assistant to Chris Carter: Joanne Service, Mary Astadourian. Production Associate: Jennifer Metcalf, Clear Hadden. Casting Associate (Vancouver): Heike Brandstatter. Postproduction Supervisor: Denise Pleune. Postproduction Sound: West Productions, Inc. Supervising Sound Editor: Mark Ridgely Crookston. Rerecording Mixers: Nello Torri, Peter R. Kelsey, Kurt Kassuke. Scoring Mixer: Larold Rebhan. Music Editor: Jeff Charbonneau. Assistant Editor: Robert Hudson. On-Line Editor: Rob Williams. DaVinci Colorist: Philip Azenzen. Visual Effects: Area 51. Visual Effects Supervision: Glenn Campbell. Visual Effects Producer: Tim McHugh. Main Title Sequence: Ramsey McDaniel/Storm Media. Processing: Gastown Post. Electronic Assembly: Encore Video. Cameras and Lenses: Clairmont Camera. Vehicles Provided by: Chrysler. Filmed on Location in: British Columbia. A Ten Thirteen Production.

EPISODE GUIDE

• First Season (1996–1997)

1. "Pilot" Written by Chris Carter; Directed by David Nutter; airdate: October 25, 1996; Guest Cast: Bill Smitrovitch (Bob Fletcher); Terry O'Quinn (Peter Watts); Brittany Tiplady (Jordan Black); Stephen J. Lang (Detective Gablehouse); Don MacKay (Jeff Meredith); Mike Puttonen (Pathologist); Jared Blancard (Young Man at Ruby Tip); Paul Dillon, Stephen E. Miller, Kate Luyben, April Telek.

Frank Black, his wife Catherine, and daughter Jordan move into their new yellow house in suburban Seattle. A former FBI agent recovering from a nervous breakdown, Frank is now profiling criminals as well as consulting for a mysterious organization called the Millennium Group. His first job involves the murder of a peep-show stripper by an unknown deviant, a poetry-spouting Frenchman. Frank tracks the killer, hoping to catch him before he strikes again ... but the police place little stock in Frank's seemingly psychic ability to see what the killer sees.

2. "Gehenna" Written by Chris Carter; Directed by David Nutter; airdate: November 1, 1996; Guest Cast: Terry O'Quinn (Peter Watts); Brittany Tiplady (Jordan Black); Bill Smitrovitch (Bletcher); Robin Gammell (Mike Atkins); Don MacKay (Jack Meredith); George Josef (Mr. Bolow); Stephen Holmes; Chris Bradford (Driver); Henry Watson (Detective); Don McWilliams (Park Guy).

The Group brings Frank out to San

Francisco to investigate the discovery of a human ear amidst a vast ash pile. Police work indicates that there are seven adult bodies in the thirty-nine pounds of ash, and Frank suspects that a strange cult which is utilizing a crematorium furnace may be responsible. An interrogation of one of the brainwashed cult members reveals an organization called "Gehenna" which is planning to control the coming (in 1998) apocalypse with everything from fear tactics to biological weaponry. A friend of Frank's gets too close a look at the cult's standard operating procedure when he is locked inside an industrial size microwave oven.

3. "Dead Letters" Written by James Wong and Glen Morgan; Directed by Thomas J. Wright; airdate: November 8, 1996; *Guest Cast:* Brittany Tiplady (Jordan Black); James Morrison (Jim Horn); Chris Ellis, Ron Halder, Garvin Cross (Patient); Anthony Harrison (Detective Jenkins); Lisa Vultaggio (Janice Sterling); Rob Morton (Lewis); Maria Louis Figura (Cindy Horn); Cooper Olson (T.C. Horn); Michelle Hart (Marjorie Holden); Fulvio Cecere (Security Guard); Andrew Laurenson (Clown); Allison Warren (Officer Sarah Stevens); Ken Shimizu (C.S.T. Member).

Little Jordan is plagued by nightmares of a demonic clown as Frank investigates a serial killer in Portland whom the Millennium Group is unwilling to profile as of yet. Frank teams with the explosive detective Horn, a man distracted from the job by marital difficulties and his own temper. Frank discovers that the killer has left behind a message on the dead woman's hair follicles: "hair today, gone tomorrow." He realizes he is dealing with a very clever perpetrator with a knack for precision and a need for adulation. Frank decides it is time to bait the obsessive killer by reporting to the press that his message to the police was misspelled, and that he is of "lower intelligence."

4. "Kingdom Come" Written by Jorge Zamacona; Directed by Winrich Kolbe; airdate: November 15, 1996; *Guest Cast:* Michael Zelnicker (Galen); Lindsay Crouse (Cohen); Laurie Murdoch (Father Schultz); Arnie Walters (Father Brown); Terence Kelly (Detective Brown); Tom McBeath (Detective Romero); Alan Lehros (Jonathan); Ed Harrington (Marcus Crane); Wanda Wilkinson (Sister); Peter Haworth (Reverend Jack Harned); Brad Wattum (Reverend); Ralph J. Alderman (Motel Manager).

Frank and an old friend and colleague, the beautiful Ardis Cohen, work overtime to stop a serial killer who is targeting men of the cloth. Frank's visions lead him to an understanding of this religious fanatic, and he attempts to talk the killer down during a dangerous hostage situation inside a church.

5. "The Judge" Written by Ted Mann; Directed by Randy Zisk; airdate: November 22, 1996; *Guest Cast:* Brittany Tiplady (Jordan Black); Bill Smitrovitch (Bletch); Marshall Bell (The Judge); John Hawkes (Mr. Bardale); Chris Ellis, Stephen James Lang (Detective Gablehouse); Brian Markinson, C.C.H. Pounder (Cheryl Adams); Michael Puttonen (Pathologist Massey); David Fredericks (Jonathan Mellen); Kirsten Williamson (Mail Room Worker); J.R. Bourne (Carl Nearman); Donna White (Anne Tisman); Eva DeViveiros (Ass't D.A. Aquila); Kate Robbins (Marilyn); Beverly Elliot (Terry); Gabe Khouth (Parcel Service Employee).

A killer strikes outside the Lucky Pins Bowling Alley in Seattle, and then overnights the victim's severed tongue to a seemingly random target, a widow. Bletch brings Frank in on the case after revealing that this type of "delivery" has occurred several times before in the last four years. The killings are the work of a lunatic who is working under the express direction of a man called "the Judge," a wacko who believes he is dispensing justice to people who have escaped the legal system. When "the Judge" is apprehended and then released for lack of evidence, he offers Frank a job in which he will also be able to dispense absolute justice.

6. "522666" Written by James Wong and Glen Morgan; Directed by David Nutter;

airdate: November 29, 1996; *Guest Cast:* Terry O'Quinn (Peter Watts); Brittany Tiplady (Jordan Black); Sam Anderson, Robert Lewis, Joe Chrest, Hiro Kanagawa (Agent Yung); William McDonald (Agent); Roger Barnes (Agent Smith); Deryl Hayes (Officer Mark Stanton).

A bar in Washington, D.C., frequented by British diplomats is destroyed in a bombing, and the Group flies Frank to the nation's capital to investigate. A code typed in on a telephone before the explosion, 522666, spells "kaboom," and Frank realizes he is dealing with one psychopath, not a foreign terrorist organization. Frank soon develops a "relationship" with the bomber through phone conversations and learns that the bomber considers himself a star, an artist whose palette is glass, blood, and fire. When the next bomb goes off, the bomber turns the tables by rescuing Frank and becoming a hero … a star.

7. "Blood Relatives" Written by Chip Johannesen; Directed by James Charleston; airdate: December 6, 1996; *Guest Cast:* Terry O'Quinn (Peter Watts); Brittany Tiplady (Jordan Black); Bill Smitrovitch (Bletch); Stephen James Long (Gablehouse); John Fleck, Sean Six, Brian Markinson, Lynda Boyd, Nicole Parker (Green Cort); Diana Stevan (Mrs. Cort); Bob Morrisey (Mr. Cort); Deanna Milligan (Tina).

Following the wake of her deceased son, a grieving mother is pulled into his open grave by a psycho and then brutally stabbed to death. While Catherine counsels the family in her capacity with Victim Services, Frank looks into the killing and determines that the murder was not about the dead woman, but about her dead, college-age son, and the grieving process. Frank also determines that the suspect is a funeral junkie who shows up at services to participate in the mourning, steal a souvenir or two, and depart, but now he seems to have crossed into a murderous rage. Frank traces the suspected killer to a refuge in a junkyard while Catherine attempts to make contact with the suspect's biological mother, who abandoned him years earlier as a strung-out teenager.

8. "The Well Worn Lock" Written by Chris Carter; Directed by Ralph Hemecker; airdate: December 20, 1996; *Guest Cast:* Paul Dooley (Joe Bangs); Michelle Joyner (Connie Bangs); Bill Smitrovitch (Bob Fletcher); J. Douglas Stewart (Larry Bangs); Shaina Tianne Unger (Sara Bangs); Campbell Lane (Joe Bangs' Attorney); Jim Fletcher (Bailiff); Steve Gatway (Judge); Christine Dunford, Lenore Zann, Sheila Moore.

In her capacity as a clinical social worker, Catherine assists a young woman who has been molested by her father, a prominent member of the chamber of commerce, for twenty plus years. Catherine discovers that the molestations occurred not just with one daughter, but all three. Political pressure mounts against Catherine for pursuing this case, and soon the misbehaving father vanishes with his youngest daughter in tow. Frank uses his gift to help end the terror, but will he be too late?

9. "Wide Open" Written by Charles D. Holland; Directed by James Charleston; airdate: January 3, 1997; *Guest Cast:* Brittany Tiplady (Jordan Black); Bill Smitrovitch (Bletch); Glynn Turman, Stephen James Lang (Gablehouse); Pablo Coffey, Nevada Ash (Patricia Highsmith); Eileen Kenney (Beverly Bunn); Sandra Ferens (Mary Kay Highsmith); David Neale (John Highsmith); Roger R. Cross (Officer Shaw).

A couple with a house for sale return home after an open house only to be bludgeoned to death by an intruder with an antique axe. Their young daughter survives this trauma in a vent, and Frank discovers her on the scene, though she is unable to help the police or Frank learn about the bloody crime she witnessed. At his home, the killer watches a video recording of the brutal crime and then mails it to the realtor who conducted the open house. When Bletch gets nowhere on the case, he considers showing the little girl the video of her parents' death, but Frank realizes that such a viewing is exactly what the killer desires: for little Patricia to relive the terror she has already experienced.

10. "The Wild and the Innocent" Written by Jorge Zamacona; Directed by Thomas J. Wright; airdate: January 10, 1997; *Guest Cast:* Terry O'Quinn (Peter Watts); Brittany Tiplady (Jordan Black); Heather McComb (Maddie Haskel); Jeffrey Donovan, John Pyper-Ferguson, Michael Hogan, Jim Gallanders (Missouri State Trooper); Steve Makaj (Arkansas Trooper Flanagen); John Tierney (Preacher); Renee Michelle (Adeline Travis); Jim Swansburg (Sam Travis).

Frank and Peter Watts head to Joplin, Mississippi, to track a fugitive murderer who Frank previously caught in 1992 (while he was still in the F.B.I.). Little does Frank realize that his dangerous perp has already been captured ... by his own victimized daughter and a volatile, gun-toting boyfriend. This duo heads to Arkansas searching for a child named Angel. Frank must stop them before they can harm Angel's adopted parents.

11. "Weeds" Written by Frank Spotnitz; Directed by Michael Pattinson; airdate: January 24, 1997; *Guest Cast:* Ryan Cutrona, Michael Tomlinson, Josh Clark, Terry David Mulligan, Brian Taylor, C.C.H. Pounder (Cheryl Andrews); Don MacKay (Jack Meredith); Joy Rinaldi (Linda Comstock); Paul Batten (Priest); Andrew Johnston (County Coroner); Fred Henderson (Lawyer); Karin Konoval (Woman).

An upper-class, gated housing community in Pierce County, Washington, is terrorized by a lunatic who subdues his victims with a cattleprod, forces them to drink his own blood, and then kills them by amputating their hands. Frank consults on the case for the Group as more victims are taken and then returned, mutilated. One night, the killer follows Frank home and leaves behind a message: a paint swatch and the number 528. While Frank tries to decipher the meaning of the clues, he realizes that the killer knows the secrets of his well-to-do neighbors and is visiting the sins of the fathers upon the children.

12. "Loin Like a Hunting Flame" Written by Ted Mann; Directed by David Nutter; airdate: January 31, 1997; *Guest Cast:* Terry O'Quinn (Peter Watts); William Lucking (detective); Hrothgar Mathews (Art Nesbitt); Harriet Sansom Harris (Maureen); Barbara Howard (Karen); Malcolm Stewart (Vic); Doug Abrahams (Detective Kent); Barry Greene (Mark); Michael Buie (Randy); Derek Hamilton (New Mel); Natassia Malthe (New Leslie); Peg Christopherson (Sylvie); Crystal Cass (New Anne); Fawnia L. Mondey (Lauri).

In Boulder, Colorado, two adults in their 20s are found dead in a pose reminiscent of the Garden of Eden, right down to an apple with two bites taken out of it. Frank looks in on the case for the Group and determines that a repressed man who wants sex to be "innocent" and uninhibited is the culprit. Soon, he kills two swingers and displays their bodies on a bench, leading Frank to believe that the killer cannot allow his victims to live outside the world of his fantasies. The killer, a pharmacist, continues to abduct people as part of his quest to consummate, for the first time, his sexual relationship with his wife of eighteen years.

13. "Force Majeure" Written by Chip Johannesen; Directed by Winrich Kolbe; airdate February 7, 1997; *Guest Cast:* Terry O'Quinn (Peter Watts); Brittany Tiplady (Jordan Black); Brad Dourif (Dennis Hoffman); Morgan Woodward (Noah); C.C.H. Pounder (Cheryl Andrew); Mitch Kosterman (Lieutenant); Sarah Strange (Maura); Kristi Angus (Lauren/Carlin); Peter Manlon (Manager); Cindy Girling (Myra); Phillip Mitchell (Uniform #1); Merrilyn Gann (Carlin's Mother); Timothy Webber.

During a freak snow storm, a college student immolates herself in what seems a ritualistic act. Catherine comforts her grieving (adopted) parents and is assisted by a mysterious man named Dennis Hoffman who claims that he works with Frank. Since Frank has no knowledge of any co-worker named Dennis, he enlists Peter Watts to help discover the truth about this man and the bizarre death. The mysterious Dennis Hoffman is a strange wanna-be profiler who believes that seven planets will align on May 5, 2000, causing extreme gravitational pressure on Earth and bringing about the end of the world through a massive flood.

14. "The Thin White Line" Written by Glen Morgan and James Wong; Directed by Thomas J. Wright; airdate: February 14, 1997; *Guest Cast:* Bill Smitrovitch (Bletch); Jeremy Roberts (Richard Allan Hanz); Scott Heindl (Jacob Tyler); Ken Tremblett (Agent Riley); Allan Harvey (Agent Johnson); Mark Holden (Agent Clark); Nancy Sivak (Anne Rothenburg); Larry Musser (Warden); Tom Heaton (Store Clerk).

When a stabbing victim is carried into the hospital, Frank recalls an incident from his days in the FBI, when he was stabbed in the hand by a psycho. The killer strikes again, killing a grocer, and Frank realizes that a monster from twenty years ago is back ... killing in pairs and leaving behind calling cards. Frank's old foe, however, is actually serving seven consecutive life sentences in a maximum security penitentiary, and his work is being carried on by his former cell-mate, whom Frank calls the "living reincarnation" of the original terror. To stop the copycat, Frank must face his fears and interview Richard Allan Hanz, the man who scarred him two decades ago.

15. "Sacrament" Written by Frank Spotnitz, Directed by Michael Watkins; airdate: February 21, 1997; *Guest Cast:* Terry O'Quinn (Peter Watts); Brittany Tiplady (Jordan); Stephen James Lang (Gablehouse); Bill Smitrovitch (Bletch); Philip Anglim (Tom Black); Dylan Haggerty (Richard Greene); Brian Markinson (Cop); Lorena Gale (Dr. Patricia Moss); Daphne Goldrick (Green's Mother); French Tickner (Store Clerk); Ken Roberts (Green's Father); Liz Bryson (Helen).

At his nephew's baptism, Frank is on the scene when his brother's wife, Helen, is abducted. Bletch asks Frank *not* to get involved in the investigation, or to allow the Millennium Group to get involved, but Frank is unable to remain on the sidelines while his family suffers. With Peter Watts' unofficial help, Frank finds a suspect, Richard Greene, a sex-

ual sadist and a mental patient formerly incarcerated at the Glen Rosa Home for the Criminally Insane. Frank's brother, Tom, snaps and confronts the killer at gunpoint, even as Frank learns that Greene is a satanist who has declared loyalty to Lucifer for all eternity.

16. "Covenant" Written by Robert J. Moresco; Directed by Roderick J. Pridy; airdate: March 21, 1997; *Guest Cast:* Brittany Tiplady (Jordan Black); John Finn (William Garry); Michael O'Neill, Sarah Koskoff (Didi Higgins); Jay Underwood, Steve Bacic, Don MacKay (Jack Meredith); Nicole Oliver (Dr. Alice Steele); Tyler Thompson (William Garry, Jr.); George Gordon (Judge Francis Maher); Karen Elizabeth Austin (Mrs. Anderson); David Abbott (Mr. Anderson); Norman Armour (Medical Examiner); Noah Heney (Charles Horvath).

A town sheriff in Ogden, Utah, is arrested for the murder of his wife, two boys, and his little girl with a skew chisel. Six months later, Frank is called in as an expert witness on cold-blooded killers to assure that William Garry is given the death penalty by the jury. After examining the crime scene, however, Frank thinks something does not add up about the murders and the murderer, and he determines that accused family man is not the killer ... despite his own confession to the contrary. To save an innocent man, Frank must discover the real killer, persuade the judge of the truth, and risk the wrath of local law enforcement.

17. "Walkabout" Written by Chip Johannesen and Tim Tankosic; Directed by Cliff Bole; airdate: March 28, 1997; *Guest Cast:* Terry O'Quinn (Peter Watts); Brittany Tiplady (Jordan Black); Stephen James Lang (Gablehouse); Bill Smitrovitch (Bletch); Zeljko Ivanek (Dr. Daniel Miller); George Itzin (Hans Ingram).

Peter Watts shows up at the Black house to inform Catherine that Frank has disappeared while working under the alias David Marx on a case. As the days pass, Frank shows up, beaten and bruised, in a dark alley, but he has amnesia and cannot remember exactly where he was or what happened to him. Frank and Peter attempt to reconstruct what transpired in Black's missing days and realize that it had something to do with a "cure" for Frank's visions, a test for an experimental drug called Proloft which treats temporal lobe anomalies. Frank remembers that somebody died during the tests, but who was the victim, who was really testing this so-called "medicine," and why?

18. "Lamentation" Written by Chris Carter; Directed by Winrich Kolbe; airdate: April 18, 1997; *Guest Cast:* Terry O'Quinn (Peter Watts); Brittany Tiplady (Jordan); Stephen James Lang (Gablehouse); Bill Smitrovitch (Bletch); Alex Diakun, Sarah-Jane Redmond (Lucy Butler); Michael David Simms.

An evil doctor who slit the throats of five nurses escapes from police custody after donating a kidney to his sister. The F.B.I. behavioral sciences division calls in Frank, who has caught the doctor once before, and Peter Watts to help apprehend the inhuman physician before he kills again. The trail leads to an evil woman named Lucy Butler, who just might be the devil, and the death of Frank's close friend, Bletch.

19. "Powers, Principalities, Thrones and Dominions" Written by Ted Mann and Harold Rosenthal; Directed by Thomas J. Wright; airdate: April 25, 1997; *Guest Cast:* Terry O'Quinn (Peter Watts); Stephen James Lang (Gablehouse); Brittany Tiplady (Jordan); Bill Smitrovitch (Bob Bletch); Richard Cox (Alistair Pepper); Robin Gammell (Mike Atkins); Rodney Eastman, Sarah-Jane Redmond (Lucy Butler); Alf Humphreys (Damon Rummer); Guy Fauchon (Martin); Dean P. Gibson (Phil Bruce); Robert Maloney (Uniformed Cop Adams); Judith Maxie (Judge Myers); Allan Franz (Medical Examiner Anderson); Bonnie Hays (A.D.A. Mills).

Frank is still recovering from his encounter with Lucy Butler and Bob Bletcher's death, but he reluctantly joins Peter Watts on a homicide case with ritualistic overtones. A

suspect is apprehended quickly, but Frank feels the case is far from over, even as he experiences a vision of Bletch, a bloody apparition who tries to warn him about something. The suspect's lawyer, Allistair Pepper, offers Frank a job at his law firm, but Frank suspects it is, literally, a deal with the devil. When the suspect confesses to murdering Bob Bletch, Frank realizes that an elaborate web, a trap, is being spun to snare him and his family ... and then he spots Lucy Butler in a grocery store.

20. "Broken World" Written by Robert Moresco and Patrick Harbinson; Directed by Winrich Kolbe; airdate: May 2, 1997; *Guest Cast:* Terry O'Quinn (Peter Watts); Jo Anderson (Claudia Vaughn); Van Quattro, John Dennis Johnston, Donnelly Rhodes, Ingrid Kavelaars (Sally Dumont); P. Adrien Dorval (Fatso); Michael Tayles (Deputy Billy); J.B. Bivens (First Deputy).

In North Dakota, a woman is assaulted in her horse stable by a budding psycho-sexual killer responsible for twenty-one horse deaths in neighboring counties. Hoping to prevent any human murders, Frank and Peter investigate the case and Black realizes that he needs to talk to this particular madman before he graduates to the murder of a human victim. Peter Watts fears that the killer has become empowered by his recent actions, and his worry proves accurate: the psycho strikes again, kicking an innocent man to death and murdering several hogs. Frank comes to see that the killer is a man who is jealous of horses, because he feels they are taking female affection away from him.

21. "Maranatha" Written by Chip Johannesen; Directed by Peter Markle; airdate: May 9, 1997; *Guest Cast:* Terry O'Quinn (Peter Watts); Bill Nunn, Boris Krutonog (Yuri); Levani (Sergei Steponovitch); Michael Aniol (Priest); Dmitri Boudrine (Andrei Petrovich Melnikov); Michael Cram (Paramedic); Bill Croft (Broadface); Brian Downey (Medical Examiner); Roger Haskett (ER Doctor); Beverly Pales (Torch Singer).

Frank travels to Brighton Beach, NY, to investigate the homicide of several Russian-

American citizens. The culprit seems to be a man named Yapochnik who in some way was involved at the Chernobyl disaster in 1986. The Russian community believes a mythical monster is involved, and was actually responsible for the nuclear accident, per Revelation, Chapter 8, verse 10. Worse, this homicidal "legend" may actually be the Antichrist, a creature who will unite the ten nations of the former Soviet Union against Israel and bring about the Last Days.

22. "Paper Dove" Written by Walon Green and Ted Mann; Directed by Thomas J. Wright; airdate: May 16, 1997; *Guest Cast:* Brittany Tiplady (Jordan); Barbara Williams, Mike Starr, Linda Sorenson, Ken Pogue, William Nunn, Frank Cassini (Agent Devlin); Judy Norton (Carol Scammel); Garry Davey (Ranger Chet); Doris Chillcott (Adele Hunziger); Paul Raskin (Figaro); Arlen Jones (Agent Emmerlich); Eric Breker (Malcolm Hunziger); Angela Donahue (Amy Lee Walker).

Frank, Catherine, and Jordan visit Catherine's parents in Arlington, Virginia, while the mysterious Polaroid-snapping killer plots to destroy him. Catherine's father asks Frank to review a case for a friend who is terminally ill and estranged from his incarcerated son. Frank believes the boy is innocent of the charge of murder and the trail leads him to a psycho who is actually a patsy for the Polaroid killer. Upon return to Seattle, Catherine vanishes at the airport.

● *Second Season (1997–1998)*

23. "The Beginning and the End" Written by Glen Morgan and James Wong; Directed by Thomas J. Wright; airdate: September 9, 1997; *Guest Cast:* Terry O'Quinn (Peter Watts); Brittany Tiplady (Jordan Black); Doug Hutchison (Polaroid Killer); Allan Zinyk (Rodecker); Judith Maxie (Finley); Drew Reichelt (Dicky Bird Parking); Mitch Kosterman (Sheriff); Alan Robertson (Elderly Man); Norman Armour (Suited Man).

Catherine is abducted from the airport by the Polaroid Killer, who is daring Frank to catch him. The killer escapes a roadblock with Catherine still in his custody, and the Millennium Group is stirred to action. The abduction of Frank's wife coincides with the passage of a comet in the night sky, and the killer suspects an omen: the comet overhead will give humankind a chance to decide how the end of the world will come about. Frank's search for his wife turns to frustration when he realizes that the killer defies all attempts at profiling and understanding.

24. "Beware of the Dog" Written by Glen Morgan and James Wong; Directed by Allen Coulter; airdate: September 26, 1997; *Guest Cast:* Terry O'Quinn (Peter Watts); Brittany Tiplady (Jordan Black); Randy Stone (Michael Peebie); R.G. Armstrong (Old Man); Brent Butt (Short Order Cook); Ralph Alderman (Nate); Anita Wittenberg (Cora); Arnie Walters (Paul Lombardo); Margaret Martin (Mary Ann Lombardo); Sally Stevens (Radio Singer).

In the remote town of Bucksnort, a couple of tourists are terrorized and murdered by vicious dogs ... which appear to be hellhounds. Though Frank is reluctant to investigate what appears to be a simple, if brutal, animal attack, the Millennium Group insists he go to Bucksnort to learn more. What Frank discovers is a strange town with no law enforcement facilities and a dread of sundown. When darkness comes and a pack of wild dogs starts to gather in town, Frank realizes there is more going on than meets the eye, and that the only person who can explain the mystery is an old man in the woods with the power to keep the dogs at bay.

25. "Sense and Anti-Sense" Written by Chip Johannesen; Directed by Thomas J. Wright; airdate: October 3, 1997; *Guest Cast:* Terry O'Quinn (Peter Watts); Stephen James Lang (Detective Gablehouse); Allan Zinyk (Rodecker); Clarence Williams, III (Patient Zero/William Kremer); Ricky Harris, Badja Djola, Brian Jensen (Wright); Chris Nelson Norris (Patterson); Peter Bryant (Editor); Forbes Angus (Dr. Pettey); Michael Vaird (Officer Ginelli).

A kind taxi driver escorts a dying man to a Seattle hospital. Sick with hemorrhagic fever, this patient escapes with the help of the cabbie, and Frank and the CDC track him down. The mystery broadens when the CDC men vanish with their prey, and Frank suspects that the sick man was telling the truth about a secret plan involving the government's exploitation of and experimentation on the black man. Frank discovers evidence of a biological study being conducted by the D.O.E. called "The Human Genome Project."

26. "Monster" Written by Glen Morgan and James Wong; Directed by Perry Lang; airdate: October 17, 1997; *Guest Cast:* Terry O'Quinn (Peter Watts); Kristen Cloke (Lara Means); Brittany Tiplady (Jordan Black); Chris Owens (Deputy Bill Sherman); Robert Wisden (Sheriff); Mary Gillis, Lauren Diewold, Gillian Barber, Fred Keating, Ken Roberts (Police Chief Jenkins); Judy Norton (Coroner); J. Douglas Stewart (Dentist); Kevin Blatch (Shoe Salesman); Thomas Miller (Billy Sherman Jr.).

The Millennium Group orders Frank to a small town to investigate charges of child abuse at Mrs. Penny's Daycare. Also there is psychic Lara Means, who teams with Frank to learn why a boy has died at the center. At home, Frank is accused of child abuse when Jordan is found to have a bad cut on her gums. Although there is little evidence of abuse in either case, a mob mentality is soon born and a witchhunt begins in full flow ... with people unaware that a five-year-old girl might represent the real evil.

27. "A Single Blade of Grass" Written by Erin Maher and Kay Reindl; Directed by Rodman Flender; airdate: October 24, 1997; *Guest Cast:* Amy Steel (Dr. Liz Michael); Michael Greyeyes, Floyd Red Crow Esterman, Garry Chalk, Doug Abrahams, Rondel Reynoldson (Coroner Hutson); Byron Chief Moon (Fenton).

In Manhattan, a feisty archaeologist uncovers a recently murdered corpse on a construction site which is also a Native American burial ground. Frank is sent to New York to help discover the identity of the dead man, and the clues lead him to the basement of a ritzy West Side Hotel. There he finds evidence of an Indian ritual which is meant to forge a contact with the spirit world. As Frank learns more, he realizes that a lost Indian tribe, thought to be mythical, has rejoined to spur a Native American version of the apocalypse.

28. "The Curse of Frank Black" Written by Glen Morgan and James Wong; Directed by Ralph Hemecker; airdate: October 31, 1997; *Guest Cast:* Brittany Tiplady (Jordan Black); Dean Winters (Lt. Detective Robert Fletcher).

On Halloween, Frank takes Jordan, dressed as Marge Simpson, trick-or-treating through the neighborhood. A fleeting glimpse of a ghost spurs Frank's memory of a Halloween from his own youth. A freak breakdown of Frank's car and cell phone then lands a lonely Frank at home at his yellow house, but it is a dark vacant place filled with ghosts of strange times. One such ghost belongs to a tortured World War II veteran who knew Frank as a child, and who has now returned from the afterlife with a dire warning.

29. "19:19" Written by Glen Morgan and James Wong; Directed by Thomas J. Wright; airdate: November 7, 1997; *Guest Cast:* Terry O'Quinn (Peter Watts); Kristen Cloke (Laura Means); Christian Hoff (Matthew Pine); Steve Rankin (Sheriff Cayce); Colleen Rennison (Jesse Cayce); David Abbott (Vernon Roberts); Kurt Evans (Deputy Jack); Drew McCreadie (Storm Chaser); Bill Marchant (Accomplice); Robyn Wood (Little Girl).

A young man who believes he can be the instrument to prevent the apocalypse abducts a bus-load of children in Broken Bow, Oklahoma. Frank and Watts pursue the kidnapper alongside an angry local sheriff whose daughter, Jesse, is among the missing. The madman leaves a message on a local radio show quoting the Bible, Revelation 19, verse 19. When Frank realizes there are eighteen abducted children he also realizes that the abductor will come back to kidnap child number nineteen, who stayed home from school sick that day.

30. "The Hand of Saint Sebastian" Written by Glen Morgan and James Wong; Directed by Thomas J. Wright; airdate: November 14, 1997; *Guest Cast:* Terry O'Quinn (Peter Watts); Phillip Baker Hall, Gottifried John, Allan Zinyk, C.C.H. Pounder (Cheryl Andrews); Stephen Dimopoulos (Detective Betzdorf); Christine Lippa (German Police Captain); Grahame Andrews (Dr. Schlossburg); Damon Johnson (Hospital Security); Stefano Giulianetti (Fugitive); Noah Heney (Provider).

Peter Watts is working on a special project, unauthorized by the Millennium Group, and he asks Frank to assist him on it in Germany. Peter, Frank, and the German police team up to investigate a thousand year old corpse preserved in a bog ... a body which dates back to the beginnings of the Millennium Group and can help Peter establish "who we are" as a race. The object of interest is the hand of St. Sebastian, a holy relic which is said to be the key to overcoming the evils of the millennium. Unfortunately, there are people and factions who are willing to kill to protect the sacred hand of St. Sebastian, and Peter is framed for a murder he has not committed.

31. "Jose Chung's '*Doomsday Defense*'" Written and directed by Darin Morgan; airdate: November 21, 1997; *Guest Cast:* Terry O'Quinn (Peter Watts); Stephen James Lang (Detective Gablehouse); Charles Nelson Reilly (Jose Chung); Dan Zukovic (Selfosophist), Richard Steinmetz, Patrick Fabian.

Writer Jose Chung peers a bit too closely into the strange new religion "selfosophy" invented by former friend and now messiah, Onan Gopta. Frank investigates the murder of a selfosophist who broke ranks and spoke with Chung about selfosophy's internal hierarchy. Chung is also writing a doomsday book and is curious about the Millennium Group, but there is also a psycho on the loose who wants him dead.

Note: This episode is a sequel, of sorts, to the *X-Files* third season episode, "Jose Chung's '*From Outer Space.*'" This episode also features a guest appearance (on posters only) by David Duchovny as Bobby Wingood, a whoring, hedonistic movie star and selfosophist who discovers the power of positive thinking.

32. "Midnight of the Century" Written by Erin Maher and Kay Reindl; Directed by Dwight Little; airdate: December 19, 1997; *Guest Cast:* Darren McGavin (Henry Black); Terry O'Quinn (Peter Watts); Brittany Tiplady (Jordan Black); Kristen Cloke (Lara Means); Allan Zinyk (Brian Rodecker); Gerry Curry (Simon); Jessica Schreier (Barbara Watts); Cheryl McNamara (Linda Black); Trevor White (Caspar); Donny Lucas (Balthasar); Tim Bissett (Melchior).

Frank prepares to spend a lonely Christmas in his new home, away from his wife and child, when he is unexpectedly contacted by his long-absent father to whom he hasn't spoken in some forty years. Worse, on the eve of her Christmas pageant, Jordan seems to be communing with Frank's dead mother, a woman who saw angels throughout her brief life. Frank seeks the help of Lara Means in understanding Jordan's visions of angels, and then decides it is time to go home and confront his father about a fateful Christmas Eve in 1946.

33. "Goodbye Charlie" Written by Richard Whitley; directed by Ken Fink; airdate: January 9, 1998; *Guest Cast:* Kristen Cloke (Lara Means); Tucker Smallwood (Steven Kiley); Stephen James Lang (Gablehouse); Deanne Henry (Eleanor); Bethor Shirkoff, Stefan Arngrim, Ally Warren (Officer Nello); Dave Hurtubise (Russ); Gina Stockdale (Tammy); David MacKay (Jeff Lubo).

A strange man, apparently a doctor, is using a suicide machine and not a wee bit of physical pressure to be sure that terminally ill patients are "assisted" to their death. Frank, Lara Means, and the Millennium Group become involved, and learn that this suicide doctor is a psycho who has taken his name from the moniker of a character from the *Marcus*

Welby TV series! As Frank and Lara narrow in on the suicide doctor, they realize that someone else may be pulling the strings from behind the scene.

34. "Luminary" Written by Chip Johannesen, Directed by Thomas J. Wright; airdate: January 23, 1998; *Guest Cast:* Terry O'Quinn (Peter Watts); Brittany Tiplady (Jordan Black); Brion James (Sheriff); Tobias Mehler, Rob Freeman, Tamsin Kelsey, Matthew Walker, Syd Van Rood (Astrologer); Gardiner Millar (Millennium Group Member); Judith Maxie (Finley); John Moore (Lecturer); Bernie Coulson (Pilot); Hagan Beggs (Doctor); Bart Anderson (Clerk); Jessica Schreier (Barbara Watts); Marke Driesscher (Weatherman).

Frank is grilled by the Group during a review of his candidacy, and he walks out of the proceedings, angry. Later, friends of Catherine ask Frank to find their eighteen-year-old son, Alex, who has gone missing in the Alaskan wilderness. When Frank goes off in search of the boy as a lone agent, Catherine enlists the help of Peter Watts, who is under strict orders from the Group *not* to help Black. Alone in the wild, Frank searches for Alex, even as his own rescue plane leaves him behind.

35. "The Mikado" Written by Michael Perry; Directed by Roderick J. Pridy; airdate: February 6, 1998; *Guest Cast:* Terry O'Quinn (Peter Watts); Allan Zinyk (Rodecker); Greg Michaels, Gillian Carfra (The Web Girl); Micah Gardener (Brandon); Tony Sampson (Anthony); Justin Wong (Danny); Rachel Hayward (Angela); Jonathan Bruce (Haverford Man); Aaron Fry (Columbus Man); Dawn Murphy (Special Agent Tully); Harrison R. Coe (San Francisco Officer); Patrick S. Phillips (Detective Brusky); Eileen Pedde ("Pain" Victim).

High school students surfing the net for porn run across a site called "The Mystery Room," where a twenty-six-year-old woman is bound to a chair and murdered by a hooded killer. One of the boys realizes what he has seen and prints a screen of the bloody death,

the only evidence that a murder has been committed. Now Frank, Peter, and Rodecker marshal the forces of the Millennium Group to find the cyberstalker as he plots to kill a second victim when his Internet site receives a certain number of "hits." As Frank gets into the mind of his opponent, he realizes he may be dealing with a psycho called "Avatar" who committed multiple-murders in the early 1980s and has now found his enthusiasm rekindled by the advent of the Internet.

36. "The Pest House" Written by Glen Morgan and James Wong; Directed by Allen Coulter; airdate: February 27, 1998; *Guest Cast:* Terry O'Quinn (Peter Watts); Melinda McGraw (Dr. Alex Stohler); Justin Louis (Edward); Michael Massee (Cainin Purdue); Darcy Laurie (Jacob Woodcock); Amber Warnat (Christie Morris); Brendan Fehr (Kevin Galbraith); C. Ernst Harth (Bear); Michael Weaver (Ted); Jada Stark (Callie); Greg Anderson (Detective Munsch); Tyronne L'Hirondelle (Brennan); John Callandar (Attendant); Holly Ferguson (Katie).

A teenager is murdered on an isolated bridge in what appears to be a re-creation of an urban legend: a killer with a hook for a hand slaughters a girl's boyfriend and then hangs the bleeding boy upside down over the roof of his car. Though Frank is reluctant to believe in a serial killer who works from urban legends, Peter and the Millennium Group suspect an inmate (with a hook for a hand) in a local sanitarium nicknamed "The Pest House" may be involved. A second crime (the murder of a young couple) suggests that more than one maniac may be on the loose, perhaps escaped patients from the Pest House. After a third urban legend killing is narrowly averted, Frank gives credence to one inmate's terrifying belief that someone is stealing the evil out of inmates' minds and transporting the urge to kill outside the installation into murderous reality.

37. "Owls" Written by Glen Morgan and James Wong; Directed by Thomas J. Wright; airdate: March 6, 1998; *Guest Cast:* Terry O'Quinn (Peter Watts); Brittany

Tiplady (Jordan Black); Kristen Cloke (Lara Means); Kimberly Patton (Claire Knight); R.G. Armstrong (The Old Man); Malcolm Stewart, Bob Dawson (Helmut Gunsche); Michael Tiernan (Millennium Group Driver); Brian Downey (Mr. Dean); Judith Maxie (Finley); John Juliani (Mr. Plunkett); Mark Holden (Amadar); Bruno Verdon (Le Fur); Gardiner Millar (Mr. Otto).

Two factions fight it out in Damascus over an unearthed holy relic: the cross of Christ's Crucifixion. Strangely, this war seems to be fought among the chapters of a divided Millennium Group: the Owls (who believe there will be a secular apocalypse in approximately 2020) and the Roosters (who subscribe to the notion that a religious, theological apocalypse is destined to occur in the year 2000 ... just 665 days away). When it looks like Group members are murdering Group members to control the cross of Christ, which promises victory to anyone who possesses it, Peter Watts brings in Frank and Lara Means to get to the bottom of what is rapidly becoming a violent civil war. Frank has had enough of the Millennium Group's secrets and lies, however, and refuses to help Peter through the crisis, even as Catherine is courted by a suspicious German company which seems to have an unhealthy interest in Frank.

38. "Roosters" Written by Glen Morgan and James Wong; Directed by Thomas J. Wright; airdate: March 13, 1998; *Guest Cast:* Terry O'Quinn (Peter Watts); Stephen James Lang (Gablehouse); Kristen Cloke (Lara Means); R.G. Armstrong (The Old Man); Kimberly Patton (Claire Knight); Ernest Lenart, Philip Baker Hall, Bob Dawson (Helmut Gunsche); Brian Downey (Mr. Dean); Judith Maxie (Finley); John Julian (Mr. Plunkett); Barry W. Levy (Driver); Gardiner Millar (Mr. Otto); Steve Griffith (Jim Ford); Charles Andre (Passenger).

As the civil war within the Millennium Group deepens, Frank is nearly gunned down by assassins who identify themselves as being within the Group. Meanwhile, a neo-Nazi organization called Odessa steals what it believes to be the cross of the Crucifixion and fosters the schism within the Group. The Old Man, the leader of Millennium, seeks the assistance of Frank and Laura when Odessa threatens his life and the future of the Group.

39. "Siren" Written by Glen Morgan and James Wong; Directed by Allen Coulter; airdate: March 20, 1998; *Guest Cast:* Terry O'Quinn (Peter Watts); Stephen James Lang (Gablehouse); Brittany Tiplady (Jordan Black); Kristen Cloke (Lara Means); Vivian Wu (Tamara Shua Fa Lee); Tzi Ma, Ricki Cheng, Fulvio Cecere (Agent Brown); Colin Foo (Lo Fat); Simon Wong (Chin); Alannah Ong (Jennifer); Ronin (Interpreter); Michael Puttonen (Coroner); Cory Dagg (Star); Eileen Pedde (Doctor); Bobby Magee (Customs Officer).

A Chinese freighter smuggling illegal immigrants into the United States is raided by the I.N.S. Jordan makes a connection with a strange Chinese woman who was chained aboard the ship and who may now hold the key to saving Frank's life. As Lara and Frank investigate, they learn how the mysterious woman came to be aboard the ship, and how this strange siren may have killed four people she seduced. The siren attempts to seduce Frank with a vision in which the Millennium Group has no role in his life.

40. "In Arcadia Ego" Written by Chip Johannesen; Directed by Thomas J. Wright; airdate: April 3, 1998; *Guest Cast:* Terry O'Quinn (Peter Watts); Missy Crider, Mary-Pat Green, David Jean Thomas, Ed Lauter, Sean Campbell (Second Guard); R. Nelson Brown (First Guard); Ronald Selmour (Ernie Shiffer); Steve Oatway (Chris Taylor); Frances Flanagan (Nurse); Marina Dufort (Warden's Assistant).

Two women prisoners — lovers — escape from captivity under violent and unusual circumstances. Frank joins the hunt to bring the women to justice but quickly determines that the couple has fled authorities to protect something of vital importance. When it is learned that one of the couple, Janette, is pregnant, Frank takes care to prevent the authorities from hurting the fugitives. The two women believe they have conceived a miraculous child, but Peter and Frank think they know the truth: that Janette was (unknowingly) raped in the infirmary by a guard.

41. "Anamnesis" Written by Erin Maher and Kay Reindel; Directed by John Kousakis; airdate: April 17, 1998; *Guest Cast:* Terry O'Quinn (Peter Watts); Kristen Cloke (Lara Means); Gwynwth Walsh (Claire McKenna); John-Pyper Ferguson, Genele Templeton, Garry Davey, Brendan Fletcher, John B. Lowe (Reverend Sam Hanes); Kimberly Warnat (Maureen); Melanie Manuel (Kelly); Eryn Collins (Shelley); Jessica Murdoch (Leslie); Jenny Mitchell (Lydia); Christopher Gray (Buddy); Angela Moore (Teacher); A.J. Bond (Sports Boy); Mia Ingimundsen (Cloaked Woman).

Five girls in Rowan have a religious vision of Mary, and Catherine Black is asked to talk to the teenagers in her capacity as a therapist. Lara Means arrives, working for Watts and the Group, and quickly comes to loggerheads over the truth of this bizarre situation. The case takes an odd turn when Catherine and Lara discover that one girl's vision was not of the Virgin Mary, but of Mary Magdalene, the first witness of the resurrection of Christ. When a local boy attempts to kill the visionary, Lara reveals a startling secret about the girl's heritage.

42. "A Room with No View" Written by Ken Horton; Directed by Thomas Wright; airdate: April 24, 1998; *Guest Cast:* Terry O'Quinn (Peter Watts); Stephen James Lang (Gablehouse); Sarah-Jane Redmond (Lucy Butler); Christopher Kennedy Masterson, Chad Todhunter, Mariangela Pino, Timothy Webber.

A high school boy dies of fright, and his best friend, who was recently voted "most likely to succeed," is abducted by a sinister force. The missing boy has been taken to a kind of horror hotel run by none other than the evil, shape-shifting Lucy Butler. Though Peter is skeptical about Lucy's involvement in the case, Frank feels the chill of her presence

at the crime scene. Lucy is attempting to steal the future by abducting promising students and torturing them so that they become "ordinary."

43. "Somehow, Satan Got Behind Me" Written and directed by Darin Morgan; airdate: May 1, 1998; *Guest Cast:* Bill Macy, Dick Bakalyan, Alex Diakun, Wally Dalton, Dan Zukovic (Censor), Gabrielle Rose, Stephen Holmes, Bill Mackenzie (Brock); Austin Basile (Donut Clerk); Fawnia Louise Mondey (Stripper); Kett Tarton (Devil Worshipper); Michael Sunczyk (Johnnie Mark Potter).

Four demons in a rundown donut shop called The Donut Hole reminisce about the good old days when evil had more character and grandeur. One demon recounts how he nudged a youngster into becoming a serial killer ... only to see his protégé apprehended by Frank Black. Another demon recalls how a human being's day-to-day existence can lead to evil and damnation. A third demonic story revolves around a hyper TV network standards and practices censor whose insanity grows and grows.

44. "The Fourth Horseman" Written by Glen Morgan and James Wong; Directed by Dwight Little; airdate: May 8, 1998; *Guest Cast:* Terry O'Quinn (Peter Watts); Brittany Tiplady (Jordan); Glenn Morshower (Richard Gilbert); Bill Dow (Pathologist); Kristen Cloke (Lara Means); Anna Hagan (Mom); Terrence Kelly (Dad); Jennifer Davis (Leslie Hopps); Bryan Vukelic (Greg Davis); David Longworth (Farmer Duffy); Lindsay Bourne (Physician #1); Max Wyman (Group Member); Fred Henderson (Agent Russell); Eileen Pedde (Dr. Miriam Greenwood).

A representative from the Trust attempts to recruit Frank into its ranks, even as Frank learns of his father's death. Later, Peter Watts brings Frank in on a case in which a man has died of a fast-acting and highly infectious disease. A pathologist determines that Peter and Frank may have been exposed to the disease, and they are whisked away to quarantine by the Millennium Group and unknowingly given an antidote to this "Marburg Variant" plague. Frank begins to realize that the Millennium Group is plotting to release this mutant strain for a planned armageddon which will leave them in control of a decimated world, and worse, Frank discovers that there is not enough antidote available to save his wife and daughter.

45. "The Time Is Now" Written by Glen Morgan and James Wong; Directed by Thomas J. Wright; airdate: May 15, 1998; *Guest Cast:* Terry O'Quinn (Peter Watts); Brittany Tiplady (Jordan Black); Glenn Morshower (Richard Gilbert); Kristen Cloke (Lara Means); Daryl Shuttleworth (Brian Dixon); David Palffy (Dr. Sorenson); Hiro Kanagawa (Team Member Lewis); Ian Robinson (Computer Monitor); Barry W. Levy (Braylock); Stephen Macht.

Frank has promised Catherine that he will leave the Millennium Group once and for all, and return with her and Jordan to their yellow house ... but events rapidly unfold which change Frank Black's life in a very dramatic way. The Marburg Variant disease is spreading now, and Lara Means is having a nervous breakdown because she has psychically witnessed the future engineered by the Group. She gives Frank her antidote serum, but as the virus spreads, Frank knows it will not be enough. The Blacks flee the city for a cabin in the woods as the outbreak gets worse, and soon Catherine becomes infected.

• *Third Season (1998–1999)*

46. "The Innocents" Written by Michael Duggan; Directed by Thomas J. Wright; airdate: October 3, 1998; *Guest Cast:* Brittany Tiplady (Jordan Black); Peter Outerbridge (Agent Barry Baldwin); Stephen E. Miller (Andy McLaren); Katy Boyer, Ken Pogue, Averie Maddox, Maxine Miller, Doris Chillcott (Elderly Woman); Judith McDowell (Dr. Luanna Chase); Francoise Yip (Flight Attendant #2); Damon Gregory (Larry Palmer); Barry W. Levy (Passenger); Garvin Cross (Trucker); Frances Flanagan (Nurse); Gerry Narini (NTSB Investigator).

A commercial airline goes down with all aboard (including twenty-three children) as a result of a strange conspiracy involving blonde women. Frank Black and his daughter Jordan have relocated to Falls Church, Virginia, after an outbreak of plague in the Pacific Northwest and the death of Catherine Black. Frank has rejoined the F.B.I. and on his first case he teams with novice agent Emma Hollis at the airplane crash site in the Sierras. There he begins to suspect that the Millennium Group was involved with the crash. Soon, another blonde woman and her child are murdered in a house bombing and Frank suspects yet another connection.

47. "Exegesis" Written by Chip Johannesen; Directed by Ralph Hemecker; airdate: October 10, 1998; *Guest Cast:* Brittany Tiplady (Jordan Black); Peter Outerbridge (Agent Barry Baldwin); Stephen E. Miller (Andy McClaren); Terry O'Quinn (Peter Watts); Katy Boyer, Ken Pogue, Averie Maddox, Maxine Miller, Doris Chillcot (Elderly Woman); William Richert (Tom Coty); Demetri Goritsas (Agent Dixon); Barry W. Levy (Millennium Group Member); Tim Dixon (Forensic Doctor); Ted Cole (Dr. Thomas); Frances Flanagan (Nurse).

Another mother and daughter are dead, and Frank believes that the unusual women are seers, oracles, who can gaze into the future. Worse, he believes they are being systematically annihilated by the Millennium Group so as to protect some kind of "end of the world" scenario. Emma Hollis and Frank learn of a CIA program called "Grillflame" in which "Remote Viewers" psychically project themselves into the minds of enemies and foreign operatives. Now these women and their daughters, descendants of the most powerful Remote Viewer, Number 512, are seeking some way to survive in a world that wants them dead.

48. "Teotwawki" Written by Chris Carter and Frank Spotnitz; Directed by Thomas J. Wright; airdate: October 16, 1998; *Guest Cast:* Brittany Tiplady (Jordan Black); Peter Outerbridge (Agent Baldwin); Stephen E. Miller (Andy McClaren); Robert Wisden

(Chris Carmody); Stephen James Lang (Gablehouse), Eric Keenleyside, Laurie Murdoch, Andrew Johnson, Michelle Skalnik, John Gingell (Carlton King); Hilary Strang (Mrs. Carmody); Jeremy Guilbaut (Brent Carmody); Sasha McLean (Tammy Meador); Keith Martin Gordey (Software Engineer).

A high school pep rally in Seattle turns terrifying when a sniper opens fire on the crowd and kills several people. The F.B.I. opens an investigation, but the stakes are higher than anyone realizes. Frank learns that Y2K and the predicted collapse of a computer-dependent American society have led some corporate executives and their high school age children to prepare for doomsday. The shooting spree may be the result of one child's feeling of hopelessness about the future ... and may be only the first such act of violence.

Note: TEOTWAWKI stands for The End of the World as We Know It.

49. "Closure" Written by Laurence Andries; Directed by Daniel Sackheim; airdate: October 23, 1998; *Guest Cast:* Garret Dillahunt (Richard Van Horn); Shelley Owens (Joanie); Michael Sunczyk (Peter); Jason Gray-Stanford (Kyle); Dee Jay Jackson (Detective Jay Cooper); Don McWilliams (Conner); Howard Siegel (Transient); Carol Alexander (Woman in Bar); Bob Dawson (Captain Kevin Mann); Tim Henry (Sheriff Taylor); Christopher R. Sumpton (Tow Driver); Robert Luft (F.P.D. Officer).

Special Agent Hollis investigates a seemingly random murder in a seedy motel wherein the shooting victim's penis has been chopped off, presumably as a trophy. The perpetrators are a pair of thugs who delight in the torment of others and even "play" at being snipers in a public park. The case strikes a special chord with Hollis, who in childhood suffered her own personal trauma and seemingly random crime when her sister, Melissa, was murdered. As Hollis struggles to understand both the crime in her past and the criminal she is pursuing, the killers claim further victims, including a hapless mountain biker who dies in a game of "William Tell."

50. "13 Years Later" Written by Michael R. Perry; Directed by Thomas J. Wright; airdate: October 30, 1998; *Guest Cast:* Jeff Yagher (Marc Bianco); Jim Pirri, Donnelly Rhodes, Matthew Walker, Kate Luyben, KISS, Stefan Arngrim (Hugo Winston); Crystal Cass (Ramona/Mary); Andre Danyliu (Major Dooley); Tanja Reichert (Ruby Dahl); Paul Stanley (Director Lew Carroll); Gene Simmonds (Hector Leachman); Ace Frehley (Sick Cop); Peter Criss (Nice Cop); Dana Grahame (Sarah Cryer); Ted Kozma (Kenny Neiderman); Morgan Brayton (Assistant Director); Guy Fauchon (Movie Sheriff); Edmond Wong and Cavan Cunningham (Gaffers).

Art imitates life when an actress on the set of a horror movie shooting in Trinity, South Carolina, is brutally murdered after a shower. Frank and Emma go to the set and Frank discovers that the film is based on a case he investigated thirteen years earlier. Thespian Marc Bianco is playing F.B.I. agent Frank Black, a bureau profiler who pursues the Madman Maniac to a KISS concert. When the case produces no useful leads, Hollis suggests that she and Frank review a selection of horror films including *Halloween*, *Psycho*, and *Friday the 13th* to help them catch the movie-obsessed psycho-killer.

51. "Skull and Bones" Written by Chip Johannessen and Ken Horton; Directed by Paul Shapiro; airdate: November 6, 1998; *Guest Cast:* Peter Outerbridge (Agent Baldwin); Arye Gross; Stephen E. Miller (Andy McClaren); C.C.H. Pounder (Cheryl Andrews); Terry O'Quinn (Peter Watts).

A freeway construction crew in Fingus, Maine, uncovers a mass unmarked grave where several skeletons are found in the mud. Peter Watts leads the investigation on behalf of the Millennium Group, but Frank also becomes involved when his section chief, McClaren, informs him that someone has sent him letters detailing several unsolved murders, with mention of Fingus. Frank tracks down the mysterious writer to Arlington, Virginia, and finds a man who has kept detailed notes about the activities of the Millennium Group for more than fifteen years.

52. "Through a Glass Darkly" Written by Patrick Harbinson; Directed by Thomas J. Wright; airdate: November 13, 1998; *Guest Cast:* Brittany Tiplady (Jordan Black); Tom McCleister (Max Brunelli); Scott Sowers, Paul Jarret, William MacDonald (Sheriff); Eileen Pedde (Karen Jarret); Karin Konoval (Dr. Angela Horvath); Ron Suave (Brunelli's Dad); Shawna Delgaty (Julie Jarret); Tiffany DesRosiers (Shannon McNulty); Michelle Hart (Casey Peterson); Jim Poyner (Judge); Marco Roy (Deputy Lucas); Anthony Ulc (Deputy Bobby).

Twenty years ago, a simpleton named Max Brunelli was arrested for abusing and murdering several adolescent girls. Now he is headed home, to the abject disgust of the community where the crimes occurred; girls are disappearing again, and Max Brunelli is the prime suspect. Frank and Emma go to the scene of the vanishing to learn the truth, but Frank becomes more and more convinced that Brunelli is innocent now ... just as he was two decades ago. Now it's a race against time to learn exactly what Brunelli knows about the real perpetrator before another innocent girl dies of starvation.

53. "Human Essence" Written by Michael Duggan; Directed by Thomas J. Wright; airdate: December 11, 1998; *Guest Cast:* Peter Outerbridge (Agent Barry Baldwin); Stephen E. Miller (Andy McClaren); Samaria Graham (Tamra Caffrey); Darryl Quon (Pulga); Rick Dobran (Johnny); Hiro Kanagawa (Detective Rondell); Winston Brown (House Staffer); Stephen Chang (Mr. Ho); Mikela J. Mikael (Elissa); Jargito D. Vargas (Young Dealer); Donald Fong (Kai Lam); David MacKay (Medical Examiner); Judi Closkey (Vancouver Trustee).

Emma Hollis is relieved of duty when she fails a random drug test for heroin. Frank is convinced his new partner is no abuser of drugs and asks for her to explain what happened. Emma refuses to talk and heads to Vancouver in search of a woman named Tamra Caffrey, whose friend died after a bad drug trip which transformed her into an in-

human-looking monster. A concerned Frank follows Emma, and between them they track down a vengeful Asian drug-trafficker who is secretly working for the U.S. government and the DEA, and putting poisoned drugs on the street.

54. "Omerta" Written by Michael R. Perry; Directed by Paul Shapiro; airdate: December 18, 1998; *Guest Cast:* Brittany Tiplady (Jordan Black); Jon Polito (Eddie Scorpino Giannini); Bob Morrissey, Tom McBeath, James DiStefano, Michelle Beauchamp, Keegan Tracy, Nelson Brown, Arthur Corber (Danny); Salvatore Sortino (Paolo Stefano); Nicole Robert (Front Desk Clerk); Patrick Keating (Dr. Rice).

At Christmas time, Frank takes Jordan on vacation to a small town where a mythical creature called Little Foot is said to exist. More bizarre than that, Frank discovers evidence of some kind of "feminine energy" in the woods, a spirit who heals those who have been killed, including a gangland hitman Eddie Giannini who was supposedly murdered on December 20, 1989. Eddie tells Frank that he is protecting a secret in the woods, but is it Little Foot, a wood sprite, or an angel who dwells in secret there? Hollis and Frank find the entrance to a secret dwelling and uncover two innocent women with extraordinary powers.

54. "Borrowed Time" Written by Chip Johannessen; Directed by Dwight Little; airdate: January 15, 1999; *Guest Cast:* Brittany Tiplady (Jordan Black); Eric Mabius (Death); Amanda Tapping (Doctor); Bill Dow (CDC Examiner); Kim Hawthorne (Nurse); Jenny Lynn Hutcheon (Little Girl); Andrea MacDonald (Girl's Mother); Tonjha Richardson (Business Woman); Colin Murdock (Business Man); Andrew Wheeler (Priest); Tom Pickett (Train Conductor); Nina Roman (Gertrude Epstein); Paul Magel (Orthodox Son); Robert Thurston (R.I.L. Director); Kerry Sandomirsky (R.I.L. Woman); David Pauls (Yuppie); Ted Cole (Paramedic); Ben Derrick (Track Controller); Ian Marsh (Track Controller); Ingrid Tesch (Mom w/Camera); Corey Storin (Patrick Varad).

In the middle of a very dry park, a woman spontaneously drowns to death. Soon, another woman suffers the same fate in equally mysterious circumstances. Frank and Emma look into the drownings and discover that both victims have survived fatal or near-fatal incidents and thereby cheated "death" of a prize. Frank suspects that "death," an evil personification, may be mad about that fact, even as Jordan, who is also living on borrowed time after surviving a bout of meningitis, has fallen ill.

55. "Collateral Damage" Written by Michael R. Perry; Directed by Thomas J. Wright; airdate: January 22, 1999; *Guest Cast:* Terry O'Quinn (Peter Watts); James Marsters (Eric Swan); Stephen E. Miller (Andy Mc-Claren); Jacinda Barrett (Taylor Watts); Art Bell (Himself); Terry David Mulligan, Brendan Fehr (Nick Carfagna); Jessica Schreier (Mrs. Watts); Bob Wilde (Mabius); Bill Merchant (David Cougar); Kaare Anderson (Raid Agent); Tony Alcantar (Chuck); David Lewis (FBI Technician); Laura Mennell (Sorority Sister #1); Kea Wong (Sorority Sister #2).

Peter Watts' daughter is kidnapped while away at college in Virginia, and Peter asks for Frank's help in rescuing her, even though there is still bad blood between them concerning the Millennium Group and Catherine's death. Frank is reluctant to help, but he and Hollis begin the search for the missing girl even as young Taylor Watts is infected with the same disease (the Marburg Variant) which killed Catherine Black and the seventy others in the outbreak in the Pacific Northwest. The culprit is a Gulf War veteran who has knowledge that the government and the Millennium Group conspired to use a deadly biological weapon against American soldiers in Kuwait, and now wants a confession from Peter Watts. The Group will not permit such an admission of guilt, so Taylor's life rests with Frank's ability to empathize with the ex-soldier.

56. "The Sound of Snow" Written by Patrick Harbinson; Directed by Paul Shapiro; airdate: February 5, 1999; *Guest Cast:* Brittany Tiplady (Jordan Black); Stephen James Lang (Detective Gablehouse); Jessica Tuck (Alice Severin); Megan Gallagher (Catherine Black); Deanna Milligan (Carol Wheatley); Christina Jastrzembrska (Mrs. Wheatley); Trevor White (Doug Scaife); Todd Ritchey (Jerry Origo); Ryan Robbins (Mailer); Mark McConchie (Home Owner).

A mysterious source is sending out static-filled audio tapes which induce hallucinations in listeners and eventually cause tragic "accidental" deaths. A woman with a secret in her past about ice and snow dies in an imaginary ice storm, and a man who was once involved with fire dies in an imagined conflagration. Frank and Emma investigate the tapes, and Frank soon receives one at his old Seattle address — at the yellow house, now painted white. As he listens to the tape, Frank finds himself reliving the outbreak near Seattle, and his last encounter with his wife, Catherine.

57. "Antipas" Written by Chris Carter and Frank Spotnitz; Directed by Thomas J. Wright; airdate: February 12, 1999; *Guest Cast:* Art Hindle (John Saxum); Stephen E. Miller (Andy McClaren); Susan Hogan (Una Saxum); Jay Brazeau (Mr. Wassanau); Rachel Victoria (Divina Saxum); Sarah-Jane Redmond (Lucy Butler); Scott Heindl (Long-Haired Man); Lloyd Berry (Gardener); Nancy Sivak (Nurse); Fulvio Cecere (Detective); John Harris (Agent); Brian Drummond (Second Agent).

Satanic Lucy Butler has found her way to the Antipas Estate of a wealthy politician hoping to become state governor. She befriends a sickly young girl, the politician's daughter, and claims to be her mother. Investigating a murder in a hotel room far away, Hollis and Frank soon find their way to Lucy in Wisconsin. Strangely, Lucy wants Frank close: she wants him to make her pregnant! In a bizarre dream, Frank is raped by Lucy ... as a horned demon ... but Lucy soon claims the opposite — that Frank was the rapist ... and she has the bruises to prove it.

58. "Matryoshka" Written by Erin Maher and Kay Reindl; Directed by Arthur Forney; airdate: February 19, 1999; *Guest Cast:*

Barbara Bain (Lily Unser); Peter Outerbridge (Agent Barry Baldwin); Dean Winters, Mark Houghton, Peter Hanlon, David Fredericks, Marie Stillin (Natalie); Wally Dalton, Matthew Walker, Terry O'Quinn (Peter Watts); Ocean Hellman (Young Lily Unser); Vince Metcalfe (General Groves); Mecca Menaro (Young Natalie); Monica Gemmer (Secretary); Tiffany Burns (Reporter); Alex Ferguson (Dr. Caton); Jim Thornburn (Agent).

An aging F.B.I. agent kills himself, leaving only the cryptic message "it must end." Emma and Frank investigate his suicide and realize it has something to do with a bizarre case from 1945, a case involving the atom bomb, murdered scientists at Los Alamos, a fledgling Millennium Group spearheaded by J. Edgar Hoover himself, and the atomic splitting of a man's good and evil qualities. Hours before Agent Lanyard committed suicide, he was visited by Peter Watts, who is once more protecting a Group secret: a scientist from 1945 sought to split his soul as he had split the atom, creating an evil doppelganger called Kroll. Now, Kroll's child has grown up to repeat her father's mistake in "playing God."

59. "Forcing the End" Written by Marjorie David; Directed by Thomas J. Wright; airdate: March 20, 1999; *Guest Cast:* Andreas Katsulas (Gorovich); Stephen E. Miller (McLaren); Juliet Landau (Jean Cohen Borenstein); Peter Wilds (Daniel Borenstein); Shae Popovich (Rachel); Terry O'Quinn (Peter Watts); Jason Emanuel (Cult Member); Klodyne Rodney (Security Guard); Anthony Santiago (Print Tech).

An expectant Jewish woman is abducted from her home in New York by a strange cult which has plans for the unborn child. The cult wants to rebuild a temple in Jerusalem (over a mosque) that will trigger the return of the messiah and bring about the end of the world, and the baby represents the future of the priesthood in the so-called third temple. Peter Watts and the Millennium Group become involved, and Hollis suspects that such involvement is evil ... but McLaren makes it clear

that such suspicions are unacceptable. Now Frank and Emma must save the newly born baby, discover the reason behind Peter Watts' interest in the case, and prevent the end of the world.

60. "Saturn Dreaming of Mercury" Written by Jordan Hawley and Chip Johannesen; Directed by Paul Shapiro; airdate: April 9, 1999; *Guest Cast:* Brittany Tiplady (Jordan Black); Michael Boishever (Will Sanderson); Colleen Winton (Jean Sanderson); Dillon Moen, Gabrielle Rose, Jane Perry (Principal Hawes); Connor Widdows (Calvin); Helen Taylor (ER Nurse); Ian Robison (ER Doctor); O'Neil Mark (Police Officer); Paul Dickson (Firefighter); Sarah Jane Redmond (Lucy Butler).

Young Jordan has a vision of a little boy named Lucas, a new classmate, in danger. She sees his father as a demonic creature and tries to warn the boy, but Lucas seems afraid of her. Frank grows worried when Jordan begins to behave badly in school and starts talking to an imaginary friend named Simon. Worse, she insists that Lucas's father is a murderer who killed a woman in Phoenix. Jordan soon enters Lucas's house illicitly and finds a weird collection of antique glass eyeballs, as well as a much darker secret.

61. "Darwin's Eye" Written by Patrick Harbinson; Directed by Ken Fink; airdate: April 16, 1999; *Guest Cast:* Peter Outerbridge (Agent Baldwin); Tracy Middendorf (Cassie Doyle); Peter Simmonds (Joe McNulty); Kevin McNulty, John Beasley, Lesley Ewen (Dr. Heath); Alfred E. Humphrey (Sheriff Randall); Alex Zahara (Dane); Kurt Evans (Clerk); Cam Chai (Ranjiti Patel); Shawna Delgaty (Young Cass).

A mute psychiatric patient named Cassie escapes from her high-security facility after seven years, leaving behind a decapitated corpse and a cell wall filled with mysterious and prophetic writings. Frank and Emma investigate both the current crime and the seven-year-old murder of Cassie Doyle's parents ... which she claims was committed by men in suits. The clue central to this case turns out to be the symbol of two wild palms … .and a secret rape from the girl's childhood also figures prominently. Meanwhile, Emma's father becomes sick and starts mailing origami palm trees to her.

62. "Bardo Thodol" Written by Virginia Stock and Chip Johannesen; Directed by Thomas J. Wright; airdate: April 23, 1999; *Guest Cast:* Brittany Tiplady (Jordan Black); James Hong (Monk); Stephen E. Miller (McLaren); Tzi Ma (Dr. Steven Takahashi); Terry O'Quinn (Peter Watts); Bob Wilde (Mabius); Trevor White (Doug Scaife); Patrick McManus (Agent); Daniel Bacon (Bio Tech); Jefferson Dylan (Harbor Cop); Hiro Kanagawa (Shopkeeper); Kevan Ohtsji (Hotel Clerk); Anees Peterman (Receptionist); Sean Millington (Guard).

Working on a supposedly routine case, Emma discovers a cooler filled with severed human hands aboard a Japanese ship, even as Frank's computer is infiltrated by a virus which warns him of a coming apocalypse. Calligraphy on the wall of the Japanese ship repeats the same cryptic warning. An F.B.I. investigation soon reveals that the human hands are growing, alive somehow, and a computer tech studying the virus reports that it is continually rewriting itself, like a snake eating its own tail (the symbol of the Millennium Group). As Frank and Emma conduct their separate investigations, they become involved with a Millennium Group organization called Emergen Corps and a project involving the transubstantiation of the human species.

63. "Seven in One" Written by Chris Carter and Frank Spotnitz; Directed by Peter Markle; airdate: April 30, 1999; *Guest Cast:* Brittany Tiplady (Jordan Black); Stephen E. Miller (McLaren); Maxine Miller (Psychologist); Bob Wilde (Mabius); Dean Norris (Boxer); Ken Pogue.

On Jordan's eighth birthday, Frank receives in the mail a series of digitally enhanced photographs depicting him dead in his own bath tub. A special F.B.I. profiler assists Frank and Emma to find the killer, and the key seems to be Frank's childhood fear of drowning. Soon, the profiler suspects that Frank is having another breakdown and that he is in fact responsible for the odd events. When Frank begins to believe he has lost his mind, he decides it is time to quit the F.B.I.

64. "Nostalgia" Written by Michael R. Perry; Directed by Thomas J. Wright; airdate: May 7, 1999; *Guest Cast:* April Telek (Liddy Hopper); Jem Griffin (Lana); Lisa Marie Caruk (Jan McCall); Jim Shield (Lee Smith); Blake Stovin (Deputy Wayne Johnson); Ron Small (Ron Hauge); Ian Brown (Minister); Paul Cehvreau (Grave Digger); Madeleine Campbell (Cora); Kaitlyn Burke (Alicia); Linnea Sharples (Alicia's Mom); R. David Stephens (Agent).

A brutal murder leads Frank and Emma back to Emma's hometown, where dangerous secrets soon spill out and cause turmoil. The recent murder can only be solved by examining a similar murder from five years ago, a case which seems to implicate many of the men on the local police force. The victim then was a promiscuous young woman, a local, and her death may have been the springboard for a serial killer who hoped to be caught and was disappointed by society when he remained free.

65. "Via Dolorosa" Written by Marjorie David and Patrick Harbinson; Directed by Paul Shapiro; airdate May 14, 1999; *Guest Cast:* Terry O'Quinn (Peter Watts); Brittany Tiplady (Jordan Black); Peter Outerbridge (Baldwin); John Beasley, Matthew Glave, Jeff Parise, Kevin McNulty, Ken Roberts (Warden); Mark Humphrey (Marcetti); Andrew Wheeler (Father Murray); Trevor White (Doug Scaife); Carla White (Cyndie Dryden); Paul Kane (John Dryden); John Mann (Detective Krebbe); Sarah Macauley (Maria Jones); Frida Betrani (Art Teacher); Khaire E. (Susan Suzie).

While Emma continues to cope with her terminally ill father, she and Frank investigate the brutal murders of a young suburban couple. After viewing the crime scene, Frank becomes convinced that the killer is actually a man whom he saw executed in the electric chair weeks earlier. Peter Watts approaches Emma with a possible cure for her father — in exchange for two things: her complicity with and loyalty to the Millennium Group, and her assistance in forcing Frank out of the FBI.

66. "Goodbye to All This" Written by Ken Horton and Chip Johannesen; Directed by Thomas J. Wright; airdate: May 21, 1999; *Guest Cast:* Brittany Tiplady (Jordan); Terry O'Quinn (Peter Watts); Peter Outerbridge (Baldwin); Stephen E. Miller (McLaren); John Beasley, Jeff Parise, Kevin McNulty, Jade Malle.

While continuing to pursue a vicious serial killer, Franks grows convinced that the Millennium Group is involved in the death of special agent Baldwin. McLaren plans to retire from the bureau, leaving Emma Hollis in charge ... but he is unaware that she is being courted by the Millennium Group. Frank confronts Peter Watts, suspecting that the Millennium Group wants him back and will do anything to get him — even trigger another mental breakdown, and even threaten the life of Jordan. Soon, a startling betrayal is in the offing, a high-ranking Millennium Group member is killed in a bloody assassination, and an unexpected flight from this paranoid, dangerous world of betrayal and shifting loyalty follows.

33

Buffy the Vampire Slayer (1997–)

CRITICAL RECEPTION

"It's *Romeo and Juliet* in black leather and mini skirts. Sarah Michelle Gellar as Buffy may have finally kicked asunder that tired cliché of the screaming maiden in distress. Here is a heroine who can be sexy without being trashy, tough without resorting to twisted variations of machismo, and funny without the forced goofiness prevalent in today's comedy. It's the best the WB has to offer ... so catch up with the narrative ... and give its horror and humor a chance ... just about the best horror show on television."— Frederick C. Szebin, *Cinefantastique*: "Horror on Television," October 1997, page 119.

"a wry satire of suburban teenage life ... and a post-feminist parable on the challenge of balancing one's personal and work life ... Buffy has vampires to kill, but she also has to find time for boys and Ben & Jerry's."— *Time Magazine*, December 29, 1997, page 137.

"a slam-bang series that prides itself on its blithe knowingness and sarcasm and just keeps getting better at juggling hilarity, gothic romance, and horror ... no show this side of *Seinfeld* loves the language of conversation (the wisecrack, the pun, the withering retort, and the muttered aside) as much ... Give series creator Joss Whedon credit; no other show balances so many elements as deftly, without a trace of corniness or melodrama."— Ken Tucker, *Entertainment Weekly*: "Ouija Broads," November 6, 1998.

"a literal scream and always a hoot. Better yet, it's smart, with unfailingly glib dialogue that's more believable than *Dawson's Creek*'s hyperbabble."— Matt Roush, *TV Guide*, January 2-8, 1999, page 23.

"she's hyper-responsible about her ... chores, a sort of Bionic Woman with a superior work ethic. It sounds odd and goofy and off-putting, this gothic drama for the Clearasil nation. But aside from the self-aware, brand-name-and-psychotherapy-rich patter, the show is the pretty traditional story of a girl in search of herself and the guy she loves."— Barbara Lippert, *New York*: "Hey There, Warrior Girl," December 15, 1997, page 25.

FORMAT

High school student, blonde bombshell, and teenage shopping queen Buffy Summers (Sarah Michelle Gellar) has learned that she is the "Chosen One," a super strong "slayer" of vampires who only comes along once in a generation. Buffy discovers her destiny not a moment too soon, because she and her single mother (Kristine Sutherland) have just moved to Sunnydale, a cheery little southern California town which happens to sit over a portal to hell known affectionately by demons as the "Hellmouth." Buffy's vampire slaying skills are required immediately, and the high school student is trained by a British "watcher," Rupert Giles (Anthony Stewart Head), who also works as the high school librarian. Along with her friends, Xander (Nicholas Brendan), a good-humored geek, Willow (Alyson Hannigan), a sweet-hearted innocent and budding witch, Cordelia (Charisma Carpenter), a rich snob, and later Oz (Seth Green), a werewolf with his own band, Buffy fights not only blood-sucking vampires, but robots ("Ted"), humanoids from the deep ("Go Fish"), parasitic puppet masters ("Bad Eggs"), fraternity cultists who serve a lizard God ("Reptile Boy"), demonic under-dwellers ("Anne"), the grim personification of death itself ("Killed by Death"), abusive Dr. Jekyll/Mr. Hyde boyfriends ("Beauty and the Beasts"), zombies ("Dead Man's Party"), and the like. In addition to these guest beasties, the intrepid Buffy has faced a recurring main villain for each of the three seasons she has been staking vampires before a TV audience. In the first season, evil was represented by a bald Nosferatu-like demon called the Master; in the second by Drusilla and Spike, a vampire *Bonnie and Clyde* team; and in the third by a Mr. Rogers like town mayor who was planning to ascend to full demonhood come graduation day in the spring. Also in the third season, Buffy faced off against her greatest, most interesting opponent yet: a fellow slayer named Faith (Eliza Dushku) who came to serve the evil mayor as the season progressed.

Of course, no description of *Buffy the Vampire Slayer* would be complete without a mention of one of its most popular and successful components: the doomed love affair between Buffy and Angel (David Boreanaz), a vampire with a (sometimes) soul. Although the flip-sounding title of this series indicates a juvenile romp, nothing could be further from the truth. This show is one of the best things to happen to the horror genre in the last thirty years. As *Forever Knight* employed vampirism as a metaphor for alcoholism and addiction, so does *Buffy* use supernatural happenings/creatures to describe the terror of adolescence and growing up. Thus Buffy learns firsthand that boys change after sex when she makes love to Angel and he consequently loses his soul, and so on. Clever, funny, and often unbelievably tragic, *Buffy the Vampire Slayer* is so much better than its title suggests.

Buffy the Vampire Slayer began airing on the new WB network in winter of 1997, and it has been a fixture of Monday and Tuesday nights ever since. Buffy will soon return for a fourth season, but format changes are in the offing: Angel and Cordelia are leaving Sunny-

dale (and the series) for their own spin-off, and therefore ending the *Romeo and Juliet* aspect of the series which has worked so beautifully for three years.

HISTORY

It is probably fair (though a little cruel) to state that not many people had high hopes for a TV series based on the film *Buffy the Vampire Slayer* (1992). The film, starring Kristy Swanson, Luke Perry, Donald Sutherland, Paul Reubens, and Rutger Hauer, was a bit of a letdown: a horror comedy that was neither particularly scary nor particularly amusing. It was a mildly fun picture, to be sure, concerning a popular but moderately dim-witted girl who found that she was the "Chosen One," a human being genetically destined to kill vampires. Still, the central joke of the film was well-constructed as one of purposeful contrasts. On one hand, Buffy was just Buffy, a vapid, selfish mall-rat who loved to shop at malls, go to dances, and attract the boys. This side of Buffy was epitomized by her chic put-down line "you are *sooo* five minutes ago."

On the other hand, Buffy was also the vampire slayer, a rather serious-sounding position with all kinds of responsibilities and dangers attached. The very title of the piece, *Buffy the Vampire Slayer*, exemplified perfectly the contrast, and the central joke, of the picture. In concept, this conceit of contrasts forced together in one package, a teenage girl, is quite good, and even artistic, but the direction and execution of the theme by director Frank Rubel Kuzui left more than a little to be desired. In particular, a flabby Rutger Hauer did not capture the right tone of menace necessary to make his master vampire seem a real danger. With no significant threat in *Buffy the Vampire Slayer,* there was no real conflict, and the movie was listless instead of rousing. Still, the picture was a modest success, even though it failed to walk the successful line of horror/comedy that *Fright Night* (1985) and *Return of the Living Dead* (1985) had so adroitly managed.

Joss Whedon, the talented writer who conceived *Buffy the Vampire Slayer*, was not particularly pleased with the finished film either. He had wanted the picture to be scary, funny, and hip, and he had the smarts and awareness to realize that not all the notes he had strived for in his screenplay had been perfectly reached by the movie. Whedon, something of a *wunderkind* for his rewrite of *Speed* (1994), his screenplay for the popular animated hit *Toy Story* (1995), and his series-reviving script for the fourth in the long-lived *Alien* series, *Alien Resurrection* (1997), thus took matters into his own hands and decided in late 1996 to revive the *Buffy* concept ... as a weekly television series. Again, it is safe to say that few held out hope that a TV show, based on a tepid movie, would be any good. Dimming expectations further, the show was slotted to air on a fledgling sixth network from Warner Brothers called the WB, a network that, unlike the UPN (which had *Star Trek: Voyager* to its credit, at least), seemed to have no dramatic programming on its schedule ... just black-culture oriented situation comedies which seemed to appeal only to the lowest common denominator.

Amazingly, through a combination of several factors, including the maligned venue of a sixth network with the patience to let its product grow, the TV series *Buffy the Vampire Slayer* emerged in early 1997 as the surprise critical and viewer success of the season. Critics understood immediately what Whedon was striving for this time, and the contrast between Buffy the teenager and Buffy the slayer of vampires was captured far more skillfully.

It is difficult to list all the myriad ways in which the TV offshoot of *Buffy* managed to surpass (by miles) the quality of the original early-'90s film. One should make mention of the fact that Joss Whedon re-imagined Buffy not as the popular queen bitch of high school, but as a sympathetic, resourceful girl whose position as vampire slayer made her every bit as much an outcast as the geek, the nerd, the band fag, or the plain Jane. That she came from a broken home with a single parent made

her even more likable and sympathetic. That her watcher became a surrogate father figure also added considerably to the human equation, which the show has generated so competently. But mostly, this reconception of the title character as a recognizable, likable (rather than snide) human being was vitally important to the success of the new series. Equally impressive was the skill and charisma of the actress who was contracted to play her. Sarah Michelle Gellar (late of the TV soap *All My Children*) brought a combination of virtues to her TV portrayal of this new hero. She combined strength, self-discipline, and determination with healthy, athletic good looks. She meshed a rapier wit with a soft, vulnerable side. She transmitted a high level of humanity to the horror stories that few young actresses could have managed. Quite simply, Gellar ended up giving a consistently superb performance in a role which had once belonged exclusively in the "dumb blonde" category. Were not most award-givers prejudiced against horror as a genre, Sarah Michelle Gellar (*I Know What You Did Last Summer* [1997], *Scream 2* [1997], *Small Soldiers* [1998]) would certainly have been nominated (and won) three Emmy Awards by now. She really is that good on this show. She *carries* the drama as easily as Buffy trades quips with vampires or changes (always fashionable) clothes. If there is a Sarah Michelle Gellar fan club out there, sign this author up!

Whedon then did something else that was brilliant when he reconceptualized *Buffy the Vampire Slayer*. He surrounded his new Buffy with likable, distinct characters who were all outcasts in the wild jungle of high school life: the nerd-geek Xander (a child of alcoholics), the smart kid Willow (neglected by her psychologist mother), and the band boy Oz (a werewolf). The audience soon came to identify with each of these outcasts as they banded together to become something meaningful: a vampire slaying brigade. Also part of the gang was the show's primary comedic relief, Cordelia Chase, a sarcastic, popular girl who resembled the Buffy character of the film. Cordelia's presence kept the wit and put-down quotient of the series high, and was a pointed contrast to the redesigned, more human Buffy. Cordelia, Xander, Buffy, Willow, and Oz have become what several sources have termed "The Scooby Gang" because they resemble the characters of the *Scooby Doo* cartoon (smart girl; pretty girl; dopey guy); but that easy hook does not encompass all the elements of these fine characters, all of whom have emerged over the years as truly interesting, likable people.

The last character in the modified *Buffy the Vampire Slayer* mix is Angel, a 244-year-old vampire who is attempting to make amends for his time as a murderer and consumer of human blood. Angel is played in angst-ridden, hunky fashion by David Boreanaz. Importantly, Angel was conceived as a vampire of the postmodern variety. Thus he looks more like a leather-jacket garbed gang member than a haughty European count, and he follows the interesting addiction model captured on television earlier by Geraint Wyn-Davies' characterization of hero Nick Knight on *Forever Knight*. What makes Angel's presence on *Buffy* so important is his personal relationship with the title character. As one of the above reviews indicates, the Angel/Buffy relationship elevated *Buffy the Vampire Slayer* above its comedy of contrasts and action-horror. The series really did become a kind of horror *Romeo and Juliet*, with two star-crossed lovers (one human, one vampire) trying to make things work. Accordingly, several episodes of the series played as modern tragedy when Buffy had to confront various facets of her relationship with Angel (including the fact that he would never grow old, that he could not face sunlight, and that he would lose his soul every time he had sex!).

Although Joss Whedon had created a format in which he could discuss almost any issue involving contemporary American teens, he had also invented an action-adventure world of intense martial-arts fights, where kicking-butt and comic book-style action was as important as Buffy's high school life (since it was the other facet of her two-sided life). Whedon once discussed what he was aiming for in his poetic, ballet of horror and how his characters were intended to be seen:

> I invoke about five genres ... I love superheroes. I was a comic-book boy. I tend to create universes with the kind of sophomoric emotional bigness that really exists only in comic books and TV. I am very old-fashioned about heart and story. I don't watch *Seinfeld*. It's the coldest show on TV ... I don't care about these people. If I'm making the emotional connection to the person ... the person ... could be an amoeba. The show [*Buffy*] is about disenfranchisement, about the people nobody takes seriously.[1]

Those people that "nobody takes seriously" were proven to be valuable commodities in Sunnydale again and again, making a clear statement to teens around America that one need not conform or buckle under to be successful or proud. *Buffy the Vampire Slayer* is really television's ultimate statement about peer pressure and the (perceived) need to be like others in high school. If Xander, Buffy, or Willow were to neglect their gifts, or hide their gifts, Sunnydale would be overrun with vampires, robots, werewolves, and other ghouls many times over. Thus *Buffy the Vampire Slayer* is a positive role model for teens, despite the fact that it has sometimes been viewed (wrongly) as encouraging violence.

As this text has hopefully explained, horror television can often be a venue through which important, relevant, or illuminating comments on modern society can be forwarded without being heavy-handed or obvious. This author considers the best horror shows to be those productions which manage to be *about* something other than blood, guts, and suspense. The science versus faith didacticism of *The X-Files*, the "nature of evil" study of *Millennium*, the fiercely individual *Kolchak: The Night Stalker*, the redemption study of *Brimstone*, the gadfly commentary of *Rod Serling's Night Gallery*, the addiction model of *Forever Knight* ... these are artistic components which really elevate the quality of the genre. *Buffy the Vampire Slayer* belongs on the select "ten best of horror" list because it sneaks in relevant points about contemporary society (specifically issues revolving around adolescence and high school) in humorous and often subtle ways. For instance, the monsters of the show are rarely just monsters. Instead, they tend to represent something more than "evil": the family interloper who wants to date Mom ("Ted"), the hypocrisy of moral watch-guards ("Gingerbread"), hidden desires released ("Doppelgangland"), abusive boyfriends ("Beauty and the Beasts"), and so forth. What this author is saying then is that Joss Whedon follows proudly in the tradition of Gene Roddenberry, Rod Serling, and Chris Carter, TV artists who take special pains to assure that their visions have relevance and importance beyond the selling of detergent or fast food. Early on, Whedon found that his social commentary was accepted, if not openly encouraged, by the venue of the show, the WB:

> They [the WB network] really let me get away with murder. They get what the show is, how strange it is, how all over the place and how sometimes very edgy it is. We've never had a story thrown out or a real disaster ... But they do get what we're doing, and that's rare.[2]

This remark would come back to haunt Whedon in the series' third season, when events in real life would have a disastrous impact on *Buffy the Vampire Slayer*. Before that lowpoint, however, *Buffy* managed to survive an abbreviated (thirteen shows) first season, and head triumphantly right into its second season. By that point, the series was garnering great reviews, and Whedon had stuck with his plan to feature a different recurring villain in each season. During the second season, the horrifying happened when Buffy had to fight her lover, Angel, who had lost his soul because of a gypsy curse. In the final show of the second season, "Becoming," Buffy had finally worked up the courage and strength to finish off her once lover (he had already killed Ms. Calendar, Giles' girlfriend) but at the last possible moment, Willow's magic spell worked and Angel returned to his previous, human, self. The story, again echoing the details and feel of *Romeo and Juliet*, turned even more tragic when Buffy was forced to kill Angel anyway.

Before returning to his "good" state, Angel had opened the doorway to hell and only his death, his blood, could now close it. Thus poor Buffy, a lonely teenager, had to sacrifice the one man she loved to save the world ... and TV drama does not get much bigger or tragic than that. "Becoming" won *Buffy* legions of fans, and set the stage for the third season.

Buffy returned in the fall of 1998 to the WB line up as part of "New Tuesday." It aired at 8:00 P.M. and was followed by the angst-ridden college drama *Felicity* (1998–). The season introduced a host of new elements: a new villain (Mayor Wilkins), the return of Angel from hell, college worries for the so-called Scooby Gang, and the addition of a sociopath (but oh so sexy!) vampire slayer named Faith who changed allegiances midseason to serve evil. By now, *Buffy* was the recipient of some major buzz. *TV Guide*'s critic, Matt Roush, was widely and loudly proclaiming that the show should be nominated for one or several Emmy Awards, and Sarah Michelle Gellar was heading straight to superstardom (though her 1999 features were greeted with mixed feelings: *Simply Irresistible* flopped, but *Cruel Intentions* hit).

While *Buffy* was riding high from its best season yet, however, tragedy struck. Far away, in Littleton, Colorado, at an affluent high school called Columbine, a duo of high school-age crazies who called themselves "The Trenchcoat Mafia" went on a killing spree. The bloody event became major news in America, and the Republican Party, realizing that it would suffer pretty dire consequences if Americans finally focused in on its right-wing ties with the National Rifle Association and its neverending push for unlimited gun availability, launched a counter-offensive at Hollywood, films, and TV. Yes, the reactionary political party which claims that they want *less* government involvement in all matters hypocritically came forward to push for heavy government involvement in what Americans see on their TV and movie screens. Sadly, *Buffy the Vampire Slayer* was a casualty of this political war, as it was the only high school horror show on the air at the time. Under pressure from various moral watchdogs, the WB pulled "Earshot" out of *Buffy*'s episode roster, fearing its guns and school theme would be misperceived as "encouraging" violence in teens. Worse than that, the final episode of the third season arc, "Graduation Day, Part II," was also yanked before broadcast. The latter decision was especially ridiculous, as the episode featured high school students of *all* cliques working together to quash the villainous mayor's ascension. Yes, the students were armed (with torches and crossbows, for heaven's sake!) but the message of teamwork was a very positive one that only Henry Hyde, Orrin Hatch, and their ilk could be dull-witted enough to misinterpret. As is usual, politicians picked the wrong target, and *Buffy* fans suffered the consequences of a witchhunt (similar to the one that the episode "Gingerbread" had dramatized the very same season!).

The Columbine incident's political fallout effectively ruined *Buffy*'s season-long, suspenseful build to a terrific, heartfelt conclusion. Fortunately, it will not happen again: Buffy is going away to college and the "dangerous" high school years of its development are now over. Still, this censorship incident again points to the fact that some people in Washington, D.C., want to control what others watch, and tend to lump all horror together as "bad" while lauding sophomoric melodrama such as *Touched by An Angel* and *7th Heaven* as "good" Christian entertainment. If just one of the loud-mouthed conservative "moral watch-guards" sat down and watched two or three episodes of *Buffy the Vampire Slayer*, they might realize what a good, solid role-model it is for teens.

This author has always believed that art imitates life, not vice versa, but many in Washington would rather blame shows like *Buffy the Vampire Slayer* for incidents such as Columbine or Jonesboro than look at the root causes of such crimes: parental neglect and the easy availability of powerful firearms. The WB, whom Whedon had once asserted was being quite supportive of *Buffy*, had responded to the Columbine incident with what Matt Roush called "too much sensitivity." *Buffy* was never the problem. Ever.

"Graduation Day, Part II" finally aired July 13, 1999, almost a full two months after its scheduled airdate in May. "Earshot" was held back even longer, more than four months, until September 21, 1999. Despite being at the center of a political nightmare, *Buffy the Vampire Slayer* did not close out 1999 in shame or under a cloud. On the contrary, fans were buoyed by the announcement that a spin-off from the show called *Angel* would appear in the fall of '99, starring Boreanaz and Carpenter. Although some fans worried that the removal of Angel and Cordelia from the *Buffy* format would spell trouble for the show, others looked forward to what Whedon promised would be a darker peek into the *Buffy* universe, set in nighttime Los Angeles.

Already a television classic that has inspired one knock-off (the inferior WB show *Charmed* [1998–]), *Buffy* and *Angel* landed for a new season on October 5, 1999. They are scheduled back-to-back, so fans could get a healthy helping of Joss Whedon's literate, funny, and endearing horror masterpiece. Perhaps it was Sarah Michelle Gellar, Buffy herself, who once described the show's appeal in the most elegant, and simple, terms:

> What I like about the show is that it reminds you it's O.K. to be different. What people think isn't necessary true. If people walk away with half of that, we've done our job.[3]

CRITICAL COMMENTARY

Joss Whedon's *Buffy the Vampire Slayer*, along with *The X-Files* and *Millennium*, may just be the best reason to watch network television as America approaches the 21st century. Though some closed-minded people may *never* take this show seriously simply because of its quasi-comedic title, *Buffy* is nonetheless a terrific excursion into terror TV, and one video voyage that is very different from the popular imaginings of Chris Carter. In a world of *The X-Files*' clones (from *Nowhere Man* and *Strange Luck* to *The Burning Zone* and *Dark Skies*), *Buffy the Vampire Slayer* is perhaps the only horror show on the air with such a high degree of originality, and its own distinctive mo-jo. It cares little about scientific explanations, or the world of rationality and enlightenment. After all, what does the high school experience have to do with reality or enlightenment?

A real (and constant) joy of *Buffy the Vampire Slayer* is its witty, razor-sharp dialogue, which is deployed not just for laughs, but to succinctly and efficiently build and reveal character. Xander's reluctant heroism is spotlighted in "The Witch" when he states, straight-faced: "I laugh in the face of danger … then I run and hide." Cordelia's innate insensitivity and selfishness is expressed through any number of funny lines, but her best quip may be the withering interrogative she first levels at Buffy in "Welcome to the Hellmouth": "God!? What is *your* childhood trauma?!" Faith's lack of conscience and abuse of slayer power is perfectly captured through her three word manifesto, heard in "Bad Girls" "Want … take … have." Epitomizing his sensitivity and dignity, Giles is told at one point in "Helpless," that he has a "father's love for the girl" (meaning Buffy). There could be no better a description of this character. The dialogue of *Buffy* is wonderfully individual, a far cry from other cookie-cutter lines on most shows.

The marvelous Buffy uses language to reveal much about herself. Her insecurity about returning to school is the focus in "Dead Man's Party" when she brings up home schooling, stating that it isn't "just for scary religious people anymore." Her love for Angel is almost tangible in "The Prom" when she earnestly declares that "I want my life to be with you," and so forth. For a would-be vapid mall-chick, Buffy manipulates the English language like a pro … and it works beautifully for this show.

Even the villains are given brilliant dialogue to utter on this series. In "Gingerbread," Buffy's mother is possessed by the spirits of Hansel and Gretel and she suddenly becomes a moral-guardian, a "reactionary" to all the vi-

olence in society. The ridiculous nature (and slippery slope) of censorship is revealed when Ms. Summers states, solemnly, of the school library: "Any student could waltz in there and get any kind of ideas!" Indeed, some people might even say that ideas are a library's stock and trade! But as Buffy's mother inadvertently reveals, some people think that ideas are dangerous and should be controlled. Other examples are equally witty. A malfunctioning, 1950s robot weaned on *Father Knows Best* backhands Buffy and then asks her "How about a nice game of Parcheesi?" in "Ted." Of her monstrous, abusive boyfriend in "Beauty and the Beasts," a teenager named Debbie states: "It's not his fault. He's not himself when he gets this way. It's nothing … it's me. I make him crazy." Talk about a perfect encapsulation of the enabling, victim mentality! Thus the writing, particularly the dialogue, of *Buffy* is clever and purposeful, a far cry from most TV dramas, where boring exposition is mixed with tepid lines lacking motivation, a voice, or even a degree of charm.

Delightfully, *Buffy* is also savagely sharp-witted in its visual jokes (which also build character)! In "Bad Girls," the evil mayor (played by Harry Groener) who is hoping to soon ascend to full demonhood, opens his office closet casually. Inside are skulls, weapons, and occult items of all varieties … as well as a box of Wet Naps! Not surprisingly, the same episode features this prissy villain checking off a "to do" list which features the odd task of "becoming invincible" alongside such mundane tasks as "pick up laundry" and "write speech." Simply put, this show is a riot. And, though its villains are sometimes treated with humor, they never lose their sense of menace. This mayor is not only funny, and scary, he is touching. In "Graduation Day, Part II" his one weakness, which Buffy capitalizes on, is his affection for Faith. On *Buffy*, even the evil sometimes feel love.

Rather than taking *The X-Files* approach of leveling social commentary at a variety of interesting topics, *Buffy* restricts its conscience, its voice, to a smaller playing field, specifically the issues involved with growing up, with the teen set. "Ted" captures perfectly the conflicting feelings a child of a single parent might experience when a new, would-be spouse enters the picture and begins to date Mom. Buffy dislikes Ted (guest John Ritter, in a hysterical guest role) not only because she feels like she is being replaced, but because she suddenly feels inferior to and less important than this nurturing, charming interloper in her family unit. It does not help Buffy to accept Ted, of course, that he is a chauvinist, Stepford Dad robot bent on creating a perfect 1950s household. "Reptile Boy" finds a metaphor for fraternity parties, date rape, and hazing by imagining a very special fraternity which is actually a cult. The cult members, all good looking college athletes and studs, drug, capture, and nearly sacrifice Cordelia and Buffy to a hungry Snake God who promises them success in their careers. Talk about moving with a fast crowd! Likewise, "The Witch" dramatizes how nostalgic parents sometimes attempt to recapture their glory days and re-experience their high school years when a nasty witch usurps her daughter's body and tries out for the cheerleading squad!

On *Buffy*, this supernatural road map to the process of growing up just keeps becoming more interesting, and more complex. In "Invisible Girl," an unpopular student who feels ignored *literally* becomes invisible after being metaphorically invisible to her classmates for years. In "Band Candy," adults regress and become teenagers, and the young protagonists are allowed to see how their erratic behavior might look from an adult perspective. At the same time, the adult cast members are reminded what it is like to be carefree, a little less uptight. Indeed, no aspect of modern high school life has been left unexamined on *Buffy*, much to the show's credit.

To wit: student rights and censorship inform "Gingerbread." That the once open-ended future might be limited because of identity and choices is a subject broached in "Lover's Walk." Postsex brush-offs are the underlying subject of "Surprise" and "Innocence," wherein Angel has intercourse with Buffy and then promptly loses his soul. Youth-

ful indiscretions like alcohol and drugs find a supernatural analogy in "The Dark Age" when Giles reveals his wild adolescence and a kind of "high" that involves dangerous demonic possession. The aforementioned "Beauty and the Beasts" is about abusive relationships and the people who stay in them for lack of self-esteem, but in this case, the "bad" boyfriend is a Dr. Jekyll/Mr. Hyde character transformed by a chemical reaction. "Go Fish" rigorously explores several teen-oriented topics: the use of steroids in high school athletics (which in this case transforms the Sunnydale swim team into sea monsters), the "win" mentality of high school authorities such as coaches, and even the special treatment that athletes receive because of their physical prowess and the trophies they bring home. On top of all that, "Go Fish" is an off-kilter homage to "B" sea monster movies of the 1950s and '60s such as *The Horror of Party Beach* (1964) and *The Creature from the Black Lagoon* (1954), as well as more recent water-based horror fare like *Jaws* (1975) and *Humanoids from the Deep* (1980). The competitive nature of high school life is bemoaned in "Homecoming," an episode in which Buffy and Cordelia wage an all-out war to win the coveted title of Homecoming Queen. As Buffy warns her opponent, "you've awakened the Prom Queen within." Impressively, the Cordelia/Buffy competition is mirrored with a slayer rivalry (Buffy and Faith) and with the "Baddies" of the week, a troop of bounty hunters who are competing against one another for the honor of killing Buffy. Other *Buffy*'s are just as interesting and as artful. The episodes deal with teen pregnancy ("Bad Eggs"), balancing responsibilities ("Never Kill a Boy on the First Date"), and even the good girl who wishes she could be bad ("Doppelgangland"). The final episode of the third season, "Graduation Day," issues the show's ultimate statement on high school life when the joyous graduates and heroes proclaim, emphatically, "*We survived.*" They are referring not just to their war with evil, but the entire high school experience. So on *Buffy*, high school equals terror. Anyone who has lived through high school and wondered if survival was a possibility knows just how potent this series equation really is.

The very worst thing this reviewer could do is to leave readers with the impression that *Buffy the Vampire Slayer* is like some whacked out *Afterschool Special*, filled with "messages." That is simply not so. First and foremost, *Buffy* is a rock 'em sock 'em action/horror series. What makes it great is simply that it uses the language of horror (vampires, werewolves, humanoids from the deep) not just to titillate or scare, but to make relevant points about a turbulent period of life that everyone must face. Because high school is a universal experience, *Buffy* is not quite the "feminist" show that some critics have called it. It is true that Buffy is a woman, and that Joss Whedon writes women extraordinarily well. However, *Buffy* is really post-feminist because sexual identity is not the main issue of the show. *Buffy* is a very beautiful, very sensitive woman, and she is also a hero. The show does not question that fact or make allowances or pronouncements based on Buffy's sex. *Buffy* is a humanist drama about a universal experience.

As for the horror elements of this series, well, they could not be better. This is *not* the metaphysical, fin de siècle horror of *Millennium*, the straight-faced scientific horror of *The X-Files* or the "bad trip" hallucination horror of *Twin Peaks*. Instead it is, as Whedon has asserted, comic book horror: fun scares coupled with a comedic flair. Still, *Buffy* manages to be quite scary when that is its end goal. In "Bad Eggs," a skittering parasite breaks out of an egg shell and hides under Buffy's bed. As Buffy looks for the wee beastie, it attacks! As is appropriate for a series toiling in youthful fears, "Bad Eggs" exploits the notion that a monster can hide in our closets, or even under our beds. When Buffy spikes the damn thing with a pair of scissors, the monster is dead, but the lingering fear of what is hidden "down there" remains.

Other horror imagery in *Buffy the Vampire Slayer* manages to be a bit more adult, and a lot more disturbing from a psychological standpoint. In "The Prom," Buffy has a dream

of her wedding to Angel. It is a vision of a future that can never be, and as the happy couple exits triumphantly from the church, a radiant Buffy, garbed in stunning white wedding gown, suddenly catches fire and burns away to ashes. This image is powerful on a variety of levels. First, it is tragedy because there will *never* be a wedding between vampire and vampire slayer, and thus there is a feeling of longing and sadness associated with the image. Secondly, the dream represents the destruction of a day that all youngsters look forward to with great anticipation: their wedding day. That "special" day when a love between two people is sealed for eternity by splendor and ceremony is thus ruined for Buffy here.

Most disturbingly, the dream climaxes with an ironic reversal: it is not Buffy who should be scorched in the harsh glare of sunlight, it is the undead Angel, a vampire! Yet it is clear why Buffy imagines herself dying instead of her lover. Her death, her destruction, is imminent because she is, despite her gifts, mortal. The plain fact is that Angel will be young and beautiful long after his lovely bride is literally ashes ... cremated after her death. The dream sequence in "The Prom" is not only about what Buffy can never have (a happy life with Angel), it is about what she knows *will* be: her own mortal end while Angel goes on, forever young.

Do not let the title of this series fool you or keep you from sampling it. *Buffy the Vampire Slayer* is certainly one of the three or four best horror series produced in the last thirty years. Its conscientious focus on high school and teen issues gives it admirable cohesion, its cast is uniformly wonderful (but Gellar is *especially* good), and the comic book horror and action is more fun than any game in town. Accept no substitutes (because they might be giant praying mantises in disguise)!

CAST AND CREDITS

Cast: Sarah Michelle Gellar (Buffy Summers); Nicholas Brendan (Xander Harris); Alyson Hannigan (Willow Rosenberg);

Charisma Carpenter (Cordelia Chase); Anthony Stewart Head (Rupert Giles); David Boreanaz (Angel); Seth Green (Oz).

Credits: Created by: Joss Whedon. *Executive Producer:* Joss Whedon. *Score:* Walter Murphy. *Theme:* Nerf Herder. *Editors (various episodes):* Christopher Cooke, Regis B. Kimble, Geoffrey Rowland, Skip Schoolnik. *Production Designer:* Steve Hardie. *Director of Photography:* Michael Gershman. *Co-Producer:* David Solomon. *Producer:* Gareth Davies. *Executive Producers:* Sandy Gallin, Gail Berman, Fran Rubel Kuzui, Kaz Kuzui. *Co-Executive Producer:* David Greenwalt. *Story Editors:* Matt Kiene, Joe Reinkemeyer, Robert Des Hotel, Dean Batali. *Unit Production Manager/Co-Producer:* Joseph M. Ellis. *First Assistant Director:* David D'Ovidio, Brenda Kalosh. *Second Assistant Director:* Mark Hanson. *Casting:* Marcia Shulman. *Costume Designer:* Susanna Puisto. *Art Director:* Carey Meyer. *Set Decorator:* David Koneff. *Leadman:* Gustav Gustafson. *Construction Coordinator:* Daniel Turk. *Property Master:* Ken Wilson. *Chief Lighting Technician:* Larry Kaster. *Key Grip:* Tom Keefer. *Camera Operator:* Russ McElhatton. *Script Supervisor:* Lesley King. *Production Sound Mixer:* David Kirshner. *Production Coordinator:* Susan Ellis. *Assistant Production Coordinator:* Claudia Alves. *Production Auditor:* Edwin L. Perez. *Assistant to Joss Whedon:* George Snyder. *Assistant to David Greenwalt:* Robert Price. *Assistant to Gareth Davies:* Marc D. Alpert. *Stunt Coordinator:* Jeff Smolek. *Transportation Coordinator:* Robert Ellis. *Location Manager:* Jordana Kronen. *Costume Supervisor:* Rita Salazar. *Makeup Artist:* Todd McIntosh. *Hair-Stylist:* Jeri Baker. *Post-production Coordinator:* Jahmani Perry. *Assistant Editor:* Kristopher Lease, Golda Savage. *Post-production Sound:* Todd-AO Studio. *Supervising Sound Editor:* Cindy Rabideau. *Re-Recording Mixers:* Kevin Patrick Burns, Jon Taylor, Todd Keith Orr. *Music Editor:* Celia Weiner. *Special Makeup Effects Created by:* John Vulich, Optic Nerve Studios. *Visual Effects Support:* Glen Campbell. *CGI Animation*: Scott Wheeler. *Main Title Design:* Montgomery/Coss. *Processing:* 4MC. *Post-production Services Provided by:* Digital Magic. *Presented by*: Mutant Enemy, in association with Kuzui Enterprises, Sandollar Television, 20th Century–Fox Television.

EPISODE GUIDE

• *First Season (1997)*

1. "Welcome to the Hellmouth" (Part I) Written by Joss Whedon; Directed by Charles Martin Smith; airdate: March 10, 1997; *Guest Cast:* Mark Metcalf (The Master); Brian Thompson (Luke); Ken Lerner (Principal Flutie); Kristine Sutherland (Mrs. Summers); Julie Benz (Darla); J. Patrick Lawlor (Thomas); Eric Balfour (Jesse); Natalie Strauss (Teacher); Mercedes McNab (Harmony); Amy Chance, Tupelo Jereme, Persia White, Deborah Brown (Girls); Jeffrey Steven Smith (Guy in Computer Class); Teddy Lane Jr. (Bouncer); Carmine D. Giovinazzo (Boy).

Buffy, the Chosen One, arrives at Sunnydale High School, which sits on an evil mystical portal called the Hellmouth. There have been a rash of killings lately, and a student turns up dead in the school gym, a victim of a vampire attack. Buffy's new watcher, British librarian Rupert Giles, fears a major mystical upheaval will soon occur, but Buffy just wants to be a regular girl, *not* a vampire slayer. On her first night in town, Buffy meets a dark stranger named Angel who warns her about the Hellmouth, and a frightening supernatural event called "the Harvest."

2. "Welcome to the Hellmouth" (Part II, aka "The Harvest") Written by Joss Whedon; Directed by John Kretchmer; airdate: March 10, 1997; *Guest Cast:* Mark Metcalf (The Master); Brian Thompson (Luke); Ken Lerner (Principal Flutie); Kristine Sutherland (Mrs. Summers); Julie Benz (Darla); Eric Balfour (Jesse).

Buffy teams up with geek Xander, computer expert and "Brain" Willow, and librarian Rupert Giles to rescue their friend Jesse from the grasp of the Master, an ancient vampire/demon who hopes to "ascend" to a position of power during the Harvest. In the underground tunnels beneath the school, Jesse is revealed to be a vampire, and Buffy and Xander seek escape. Later, the Master's vessel, Luke, and his minions attack party-goers at the Bronze in an effort to claim more souls for the Master and thereby open the door to the Hellmouth. Buffy and friends rush to a confrontation which could end in the subjugation and termination of the human race.

3. "The Witch" Written by Dana Reston; Directed by Stephen Cragg; airdate: March 17, 1997; *Guest Cast:* Kristine Sutherland (Joyce Summers); Elizabeth Anne Allen (Amy Madison); Robin Riker (Catherine "The Great" Madison); Jim Doughan (Mr. Polc); Nicole Prescott (Lishanne); Amanda Wilmshurst (Senior Cheerleader); William Monaghan (Dr. Gregory).

Giles is upset when Buffy tries out for the Sunnydale High cheerleader squad because he fears her attention will be diverted from slaying, but things take an uglier turn when a popular cheerleader almost spontaneously combusts during a rehearsal. While Buffy and the gang contemplate this bizarre incident, Buffy realizes that her relationship with her mother is not as close as that of friend Amy and her mother, a woman who was once a very popular cheerleader herself. When Amy fails to make the cheerleading squad, her mother retaliates with witchcraft and even blinds Cordelia with a nasty spell. Soon, cheerleaders are dropping like flies and Buffy is the next target.

4. "Teacher's Pet" Written by David Greenwalt; Directed by Bruce Seth Green; airdate: March 25, 1997; *Guest Cast:* Ken Lerner (Principal Flutie); Musetta Vander (Ms. French); Jackson Price (Blayne); Jean Speegle Howard (Old Ms. French); William Monaghan (Dr. Gregory); Jack Knight (Homeless Person); Michael Robb Verona (Teacher); Karim Oliver (Bud #1).

Sunnydale's newest substitute (science) teacher is also Sunnydale's newest creature: a walking-talking praying mantis who murdered the regular biology teacher. Xander starts falling for Mrs. French, even as other boys who have been seen with her start to vanish.

Xander loses his virginity, but finds that his lover is a monster.

5. "Never Kill a Boy on the First Date" Written by Rob Des Hotel and Dean Batali; Directed by David Semel; airdate: March 31, 1997; *Guest Cast:* Mark Metcalf (The Master); Christopher Wiehl (Owen Thurman); Geoff Meed (Man on Bus); Robert Mont (Van Driver); Andrew J. Ferchland (Boy/The Anointed One).

The Master hatches another plan to further the aims of evil, this time by enlisting the services of a supernatural warrior called the Anointed One, who it is written can lead the Slayer to hell. Meanwhile, Buffy goes out with Owen, an Emily Dickinson fan and high school hunk. As Buffy attempts to balance her job responsibilities as a slayer and the demands of her social life, the Order of Aurelius works to resurrect the Anointed One ... a resurrection which can only come about through the deaths of five innocent people.

6. "The Pack" Written by Matt Kiene and Joe Reinkmeyer; Directed by Bruce Seth Green; airdate: April 7, 1997; *Guest Cast:* Ken Lerner (Principal Flutie); Jeff Maynard (Lance); James Stephens (The Zookeeper); David Brisbin (Mr. Anderson); Barbara K. Whinnery (Mrs. Anderson); Gregory White (Coach Herrold); Justin Jon Ross (Joey); Jeffrey Steven Smith (Adam); Paltrese Borem (Young Woman); Eion Bailey, Michael McRaine, Brian Gross, Jennifer Sky (The Pack).

A field trip goes bad for Buffy's class when a bunch of the boys become inhabited by wild animal spirits. Even Xander is affected by the vicious "pack" mentality in Sunnydale, and it is up to Buffy to save her friend and stop the wilding spree in her high school. Among the victims of "the pack" are Principal Flutie and the school mascot.

7. "Angel" Written by David Greenwalt; Directed by Scott Brazil; airdate: April 14, 1997; *Guest Cast:* Mark Metcalf (The Master); Kristine Sutherland (Joyce Summers); Julie Benz (Darla); Andrew J. Ferchland (Collin/

The Anointed One); Charles Wesley (Meanest Vampire).

The Anointed One is not really dead: he is a boy, a child, who is destined to lead an unknowing Buffy straight to hell. Meanwhile, Buffy starts to develop an attraction to the mysterious Angel, especially after he saves her life from three warrior vampires of an ancient caste. As Angel starts to reciprocate Buffy's feelings, she learns that he is actually a 240-year-old vampire who has been cursed with a soul, which means that he feels remorse and regret for all his evil actions. The Master sends vampire bitch Darla to kill Buffy's Mom, but Buffy becomes convinced that Angel, who was invited into her home, is actually the attacker.

8. "I Robot — You Jane" Written by Ashley Gable and Thomas A Swyden; Directed by Stephen Posey; airdate: April 28, 1997; *Guest Cast:* Robia La Morte (Jenny Calendar); Chad Lindberg (Dave); Jamison Ryan (Fritz); Pierrino Mascarino (Thelonius); Edith Fields (School Nurse); Damon Sharp (Male Student); Mark Deakins (Moloch).

The naive Willow has made friends with a boy over the Internet, but in this case, she has really accessed the chat room from hell. A demonic creature called Moloch has been conjured up from Giles' library and is now in the Sunnydale high computer system, working towards murderous and deadly ends. In the end, Buffy is forced to put Willow's would-be love, a seven-foot-tall robot predator, on the scrap heap.

9. "The Puppet Show" Written by Dean Batali and Rob Des Hotel; Directed by Ellen Pressman; airdate: May 5, 1997; *Guest Cast:* Kristine Sutherland (Joyce Summers); Richard Werner (Morgan); Burke Roberts (Marc); Armin Shimerman (Principal Snyder); Lenora May (Mrs. Jackson); Chasen Hampton (Elliot); Natasha Pearce (Lisa); Tom Wyner (Sid); Krissy Carlson (Emily/Dancer); Michelle Miracle (Locker Girl).

Giles is forced to run the High School Talent(less) Show, much to the amusement of Buffy, Willow, and Xander. New school principal Snyder has the last laugh, however, when

he forces the trio to participate in the show as well. Little do these new "talents" realize that they will be sharing the stage with Sid, a very lively and quite terrifying ventriloquist's dummy who desires to be "Flesh." Worse, the dummy believes that by murdering Buffy, a girl of great strength and power, he can accomplish this goal.

10. "Nightmares" Story by Joss Whedon; Written by David Greenwalt; Directed by Bruce Seth Green; airdate: May 12, 1997; *Guest Cast:* Mark Metcalf (The Master); Kristine Sutherland (Joyce Summers); Jeremy Foley (Billy Palmer); Andrew J. Ferchland (Collin); Dean Butler (Hank Summers); Justin Urich (Wendell); J. Robin Miller (Laura); Terry Cain (Ms. Tishler); Scott Harlan (Aldo Gianfranco); Brian Pietro (Coach); Johnny Green (Way Cool Guy); Patty Ross (Cool Guy's Mom); Dom Magwili (Doctor); Sean Moran (Stage Manager).

Sunnydale is going to hell, literally, when dreams and nightmares start to supplant everyday reality. A killer clown, a collection of nerds, a day without clothes, a fear of vampires, the death of loved ones, a fear of responsibility — these are the subconscious images manipulated for evil purposes by a hidden villain. Buffy's friendship with a youngster may be the key to this world gone crazy, but her own fears could jeopardize the entire town's future.

11. "Invisible Girl" Story by Joss Whedon; Written by Ashley Gable and Thomas A. Swyden; Directed by Reza Badiyi; airdate: May 19, 1997; *Guest Cast:* Clea Duvall (Marcie Ross); Armin Shimerman (Principal Snyder); Ryan Bittle (Mitch); Denise Dowse (Ms. Miller); John Knight (Bud #1); Mercedes McNab (Harmony); Mark Phelan (Agent Doyle); Skip Stellrecht (Agent Manetti); Julie Fulton (FBI Teacher).

A lonely, unpopular girl at Sunnydale High becomes an unexpected menace when she recedes into the woodwork, becoming invisible to others. The popular crowd takes it on the chin from the invisible Marcie as she wreaks revenge for all the licks she has taken in high school over the years. Buffy and friends must put their own wounds aside to help Cordelia's clique before the battle between the snobby and the transparent turns fatal — with the ultra-snooty Cordelia the ultimate target.

12. "Prophecy Girl" Written and directed by Joss Whedon; airdate: June 2, 1997; *Guest Cast:* Mark Metcalf (The Master); Kristine Sutherland (Mrs. Joyce Summers); Robia La Morte (Jenny Calendar); Andrew J. Ferchland (Collin); Scott Gurney (Kevin).

Giles comes across a disturbing prophecy in one of his texts: the Slayer is to be murdered by the villainous head vampire, The Master. Buffy learns of her unpleasant fate as Xander contemplates asking her to an important spring dance. To the dismay of all her friends in school, the prophecy comes true as Buffy is killed by the Master.

• *Second Season (1997–1998)*

13. "When She Was Bad" Written and directed by Joss Whedon; airdate: September 15, 1997; *Guest Cast:* Kristine Sutherland (Joyce Summers); Dean Butler (Hank Summers); Robia La Morte (Jenny Calendar); Andrew J. Ferchland (Collin); Tamra Braun (Tara); Armin Shimerman (Principal Snyder); Brent Jennings (Absalom).

After being revived from the dead and going off for a summer vacation, Buffy the Vampire Slayer of Sunnydale returns to high school with a sizable chip on her shoulder. At the same time, evil forces attempt to revive the dead Master for one more go round with the Chosen One. If Buffy cannot get her act together in time, the evil she conquered once will return to rule the day.

14. "Some Assembly Required" Written by Ty King; Directed by Bruce Seth Green; airdate: September 22, 1997; *Guest Cast:* Robia La Morte (Jenny Calendar); Michael Bacall (Eric); Angelo Spizzirri (Chris); Ingo Neuhaus (Daryl); Melanie MacQueen (Mrs. Epps); Amanda Wilmshurst (Cheerleader).

Grave robbing is the activity of the week

as a modern day Frankenstein (and fellow high school student) starts to assemble a bride for his dead brother, who has also been brought back from the dead out of spare parts. While Giles romances computer teacher Mrs. Calendar, Buffy investigates the disappearance of several cheerleader body parts ... and comes upon the deadly Frankenstein scenario. Can she stop the evil before Cordelia becomes part of the mix-n-match bride of a modern Frankenstein?

15. "School Hard" Written by David Greenwalt; Directed by John Kretchmer; airdate: September 29, 1997; *Guest Cast:* Kristine Sutherland (Joyce Summers); Robia La Morte (Jenny Calendar); Andrew J. Ferchland (The Anointed One); James Marsters (Spike); Juliet Landau (Drusilla); Alexandra Johnes (Sheila); Armin Shimerman (Principal Snyder); Alan Abelew (Brian Kirch); Keith MacKechnie (Parent); Joanie Pleasant (Helpless Girl).

Two new vampires come to Sunnydale: the punk rocker Spike and his evil lover, the bizarre and sometimes psychic Drusilla. While Buffy works to bring off parent-teacher night at school to raise her grade point average, the Anointed One joins forces with Spike and Drusilla to kill the Slayer who offed the Master. Before long, Spike and his minions have attacked the school on parent-teacher night and Buffy must not only save the day, but keep her secret identity as the Chosen One from her mother.

16. "Inca Mummy Girl" Written by Matt Kiene and Joe Reinkemeyer; Directed by Ellen Pressman; airdate: October 6, 1997; *Guest Cast:* Kristine Sutherland (Joyce Summers); Ara Celi (Ampata/Mummy); Samuel Jacobs (Peruvian Boy); Kristen Winnicki (Gwen); Jason Hall (Devon); Gil Birmingham (Peru Man); Henrik Rosvall (Sven); Joey Crawford (Rodney); Danny Strong (Jonathan).

Xander falls in love again, this time with a vicious Peruvian mummy masquerading as an exchange student. The mummy, once a slayer in her own culture, must kill to stay alive and she commits her misdeeds with a deadly kiss, of all things. Now Buffy must save Xander from a fate worse than death, but in the final battle, it is Xander who ends up doing the saving.

17. "Reptile Boy" Written and directed by David Greenwalt; airdate: October 13, 1997; *Guest Cast:* Todd Babcock (Tom Warner); Greg Vaughan (Richard); Jordana Spiro (Callie).

Cordelia is dating a fraternity boy with a dark secret: his brotherhood is sacrificing high school girls to a reptilian, subterranean demon called Makita. Buffy joins Cordelia at a frat party after she and Angel have a fight, and learns the unpleasant truth about this fraternity. Xander crashes the party and is mistaken for a new pledge at the same time Buffy is drugged by the boys of Delta Zeta Kappa and lined up to be sacrificed.

18. "Halloween" Written by Carl Ellsworth; Directed by Bruce Seth Green; airdate: October 27, 1997; *Guest Cast:* James Marsters (Spike); Juliet Landau (Drusilla); Armin Shimerman (Principal Snyder); Robin Sachs (Ethan).

Halloween is supposed to be a slow night for Buffy and Sunnydale because vampires tend to stay in, but this year turns out to be anything but quiet. An evil spell which invokes the name of Janus, the two-faced Roman god, changes the identities of the trick-or-treaters to match the costumes they are wearing. Xander, in fatigues, becomes a macho soldier; Willow, as a ghost, becomes an apparition, and Buffy, in 1770s gown, becomes a shrinking violet. Normally, such a switch would be a nuisance but not fatal, yet on this Halloween, Spike is on the prowl, and the services of a slayer are desperately required.

19. "Lie to Me" Written and directed by Joss Whedon; airdate: November 3, 1997; *Guest Cast:* Robia La Morte (Jenny Calendar); James Marsters (Spike); Juliet Landau (Drusilla); Jason Behr (Billy Fordham); Jarrad Paul (Marvin Diego); Julia Lee (Chanterella); Will Rothhaar (James).

An old flame of Buffy's named Billy "Ford" Fordham comes to Sunnydale to rekindle the affair, but in secret he is planning to give Buffy's life to Spike in exchange for the immortal life of a vampire. Angel and Willow suspect that something is not right with "Ford," and attempt to convince Buffy that her old boyfriend has ulterior motives. As it turns out, Billy is dying of a terminal illness and he thinks that vampirism is his only chance to outlive the disease growing inside him.

20. "The Dark Age" Written by Dean Batali and Rob Des Hotel; Directed by Bruce Seth Green; airdate: November 10, 1997; *Guest Cast:* Robia La Morte (Jenny Calendar); Robin Sachs (Ethan Rayne); Wendy Way (Dierdre Page); Stuart McLean (Philip Henry); Michael Earl Reid (Custodian); Tony Sears (Morgue Attendant); Daniel Henry Murray (Creepy Cult Guy); John Bellucci (Man).

Giles' youthful indiscretions come back to haunt him when he learns that many of his friends in London, and one here in the U.S., are being killed. As it turns out, Giles experimented with demonic possession when he was an adolescent, and the same demon he once conjured is now jumping bodies and killing his friends ... while simultaneously framing him for the crimes. Before long, the demon has entered the body of Giles' lover, Mrs. Calendar. Buffy and her friends must find a way to clear Giles of any suspicion, and save Ms. Calendar before it is too late.

21. "What's My Line?" (Part I) Written by Marti Noxon and Howard Gordon; Directed by David Solomon; airdate: November 17, 1997; *Guest Cast:* James Marsters (Spike); Juliet Landau (Drusilla); Armin Shimerman (Principal Snyder); Eric Saiet (Dalton); Bianca Lawson (Kendra); Norman Pfister (Kelly Connell); Michael Rothhaar (Suitman); P.B. Hutton (Mr. Kalish).

Buffy is depressed during career week because her "job" has already been chosen without her consent: she is the slayer, always and forever. Willow's future options look considerably brighter, but even that bit of good news cannot cure Buffy's blues, especially when Spike summons a group of bounty hunters to kill her. Just when things look like they can't get any worse, a new arrival in town changes the status quo: Kendra, a fellow vampire slayer.

22. "What's My Line?" (Part II) Written by Marti Noxon; Directed by David Semel; airdate: November 24, 1997; *Guest Cast:* James Marsters (Spike); Juliet Landau (Drusilla); Bianca Lawson (Kendra); Saverio Guerra (Willy); Danny Strong (Hostage Kid); Spice Williams (Patrice).

Kendra, the vampire slayer, has come to Sunnydale to replace Buffy, who actually "died" during her confrontation with the Master some time back. Angel is captured by Drusilla and Spike and is to be fodder in a ritual which will cure the sick Dru forever. Buffy feels useless, now that her skills are redundant, and even grows jealous as Giles and Kendra form a bond which threatens Buffy's own relationship with her watcher. Buffy must save Angel before she loses him forever.

23. "Ted" Written by David Greenwalt and Joss Whedon; Directed by Bruce Seth Green; airdate: December 8, 1997; *Guest Cast:* Kristine Sutherland (Joyce Summers); Robia La Morte (Jenny Calendar); John Ritter (Ted Buchanan); James G. MacDonald (Detective Stein); Ken Thorley (Neal); Jeff Langton (Vampire).

Buffy has trouble coping with her mother's smarmy new boyfriend, Ted. Making matters worse, everyone else seems to love the guy, a salesman and computer wiz. Ted shows his true colors to Buffy at a miniature golf game, proving to be an uptight, controlling, disciplinarian ... but no one believes her. Ted and Buffy come to blows over their different approaches to domestic bliss, and Ted is believed dead until revealed to be a malfunctioning robot.

24. "Bad Eggs" Written by Marti Noxon; Directed by David Greenwalt; airdate: January 12, 1998; *Guest Cast:* Kristine Sutherland (Joyce Summers); Jeremy Ratch- ford (Lyle Gorch); James Parks (Tector Gorch); Rick Zeiff (Mr. Whitmore); Danny Strong (Jonathan).

Buffy's mother thinks Buffy needs a lesson in responsibility, and Sunnydale high's health teacher, Mr. Whitmore, comes up with a plan: Buffy and all her classmates will each take care of an offspring, an egg, and treat it like a human baby for a week. Unfortunately, these are no ordinary eggs, and each one contains a deadly parasitic lifeform which can control a human host through a process called "neural clamping." The parasites serve a larger, prehistoric mother organism which dwells beneath the school and is enslaving the human populace of Sunnydale.

25. "Surprise" Written by Marti Noxon; Directed by Michael Lange; airdate: January 19, 1998; *Guest Cast:* Kristine Sutherland (Joyce Summers); Robia La Morte (Jenny Calendar); Brian Thompson (The Judge); Vincent Schiavelli (Jenny's Uncle); James Marsters (Spike); Juliet Landau (Drusilla); Eric Saiet (Dalton).

Buffy contemplates consummating her relationship with Angel, with all the angst that goes along with the decision to have sex. Meanwhile, Drusilla and Spike are up to their old tricks, planning once more to off the slayer. Buffy and Angel finally sleep together, but something awful is borne of their union.

26. "Innocence" Written and directed by Joss Whedon; airdate: January 20, 1998; *Guest Cast:* Ryan Francis (Soldier); James Lurie (Teacher); Parry Shen (Student); Carla Madden (Woman).

Angel loses his soul after one night of love with Buffy, and one moment of pure happiness. This horrible event is a result of an ancient gypsy curse, but it bodes trouble for Sunnydale. Now Angel is a dark, evil vampire, far more dangerous even than Drusilla or Spike. Soon, Buffy realizes she will have to contemplate the impossible: killing the only man she has ever loved. When Angel teams with Spike and Dru, Buffy must bring out the big guns to stop the killer trio.

27. "Phases" Written by Rob Des Hotel and Dean Batali; Directed by Bruce Seth Green; airdate: January 27, 1998; *Guest Cast:* Jack Conley (Cain); Camilla Griggs (Gym Teacher); Larry Baby (III); Meghan Perry (Theresa Klusmeyer); Keith Campbell (Werewolf).

A werewolf is on the loose in Sunnydale, and it is up to Buffy and her friends to discover the identity of the offending monster. Xander thinks he knows the answer, but instead "outs" a gay classmate. The werewolf in questions turns out to be none other than Oz, Willow's boyfriend and a cool band member.

28. "Bewitched, Bothered and Bewildered" Written by Marti Noxon; Directed by James A. Contner; airdate: February 10, 1998; *Guest Cast:* Kristine Sutherland (Joyce Summers); Robia La Morte (Jenny Calendar); Elizabeth Anne Allen (Amy); Mercedes McNab (Harmony); Jason Hall (Devon); Jennie Chester (Kate); Kristen Winnicki (Cordette); Scott Hamm (Jock); Tamara Braun (Frenzied Girl); James Marsters (Spike); Juliet Landau (Drusilla); Lorna Scott (Miss Beakman).

Xander is dumped at the Valentine's Day dance by the fickle Cordelia, leaving him fuming with anger. Xander asks the local witch, Amy, for a potion which will make him irresistible to Cordelia. The spell goes wrong badly, leaving Cordelia still feeling indifferent over him. On the other hand, every other woman in Sunnydale, from Mrs. Summers to a bevy of vampires, find Xander absolutely irresistible.

29. "Passion" Written by Ty King; Directed by Michael E. Gershman; airdate: February 24, 1998; *Guest Cast:* Kristine Sutherland (Joyce Summers); Robia La Morte (Jenny Calendar); James Marsters (Spike); Juliet Landau (Drusilla).

The evil Angel is bound and determined to kill Buffy, the woman he once loved. As Angel's torments become increasingly dangerous, threatening Buffy's friends and even her Mother, Mrs. Calendar, a gypsy herself, works desperately to undo the curse that has robbed Angel of his soul. In response to this act of kindness, Angel kills the beloved teacher, sending poor Giles into mourning.

30. "Killed by Death" Written by Rob Des Hotel and Dean Batali; Directed by Deran Sarafian; airdate March 3, 1998; *Guest Cast:* Kristine Sutherland (Joyce Summers); Richard Herd (Dr. Stanley Backer); Willie Garson (Security Guard); Andrew Ducote (Ryan); Juanita Jennings (Dr. Wilkes); Robert Munic (Intern); Mimi Paley (Little Buffy); Denise Johnson (Celia); James Jude (Courtney).

Buffy is sick with the flu, but she insists on challenging the demonic Angel anyway. After Xander, Willow, and Cordy save her life in battle, Buffy is sent to a hospital to recuperate. Buffy has always had a deep-seated fear of hospitals, ever since her cousin Celia died in one, and now Buffy learns why: sick children are being terrorized and murdered by an invisible personification of death that only the young can see. When a doctor attempting to save the children is slashed, killed, and dragged away by death, Buffy decides to remain in the hospital to protect the children and fight the demon.

31. "I Only Have Eyes for You" Written by Marti Noxon; Directed by James Whitmore Jr.; airdate: April 28, 1998; *Guest Cast:* James Marsters (Spike); Juliet Landau (Drusilla); Armin Shimerman (Principal Snyder); Christopher Gorham (James Stanley); Meredith Salinger (Grace Newman); Miriam Flynn (Ms. Frank); John Hawkes (George); Sarah Bib, Brian Poth (Fighters); Anna Coman-Hidy and Vanessa Bodnar (50s Girls); Brian Reddy (Policeman); James Lurie (Mr. Miller); Ryan Taszreak (Ben).

Sunnydale High is haunted on the eve of the Sadie Hawkins' dance by one, perhaps two, restless spirits. A dejected Giles suspects that Mrs. Calendar is haunting the school, but the facts of the case bear out a different conclusion. In the mid-1950s a teacher and her student lover both died violently after a torrid love affair. Now, Buffy and Angel are possessed by these spirits and find themselves acting out the moments leading up to the tragic deaths.

32. "Go Fish" Written by David Fury and Elin Hampton; Directed by David Semel airdate: May 5, 1998; *Guest Cast:* Armin Shimerman (Principal Snyder); Charles Cyphers (Coach Marin); Conchata Ferrell (Nurse Greenleigh); Jeremy Garrett (Cameron Walker); Wentworth Miller (Gage Petronzi); Jake Patellis (Dodd McAlvy); Shane West (Sean); Danny Strong (Jonathan).

Sunnydale's winning swimming team faces a new challenge when members of its team start to die, seemingly devoured by green-scaled monster-humanoids from the sea. Buffy and friends look into the killings, and Xander goes undercover by joining the swim team. Buffy soon learns that the sea monsters are not devouring team members ... they *are* the team-members, transformed into beasts! The catalyst for this nefarious change is a Russian experimental steroid being administered by the team coach in the steam of the team's daily sauna.

33. "Becoming" (Part I) Written and directed by Joss Whedon; airdate: May 12, 1998; *Guest Cast:* Kristine Sutherland (Joyce Summers); James Marsters (Spike); Juliet Landau (Drusilla); Armin Shimerman (Principal Snyder); Bianca Lawson (Kendra); Julie Benz (Darla); Jack McGee (Curator); Richard Riehle(Assistant); Shannon Wellese (Gypsy Woman); Zitto Kazaan (Gypsy Man); Ginger Williams (Girl); Nina Gervitz (Teacher).

Even as final exams loom close, Buffy is worried about how and when to finish things with the murderous Angel once and for all. Meanwhile, Giles examines an ancient artifact recently unearthed near the Hellmouth, a statue which when activated properly via occult methods can open the doorway to hell and suck all life on planet Earth into that nether region. While studying chemistry, Willow and Buffy find a spell belonging to the late Ms. Calendar which can restore Angel's lost soul. Kendra is killed in action while Willow tries to use the spell; the library is attacked by Drusilla, and Giles is kidnapped.

34. "Becoming" (Part II) Written and directed by Joss Whedon; airdate: May 19, 1998; *Guest Cast:* Kristine Sutherland (Joyce Summers); Robia La Morte (Jenny Calendar); James Marsters (Spike); Juliet Landau (Drusilla); Armin Shimerman (Principal Snyder); James G. MacDonald; Susan Leslie and Thomas G. Waites (Cops).

Giles has been kidnapped, Kendra is dead, and Buffy is now a fugitive from the law. When the Slayer learns that Willow is in the hospital in a coma, she realizes it is finally time to end things with the soulless Angel. Buffy finds an unexpected ally in Spike, who is desperate to win Drusilla back from Angel. In a final gambit to rescue Giles and save the world, Buffy locks horns and swords with Angel, only to be faced with the most difficult and heart-wrenching task in her life.

● *Third Season (1998–1999)*

35. "Anne" Written and directed by Joss Whedon; airdate: September 29, 1998; *Guest Cast:* Kristine Sutherland (Joyce Summers); Julia Lee (Lilly); Carlos Jacott, Mary-Pat Green, Chad Todhunter, Larry Bagby III (Larry); Michael Leopard (Roughneck); Harley Zumbrum (Demon Guard); Barbara Pilavin (Old Woman); Harrison Young (Old Man); Alex Toma (Aaron); Dell Yount (Truck Guy).

With Buffy out of town, despondent over her choice to send Angel to hell, Xander, Willow, and Oz try to fill her shoes in Sunnydale as slayers. Meanwhile, Buffy is in Los Angeles working at a greasy spoon under the name "Anne." She discovers there that teenage runaways are disappearing to a hellish underground where evil demons are using the humans as slave labor. Buffy descends to the underworld to save the captured teenagers, but she must act fast, lest she be prematurely aged in the bubble of "quick" time below the surface.

36. "Dead Man's Party" Written by Marti Noxon; Directed by James Whitmore Jr.; airdate: October 6, 1998; *Guest Cast:* Kristine Sutherland (Joyce Summers); Nancy

Lenehan (Pat); Armin Shimerman (Principal Snyder); Danny Strong (Jonathan); Jason Hall (Devon); Paul Morgan Stetler (Young Doctor); Chris Garnant (Stoner #1).

Buffy returns home to Sunnydale to find that her friends have taken up slaying, and that her Mom has added an unusual decoration to the house: a strange Nigerian mask. When Buffy has a difficult time rebonding with her alienated friends and schoolmates, Buffy's Mom invites her friends over for a party. Willow and Xander's feelings of abandonment (by Buffy) come to the fore of the party, but soon Buffy must contend with the Nigerian mask, an evil artifact which is capable of reanimating the dead.

37. "Faith, Hope and Trick" Written by David Greenwalt; Directed by James A. Contner; airdate: October 13, 1998; *Guest Cast:* Kristine Sutherland (Mrs. Summers); K. Todd Freeman (Mr. Trick); Fab Filippo (Scott); Jeremy Roberts (Coquistos); Eliza Dushku (Faith); Armin Shimerman (Principal Snyder); John Ennis (Manager).

While Buffy has recurring nightmares about Angel's death, a new vampire named Mr. Trick comes to town in the service of a vampire master called Coquistos, a beast so old his feet and hands are cloven. Another new arrival in town is the beautiful Faith, a second and highly unorthodox slayer. Mr. Trick and his Master are out to kill Faith in revenge for a scar she branded Coquistos with, and now Buffy gets dragged into the conflict.

38. "Beauty and the Beasts" Written by Marti Noxon; Directed by James Whitmore Jr.; airdate: October 20, 1998; *Guest Cast:* Fab Filippo (Mr. Platt); John Patrick White (Scott); Danielle Weeks (Debbie); Phil Lewis (Pete); Eliza Dushku (Faith).

Someone or something is killing people by night in Sunnydale, and Buffy fears it is Angel (returned from hell), and Willow fears the culprit is Oz (a werewolf because of the full moon). While the girls worry about their respective men, the real answer lays with an experiment gone wrong. A high school kid named Pete is so insecure about his manhood

that he has created a special formula to make him more macho ... a formula which has also turned him into a monster and an abusive boyfriend.

39. "Homecoming" Written and directed by David Greenwalt; airdate: November 3, 1998; *Guest Cast:* K. Todd Freeman (Mr. Trick); Fab Filippo (Scott); Ian Abercrombie (German); Harry Groener (Mayor Wilkins); Eliza Dushku (Faith); Jeremy Ratchford (Gorch); Jennifer Hetrick (Teacher); Danny Strong (Jonathan); Robert Treveiler (Gary); J.C. Quinn (Lone Customer).

Boyfriend Scott dumps Buffy on the eve of the Homecoming Dance and out of despair she decides to run for Homecoming Queen against Cordelia. At the same time, a slew of assassins arrive in town to off Buffy in what Mr. Trick calls "Slayerfest '98." On the way to the dance, Buffy and Cordelia are hijacked in their limo by the assassins, and the girls must stay alive while simultaneously settling their differences.

40. "Band Candy" Written by Jane Espenson; Directed by Michael Lange; airdate: November 10, 1998; *Guest Cast:* K. Todd Freeman (Mr. Trick); Kristine Sutherland (Joyce Summers); Robin Sachs (Ethan); Harry Groener (Mayor Wilkins); Armin Shimerman (Principal Snyder); Jason Hall (Devon); Peg Stewart (Mrs. Barton).

Principal Snyder orders Buffy and friends to sell candy to raise money for the Sunnydale High marching band. Unfortunately, the band candy has the unusual side effect of turning all of the adults in town, including Giles, Mrs. Summers, and Snyder, into rampaging, rebellion-crazed adolescents. The contaminated candy is the latest evil plan sponsored by Mayor Wilkins and his new majordomo, Mr. Trick. A teenage-acting Giles realizes his cultist former friend Ethan is also working on the contaminated candy.

41. "Revelations" Written by Douglas Petrie; Directed by James A. Contner; airdate: November 17, 1998; *Guest Cast:* Serena Scott

Thomas (Gwendolyn Post); Eliza Dushku (Faith).

While Buffy continues to keep Angel's return to Sunnydale a secret, Faith's new watcher, Mrs. Gwendolyn Post, arrives in town. Post warns that a demon called Logos is seeking the all-powerful glove of Miligon, an occult object. Now Buffy and Faith must keep the artifact from falling into the wrong hands, but all is not as it seems on this particular hunt. Worse, Xander discovers that Angel is back in town, and with the help of Willow, Oz, Giles, and Cordelia, he stages an intervention for Buffy.

42. "Lovers Walk" Written by Dan Vebber; Directed by David Semel; airdate: November 24, 1998; *Guest Cast:* Kristine Sutherland (Joyce Summers); Harry Groener (Mayor Wilkins); James Marsters (Spike); Jack Plotnick (Deputy Mayor); Marc Burnham (Lenny); Suzanne Krull (Clerk).

Buffy and the crew get their SAT score results, and Spike returns to Sunnydale, lovelorn and despairing for Drusilla. While Giles is away at a Druidic camp getaway, Buffy weighs her options for the future and wonders if she should leave town to go to college. Spike abducts Willow and forces her to conjure a love spell that he can use on Drusilla, who jilted him for a chaos demon. In rescuing Willow, Cordelia and Oz discover that Willow and Xander have become romantically entangled behind their backs.

43. "The Wish" Written by Marti Noxon; Directed by David Greenwalt; airdate: December 8, 1998; *Guest Cast:* Mark Metcalf (The Master); Mercedes McNab (Harmony); Nicole Bilderback (Cordette #1); Nathan Anderson (John Lee); Mariah O'Brien (Nancy); Gary Imhoff (Teacher); Robert Covarrubias (Caretaker).

An angry Cordelia, still smarting over Xander's infidelity with Willow, uses the powers of a magical "wish" necklace belonging to a student named Anya. Cordelia wishes that Buffy Summers had never come to Sunnydale, and reality suddenly alters drastically. Cordelia finds herself in a town overrun with vampires

(including an undead Xander and Willow, and an "ascended" Master). Attacked by Xander, an injured Cordelia finds herself in the care of Giles, who is fighting vampires even in this dimension, and she warns him that this is not the way things are supposed to be.

44. "Amends" Written and directed by Joss Whedon; airdate: December 17, 1998; *Guest Cast:* Kristine Sutherland (Mrs. Summers); Eliza Dushku (Faith); Robia La Morte (Jenny Calendar); Shane Barach (Daniel); Saverio Guerra, Edward Edwards, Cornelia Hayes O'Herlihy, Mark Kriski (Weatherman); Tom Michael Bailey (Tree Seller Guy).

As Christmas approaches, Angel is tortured by memories of victims he has taken throughout his long life, including his friends in 1838 Dublin. Meanwhile, Oz and Willow reconcile, and Buffy invites Faith to spend Christmas at her house. Angel seeks help with his plight from Giles, who simply cannot forgive Angel for the death of his true love, Jenny Calendar. As Angel's behavior grows more erratic, Buffy realizes that in order to save the angst-ridden vampire she will have to face down a monster beyond sin, beyond damnation: a creature of the darkness called "The First Evil."

45. "Gingerbread" Written by Jane Espenson; Story by Thania St. John and Jane Espenson; Directed by James Whitmore Jr.; airdate: January 12, 1999; *Guest Cast:* Kristine Sutherland (Joyce Summers); Elizabeth Ann Allen (Amy); Harry Groener (Mayor Wilkins); Jordan Baker (Sheila Rosenberg); Armin Shimerman (Principal Snyder); Lindsay Taylor (Little Girl/Gretel); Shawn Pyfrom (Little Boy/Hansel); Blake Swendson (Michael); Grant Garrison (Roy); Roger Morrissey (Demon); Daniel Tanim (Mooster).

Buffy's mom joins Buffy for a night of slaying and is horrified by the brutal deaths of two young children in a playground. In response to this tragedy, Joyce organizes a group railing against occult-oriented violence, known as M.O.O. (Mothers Opposed to the Occult). This organization promptly confiscates inappropriate books from Giles' library and conducts searches of student lockers. Soon, witches in town (including Willow) are being scapegoatted and bullied, and Buffy must face down her mom before Sunnydale becomes a fascist state bent on destroying all freedom and liberty.

46. "Helpless" Written by David Fury; Directed by James A. Contner; airdate: January 19, 1999; *Guest Cast:* Kristine Sutherland (Joyce Summers); Jeff Kober (Zachary Craylag); Harris Yulin (Quentin Travers); Dominic Keating (Blair); David Haydn-Jones (Hobson); Nick Cornish (Guy); Don Dowe (Construction Worker).

As Buffy turns 18, she faces two disappointments: her father cancels his visit to town, and she loses all of her slaying abilities. Giles proves unhelpful in solving the latter problem and is, in fact, behind the vanishing powers. At the behest of the Council of Watchers, Buffy is to be part of a slayer "rite of passage" in which she must kill a vampire while virtually defenseless and powerless. Locked in a tomb with a vicious vampire, Buffy must prove herself or die.

47. "The Zeppo" Written by Dan Vebber; Directed by James Whitmore Jr.; airdate: January 26, 1999; *Guest Cast:* Saverio Guerra, Channon Roe (Jack O'Toole); Michael Cudlitz ("Big" Bob); Eliza Dushku (Faith); Darin Heames (Parker); Scott Torrence (Dickie); Whitney Dylan (Lysette); Vaughn Armstrong (Cop).

Xander is tired of being the "zeppo," the useless part of the slaying group, and he buys a car to help distinguish himself. Unfortunately, notoriety is the last thing Xander needs when he hooks up with three undead gang boys who plot to detonate an explosive in the high school boiler room! While Xander contends with his problem, an apocalypse cult attempts to open the Hellmouth. Xander unexpectedly hooks up with the tempestuous Faith and proves his worth in more ways than one.

48. "Bad Girls" Written by Douglas Petrie; Directed by Michael Lange; airdate: February 9, 1999; *Guest Cast:* Kristine Sutherland (Joyce Summers); Harry Groener (Mayor Wilkins); K. Todd Freeman (Mr. Trick); Jack Plotnick (Deputy Mayor); Alexis Denisof (Wesley Windom Price); Christian Chlemenson; Eliza Dushku (Faith); Alex Skuby (Vincent); Wendy Clifford (Mrs. Taggart); Ron Rogge (Cop).

A new watcher is in town to take over for Giles, but nobody likes the prissy, arrogant young Brit. At the same time, a 15th-century vampire cult serving an obese, fleshy demon called Balthazar also arrives in town to reclaim a powerful, magical amulet. While Faith and Buffy go in search of the ancient vampire cult, Faith encourages a more loose, rebellious attitude in Buffy. This new tenor has deadly consequences for the Sunnydale Slayers when one of them accidentally kills a mortal with a stake through the heart.

49. "Consequences" Written by Marti Noxon; Directed by Michael Gershman; airdate: February 16, 1999; *Guest Cast:* Kristine Sutherland (Joyce Summers); Harry Groener (Mayor Wilkins); K. Todd Freeman (Trick); Alexis Denisof (Wesley Windom Price); Eliza Dushku (Faith); Jack Plotnick (Deputy Mayor); James G. MacDonald, Amy Powell (TV News Reporter); Patricia Place (Woman).

Faith lies and tells Giles that Buffy murdered an innocent human while out slaying. This complicates things for Buffy, who has been assigned by Wesley to investigate the dead man's — the deputy mayor's — death. Soon, the police are involved and questioning Faith and Buffy about the unsolved murder. Matters go from bad to worse when Wesley kidnaps Faith from Angel's care and threatens to take her back to England to stand trial before the Watcher's council.

50. "Doppelgangland" Written and Directed by Joss Whedon; airdate: February 23, 1999; *Guest Cast:* Harry Groener (Mayor Wilkins); Alexis Denisof (Wesley Windom Price); Emma Caulfield (Ananka/Anya); Ethan Erickson (Percy); Eliza Dushku (Faith); Armin Shimerman (Principal Snyder); Jason Hall (Devon); Michael Hagy (Alfonse); Andy Umberger (O'Hoffryn); Megan Gray (Sandy);

Norma Michaels (Older Woman); Corey Michael Blake (Waiter); Jennifer Nicole (Body Double Willow).

Ananka, the wish demon who once granted Cordelia a devastating wish to change the fabric of creation, seeks to regain her power base. Meanwhile, Buffy and Faith go through a rigorous physical and mental evaluation at the hands of the new watcher, and Willow is "asked" by Principal Snyder to tutor a flunking athlete. Ananka masquerades as a normal high school student and enlists Willow's assistance in casting a spell which will bring the wish necklace back in her grasp. In the act, the alternate Willow, a vampire from the other dimension, appears to confront the real Willow in this dimension.

51. "Enemies" Written by Douglas Petrie; Directed by David Grossman; airdate: March 16, 1999; *Guest Cast:* Kristine Sutherland (Joyce Summers); Harry Groener (Mayor Richard Wilkins III); Alexis Denisof (Wesley Windom Price); Eliza Dushku (Faith); Michael Mannasseri, Gary Bullock.

After Buffy and Angel see a movie together and confront the fact that they can never be together sexually without compromising Angel's immortal soul, Buffy and Faith meet with a demon who offers to sell them the "Books of Ascension," before Mayor Wilkins himself "ascends" on "Graduation Day." Worried, the mayor orders the double-agent Faith to kill the demon before Buffy can get the books, and then Faith seeks solace from Angel for her wayward behavior. Buffy witnesses Faith and Angel in an embrace and mistakes his attentions, even as the mayor determines it is time to rid Angel of his soul once more. Faith and a converted, evil, Angel kidnap Buffy and plot to torture her as the mayor's big day approaches.

52. "Earshot" Written by Jane Espenson; Directed by Regis Kimble; airdate: September 21, 1999; *Guest Cast:* Kristine Sutherland (Joyce Summers); Alexis Denisof (Wesley Windom Price); Ethan Erickson, Danny Strong, Larry Bagby III (Larry); Keram Malicki-Sanchez (Freddy Iverson); Justin Doran (Hogan); Lauren Roman (Nancy); Wendy Worthington (Lunch Lady); Robert Arce (Mr. Beach); Molly Bryant (Ms. Murray); Rich Muller (Student); Jay Michael Ferguson (Another Student).

Buffy vanquishes one of two new (mouthless) demons in town and then inherits one of the dead demon's "aspects," specifically, his ability to read minds. Soon, Buffy is hearing the thoughts of all her friends (excluding Angel, who is immune because he is a vampire) and starting to go crazy from the din. Then, in the cafeteria, Buffy hears the thoughts of a disaffected person who is planning to kill everybody in school the next day. The trail to the killer takes Buffy to the school newspaper editor, sad little Jonathan, and finally, to a hulking cafeteria worker.

Note: "Earshot" was scheduled to be aired on April 27, 1999, but it was shelved before airtime because of the tragic shootings at Columbine High School in Littleton, Colorado. The show was rescheduled for airing, some five months later! Strangely, "Earshot," filmed before Littleton, makes reference to Littleton-style events with sensitivity and wit. Because the episode really never shows a student gunning down classmates, it is hard to understand why this particular episode was targeted and then banned for so long.

53. "Choices" Written by David Fury; Directed by James A. Contner; airdate: May 4, 1999; *Guest Cast:* Kristine Sutherland (Joyce Summers); Harry Groener (Mayor Wilkins); Alexis Denisof (Wes); Eliza Dushku (Faith); Armin Shimerman (Principal Snyder).

The mayor sends Faith to the airport to retrieve a trunk from a Central American flight which he says is crucial to his ascension. Meanwhile, Buffy's mother wants her to go away to college at Northwestern, and Buffy realizes she wants to go too ... which means stopping the mayor's ascension before graduation. Buffy learns that the important crate is the Box of Gavrok, a container of more than fifty billion carnivorous hell spiders. Buffy and friends stage a daring *Mission: Impossible*-style operation to steal the Box of Gavrok, but things go wrong when Faith captures Willow.

54. "The Prom" Written by Marti Noxon; Directed by David Solomon; airdate: May 11, 1999; *Guest Cast:* Kristine Sutherland (Joyce Summers); Alexis Denisof (Wes); Emma Caulfield (Anya); Brad Kane, Danny Strong (Jonathan); Bonita Friedericy (Mrs. Finkle); Andrea E. Taylor (Sales Girl); Mike Kimmel (Harry); Tove Kingsbury (The Boy); Michael Zlabinger (Student at Mic); Monica Serene Garnich (Pretty Girl); Joe Howard (Priest); Damien Eckhardt (Jack Mayhew); Stephanie Denise (Tux Girl).

Anya, the wish demon trapped in teenage human form, asks Xander to the senior prom, and he accepts. Buffy's Mom goes to visit Angel because she is concerned that Buffy and Angel are from very different worlds. With the prom looming, Angel worries that he and Buffy cannot possibly share a future together, and he decides to leave Sunnydale for good. Meanwhile, three vicious hell beasts try to crash the prom.

55. "Graduation Day" (Part I); Written and directed by Joss Whedon; airdate: May 18, 1999; *Guest Cast:* Kristine Sutherland (Joyce Summers); Harry Groener (Mayor Wilkins); Alexis Denisof (Wesley Windom Price); Mercedes McNab (Harmony); Ethan Erickson (Percy); Emma Caulfield (Anya); Eliza Dushku (Faith); Armin Shimerman (Principal Snyder); James Lurie (Mr. Miller); Hal Robinson (Lester); Adrian Neil (Vampire Lackey #1); John Rosenfield (Vampire Lackey #2).

Graduation day and the mayor's ascension of evil approach rapidly and Xander fears his number is finally up. Meanwhile, Faith murders a professor for the mayor who may have the knowledge how to stop the ascension. Anya, the only Sunnydale resident, human or otherwise, to ever witness an ascension, provides some pertinent information on the subject even as the mayor prepares for his hellish commencement. Meanwhile, Faith shoots Angel with a poison arrow and the only cure is the blood of a slayer.

56. "Graduation Day" (Part II) Written and directed by Joss Whedon; original airdate (delayed): May 25, 1999; ultimate airdate: July 13, 1999; *Guest Cast:* Harry Groener (Mayor Wilkins); Alexis Denisof (Wesley); Danny Strong (Jonathan); Larry Bagby, III (Percy); Mercedes McNab (Harmony); Ethan Erickson, Eliza Dushku (Faith); Armin Shimerman (Snyder); Paulo Andres (Dr. Powell); Susan Chuang (Nurse); Tom Bellin (Dr. Gold); Samuel Bliss Cooper (Vamp Lackey).

Buffy fails to bring Faith home to Angel, who requires her blood, the blood of a slayer, to survive the poison. Buffy offers herself to Angel and, desperate, he accepts. Buffy ends up in the hospital just down the corridor from Faith and has a strange encounter with her on the dream plane. Soon, both the mayor and Buffy are formulating strategies for their mutual commencements, ascension, and graduation, the day when good and evil in Sunnydale will clash once and for all.

34

Sleepwalkers (1997)

CRITICAL RECEPTION

"despite its B-movie feel, *Sleepwalkers* is surprisingly smart in its technogimmickry and its talk about the mythology of the subconscious ... If the show toned down its lurid element, it would deserve a chance to dream on."— Will Joyner, *The New York Times*: "For Harrowing Horror Tales, Dreams Are a Fertile Field," November 1, 1997.

"these pj warriors are nothing if not deadly serious, although apparently it hasn't occurred to any of them that the inability to distinguish between dreams and reality is, in fact, psychotic ... Freud as an action adventure series."— Stacey D'Erasmo, *US*: "Hot TV," October 1997, page 82.

"Fanciful, played with a straight-face and directed by David Nutter with an impressive eye to detail and effects ... at least imagination's at work, and that's entertaining."— Tony Scott, *Variety*, October 27, 1997, page 32.

FORMAT

Neurophysiologist Nathan Bradford (Bruce Greenwood), together with his elite staff, including Vincent (Abraham Benrubi), a polysomnographic technician, and Dr. Kate Russell (Naomi Watts), a dream interpreter and clinical psychologist, works at the Morpheus Institute, a government installation dedicated to deciphering the dream plane. Bradford and his co-workers have mastered a scientific technique by which they can enter the "nocturnal world" of their troubled patients, and administer therapy right there, as well as diagnose psychological impairments.

In each adventure of this briefly-aired NBC network drama, Bradford and his staff journey into the dreams of their patients, and face a world which melds fantasy, reality, and, of course, nightmares. This is a dangerous "mission" for Bradford and company because, as all fans of *A Nightmare on Elm Street* will recall, if you die or are hurt in your dreams, you will awake facing the same injury in your waking existence. The human connection in *Sleepwalkers* came from Dr. Bradford's personal and tragic relationship to his work. In one of his "sleep cradles" lies his wife Gail, trapped perpetually in a coma. His only way to reach his true love is through the hyper-REM process which allows him to walk in the slumber of others.

HISTORY

Billed by NBC as part of its "thrillogy," the short-lived *Sleepwalkers* very briefly inherited the Saturday night time slot vacated when *Dark Skies* was canceled, and the schedule reshuffled. It aired between *Pretender* and *Profiler*, two borderline genre series, and starred Bruce Greenwood, the charismatic hero of *Nowhere Man* and star of such films as Atom Egoyan's *The Sweet Hereafter* (1997). Although the mold of *Sleepwalkers* was clearly patterned after *The X-Files* mix of science and frightening "extreme possibilities," the focus of *Sleepwalkers* was "dreams," which made the series quite different from competition such as *Millennium* and *Buffy the Vampire Slayer*. Although dreams (usually premonitory) had been an element of shows such as *One Step*

Beyond, The Next Step Beyond, Freddy's Night-mares, Beyond Reality, and films like *Dream-scape* (1985), and Wes Craven's *A Nightmare on Elm Street* (1984), *Sleepwalkers* represented the first time that the landscape of our slumber would be the fodder for weekly horror con-templations.

Prominent guest stars on *Sleepwalkers* in-cluded Harry Groener, the evil mayor of Sun-nydale on *Buffy the Vampire Slayer,* as the equally evil "Smiling Man," and Ray Wise, who was Leland Palmer and the host to "Killer Bob" in *Twin Peaks.*

Sleepwalkers became notorious as one of the most expensive and short-lived series of the 1997 season. NBC canceled the series after only two prime airings. For at least a year, this was a record, until UPN trashed *Mercy Point* after two shows and ABC dropped *Strange World* with equal speed (just three airings). *Sleep-walkers* has been aired in its entirety overseas, but not yet in the United States. Because of its brief life and relative obscurity, episodes are not currently available for this author to review.

Cast and Credits:

Cast: Bruce Greenwood (Dr. Nathan Bradford); Kathrin Nicholson (Gail Brad-ford); Jeffrey D. Sams (Ben Costigan); Naomi Watts (Kate Russell); Abraham Benrubi (Vin-cent).

Credits: Executive Producers: Stephen Kronish, David S. Goyer. *Created by:* Stephen Kronish, David S. Goyer. *Co-Executive Pro-ducer:* David Nutter. *Co-Producers:* Sara Charno, Stephen Gaghan, Harker Wade, Robert Parigi. *Supervising Producer:* Steve Beers. *Casting:* Susan Booker. *Music:* Jeff Rona. *Editor:* Randy Jori Morgan; *Art Direc-tor:* Alex Hajdu. *Sound:* Tom Allen. From NBC Studios in association with Columbia TriStar Television.

Episode Guide (1997)

1. "Pilot" Written by David S. Goyer and Stephen Kronish; Directed by David

Nutter; airdate: November 1, 1997; *Guest Cast:* Lewis Arquette, Michael Watson (Steve); Bobbi Sanders (Jill); David Kirkwood, Chris-tian Copelin, Jeffrey Noah, Carla Capps.

At the Morpheus Institute, a team of sci-entists investigating the "dream world" put their technology to use to help an ex-air force pilot cope with his nightmares.

2. "Night Terrors" Written by Stephen Gaghan; Directed by Kristoffer Tabori; air-date: November 8, 1997; *Guest Cast:* Michael Watson (Steve); Ray Wise, Harry Groener (The Smiling Man); Anna Gunn (Angie); Pep-per Sweeney (Deacon).

A boy's sudden change in demeanor sig-nals to his parents the fact that something is terribly wrong with him on a subconscious level. Dr. Bradford soon finds an evil charac-ter influencing the boy's dreams.

Unaired Episodes

3. "Forlorn" Written by Todd Ellis Kessler; Directed by Jeffrey W. Woolnaugh; unaired; *Guest Cast:* Michael Watson (Steve); Timothy Webber, Brooks Almy, Devon Odessa, Matthew Walker.

An erotic dream with disturbing over-tones captivates the inhabitants of a typical American town.

4. "Eye of the Beholder" Written by Sara B. Charno; Directed by James Whitmore Jr.; unaired; *Guest Cast:* Michael Watson (Steve); Daphne Ashbrook, Robert Wisden, Lorena Gale.

A woman who has recently had an organ transplant begins to experience strange dreams which she fears may belong to the organ's orig-inal owner.

5. "Counting Sheep" Written by David S. Goyer; Directed by William Malone; un-aired; *Guest Cast:* Michael Watson (Steve); Romy Rosemont, Jeff Doucette, Patrick Kil-patrick.

Further information unavailable.

6. "Passed Imperfect" Written by Jonathan Robert Kaplan; Directed by Lee

Bonner; unaired; *Guest Cast:* Harry Groener (The Smiling Man); Paul Dooley, Gillian Barber.

Dr. Bradford's dream nemesis, the villainous "Smiling Man," returns.

7. "A Matter of Fax" Written by Stephen Kronish; Directed by James Whitmore, Jr.; unaired; *Guest Cast:* Michael Watson (Steve); Ray Wise.

Further information unavailable.

35

Prey (1998)

CRITICAL RECEPTION

"While the show boasts both an intriguing premise and a comely lead in Debra Messing ... [it] doesn't quite draw you in ... A peek at future segment indicates the lameness quotient stands to rise considerably ... What tends to boost *Prey* is the unsettling sense that practically anyone on-screen might be one of the DNA blessed since they essentially look normal ... the elimination of the monster angle feels like an original approach." — Ray Richmond, *Variety*, January 12–18, 1998, page 100.

"surprisingly lively ... Silly at its core and straight-faced in its delivery, *Prey* is also effective as a thriller and a sly science fiction story ... the show's real strength is its creepy *X-Files* paranoia." — Caryn James, *The New York Times*: "Humanoids Make Scientists Paranoids," January 15, 1998, page E5.

"First, nobody knows the other race exists, until Parker discovers them through blood testing. Yet the new species seems to be organized enough to have developed a cohesive philosophy ... The entire notion, I'm afraid, of a new species springing into place, achieving adulthood, and developing a group identity overnight without being noticed, even in Southern California, is very illogical ... There's as much chance of this show surviving as my ever seeing a return of *Ned and Stacey* to prime-time TV." — Peter Huston, *Skeptical Inquirer*: "ABC's *Prey*— Not Exactly the Science Adventure Promised," May-June 1998, page 9.

FORMAT

Hoping to prove that the brutal murder of her superior and mentor Anne Coulter is related to the killing spree of the unrepentant, incarcerated serial killer, Randall Lynch, beautiful geneticist Dr. Sloan Parker (Debra Messing) uncovers a startling and quite unexpected fact. Randall Lynch is not human. He is 1.6 percent different from the rest of us, more different, in fact, than human beings are from chimpanzees. Sloan's discovery of this new species is amazing and frightening, and Sloan shares the news not only with police detective Ray Peterson (Frankie Faison), but with fellow geneticist Ed Tate (Vincent Ventresca). Sloan is then approached by the F.B.I. regarding the newly discovered species, but her contact, agent Tom Daniels (Adam Storke), has a secret of his own. He is not human: he is one of the new species as well, though he is not hostile to human beings and is even beginning to experience emotions (a facet of humanity his cohorts lack).

As the series continues, Sloan makes further discoveries about the new and hostile race sharing our planet. The *Homo dominants* (as they are later named) sleep on strange, black monolith-like beds, they may be telepathic, they have an incredibly hyperactive metabolism, they are super strong and super intelligent. Although Sloan shares all this data with her new lab administrator, Dr. Attwood (Larry Drake), he may not be a friend at all. In fact, he seems to be in cahoots with an "Attractive Woman" (Alexandra Hedison), whose motives and agenda remain unclear.

As *Prey* progresses, Sloan works with Tom to learn more about his secretive species, but there is danger around every corner. Part of this danger stems from the fact that Tom and his brethren appear human, and are difficult to detect. This fact makes establishing trust difficult for Sloan. Still, she begins to develop strong romantic feelings for Tom.

Fast paced, this short-run ABC series unfolds rapidly and ends with an (as yet) unresolved cliffhanger.

HISTORY

A surprisingly inventive series, *Prey* landed on our TV sets in 1998 and scared the heck out of viewers who took the time to stick with it. Its premise, that a more advanced but lookalike species is existing in man's world undetected, was daring and different enough for the series to avoid the dreaded *X-Files* "rip-off" label which had sunk *Dark Skies, Strange Luck, The Burning Zone*, and would later plague the interesting *Strange World*. Lending dynamic support to the series was lead actress Debra Messing, later a superstar courtesy of her role on the breakthrough sitcom *Will & Grace*, who created a memorable female character and fierce fighter in Dr. Sloan Parker. Together with an enigmatic Larry Drake, *Dr. Giggles* (1992) himself, and a stoic Adam Storke as a human sympathizer among the new breed, Messing managed to explore in just thirteen episodes what became one of terror TV's best modern mysteries, and uncovered the identities and plans of this malevolent new species.

Directors on *Prey* included *Star Trek: The Next Generation* veteran Winrich Kolbe, and *X-Files* regulars Jim Charleston and Vern Gillum. Guest stars included Natalija Nogulich (*Dark Skies*: "Mercury Rising," *Star Trek: The Next Generation*: "Chain of Command"), Susanna Thompson (the Borg Queen of *Star Trek Voyager*: "Dark Frontier"), James Morrison (of *Space: Above and Beyond*) and Roger Howarth as the psychotic *homo dominant* terrorist named Randall Lynch.

Of all modern TV horrors, *Prey* was perhaps the one which felt most like a visual novel, as storyline ran directly into storyline

and each succeeding chapter revealed a new element of the *Homo dominant* psychology, as well as plans to resist the subjugation of the human species. The series started off with a mystery ("Existence"), ballooned into the discovery of the new species ("Discovery"), went to the home land of the enemy ("Origins"), revealed the history of Tom the turncoat ("Veil"), explored various plans to destroy humanity ("Collaboration," "Sleeper"), looked gravely to the future ("Progeny") and seemed to be building towards a dynamic conclusion in its season-ending (unresolved) cliffhanger ("Deliverance"). Cohesive, compelling, and complex, *Prey* represented terror TV at its best, a kind of quirky combination of *Invasion of the Body Snatchers* (no one knows who is human anymore), and *Star Trek* (with Tom as a stoic Spock-like hero attempting to experience human emotions), with some spicy romance between attractive leads thrown in for good measure.

Despite *Prey's* promising qualities, not many people tuned into this neglected ABC hour, which premiered in mid-January of 1998, the so-called "second season" of the networks when new series not deemed strong enough for the fall are given a trial run. Although the "you've just been bumped down the food chain" ad line of *Prey* was heavily promoted, ABC did this William Schmidt-created series no favors by scheduling it at 8:00 P.M. on Thursday nights against the NBC sitcom powerhouse, *Friends*. Faced with such stiff competition, *Prey* was hunted to the brink of extinction, landing only 9 million or so viewers on a good night, and ranking no higher than 67th place in the Nielsen ratings.

Predictably, ABC responded to the low ratings by making *Prey* even harder to find. It was taken off the air completely for the months of April and May, and then ABC dumped the last five episodes during the dog days of summer (June and July) at an even worse time slot: Thursday nights at 9:00 P.M. This time around, *Prey* was pitted against the final season on *Seinfeld*, just about the only series on TV *more* popular than *Friends*! Not surprisingly, *Prey* aired its final episode on July 9,

1998, and has not been heard from or much remembered since. ABC learned nothing from the debacle and treated its 1999 horror show *Strange World* in much the same haphazard fashion. At least in the case of *Prey* it was able to air all of its filmed episodes before being moth-balled.

CRITICAL COMMENTARY

Similar to *Millennium* before it, *Prey* expertly trades on what could be the ultimate scare scenario: humankind's fall from grace. In this case, it is not the end of the world that sparks the terror however, but rather humankind's involuntary replacement at the hands of superior species, right here in our very own cities and neighborhoods. The thing that makes this series of recent vintage so compelling is that it is not aliens, monsters, or even conspiracies that must be defeated if the battle is to be won, but evolution, Mother Nature herself. Since Darwin and his theories are the playing ground of this series, much as Sigmund Freud was the incipient force behind *Sleepwalkers*, *Prey* raises many provocative questions about concepts such as "survival of the fittest," humankind's own prehistory (we supplanted the Neanderthals some 40,000 years ago, so why shouldn't another species do the same to us?), and of course, our assumed destiny as the dominant life form on the planet. Each episode of *Prey* obliquely handles these questions and others, making it a series which is obsessed, for one thing, with what it really means to be a human being. For instance, emotions do not exist in the *Homo dominants*. Does this fact reveal that emotions are destructive, an impediment to human survival, and therefore bred out of our successors? Or, does the lack of emotion in the new species signal the fact that *Homo dominants* represent only a blind alley, genetically speaking, a creature less perfect than the one who came before?

These ideas are played out on a stage filled with paranoia and dark conspiracies. The *Homo dominants* look just like humans, so they can infiltrate government agencies, hospitals, local bureaucracies, schools, even the highest levels of human society, and blend in totally unnoticed as they do grave damage to human institutions, history, and ideals. *Prey* remembers that the one essential fact of the human existence is that all persons, in the end, stand alone and separate in their own head. We do not know what other people are thinking because we are individual, lonely organisms who depend on clumsy tools like the written word, or vocal language, to convey ideas. *Prey* exploits this fact by putting its human heroes into situations where it is difficult, if not impossible, to guess who is the real enemy. It is a paranoia trip to be sure (the best since *Nowhere Man*), but it is worthy, and even optimistic too. This show argues persuasively that human emotions, relationships, and thus humanity itself, are all worthwhile. The character of Tom, the alien who sides with the humans, nicely establishes that humankind has pluses to go hand-in-hand with the obvious negatives.

None of this dialogue about the series is meant to suggest, however, that *Prey* is without flaws. For one thing, the scientists dramatized on this program are all incredibly good-looking and young (and very fit!) men and women, and they all seem to be fully versed in various schools of study which, in reality, would take several lifetimes to accumulate. Thus it is a bit difficult to accept that Ed Tate (the hunky blond surfer scientist) is equally comfortable with archaeology, laser machinery, and foreign languages as he is with genetic DNA examinations. And, for all of its own intelligence, *Prey* has the annoying habit of repeating for viewers the same clue again and again (sometimes in slow motion, sometimes in flashback, sometimes in black-and-white), just to make sure that we get "it." This was an element that slowed down *Poltergeist: The Legacy*, and it has a similar effect here. Horror shows would do well to remember that modern audiences are not stupid. They understand the plots and details of these stories without being bludgeoned by "flashbacks."

Believability is also a major problem at points because in the world of *Prey*, the media has "officially" announced to the United States population the existence of the nonhuman but human-looking predators, yet there is no public panic, no outcry, no critical shift in resources to combat this new enemy, nor even much worry. Were MSNBC or CNN to broadcast such an announcement in reality, the face of America would transform in seconds. We would become even more wary and suspicious of our neighbors, of those who seem different or hostile. *Prey* missed out on a good bet by failing to dramatize truthfully how our human world would respond to such important news, to such an immediate crisis. For example, what would the major religions, who all tend to believe that man is created in God's image, think of news that a new master race walks God's green earth? Would it be assumed that humankind has fallen from grace? Would the *Homo dominants* be worshipped as evidence of God's hand and master plan, or feared as the work of Satan? These are just a few notions that could have been investigated had *Prey* thought to fully exploit its paranoid central concept.

There are situational gaffes too. Weird alien beds are encountered by Sloan as early as episode #2, "Discovery," but she never asks Tom what specific physiological function these beds fulfill for the *Homo dominants*. It is a nice visual joke that these beds are designed to resemble the black monoliths of *2001: A Space Odyssey*, which also spurred evolutionary changes (and which also featured the word *Discovery* as the name of a spaceship), but it is illogical that the resourceful, curious Sloan would fail to follow up on what seems so important a piece of the new species' puzzle. Again, as with the flashbacks, viewers are way ahead of the characters in the drama. Viewers screamed to know about those beds, but the "brilliant" Sloan did not think to bring them up!

Despite these flaws, *Prey* really worked well more often than not, even if its premise may have been scientifically preposterous. One of the most interesting episodes, "Progeny," even featured some social commentary to go side-by-side with the terror. In this story,

Sloan and Tom investigate the unexpected escalation of child violence in schools around the United States, and proceed to discover that the *Homo dominants* are fathering children with human mothers. As the story develops, one is reminded of Jonesboro or the more recent Littleton school disasters, and *Prey* does not take the easy way out in explaining this upsurge of juvenile violence. The show is, in fact, an essay about what it means to grow up, and the sometimes unpleasant necessity of parents to practice impulse-control among the disenfranchised young. "Progeny" is a latter day version of *Star Trek*'s "Charlie X," with a violent boy (influenced by nonhumans) facing a choice in his adolescence: whether to be a moral human or a sociopathic monster. In nice, if ambiguous terms, *Prey* sets up the argument that the boy can always *choose* to be either good or bad, either victim or predator, a monster or a man, even if his genetic makeup points him in one specific direction. The show also set up a chilling climax. A group of the amoral children boarded a school bus together, like a scene out of *Village of the Damned* (1960), and were shuttled away to a future where their violence might one day erupt again.

The prominent romance between Tom and Sloan on *Prey* also had some socially redeeming value. It was clearly meant to be a metaphor for interracial romance in our society, and one episode ("Veil") reveals how Tom's *Homo dominant* mother disdains humans and looks down her nose at Tom for betraying his own kind. Prejudice, it seems, does not belong solely to the evolutionarily challenged human beings. The series is no morality play, but socially relevant themes were brought up in entertaining ways.

Lest one think that *Prey* is all paranoia and social commentary, it is helpful to remember that the series is packed with slow motion fight sequences between Tom and other *Homo dominants* (à la the bionic shows of the mid-1970s), car chases, and gun fights. The traditional horror accouterments such as ghoulish makeup and prosthetics, monsters, and even gore, are all missing in action, but the central concept, adapted straight from *Invasion of the Body Snatchers* (1978) or John Carpenter's remake of *The Thing* (1982), successfully make *Prey* a scary show in a different way. It is decidedly different from *The X-Files*, *Dark Skies*, and its modern brethren, and that alone gives the show some room to maneuver and experiment.

CAST AND CREDITS

Cast: Debra Messing (Sloan Parker); Vincent Ventresca (Dr. Ed Tate); Adam Storke (Tom Daniels); Frankie Faison (Detective Ray Peterson); Larry Drake (Dr. Walter Attwood).

Credits: Executive Producer: Charlie Craig. *Producer:* Donald Marcus. *Supervising Producer:* Jeremy R. Littman. *Executive Producer:* William Schmidt. *Producer:* Phil Parslow. *Created by:* William Schmidt. *Editors (various episodes):* Lee Haxell, Anthony Pinker. *Music:* Mark Morgan. *Director of Photography:* Ronn Schmidt. *Associate Producer:* Drew Matich. *Executive Story Editor:* Laurence Andries. *Production Designer:* James J. Agazzi. *Unit Production Manager:* Neal Ahern. *First Assistant Director:* Stephen Lofaro. *Second Assistant Director:* Cynthi Stefannoni. *Executive in Charge of Casting:* Barbara Miller. *Casting:* Lorna Johnson. *Costume Designer:* Betty Madden. *Costume Supervisor:* Tina Ficaro. *Makeup Artist:* Tim Miguel, Melanie Levitt. *Hairstylist:* Dianne Roberson. *Set Decorator:* Kristin Peterson. *Property Manager:* Lynda Reiss. *Sound Mixer:* Walter Anderson. *Camera Operator:* Rich Cantu. *Postproduction Supervisor:* Tim Scanlon. *Rerecording Mixer:* Neil Brady, Joe Citarella. *Music Editor:* Chris McGeary. *Supervising Sound Editor:* Bob Redpath. *Lab Equipment Provided by:* Beckman Instruments, Inc. *Color:* Four Media Inc. Lars Thorwald, Inc., Edelson Productions in association with Warner Brothers Television.

EPISODE GUIDE

1. "Existence" Written by William Schmidt; Directed by Peter O'Fallon; airdate: January 15, 1998; *Guest Cast:* Roger Howarth (Randall Lynch); Natalija Nogulich (Dr. Ann Coulter); Don Martin (Prosecutor); Joyce Guy (Judge); Ivon Allen (Defense Attorney); Nathan Dono (Guard); Robert Lynch (Cop); Catherine Grace (Receptionist); Scott Wolff (Officer); Mark Ankeny (FBI Agent).

Randall Lynch, a serial killer and rapist, is apprehended by the police after a string of bloody murders. Scientists Sloan Parker, Ed Tate, and world-famous geneticist Ann Coulter discover a genetic anomaly in Lynch's blood, and Dr. Coulter is soon found murdered in her genetics lab at Whitney University. Sloan, Coulter's apprentice, suspects that Lynch is somehow responsible for the murder, but stumbles into something much more important: the inmate is actually a member of a new species, one with a 1.6 percent difference from human beings. Soon, Sloan and Ed find themselves looking over their shoulders at FBI agents, policemen, and others who may or may not be part of this new, dangerous, and apparently emotionless species.

2. "Discovery" Written by Chris Levinson; From a story by Charlie Craig and Jeremy R. Littman; Directed by Dan Lerner; airdate: January 22, 1998; *Guest Cast:* Alexandra Hedison (Attractive Woman); Roger Howarth (Randall Lynch); Steven Burr (Detective Masters); Christopher Michael (SWAT Officer); Kathryn Joston (Landlady); Bari K. Willerford (Guard); Michelle Durham (Cute Girl); Christopher Titus (Marksman); Anna B. Choi (Reporter #1); Sonja Parks (Reporter #2); Tom Bailey (Guard); Lawrence McNeal III (Hospital Security Guard).

After meeting with Tom Daniels, a turncoat among the new species who seems to be developing human emotions, Sloan attempts to get some answers out of the incarcerated Randall Lynch. When her interrogation fails, Dr. Attwood goes behind her back to conduct a physical examination of the prisoner and announce the existence of the new species to the world. Lynch murders another doctor and then escapes captivity. Meanwhile, Attwood's tests prove that Lynch and his kind have a high metabolism, and possibly ESP.

3. "Pursuit" Written by Laurence Andries; Directed by Stephen Cragg; airdate: January 29, 1998; *Guest Cast:* Roger Howarth (Randall Lynch); Alexandra Hedison (Attractive Woman); Marc Gomes, Amy Daniels (Dark-Haired Girl); Megahn Perry (Timid Girl); Nynno Ahli (Muscular Man); Skip Stellrecht (Attendant); Elizabeth Maynard (News Anchor).

Randall Lynch is still on the loose, and Sloan has learned from Tom that the new species' goal is not just survival, but the total domination of humanity. Sloan also gets definitive proof of the new species' sixth sense: one in which they can detect the neural impulses and emotions of humans nearby. Lynch steals a pick-up truck, captures two teenage hitchhikers, and takes them to a mountain hideaway where his people kill humans and horde their clothes, watches, glasses, and other accouterments. Ed, Tom, and Sloan rescue the terrified teen girls and briefly capture Randall Lynch before he promises that this "is only the beginning," and then immolates himself.

4. "Origins" Written by Donald Marcus; Directed by Bill Corcoran; airdate: February 5, 1998; *Guest Cast:* Susanna Thompson (Tom's Mother); Alexandra Hedison (Attractive Woman); Al Rodrigo (Tony); David Soderholm (Bill).

Ed, Tom, and Sloan fly to Qaxaco in southern Mexico, the birthplace of the new master species, after Tom's people flee L.A., causing 108 fires in the process. In the desert, the trio digs up a corpse of a young, nonhuman female with four uteruses! Later that night, Tom unearths a strange, cylindrical pillar in the desert floor (really an entrance to a subterranean village founded in 1964) at the same time he experiences flashbacks of a beautiful woman in a white gown. Dr. Attwood soon rescues Ed and Sloan from a nighttime attack and reveals he has been working for the federal government, while Tom seeks to sort out his visions and ends up coming face-to-face with a mother he last saw some sixteen years ago.

5. "Revelations" Written by Laurence Andries and Chris Levinson; Directed by Jim Charleston; Airdate: February 19, 1998; *Guest Cast:* Vanessa Bell Calloway (Grace Peterson); Alexandra Hedison (Attractive Woman); Shelley Morrison, Irene Olga Lopez, James Handy (Lieutenant Quinn); Aymore De Llano (Danielle); Lucky Luciano (Man); Robert Keith (Man #2); Robert Madredi (Truck Driver).

Sloan cares for Tom after he has learned that the tattoo on his back symbolizes that he has been chosen as a leader of his kind. Meanwhile, Attwood has recovered the strange pillar from the desert, what Sloan refers to as the "Rosetta stone" of the new species. Sloan and Ray search out immigrants from Qaxaca who may not be human, and are nearly killed in a drive-by shooting while Ed and Tom become friends. They examine the pillar together, discover an energy source emanating from inside it, and realize that the artifact marks certain important celestial positions.

6. "Infiltration" Written by Charlie Craig and Jeremy R. Littman; Directed by Winrich Kolbe; airdate: March 5, 1998; *Guest Cast:* Vanessa Bell Calloway (Grace Peterson); Dwier Brown (Roer Young); James Handy (Lt. Quinn); James Morrison (Lewis); Megahn Perry (Kelly); Jennifer Sommerfield (Lisa); Bart McCarthy (Alley Man); Lawrence A. Mondley (Negotiator); Elizabeth Maynard (News Reporter #1); Lara Newton (News Reporter #2).

The pillar has been destroyed by its builders, but not before Ed has deciphered a portion of the artifact which indicates that something big is being planned for the second week of October — to coincide with the passage of a comet. At the same time, the new species launches a campaign of terror by blowing up a city bar utilizing a new explosive compound. While Tom and Sloan try to track down a reporter who may have information on the new species, Ed talks down a suicidal girl, Kelly, who had a run-in with Randall Lynch at the cave prior to his immolation. Tom realizes that a new species "mentor," a particularly vicious man called Lewis, is behind the recent murders and he suggests using the reporter as bait to eliminate the threat.

7. "Transformations" Written by Donald Marcus; Directed by Jim Contner; airdate: March 12, 1998; *Guest Cast:* James Morrison (Lewis); Susanna Thompson (Tom's Mother); Jennifer Sommerfield (Lisa); Alexandra Hedison (Attractive Woman); Megahn Perry (Kelly Hammond); Maria Rangel (Anna DeLeon); Jordan Lund (Martin); Thomas Mills (Guard).

Sloan is kidnapped by Tom's mentor, Lewis, and a trap is set for the turncoat Tom. Ed discovers that Kelly's DNA has been altered after discovering a rash on her neck. Instead of murdering his captives, Lewis frames Sloan and Tom for murder, forcing them to go on the run. Despite Ed's best efforts, Kelly dies after her genetic structure has been altered to mimic that of the new species.

8. "Veil" Written by Charlie Craig and Jeremy R. Littman; Directed by Martha Mitchell; airdate: March 19, 1998; *Guest Cast:* Susanna Thompson (Tom's Mother); Michael Bofshever (Mr. Hammond); Wendy Schenker (Mrs. Hammond); James Morrison (Lewis); Megahn Perry (Kelly); Maree Cheatham.

Sloan and Tom flee from the law after being set-up by Lewis, and Ed Tate discovers at Kelly's funeral that something is still alive inside the teen's body. Tom and Sloan almost become intimate, but the police break into their motel room and apprehend Sloan. Attwood and Tate conduct an autopsy on Kelly and learn of a parasite inside her brain which is inching towards her ear. A posthypnotic suggestion from Lewis turns Tom's loyalties away from Sloan and the lab at the same time that Attwood determines that the parasitic tick inside Kelly is capable of conducting gene therapy which can turn the human host into a member of the new species.

9. "Collaborations" Written by Laurence Andries and Chris Levinson; Directed by Ian Toynton; airdate: June 11, 1998; *Guest Cast:* Sam Anderson (Ian Copeland); Alexan-

dra Hedison (Attractive Woman); Kaj-Erik Eriksen (Shane); Cristine Rose (Principal Cook); Hayley Palmer (Little Girl).

While Ed and Sloan visit a school in Bardsdale where school children are being altered by the new species, Tom meets the "Attractive Woman" and learns that she and Attwood are being provided insider information from an unknown confederate of the new species. Ed finds evidence of genocide when he discovers the children's immune systems are being destroyed so as to kill the next generation of humans. The damage is being wrought by highly advanced bio-technology and nanites spread through Orange Max juice boxes.

10. "Sleeper" Written by Donald Marcus; Directed by Vern Gillum; airdate: June 18, 1998; *Guest Cast:* Sam Anderson (Ian Copeland); Kaj-Erik Eriksen (Shane); Dorian Gregory (New Species); Jessica Cushman (Dr. Kristen Hale); Dennis Bailey.

Ed has been abducted by Professor Copeland, a member of the new species who has developed the immune system-destroying nanite. Copeland has taken Ed to a base in the Alaskan tundra, where he shows him his laboratory. Ed escapes from captivity, and Sloan, Tom, and Attwood trace him there. Tom and Sloan are captured after discovering Copeland's plan to revive Spanish influenza, which in 1918 killed thirty million people. The deadly flu begins to claim lives in Alaska, including members of the new species, and Copeland proposes a truce to develop a vaccine.

11. "Vengeance" Written by Laurence Andries; Directed by Bill Corcoran; airdate: June 25, 1998; *Guest Cast:* Roger Howarth (Randall Lynch/John Doe); Jordan Lund (Martin); Rob Eld (Guard #1); Melissa Chan (Reporter #1); David F. Willis (Reporter #2).

While visiting Ed in the hospital, Sloan learns from Attwood that Tom has been murdered by his own kind. When Attwood suggests taking the war to the new species, Sloan sees it as an opportunity for revenge. Amazingly, Tom shows up alive and well at Sloan's apartment, which leads the team to conclude that somehow the new species has mastered an advanced cloning technique. The person behind the death of the Tom clone may be none other than Randall Lynch, or a Randall Lynch clone, which means that the new species has had cloning capability for at least thirty years.

12. "Progeny" Written by Donald Marcus; Story by James Halpern; Directed by Terence O'Hara; airdate: July 2, 1998; *Guest Cast:* Michelle Joyner (Rachel Taylor); Vincent Berry, Patrick Corman, Brian McNamara, Tim Redwine (Todd Cameron); Elizabeth Maynard (Lydia Holcomb); Garrett Finley (Willie Reynolds); John Kidwell (Joey Luck).

Little Kevin is tired of being picked on by bigger kids and one afternoon he suddenly goes on the offensive: utilizing his new species' strength to help him commit horrible violence. At the lab, Attwood worries that the national escalation of violence in elementary age children may be a secret plot to destroy humanity, so Sloan and Tom investigate and meet Kevin's parents. DNA testing reveals that Kevin is of the new species, even though both of his parents are human. Soon however, Sloan learns that Mr. Taylor isn't Kevin's real father, and Attwood finally names the new species: *Homo dominants.*

13. "Deliverance" (Part I) Written by William Schmidt; Directed by Bill Corcoran; airdate: July 9, 1998; *Guest Cast:* Alexandra Hedison (Attractive Woman); D.B. Woodside (Mark); Timothy Dale Agee (Jerry).

The *Homo dominant* grows more bold in its plans for the eradication of the human race as loyalties are tested, revealed, and twisted.

36
Charmed (1998–)

CRITICAL RECEPTION

"Divide three cool powers: bitchiness, wit and flakiness ... Each episode a new opportunity to sort out family dysfunctions, while incidentally quashing villains with inferior hairdos."—*Newsweek*: "Hollywood's Real Witch Hunt," November 2, 1998, page 8.

"a rather damp affair, a bland mixture of *Beverly Hills 90210* and *Buffy the Vampire Slayer* that struggles unsuccessfully to find a personality of its own. *Charmed* has witchcraft, but precious little magic ... the three actresses come across as interchangeably snippy."— Robert Bianco, *U.S.A. Today*: "*Charmed* Looks for Magic in Stars," October 7, 1998, page 3D.

"*Charmed* is almost quaint, with Doherty acquitting herself well and the production playing with an engaging spark ... *Charmed* has an entertaining little way about it, with Spelling and company mostly striking a solid balance between escapist slap-shtick and mild horror ... [it] isn't terribly concerned with issues of believability, relatability and self parody..."— Ray Richmond, *Variety*, October 5–11, 1998, page 33.

"you don't need any special powers to see why *Charmed* is a hit. It has the campy sci-fi vibe and the girl-power message of *Buffy the Vampire Slayer* mixed with the soapy sexiness of *Melrose Place*."— Janet Weeks, *TV Guide*: "Charmed Life," December 12–18, 1998, page 23.

FORMAT

Described aptly by many critics as *Charlie's Angels* (1976-81) meets *Buffy the Vampire Slayer*, Aaron Spelling's *Charmed* is an hour-long light-hearted horror program following the adventures of the three Halliwell girls (all in their mid-20s) who discover in the premiere episode ("Something Wicca This Way Comes") that they are actually powerful witches known as "the Charmed Ones" who must "protect the innocent." Along with its overt horror notes, *Charmed* highlights the day-to-day and romantic adventures of its three beautiful leads.

The *Charmed* story opens as Prue (Shannen Doherty) and Piper (Holly Marie Combs) welcome their errant sister Phoebe (Alyssa Milano) back to San Francisco and their gorgeous Victorian home (which belonged to their grandmother). The curious Phoebe soon discovers the mysterious "Book of Shadows" in the attic and before long all three Halliwells learn they possess special powers of witchcraft. The ditzy, visionless Phoebe now has the power of prophecy and premonition. The aggressive, defensive Prue is armed with telekinesis, and the kindhearted go-between and peace-making Piper is capable of freezing time for a few seconds. Adjusting to their new lives as witches is difficult for the Halliwell women, and made more so by the fact that Prue is dating a San Francisco police inspector, Andy Trudeau (T.W. King)!

Each week on *Charmed*, a WB Network "original drama," the three girls must battle all forms of evil including warlocks ("Something Wicca This Way Comes"), youth-sucking demons ("I've Got You Under My Skin"), fear-sucking demons ("From Fear to Eternity"), evil witches ("The Fourth Sister," "The Witch Is Back"), as well as protect the innocent both living ("The Wedding from Hell") and deceased ("Dead Man Dating"). Against this supernatural backdrop, the Halliwell sisters learn dramatic life lessons. In "From Fear to Eternity," the emotionally-stingy Prue learns to say "I love you" to her sisters, and in "Thank You for Not Morphing" all three girls must forgive the absentee father who abandoned them, and so on.

Charmed, which first aired Wednesday nights at 9:00 P.M. in the 1998–1999 season, features some predictable elements week-to-week. Each opening sequence (following the first commercial) features popular songs from notable and "hip" recording artists such as Jewel ("The Wendigo"), Natalie Imbruglia ("I've Got You Under My Skin"), Sarah McLachlan, Royal Crown Revue, Eve ("Feats of Clay"), Brooke Ramel, Chasing Furies, Khaleel ("From Fear to Eternity"), the Cranberries, Citizen King ("Déjà Vu All Over Again"), and Elysian Fields and Uma ("The Fourth Sister"). This blending of pop TV with pop music was also an important element of other contemporary WB hits in the late '90s including *Dawson's Creek* and *Buffy the Vampire Slayer*. In additions to the requisite top forty tune, audiences of *Charmed*'s first season could always expect Andy and his partner Morris (a wasted Dorian Gregory of *Prey*) to become involved on whatever case the Halliwells were currently embroiled in. One nice running joke on the program involves the flighty Phoebe, who cannot hold down a steady job to save her life. She was a waitress in "I've Got You Under My Skin," a hotel lobby psychic in "Dead Man Dating," a catering assistant in "The Wedding from Hell," Prue's underling at the auction house in "The Wendigo" and a real-estate office receptionist in "From Fear to Eternity."

Recurring settings on Year One of *Charmed* include "Quake," the busy and trendy restaurant Piper manages, and Buckland's Auction House, where Prue found a job after the pilot. Recurring characters in the first season include Leo (Brian Krause), the hunky handyman to the Halliwell sisters who is actually a male witch known as a "White Lighter," and Prue's evil employers: Rex Buckland (Neil Roberts) and Hannah (Leigh Allyn-Baker). In the second season, Piper will reportedly have her own club to manage, so settings are changing.

HISTORY

If ever a TV show could be accused of opportunism, Aaron Spelling's 1998 horror-drama *Charmed* would be at the top of the list. This WB horror series takes no chances with originality or progressive concepts. Instead, it trades almost exclusively on fads, trends, and the good looks of its beautiful stars. It echoes the in-vogue '70s nostalgia sweeping the nation (evidenced by the 1998 Fox series *That '70s Show*) by regurgitating rather precisely the character troika of Spelling's seventies jiggle classic *Charlie's Angels* (with three beautiful women combating the forces of evil) and even setting an episode in that "hip" decade ("That '70s Episode").

Furthermore, *Charmed* exploits the trendy late '90s popularity of witchcraft and the occult by joining the ranks of productions such as the feature films *The Craft* (1996) which also featured sexy young witches in the persons of Neve Campbell and Fairuza Balk, *Practical Magic* (1998) starring Sandra Bullock, Aidan Quinn, and Nicole Kidman, *Simply Irresistible* starring Sarah Michelle Gellar, and the highly successful TV series *Sabrina the Teenage Witch* (1996–).

Lastly, *Charmed* picks up none too subtly on the "girl power" themes of Joss Whedon's exemplary *Buffy the Vampire Slayer*, a kindred spirit on the WB network, and *Charmed* even hired *Buffy* monster makeup man John Vulich to create its weekly demons. In TV, similarity does not breed contempt so much as it breeds success, and *Charmed*'s familiar formula almost instantly created a hit. When the series premiered in the fall of 1998, it drew the WB's highest ratings for a regular program premiere, even out-drawing the second season opening of Kevin Williamson's talky coming-of-age saga, *Dawson's Creek*.[1] As of this writing, *Charmed* has also been renewed for a second season when far worthier shows such as *Millennium, Strange World*, and *Brimstone* failed to survive the grueling 1998–1999 season.

Much of the early publicity concerning *Charmed* involved casting. Shannen Doherty, former star of *Beverly Hills 90210* (1990–) had become famous for her on-and-off-stage shenanigans, and rumors had flown fast and loose that she had been fired from the *90210* series by producer Aaron Spelling. So, when Spelling and Doherty joined forces again for *Charmed*, it was a pop-culture media event the equivalent of an Arafat-Netanyahu handshake, as each party bent over backwards to suggest that there had *never* been any real animosity between them. The fact that Shannen Doherty, a perceived Hollywood witch, would be playing a real witch on TV was an irony not lost on several reporters, and much of the early buzz suggested that *Charmed* might very well be a camp hoot.

Charmed faced another brief casting problem in its early days. Actress Lori Rom, who was to have played Phoebe, was replaced after the pilot (which had to be reshot) by the more well-known Alyssa Milano. With Milano in place as the third in the troika, *Charmed* boasted a line-up worthy of the original *Charlie's Angels*: Shannen Doherty, Holly Marie Combs (of *Dr. Giggles* [1992] and *Picket Fences* [1992-96]), and Milano.

In part, *Charmed* slid through its first season on its good looks. In addition to its beautiful leads, it was smart enough to cast interesting cult guest stars to add visual support to the beautiful main trio. A bevy of lovely (and familiar) women graced the series including *Halloween IV: The Return of Michael Myers* and *Halloween V: The Revenge of Michael Myers* star Danielle Harris in "The Fourth Sister," Stacy Haiduk (*Kindred: The Embraced, Brimstone*) in "Feats of Clay," *American Gothic*'s sultry Brenda Bakke in "The Power of Two," and *General Hospital*'s Finola Hughes in "That '70s Episode." *Charmed* was also packed wall-to-wall with testosterone-laden hunks for the Halliwell girls to romance. Brian Krause (*Sleepwalkers* [1992]) had the recurring role of Leo, and Billy

Wirth ("The Witch Is Back"), Victor Brown ("Feats of Clay"), Shawn Christian ("Is There a Woogy in the House?"), and Raphael Sbarge ("Blind Sided") all showed off their handsome wares just enough to make the teenage female audience swoon. Billy Drago, David Carradine, and Jeff Kober (*Kindred: The Embraced*) took the opposite route and showed up to menace the Charmed Ones. All in all, *Charmed*'s first season went by smoothly, and the series was an uninteresting, uncontroversial venture not dissimilar in tone to *The Bionic Woman, Wonder Woman*, or any other seventies adventure in which beautiful women hid a funny secret about "super powers."

Although 1998–1999 saw much attention focused on horror and occult in the media, and *Buffy the Vampire Slayer* even had two episodes yanked from the air ("Earshot" and "Graduation Day, Part II") following the Columbine tragedy, *Charmed* avoided any such controversy by charting its own rather bland and unchallenging course. Each week, the Halliwell girls protected the innocent, romanced the hunks, and defeated showy demons in a neat special effects finale. Even though the protagonists were witches, *Charmed* escaped focus from censoring media watchers because the show reduced witchcraft to an inoffensive, "magic" power that could be harnessed at the right moment and ignored the rest of the time. One episode, "I've Got You Under My Skin," even made a special point of demonstrating that the Halliwell girls, despite their true nature as witches, were still *good Christians* who could walk into a church unharmed and undisturbed. Although spells were harnessed to vanquish evil on *Charmed*, they had more the feel of a home economics project (as they were often whipped up in the Halliwell kitchen!) than any significant mingling with "dark" or elemental forces. Perhaps this was the intention, however. By being so resolutely flat, *Charmed* opened the doorway (just a little) for the mass acceptance of the wiccan way as a legitimate "alternate life style." As creator Connie Burges stated, regarding the wicca connection and its acceptance in modern America:

In my mind, I like to think we are all becoming more open to entertaining things in our world. Maybe we're on the path to becoming better people.[2]

Whatever the intention, *Charmed* was so black-and-white a drama (gorgeous good girls beat ugly, evil bad guys), that none but the most ardent arch-conservative could have objected to the proceedings. In this case, beautiful faces, beautiful bodies, beautiful fashions, and excellent special effects made up for the uninspired writing from the likes of frequent *Tales from the Darkside* scribe Edithe Swensen, and *Charmed* thrived. At the end of the first season, it appeared some changes were in the offing, as Andy was killed off, and Piper quit her job at Quake. Schedule-wise, *Charmed's* second season is to air on WB Thursday nights instead of Wednesdays. That placement could be as dangerous to the Halliwell witches as warlocks, because the show will be pitted against the NBC powerhouse, *Friends*.

CRITICAL COMMENTARY

Charmed recalls that old axiom that there are no new stories under the sun, only old ones that can be combined and shuffled in new ways. Unfortunately, the witch's brew here, a concoction of oft-told tales, seems more derivative than innovative even after the contents of the cauldron have been thoroughly stirred. *Charmed's* major weakness is its derivative scripts, and the first season aptly demonstrates an alarming trend towards rehashing the plots of popular movies. Specifically, "Dream Sorcerer" pits the stalwart Halliwells against a killer who stalks Prue in her dreams. The kicker is that the wounds picked up in dreams materialize in reality, and that if you die in your dream, you die in "real" life as well. Of course, this is the central idea informing Wes Craven's classic *A Nightmare on Elm Street* (1984). The Dream Sorcerer of *Charmed* is a poor substitute for Freddy Krueger, and this episode of *Charmed* even has the audacity to set a scene at a dream clinic, an exact repeat of a similar scene in *Elm Street*! "The Witch Is Back" takes the plot of

the Julian Sands horror film *Warlock* (1989) as its template, featuring the story of a witch-hunter who follows a witch through the ages, into the present. In *Charmed*, the dynamic of *Warlock* is flip-flopped and the witch is the protagonist rather than the antagonist, which is a representation of what passes for inspiration on this show. Perhaps the most blatant steal of all is seen in the episode "The Truth Is Out There ... And it Hurts." In this entry, a villain returns to the present from the future to kill an unborn child before he can grow up to become the savior of mankind. If this sounds familiar, it should ... it is the exact plot of James Cameron's *The Terminator* (1984)!

In a much more general way, *Charmed* attempts to ape the sly, self-referential style of the *Scream* films by throwing in, seemingly willy-nilly, jokes about various popular films and television programs. In the first season, *Evil Dead 2: Dead by Dawn* ("I've Got You Under My Skin"), *Touched by an Angel* ("Wedding from Hell"), *Twin Peaks* ("Is There a Woogy in the House?") and even *Jaws* ("That '70s Episode") all get nods, but the humor is missing from these references because of awkward placement. The faux-witty dialogue falls flat from flaccid delivery, as if the stars of the series don't quite get the jokes. And, sadly, acting is a problem here. Milano, Doherty, and especially Combs are competent performers who have done good work in the past (again, especially Combs), but they are not served well by the scripts in this series. Doherty gets to play defensive and angry, Milano plays ditzy and sarcastic, and Combs is frequently seen to be harried and irritable, but beyond these very superficial qualities, the characters remain empty, lacking the resonance of a Buffy and Willow, or even an Ian and Randi.

Perhaps most disturbingly, *Charmed* credits its three heroines with virtually no intelligence whatsoever. They are depicted as powerful witches, but they have to do almost nothing to defeat evil but read passages from the Book of Shadows. *Charmed* is alarmingly like "Witchcraft for Dummies," without any real interest or curiosity in the breadth of the wiccan way or witchcraft in general. Indeed, rhymes from the Book of Shadows ("the power of three will set us free...") vanquish villains with a minimum of tussling (or conflict) in "Something Wicca This Way Comes," "I've Got You Under My Skin," "Thank You For Not Morphing," "Love Hurts," "Déjà Vu All Over Again" and others. Buffy Summers is a likable character whom audiences root for because she *acts* in a heroic manner. She confronts evil and defeats it by physical prowess, strength of will, strategy, and plenty of determination. Mulder and Scully are praiseworthy and likable heroes because they question, prod, and push their way towards a victory over evil by using their (vastly opposite) smarts. Even the sometimes enigmatic Frank Black of *Millennium* seems heroic and active because he must interpret the visions he experiences if he is to prevent another terrible crime. The girls of *Charmed* fail in this regard. They must simply know how to navigate a book index if they are to succeed over evil! They use their all-powerful book, lock their hands together and in rote, almost cheerleaderlike fashion, recite a pertinent passage. With such a passive act of heroism, the special effects show then commences and takes over, but there is rarely any real excitement or suspense in *Charmed* because it all seems too easy and convenient. Witchcraft for dummies indeed.

Charmed is also unduly formulaic, which succeeds only in fostering boredom. Every episode commences with a lovely but time-consuming montage of San Francisco, usually the same five or six views of the Golden Gate Bridge, the trolleys, and the Halliwell house, but edited in a different sequence. Every show includes some cliché police procedural scene in which Andy and Morris puzzle over a crime scene which is obviously related to a supernatural event. And finally, every episode inevitably brings in a new hunk, who for one reason or another, cannot sustain a relationship with the beautiful Halliwells. On top of this basic plot is overlaid the horror, almost as an afterthought: an innocent to be protected, a demon to be vanquished. Four of five times,

this works, but repetition really sinks *Charmed*.

When *Scream* was released in 1996, film executives all over Hollywood took notice that teenage girls comprised much of the repeat audience. It is not hard to see why that is so: Neve Campbell played a strong, attractive, heroic role model. She was a young woman who faced personal adversity and real danger with composure and wit. Joss Whedon's *Buffy* is imbued with many of the same qualities, only more so. She balances the demands of life (school, work, home) adroitly and intelligently, yet never gives up her right to "girlhood." *Charmed* attempts to strike the same empowering chord but is much less successful. Though the stated theme of the series is that sisters must stick together through thick and thin, the real message seems far less positive than that.

What each episode of *Charmed* is really about is the search for a man. Week in and week out, the Halliwells struggle with the fact that they have no regular men in their lives. That yearning suggests, at least in part, that a man is required if a woman is to feel whole or complete. Is that any kind of "girl power" message to send to the next generation? If changes in its format really are in the offing for *Charmed*'s second season, one can only hope that the writers go back to *Buffy the Vampire Slayer* or *Scream* or even *The X-Files* to remember what makes those productions work so well.

Charmed is a horror show with almost no real horror, despite the presence of warlocks and monsters almost every week. Suspense, scares, surprise, shocks, and terror are all missing from this brew. Each episode features some genuinely amazing special optical effects (watch the incredible destruction of the Grimlocks in "Blind Sided," for instance) and demon makeup, but the edgy, biting, and genuinely horrific moments of a show like *Buffy the Vampire Slayer* have not been adopted in any kind of successful or even intriguing way on this Aaron Spelling production. *Charmed* lives to a second season, but that is not necessarily a good thing.

CAST AND CREDITS

Cast: Shannen Doherty (Prue Halliwell); Holly Marie Combs (Piper Halliwell); T.W. King (Inspector Andy Trudeau); Dorian Gregory (Morris); Alyssa Milano (Phoebe Halliwell).

Credits: Created by: Constance M. Burge. *Coordinating Producer:* Robert Del Valle. *Producers:* Sheryl J. Anderson, Les Sheldon. *Executive Producers:* Brad Kern, Constance M. Burge, Aaron Spelling, E. Duke Vincent. *Consulting Producers:* Jonathan Levin, Tony Blake, Paul Jackson. *Executive Story Editors:* Javier Grillo-Marxuach, Michael Perricone, Greg Elliot. *Story Editors (various episodes):* Chris Levinson, Zack Estrin, Edithe Swensen. *Associate Producer:* Peter Chomsky. *Music (various episodes):* Jay Gruska, Tim Truman. *Casting:* Victoria Huff. *Directors of Photography (various episodes):* Tom Del Ruth, Michael Negrin, Geoff Schaaf. *Production Designer:* Dean Mitzner. *Editors (various episodes):* Derek Berlatsky, Dianne Ryder-Rehnolds, Alan Shefland, William Turro. *Unit Production Manager:* Patrick McKee, Robert Dell Valle. *First Assistant Director:* Richard Denault, Timothy Lonsdale. *Key Second Assistant Director:* Nancy Henkle Green, Marty Mericka. *Camera Operator:* Buddy Fries. *First Assistant Camera:* Lex Rawlings. *Chief Lighting Technician:* Walter Stewart. *Assistant Chief Lighting Technician:* Mark Meisenheimer. *Set Designer:* Cate Bangs. *Set Decorator:* Donald W. Crafft. *Leadperson:* Rocky Slaymaker. *Property Master:* Roger Montesano. *Assistant Property Master:* Christy McGeachy. *Script Supervisor:* Susan Lowitz. *Sound Mixer:* James LaRue. *Location Manager:* Bob Boyle. *Transportation Coordinator:* Dave Bassett. *Production Coordinator:* Jill Barnet Taylor. *Production Accountant:* Sharon Taksel. *Key Grip:* Marlin Hall. *Costume Designer:* Holly Harris Campbell. *Costumer Supervisor:* Jake Jacobs. *Key Makeup Artist:* Kathryn Miles Kelly. *Key Hairstylist:* Enid Arias. *Special Effects Makeup:* John Vulich. *Best Boy Grip:* Ray Michels. *Construction Coordinator:* Michael Caiozzo. *Stunt Coordinator:* Ernie Orsatti. *Special Effects Coordinator:* John Gray. *Executive Assistant:* Renate Kamer. *Casting Associate:* Jeffrey Roth. *Assistant to Executive Producers:* Aviva Barraclough, Max Joffe, Chele Knapp. *Assistant Editor:* Wendi Raderman. *Music Editor:* Nino Cenutiron. *Supervising Sound Editor:* Rich Steven. *Rerecording Mixers:* Larry Benjamin, Bruce Michaels, Eddie Gilroy. *Film and Electronics Laboratory:* Laser Pacific Media. *Lenses and Panaflex Cameras:* Panavision. *Digital Sound Editing and Mixing:* Laser Pacific Media. *Digital Visual Effects:* Encore Video, CBS Animation Group. *Executive in Charge of Production:* Gail M. Patterson. *Executive in Charge of Postproduction:* Kenneth Miller. *From:* Spelling Television, a Subsidiary of Spelling Entertainment Group, Inc.

EPISODE GUIDE

1. "Pilot" / "Something Wicca This Way Comes" Written by Constance M. Burge; Directed by John T. Kretchmer; airdate: October 7, 1998; *Guest Cast:* Eric Scott Woods (Jeremy Burns); Matthew Ashford (Roger); Chris Flanders (Chef Moore); Lonnie Partridge (Woman); Charmaine Cruz (Admitting Nurse); Hugh Holub (Pharmacist); Francesca Cappucci (News Reporter).

In scenic San Francisco, a cloaked murderer is killing witches with a ceremonial dagger which is said to steal their powers. Elsewhere in town, the beautiful Halliwell sisters Prue and Piper are surprised by the return of their flaky sister, Phoebe, who was living in New York City. The three Halliwells share space in their deceased grandmother's Victorian home and learn that they are powerful witches with the power to freeze time (Piper), see the future (Phoebe), and move objects telekinetically (Prue). The serial killer is actually a warlock out to steal the power of the Halliwell sisters, but the girls defend themselves with the mysterious Book of Shadows and the "power of three."

2. "I've Got You Under My Skin" Written by Brad Kern; Directed by John T. Kretchmer; airdate: October 14, 1998; *Guest Cast:*

Michael Philip, Neil Roberts (Rex Buckland); Leigh-Allyn Baker (Hannah); Marc Schelton, Bailey Luetgert, Barbara Pilavin, Cynthia King, Julie Araskog (Darlene); Tamara Lee Krinsky (Tia); Ben Caswell (Max Jones); Ralph Manza (Elderly Man); Todd Feder (Clerk); Lou Glenn (Carpenter).

Although the Halliwell sisters have promised not to use their special abilities, Phoebe has been using the power of premonition to target possible boyfriends at the restaurant where Piper works as a chef. While Prue renews her sexual relationship with Andy, Piper fears that her status as a witch will prevent her from entering a church without being struck down by lightning. Meanwhile, four women have been abducted in town and Prue lands a job at Buckland Auction House. Phoebe finds herself dating a professional photographer named Stefan who also happens to be a youth-sucking demon called Javna.

3. "Thank You For Not Morphing" Written by Chris Levinson and Zack Estrin; Directed by Ellen Pressman; airdate: October 21, 1998; *Guest Cast:* Markus Flanagan (Marshall); Eric Matheny (Fritz); Mariah O'Brien (Cinda); Jimes Dineen; Brian Krause (Leo); Tony Denison (Victor Halliwell).

Three nasty shapeshifters are in town to steal the Book of Shadows. At the same time, the girls' father, Victor Halliwell, returns home. He abandoned the family many years ago and Prue has not forgiven him for missing out on her childhood. While the sisters work out their feelings for their errant, con-man father, the shapeshifters get closer to reaching their goal.

4. "Dead Man Dating" Written by Javier Grillo-Marxuach; Directed by Richard Compton; airdate: October 28, 1998; *Guest Cast:* John Cho (Mark); Patricia Harty (Woman in Hotel); Elizabeth Sung (Berlitz); William Francis McGuire (Man in Hotel); Joe Hoe (Tony Wong); Todd Newton (News Man); Sherrie Rose (Susan Trudeau); Rendelle Granachia (Frankie).

While Andy and Prue plan a romantic getaway for her birthday, a young man named

Mark from Chinatown is murdered by Chinese thugs. As a spirit, he seeks out Piper's assistance in bringing to justice the men who killed him. At the same time, Phoebe (in *I Dream of Jeannie* outfit) spends time as a hotel lobby psychic and ends up assisting a cranky married couple who don't really want to be helped. Prue is irritated to learn that Andy was once married, and Piper tries to save her astral friend before the Gatekeeper to hell can claim his soul.

5. "Dream Sorcerer" Written by Constance M. Burge; Directed by Nick Marck; airdate: November 4, 1998; *Guest Cast:* Neil Roberts (Rex Buckland); J. Robin Miller (Skye Russell); Alex Mendoza (Whitaker Berman); Tim Herzog (Hans); James O'Shea (Guy #1); Bo Clancy (Businessman); James Howell (Technician #1); Marie O'Donnell (Dr. Black); Todd Howk (ER Nurse); Trish Suhr (Paramedic #1); Douglas Spearman (Nurse).

A man relegated to a wheelchair can control the dreams of others, and even murder people while they sleep. When Prue rejects his romantic advances, the dream wizard starts to stalk her as well. Meanwhile, Phoebe and Piper, who are tired of being single, cast a spell: how to attract a lover. While Morris and Andy try to solve the mysterious murders of three women who have died in their sleep, the dream sorcerer gets closer to Prue ... and lands her in the hospital.

6. "The Wedding from Hell" Written by Greg Elliott and Michael Perricone; Directed by R.W. Ginty; airdate: November 11, 1998; *Guest Cast:* Sara Rose Peterson, Barbara Stock, Deeny Consiglio, Neil Roberts (Rex Buckland); Christie Lynn Smith, Leigh-Allyn Baker (Hannah); Todd Cattell, Jeffrey Hutchinson, David Moreland (Butler); James Geralden (Justice of the Peace); Bill Ferrell (Security Guard); Phoenix Nugeny (Seamstress); Roy Abramsohn (Doctor); Thomas Crawford (Security Guard #2); Jennifer S. Badger (Bridesmaid #1); Eileen Weisinger (Bridesmaid #2); Leon Franco (Male Stripper).

Twenty years ago, Mrs. Spencer made a

deal with a demon called Jade, really Hecate of the Underworld: wealth and power in exchange for the hand of her son, Elliott, in marriage. Now Elliott is planning to marry Allison, but that changes when he is bewitched by Jade, who requires a human male to produce a normal-looking demon child. Piper is catering the Spencer wedding and facing her own problem — she fears she is pregnant with Jeremy's warlock baby. Now the Halliwell sisters must stop the wedding from hell before it is too late.

7. "The Fourth Sister" Written by Edithe Swensen; Directed by Gil Adler; airdate: November 18, 1998; *Guest Cast:* Danielle Harris (Aviva); Brian Krause (Leo); Rebekah Carlton (Kali); Rebecca Balding (Aunt Jackie); Michael Le Blanc (Video Clerk).

While Phoebe and Piper compete for the romantic attention of Leo, their hunky handyman, a fledgling witch being controlled by a demonic force seeks to insinuate herself with the Halliwell sisters by returning their missing cat (whom she stole). The witch, Aviva, wants to be part of the family but her evil mistress, Kali, wants the Halliwell wicca powers under her command. Aviva befriends Phoebe, hoping to use her insecurities to split the power of three and replace Prue as the leader of the Charmed Ones. When her assassination attempt fails thanks to Phoebe's power of premonition, Aviva is possessed by Kali and Prue, Piper, and Phoebe must save her.

8. "The Truth Is Out There ... And It Hurts" Written by Zack Estrin and Chris Levinson; Directed by Jim Contner; airdate: November 25, 1998; *Guest Cast:* Brad Greenquist (Warlock); Michelle Brookhurst (Tonya Parker); Brian Krause (Leo); Leigh-Allyn Baker (Hannah); Neil Roberts (Rex Buckland); Jason Stuart, Richard Gilbert-Hill, Craig Thomas (Alex Pearson).

While Piper and Phoebe compete for Leo's affections and Prue mourns the end of her relationship with Andy, a strange murderer arrives in San Francisco with knowledge of the future. Knowing that the truth about her identity as a witch is standing between her and Andy, Prue casts a truth spell which makes it impossible for Piper, Phoebe, and all those people the Halliwells have contact with, to lie. Phoebe attempts to save a sandwich delivery girl named Tonya, whom the killer from the future is stalking for some unknown reason. Phoebe learns that the killer is a warlock who wants to kill Tonya's unborn baby before he can grow up and develop a vaccine which will destroy all warlocks.

9. "The Witch Is Back" Written by Sheryl J. Anderson; Directed by Richard Denault; airdate: December 13, 1998; *Guest Cast:* Billy Wirth (Matthew Tate); Tyler Layton (Melinda Warren); Brian Krause (Leo); Neil Roberts (Rex Buckland); Leigh-Allyn Baker (Hannah); Terry Bozeman, Michael Mitz, Catherine Kwong (Waitress); Jodi Fung (TV Reporter).

In Salem in the 1600s, a beautiful witch vanquishes a sorcerer who tried to steal her powers. More than three hundred years later, Prue opens a locket which releases the devilish warlock, Matthew Tate. Now he wants the power of all three Halliwell girls and will stop at nothing to get them. Tate conspires with Rex Buckland and his assistant Hannah, both of whom have sinister ties to the occult, and the Halliwells summon the author of the Book of Shadows, Melinda Warren, to defend them.

10. "Wicca Envy" Written by Brad Kern and Sheryl J. Anderson; Directed by Mel Damski; airdate: January 13, 1999; *Guest Cast:* Neil Roberts (Rex Buckland); Leigh-Allyn Baker (Hannah); Brian Krause (Leo); Al Rodrigo (Jamie); Tim Stark (Super).

Rex and Hannah attempt to frame Prue for the theft of a tiara, so they can finally be rid of her. When that fails, they next try to frame her for murder. Meanwhile, Phoebe goes out on a date with Rex, and is surprised when she returns to his apartment to find that it is not exactly what it appears to be.

11. "Feats of Clay" Written by Michael Perricone, Greg Elliot, Chris Levinson and Zack Estrin; From a story by Javier Grillo-Marxuach; Directed by Kevin Inch; airdate:

January 20, 1999; *Guest Cast:* Stacy Haiduk (Guardian of the Urn); Victor Browne (Clay); Eddie Bowz (Palmer); Allen Cutler (Doug); Niklaus Lange (Welsey); Carolyne Lowery (Shelley); Ming Lo; Cristine Rose (Claire Price); Season Moran (Customs Officer); Allan Hunt (Auctioneer);

In Cairo, Phoebe's old boyfriend Clay and two partners steal a valuable Egyptian urn ... and a curse is born. The beautiful Guardian of the Urn kills one partner, Wesley, and then pursues Clay to San Francisco and the Halliwells. Meanwhile, Piper practices her matchmaking skills on Doug and Shelley, two employees at Quake. Phoebe sticks by Clay even as Prue learns that he is a thief, and the Guardian prepares to punish him for his greed.

12. "The Wendigo" Written by Edithe Swensen; Directed by James L. Conway; airdate: February 3, 1999; *Guest Cast:* Jocelyn Seagrove (Special Agent Fallon); Billy Jayne (Billy); J. Karen Thomas (Harriet Lake); Charles Chun (Health Inspector); Cristine Rose (Claire Price); Richard S. Wolf (Auctioneer); Christina Milian (Terri Lake); William Dixon (E.R. Doctor).

When Piper's car breaks down near the park, she is scratched by a Wendigo, a horrible monster which devours the hearts of those whose blood is AB negative. Special Agent Fallon of the F.B.I. shows up to investigate the case with Andy at the same time that young Billy arrives in town to kill it. His fiancée, Laura, was murdered by the Wendigo, and he has learned that it fears fire. While the Wendigo seeks out new victims in the park, including Andy, Piper begins to transform into a Wendigo herself.

13. "From Fear to Eternity" Written by Tony Blake and Paul Jackson; Directed by Les Sheldon; airdate: February 10, 1999; *Guest Cast:* Billy Drago (Demon of Fear); Kimberly Kates (Tangela); Steve Wilder (Lucas Devane); Jodie Hanson (Zoe); Allen Cutler (Doug); Dailyn Matthews (Susan); Evan D'Meara (Richard).

Once every thirteen hundred years, there is a universal convergence of negative energy on Friday the 13th ... and this is that year. A demon materializes in San Francisco who can kill witches by materializing their worst fears. If the demon can kill thirteen unmarried witches before midnight, he will be able to leave the underworld and wreak havoc on Earth every day of the year. Prue, Piper, and Phoebe try to warn the other witches of San Francisco before it's too late, while Prue attempts to overcome her fear of drowning.

14. "Secrets and Guys" Written by Constance M. Burge and Sheryl J. Anderson; Story by Brad Kern and Constance M. Burge; Directed by James A. Contner; airdate: February 17, 1999; *Guest Cast:* Brian Krause (Leo); Robert Gossett, Brad Tatum, David Netter, Will Stewart, Richard Cody.

A young boy named Max who has been kidnapped uses his powers to telepathically request help from the Halliwells. While they try to find out who and where he is, Leo returns for a visit and Prue seeks Andy's assistance on the case. Phoebe discovers that Leo is a good witch called a "White Lighter," even as Max's kidnappers force him to use his powers on a high-tech robbery. Leo has been sent back to San Francisco by his superiors, the mysterious "Founders," to help Max, but the boy's rescue is actually left to Prue.

15. "Is There a Woogy in the House?" Written by Chris Levinson, Zack Estrin; Directed by John T. Kretchmer; airdate: February 24, 1999; *Guest Cast:* Shawn Christian (Josh); Richard McGonagle (Doug); Cristine Rose (Claire Price), Nancy Moonves, Michael Mantell, Jennifer Rhodes (Gramms).

A workman comes to check out the Halliwell house after an earthquake and is possessed by an evil spirit he has inadvertently freed. The dark force possesses Phoebe as Prue prepares for an important dinner at the house. The evil "Woogyman" commands Phoebe to use a deadly new power, the instant materialization of objects, against her unsuspecting sisters. As the dinner party commences, the Halliwell house manifests signs of serious poltergeist inhabitation.

16. "Which Prue Is It, Anyway?" Written by Javier Grillo-Marxuach; Directed by John Behring; airdate: March 10, 1999; *Guest Cast:* Alex McArthur (Gabriel Statler); Shannon Sturges (Helena Statler); Bernie Kopell (Coroner); Cristine Rose (Claire Price); Mongo Brownlee (Luther Stubbs); Susan Chuang (Monique).

An evil Lord of War kills a boxing champion and drains his strength with a mystical sword. Phoebe has a vision of the same warlord killing Prue, running her through with the sword, and thereby stealing the energy of a firstborn witch. Now Phoebe and Piper must keep Prue safe, even if it means casting a special spell to increase Prue's powers. The spell has quite a different effect, however, and creates two exact duplicates of Prue.

17. "That '70s Episode" Written by Sheryl J. Anderson; Directed by Richard Compton; airdate: April 7, 1999; *Guest Cast:* Finola Hughes (Patty Halliwell); Andrew Jackson (Nicholas); Jennifer Rhodes (Gramms); Jake Sakson (Little Andy); Megan Corletto (Little Piper); Emmalee Thompson (Little Prue); Sally Ann Brooks (Officer in Jail); Rey Silva (Officer in Park).

A warlock claims that the girls' mother bargained away their future powers to save their lives, some twenty-four years ago. To escape the powerful villain, Piper, Prue, and Phoebe cast a spell which propels them back in time to the year 1975 and to a Halliwell house inhabited by Gramms, their mother, and their younger selves. The Halliwell sisters must now convince their mother not to make the pact with the warlock, or they may not be able to find a way back to the present. To make matters worse, their powers do not work in the past, and they must find a way to defend against Nicholas, the powerful warlock with a deadly power ring.

18. "When Bad Warlocks Go Good" Written by Edithe Swensen; Directed by Kevin Inch; airdate: April 28, 1999; *Guest Cast:* Shawn Christian (Josh); Nick Kokotakis (Brendan Rowe); David Kriegel (Greg Rowe); Frank Birney, Michael Weatherly, Andrea E. Taylor (Girl Victim); Stacie Chan (Little Girl); Ethan Hooper (Officer); Anne Vareze (Nun).

A warlock named Brendan faces the wrath of his brethren when he goes to a church and renounces his evil heritage. The Halliwell witches use their powers to rescue Brendan from his warlock siblings, and learn that he is an essential component of an all-powerful warlock trio. Now the warlocks must reconvert Brendan to evil before he is ordained as a priest, or see to it that he dies. Andy becomes involved in the case after Father Austin is attacked by the warlocks in church, and he learns of Prue's involvement.

19. "Blind Sided" Written by Tony Blake and Paul Jackson; Directed by Craig Zisk; airdate: May 5, 1999; *Guest Cast:* Shawn Christian (Josh); Scott Plank (Eric Loman); Raphael Sbarge (Brent Miller); Scott Terra, Matt George, Maureen Muldoon (Dee); Michael O'Connor (Jerry Cartwright); Dennis Keiffer (Grimlock #2); Lucy Rodriguez (Housekeeper).

Prue attempts to save a little boy from a bald "grimlock," but the monster escapes with his prey into some kind of dimensional portal. Worse, a passerby, who just happens to be an investigative reporter, observes Prue's powers and now intends to "out" her on videotape. While Prue copes with the publicity-desperate reporter, Phoebe and Piper enlist the services of a blind man to help stop the demons, who steal the eyesight of children and then use that ill-gotten vision to determine who has a "good" aura and destroy it. The reporter tells Andy about Prue's power, spurring a confrontation between Andy and Prue.

20. "The Power of Two" Written by Brad Kern; Directed by Elodie Keene; airdate: May 12, 1999; *Guest Cast:* Jeff Kober (Jackson Ward, "The Ghost of Alcatraz"); Brenda Bakke (Soultaker); Cristine Rose (Clair); Carlos Gomez, Sean Hennigan, Susan Chuang (Monique); Don Brunner (Inspector Anderson); Lesley Woods (Iris Beiderman); Jack Donner (Judge Renault); Michelle Harrell (Inspector Blakely); Gregg Monk (Officer); Jim Hanna (Detective); Victoria

Fang (Marianne); Yuji Hasegawa (Banker Yakuhama).

Phoebe runs afoul of an astral projecting ghost on Alcatraz, and Prue is told to limit family emergencies if she wants to keep her job at the auction house. Andy conducts a murder investigation in which it appears that the killer is Phoebe's ghost of Alcatraz, a man who died thirty-five years ago! To stop the evil spirit, it must be combated on the astral plane ... which means that one of the Halliwell girls must die!

21. "Love Hurts" Written by Chris Levinson, Zack Estrin, Javier Grillo-Marxuach; Directed by James Whitmore; airdate: May 19, 1999; *Guest Cast:* Brian Krause (Leo); Michael Trucco (Alec); Carlos Gomez (Rodriguez); Lisa Robin Kelly (Daisy); Don Brunner (Inspector Anderson); Tom Vi (Motel Manager).

Leo returns to San Francisco to help a witch being stalked by a warlock known as a "Dark Lighter." Poisoned by the warlock, Leo seeks the help of the Halliwells as they prepare for a vacation. There is no cure for the Dark Lighter's evil venom, and Leo faces death even as Prue tries to defend Daisy. Piper conducts a "power switch" spell to save Leo with his own healing powers, but she ends up jumbling Phoebe's and Prue's powers. Under pressure from Internal Affairs, Andy resigns from the force.

22. "Déjà Vu All Over Again" Written by Brad Kern and Constance M. Burge; Directed by Les Sheldon; airdate: May 26, 1999; *Guest Cast:* David Carradine (Tempus); Carlos Gomez (Rodriguez); Wendy Benson (Joanne Hertz).

Inspector Rodriguez of Internal Affairs is actually a demon sent to defeat the Charmed Ones, and now he is assisted in his efforts by a powerful demon called "Tempus" who can replay time again and again. Rodriguez sets a trap for the Halliwell sisters using Andy's life. In the first attack, Phoebe is killed, but Tempus wants a total victory, so he reverses time and allows Rodriguez to make a second attempt. In the next go round, Piper and Phoebe are both killed, but then time resets again and it all starts over one more time ... but finally the catastrophic consequences cannot be avoided, and a beloved friend dies.

Brimstone (1998–1999)

CRITICAL RECEPTION:

"*Brimstone* is so dark and paranoid, it almost makes *Millennium* look cheerful ... shot in a weird fluorescent glow that makes everything bleach out, *Brimstone* is as pretentious as it is dreary ... the show is beyond salvation." — Robert Bianco, *U.S.A. Today*: "Hellfire Without Heat," October 23, 1998, page 9E.

"... dark, implausible yet surprisingly watchable hour thriller ... Horton flashes enough hangdog expressions and dispenses sufficient soulful wisdom to make viewers care about his bizarre predicament. Glover is terrific ... while helmer/director of photography Felix Enriquez Alcala lends ... an agreeably foreboding, shadowy ambiance." — Ray Richmond, *Variety*, October 5–11, page 33.

"... *Brimstone* earns points for visual flair; Co-executive producer and director ... Alcala gets a lot out of framing Horton against rain-wet street corners. In turn, the actor responds to his surroundings by assuming the classic hard-boiled posture of clipped speech and sudden, violent actions." — Ken Tucker, *Entertainment Weekly*: "Super Freaks," November 13, 1998.

"... *Brimstone* launches with one of the best pilots filmed for television ... This one kicks the flames high from the beginning with a great premise that's compellingly presented. There's subtle acting and dark-but-witty writing, ... quick and jerky camera work that adds nervous texture, and a scratchy, nasty soundtrack. As Stone, Peter Horton is a smashing standout ... a superb anti-hero." — Tamara L Hladik, *Sci-Fi Weekly* (Internet Review): "NYPD Brimstone," October 1998.

"This show is so high concept its many concepts collide ... The show is partly *The Fugitive* and partly time travel. It's about good and evil and *The Twilight Zone*. But always, it is dull ... any sign of life would have been an improvement." — Caryn James, *The New York Times*, October 23, 1998, page E32.

FORMAT

Tough-talking but tender-hearted Ezekial Stone (Peter Horton) is a Manhattan cop who made a bad mistake. When his beautiful wife, Rosalyn, was raped by a psycho named Gilbert Jax, he took the law into his own hands and killed the rapist. Two months later, Stone was killed in the line of duty and he went straight to Hell for his crime. That's where he's been for the last fifteen years, since 1983 actually. However, sometime in 1998, 113 of the most "vile" criminals in Hell manage a daring jailbreak and return to Earth. The Devil (John Glover), a wisecracking and witty fellow, recruits Detective Stone to pursue the fugitives and send them back to Hell. Stone's reward for doing so is a second shot at human life and happiness ... redemption. Every time Stone dispatches a villain from Hell, a runic tattoo (representing a specific convict) disappears from his body.

Such is the plot of *Brimstone*, an hour-long horror drama which aired on Fox TV in late 1998 and early 1999. In addition to central characters Stone and the Devil, *Brimstone* features a large cast of supporting/recurring characters. On the side of good are Father Horne (Albert Hall), a blind priest who knows the truth about Stone, Max (Lori Petty), the smart-talking landlord in Stone's fleabag building, and a kindly waitress (Maria Costa) who serves Stone his favorite artery-clogging foods in an oft-seen greasy spoon diner. Seen frequently as well are Fraker (Scott Lawrence) an L.A. cop with no love for Stone, and Ezekial's lovely widow, Rosalyn (Stacy Haiduk). Representing first friendship and then danger on the series is Detective Sergeant Ashe (Teri Polo), a cop who changes loyalty as the series progresses, and eventually reveals a dark secret.

Brimstone is among the most visually distinctive series of the Terror TV pantheon. Jammed with slow-motion photography, disturbing jump cuts, and grainy, gritty images, the series is always a treat to watch. Although the formula is repetitive (Stone goes after a fugitive, catches the fugitive, and sends the fugitive back to Hell), Brimstone is nonetheless a remarkably cohesive series. Each and every episode of Brimstone explores the yin and yang of human existence, and meditates on the nature of evil.

Villains featured on the series include an unrepentant rapist ("Encore"), a shape-shifting multiple personality ("Faces"), a neo-Nazi ("Ashes"), a sexy love-starved convict who kills the ones she loves ("Heat"), and even a *Bonnie and Clyde* pair of Hell thugs trying to relive their doomed romance ("The Lovers").

Though Stone is a New York cop, the series is set in Los Angeles.

HISTORY

Brimstone emerged from the minds of Ethan Reiff and Cyrus Voris, two horror writers who had combined forces to pen the successful *Tales from the Crypt: Demon Knight* (1995) motion picture. Ironically, *Brimstone* was originally a movie concept, but the mid-nineties proved to be a bad time for horror films at the box office (this was pre-*Scream* [1996]). However, horror was really flourishing on TV for the first time with the wildly successful *The X-Files*, and Voris and Reiff soon tailored their concept to the small screen.

An early controversy concerning *Brimstone* involved the Voris/Reiff format. Some fans/critics openly complained that the central idea of *Brimstone* cribbed too much from Todd McFarlane's *Spawn*, a popular comic/film/cartoon/toy franchise which centered around a warrior returning to Earth from Hell to combat the forces of evil. It was a moot point, however, as *Spawn* was an adolescent wish-fulfillment adventure about a cool superhero with a bad ass attitude and neat superweapons, and *Brimstone* emerged almost immediately as an adult meditation on evil's role in the heart of man.

Fox TV, which had seen good luck with *The X-Files*, decent luck with *Millennium* and *Werewolf*, and not so good luck with *Space: Above and Beyond*, *Strange Luck* and *The Visitor*, green-lighted production of the 13 episodes of *Brimstone* with *Thirtysomething* star Peter Horton playing Ezekial Stone and John Glover (*Gremlins 2: The New Batch* [1990], *Tales from the Crypt*: "Undertaking Pallor") essaying the role of the Devil. Lori Petty (*Point Break* [1991], *Tank Girl* [1994], *Star Trek Voyager*: "Gravity"), and familiar face Stacy Haiduk (*Superboy*, *SeaQuest DSV*, *Kindred: The Embraced*, *Charmed*: "Feats of Clay") brought additional charm and talent to the gritty series, as the two "good" women in Stone's (after) life.

Brimstone was originally scheduled to premiere on Tuesday, October 27, 1998, at 9:00 P.M., but was bumped from the Fox schedule and moved to an earlier time slot, October 23rd at 8:00 P.M., with almost no warning. The move was made for two reasons. First, Fox had canceled two sitcoms (*Living in Captivity* and *Getting Personal*) which aired on Friday nights as a lead-in for Chris Carter's troubled second series, *Millennium*. Secondly, Fox had seen good ratings emerge from several episodes of the "reality based" series *Guinness World Records: Prime Time* on Tuesday nights, and did not wish to bump it from a successful time slot.[1] The upshot of this arrangement was that many people who were eagerly awaiting the premiere of *Brimstone* simply could not find it. The move came at such a late date that commercials had already aired heralding the premiere of the show on the 27th. This last minute shift to an earlier time (the Friday before the scheduled first Tuesday) resulted in lower-than-expected ratings for *Brimstone* right out of the gate. Generally well-reviewed, however, *Brimstone* delighted critics (who found it) because, like *The X-Files*, it successfully incorporated humor into its horrific format. Creators Reiff and Voris, along with series producers, referred to their new show as *Touched by a Devil*, and the writers successfully utilized humor to break the tension. As Reiff and Voris described it:

> There are a lot of little one-liners and little things Peter did so well (in the pilot), and we're going to keep pushing that.[2]

Despite the humor, the visual flair, stylish action sequences, excellent performances by Horton and Glover, and a compelling unity of mood and content unusual in so young a series, *Brimstone* did not succeed in the ratings game on Friday night even though it aired before the similarly horrific *Millennium*. Generally, the Reiff/Voris series captured 4.0–4.3 million viewers per week (the same audience numbers, essentially, for *Charmed* on the WB or *Star Trek: Voyager* on UPN), but that tally was not nearly enough for Fox to grant a renewal. In spite of several excellent episodes, *Brimstone* was canceled after the initial guarantee of thirteen episodes. By February 12, 1999, all 13 shows had been aired, and Fox was already exploring other ratings gambits (such as a rerun of "Triangle," the Bermuda Triangle episode of *The X-Files*, and the broadcast network premiere of the 1995 feature film, *Seven*).

Although Fox could point to the ratings failure of the series to validate the cancellation of *Brimstone*, it was (and is) still quite difficult to understand the network's lack of commitment. What series could have proven to be a better lead-in for *Millennium*? Two sitcoms had already failed there, so it is highly unlikely that two *different* sitcoms would do the trick. If Fox had just been patient (as they had been with *The X-Files* and *Millennium*), the powers-that-be may have realized that they had in *Brimstone* the perfect successor to the rapidly aging (six years and counting) *X-Files*.

Compelling stories, good acting, fine guest stars including Alex Datcher (*John Carpenter's Body Bags* [1993]), Lindsay Crouse (*Iceman* [1985]), Louise Fletcher (*Invaders from Mars* [1986], *Star Trek: Deep Space Nine* [1993–1999]), William McNamara (*Copycat* [1995]), Michelle Forbes (*Kalifornia* [1993], *Star Trek: The Next Generation*), and veteran Jeff Corey, as well as oodles of visual flourishes all assure *Brimstone*'s position as one of the ten best modern terror TV offerings, even if the network which aired it did not give a damn about it.

Brimstone is currently the hub of a very large fan base, a group of dedicated aficionados who are working to bring the series back into production.

CRITICAL COMMENTARY

The episodic nature of television often precludes a true feeling of consistency in dramatic, and especially horror, series. The anthologies, by definition, resist consistency and unity: each week a new story, new characters, new performers, and often new directors and writers are featured. But even programs with continuing characters sometimes find it difficult to be consistent because of the need to throw something new and different out to the fickle masses. Consider *Millennium*, a series which aired for three years. It has also had three different formats, because some audiences apparently felt that something was missing, or needed to be tweaked.

On the other hand, a dramatic series can also falter because it is simply too consistent (and repetitive), so as to actually become boring. *Brimstone* is that unique television (and genre) jewel, a series which brilliantly mixes style, cinematic technique, strong stories and fine acting to create a large and meaningful single tapestry, in this case once concerning "the nature of evil" and man's relationship to that "nature."

At first blush, *Brimstone* feels like a perfect candidate for the aforementioned boredom/repetition factor. Like the lackluster mid-80s series *Friday the 13th: The Series* (in which antiques were slavishly and boringly recovered week in and week out for some 70 episodes), *Brimstone* threatened tedium by appearing single-minded. After all, everybody knew that each week there would be a fugitive from Hell with incredible superpowers (a woman who burns up those she makes love to in "Heat"; a woman who kills lovers with a fatal kiss in "Carrier"; a man who shoots electricity from his hands in "Executioner"; an evil Carthaginian warrior who can move like the wind in "Slayer") who would wreak terror for nearly an hour, until Stone banishes them to Hell (by destroying the windows to their souls: the eyes). Thirteen weeks of such a rigid, unvarying formula could represent a kind of Hell all its own. But *Brimstone* grew nicely from week-to-week, until the hellish antagonist of the week was almost unimportant, except in how he or she affected Stone on a personal, introspective level. And how did this gallery of villains affect the hero? In very interesting ways, actually.

The Devil held up each of these nefarious criminals to Stone as a kind of twisted reflection of the detective, himself. The villain in "Heat," for instance, was a beautiful young girl named Gwendolyn who had lived during the Middle Ages. One day, she was raped by a gang of wealthy would-be knights. Her crime? She killed them all in an act of bloody vengeance. In other words, Gwendolyn was guilty (essentially) of the same crime which Stone had committed (and had been damned to Hell for). Stone saw the parallel, and realized that he did not want to kill this particular fugitive. He identified with her, understood her pain, and her villainy evolved from the realm of the comic book to one of human tragedy.

The same is true of "Repentance," a story in which a Nazi war criminal returns to Earth and, amazingly, decides to do good. He performs good works, and attempts to atone for the conspicuous evils of his previous existence. Although Stone must still dispatch this char-

acter to the underworld, the question is successful raised: is eternal suffering an appropriate punishment for someone with a finite life span, for someone who still has the seeds of goodness within him? Does a second chance make a difference, or is damnation really and truly for "all eternity" with no second chances, no opportunities for reflection, or a change in judgment? The "draconian" nature of Christian theology is thus questioned.

Commendably, Stone is able to review the ups and downs of his own life in a *Brimstone* story entitled "It's a Helluva Life." In this, perhaps the finest episode of the *Brimstone* roster, Stone is given a tour of his life by both the Devil and a lookalike angel (John Glover). The audience sees Stone as a child, his oft-mentioned abusive father, and even his life as a rule stretching, hell-bent police officer. Again, the nature of good and evil is explored in a significant and interesting way. One man who Stone sent to jail (by manufacturing evidence against him!) was subsequently murdered in prison. So, was Stone responsible for that death? Or, was he to be rewarded because by planting false evidence he actually saved a family of vacationers who would have crossed paths with the drug-addicted perp had he still been free? *Brimstone* works so well because it examines critically what "evil" in human nature is really about. Can it ever be mitigated by extenuating circumstances (like environment and upbringing), or is evil simply a deed which once done cannot be undone? On this "walking tour" of Stone's sins, the Devil tells Ezekial that it is "the thought that counts," the thought of evil which poisons a soul. Yet no less a source than an angel suggests otherwise. This minion of Heaven reveals (conversely) that even Universal law is open to mitigating circumstances. So, what the narrative of *Brimstone* has accomplished in its brief run is rather impressive. It is a show that exists in the universe of absolutes and black and whites (Good and Evil; Heaven and Hell); yet it is obsessed with moral relativism, the notion that evil is *caused* sometimes through ignorance, passion, or other human foibles. Some people might say that Stone is "evil" for planting evidence and breaking the law (and, indeed, that is how the universe has finally judged him), but at the same time, that very same evil has generated a great good (the survival of other innocents). "It's a Helluva Life" examines this contradiction in some beautiful ways, and it was not the only episode to do so.

The moral relativism of *Brimstone* has been incorporated throughout the series in beautiful and rather poetic ways. In "Executioner" Stone is again judged "evil," because, like the villain of the week, he once put himself above the law (in murdering Gilbert Jax) and had become judge, jury and executioner. Art can do two things for a viewer: it can compare (show similarities) or contrast (expose differences). "Executioner" landed two characters in mortal conflict, but compared the contestants and found that they were like-minded. Those who watch it attentively will understand the message, even though it is not enunciated in typical TV fashion (with flashbacks or heavy-handed dialogue).

"Faces" asks the age-old question: can children be evil? It then refers to the topical subject of the juvenile killing sprees in Jonesboro and elsewhere. The same episode also gives Stone the chance to be a father for a short while, an experience which he missed because of his interrupted life. "Mourning After" takes another tact all together, asking Stone to contemplate whether his love of wife Rosalyn is selfish since it keeps putting her in harm's way. The longer *Brimstone* lasted, the more obvious it became that the show was not about superpowered criminals from Hell, but the soul of one tortured man. The criminals were but looking glasses through which Stone could view himself.

Brimstone is well-written not just because of its debates on morality, but because the writers permit the show to develop in a believable and fun manner. One continuing storyline saw Stone as a kind of befuddled fish-out-of-water as he attempted to cope with fifteen years of technological and societal changes on Earth. He learned about *69 in "Heat," the Internet and websites in "Repen-

tance," screen savers in "Executioner," computer files in "Ashes," Rollerblades in "The Lovers" and fax machines in "Faces." He longed for Reggie Bars in "Repentance," and so forth. This subplot granted *Brimstone* permission to veer effortlessly into humorous terrain without seeming hokey. The writers were also exceptionally gifted at defining concepts which are sometimes difficult to pin down in concrete terms.

For instance, Hell is tantalizingly described (in "Heat") as a place where "everything you want is just out of reach ... you're stuck in mud." That account of the realm is more effective than the sight of bright licking flames and pools of fire because it immediately establishes the emotional impact of damnation. Stone himself provides a touching definition of love in "Mourning After," commenting that it is "binding, euphoric ... but torture. It's painful, but you don't want it to stop." Again, Stone's description manages to explain his feelings for his wife in a manner that a flashback to a "happy" time for the couple might not have managed so eloquently. *Brimstone* is one series which remembers that what is intimated, what is merely suggested, can be far scarier or more powerful than what is actually depicted on screen. *Brimstone* never actually went to Hell, but the Devil, Stone, and the parade of fugitives all provide eye-witness testimony about its horrors, accounts which are ever more convincing than any matte painting or optical effect could prove to be.

Modern TV has all but forgotten that camera angles are supposed to mean something, that how the audience sees an image is as important as the subject of the image itself. *The X-Files* and *Space: 1999* are two examples of TV programming which use the language of film to evoke terror and generate feelings of heightened suspense and involvement in viewers. Thankfully, *Brimstone* is another latter day example. The entire series uses images in an eerily effective way. Firstly, every episode is lensed in a kind of faded, icy blue hue. Blue is traditionally the color (or pallor) of death, and the world of *Brimstone* is very much a dead one to Stone. He is (technically) dead, his connection to his past life is dead for all intents and purposes, and though his emotions are alive, he has little connection with the world. The grainy, gritty visuals and the overall ashen look of the series reinforce this feeling of remoteness. The pervasive jump cuts (seen in all episodes) keep a viewer on edge in an avant-garde kind of way, and one leaves a typical viewing of this show with a nasty case of the jitters. Murderous actions are forecasted, unexpectedly repeated, and time flashes backward and forward in herky-jerky style. It is *film noir* for TV, and for once the visuals actually reflect content.

The episode "Carrier" opens with an extended slow-motion dance sequence. Sally Ann McGee, a Prohibition era lass who died after spending years isolated from humanity because she was a carrier of typhoid, dances expressively on the floor of a 1990s night club called *Writhe*. The slow motion technique reveals to the audience how much Sally revels in her new physicality (having recently returned from Hell), as well as how dearly this woman adores the spotlight and the attention of others ... a facet of humanity which her quarantine in an earlier life denied her. At the same time, the slow motion alerts viewers to the fact that this particular girl is not quite right. Her moves are different, slightly out-of-synch, because they come from another era: the roaring '20s. As this is the opening sequence of the episode, all of this data is conveyed visually in a *tour de force* of editing and filmic style.

"Carrier" is not alone in exploiting visuals to sell a storyline. In "Mourning After," Stone's memories are seen in stark black and white (like flashbacks on any number of shows, from *Poltergeist: The Legacy* to *Prey*) but the little glass snow globes which Rosalyn collects are seen in contrast, in bold color. In other words, the globes are an emotional connection to a colorful past, and are alive to Stone in a way that his memories can never be. The creators and cinematographers of *Brimstone* thus manage what few others have seen fit to do of late: they reinforce their episodes with a powerful (and unifying) visual conceit.

Icy blues, jagged jump cuts, slow motion, black and white versus color photography ... all these things can mean something when deployed for a purpose, and *Brimstone* remembers that.

Beyond the thematic and visual delights, *Brimstone* is successful because it manages to create "real" people. Peter Horton gives a gruff-voiced, understated performance throughout. His soulful eyes express volumes about his character's inner life, and when he is finally pushed to anger Stone becomes unpredictable, explosive and dangerous. A rumpled detective, a man with an edge, a soul looking for redemption, and a fish out-of-water trying to understand his world and time — Stone is all of these things and Horton hits every note with incredible precision. His Ezekial Stone ranks with David Duchovny's Mulder, Darren McGavin's Kolchak, Lance Henriksen's Frank Black and Sarah Michelle Gellar's Buffy as one of the greatest and most memorable of horror heroes.

John Glover is equally delightful as the Devil, and shows some real chemistry with Horton. Playful, deceitful, bitter and even mischievous, Glover makes the Devil an unforgettable individual. Whether cracking wise ("I say stop and smell the blood of sinners"), reflecting on the vicissitudes of Mother Nature ("Carrier") or hiding an embarrassing character flaw like love ("Ashes"), Glover is consistently charismatic as this most evil of evil characters. Together, the two lead performers of *Brimstone* challenge each other, and the resulting acting fireworks and verbal fencing enliven every story. Like Villa and Avon on *Blake's 7*, Spock and Bones on *Star Trek*, and even Mulder and Scully on *The X-Files*, Stone and the Devil on *Brimstone* share a dynamic love/hate relationship and opposite points of view which make their relationship ever fascinating and ever stimulating. Wit, irony, and delight are on display whenever Glover and Horton share a scene.

Perhaps *Brimstone* is a great series because, in the end, it is really just a tragic love story. As *Titanic* (1997) proved so dramatically, doomed love is pretty hard for human beings to resist. Along with the debate on evil and the stylistic flourishes, *Brimstone* is about one man's love for his wife. Even the torments of Hell cannot prevent Ezekial Stone from loving Rosalyn, and that fact (or flaw, as the Devil might say) makes the series seem very human. As the series inched towards cancellation, it was also moving directly toward an epiphany about Stone and his wife.

Rosalyn was a featured player in the last two stories ("It's a Helluva Life" and "Mourning After") and it seemed that she was becoming ever more aware of her husband's (sometimes distant) presence. This proved interesting, because early in the series Stone was obsessed with finding her ("Heat," "Encore"), but that obsession dwindled when he saw that his actions were putting his wife in danger. Oppositely, Rosalyn had no knowledge that Stone was alive in the early shows, but indications were that she was clued in to that strange fact by the climax of the last episode. So Stone and Rosalyn were really star-crossed lovers, never at the same point at the same time, never quite making contact with one another again. It was sad, and it was impossible to resist.

Brimstone had everything going for it except strong ratings. It is a quality program which excels in every avenue of production from acting and visualization to writing. If it had any weakness at all, it was that Ezekial Stone was sometimes unforgivably slow on the draw. In several episodes, he hesitated when he should have just blown away the bad guy … and his moment of indecision resulted in another half-hour of carnage as the bad guy escaped and killed mortals. Still, this was a very minor flaw in an excellent series, and one can even argue that Stone's hesitation was dramatically motivated. Unlike some TV cops or heroes, Stone was an angst-ridden guy who had to consider the weight of destiny and the afterlife every time he pulled the trigger and killed somebody. If only Fox TV had been so considerate when determining whether or not to blast *Brimstone* from its prime time schedule.

Cast and Credits

Cast: Peter Horton (Detective Ezekial Stone).

Credits: Created by: Ethan Reiff, Cyrus Voris. *Brimstone Theme:* Peter Gabriel. *Producers:* Peter Horton, Phil Parslow. *Co-Executive Producers:* Felix Enriquez Alcala, Ethan Reiff, Cyrus Voris. *Music (various episodes):* Mark Morgan, David Schwartz. *Editors (various episodes):* Victor Dubois, Kevin Krasny. *Director of Photography (various episodes):* Felix Enriquez Alcala, Herbert Davis. *Associate Producer:* Steve Turner. *Executive Story Editor:* Scott A. Williams. *Story Editors:* Angel Dean Lopez, Janis Diamond, Fred Golan. *Production Design:* Jonathan Carlson. *Unit Production Manager:* Jeffrey M. Zeitlin. *First Assistant Director:* Richard Peter Schroer. *Second Assistant Director:* Bob Kozicki. *Executive in Charge of Casting:* Barbara Miller. *Casting:* Penny Perry. *Costume Designer:* Tom McKinley. *Set Decorator:* Kristin Peterson. *Property Master:* Tom Cahill. *Costume Supervisor:* Wingate Jones. *Key Makeup Artist:* Barbie Palmer. *Key Hairstylist:* Susan Kelber. *Sound Mixer:* Bill Fiege. *Re-recording Mixer:* Dan Hiland, Gary D. Rogers. *Music Editor:* David Bondelevitch. *Supervising Sound Editor:* Jain Sekuller. *Production Coordinator:* Lisa Martley. *Film and Electronic Labor:* LaserPacific. *Special Visual Effects:* Stargate Films, Inc.

Episode Guide

1. "Pilot" Written by Ethan Reiff and Cyrus Voris; Directed by Felix Enriquez Alcala; airdate: October 23, 1998; *Guest Cast:* Peter Woodward (Father Salinas); Albert Hall (Father Horne); Michael Harney (William Kane); Currie Graham, Gene Mack (Tibbetts); Maria Ricossa (The Curator); Jack Duffy (Dollinger); Brian Miranda (Christopher); Kristen Booth (Teacher); Lindsey Connell (Desk Clerk); Peter Windrem (Jax); Jean Daigle (Tourist); Genevieve Langlois (Rosalyn); Adrian Griffin (Sketch Artist); Austin Di Iulio, Brandon Bone, Jesse Cairns (Altar Boys).

New York Detective Ezekial Stone murdered his wife's rapist in 1983, and then was killed on the job himself, two months later. Since then, Stone has been languishing in eternal torment in Hell. When 113 criminals escape from Hell, the Devil recruits Stone to bring them back to his tender embrace ... in return for a second shot at life on Earth. Stone's first case involves a 19th century priest who is killing altar boys as part of a bizarre ritual. Stone teams with a New York cop to return the criminal to eternal torment at the same time that he determines to discover the fate of his wife, Rosalyn.

2. "Heat" Written by Janis Diamond; Directed by Jesus Trevino; airdate: October 30, 1998; *Guest Cast:* John Glover (The Devil); Teri Polo (Detective Ashe); Holly Fields (Gwendolyn DuBar); Chad Morgan, Tim Dekay, Eric Saiet, Lindsey Crouse, Matt Reid (Todd); Larry Williams (Lawyer); Alex Sol (Nice Guy); Miguel Perez (Officer); J.F. Pryor (Carl); Karine Logue (Eileen); Carmen Mormino (Lean Cop).

Stone is hot on the trail of another Hell escapee, this time a beautiful young woman who burns her chosen lovers by touch. Her latest victim is a professor of medieval studies at a nearby University who started an affair with her but got too close. The woman, Gwendolyn DuBar, is actually a bitter serf who grew up in the unjust Middle Ages: three squires burned her home and raped her, so she killed them and ended up in Hell for her crime. Now Gwendolyn is free and Zeke must send her back ... but it is not a task he cherishes since he too is guilty of murdering a rapist.

3. "Encore" Written by Scott A. Williams; Directed by Felix Enriquez Alcala; airdate: November 6, 1998; *Guest Cast:* John Glover (The Devil); Stacy Haiduk (Rosalyn Stone); Albert Hall (Father Horne); William McNamara (Gilbert Jax); Louise Fletcher (Mrs. Jax); Kristin Minter (Janice Nowack); Michael Raynor, Alex Datcher (Laura Miller); John Cassini, Bruce Nozicki, Elizabeth Barris (Viv); Eileen Weisinger (Marie Tepekian);

Joleen Lutz (Woman); Stephen Walsh (Groundskeeper); Lori New (Waitress); Kate McIntyre (Neighbor); A.J. Marton (Boy); Joseph Della Sorte (Gardener).

Stone is forced to remember the unhappy past when he finds himself hunting the Hell escapee who raped his wife, Rosalyn. The diabolical Gilbert Jax has returned to Earth to rape more women, and his overjoyed mother is harboring him because she believes he has returned from Heaven. Stone is soon on the trail of the rapist, but is overcome with anger when he realizes who he is tracking this time. Stone soon discovers that to kill Jax he must do more than shoot out his eyes.

4. "Repentance" Written by Fred Golan; Directed by Terence O'Hara; airdate: November 13, 1998; *Guest Cast:* John Glover (The Devil); Albert Hall (Father Horne); Lori Petty (Max); Norbert Weisser (Martin Benedict); David Proval (Harry); Geoffrey Blake (Toby Cole); Maria Costa (Waitress); Curtis Armstrong (Jimmy G.); Adina Porter (Rachel); Scott Lawrence (Fraker); Harris Shore (Tailor); Bart Braverman (Man); Amy Reece (Aide); Tracy Walter (Knapsack); David Stifel (Bandana).

A homeless person traversing a bridge at night sees a man kill another man by removing his eyes. At the Devil's behest, Stone investigates the crime and discovers, to his surprise, a brass pin from a Dutch SS Nazi uniform. He soon learns that it belongs to a folk hero whom homeless folks in the area are referring to as the "Angel of Mercy," but who is actually a Nazi criminal escaped from Hell and making restitution for his sins. Stone grapples with his own conscience as he determines if this sinner turned saint is committing murder, or if there is another culprit out there.

5. "Poem" Written by Ethan Reiff and Cyrus Voris; Directed by Felix Enriquez Alcala; airdate: November 20, 1998; *Guest Cast:* Teri Polo (Detective Ashe); Roger Yuan (Mr. Po); Rosalind Chao (Ms. Chow); Ntare Mwine; Will Yun Lee (Roger); Kiva Dawson (Girl at Club); Diana Campaneau (Romanian Girl); Robert Gallo (Desk Sergeant); Beulah

Quo (Landlady); John Lepard (Assistant D.A.); Randall Rapstein (Assistant Coroner); June 2ujimoto (Waitress); Mike Sun (Charles); Charles Shen (Wing); Nikolai Stoilov (Romanian Guy); Stephanie Han (Wei Yei Bring); Albert Wong (Chinese Homeless Man); Melissa Chan (Teaching Assistant).

Another Hell escapee, this time a Chinese man who died a thousand years ago, is on the loose in Los Angeles. Po once committed a horrible crime against a member of a royal family, and now he is murdering innocent women as part of an epic poem to atone for his long ago deed. Stone butts heads again with Detective Ashe at the same time he seeks the assistance of a pretty teacher in sending this villain back to the nether region.

6. **"Executioner"** Written by Scott A. Williams; Story by Fred Golan; Directed by Dan Lerner; airdate: December 4, 1998; *Guest Cast:* John Glover (The Devil); Teri Polo (Detective Ashe); Lori Petty (Max); Michelle Forbes (Julia Trent); Robert Knepper (Stuart Lambert); John Hawkes (Frederick Wilcott Graver); Maria Costa (Waitress); Scott Lawrence (Fraker); Tim DeZarn, Jeff Corey, Frank Ozzolino, Laura Lee Botsacos, Dino Menninger, Bob Bonds, Gary Anthony Williams.

When the Devil pops up on a public access TV show and sits in on a panel with a man from the Southland Metaphysical Foundation who believes that people are spontaneously combusting, Stone takes on a new and bizarre case. The last victim of a "freak electrical accident" as the authorities are calling it, was an attorney named Errol Lichter. Stone follows the trail to a beautiful D.A. named Julia Trent, and learns that there have been five murders in four months ... all associated with electricity. Using the Internet with Max, Stone tracks the perp down and discovers he is a Hell escapee who takes a special glee in putting folks in the electric chair.

7. **"Slayer"** Written by Angel Dean Lopez; Story by Ethan Ruff and Cyrus Voris; Directed by Vern Gillum; airdate: December 11, 1998; *Guest Cast:* John Glover (The Devil);

Teri Polo (Detective Ashe); Albert Hall (Father Horne); Lori Petty (Max); Maria Costa (Waitress); Richard Brooks, Lisa Akey, Danielle Nicolet, Aaron Lustig, Ntare Mwine, Diane Robin, Joey Dente (Bartender); Michael Li (Uniform Cop); Eddie Watkins (Uniform Officer); Saida Pagan (Field Reporter).

A fierce warrior, Hazrable Scarus, returns to Earth and challenges Stone, whom he realizes is duty-bound to dispatch him back to Hell. The soldier knows that Stone will protect the innocent, but he fought in the Punic Wars for Carthage and delights in the murder of bystanders. Now the warrior from the past and the cop from the present must lock horns over a would-be alliance. Scarus wants to team up with Stone and rule the world, and he is killing innocent victims, the widows of slain police officers, to get what he wants.

8. **"Ashes"** Written by Angel Dean Lopez; Directed by Larry Carroll; airdate: December 18, 1998; *Guest Cast:* John Glover (The Devil); Teri Polo (Detective Ashe); Scott Lawrence (Fraker); Michael Bowen, Wayne Pere, Mark Pelligrino, Carlos La Camara, Nameer El Kadi (Al Samaysir); E.E. Bell (Mailman); Breck Charles White (Cop); Hershel Fox (Praying Man).

After the Devil shows up in his bed and admonishes him to go to church, Detective Stone looks into a series of church fires in L.A. Stone meets with a rabbi who has been monitoring the destruction of mosques, churches and synagogues, and he has found 4,000 year old Canaanite knives at each crime scene. Stone and Detective Ashe track the knives to a neo-Nazi and then an arsonist named Lee Varner. Ashe and Stone become emotionally involved as they work together to stop the arsonist ... but Ashe is not who she seems to be.

9. **"The Lovers"** Written by Chris Bertolet; Directed by John Kretchmer; airdate: January 8, 1999; *Guest Cast:* John Glover (The Devil); Jesse Borrego (Paco Gomez); Shannon Sturges (Jocelyn Paige); Lori Petty (Max); Scott Lawrence (Fraker); Maria Costa (Waitress); Castulo Guerra, Kevin Cooney, Mel

Winkler, Laurence Lau, Betty Carvalho, Brian Senter, Harry S. Murphy.

Stone needs a set of wheels, so after a brief flirtation with Rollerblading, he purchases a car from the Devil for $36.22 — all the money he has left in the world. The car comes in handy in tracking down a couple of Hell escapees, Paco and Jocelyn, both of whom died thirty years ago. Now they're reliving their glory days, trying to steal her aunt Ruth's money, and burning up the hearts of those who stand in their way. Stone first sends Paco back to Hell (with the help of a pointed hood ornament) and then turns his attention to the spoiled Jocelyn.

10. "Carrier" Written by Janis Diamond; Directed by Jesus Salvador Trevino; airdate: January 15, 1999; *Guest Cast:* John Glover (The Devil); Lori Petty (Max); Alexandra Powers (Sally Ann McGee); Lauren Sinclair (Dr. Maria Geyser); Maria Costa (Waitress); Dax Griffin, Kari Wiedergott, Steven Culp, Christian Bocher, David Correi, Craig Allen Wolf, Ray Proscia (Manager); Miriam Parrish (Christine); Jerry Hauck (Blue Collar Bartender); Devin Kamin (Drunken Party Guest).

A beautiful flapper, escaped from Hell, kills those she kisses because of an internal disease she has been incubating in the burning nether region for more than 75 years. Stone and a biological containment team led by Dr. Maria Geyser try to solve a murder at Writhe, the night club where the flapper struck. Then, the flapper, a salmonella typhoid carrier, manages to cause a disease outbreak at a party. Stone tracks down Sally Ann McGee, the killer, but she pulls a fast one on him and plants a big wet, juicy ... disease-ridden ... kiss on his eyes ...

11. "Faces" Written by Fred Golan; Directed by Larry Carroll; airdate: January 29, 1999; *Guest Cast:* John Glover (The Devil); Lori Petty (Max); Stefan Gierasch (Charles Reid); Jerry Hardin (Judge Thurston Bristol); Billy O'Sullivan, Greg Ellis, Joanna Canton, Timilee Romolini, Heidi Kling, Taffy Wallace, Billy Sly Williams, Michael C. Mahon

(Carl); Octavia L. Spencer (Duty Nurse); Barbara K. Whinnery (Katherine); John Apicella (Donny); Rawnie Leigh (Granddaughter).

The Devil directs Stone to 153 Green Street, a suburban street address, where a husband has just been murdered by an apparently schizophrenic escapee from Hell. Stone befriends one of the multiple personalities, a helpless teenage boy named Brian, and questions him about his "friends," the violent Vic and the protective Tammy. Stone soon learns that the boy was the subject of a book called *Beaten Down* (written in 1957) and that he went to Hell for murder ... but now he's returned to finish off his abusive stepdad.

12. "It's a Helluva Life" Written by Janis Diamond and Scott A. Williams; Directed by Felix Enriquez Alcala; airdate: February 5, 1999; *Guest Cast:* John Glover (The Devil/Angel); Stacy Haiduk (Rosalyn Stone); Ralph Seymour, Steven Durham, Jane Leigh Connelly, Vincent Berry, John Casini, Kevin Frye, Marisa Parker, Cody McMains, Rick Ike Jones (Bank Guard); Brett Walkow (Marvin); Alberto Vasquez (Carlin); Saida Pagan (Reporter).

Stone unexpectedly spots his wife, Rosalyn, during his pursuit of a bank-robbing Hell escapee, and then debates with the Devil about the course of his life. The Devil says that Stone was always a bad and unredeemable man, and then takes the detective on a tour of his life. Zeke and the Devil have ringside seats to review his short life: the neglect of his wife, the broken rules, the hurt inflicted on an innocent child during his own childhood, and so forth. Later, Stone is visited by an angel who looks just like the devil and tells him that there is an upside to his life.

13. "Mourning After" Written by Ethan Reiff and Cyrus Voris; From a story by Angel Dean Lopez; Directed by Dan Lerner; airdate: February 12, 1999; *Guest Cast:* John Glover (The Devil); Teri Polo (Ashe); Lori Petty (Max); Stacy Haiduk (Rosalyn Stone); Mark Valley (Barry Sinisa); Staci Greason, Esther Scott, Brooke Davis, Kay E. Kuter.

On Valentine's Day, a lonely Stone reminisces about his life with his wife, Rosalyn. He follows her home one night, unable to resist the temptation to be close to her, only to discover that there is another man in her life: a real estate agent named Barry. Stone drowns his sorrows at a bar with Max, who is also depressed about love, and then investigates a series of snake attacks near Rosalyn's house in Highland Park. As Stone gets closer to Rosalyn, he is confronted with a surprise: Barry is actually a shape-shifting and vengeful Ashe.

38

Strange World (1999)

CRITICAL RECEPTION

"Like a fourth-generation copy of a clever concept, this grim *X-Files* wannabe has the basic elements, but it's all a little garbled and hard to decipher. Tim Guinee stars as ... Paul Turner, a combat veteran battling the lethal effects of Gulf War Syndrome. He's kept alive by a series of vaccinations provided by a mysterious woman who warns him not to investigate too closely the origins of his illness ... Sound familiar? It should. Creator and executive producer Howard Gordon worked for four years on *The X-Files*." — *E Online Review*, "The Midseason Lineup," March 1999.

"The disturbingly derivative *Strange World* illustrates what *The X-Files* might have played like had it revolved around Gulf War Syndrome rather than the supernatural ... which isn't necessarily a solid foundation on which to build an action series ... It's hard to envision where *Strange World* will travel from here as it weaves a scenario in which it's left to one scientist with a battle-related illness to save mankind from itself ... Tech credits are fine, save for lighting that appears to have suffered from budget cutbacks." — Ray Richmond, *Variety*, March 9, 1999.

"Another *X-Files* clone ... Our advice? Skip your meds, doc, and get out of this dreary world." — Marc Bernardin, *Entertainment Weekly*, March 12, 1999.

FORMAT

Strange World is the chronicle of Dr. Paul Turner (Tim Guinee), an M.D. exposed to a deadly toxin during the Gulf War. In 1991, he returned home to the United States to die, only to discover that he was being kept alive by a mysterious antidote, administered by a secret conspiracy. For eight years, he did not know who was supplying him with the medicine to keep his acute aplastic anemia in remission, but in early 1999 Turner discovered the answer. A mysterious Japanese Woman (Vivian Wu) and a large pharmaceutical company had invested a great deal of money in him and his "cure," and were now bent on using him as a secret agent for their own, enigmatic agenda. At the same time, Turner's commanding officer from the army, Major Lynne Reese (Saundra Quartermain) recruits Turner to work for US ARMIID (United States Army Medical Institute for Infectious Diseases) to investigate the criminal abuses of science in the United States, permitted by Charter 44.

Turner is helped in his quest to learn more about his disease and his benefactors by his lover and former physician, a Yale educated M.D., Sydney MacMillan (Kristin Lehman).

Strange World is an hour-long action-adventure horror series from the talented Howard Gordon, longtime writer and producer for *The X-Files*. The series premiered in the early months of 1999. It was only broadcast three times before being canceled by its host network, ABC.

HISTORY

Strange World came out of nowhere and vanished to nowhere in a blink of an eye. Early in 1999, the ABC network began to publicize the imminent airing of what it called an "exclusive limited series," a title which in retrospect was an indicator that the network was not committed to either the series' success or its longevity. Created by Howard Gordon with Tim Kring, the TV series concerned one man's pursuit of the truth, and his continuing mission to expose "crimes of science" in turn-of-the-21st-century technological America. Like *The X-Files*, *Strange World* is steeped in paranoia and conspiracies, and like *The Burning Zone*, it has a strong biological/medical slant to its stories. Tim Guinee (*John Carpenter's Vampires* [1998], *Blade* [1998]) essayed the lead role of the "true believer," Paul Turner, and he did an excellent job of playing a hyperintense, hyperintelligent young man who has become a puppet for the "forces that be" thanks to a deadly disease and a mysterious cure. Despite his fine turn as Turner, most critics saw Guinee's character as a Fox Mulder knock-off, a comparison made worse by the fact that Guinee is physically appealing in much the same manner as David Duchovny … kind of an athletic/intellectual hunk. Also lending some confusion to this 1999 affair is the fact that its early guest stars all seem to be culled directly from recent *X-Files* and *Millennium* episodes, with Sarah-Jane Redmond ("Schizogeny," "Lamentation," "A Room with No View," "Antipas"), John Finn ("Redux," "Redux II," "Covenant") and William MacDonald ("Through a Glass Darkly") making prominent appearances. Because ABC so prominently advertised the behind-the-scenes connection to *The X-Files*, some viewers of *Strange World* were left confused … wondering if these familiar performers were supposed to be essaying the same roles as they had on the twin Chris Carter series.

Strange World began its abbreviated prime time run on Monday, March 8, 1999, at 10:00 P.M. It then moved to its regular time slot on Tuesday nights at 10:00 (briefly filling in for the hit cop show *NYPD Blue*). The show was only broadcast twice in its Tuesday slot before being eliminated by ABC. The network had originally planned to run five of the thirteen episodes it had ordered in that sortie, but the March 23 episode ("Spirit Falls") and the

March 30 episode ("Skin") were replaced by *NYPD Blue* and the series was canceled. Ironically, the last episode of *Strange World* broadcast on ABC ("Azrael's Breed") had featured a trailer for "Spirit Falls," an episode that was destined never to be shown! Loyal viewers (all five of them!) tuned in the following week only to be surprised that *Strange World* had vanished as quickly as it had come.

There was some talk of *Strange World* returning in either the fall of 1999 or as a midseason replacement in 2000, but those proved to be unfounded rumors and *Strange World* seems to be a "dead" property at this time, especially with producer Howard Gordon working on the *Buffy the Vampire Slayer* spin-off, *Angel*.

A horror show based in science and medicine, *Strange World* is another example of a series that was never given time to breathe or develop adequately. All the episodes aired showed considerable promise (certainly more promise than a whole season of *Charmed*). This could have been an excellent TV series if ABC (the network which had also trashed the promising *Prey*) had shown the same faith in it they had lavished on the once-low rated drama *The Practice*. *Strange World* qualifies as horror because even in its short run, it focuses on the terrifying side effects of unwarranted and unapproved scientific experiments. In the pilot, a boy is kidnapped and his parents discover that he is a clone … a fact made more hideous by the appearance of a bad Xerox copy of the boy (suffering the effects of replicative fading). In "Lullaby," babies are ripped from their mother's wombs, and the expectant women find, to their horror, that there were no babies there at all. Instead, their stomachs were simply a planting ground for organs to be harvested by a shadowy conspiracy! And, in "Azrael's Breed," a lunatic neurologist explores the boundaries of death by injecting brain cells from dead people into the minds of the living. These "death memories" become like a narcotic high for those who experience them, but they also are highly addictive. These are horror stories in the vein of Mary Shelley's novel *Frankenstein*: they raise questions about science, its applications, and its misuse, in a frightening and thought-provoking manner.

As odd as *Strange World* was, it could never survive in a much stranger world: the universe of TV ratings. As someone who watched it pass in the blink of an eye, this critic will miss its intelligence and its intensity. This one could have been a contender.

CRITICAL COMMENTARY

Even though it aired less than a third of all its episodes before facing the razor-sharp axe of hiatus, *Strange World* promptly delivered on its format promise to investigate "the criminal abuses of science." The pilot episode touched on the moral issues and ramifications of cloning, and whether or not an individual has the right to strive for immortality by re-creating himself as a youngster. The second story, "Lullaby," tackles the controversial concept of surrogate motherhood and the far more troubling idea of harvesting living organ banks so that people in need of donor organs will not have to wait so long. The third and most impressive episode, "Azrael's Breed," is a thinly veiled story about drug addiction. In this case, however, the narcotic to which people are addicted is the chemical memories of recently dead people. Like adrenaline junkies, the folks addicted to this new drug go out and kill for the excitement ... just so they can relive it later ... through a needle. There are withdrawal symptoms, scenes of people shooting up with hypodermics, and even a subplot about a promising young poet who drops out of school and loses her life and her potential — all over her addiction to this most unusual of drugs.

These are good stories, well-told, and Tim Guinee manages to be focused and concentrated throughout, serving as the viewer's tour guide to a world of conspiracies and medical and ethical dilemmas. As he states in the pilot, "science is changing everything — a lot faster than we expected." That is the bailiwick of *Strange World*, and a concept whose time has come. It plays on people's fears that science is running out of control, playing God, and tampering with our lives in ways that are frightening. And, as all horror fans know, horror works best when it is related to a real life fear. In this case, our fears of science are perfectly matched for the substance of this series.

Like *Brimstone*, *Strange World* acquits itself well from a visual standpoint. Some attempt has been made to make the show stand out, imagery-wise, from others. It has a dark, grainy-look, not quite burned-out, but low key and menacing. Perhaps what is best about *Strange World* is the fact that it realizes that horror is at its best when it is smart. So, in fast succession the audience is expected to understand things like Munchausen-by-Proxy syndrome, growth hormones, variable dosing, nerve cell regeneration, and the like. Unlike *Prey*, a good show that would often stop to rehash the scientific data presented by the leads (ostensibly so the viewers could keep up), *Strange World* never assumes that its audience was anything less-than-knowledgeable and well-versed in its lingo. It is not the first series that has failed because it aimed too high. Where *Millennium* mined "end of the world" scenarios successfully for three years, *Strange World* should have been allowed to do the same about science-generated monstrosities.

On the other hand, some of *Strange World* is a little bit *X-File*-like. The mysterious "Asian Woman," for instance, is but a shadow of the complex Cigarette Smoking Man on the former series. She is a caricature here, and her relevance to the overall story of *Strange World* is not made obvious in the series' short run. It is also derivative and troubling to see another man/woman investigative team in Turner/Sydney. Like Mulder, Turner is the believer (he even subscribes to Gulf War Syndrome internet sites) and like Scully, Sydney is a reality-grounded physician. This kind of imitative coupling failed on *Dark Skies*, and *The Burning Zone*, and it is both troubling and sad to see it resurrected once more for *Strange World*. Partners are fine, but why must the dynamic always be so derivative of Scully and Mulder? Why cannot the woman be the action lead, the believer, and the man be the skeptic for a change? Or is that too obvious also?

It is always dangerous to review a series that lives for such a short time. It is quite possible that *Strange World* would have answered successfully all the questions it raised during its first three episodes. On the other hand, it might have always remained confusing and derivative. The fact is, viewers and critics shall never know for sure. But when performances, stories, concepts, and production values are this good so early, there is sufficient reason to hope. *Strange World* should have been allowed to survive. At the very least, it should have been permitted to air all thirteen episodes in its roster.

CAST AND CREDITS

Cast: Tim Guinee (Dr. Paul Turner); Saundra Quartermain (Major Lynne Reese); Vivian Wu (Asian Woman/Japanese Woman/Mysterious Woman); Kristin Lehman (Dr. Sydney MacMillan).

Credits: Created by: Howard Gordon and Tim Kring. *Supervising Producer:* Harvey Frand. *Production Designer:* Lance King. *Executive Producer:* Howard Gordon. *Editor:* Lori Jane Coleman. *Music:* Michael Hoenig. *Directors of Photography (various episodes):* Jon Joffin, Peter Wunstorf. *Consulting Producer:* Mick Johnson. *Co-Producer:* Ron French. *Producer:* Tim Mincar. *Co-Executive Producer:* Manny Coto. *Story Editor:* John Chambers. *Associate Producer:* Tracey D'Arcy. *Original Casting:* Nan Dutton. *Additional Casting:* Coreen Mayrs. *Production Manager:* Ron French. *First Assistant Director:* Vladimir Stefoff. *Second Assistant Director:* Mark Currie. *Set Decorator:* Dominique Fouquel-Lemaitre. *Art Director:* Eric Norlin. *Property Masters:* Brent Lane, Alex Kutschera. *Costume Designer:* Jenni Gullett. *Key Hair:* Sanna Seppanen. *Key Makeup:* Connie Parker. *Special Effects Makeup:* Lindala Make-Up Effects, Inc. *Assistant to Mr. Gordon:* Shayne Wilson, Jose Molina. *Assistant to Mr. Coto:* Meredyth Smith. *Assistant to Harvey Frand:* Nancy Mosher. *Script Coordinator:* Neil H. Levin. *Writer's assistant:* Daniel Bolon. *Rerecording Mixers:* Larry Stensvold, Peter Elia. *Sound Mixer:* Tim Richardson, Gordon Anderson. *Script Supervisor:* Susan Lambie. *Technical Advisor:* Dr. Seke Emmai. *DaVinci Colorist:* Phil Azenzer. *Associate Editor:* Lisa Lessek. *Postproduction Coordinator:* Erica Bord. *Supervising Sound Editor:* Victor Torillo. *Music Editor:* Marty Woroski. *Special Effects Coordinator:* Andy Chamberlayne. *Stunt Coordinator:* J.J. Makaro. *Transportation Coordinator:* Mike Sassen. *Construction Coordinator:* Peter Grace. *Location Manager:* Scott Walden. *Production Coordinator:* Anita Mechon Truelove. *Assistant Production Coordinator:* Justin Peterson. *Camera Operator:* Mark Willis. *Gaffer:* Peter Slatter. *Key Grip:* Kim Olsen. *L.A. Casting Associate:* Anna Marie Donaghue. *Film Lab:* Rainmaker Digital Pictures. *Postproduction Audio:* Westwind Media. *Electronic Assembly:* Encore Video. Teakwood Lane Productions.

EPISODE GUIDE

1. "Pilot" Written by Howard Gordon and Tim Kring; Directed by Mick Jackson; airdate: March 8, 1999; *Guest Cast:* Michael Moriarty (General Conway); Bill Sage (Nathan Burke); Arnold Vosloo (Assassin); Sarah-Jane Redmond (Cynthia Ballard); William MacDonald (Mr. Ballard); Sheila Moore (Norma Burke); John Finn (Agent Hoffmann); Michael Mantell, Fulvio Cecere (Officer); Robert Lewis (F.B.I. agent); Jane Perry (Nurse).

Eight years ago, during the Gulf War, two U.S. soldiers, Turner and Burke, investigated a "hot zone" where American forces had bombed an Iraqi biological weapon site ... and the two men were subsequently contaminated. In the present, Turner has survived the deadly disease (acute aplastic anemia) because a mysterious organization has secretly been providing him with an unknown, untested antidote. Now the military and the organization want Turner to investigate a kidnapping apparently perpetrated by Turner's old partner, Burke. Turner soon uncovers layers of conspiracy to determine that the kidnapped child, Jeremy Ballard, is in fact a clone of Burke, who, because of his disease, is still trying to stay alive and even achieve immortality of a sort.

2. "Lullaby" Written by Tim Minear; Directed by Joseph Scanlon; airdate: March 9, 1999; *Guest Cast:* John Finn (Agent Richard Hoffmann); Monet Mazur, Randle Mell.

A teacher is rushed to the hospital during the last trimester of her pregnancy and is informed that her baby has died, when in fact *something* has been taken away from her. Later, another woman expecting a baby is afraid that her child will be abducted or killed too, and Sydney and Paul investigate her doctor. He informs them that the mother-to-be is paranoid, and a surrogate mother to boot! Turner soon uncovers a conspiracy in which surrogate mothers are implanted not with children, but with healthy human organs, which are then removed from the womb and sold on the black market at high prices.

3. "Azrael's Breed" Written by Manny Coto; Directed by Vern Gillum; airdate: March 16, 1999; *Guest Cast:* Lauren Velez (Detective Arias); Robert Knepper (Gil Sandefur); Melissa Crider (Celia Monroe); Mikela J. Mikela (Dana Monroe); Ron Souva (Larry Moses); Ryan Robbins (Bledsoe); Jenny Mitchell (Janice); Conor Topley (Chunky Kid); Shayn Solberg (Pony-Tailed Kid); Dalios Blake (Police Officer #1); Kristine Petzold (Nurse); Alessandro Julian (Ennis).

A series of "accidental" deaths are suspected to be murder when evidence of hypodermic injections in the nasal passages is found in each of the victims. Turner investigates the case with a cop and suspects that a prominent neurologist, Gil Sandefur, is experimenting with sensory neuron grafts which can transfer memory from one being to another. A girl involved with Gil is a former poet who experiences a rush from reliving the dying moments of other people's lives, and Turner hopes this memory "junkie" can lead them to Sandefur. Turner tracks down Sandefur, but as it turns out, Sandefur is already pursuing Turner, and hoping to give Paul a taste of this unusual "high."

Unaired Episodes

4. "Spirit Falls" Written by Todd Kessler and Tim Minear; Directed by Peter Markle; unaired.

Turner travels to the midwest to investigate the Jonestown-style mass-suicide of a "quiet" country town.

Note: This episode was originally to be aired on Tuesday, March 23, 1999, at 10:00 P.M., but was pulled from the schedule after *Strange World*'s cancellation.

5. "Skin" Written by Jessica Scott and Mike Wollaeger; Directed by Brett Dowler; unaired.

One of Sydney's former patients shows up at the hospital suffering from a rare and bizarre epidermal condition.

Note: This episode was originally to be aired on Tuesday, March 30, 1999, at 10:00 P.M., but was pulled from the schedule after *Strange World's* cancellation.

6. "Man Plus" Written by Howard Gordon and Thania St. John; Directed by Peter Markle; unaired.

7. "The Devil Still Holds My Hand" Written by John Chambers; Directed by Tucker Gates; unaired.

8. "Rage" Written by Manny Coto; Directed by James Whitmore, Jr.; unaired.

9. "Aerobe" Written by Manny Coto and Hans Tobeason; Directed by Dan Lerner; unaired.

10. "Food" Written by John Chambers; Directed by Tucker Gates; unaired.

11. "Eliza" Written by Tim Minear; Directed by Vern Gillum; unaired.

12. "Down Came the Rain" Written by Manny Coto and Jose Molina; Directed by Ian Toynton; unaired.

13. "Age of Reason" Information unavailable; unaired.

39

G vs E (1999–)

CRITICAL RECEPTION

"the best new show of the summer ... It's sort of 'Touched by an Angel to Kick Butt' ... *G vs E* has a smashing visual style — oddball camera placements, tinted colors seeping into the scenes, jump cuts that would make Jean-Luc Godard's neck snap ... and Brooks is a hoot ... a modern-day Shaft with end-of-the-century smarts and irony." — Ken Tucker, *Entertainment Weekly*, July 20, 1999.

"wildly eccentric comedy-thriller that breaks from the gate feeling uncommonly hip and clever ... The actors play it all to deadpan perfection ... Tech credits are spiffy, particularly the artistically ambitious photography and makeup that help make for some agreeably cheesy f/x." — Ray Richmond, *Variety*, July 16, 1999.

"best described as *Brimstone* goes goofy ... The overly violent show has some trouble being gritty and crazy at the same time, but the G in it outweighs the E ... Bottom line: can be devilishly funny." — Erik Meers, *People*, July 26, 1999, page 27.

"An oh-so-droll comedy thriller ... the twin brothers Pate shrink from blatant sentimentality of the *Touched by an Angel* and *Highway to Heaven* sort, occasionally going a little too far to prove that they laugh in the face of death ... but it all makes for devilish fun." — Barbara D. Phillips, *The Wall Street Journal*: "TV: Touched by the Devil," July 12, 1999, page A26.

FORMAT

When washed-up journalist Chandler Smythe (Clayton Rohner) is killed by demons in a dark alley (on his birthday of all days), he leaves behind an unfinished life. He has not squared things with his delinquent teenage son, and there is a very good chance he could go to hell because he is an absentee father. Chandler is rescued from this unpleasant fate by the Corps, a top secret organization run by the Big Man, God! Chandler will have a second chance at life as an agent for the Corps so long as he combats the dark forces of evil.

It will not be an easy life, however. Chandler will have no superpowers, he is not allowed to have sexual intercourse, and worst of all, he is not able to contact anyone from his previous life ... not even his son. Operating out of a secret Corps headquarters/squad room inside Geraldo's Casa De Tires, Chandler and his new partner, a jive-talking, afro-wearing refugee from the 1970s named Henry McNeil (Richard Brooks), fight the morlocks (mortals/warlocks), demonic villains attempting to sway human beings to the darkside. Hollywood happens to be the center of the action for morlocks and Emmanuel Lewis, Gavin McLeod, LeAnn Rimes, and Orrin Hatch, are all known morlocks. This evil busting duo must also keep people called "Faustians" from making deals with the aforementioned morlocks. On occasion, Chandler and Henry are also helped by their put-upon superiors, Ford (Marshall Bell) and Decker (Googy Gress).

Such is the format of the USA Network hour-long horror comedy *G vs E*. What the above recapitulation of the series does not express, however, is that on this show, style is *all*. It is hip times three. *G vs E* relishes in split screens (sometimes as many as three per shot), jump cuts, askew angles, slow-motion photography, freeze-frames, and the like. The interrogation sequence which opens the premiere, "Orange Volvo," is a sly parody of all those police "interview" sessions on *NYPD Blue*, right down to the shaky hand-held camera work. Premiering on Sunday nights at 8:00 in the summer of 1999, the slick and sassy *G vs E* almost instantly became a darling of critics and audiences alike for its audacious, stylish, and rambunctious mix of humor, hipness and horror. Hopefully, this battle between good and evil will be with us for a long time.

HISTORY

In 1996, the Pate Brothers made a big splash with their low-budget film *The Grave*, a favorite of the independent film circuit, and it was not long before this talented duo was recruited by an ever-watchful Hollywood. The dramatic (and comedic) horror series *G vs E* is their first "establishment" effort, and it is a hoot through and through. Following in the tradition of *Forever Knight*'s third season, the series has been produced for airing on the cable network, USA, and the series started broadcasting first-run, hour-long episodes during the summer of 1999. Scheduled at 8:00 P.M. on Sunday nights, before other first-run dramas such as *Pacific Blue* and the popular *La Femme Nikita*, *G vs E* stars Clayton Rohner (*Star Trek: The Next Generation:* "Too Short a Season," *The Relic* [1997], *The X-Files*: "Rain King") as a man who returned from the grave to fight in the "Corps" against demons.

According to Josh Pate, this idea came from an unlikely source.

> It all started with a dream ... One morning, my brother [Jonas] called me up and told me about this dream he had where he was killed in an alleyway and these people come and offer him a deal where he could stay on Earth and fight this secret war.[1]

If that (very) brief plot summary sounds somewhat reminiscent of *Brimstone*, the late lamented Fox 1998 cult show, it is deceptive. Instead of being a grim, atmospheric, graphic novel for television, *G vs E* is a hyper, silly throwback to the 1970s. With an opening credits sequence straight out of *Charlie's Angels* (down to the split screens and freeze frames), it is horror-hip rather than horror-dark. There is no moral relativism here, thank you very much! Drunk with its own cleverness, the series quickly became the highlight of the summer of 1999 (at least until *The Blair Witch Project* made such a splash), and it has been warmly received by critics who appreciate its knowing, self-reflexive humor and acid wit. The series has also snagged an important victory in the Nielsen ratings. Its debut in July of 1999 catapulted USA into the number one most watched basic cable station position. The first two episodes of the series also showed a 56 percent increase in viewership on the USA network for that time period.

Although only about seven episodes have aired by the time of this writing, it is safe to say that *G vs E* has found a niche by alluding simultaneously to 1970s cinematic and TV style and 1990s post-*Scream* post-modernism. A trademark (thus far) of the show has been its eccentric, comedic casting: Emmanuel Lewis (*Webster*) as an agent of evil in "Buried," Dawn Wells (*Gilligan's Island*), Charlene Tilton (*Dallas*) and Erin Moran (*Happy Days*) as co-conspirators in "Gee, Your Hair Smells Evil," and so forth. Deacon Jones also has a recurring bit part as the Corps training expert, and at the end of each episode he demonstrates (usually on a live candidate) offensive tactics such as "The Head Slap" and "The Rip Up," both of which could be employed against the Morlocks. Also adding to *G vs E*'s cool veneer is a bevy of weird musical artists who contribute songs to the episodes, including Boards of Canada ("Music Has the Right to Children"), Burger/Ink ("Las Vegas"), Come ("Gently Down the Stream"), Guided by Voices ("Mag Earwhig") and Nightmares on Wax ("Carboot Soul").

A kind of *Shaft* meets *Charlie's Angels* meets *Brimstone* meets *Touched by an Angel* meets *Starsky and Hutch* meets *The Prophecy*, the young *G vs E*, at least at this early date, seems destined for greatness in the Terror TV hall of fame. If it survives its first season and continues to so successfully mix scares with laughter, *G vs E* just might remain a memorable entry in the Terror TV Valhalla. Tune in.

CRITICAL COMMENTARY

Proving that the turn of the century is a great time for the horror genre, *G vs E* has blasted its way onto our airwaves and really shaken things up. Like *The X-Files, American Gothic, Millennium*, or *Brimstone*, this is a contemporary series which can rightfully make the claim that it is as artistic as it is entertaining. Wes Craven, the director of numerous horror films, once made the point that horror and comedy are two genres which are intertwined, since both depend heavily on suspense, pacing, and timing. The end result may be different, a laugh rather than a gasp, but the mechanisms which deliver the gut punch or the punch line are identical. *G vs E* has taken that lesson to heart, a fact which results in one of the most amusing genre series to come this way in a long, long time.

The *Pulp Fiction* (1994) of modern terror television, *G vs E* has an uncanny knack to deliver laughs and chills at exactly the right moments and in the right proportions. Amazingly, it does so not only with its dead-on performances from series leads (the cool Brooks and the immensely likable Rohner) and good, amusing scripts, but through its very bizarre, very clever narrative structure. In particular, *G vs E* utilizes time and time's passage to its advantage like no other series in history. It has no devotion to linear storytelling (hence the *Pulp Fiction* reference above) and instead manipulates time to heighten suspense, generate laughs, or involves viewers in the predicament of the week.

"Evilator" is a perfect example of this tendency. This episode opens with a bravura action sequence high inside a morlock-controlled sky rise, and a spectacular danger: Henry and Chandler become trapped in an elevator that has been "dropped" and is careening towards the ground ... and disaster. As the floors race by at a dizzying speed and the suspense is at an apex, the "Evilator" tele-

play (by Marshall Page) shifts gears and gives us a flashback explaining how the agents found themselves in this unusual predicament. By cutting between deadly present and explanatory past, the creators of *G vs E* manage to lengthen the level of suspense throughout much of the hour. Where a falling elevator might be a two minute set-piece (at most) on most ordinary shows, *G vs E* manages to turn the situation into an episode-long threat! The story keeps flashing backwards and forwards so fast, sometimes for just a minute of nonsensical exposition, that heads are nearly spinning. Another good early show, "Airplane," does the same thing: marooning Chandler and Henry on a doomed airliner and then working backwards to the beginning of the drama before, finally, resolving the teaser's heart-pounding dilemma.

"Buried" is another show which utilizes time in an unusually effective manner. Henry is seen relaxing at home when he gets a call from Chandler requesting help. Chandler has been buried alive in a coffin, and water is leaking in from somewhere. For the rest of the episode, Henry goes in search of Chandler, trying to find his partner before he drowns or asphyxiates in his own coffin. Making matters worse, Chandler has no idea where he is, because he lost consciousness after an encounter with a morlock. In this case, the threat is immediately established, and the remainder of the hour-long show cross-cuts mercilessly between Henry's very unlucky search for Chandler (which involves, of all things, a transsexual dominatrix) and Chandler's ever-worsening plight, trapped in the death box. Unwilling to go gently, Chandler keeps reinserting himself in the picture (literally — via split screen) by phoning Henry at inopportune times, and the fast-paced suspense becomes unbearable. This is a "ticking clock" show, with every moment leading savagely to the point when Chandler either suffocates or drowns in his coffin. As Henry takes each step toward finding Chandler, he is dealt a reverse, and the camera cuts back obligingly to Chandler's woes: he is up to his neck, then up to his eyeballs in water! Yikes! Besides the "ticking clock" premise of "Buried," which lends it incredible tension, this episode also has the audacity to cast Emmanuel Lewis as a morlock ... and then blow him to smithereens!

Episodes of *G vs E* move at warp speed, like *Brimstone* on acid, because sometimes four things are happening at once: the screen is literally "split" into four scenes, each one depicting various perspectives and various characters. In "Gee, Your Hair Smells Evil" Chandler is wired with a camera by an evil morlock and forced to invade Corps Headquarters. The pace grows frenetic as the episode shows us (simultaneously): Chandler entering the establishment and "gliding" through the office (mimicking a trick seen in many Spike Lee films), the camera's (i.e., Chandler's) perspective as he enters the building; the morlock agent watching this information on a monitor; and, finally, poor Henry being tortured on a gazebo (?), being jolted with electric shocks. Thus, on one TV screen, these four viewpoints manage to give the audience an overload of important and relevant plot/character information. The close shot on Chandler's entrance in the Corps shows his trepidation as he is forced to become a traitor to the cause. The shot from the hidden "Chandlercam" tells the audience where the agent is heading, and reveals the obstacles in his way. The shot of the morlock reminds us who is behind the treachery, and that there is no opportunity to back out of it. And, finally, the shot of Henry in danger clarifies the reason why Chandler has turned double agent. This kind of sensory overload is challenging, brilliantly done, and fast-paced.

So often, television fails by assuming that the audience is stupid, or simply unable to grasp important plot details. *Poltergeist: The Legacy* and *Prey* are two series, both good — all considered — which tell the audience everything at least twice. Flashbacks (in black and white) are inserted in both shows to remind viewers who the bad guys are, or to clarify bits of data, and background detail that is obvious to any viewer who is not catatonic. In one episode of *Prey*, the new species member named Tom leaves behind an article of cloth-

ing in Sloan's apartment. The camera showed us this action once (in master shot), then provided a black and white flashback of the same action so the audience would be *sure* to understand where Sloan found the clothing, which she then used to analyze Tom's DNA. *G vs E* very commendably takes the opposite approach. It overloads the audience with so much information that viewers are literally dared to keep up. This show *moves*, and it does so with sure footing.

At the same time that *G vs E* brilliantly deploys jump cuts, freeze frames, slow-motion photography, split screens, high and low angles, and the like, it also manages to be dead-on with its satirical commentary. One episode, "To Be or Not to Be ... Evil," takes on the career of Kevin Williamson, the writer who rose to fame with the screenplay for *Scream* (1996), cemented that fame by writing *I Know What You Did Last Summer* (1997), and then established what will undoubtedly be a long career in the industry by creating the teen-angst TV series *Dawson's Creek* (1998–). By *G vs E*'s way of thinking, the only *possible* way that someone could manage this degree of instant success would be by signing a Faustian deal with the devil! The episode mocks Williamson's trademark brand of "chic" slasher pictures by showing five "fashionable" (yet strangely identical ...) posters for each of the sequels to *I Saw What You Did Last Winter* (about a killer janitor who mutilates teenagers with a shovel). The episode also dramatizes a scene from an insipid, psycho-babble-laden *Dawson's Creek*-style TV drama called *Dunbar's Lake*, and even shows the Williamson stand-in (named Todd Charleston) to be an egomaniacal little tyro. At the same time that "To Be or Not to Be ... Evil" pokes fun at Kevin Williamson's meteoric rise to fame, it takes aim at America's culture of celebrity.

To wit: A tempted Harry signs a Faustian deal with the Devil after getting a taste of how "rewarding" it is to be popular, rich, and part of the Hollywood elite. In a culture where everybody wants to be a star, and everybody gets their "fifteen minutes of fame," *G vs E* reminds us, in its own light-handed fashion, that there is a price to pay for laying down alongside the insipid elite of the jet set.

G vs E takes punches at other figures and productions with equal vigor. Its opening episode, "Orange Volvo," begins with a long "police" interrogation scene of the deceased Chandler Smythe that mimics in style the umpteen Sipowitz/Simone interviews of perps in the popular but tiring *NYPD Blue*. The herky-jerky, hand-held camera; the deal laid out for the perp; the heavyset cop acting tough while the thinner one is more sympathetic ... all these clichés are carried over to *G vs E* with hysterical results. At the same time, this *NYPD Blue*-style informs the audience immediately about the content of the show. In one sense, *G vs E* is a police procedural and partner show, just like the cop drama it mimics. On the other hand, as in this interview sequence, it will take those ideas (partners/cops/bad guys on the street) and reinvent them.

The ingenuity of *G vs E* is sometimes simply startling. In one episode, Chandler, Henry, Ford, and Decker are eating french fries at an L.A. burger joint when a morlock stages a drive-by shooting. The heroes of the series are splattered not with red blood ... but with the red ketchup from their fries, though the result looks very much the same. In the aforementioned "Evilator," a young girl is a double agent for the morlocks and Decker gets her to confess by dismembering and decapitating her collection of Barbie dolls! This show is weird, but fun.

Another of *G vs E*'s many delights is its celebrity cameo appearances. Erin Moran, a former *Happy Days* cast member who once came out in the press to "pray" for her former co-workers, plays an agent of evil in "Gee, Your Hair Smells Evil," along with Charlene Tilton, Jill Whelan, and Dawn Wells. Emmanuel Lewis and film star Theresa Russell have also shown up ... as morlocks and Faustians, naturally, to good comedic effect. These cameos never threaten to overtake the show, but they do add an additional degree of fun to the bizarre proceedings.

Although it may be a bit early to make such a declaration, *G vs E* is one of modern Terror TV's ten best series. Its vivid imagery, its great performances, its whacked vision of the world, its celebrity cameos, and its brilliant use of film technique make it a superb series that deserves to live a long life.

CAST AND CREDITS

Cast: Clayton Rohner (Chandler Smythe); Richard Brooks (Henry McNeil); Marshall Bell (Ford); Googy Gress (Jack Decker).

Credits: Created by: Josh and Jonas Pate. *Casting:* Jennifer Fishman, Amy McIntyre-Britt, Anya Colloff. *Music:* Will Thomas. *Production Design:* Mark Hutman. *Editor:* Joshua Butler. *Director of Photography:* Michael Grady. *Associate Producer:* Barclay Dereau. *Co-Producer:* Mark T. Hyatt. *Executive Producers:* Jonas and Josh Pate, Paul Biddle. *Unit Production Manager:* Nancy Noever. *First Assistant Director:* Tony Steinberg. *Second Assistant Director:* Valerie Ann Bleth. *Location Manager:* Douglas Dresser. *Production Coordinator:* Paul A. Lucero. *Set Decorator:* Jennie Harris. *Lead Man:* J.M. Vasquez. *Set Dressers:* Graeme Perez, Justin Mulchy, Chad Vachter. *Costume Designer:* Erik LeMass Pattner. *Property Master:* Matthew Cavaliero. *Visual Consultant:* Austin Gorg. *Script Supervisor:* Gene Babcock. *Camera Operator:* Patrick Rouisseau. From Rockfish Films/USA Network.

EPISODE GUIDE

1. "Orange Volvo" Written and directed by the Pate Brothers; airdate: July 18, 1999; *Guest Cast:* Tony Denman, Deacon Jones (Himself); Susie Parks, Blake Heron, Ashley Rogers, Troy Evans,

Reporter Chandler Smythe is murdered by a demon in an alley after attending his own birthday party. He awakens to find himself in the headquarters for the Corps, and is given a chance to redeem himself by becoming an

Agent for Good, a warrior in the battle against evil. Chandler meets his new partner, Henry, and then is assigned his first task: to determine who really killed a cop, even though a Russian shopkeeper was framed for the crime. After a sting at L.A. Burger ends in sniper fire and Henry's car is stolen (by Chandler's delinquent son), other means of solving the case and stopping a demon called El Aurens are required.

2. "Men Are from Mars, Women Are Evil" Written by Bill Wolff; Directed by Josh Pate; airdate: July 25, 1999; *Guest Cast:* Deacon Jones (Himself); Shannon Elizabeth (Cherry Vallance); Mariah O'Brien (Marcy); Ron Marasco, Michael Cudlitz, Bart Braverman, Lorna Scott, Lisa Boyle (Gigi Peaks); Dana Patrick (Candy Striper); David Stifel (Mel Scheinberger); Kimberly Huie (Nisco); Chris Owens (Trekkie); James Brown-Orleans (South African); Christopher Neiman (Cop #1); Adam Ritz (Cop #2); Phyllis Franklin (Neighbor).

Chandler is arrested for the murder of Cherry Vallance, a beautiful red-headed stripper who was really killed by a Faustian-turned-morlock named Dr. Love. Chandler met with Cherry at the House of Pies and was charmed by her sweet nature, but he had to be careful not to break the Corps edict about having sexual intercourse. The cops grill Chandler about his role in the murder, aware of his suspicious visit to Ye Olde Porn and Comic Shoppe to find the exact brand of "Death" card left on the scene of the crime by Dr. Love. Henry springs Chandler from police custody to lay a trap for Dr. Love.

3. "Buried" Written and directed by Josh Pate; airdate: August 1, 1999; *Guest Cast:* Deacon Jones (Himself); Emmanuel Lewis (Himself); Tony Denman, Susie Park, Reno Wilson, Michael Paul Chan, Frank Roman, Thomas Burr; Ruben Madera, Wells Rosales, Franklin Hernandez, Marco Roe (Gang Members).

A claustrophobic Chandler awakens after working on the Culpepper case to find himself in a coffin, buried alive, with water leaking in! While Chandler recounts (on his cell phone) how he came to be in this dire situation after trying to prevent professional boxer Terry Culpepper from making a deal with the Devil, Henry searches in vain for his missing partner. A comedy of errors ensues as the moments tick away and Harry finds himself besieged by bad drivers, thrown into a car trunk, captured by Latino thugs, and prepared for human sacrifice by a satanist drag queen. Henry learns that the morlocks want to exchange Chandler for the freedom of a vicious morlock leader: Emmanuel Lewis.

4. "Gee, Your Hair Smells Evil" Written by Josh and Jonas Pate; Directed by Jonas Pate; airdate: August 8, 1999; *Guest Cast:* Deacon Jones (Himself); Susie Park (Walker); Cyd Strittmatter, Pedro Balmaceda, Ray Proscia, Dawn Wells (Herself); Charlene Tilton (Herself); Erin Moran (Herself); Jill Whelan (Herself).

Ford is criticized by his superior, Koslo, even though Faustian renunciation is on the rise in Hollywood. In response, Ford sends Chandler and Henry to get a renunciation out of Gregor, a man who went from flunking cosmetology school to being the hair-stylist to the rich and famous. Not only must the duo help this Faustian, they must target his morlock, the villainous Morgan Le Fay, and defeat her evil plans for world domination. When a renunciation goes bad, Henry is captured and forced to endure the brutal "Torture-Lux" while Le Fay forces Chandler to transmit footage of the secret Corps headquarters and steal the agent register.

5. "Airplane" Written and directed by Josh Pate; airdate: August 15, 1999; *Guest Cast:* Deacon Jones (Himself); Fred Willard (Sam Kleinhouser); Pat Skipper (Ray Lee Morris); Marianne Filali (Esmerelda); Ric Sarabia (Farley Pollat); Kyle Colderidge-Kruge, Jan Hoag, Shelly Malil, Colin Campbell, Caren Saiet, Brad Miller (Tony Collins); Dora Rowe (Jenny); Michelle Ruben (Groupie); Foofer Beachwood (Bonnie Smythe); Brian Card (Middle Agent Man #1); Doug Tempos (Middle Agent Man #2).

Henry and Chandler board a plane with a morlock assassin in their custody. In midair, the minion of evil breaks free, kills the pilot, and parachutes from the plane. The Corps tries to talk Chandler out of the deadly inflight situation, but he accidentally dumps all remaining fuel, worsening the situation. Knowing the end is near, Henry breaks Corps laws and gets laid by a beautiful Spanish agent named Esmerelda, even as Chandler realizes there are still two parachutes aboard.

6. **"Evilator"** Written and directed by Marshall Page; airdate: August 22, 1999; *Guest Cast:* Deacon Jones (Himself); Mary Mara (Leona); Marianne Filali (Esmerelda); Nicolette Little (Sandy Blair); Joseph Campanella (Dr. Townsend); Shaun Toub, Carl Anthony Payne II, Ezra Buzzington, Jay Michael Ferguson.

During a botched rescue attempt for the Corps, Henry, Chandler and a female hostage are trapped inside an elevator in the Magog Pharmaceutical Company. The hostage is Leona, the best Corps agent in the business, an operative who has been working undercover to stop production of a pill which would cloak the gruesome appearance of the morlocks. In response to the incursion, the morlocks, commanded by Dr. Townsend, drop the elevator in the massive skyrise, sending Henry, Chandler, and Leona spiraling downwards to their doom. With only a few seconds left to live, Chandler suggests that they depend on an old urban legend and jump at the final moment of elevator impact.

7. **"To Be or Not to Be ... Evil"** Written by David A. Kleiler; Directed by Dan Ireland; airdate: August 29, 1999; *Guest Cast:* Deacon Jones (Himself); Susie Park (Walker); Walter Olkewitz (Gus Wine); T.J. Thyne (Todd); Ian Abercrombie (Ray); Jessica Harper, David Deluise, Barry Sobel, Andy Milder, Jean Kasem, Theresa Russell (Resa Tussle); Richard Stuart (Dunbar); Holly Towne (Doomed Blonde); Sticky Fingaz (Rapper); Linda Porter (Mather); Paul Bartel (Photographer); Daphney Damareaux (Sitcom Wife).

Henry and Chandler become extras on the set of a hospital show called "On Call" to find out if a guest star, Gus Wine, has made a Faustian deal in exchange for his newfound stardom. On the set, Henry is asked to audition for a morlock producer responsible for the slasher franchise *I Saw What You Did Last Winter* and the teen psychobabble drama "Dunbar's Lake." After a successful callback, Henry becomes enamored with the possibility of fame and signs a Faustian blood contract. When Henry becomes a big star, he claims he is simply under "deep cover," but Chandler is afraid he has lost his friend and partner to the morlocks.

Postscript: After its summer run on USA, *G vs E* was renamed *Good Versus Evil*, toned down to be more traditional, sold to the Sci-Fi Channel ... and promptly cancelled. Ahead of its time, *G vs E* is nonetheless a memorable, high quality production in its first incarnation.

40

Angel (1999–)

CRITICAL RECEPTION

"… riskier … more audacious from the norm … an atmosphere entirely different from *Buffy*'s … fully satisfying across a whole range of emotions."— Ken Tucker, *Entertainment Weekly*, December 3, 1999.

FORMAT

In Joss Whedon's sequel to *Buffy the Vampire Slayer*, Angel, the vampire with a soul (played by David Boreanaz), opens up his own detective agency in Los Angeles. His mission: to help lost souls fight evil, and find his own redemption in the process. Angel is aided in this quest by Cordelia Chase (Charisma Carpenter) and Doyle (Glenn Quinn), a demon with prophetic visions. Angel also frequently crosses paths with L.A.P.D. officer Kate Lochley (Elizabeth Rohm). After Doyle is killed in the middle of the first season, his powers of prophecy are passed on to Cordelia, and former Vampire-Watcher, Wesley Price (Alexis Denisof), joins the team. During the course of the first season, Angel butts head with an evil law firm called Wolfram & Hart, renegade slayer Faith (Eliza Dushku), and a variety of demons with unique powers.

HISTORY

During *Buffy the Vampire Slayer*'s well-received third season on the air, Whedon announced that Angel, the angst-ridden 244-year-old vampire, would soon be featured in a spin-off of the popular WB hit. The series

was to pick up with Angel moving to Los Angeles (and leaving behind the love of his very long life, Buffy Summers). Angel's overriding goal would be to make "amends" for his centuries on Earth as a brutal, murderous vampire.

As the fall of 1999 neared, rumors flew fast and thick about the details of *Angel*. The first was that the series was going to be a variation on *Charlie's Angels* with Angel operating behind the scenes and directing the action of three lovely ladies (during the daytime): Cordelia, Kate and Faith (Eliza Dushku), the slayer who had turned "bad" during *Buffy*'s third year. When Eliza Dushku turned down a continuing role on the series, most people figured that the *Charlie's Angels* format was out, even though Cordelia has been described in press reports as being Angel's "Girl Friday."

Another change came rapidly. The character named Whistler, who had been seen from time to time on *Buffy the Vampire Slayer*, was removed. Replacing Whistler, Whedon created a character named Doyle—a friendly demon. To the dismay of many fans, Doyle would not survive the first year.

Lensed at night in L.A., Sarah Michelle Gellar, Eliza Dushku, James Marsters and Seth Green all made exciting, provocative appearances on *Angel*, and reminded viewers of the connection between Joss Whedon ventures.

Angel has been termed a darker, more adult version of *Buffy the Vampire Slayer*, one that labors on the idea of redemption. This is an interesting idea, as Buffy and her friends ascend to college and a brighter tomorrow … and Angel continues, forever, in the dark. The focus on Angel making "amends" also rings of the Nick Knight syndicated melodrama, *Forever Knight*.

Angel faces a challenge in its second season from James Cameron's FOX series *Dark Angel*, airing opposite it on Tuesday. Perhaps *Angel* has little to worry about, since *TV Guide*'s critic Matt Roush named it one of the best new shows of the 1999-2000 season.

CRITICAL COMMENTARY

Though *Angel*'s first season only sometimes featured the perfect blend of humor and action so evident in *Buffy*, overall the series seems to be on solid ground. David Boreanaz is an interesting, talented lead, and the moments wherein he breaks out of "solemn" mode to unexpectedly dance at a party or sing karaoke, really grant the show great humor and vitality. It is the old Mr. Spock principle. The best moments on *Star Trek*, inevitably, were those when the logical Vulcan broke out of dour mode to reveal emotion. The same thing applies to *Angel*. Boreanaz really understands both sides of the character: the pathos and the humor. *Angel* is the stronger for this actor's insightful approach to what could have been a cardboard "super hero" role. Charisma Carpenter's Cordelia retains her hard, sarcastic edge on this series, and Alexis Denisoff is an effective surrogate for *Buffy*'s Giles. No doubt, the team is a good one, and it gels better in each successive episode.

Angel has also staked out separate ground from *Forever Knight*, with something *Forever Knight* lacked: real wit, and real humor. Hopefully *Angel* will live for many seasons; it's already well on its way...

CAST & CREDITS

Cast: David Boreanaz (Angel); Charisma Carpenter (Cordelia Chase); Glenn Quinn (Doyle); Elizabeth Rohm (Kate Lochley); Alexis Denisof (Wesley).

Credits: Created by: Joss Whedon and David Greenwalt. *Consulting Producer:* Marti Noxon. *Producers:* Tim Minear and Kelly Manners. *Co-Producer:* James. A. Contner, Skip Schoolnik. *Executive Producers:* Sandy Gallin, Gail Berman, Fran Rubel Kuzui, Kaz Kuzui, Joss Whedon, David Greenwalt. *Consulting Producer:* Howard Gordon. *Associate Producer:* R.D. Price. *Director of Photography:* Herbert Davis. *Production Designer:* Stuart Blatt. *Editor:* Mark Goldman.

EPISODE GUIDE

1. "City of" Written by Joss Whedon and David Greenwalt; Directed by Joss Whedon; airdate: October 5, 1999.

Angel moves to Los Angeles, and teams up with unemployed actress (and ex–Sunnydale resident) Cordelia Chase. Together, they work with good-guy demon Doyle to form a detective agency and fight evil.

2. "Lonely Hearts" Written by David Fury; Directed by James A. Contner; airdate: October 12, 1999.

Angel stakes out a bar to find a killer who targets lonely hearts, teaming up with beautiful cop, Kate Lochley.

3. "In the Dark" Written by Douglas Petrie; Directed by Bruce Seth Green; airdate: October 19, 1999.

Two visitors from Sunnydale spell trouble for Angel when they grapple over an artifact that allows vampires to walk in the sunlight.

4. "I Fall to Pieces" Written by David Greenwalt; Directed by Vern Gillum; airdate: October 26, 1999.

Angel must protect a woman from a killer who can disassemble and re-assemble his own body parts.

5. "Room w/a Vu" Written by Jane Espenson; Directed by Scott McGinnis; airdate: November 2, 1999.

Cordelia moves into an apartment inhabited by a ghost.

6. "Sense and Sensitivity" Written by Tim Minear; Directed by James A. Contner; airdate: November 9, 1999.

7. "The Bachelor Party" Written by Tracey Stern; Directed by David Straiton; airdate: November 16, 1999.

Doyle attends the bachelor party of his ex-wife's new fiancée ... and finds out that he will be the "guest of honor."

8. "I Will Remember You" Written by David Greenwalt and Jeannine Renshaw; Directed by David Grossman; airdate: November 23, 1999.

Buffy visits Los Angeles just as Angel unexpectedly becomes fully human, infected by the blood of an unusual demon.

9. "Hero" Written by Howard Gordon and Tim Minear; Directed by Tucker Gates; airdate: November 30, 1999.

Doyle gives his life to save homeless demons from a fascist, demonic army and their doomsday weapon.

10. "Parting Gifts" Written by David Fury and Jeannine Renshaw; Directed by James A. Contner; airdate: December 14, 1999.

Cordelia inherits Doyle's ability to read visions from the Powers that Be, while Wesley, a "rogue demon hunter," joins the team.

11. "Somnambulist" Written by Tim Minear; Directed by Winrich Kolbe; airdate: January 18, 2000.

12. "Expecting" Written by Howard Gordon; Directed by David Semel; airdate: January 25, 2000.

Cordelia awakens from a one-night stand with a human-appearing demon to find herself pregnant.

13. "She" Written by David Greenwalt and Marti Noxon; Directed by David Greenwalt; airdate: February 8, 2000.

Angel helps a beautiful warrior as she frees her own kind from male subjugation on a trans-dimensional underground railroad.

14. "I've Got You Under My Skin" Written by Jeannine Renshaw; Directed by R.D. Price; airdate: February 15, 2000.

15. "The Prodigal" Written by Tim Minear; Directed by Bruce Seth Green; airdate: February 22, 2000.

Angel runs afoul of Kate's father, a retiring police officer.

16. "The Ring" Written by Howard Gordon; Directed by Nick Marck; airdate: February 29, 2000.

Angel is forced to fight in gladiatorial games.

17. "Eternity" Written by Tracey Stern; Directed by Regis B. Kimble; airdate: April 4, 2000.

18. "Five by Five" Written by Jim Kouf; Directed by James A. Contner; airdate: April 25, 2000.

Angel is haunted by his existence as an evil vampire, and Faith arrives in Los Angeles ... to assassinate him.

19. "Sanctuary" Written by Tim Minear and Joss Whedon; Directed by Michael Lange; airdate: May 2, 2000.

Angel seeks to reform Faith — an idea the visiting Buffy Summers can't stomach.

20. "War Zone" Written by Garry Campbell; Directed by David Straiton; airdate: May 9, 2000.

Angel teams with an African-American hero, Gunn, who fights vampires in the seedier parts of L.A.

21. "Blind Date" Written by Jeannine Renshaw; Directed by Thomas J. Wright; airdate: May 16, 2000.

A blind assassin arrives in L.A. to kill Angel, and Angel steals a prophetic scroll from Wolfram & Hart.

22. "To Shanshu in L.A." Written and directed by David Greenwalt; airdate: May 23, 2000.

Angel learns that he will one day become human, even as his enemies at Wolfram and Hart seek to resurrect a deadly opponent: Darla.

PART II

If It Looks Like Horror,
Sounds Like Horror…

In addition to the forty programs already studied in this text, there are several other TV series which include some horrific components along with other, perhaps more significant, elements. For instance, *Amazing Stories* (1985-87), the new *The Twilight Zone* (1985-87; 89), and the new *Outer Limits* (1995–) are all genre anthologies which highlight science fiction, fantasy, and, from time-to-time, horror as well. *Psi Factor* (1996–) and *Sightings* (1994-97) both purport to dramatize "real" paranormal happenings, and both feature hosts (Dan Aykroyd and Tim White, respectively) relating the events from complex control rooms that appear to be lifted from the production of *Rescue: 911. Sabrina the Teenage Witch* (1996–) and *The Munsters Today* (1988-91) openly include such classic horror elements as witchcraft and "monsters," respectively, but few would argue that these frivolous sitcoms deserve a place on the mantle beside *Kolchak: The Night Stalker* or *Buffy the Vampire Slayer*. However, for the sake of argument, this final, "catch all" chapter does list several series which feature horrific elements and motifs, but about which this author nonetheless feels queasy putting on a par with *Brimstone, The X-Files, Millennium*, and the like.

There are five basic categories for this section: The Anthologies; "Man-on-the-Run" Series; Horror Lite; Pseudo-Reality TV; and finally, Space ... The Horrific Frontier.

The Anthologies

1. AMAZING STORIES (1985–1987)

CRITICAL RECEPTION

"The first of Steven Spielberg's *Amazing Stories* on NBC wasn't very amazing. The other early installments of the series I have seen were also decidedly underwhelming. 'Appalling Stories' would be a more apt title for this century's most ballyhooed TV arrival." — Marvin Kitman, *The New Leader*: "Spielberg's Appalling Disgrace," October 7, 1985, page 21.

"a spotty skein of clichés, sentimentality and ordinary hokum ... special effects and production values are doubtless enticing, but too often they are used in the service of mushy sentimentality and questionable readings of the world we live in ... *Amazing Stories* turns out to be not so much monumentally dreadful as consistently disappointing. Skimpy story ideas ... don't look weightier when dressed up in big budgets..." — John J. O'Connor, *The New York Times*: "A Skimpiness Undermines *Amazing Stories*," January 5, 1985, page H25.

"This is one of the worst ten shows of all time, in any category. It's a disappointment every week. You tune in and expect something, and get nothing ... It's incredibly over-cute and over-produced ... with primitive premises about ... things that children could make up." — Tom Shales, *The Washington Post* (reprinted in *The Best of Sci Fi TV*), Harmony Books, 1987, page 39.

"it is depressingly obvious that quality — along with the sense of adventure and spontaneity that the series promised — is in fairly short supply ... There is no denying that *Amazing Stories* ... looks good. Its content, however, is predictable and clichéd ... While nearly everything Spielberg does is, to a degree, apparently derivative of something he saw in his formative moviegoing years, the problem with *Amazing Stories* is that few of Spielberg's episode concepts have been adequately thought out." — Bill Kelley, *Cinefantastique*, Volume 16, number 2: "*Amazing Stories*: Handsomely Mounted Stories Prove Predictable and Clichéd," May 1986, page 36.

CAST AND CREDITS

Created by: Steven Spielberg. *Presented by:* Universal Studios and Amblin Entertainment. *Executive Producer:* Steven Spielberg. *Production Executives:* Kathleen Kennedy, Frank Marshall. *Producer:* David E. Vogel. *Supervising Producers:* Joshua Brand, John Falsey. *Associate Producers:* Steve Starkey, Stephen Semel, Skip Lusk. *Story Editors:* Peter Orton, Mick Garris. *Production Designer:* Rick Carter. *Editors (various episodes):* Joe Ann Fogle, Steven Kemper. *Unit Production Manager:* Kevin Donnelly, Joan Bradshaw. *First Assistant Director:* David L. Beans, John Liberti. *Second Assistant Director:* Martha Elcar, Jerry Ketchum. *Theme Music:* John Williams. *Additional Music (various episodes):* Michael Kamen, Billy Goldenberg, Fred Steiner. *Casting:* Johanna Ray, Mike Fenton. *Art Directors:* Richard B. Lewis, Lynda Paradise. *Set Decorators:* Catherine Arnold, Greg Garrison. *Main Title:* Ron Cobb. *Special Visual Effects:* Dream Quest Images. *Stunt Coordinator:* Roydon Clark. *Titles and Opticals:* Universal Title.

THE DETAILS

"The bigger they are, the harder they fall" is a truism that immediately springs to mind when remembering the 1985-1987 network anthology series, *Amazing Stories*. This is one TV project that boasted every advantage from the get-go. NBC executive Brandon Tartikoff had promised executive producer and series creator Steven Spielberg, once a director on *Rod Serling's Night Gallery*, a two year, prime time network commitment (forty-four half-hour episodes), the exact time-slot he desired (Sunday nights at 8:00 P.M.), not to mention complete creative control over his own series with no network interference. Even more impressively, the NBC series was budgeted at a whopping $800,000 budget per half-hour, and its advertising budget alone could have paid for a feature film! Prominent film directors such as Martin Scorsese, Clint Eastwood, Peter Hyams, Danny DeVito, and Spielberg himself were recruited to helm the various episodes, another fact which seemed to promise high quality. At a press conference, Spielberg described the ideas underlining his new series:

> We're not playing it safe. A couple of the shows are really rather wiggy ... And other shows are action-packed and very visual ... *Amazing Stories* is a really mixed bag. It's science fiction, it's adventure, it's comedy ... our shows really, really vary and you have to sample a few of them to see how similar we are to the old anthologies, and at the same time how unlike them we are too.[1]

Unfortunately, what emerged from this ideal set of circumstances was but an object lesson in humility, a recapitulation of yet another old Hollywood truism: "if it isn't on the page, it isn't on the stage." Specifically, the stories on *Amazing Stories* (most from the mind of Steven Spielberg) proved to be dreadful retreads, one-note jokes, or special effects extravaganzas lacking a worldview, appealing characters, or even a rudimentary moral standpoint. So bad was this series, this juggernaut of a production, that it is now widely considered one of the worst (and most heavily hyped) anthologies in television history. Fortunately, horror is not the genre which owns *Amazing Stories*. On the contrary, the series only rarely strayed into Terror TV terrain, which is why it is covered (briefly) in this section rather than in detail elsewhere in the text.

Frankly, most of the almost four dozen stories on *Amazing Stories* defy categorization within any specific genre. "Mummy, Daddy" is an atrocious one-joke production in which a horror movie actor dressed as a Mummy faces misadventures in his costume of bandages as he races to the hospital to see his newly born child. Predictably, he is mistaken for a real monster by ignorant locals and pursued all over the countryside in a slapstick chase.

"Fine Tuning" finds potato-headed alien tourists landing on Earth (with cameras) to see their favorite TV stars and visit Hollywood. "Miscalculations," perhaps the most juvenile of all the *Amazing Stories* episodes, finds teenager John Cryer accidentally spilling chemicals on a centerfold picture and bringing her to life. "The Mission" is an hour-long suspense yarn about an American bomber in World War II which loses its landing gear during mid-air combat. The plane and crew (including Kevin Costner!) are saved when a budding cartoonist draws the plane with bright yellow "cartoon" wheels on an illustration of the aircraft. Amazingly, the real life plane sprouts the cartoon wheels and lands safely.

When the stories were not as blatantly childish as those listed above, they are simply rehashes of other, better, anthology shows. "Ghost Train," the *Amazing Stories* premiere, is a story about a sensitive grandpa's dying wish: to be taken aboard a train which once crossed through the land where his grandson's house now stands. In conception and story, this (premiere) episode of *Amazing Stories* mimicked *One Step Beyond's* 1961 episode "Goodbye Grandpa," which also involved an old man and a "ghost" train. Spielberg's episode has the (enormous) budget to dramatize the spectral locomotive destroying the living room of a suburban house in a highly destructive action set-piece, but it lacks the humanity and elegant simplicity of the far more memorable *One Step Beyond* episode.

The most horrific *Amazing Stories* episode, perhaps, is "Mirror, Mirror" starring Sam Waterston and *Poltergeist: The Legacy*'s Helen Shaver and directed by film-great Martin Scorsese. The story revolves around a horror writer who claims not to possess any fear of the monsters and villains featured in his own best-selling novels. The author learns a lesson in fear when he starts seeing a devilish, *Phantom of the Opera*-like apparition haunt him in reflective surfaces such as mirrors and table-tops.

The direction and suspense generated by this situation are tangible, but, as usual for this white bread series, the narrative ultimately goes wrong in any number of ways. First, the very concept of a killer seen only in mirrors and other reflective surfaces is also reminiscent of a *One Step Beyond* installment, in this case an episode called "The Clown." Secondly, the *Amazing Stories* venture ends confusingly, with the haunted and hunted writer inexplicably turning into the monstrous apparition and throwing himself out of a window while screaming in abject horror. This conclusion makes no dramatic sense whatsoever, especially since the character played by Waterston is delineated in only the most rudimentary terms. He is arrogant and rude, but hardly a bad enough guy to merit such a grim fate. And how, exactly, is such a transformation accomplished? There is no mechanism, as in *The Twilight Zone*, to explain such a bizarre happening.

Although Clint Eastwood's "Vanessa in the Garden" manages to be almost poetic in its visual imagery, most of the *Amazing Stories* canon generate only a half-hearted "huh?" from audiences who sense immediately that most of the stories fail to connect with them on any kind of meaningful dramatic level. Typical of this problem is "Life on Death Row," an installment about a convict destined to be executed. The convict (Patrick Swayze) is struck by lightning during an escape attempt and miraculously granted the power to heal others, including a blind girl (the daugh-

ter of the prison warden). Despite this great gift, the inmate is still executed by the state. Then, after the electrocution is complete, he awakes, resurrected … and the episode just stops … as if the reels needed to be changed. There is no viewpoint on hand, no final irony to punctuate the action, no twist ending to put a spin on the story's events, no comment at all on the preceding adventure. It is as if the show literally ran out of ideas as it went. What were audiences to feel about Swayze's hardened convict? Did he deserve to live? To die? Had his gift reformed him? Could one great good repair a great evil? What were viewers to take from this particular "amazing" story?

Sadly, "Life on Death Row" is not alone in its dramatic failures. The best anthologies are inevitably those which feature some kind of narration, a voice to put a perspective on the adventure. *Amazing Stories* is conspicuous in its absence of a narrator. What would he or she have said in the case of "Life on Death Row," "The Mission," "Miscalculations," or "Mummy, Daddy?" The stories are so empty, so banal, that no coherent or meaningful worldview could be imposed upon them. There is no evidence of a great thinker, a Rod Serling here, and that is one reason why there is no narrator. A narrator would have to give the series a sense of cohesion, and there is no cohesion.

Another pseudo-horrific story on *Amazing Stories* is "The Amazing Falsworth," a little potboiler about a blindfolded "touch" psychic (Gregory Hines) who makes contact with a serial killer (Richard Masur) hiding out in his audience. Again, the suspense is wrung for everything it was worth by director Peter Hyams, but the writing functions on a dumb, basic TV level. Falsworth manages to repeat his mantra, that his paranormal power is all "in the hands" at least five times during the half-hour, thus setting up the final punch line, a post-violence recitation of that supposedly "ironic" line. In the final moments, the psychic uses his fingers to pull the trigger on a shotgun, blowing apart the serial killer during a deadly scuffle. At this point, the recitation of "it's all in the hands" is an obvious nudge, and a patronizing attempt to forward the story's point. It's all in the hands. IT'S ALL IN THE HANDS!! Get it? GET IT?

Amazing Stories was canceled by NBC the moment its two-year commitment was over, an expensive and much-hated failure. It is an anthology series with lavish production values and good casts, but its failure should remind producers that good stories make a show a success, whereas good production values only make for big expenses.

Episode List

• *First Season (1985-1986)*

1. **"Ghost Train"** Written by Frank Deese; Story by Steven Spielberg; Directed by Steven Spielberg; airdate: September 29, 1985.

2. **"The Main Attraction"** Written by Brad Bird and Matthew Robins; Story by Steven Spielberg; Directed by Matthew Robins; airdate: October 6, 1985.

3. **"Alamo Jobe"** Written by Joshua Brand and John Falsey; Story by Steven Spielberg; Directed by Michael Moore; airdate: October 20, 1985.

4. **"Mummy, Daddy"** Written by Earl Pomerantz; Story by Steven Spielberg; Directed by William Dear; airdate: October 27, 1985.

5. **"The Mission"** Written by Menno Meyjes; Story by Steven Spielberg; Directed by Steven Spielberg; airdate: November 3, 1985.

6. **"The Amazing Falsworth"** Written by Mick Garris; Story by Steven Spielberg; Directed by Peter Hyams; airdate: November 5, 1985.

7. **"Fine Tuning"** Written by Earl Pomerantz; Story by Steven Spielberg; Directed by Bob Balaban; airdate: November 10, 1985.

8. **"Mr. Magic"** Written by Joshua Brand and John Falsey; Directed by Donald Petrie; airdate: November 17, 1985.

9. **"Guilt Trip"** Written by Gail and Kevin Parent; Directed by Burt Reynolds; airdate: December 1, 1985.

10. **"Remote Control Man"** Written by Douglas Lloyd McIntosh; Story by Steven Spielberg; Directed by Bob Clark; airdate: December 8, 1985.

11. **"Santa '85"** Written by Joshua Brand and John Falsey; Story by Steven Spielberg; Directed by Phil Joanou; airdate: December 15, 1985.

12. **"Vanessa in the Garden"** Written by Steven Spielberg; Directed by Clint Eastwood; airdate: December 29, 1985.

13. **"The Sitter"** Written by Mick Garris; Story by Joshua Brand and John Falsey; Directed by Joan Darling; airdate: January 5, 1986.

14. **"No Day at the Beach"** Written by Mick Garris; Story by Steven Spielberg; Directed by Lesli Linka Glatter; airdate: January 12, 1986.

15. **"One for the Road"** Written by James Bissell; Directed by Thomas Carter; airdate: January 19, 1986.

16. **"Gather Ye Acorns"** Written by Stu Krieger; Story by Steven Spielberg; Directed by Norman Reynolds; airdate: February 2, 1986.

17. **"Boo"** Written by Lowell Ganz and Babaloo Mandell; Directed by Joe Dante; airdate: February 16, 1986.

18. **"Dorothy and Ben"** Written by Michael De Guzman; Story by Steven Spielberg; Directed by Thomas Carter; airdate: March 2, 1986.

19. **"Mirror, Mirror"** written by Joseph Minion; Story by Steven Spielberg; Directed by Martin Scorsese; airdate: March 9, 1986.

20. **"Secret Cinema"** Written and directed by Paul Bartel; airdate: April 6, 1986.

21. **"Hell Toupee"** Written by Gail and Kevin Parent; airdate: Irvin Kershner; airdate: April 13, 1986.

22. "The Doll" Written by Richard Matheson; Directed by Phil Joanou; airdate: May 4, 1986.

23. "One for the Books" Written by Richard Matheson; Directed by Lesli Linka Glatter; airdate: May 11, 1986.

24. "Grandpa's Ghost" Written by Michael De Guzman; Story by Timothy Hutton; Directed by Timothy Hutton; airdate: May 25, 1986.

• Second Season (1986-1987)

25. "The Wedding Ring" Written by Stu Krieger; Story by Steven Spielberg; Directed by Danny DeVito; airdate: September 22, 1986.

26. "Miscalculations" Written by Michael McDowell; Directed by Todd Holland; airdate: September 29, 1986.

27. "Magic Saturday" Written by Richard Christian Matheson; Directed by Robert Markowitz; airdate: October 6, 1986.

28. "Welcome to My Nightmare" Written and directed by Todd Holland; airdate: October 13, 1986.

29. "You Gotta Believe Me" Written by Stu Krieger; Story by Steven Spielberg; Directed by Kevin Reynolds; airdate: October 20, 1986.

30. "The Greibble" Written by Mick Garris; Story by Steven Spielberg; Directed by Joe Dante; airdate: November 3, 1986.

31. "Life on Death Row" Written by Rockne S. O'Bannon; Story by Mick Garris; Directed by Mick Garris; airdate: November 10, 1986.

32. "Go to the Head of the Class" Written by Tom McLoughlin, Bob Gale and Mick Garris; Story by Mick Garris; Directed by Robert Zemeckis; airdate: November 21, 1986.

33. "Thanksgiving" Written by Robert C. Cox and Pierre R. Debs; Story by Harold Rolseth; Directed by Todd Holland; airdate: November 24, 1986.

34. "The Pumpkin Competition" Written by Peter Orton; Directed by Norman Reynolds; airdate: December 1, 1986.

35. "What If…" Written by Anne Spielberg; Directed by Joan Darling; airdate: December 8, 1986.

36. "The Eternal Mind" Written by Julie Moskowitz and Gary Stephens; Directed by Michael Riva; airdate: December 29, 1986.

37. "Lane Change" Written by Ali Marie Matheson; Directed by Ken Kwapis; airdate: January 12, 1987.

38. "Blue Man Down" Written by Jacob Epstein and Daniel Lindley; Story by Steven Spielberg; Directed by Paul Michael Glaser; airdate: January 19, 1987.

39. "The 21 Inch Sun" Written by Bruce Kirschbaum; Directed by Nick Castle; airdate: February 2, 1987.

40. "The Family Dog" Written and directed by Tim Burton; airdate; February 16, 1987.

41. "Gershwin's Trunk" Written by Paul Bartel and John Meyer; Directed by Paul Bartel; airdate: March 13, 1987.

42. "Such Interesting Neighbors" Written by Mick Garris and Tom McLoughlin; Story by Jack Finney; Directed by Graham Baker; airdate: March 20, 1987.

43. "Without Diana" Written by Mick Garris; Directed by Lesli Linka Glatter; airdate: March 27, 1987.

44. "Moving Day" Written by Frank Kerr; Directed by Robert Stevens; airdate: April 3, 1987.

45. "Miss Stardust" Written by Thomas Szollosi and Richard Christian Matheson; Story by Richard Matheson; Directed by Tobe Hooper; airdate: April 10, 1987.

2. THE TWILIGHT ZONE (1985–1987; 1988–1989)

CRITICAL RECEPTION

"The series gets off to a strong start ... technically far superior to anything that could be done on television 25 years ago."—John J. O'Connor, *The New York Times:* "Premieres of *Twilight Zone* and *MacGyver*," Friday, September 27, 1985.

"less well-written, conceived, plotted and narrated than its predecessor. Although the original was stronger, I must admit I found the copy scary ... What I miss most in the new version is Rod Serling's voice."—Marvin Kitman, *The New Leader*, October 7, 1985, page 22.

CAST AND CREDITS

Cast: Charles Aidman (Narrator)/CBS; Robin Ward (Narrator)/Syndicated

Credits: Executive Producer: Phil De Guere. *Producer:* Harvey Frand. *New* Twilight Zone *Theme Music:* The Grateful Dead and Merl Saunders. *Original* Twilight Zone *Theme Music:* Marius Constant. *Creative Consultant:* Harlan Ellison. *Story Editor:* Rockne O'Bannon. *Art Director:* Jeffrey L. Goldstein, John Mansbridge. *Narrator:* Robin Ward. *Director of Photography:* Bradford May. *Editor:* Gary Blair. *Music:* William Goldstein. *Executive in Charge of Casting:* Bob Weiner. *Casting:* Gary M. Zuckerbrod. *Production Manager and Associate Producer:* Ken Swor. *Unit Production Manager:* Paul Wurtzel. *Associate Producer:* Mark Michaels. *Set Dressers:* Robert Zilliox, Rochelle Moser. *Property Master:* Jim Zemansky. *Script Supervisor:* Kenneth Gilbert. *Costume Designer:* Robert Moore. *Costume Supervisor:* Judith Grant. *Sound Design:* Mickey Hart. *Acoustic Consultant:* Betsy Cohen. *Production Sound Mixer:* Lowell Harris. *Rerecording Mixer:* Phillip Seretti. *Sound Editor:* Jeremy Hoenack. *Music Editor:* Robert Y. Takagi. *Music Supervision:* Robert Drasnin. *Lenses and Panaflex Camera:* Panavision. *Visual Effects:* Don Lee, Price Pethel, Kevin Cox, Maury Rosenfield, Peter Sternlight, Rioch Thorne. *Main Title Designed and Produced by:* Colossal Pictures. *Post Production Executive:* Cosmas P. Bolger. CBS Entertainment Productions; In Association with London Films; in cooperation with Persistence of Vision; distributed by MGM/UA Telecommunications.

THE DETAILS

Though it is a series with no continuing characters or ongoing storyline, Rod Serling's original *Twilight Zone* (1959-64) has managed to become an American TV classic, right alongside *Star Trek*, *I Love Lucy*, or *The Honeymooners*. It is a perennial: a show which speaks powerfully to multiple generations and is so popular and ubiquitous that its stories are known by a kind of conversational shorthand. Remember the one where Burgess Meredith was a bookish little guy who survived a nuclear war, but his glasses broke? Remember the one where Agnes Moorehead was fighting those tiny little aliens who were really space-suited human beings? Or the one with William Shatner fighting that gremlin on the wing of the plane? These classic TV stories are now part of our collective modern mythology.

By the time of this 1980s revival version of *The Twilight Zone*, there had been a 1983 feature film (produced by Steven Spielberg), a regular *Twilight Zone* magazine (shepherded by Serling's wife, Carol), and even comic books celebrating Serling's long-lived creation. Since Serling had passed away in 1975, shortly after the cancellation of his second anthology, *Rod Serling's Night Gallery*, the new *Twilight Zone* was populated by a different array of artists. Executive producer Philip De Guere, story editor Rockne O'Bannon, and creative consultant Harlan Ellison provided the heart of the second team. They expressed their desire to see the series focus on "the mortal dreads ... the things we fear on a day-to-day basis translated into fantasy terms."[2] That explanation clarifies the reason *The Twilight*

Zone is reviewed in this section, rather than in a chapter with the other "terror" series listed in this book: it is really only one part horror. It is also, in turns, science fiction, drama, and fantasy. One week the show is tongue-and-cheek ("Take My Life ... Please!"), one week it visits another planet ("The Star"), and then another week, it does manage to generate some scares ("The After Hours"). On the whole however, the second *Twilight Zone* enterprise seems much less concerned with generating thrills than was its predecessor. Because of this fact, and because the new creative voices are so strong, the new *Twilight Zone* has much less of Rod Serling in it than does *Night Gallery*, a far superior series to this less-than-perfect remake.

The revival version of *The Twilight Zone* began filming at CBS/Studio City, Stage Eight, on March 11, 1985,[3] and lasted for two years before being canceled by CBS because of low ratings. Its format was different from the 1959-1964 series in that each episode was an hour long and featured as many as three stories per sixty minutes (shades of *Night Gallery*). Early into the show's Friday night run, Harlan Ellison left the project because of network interference over story content. Still, two years on CBS was not to be the end of the legend either: a syndie version of *The Twilight Zone* materialized in 1988, this one guided by *Babylon 5*'s future creator, J. Michael Straczynski. Ironically, this version of *The Twilight Zone* was done on the cheap (filmed in Canada), with its primary intention being to produce enough episodes (thirty to be exact) to make the earlier CBS two-year remake profitable in syndicated reruns. As Norman Horwitz, president of MGM/UA Telecommunications, commented on the situation:

> It was a question of "Can we make more money?" ... And I'm paid to make money for the company. Our decision to do *The Twilight Zone* is based on history. It's a memorable name and it gives us a leg up, a genuine marketing advantage ... People would rather buy something they know, that gives them comfort, rather than something innovative and different.[4]

Rod Serling must have spun in his grave over that comment. *The Twilight Zone*, the great anthology of television and a genuine work of art, was now being sold as a "comfortable" series with "name recognition" rather than "innovative" or challenging series of good stories and artistic intent. Infuriated by the tenor of the Horwitz interview (for *Starlog*), new producer Straczynski quickly arrived on the scene to extol the merits of *his* version of a classic series:

> It's a hundred percent closer to the old *Twilight Zone*, in terms of tone or atmosphere, than to the network version. What we've done is gone back and asked ourselves, "What would Rod do?" What made Serling's show so different from anything on television is that he dealt so deeply with humanistic qualities and primal emotions. We're definitely pointing the new episodes toward getting back to Rod's vision.[5]

Unfortunately, this was public relation hyperbole. The third incarnation of *The Twilight Zone* was the worst series of the lot, a show featuring dreadful thirty-minute episodes that could have come straight from the USA version of *The Hitchhiker* or *Alfred Hitchcock Presents*. In fact, some of the same behind-the-scenes "talent" from these less-than-stellar series was used on Straczynski's *The Twilight Zone*! Cheap, poorly-written, and designed solely to make a syndicated rerun of *The Twilight Zone* profitable, this third incarnation was nonetheless a stepping-stone for Straczynksi to create *Babylon 5*.

Still, the new *Twilight Zone* (network) version, did manage to generate a few interesting terror stories during its two years on the air, and it was certainly far better than its network competitor, *Amazing Stories*. At least it was not an embarrassment, like Straczynksi's low-budget version. Among the more horror oriented stories were: "Shatterday," written by Harlan Ellison and directed by Wes Craven, which featured a young Bruce Willis facing down an evil doppelganger, "Small Talent for War" about alien invaders confronting the United Nations, and "The After Hours," a remake of the famous mannequin episode of the original *Twilight Zone*, with *Star Trek: Deep Space Nine*'s Terry Farrell in the Anne Francis role. "Gramma," a frightening Stephen King story, was also adapted for the series by Harlan Ellison, to genuinely frightening effect.

Before the series passed to syndication (and then ultimately, to reruns on TBS), it offered work to a variety of horror and genre directors including Wes Craven (*A Nightmare on Elm Street* [1984], *Scream* [1996]), Peter Medak (*The Changeling* [1981], *Species II* [1998]), William Friedkin (*The Exorcist* [1973]), Joe Dante (*Gremlins* [1984]), and Jeannot Szwarc (*Rod Serling's Night Gallery*, *Jaws II* [1979]). Guest stars on the new *Twilight Zone* were also quite notable with Melinda Dillon ("A Little Peace and Quiet"), Annie Potts ("Wordplay"), Meg Foster ("Dreams for Sale"), Terry O'Quinn ("Chameleon"), Adrienne Barbeau ("Teacher's Aide"), Piper Laurie ("The Burning Man"), Helen Mirren ("Dead Woman's Shoes"), Martin Landau ("The Beacon"), Gary Cole ("Her Pilgrim Soul"), Jonathan Frakes ("But Can She Type?"), Donald Moffat ("The Star"), Elliott Gould ("The Misfortune Cookie"), Jenny Agutter ("The Last Defender of Camelot"), Tom Skerritt ("What Are Friends For?"), and Terry Farrell ("The After Hours") making memorable appearances.

EPISODE LIST

• *First Season (1985–1986)*

1A. "Shatterday" Written by Alan Brennert; Story by Harlan Ellison; Directed by Wes Craven; airdate: September 27, 1985.

1B. "A Little Peace and Quiet" Written by James Crocker; Directed by Wes Craven; airdate: September 27, 1985.

2A. "Wordplay" Written by Rockne S. O'Bannon; Directed by Wes Craven; airdate: October 4, 1985.

2B. "Dreams for Sale" Written by Joe Gannon; Directed by Tommy Lee Wallace; airdate: October 4, 1985.

2C. "Chameleon" Written by James Crocker; Directed by Wes Craven; airdate: October 4, 1985.

3A. "Healer" Written by Alan Brennert; Directed by Sigmund Neufeld; airdate: October 11, 1985.

3B. "Children's Zoo" Written by Chris Hubbell and Gerrit Graham; Directed by Robert Downey; airdate: October 11, 1985.

3C. "Kentucky Rye" Written by Richard Krzemien and Chip Duncan; Directed by John Hancock; airdate: October 11, 1985.

4A. "Little Boy Lost" Written by Lynn Barker; Directed by Tommy Lee Wallace; airdate: October 18, 1985.

4B. "Wish Bank" Written by Michael Cassutt; Directed by Rick Friedberg; airdate: October 18, 1985.

4C. "Nightcrawlers" Written by Phil De Guere; Story by Robert R. McCammon; Directed by William Friedkin; airdate: October 18, 1985.

5A. "If She Dies" Written by David Bennett Carren; Directed by John Hancock; airdate: October 25, 1985.

5B. "Ye Gods" Written by Anne Collins; Directed by Peter Medak; airdate: October 25, 1985.

6A. "Examination Day" Written by Philip De Guere; From a story by Henry Slesar; Directed by Paul Lynch; airdate: November 1, 1985.

6B. "A Message from Charity" Written by Alan Brennert; Directed by Paul Lynch; airdate: November 1, 1985.

7A. "Teacher's Aide" Written by Steven Barnes; Directed by Bill Norton; airdate: November 8, 1985.

7B. "Paladin of the Lost Hour" Written by Harlan Ellison; Directed by Alan Smithee; airdate: November 8, 1985.

8A. "Act Break" Written by Haskell Barkin; Directed by Theodore J. Flicker; airdate: November 15, 1985.

8B. "The Burning Man" Written by J.D. Feigelson; From a story by Ray Bradbury; Directed by J.D. Feigelson; airdate: November 15, 1985.

8C. "Dealer's Choice" Written by Donald Todd; Directed by Wes Craven; airdate: November 15, 1985.

9A. "Dead Woman's Shoes" Written by Lynn Barker; Story by Charles Beaumont; Directed by Peter Medak; airdate: November 22, 1985.

9B. "Wong's Lost and Found Emporium" Written by Alan Brennert; From a story by William Wu; Directed by Peter Lynch; airdate: November 22, 1985.

10A. "The Shadow Man" Written by Rockne O'Bannon; Directed by Joe Dante; airdate: November 29, 1985.

10B. "The Uncle Devil Show" Written by Donald Todd; Directed by David Steinberg; airdate: November 29, 1985.

10C. "Opening Day" Written by Gerritt Graham and Christopher Hubbell; Directed by John Milius; airdate: November 29, 1985.

11A. "The Beacon" Written by Martin Pasko and Rebecca Parr; Directed by Gerd Oswald; airdate: December 6, 1985.

11B. "One Life, Furnished in Early Poverty" Written by Alan Brennert; From a story by Harlan Ellison; Directed by Don Carlos Dunaway; airdate: December 6, 1985.

12A. "Her Pilgrim Soul" Written by Alan Brennert; Directed by Wes Craven; airdate: December 13, 1985.

12B. "I of Newton" Written by Alan Brennert; From a story by Joe Haldeman; Directed by Ken Gilbert; airdate: December 13, 1985.

13A. "Night of the Meek" Written by Rockne S. O'Bannon; Story by Rod Serling; Directed by Martha Coolidge; airdate: December 20, 1985.

13B. "But Can She Type?" Written by Martin Pasko and Rebecca Parr; Directed by Shelley Levinson; airdate: December 20, 1985.

13C. "The Star" Written by Alan Brennert; From a story by Arthur C. Clarke; Directed by Gerd Oswald; airdate: December 20, 1985.

14A. "Still Life" Written by Gerritt Graham and Chris Hubbell; Directed by Peter Medak; airdate: January 3, 1986.

14B. "The Little People of Killany Woods" Written and directed by J.D. Feigelson; airdate: January 3, 1986.

14C. "The Misfortune Cookie" Written by Steven Rae; From a story by Charles Fritch; Directed by Allan Arkush; airdate: January 3, 1986.

15A. "Monsters!" Written by Robert Crais; Directed by Bill Norton; airdate: January 24, 1986.

15B. "Small Talent for War" Written by Carter Scholz and Alan Brennert; Directed by Claudia Weill; airdate: January 24, 1986.

15C. "A Matter of Minutes" Written by Rockne S. O'Bannon; From a story by Theodore Sturgeon; Directed by Sheldon Larry; airdate: January 24, 1986.

16A. "The Elevator" Written by Ray Bradbury; Directed by Ralph Thomas; airdate: January 31, 1986.

16B. "To See the Invisible Man" Written by Steven Barnes; From a story by Robert Silverburg; Directed by Noel Black; airdate: January 31, 1986.

16C. "Tooth and Consequences" Written by Haskell Barkin; Directed by Robert Downey; airdate: January 31, 1986.

17A. "Welcome to Winfield" Written by Les Enloe; Directed by Bruce Bilson; airdate: February 7, 1986.

17B. "Quarantine" Written by Alan Brennert; From a story by Philip De Guere and Steven Bochco; Directed by Martha Coolidge; airdate: February 7, 1986.

18A. "Gramma" Written by Harlan Ellison; From a story by Stephen King; Directed by Bradford May; airdate: February 14, 1986.

18B. "Personal Demons" Written by Rockne O'Bannon; Directed by Peter Medak; airdate: February 14, 1986.

18C. "Cold Reading" Written by Martin Pasko and Rebecca Parr; Directed by Gus Trikonis; airdate: February 14, 1986.

19A. "The Leprechaun Artist" Written and directed by Tommy Lee Wallace; airdate: February 21, 1986.

19B. "Dead Run" Written by Alan Brennert; From a story by Greg Bear; Directed by Paul Tucker; airdate: February 21, 1986.

20A. "Profile in Silver" Written by J. Neil Schulman; Directed by John Hancock; airdate: March 7, 1986.

20B. "Button, Button" Written by Logan Swanson; From a story by Richard Matheson; Directed by Peter Medak; airdate: March 7, 1986.

21A. "Need to Know" Written by Mary Sheldon; From a story by Sidney Sheldon; Directed by Paul Lynch; airdate: March 21, 1986.

21B. "Red Snow" Written by Michael Cassutt; Directed by Jeannot Szwarc; airdate: March 21, 1986.

22A. "Take My Life ... Please!" Written by Gordon Mitchell; Directed by Gus Trikonis; airdate: March 28, 1986.

22B. "Devil's Alphabet" Written by Robert Hunter; Directed by Ben Bolt; airdate: March 28, 1986.

22C. "The Library" Written by Anne Collins; Directed by John Hancock; airdate: March 28, 1986.

23A. "Shadow Play" Written by James Crocker; From a story by Charles Beaumont; Directed by Paul Lynch; airdate: April 4, 1986.

23B. "Grace Note" Written by Patrice Messina; Directed by Peter Medak; airdate: April 4, 1986.

24A. "A Day in Beaumont" Written by David Gerrold; Directed by Philip De Guere; airdate: April 11, 1986.

24B. "The Last Defender of Camelot" Written by George R.R. Martin; From a story by Roger Zelazny; Directed by Jeannot Szwarc; airdate: April 11, 1986.

• *Second Season (1986–1987)*

25A. "The Once and Future King" Written by George R.R. Martin and Bryce Maritano; Directed by Jim McBride; airdate: September 27, 1986.

25B. "A Saucer of Loneliness" Written by David Gerrold; From a story by Theodore Sturgeon; airdate: September 27, 1986.

26A. "What Are Friends For?" Written by J. Michael Straczynski; Directed by Gus Trikonis; airdate: October 4, 1986.

26B. "Aqua Vita" Written by Jeremy Finch and Paul Chitlik; Directed by Paul Tucker; airdate: October 4, 1986.

27A. "The Story Teller" Written by Rockne O'Bannon; Directed by Paul Lynch; airdate: October 11, 1986.

27B. "Nightsong" Written by Michael Reaves; Directed by Bradford May; airdate: October 11, 1986.

28A. "The After Hours" Written by Rockne O'Bannon; From a story by Rod Serling; Directed by Bruce Malmuth; airdate: October 18, 1986.

28B. "Lost and Found" Written by George R.R. Martin; From a story by Phyllis Eisenstein; Directed by Gus Trikonis; airdate: October 18, 1986.

28C. "The World Next Door" Written

by Lan O'Kun; Directed by Paul Lynch; airdate: October 18, 1986.

29. "The Toys of Caliban" Written by George R.R. Martin; Directed by Thomas J. Wright; airdate: December 4, 1986.

30. "The Convict's Piano" Written by Patrice Messina; Directed by Thomas J. Wright; airdate: December 11, 1986.

31. "The Road Less Traveled" Written by George R.R. Martin; Directed by Wes Craven; airdate: December 18, 1986.

32A. "The Card" Written by Michael Cassutt; Directed by Bradford May; airdate: February 21, 1987.

32B. "The Junction" Written by Virginia Aldridge; Directed by Bill Duke; airdate: February 21, 1987.

33A. "Joy Ride" Written by Cal Willingham; Directed by Gil Bettman; airdate: May 21, 1987.

33B. "Shelter Skelter" Written by Ron Cobb and Robin Love; Directed by Martha Coolidge; airdate: May 21, 1987.

33C. "Private Channel" Written by Edward Redlich; Directed by Peter Medak; airdate: May 21, 1987.

34A. "Time and Teresa Golowitz" Written by Alan Brennert; From a story by Parke Goodwin; Directed by Shelley Levinson; airdate: July 10, 1987.

34B. "Voices in the Earth" Written by Alan Brennert; Directed by Curtis Harrington; airdate: July 10, 1987.

35A. "Song of the Younger World" Written by Anthony Lawrence and Nancy Lawrence; Directed by Noel Black; airdate: July 17, 1987.

35B. "The Girl I Married" Written by J.M. DeMatteis; Directed by Philip De Guere; airdate: July 17, 1987.

• *Third Season (1988–1989)*

Note: The third season of the new *Twilight Zone* was syndicated throughout America, and aired on different dates, and different times from city to city. Thus airdates have not been included below.

36. "The Curious Case of Edgar Witherspoon" Written by Haskell Barkin; Directed by Rene Bonniere.

37. "Extra Innings" Written by Tom Palmer; Directed by Doug Jackson.

38. "The Crossing" Written by Ralph Phillips; Directed by Paul Lynch.

39. "The Hunters" Written by Paul Chitlik and Jeremy Finch; Directed by Paul Lynch.

40. "Dream Me a Life" Written by J. Michael Straczynski; Directed by Alan King.

41. "Memories" Written by Bob Underwood; Directed by Richard Bugajski.

42. "The Hellgrammite Method" Written by William Selby; Directed by Gilbert Shilton.

43. "Our Selena Is Dying" Written by J. Michael Straczynski; From a story by Rod Serling; Directed by Bruce Pittman.

44. "The Call" Written by J. Michael Straczynski; Directed by Gilbert Shilton.

45. "The Trance" Written by Jeff Stuart and J. Michael Straczynski; Directed by Randy Bradshaw.

46. "Acts of Terror" Written by J. Michael Straczynski; Directed by Brad Turner.

47. "20/20 Vision" Written by Robert Walden; Directed by Jim Purdy.

48. "There Was an Old Woman" Written by Tom J. Aisle; Directed by Otta Hanus.

49. "The Trunk" Written by Paul Chitlik and Jeremy Finch; Directed by Steve DiMarco.

50. "Appointment on Route 17" Written by Haskell Barken; Directed by Rene Bonniere.

51. "**The Cold Equations**" Written by Alan Brennert; Directed by Martin Lavut.

52. "**Stranger in Possum Meadows**" Written by Paul Chitlik and Jeremy Bertrand Finch; Directed by Sturla Gunnarsson.

53. "**Street of Shadows**" Written by Michael Reaves; Directed by Richard Bugajski.

54. "**Something in the Walls**" Written by J. Michael Straczynski; Directed by Allan Kroeker.

55. "**A Game of Pool**" Written by George Clayton Johnson; Directed by Randy Bradshaw.

56. "**Room 2426**" Written by Jeremy Finch and Paul Chitlik; Directed by Richard Bugajski.

57. "**The Wall**" Written by J. Michael Straczynski; Directed by Atom Egoyan.

58. "**The Mind of Simon Foster**" Written by J. Michael Straczynski; Directed by Doug Jackson.

59. "**Cat and Mouse**" (written by Christy Marx; Directed by Eric Till.

60. "**Many Many Monkeys**" Written by William Froug; Directed by Richard Bugajski.

61. "**Rendezvous in a Dark Place**" Written by J. Michael Straczynski; Directed by Rene Bonniere.

62. "**Special Service**" Written by J. Michael Straczynski; Directed by Randy Bradshaw.

63. "**Love Is Blind**" Written by Cal Willingham; Directed by Gilbert Shilton.

64. "**Crazy as a Soup Sandwich**" Written by Harlan Ellison; Directed by Paul Lynch.

65. "**Father and Son Game**" Written by Paul Chitlik and Jeremy Finch; Directed by Randy Bradshaw).

3. THE OUTER LIMITS (1995–2000)

CRITICAL RECEPTION

"*The Outer Limits*, nineties-style can never hope to claim the same hallowed corner in our TV attic … much sexier than its aged ancestor … this update has actually moved closer to that *other* big anthology series of the era — *The Twilight Zone*. Some stories are intended to scare, but all are meant to make us think — morality tales, wrapped up with a homespun 'thought of the week.' That's the only flaw in what is otherwise a largely entertaining series."— Roger Fulton, and John Betancourt, *The Sci-Fi Channel Encyclopedia of TV Science Fiction*, Warner Books, New York, New York, 1997, page 336.

CAST AND CREDITS

Credits: Executive Producer: Pen Densham, Richard B. Lewis, John Watson. *Co-Executive Producer:* Jonathan Glassner. *Producer:* Brent Karl Clackson. *Supervising Producer for Atlantis:* Sue Valencia. *Senior Executive Story Consultant:* Chris Ruppenthal, Sam Egan. *Executive Story Consultant:* Naren Shankar. *Executive Consultant:* Joe Stefano. *Associate Producer:* Ben Brafman. *Casting:* Mary Jo Slater, Paul Weber. *Additional Casting:* Bette Chadwick. *Production Manager:* Lynn Barr. *First Assistant Director:* Shirley-Anne Parsons. *Second Assistant Director:* Ella Kutschera. *Theme:* Mark Mancina, John Van Tongeren. *Music:* John Van Tongeren, Randy Miller. *Director of Photography:* Rick Wincenty. *Production Designer:* Stephen Geaghan. *Editor:* Brad Rines. *Costume Designer:* Stephanie Nolin. *Art Director:* Susan Parker. *Set Decorator:* Barry Brolly. *Construction Coordinator:* Harry Griffin-Beale. *Property Master:* Jim Le Blane. *Special Effects:* Dave Allinson. *Camera Operator:* Paul Mitchnick. *Makeup Artist:* Fay Von Schroeder. *Hairstylist:* Susan Boyd. *Extras Casting:* Sandra Couldwell. *Chief Lighting Technician:* Ray Boyle. *Key Grip:* Dave Dawson. *Stunt Coordinator:* John Wardlow. *Production Coordinator: Nancy Carrow. *Location Manager:* Greg Jackson. *Script Supervisor:* Lisa Wilder. *Sound Mixer:* Bill Skinner. *Transportation Coordinator:* Darla Nathorst. *Head Painter:* Roland Gervais. *Production Assistant:* Victoria James. *Script Coordinator:* Kathie Mackie. *Assistant to Producers:* Julie Fitzgerald, Robin Belk. *Production Accountant:* Gordon Smith. *Postproduction Supervisor:* Michael S. McLean. *Visual Effects Supervisor:* Steve Anker. *Makeup Effects, Design and Construction:* Tibor and Company. *Main Title Photography:* Jerry Uielsmman. *3D Animation:* Lost Boys Studios. *Visual Effects Executive:* Robert Habros. *Main Title*: Complete Post Visual Effects and Design. Produced in association with Global, A CanWest Company and Superchannel, Canada. Filmed on location in British Columbia, Canada. A Trilogy Entertainment Group and Atlantis Films Limited Production.

THE DETAILS

The Outer Limits is another remake of a classic, in this case, of the Joe Stefano/Leslie Stevens collaboration of the mid-sixties. The original *Outer Limits* (1963-65) may rightly be named one of the greatest horror series of all time, although it pre-dates 1970, the starting point of this text. *The Outer Limits* featured great performances from recurring guests such as Robert Culp and Martin Landau, superb direction by Gerd Oswald and Byron Haskin, and creepy stories by the likes of Meyer Dolinsky ("The Architects of Fear"), Joe Stefano ("A Feasibility Study," "Nightmare," "The Zanti Misfits," "It Crawled Out of the Woodwork"), and Harlan Ellison ("Demon with a Glass Hand," "Soldier").

Although all of these talents were quite remarkable, what actually made the original *Outer Limits* something of a TV landmark was its black and white, *film noir*-style photography. Eerie, moody, dark, and menacing, *The Outer Limits* of the 1960s was as much a "scare" show as a science fiction one. Each episode featured what the producers termed a "bear," a monster-of-the-week, and these

menacing creations often came lumbering out of the shadows to scare the living hell out of viewers. Sometimes the bears were stop-motion creations ("The Zanti Misfits"), sometimes they were puppets ("The Invisible Enemy") and sometimes they were men in suits ("The Architects of Fear"). In whatever form they came, these monsters were always well presented; supported by ominous "mood" music and exquisite lighting. Besides these "bears," the story focus in the original series was on how humans' innovations in technology could open up a whole new realm of terror. A machine made evolution go wild in "The Sixth Finger," a strange device landed a seemingly benevolent alien on Earth in "The Bellero Shield," and scientists planned a dangerous and frightening conspiracy in "The Architects of Fear." Sometimes, science was even left out of the equation entirely, in gothic horror stories such as "The Guests," about a haunted house that was actually an alien brain, or "monster" shows such as "The Invisible Enemy," concerning a school of carnivorous sand sharks inhabiting the surface of Mars. The emphasis of the original *Outer Limits* was definitely "tolerable terror." Terror was to be generated, but not in such a visceral way that would leave children unable to sleep at nights.

The remake of *The Outer Limits*, though longer-lived than its predecessor, is not in the same ballpark. A product of the 1990s genre glut, it is filmed in bland color, in the same humdrum manner as *Star Trek: Deep Space Nine, Babylon 5,* or *First Wave*. In other words, the images of *The Outer Limits* are not captured in any meaningful or artistic manner. Instead of being a new *film noir* masterpiece, it is an example of typical TV drama: lacking perspective, an overall worldview, and the skills to support its storylines with appropriate visuals. The vocabulary, the very grammar of film, is not being used effectively by this TV series, and it has forsaken terror along with black-and-white photography. Produced by Trilogy, the same company responsible for *Poltergeist: The Legacy*, the new *Outer Limits* is yet another Canadian production produced cheaply.

The Outer Limits began its new life with Showtime, the premium cable channel, before seeing its episodes shunted to syndication. The Showtime deal, as with *Poltergeist*, allows *The Outer Limits* creative personnel to utilize more gore and more nudity than network television would allow, but again, this kind of freedom results not in more provocative stories, only in more T & A. "Caught in the Act" is a prime example of the gratuitous nature of this creative "freedom." In this story, a comely coed (Alyssa Milano of *Charmed*) becomes a nymphomaniac once affected by an alien object which lands, appropriately, in her bedroom. As Milano goes about having sex with handsome young men, there are plenty of opportunities for her to take her clothes off. In the end of this particular story, the moralizing, heavy-handed side of *The Outer Limits* comes to the forefront. The Milano/alien hybrid kills men with whom she has sex, until she finally makes love to her boyfriend. The emotion of "love" in the sex equation is enough to force the alien possessor out of Milano. Cue the violins, please.

For the most part, the writing on the new *Outer Limits* has been unexceptional, and the direction (from the likes of Paul Lynch, Timothy Bond, Joseph L. Scanlon, and Brad Turner), competent if uninspired. The filmic style of the original show is missing in action, and it has been replaced with an unnecessarily heavyhanded "straight" approach to the science fiction genre. Although it is terrific to see Larry Drake, Nana Visitor, Beau Bridges, Michael Dorn, Brent Spiner, Robert Patrick, Wil Wheaton, Helen Shaver, Saul Rubinek, Rene Auberjonois, and other genre celebrities stretching their talents in the anthology format, the new *Outer Limits* has a bland, dull feel to it. Worse than that, it has picked up on one of *Poltergeist: The Legacy*'s worst ideas: it has featured several of the dreaded "clip shows," wherein sequences from various stories are blended and passed off as a "new" adventure.

EPISODE LIST

● *First Season (1995)*

1. "Sandkings" (Parts I and II) Written by Melinda Snodgrass; Story by George R.R. Martin; Directed by Stuart Gillard; airdate: March 26, 1995.

2. "Valerie 23" Written by Jonathan Glassner; Directed by Timothy Bond; airdate: March 31, 1995.

3. "Blood Brothers" Written by Brad Wright; Directed by Tibor Takacs; airdate: April 7, 1995.

4. "The Second Soul" Written by Alan Brennert; Directed by Paul Lynch; airdate: April 14, 1995.

5. "White Light Fever" Written by David Kemper; Directed by Tibor Takacs; airdate: April 21, 1995.

6. "The Choice" Written by Ann Lewis Hamilton; Directed by Mark Sobel; airdate: April 28, 1995.

7. "Virtual Future" Written by Shawn Alex Thompson; Directed by Joseph L. Scanlon; airdate: May 7, 1995.

8. "Living Hell" Written by Pen Densham and Melinda Snodgrass; Directed by Graeme Campbell; airdate: May 14, 1995.

9. "Corner of the Eye" Written by David Schow; Directed by Stuart Gillard; airdate: May 21, 1995.

10. "Under the Bed" Written by Lawrence Meyers; Directed by Rene Bonniere; airdate: May 28, 1995.

11. "Dark Matters" Written by Alan Brennert; Directed by Paul Lynch; airdate: June 2, 1995.

12. "The Conversion" Written by Brad Wright; Story by Richard B. Lewis; Directed by Rebecca De Mornay; airdate: June 9, 1995.

13. "Quality of Mercy" Written by Brad Wright; Directed by Brad Turner; airdate: June 16, 1995.

14. "The New Breed" Written by Grant Rosenberg; Directed by Mario Azzopardi; airdate: June 23, 1995.

15. "The Voyage Home" Written by Grant Rosenberg; Directed by Tibor Takacs; airdate: June 30, 1995.

16. "Caught in the Act" Written by Rob Forsyth; Directed by Mark Sobel; airdate: July 1, 1995.

17. "The Message" Written by Brad Wright; Directed by Joseph L. Scanlon; airdate: July 16, 1995.

18. "I, Robot" Written by Alison Bingeman; Story by Otto Binder; Directed by Adam Nimoy; airdate: July 23, 1995.

19. "If These Walls Could Talk" Written by Manny Coto; Directed by Tibor Takacs; airdate: July 30, 1995.

20. "Birthright" Written by Michael Berlin and Eric Estrin; Directed by William Fruet; airdate: August 13, 1995.

21. "Voice of Reason" Written by Brad Wright; Directed by Neill Fearnley; airdate: August 20, 1995.

• *Second Season (1996)*

22. "A Stitch in Time" Written by Steven Barnes; Directed by Mario Azzopardi; airdate: January 14, 1996.

23. "Resurrection" Written by Chris Brancato; Directed by Mario Azzopardi; airdate: January 14, 1996.

24. "Unnatural Selection" Written by Eric A. Morris; Directed by Joseph L. Scanlon; airdate: January 19, 1996.

25. "I Hear You Calling" Written by Scott Shepherd; Story by Catherine Weber; Directed by Mario Azzopardi; airdate: January 26, 1996.

26. "Mind Over Matter" Written by Jon Cooksey and Ali Marie Matheson; Directed by Brad Turner; airdate: February 2, 1996.

27. "Beyond the Veil" Written by Chris Brancato; Directed by Allan Eastman; airdate: February 9, 1996.

28. "First Anniversary" Written by Jon Cooksey and Ali Marie Matheson; Story by Richard Matheson; Directed by Brad Turner; airdate: February 16, 1996.

29. "Straight and Narrow" Written by Joel Metzger; Directed by Joseph L. Scanlon; airdate: February 23, 1996.

30. "Trial by Fire" Written by Brad Wright; Directed by Jonathan Glassner; airdate: March 1, 1996.

31. "Worlds Apart" Written by Chris Dickie; Directed by Brad Turner; airdate: March 22, 1996.

32. "The Refuge" Written by Alan Brennert; Directed by Ken Girotti; airdate: April 5, 1996.

33. "Inconstant Moon" Written by Brad Wright; Story by Larry Niven; Directed by Joseph L. Scanlon; airdate: April 12, 1996.

34. "From Within" Written by Jonathan Glassner; Directed by Neill Fearnley; airdate: April 28, 1996.

35. "The Heist" Written by Steven Barnes; Directed by Brad Turner; airdate: May 5, 1996.

36. "Afterlife" Written by John Whelpley; Directed by Mario Azzopardi; airdate: May 19, 1996.

37. "The Deprogrammers" Written by James Crocker; Directed by Joseph L. Scanlon; airdate: May 26, 1996.

38. "Paradise" Written by Jonathan Walker and Chris Dickie; Directed by Mario Azzopardi; airdate: June 16, 1996.

39. "The Light Brigade" Written by Brad Wright; Directed by Michael Keusch; airdate: June 23, 1996.

40. "Falling Star" Written by Michael Bryant; Directed by Ken Girotti; airdate: June 30, 1996.

41. "Out of Body" Written by James Crocker; Directed by Mario Azzopardi; airdate: July 14, 1996.

42. "Vanishing Act" Written and directed by Jonathan Glassner; airdate: July 21, 1996.

43. "The Sentence" Written by Melissa Rosenberg; Directed by Joseph L. Scanlon; airdate: August 4, 1996.

● **Third Season (1997)**

44. "Second Thoughts" Written by Sam Egan; Directed by Mario Azzopardi; airdate: January 19, 1997.

45. "Re-Generation" Written by Tom Astle; Directed by Brenton Spencer; airdate: January 19, 1997.

46. "Last Supper" Written by Scott Shepherd; Directed by Helen Shaver; airdate: January 24, 1997.

47. "Stream of Consciousness" Written by David Shore; Directed by Joe Nimziki; airdate: January 31, 1997.

48. "Dark Rain" Written by David Braff; Directed by Mario Azzopardi; airdate: February 7, 1997.

49. "The Camp" Written by Brad Wright; Directed by Jonathan Glassner; airdate: February 14, 1997.

50. "Heart's Desire" Written by Alan Brennert; Directed by Mario Azzopardi; airdate: February 21, 1997.

51. "Tempests" Written by Hart Hanson; Directed by Mario Azzopardi; airdate: February 28, 1997.

52. "The Awakening" Written by James Crocker; Directed by George Bloomfield; airdate: March 7, 1997.

53. "New Lease" Written by Sam Egan; Directed by Jason Priestley; airdate: March 14, 1997.

54. "Double Helix" Written by Jona-than Glassner; Directed by Mario Azzopardi; airdate: March 21, 1997.

55. "Dead Man's Switch" Written by Ben Richardson; Directed by Jeff Woolnough; airdate: March 28, 1997.

56. "Music of the Spheres" Written by Steven Barnes; Directed by David Warry-Smith; airdate: April 4, 1997.

57. "The Revelations of Becky Paulson" Written by Brad Wright; Story by Stephen King; Directed by Steven Weber; airdate: May 9, 1997.

58. "Bodies of Evidence" Written by Chris Dickie; Directed by Melvin Van Peebles; airdate: June 6, 1997.

59. "A Special Edition" Written by Naren Shankar and Jonathan Glassner; airdate: Mario Azzopardi; airdate: June 20, 1997.

60. "Hearts and Minds" Written by Naren Shankar; Directed by Brad Turner; airdate: July 11, 1997.

61. "In Another Life" Written by Naren Shanker; Directed by Allan Eastman; airdate: July 25, 1997.

● **Fourth Season (1998–1999)**

62. "Criminal Nature" Written by Brad Markowitz; Directed by Steve Anker; airdate: January 23, 1998.

63. "The Hunt" Written by Sam Egan; Directed by Mario Azzopardi; airdate: January 30, 1998.

64. "In the Zone" Written by Naren Shankar; Story by Jon Povill; Directed by David Warry-Smith; airdate: February 6, 1998.

65. "Rite of Passage" Written by Chris Dickie; Directed by Jimmy Kaufman; airdate: February 16, 1998.

66. "Relativity Theory" Written by Carleton Eastlake; Directed by Ken Girotti; February 23, 1998.

67. **"Josh"** Written by Chris Ruppenthal; Directed by Jorge Montesi; airdate: March 6, 1998.

68. **"Glyphic"** Written by Naren Shankar; Directed by Catherine O'Hara; airdate: March 20, 1998.

69. **"Identity Crisis"** Written by James Crocker; Directed by Brad Turner; airdate: March 27, 1998.

70. **"The Vaccine"** Written by Brad Wright; Directed by Neill Fearnley; airdate: April 3, 1998.

71. **"Fear Itself"** Written by Sam Egan; Directed by James Head; airdate: April 10, 1998.

72. **"The Joining"** Written by Sam Egan; Directed by Brad Turner; airdate: April 17, 1998.

73. **"To Tell the Truth"** Written by Lawrence Myers; Directed by Mario Azzopardi; airdate: April 24, 1998.

74. **"Mary 25"** Written by Jonathan Glassner; Directed by James Head; airdate: May 29, 1998.

75. **"Final Exam"** Written by Carleton Eastlake; Directed by Mario Azzopardi; airdate: June 26, 1998.

76. **"Lithia"** Written by Sam Egan; Directed by Helen Shaver; airdate: July 3, 1998.

77. **"Monster"** Written by Chris Ruppenthal; Directed by Allan Eastman; airdate: July 10, 1998.

78. **"Sarcophagus"** Written by Bill Froehlich; Directed by Jeff Woolnough; airdate: August 5, 1998.

79. **"Nightmare"** Written by Sam Egan; Story by Joseph Stefano; Directed by James Head; airdate: August 12, 1998.

80. **"Promised Land"** Written by Brad Markowitz; Directed by Neill Fearnley; airdate: August 18, 1998.

81. **"Origin of the Species"** Written by Naren Shankar; Directed by Brad Turner; airdate: August 26, 1998.

82. **"The Balance of Nature"** Written by Derek Lowe; Directed by Steve Johnson; airdate: September 2, 1998.

83. **"Phobos Rising"** Written by Garth Wilson; Directed by Helen Shaver; airdate: October 26, 1998.

84. **"Black Box"** Written by Brad Markowitz; Directed by Steven Weber; airdate: May 10, 1999.

85. **"In Our Own Image"** Written by Naren Shankar, Carleton Eastlake, Chris Ruppenthal, Brad Markowitz; Directed by Steve Anker; airdate: May 17, 1999.

4. *THE RAY BRADBURY THEATER* (1985–1992)

By 1985, the anthology wars were in full swing. *Amazing Stories, Alfred Hitchcock Presents, The Twilight Zone, Tales from the Darkside,* and *The Hitchhiker* were locked in fierce battle for a slice of the ratings pie. HBO, the premium cable network which had received some nice buzz, as well as numbers victories, with the sex and horror mix of *The Hitchhiker*, envisioned a more highbrow anthology as their second gambit. The channel's tactic this time around was to hire one of the world's most famous and talented genre authors and give him his own anthology series. In this case, Ray Bradbury became the star and host, and *The Ray Bradbury Theater* became HBO's latest soldier in the anthology fracas. Three episodes aired in the summer of 1985, and drew critical raves. William Shatner starred in "The Playground," Nick Mancuso starred in "The Crowd," and Leslie Nielsen starred in "Marionettes, Inc." Well-cast, sumptuously shot, and well-written, *The Ray Bradbury Theater* looked destined for a long HBO run. However, by 1986 the anthology wars were all but over, and the final tally was miserable: there had been no winners, only victims. *Alfred Hitchcock Presents* was canceled and both the new *Twilight Zone* and Steven Spielberg's

Amazing Stories, were low rated ... barely surviving to second seasons. HBO decided it was time to bow out of the battle, and *The Ray Bradbury Theater* became a casualty. Its second season of three episodes (which included "The Town Where No One Got Off" with Jeff Goldblum, "The Screaming Woman" with Drew Barrymore" and "Banshee" with Peter O'Toole) was aired, or dumped, into a ninety-minute special rather than run in individual time slots on different nights. Although the second series was just as well received (*Cinefantastique* quickly labeled the show the best "fantasy anthology series on TV"), the show was canceled.

Fate intervened for Mr. Bradbury and his series when the USA Network, a basic cable station, bought the rights to the series in 1988 (as it had done with *Alfred Hitchcock Presents* and *The Hitchhiker*) and renewed it for twelve episodes. So successful was this sortie that *The Ray Bradbury Theater* ran three more seasons (two seasons of twelve episodes; one season of twenty-four episodes). In the end, there were sixty-five episodes to the series credit, which made it a perfect bet for syndication. Not surprisingly, USA then quickly shipped the series over to its network companion, the Sci-Fi Channel, and reruns of the show soon commenced.

The Ray Bradbury Theater, alas, suffered from low budgets and poor production values. Though Bradbury himself made for an amiable host and his stories were genuinely interesting, he was not well-served by a production company which shot in New Zealand, Canada, and France — any locale where labor was cheap — and the series was consequently filled with undistinguished casts and minimalist, low-budget sets. *The Ray Bradbury Theater*, USA version, is indistinguishable from *The Hitchhiker* or *Alfred Hitchcock Presents* (USA versions) and is thus a lesser light in the fierce anthology competition.

5. NIGHTMARE CLASSICS (1989)

Shelley Duvall's (*The Shining* [1980]) *Fairie Tale Theater* had become one of the biggest hits on the Showtime network in the late '80s. A sweet and often amusing series aimed primarily at children, *Fairie Tale Theater*, produced by Think Entertainment, had become a popular place for Hollywood celebrities to drop in and do a crazy, high-profile guest role (à la *Batman* [1966-69]). The success of this series (and her second series *Tall Tales and Legends*), inspired Duvall to tackle the realm of literary horror. What she came up with the third time around was *Nightmare Classics*, a short-run (four episodes) anthology which adapted famous gothic novels and stories from the last two centuries. Linda Hunt introduced each show, quoting from Edgar Allan Poe, and prominent genre writers were brought in to adapt stories.

J. Michael Straczynski adapted Robert Louis Stevenson's "The Strange Case of Dr. Jekyll and Mr. Hyde," Art Wallace, a writer on *Star Trek* and *Dark Shadows*, adapted "The Eyes of the Panther" by Ambrose Pierce, and the remaining two stories came from Henry James ("The Turn of the Screw") and Joseph Sheridan Le Fanu ("Carmilla"). The show was impeccably cast, with Roddy McDowall, Amy Irving, Meg Tilly, Roy Dotrice, Laura Dern, and Daphne Zuniga all turning up. *Nightmare Classics* aired from late-summer 1989 to November of the same year, and quietly disappeared after its quartet of shows.

6. WELCOME TO PARADOX (1998)

This 1998 genre anthology ran on the Sci-Fi Channel for thirteen episodes, approximately half-a-season. It aired Monday nights at 10:00 P.M. in the fall of 1998, and was the equivalent of that old "be careful what you wish for" horror trope exploited so successfully in several old *Twilight Zone* episodes and more recently in the *Wishmaster* film series. Each story in this anthology featured a character who *wished* for something, only to have the results of that desire turn out to be less-than-wonderful. What made this series unusual and noteworthy, however, was its setting. Every episode of *Welcome to Paradox* was part of a futuristic anthology set in the incredible metropolis of Betaville, a "utopian," technology-ridden city of the distant future. Thus the series was horrific in its view of the future, with rampant technology being the villain of the show, week-in and week-out. Filmed in Vancouver (again!), the series was produced by Lewis Chesler (of *The Hitchhiker*) and the host was a character called "Paradox." Stories were adapted from Alan Dean Foster, and guest stars included Ice Tea and Rodney Rowland, the latter of *Space: Above and Beyond*.

Though *Welcome to Paradox* was set in the future and concerned with technology, thus science fiction, an argument might also be made that it was horrific in intention since it preached the dangers of technology and usually had a moralistic, O'Henry-style ending. Each week, a specific question (of technology) was asked on *Welcome to Paradox*? What if you couldn't feel pain? What would prisons of the future be like? What if you wouldn't grow old? What if you could have a perfect body? The answers to these questions were frequently thought-provoking, and more than a little bit disturbing.

Though the show was generally well received, and Patrick Lee of *Sci Fi Weekly* on the Internet noted that "the storylines were intriguing and the acting ... was on a uniformly high level," the show did not survive for a second season, as the Sci-Fi Channel went a different way with its new prime time block called "Sci-Fi Prime."

"Man-on-the-Run" Series

1. DEAD AT 21 (1994)

CRITICAL RECEPTION

"a fast-paced, lively and colorful political/scientific atmosphere created of video quick cuts, and rock music rhythms and refrains ... Dumb as it is ... this show has an edge worth traveling along ... rooted in a deep, emotionally powerful sense of skepticism and rebelliousness ... it is technologically, culturally, and stylistically hip."—Elayne Rapping, *The Progressive*: "Cult TV with a Twist," January 1995, pages 34-36.

"heads straight for rampant paranoia, skillfully escalating a general uneasiness into full-fledged terror ... The special effects used for Ed's freakish dreams are fairly standard issue, lots of spinning cameras and strobe lights. But with some driving music and sharp directorial pacing, *Dead at 21* gives its universe of seeming conspiracy a solidly menacing spin. The performances of Mr. Noseworthy ... and Ms. Ryan are appealingly attuned to the youthful angst of Ed and Maria ... summer's first real television blast."—John J. O'Connor, *The New York Times*: "One Year to Disarm a Killer in the Brain," June 15, 1994, C16.

CAST AND CREDITS

Cast: Jack Noseworthy (Edward Bellamy); Lisa Dean Ryan (Maria Cavalos); Whip Hubley (Winston).
Credits: Associate Producers: John A. Jacobson, Bruce A. Taylor. *Supervising Producer:* P.K. Simonds. *Producer:* Steve Ecclesine. *Executive Producer:* Roderick Taylor. *Executive in Charge of Production:* Tom Campbell. An MTV Production in association with Qwerty Inc.

THE DETAILS

Call this short-lived series *The Fugitive* meets *A Rebel Without a Cause*. Motorcycle riding slacker Edward Bellamy (Jack Noseworthy of *Event Horizon* [1997]) discovers on the eve of his 20th birthday that he is actually a failed government experiment and worse ... that he has a built-in expiration date. A computer chip in his brain will kill him at the age of 21, in exactly one year, unless he finds his "creator," Dr. Heisenberg, and receives some kind of medical treatment. Edward has also been framed for a crime he did not commit: the murder of a man who shared "the truth" with him. Along for the ride on Edward's cross-country search for his real identity is the beautiful Maria. Winston is the "Hapless Pursuer," in this case, the government agent bent on catching his prey.

Dead at 21 was a youth-oriented (but not child's) series which aired on MTV, the popular music cable station, during the summer of 1994. MTV's first continuing "adventure" series (*The Real World* doesn't count!), the show ran for thirteen half-hour long episodes, and has never been rerun.

EPISODE LIST

1. "Pilot" Written by John Sherman; Directed by Ralph Hemecker; airdate: June 15, 1994.

2. "Brain Salad" Written by Roderick L. Taylor and Bruce A Taylor; Directed by Ralph Hemecker; airdate: June 22, 1994.

3. "Love Minus Zero" Written by P.K. Simonds; Directed by Charles Winker; airdate: June 29, 1994.

4. "Shock the Monkey" Written by Roderick L. Taylor and Bruce A. Taylor; Directed by Ralph Hemecker; airdate: July 6, 1994.

5. "Gone Daddy Gone" Written by Manny Coto; Directed by Kari Skogland; airdate: July 13, 1994.

6. "Use Your Illusion" Written by Manny Coto; Directed by Ron Oliver; airdate: July 20, 1994.

7. "Live for Today" Written by Jon Sherman; Directed by Mark Jean; airdate: July 27, 1994.

8. "Tie Your Mother Down" Written by Jon Sherman; Directed by Jeff Kibbee; airdate: August 3, 1994.

9. "Cry Baby Cry" Written by Manny Coto; Directed by Terence O'Hara; airdate: August 10, 1994.

10. "Life During Wartime" Written by Manny Coto; Directed by Jeff Kibbee; airdate: August 17, 1994.

11. "Hotel California" Written by Roderick L. Taylor and Bruce A. Taylor; Directed by Ralph Hemecker; airdate: August 24, 1994.

12. "In Through the Out Door" (Part I) Written by Roderick L. Taylor and Bruce A. Taylor; Directed by Ralph Hemecker; airdate: August 31, 1994.

13. "In Through the Out Door" (Part II) Written by Roderick L. Taylor and Bruce A. Taylor; Directed by Ralph Hemecker; airdate: September 7, 1994.

2. NOWHERE MAN (1995-1996)

CRITICAL RECEPTION

"This type of paranoid scenario (predecessors include *The Prisoner* and ... *VR.5*) is hard to sustain as a series without either sharp focus or boundless imagination. And *Nowhere Man*, an intriguing if thin show, isn't sufficiently flush in either category." — David Hiltbrand, *People*, August 28, 1995, page 14.

"With a solid lead in Greenwood and spooky direction from *Poltergeist*'s Tobe Hooper, *Nowhere* could go somewhere." — *Entertainment Weekly*, August 25, 1995, page 98.

"the best paranoia trip TV has seen in years ... a passionate defense of the individual in the face of overwhelming odds." — Roger Fulton, and John Betancourt, *The Sci-Fi Channel Encyclopedia of TV Science Fiction*, Warner Books, New York, New York, 1997, page 304.

CAST AND CREDITS

Cast: Bruce Greenwood (Thomas Veil).
Credits: Creator: Lawrence Hertzog. *Executive Producer:* Lawrence Hertzog. *Producer:* Peter Dunne. *Supervising Producer:* Joel Surnow. Filmed on location in Portland, Oregon. Created by Lawrence Hertzog Productions, in association with Touchstone Television.

THE DETAILS

The incredible success of *The X-Files* on Fox was an example for UPN when it greenlighted production on Lawrence Hertzog's series, *Nowhere Man*. Interestingly, *Nowhere Man* did not concern itself with aliens, monsters, or the like, only with one popular *X-Files* element: a vast conspiracy. In this case, the story involved photographer Thomas Veil (Bruce Greenwood, later of *Sleepwalkers* [1997]), and his photo "Hidden Agenda." The picture was perfectly named, for some powerful force with a hidden agenda did not like the picture, and wanted it destroyed. To do so, the agents of the conspiracy set about to "erase" the photographer, Veil, from the face of the world. Thus, in one night, Veil's whole identity was taken away. His wife (*Millennium*'s Megan Gallagher) claimed she no longer recognized or knew him, and all of his contacts with the world were removed, taken away with miraculous speed and ease. With a copy of "Hidden Agenda," Veil then set out across the United States to expose the conspiracy and discover the truth about "Hidden Agenda" and his own identity.

A "man-on-the-run" series with similarities to the formats of *The Fugitive*, *The Phoenix*, *The Immortal*, *The Incredible Hulk*, and *Starman*, *Nowhere Man* was also similar to the late-60s Patrick McGoohan production, *The Prisoner*. In this case, the lead character was not trapped in a bizarre village, but a global village: the world. No matter where he ran, Veil could not seem to get to the truth and discover what had happened to his life, his very history. This exciting, paranoid premise made *Nowhere Man* one of the most involving and high-profile shows of the 1995-96 season. Airing on Monday nights after *Star Trek Voyager*'s first year, the show quickly generated an enormous (and still active) fan following. Tobe Hooper directed several episodes of the series, and the guest list was impressive, with Michael Tucker, Carrie-Anne Moss (of *The Matrix* [1999]), Raphael Sbarge, Dean Stockwell, Dwight Schultz, and Hal Linden taking part in the massive "cover-up." Veil's one season odyssey took him from a mental hospital to a "village" set up by the conspiracy, and the final episode brought all these elements to a stunning conclusion, which will not be revealed here.

Nowhere Man was canceled after one season, and UPN offered the dreadful *The Burning Zone* in its stead. *Nowhere Man* would seem a prime candidate for the Sci-Fi Channel to pick up as part of its "Conspiracy Sunday," but so far the channel has resisted such an idea. Sadly, *Nowhere Man* has not been rerun since its original network airing, almost five years ago.

Episode List

1. "**Absolute Zero**" Written by Lawrence Hertzog; Directed by Tobe Hooper; airdate: August 28, 1995.

2. "**Turnabout**" Written by Lawrence Hertzog; Directed by Tobe Hooper; airdate: September 4, 1995.

3. "**The Incredible Derek**" Written by Joel Surnow; Directed by James Darren; airdate: September 11, 1995.

4. "**Something About Her**" Written by Lawrence Hertzog; Directed by James Whitmore Jr.; airdate: September 18, 1995.

5. "**Paradise on Your Doorstep**" Written by Lawrence Hertzog; Directed by Thomas J. Wright; airdate: September 25, 1995.

6. "**The Spider Webb**" Written by Joel Surnow; Directed by Thomas Wright; airdate: October 9, 1995.

7. "**A Rough Whimper of Insanity**" Written by Joel Surnow; Directed by Guy Magar; airdate: October 23, 1995.

8. "**The Alpha Strike**" Written by Erica Byrne; Directed by Steven Robman; airdate: October 30, 1995.

9. "**You Really Got a Hold on Me**" Written by Jake and Mike Weinberger; Directed by Michael Levine; airdate: November 6, 1995.

10. "**Father**" Written by Art Montarestelli; Directed by Guy Magar; airdate: November 13, 1995.

11. "**The Enemy Within**" Written by Peter Dunne; Director Ian Toynton; airdate: November 20, 1995.

12. "**It's Not Such a Wonderful Life**" Written by Lawrence Hertzog; Directed by Tim Hunter; airdate: November 27, 1995.

13. "**Contact**" Written by Lawrence Hertzog; Directed by Reza Badiyi; airdate: January 15, 1996.

14. "**Heart of Darkness**" Written by David Ehrman; Directed by Stephen Stafford; airdate: January 22, 1996.

15. "**Forever Jung**" Written by Joel Surnow; Directed by Stephen Stafford; airdate: February 5, 1996.

16. "**Shine a Light on You**" Written by Art Montarestelli; Directed by Stephen Stafford; airdate: February 12, 1996.

17. "**Stay Tuned**" Written by Lawrence Hertzog; Directed by Mel Damski; airdate: February 19, 1996.

18. "**Hidden Agenda**" Written by David Ehrman; Directed by Michael Levine; airdate: February 26, 1996.

19. "**Doppelganger**" Written by Schulyer Kent; Directed by Ian Toynton; airdate: March 18, 1996.

20. "**Through a Lens Darkly**" Written by Art Montarestelli; Directed by Ian Toynton; airdate: April 8, 1996.

21. "**The Dark Side of the Moon**" Written by David Ehrman; Directed by James Whitmore Jr.; airdate: April 15, 1996.

22. "**Calaway**" Written by Joel Surnow; Directed by Ian Toynton; airdate: April 29, 1996.

23. "**Zero Minus Ten**" Written by Jane Espenson; Directed by James Whitmore Jr.; airdate: May 6, 1996.

24. "**Marathon**" Written by Art Montarestelli; Directed by Stephen Stafford; airdate: May 13, 1996.

25. "**Gemini**" Written by Lawrence Hertzog and Art Monterastelli; Directed by Steven Stafford; airdate: May 20, 1996.

Horror Lite

1. TUCKER'S WITCH (1982-1983)

CRITICAL RECEPTION

"Mix a little bit of *Mr. and Mrs. North* with a dash of *Bewitched* and you know what *Tucker's Witch* was like." — Tim Brooks and Earle Marsh, *The Complete Directory of Prime Time Network TV Show*, 1946-Present, page 869.

"A wonderful show that never caught on with viewers. The cast is witty and delightful ... Unfortunately, because of the few episodes made the series has never re-aired in syndication, although it has aired overseas." — William E. Anchors, *Epilog* #17, April 1992, page 69.

CAST AND CREDITS

Cast: Catherine Hicks (Amanda Tucker); Tim Matheson (Rick Tucker); Barbara Barrie (Ellen/"Mom"); Alfre Woodard (Marsha Fullbright); Bill Morey (Lieutenant Fisk).
Credits: Executive Producers: Leonard Hill, Phil Mandelker, Steve Kline. *Created by:* Bill Bast. *Music:* Brad Fiedel. *Writers:* Bill Bast and Paul Huson.

THE DETAILS

In fall of 1982, CBS fostered high hopes for *Tucker's Witch*, a romantic detective drama which was to include an element of the supernatural (which thus qualifies the series for mention in this text). In particular, the protagonist of *Tucker's Witch*, Amanda Tucker, was a witch with special "powers" that some-

times worked and sometimes ... did not. Assisting Amanda in the development of her unusual powers was the family cat, a "familiar" named Dickens who was once described as a "furry crystal ball through which Amanda receives her psychic fixes."[6] The series was also romantic comedy in conception, with Amanda and Rick's detective skills at the Tucker Agency frequently clashing (his powers were deductive; hers psychic). *Tucker's Witch* was also a traditional crime series in that the villains were *not* supernatural, but mortal, as opposed to *Charmed*, wherein the villains are all demons and the like. Additionally, and a bit tediously, the show might also be described as a family drama because Amanda's mother Ellen was featured frequently and scenes often took place at the Tucker homestead.

Unfortunately, many elements in *Tucker's Witch* seemed confusing or ill-considered. Although a cat is often the companion of a witch in mythology and occult texts, Amanda's powers seemed more paranormal than occult-based. Amanda acted more like a psychic than a wiccan, and the series did not seem to understand the difference.

One of only six new series on CBS's schedule for the '82-'83 season, *Tucker's Witch* faced its share of problems. Early on, the original cast (Kim Cattrall as Amanda Tucker; Art Hindle as Rick Tucker) was replaced by Catherine Hicks (*Star Trek IV: The Voyage Home* [1986]; *Child's Play* [1988], *7th Heaven* [1996–]) and Tim Matheson. Also notable in the cast (as the detective agency Girl Friday) was a young Alfre Woodard, one of today's truly great actresses, seen recently in *Star Trek: First Contact* (1996).

When *Tucker's Witch* aired during its regular Wednesday night time slot at 10:00 P.M., the show followed a weak lead-in (a sitcom called *Filthy Rich* [1982-83] starring Dixie Carter and Delta Burke) and faced competition from powerhouses such as *Dynasty* (1981-88) and even the '82 World Series. Ratings were low, the show had creative problems, and CBS pulled the show from the air after just six episodes were broadcast. In March of 1983, CBS aired the last six episodes of *Tucker's Witch* on Thursday nights but by then the verdict was in and the show was officially canceled. In an interview with *The New York Times*, producer Len Hill explained why he felt that this witches' brew of romance/comedy/crime/supernatural failed to grab an audience:

> The mysteries were too fragile and not well enough thought out ... Our story ideas were too conventional. We relied too often on convenience to catch the killer and we didn't maximize the unique aspects of the relationship between our lead characters.[7]

Guest stars on *Tucker's Witch* included Ted Danson, Marj Dusay, Kenneth Mars, Liz Torres, Tracy Scoggins, and Simon Oakland. Though *Tucker's Witch* did not live long (and has never been rerun in syndication because it produced so few episodes), it did form a critical link in the "witch" chain from *Bewitched* to *Charmed* (1998–) and *Sabrina the Teenage Witch* (1996–), specifically in highlighting the activities of a beautiful witch and a cat.

EPISODE LIST

1. **"The Good Witch of Laurel Canyon"** Written by Bill Bast and Paul Huson; Directed by Peter Hunt; airdate: October 6, 1982.

2. **"Big Mouth"** Written by Bill Bast and Paul Huson; Directed by Rod Daniel; airdate: October 13, 1982.

3. **"The Corpse Who Knew Too Much"** Written by Steve Kline; Directed by Harry Winer; airdate: October 20, 1982.

4. **"The Case of the Toltec Death Mask"** Written by Maryanne Kasica and

Michael Scheff; Directed by Harry Winer; airdate: October 27, 1982.

5. **"Terminal Case"** Written by Lee Sheldon; Directed by Randa Haines; airdate: November 3, 1982.

6. **"Abra Cadaver"** Written by Bernie Kukoff; Directed by Rod Daniel; airdate: November 10, 1982.

7. **"Dye Job"** Written by Marc Rubin; Directed by Harvey Laidman; airdate: March 31, 1983.

8. **"Psych Out"** Written by Steve Kline; Directed by Peter Hunt; airdate: April 7, 1983.

9. **"Rock Is a Hard Place"** Written by Lee Sheldon; Directed by Corey Allen; airdate: April 14, 1983.

10. **"Formula for Revenge"** Written by Bill Bast and Paul Huson; Directed by Harvey Laidman; airdate: April 28, 1983.

11. **"Living and Presumed Dead"** Written by Steve Kline; Directed by Corey Allen; airdate: May 5, 1983.

12. **"Murder Is the Key"** Written by Bernie Kukoff; Directed by Victor Lobl; airdate: May 26, 1983.

2. *SHADOW CHASERS* (1985–1986)

CAST AND CREDITS

Cast: Trevor Eve (Professor Jonathan MacKensie); Dennis Dugan (Edgar "Benny" Benedek); Nina Foch (Dr. Julianne Moorhouse).

Credits: Executive Producers: Brian Grazer, Kenneth Johnson. *Created by:* Brian Grazer, Kenneth Johnson. *Music:* Joe Harnell, Marc Tanner.

THE DETAILS

Billed as a "comedic adventure into the strange and unexplained," *Shadow Chasers* might best be described as an early, funny version of *The X-Files*. Created by Brian Grazer and Kenneth Johnson, the mastermind behind *Alien Nation* (1988) as well as *Cliffhangers*

(1979), the series has also been labeled "a fantasy/comedy," a moniker which does not explain its placement in a book about terror TV. Specifically, *Shadow Chasers* is included here because it manages to feature (albeit in comedic fashion) a variety of horror tropes including cults ("The Spirit of St. Louis"), the Bermuda Triangle ("The Middle of Somewhere"), ghosts ("Amazing Grace," "Phantom of the Galleria"), zombies ("Parts Unknown"), and even deals with the devil ("Let's Make a Deal"). Some sources have also described *Shadow Chasers* as a variation on the popular 1984 hit feature film, *Ghostbusters*, and that seems pretty apt as well.

Shadow Chasers, again like the *X-Files*, features two partners investigating occult, paranormal happenings. In this case, however, the partners are not intrepid F.B.I. agents but a stumbling university professor (Eve) and an equally inept tabloid reporter (Dugan).

Shadow Chasers aired from November 14, 1985, to January 16, 1986. Like many genre shows over the years, this ABC show was scheduled against stiff competition. Because it aired on Thursday nights (from 8:00–9:00), the series was trounced by two of the biggest hits of the decade: *Magnum, P.I.* on CBS and the killer combo of *The Cosby Show* and *Family Ties* on NBC. Not surprisingly, *Shadow Chasers* only aired ten times before being canceled. It has been occasionally rerun on The Sci-Fi Channel as part of the "Series Collection," alongside *She Wolf of London*, *Nightmare Cafe*, and the like.

EPISODE LIST

1. "Shadow Chasers" (2 hours) Written by Kenneth Johnson and Brian Grazer; Directed by Kenneth Johnson; airdate: November 14, 1985.

2. "Spirit of St. Louis" Written by Craig Buck; Directed by Victor Lubl; airdate: November 21, 1985.

3. "Amazing Grace" Written by Susan Goldberg and Bob Rosenfarb; Directed by Barbara Peters; airdate: November 28, 1985.

4. "The Middle of Somewhere" Written by Renee and Harry Longstreet; Directed by Chuck Braverman; airdate: December 5, 1985.

5. "Parts Unknown" Written by Linda Campanelli and M.M. Shelly Moore; Directed by Bob Sweeny; airdate: December 12, 1985.

6. "The Many Lives of Jonathan" Written by Richard Manning and Hans Beimler; Directed by Cliff Bole; airdate: December 19, 1985.

7. "The Phantom of the Galleria" Written by Peggy Goldman; Directed by Alan Myerson; airdate: December 26, 1985.

8. "How Green Was My Murder" Written by Susan Goldberg and Bob Rosenfarb; Directed by Tony Mordente; airdate: January 9, 1986.

9. "Let's Make a Deal" Written by Peggy Goldman; Directed by Barbara Peters; airdate: January 16, 1986.

UNAIRED EPISODES

10. "Ahead of Time" Written by Renee and Harry Longstreet; Directed by Tony Mordente.

11. "Blood and Magnolias" Written by Maryanne Kasica and Michael Scheff; Directed by Chuck Bowman.

12. "Cora's Stranger" Written by Diane Frolov; Directed by Alan Myerson.

13. "Curse of the Full Moon" Written by Maryanne Kasica and Michael Scheff; Directed by Bob Sweeney.

3. THE MUNSTERS TODAY (1988–1991)

THE DETAILS

The Munsters (1964–66) was a short-lived, black-and-white CBS sitcom about a family of suburban ghouls who happened to look just like the famous monsters of Universal Studios during the 1940s. Father Herman Munster (Fred Gwynne) was the Frankenstein Munster, Grandpa (Al Lewis) was a caped vampire, Lily (Yvonne De Carlo) was the bride of Frankenstein, and little Eddie Munster (Butch Patrick) was a werewolf with pointed ears and a widow's peak. The Munsters lived in a big old gothic mansion (at 1313 Mockingbird Lane) with normal daughter Marilyn (first Beverly Owen, then Pat Priest) and their pet dragon, Spot, for two seasons. The show was initially conceived as an *Addams Family* (1964-66) rip off, but it soon achieved everlasting fame after extensive syndicated reruns in the early and mid-1970s. Today *The Munsters* is one of those perennial "rerun" comedies, like *I Love Lucy*, *The Brady Bunch*, or *Gilligan's Island*. Everybody remembers it, everybody loves it. In 1992, *The Ben Stiller Show* even acknowledged the show's popularity with a take-off/homage of *The Munsters* called *Cape Munster*. It featured a grown Eddie Munster fulfilling the Robert De Niro role of *Cape Fear* (1991).

In 1988, the Arthur Company took a stab at reviving *The Munsters* legend with a sitcom remake entitled *The Munsters Today*. Sold to New York, Philadelphia, San Francisco, Detroit, Dallas, Washington, D.C., and other major American cities as part of the genre syndication glut of the late '80s (along with *Monsters, Friday the 13th: The Series, Freddy's Nightmares, War of the Worlds,* and *The Untouchables*), *The Munsters Today* featured an all-new cast in a color version of the series. The concept underlying the revamp was that the Munsters had been "asleep" for twenty-two years and had only just awakened to find themselves in the fast-and-furious late '80s and early '90s. The new cast included John Schuck as Herman Munster, former Miss America Lee Meriwether as Lily, Howard Morton (of *Gimme a Break* [1981-85]) as Grandpa, James Marsden as a still young Eddie, and a miraculously younger version of Marilyn than had been seen before (this time played by Hilary Van Dyke). Actor John Schuck explained to *Star-*

log his reasons for being involved in the *Munsters* remake:

> … I thought that Herman Munster is an unusual creation, one I could do many wonderful things with … I like the concept of a show that deals with a family unit. I also realized we were going to be much different from the first one, which was wonderful. Then, it proved to be a challenge: How can I create my *own* Herman?[8]

Schuck, who has done everything from *Star Trek* films (*The Voyage Home* [1986], *The Undiscovered Country* [1991]) to *Holmes and Yoyo* (1976) played a blue-skinned Herman to comedic effect, even when the basic sitcom stories failed to utilize his full potential as an actor.

The Munsters Today lasted for three seasons, seventy-two episodes in all, and in the process featured guest appearances by Jonathan Brandis (*SeaQuest DSV* [1993-95]), Robbie Rist (*Galactica: 1980* [1980]), Zsa Zsa Gabor, Dr. Joyce Brothers, Donny Most, and Ruth Buzzi. As a horror program, the show was inconsequential for all intents and purposes. Instead, *The Munsters Today* was merely a family-oriented situation comedy which utilized (some might say "exploited") horror icons (Dracula, Frankenstein, the Wolfman) as central character types. Some horrific aspects came into play in certain episodes, but always with funny rather than scary results. Demons appeared in "Genie from Hell" (with Billy Barty) and "Melting Pot," a Mummy friend showed up in "Green Eyed Monsters," and a would-be werewolf was highlighted in "Don't Cry Wolfman." The monster shtick, which was carried off with at least a degree of humor, if not sophistication, in the original series, seemed far more tired and old in this low budget remake, even though the new cast was arguably as good as the original one. *The Munsters Today* is included in this book because, way back in 1970, *Rod Serling's Night Gallery* also satirized famous movie monsters during Jack Laird's sometimes notorious "black-outs." Not surprisingly, *The Munsters Today* plays like extended versions of these *Night Gallery* shows, essentially a one-joke show that exists in the world of horror without being horrific (except in its lack of quality).

The Munsters Today is rarely rerun on the eve of the 21st century, perhaps because of its low production values. When most people think of The Munsters, they remember the black and white 1960s series rather than this rather forgettable, color remake.

4. FREE SPIRIT (1989–1990)

THE DETAILS

Before Sabrina the Teenage Witch (1996–) and well after Bewitched (1964-67), there came this forgettable entry in the witch-sitcom genre, Free Spirit. An ABC situation comedy which aired on Friday nights (the same night Sabrina would inherit six years later!), the series starred Corinne Bohrer as a witch cum housekeeper/nanny who was hired to care for the typically suburban Harper family. Her special powers often came into play to save the day or avert domestic disasters. This family "situation" was a format component which made Free Spirit resemble a Who's the Boss or The Nanny variation as much as a supernatural-oriented comedy. One of Bohrer's young wards eventually came into her own, however, in the late '90s. Alyson Hannigan, who played Jessica or "Jessie" Harper on Free Spirit, became famous for playing Willow, a witch herself, on Joss Whedon's Buffy the Vampire Slayer.

Free Spirit ran for just half-a-season (thirteen episodes) before being canceled by ABC. Because the series was a two-camera sitcom, technical and acting credits were mostly unmemorable, but Robert Reed and Florence Henderson of The Brady Bunch (1969-74) did reteam for one episode, and Michael Constantine (a Terror TV hall of famer for appearances on Darkroom, Friday the 13th, and Night Gallery) appeared in another.

5. SABRINA THE TEENAGE WITCH (1996–)

CRITICAL RECEPTION

"strictly lighthearted froth rather than Stephen King-style horror ... the show's genial loopiness harks back to Bewitched." — Jill Gerston, The New York Times: "A 'Normal Kid' with Magical Properties," October 6, 1996, page 18.

"there's the fun of flying and turning people into poodles and doing all the other things that teenagers would like to do when stumbling and fumbling through an awkward age ... these characters are pleasantly odd, down to their curious conversations with a cat named Salem." — John J. O'Connor, The New York Times: "The Latest Member of the Coven," April 10, 1996, page C18.

CAST AND CREDITS

Cast: Melissa Joan Hart (Sabrina); Beth Broderick (Aunt Zelda); Caroline Rhea (Aunt Hilda); Nate Richert (Harvey); Jenna Leigh Green (Libby); Michelle Beaudoin (Jenny); Paul Feig (Mr. Pool); Nick Bakay (Salem the Cat).

Credits: Executive Producers: Paula Hart, Barney Cohen, Kathryn Wallack. Created by: Nell Scovell. Based on Characters in: Archie Comics. Producers: Richard Davis and Alana H. Lambros. Produced by Viacom in association with HartBreak Productions.

THE DETAILS

Perhaps the most popular "witch" sitcom ever, Sabrina the Teenage Witch has been delighting teen audiences since it first aired as a Showtime TV movie in April of 1996. The network series, starring the perky Melissa Joan Hart (Clarissa Explains It All), began airing the following October, and has been a mainstay of the ABC Friday prime time schedule ever since. It is credited (along with Buffy the Vampire Slayer) as creating a new generation of occult-oriented but nonetheless positive role models for young women. *Charmed*, for instance, is often described as *Sabrina* meets *Buffy*.

As older viewers may be aware, Sabrina is not a new character. This sixteen-year-old witch was one of the main characters in *Archie Comics* long before she came to TV and the so-called T.G.I.F. line-up. On TV, Sabrina is less sexy, and more innocent than her comic-book counterpart, but just as mischievous. There is not much new or exciting in this TV series, and not much horror to write about either, but the show still manages to generate some magic of its own through Hart's infectious and charming portrayal of a witch-in-training. As Hart has stated, the show is not intended to scare anyway, merely to amuse:

> It's a fun show about a normal kid who just happens to be a witch ... We don't deal with heavy stuff like drugs and divorce or black magic and killing people. It's pure entertainment.[9]

Indeed, for all the "horror" included in this show, Sabrina might as well be Barbara Eden on *I Dream of Jeannie*. Although *Sabrina the Teenage Witch* is about a horror-type character (a witch with — again — a talking cat), it is pure sitcom. It is included here only because this author finds it fascinating that horror characters such as witches, ghouls, and vampires often turn up on TV played for laughs.

Sabrina the Teenage Witch has featured appearances by Frank Conniff (TV's Frank of *Mystery Science Theater 3000* [1989-99]), Robby Benson, Martin Mull, Kathy Ireland, Ed Begley Jr., Jack Wagner, and other notable stars, but it is for Hart's heart-filled performance that the show remains most special. Interestingly, Hart looks ready to shed her "teenage" image and in late 1999 posed for a series of very provocative photographs in the men's magazine, *Maxim*. What would Salem the cat think of that?

6. *BAYWATCH NIGHTS* (1996)

Cast: David Hasselhoff (Mitch Buchanon); Greg Alan Williams (Garner Ellerbee); Angie Harmon (Ryan McBride).

THE DETAILS

Okay. You've got me. This is not a comedy, "horror lite" series at all. At least it is not supposed to be. Instead, this unintentionally hilarious spin-off from the popular *Baywatch* is a failed attempt to make a serious horror show in the vein of *The X-Files*. Airing in syndication, it lasted one short season, pitting surfer and lifeguard Mitch Buchanon (David Hasselhoff) against witches, cults, and UFOS. Its slogan was "nights will never be the same," and its intent was to show Buchanon's nocturnal life as an occult investigator, protecting the boardwalk and such from supernatural interlopers. As that description sounds, it is a fool's errand to merge the jiggle world of *Baywatch* with the paranormal, supernatural overtones of *The X-Files*, and this show manages to make a hash out of both premises. *Baywatch Nights* is executed with just enough naive stupidity to make it the campiest, funniest show to hit the airwaves in a long time. This must be the worst show to be inspired by *The X-Files*, even if it is really, really funny.

Pseudo-Reality TV

1. *SIGHTINGS* (1994–1997)

CAST AND CREDITS

Cast: Tim White (Host)

Credits: Executive Producers: Henry Winkler, Ann Daniel. *Correspondent:* Carla Wohl. *Co-Executive Producers:* Stephen Kroopnick. *Director:* George Cooke. *Supervising Producer:* Michaelle A. Davis. *Senior Segment Director:* Richard L. Schmidt. *Segment Producers:* Laura Aka, Craig Armstrong, Philip Davis, Joyce Goldstein, Ruth Rafidi, Rob Sharkey. *Head of Research and Development:* Lesley Taylor. *Researchers:* Candice Cephas-Diaz, Curt Collier, Michael Kriz, Matt Van Wagener. *Production Manager:* Lisa Blackwood. *Production Coordinator*: Chris Emhardt. *Post-production Supervisor:* Cole Metcalf. *Editors:* Mary Ann Benson, Paul Broz, Kelly Coskran, John Moore, Steven Uhlenberg, David Vernon. *Postproduction Audio:* Ron Miller, Craig Plachy. *Original Music:* Alan Ett. *Main Title Theme:* Bill Bodine. *Clip Clearance:* Gregory Fein, Kristi Dixon. *Online Producer:* Joe Fairbrother. *First PA:* Richard Brandt. *Production Assistant:* Derek McDaniel, Christopher Reidy, Trista Switzer. *Post Production:* Blake Grant, Alicia Jabin. *Wardrobe*: Brenda Maben. *Makeup:* Renee Napolitano. *Stage Manager:* Michael Malone. *Technical Director:* Jay Larkins. *Lighting Director:* James Moody. *Newsroom Designer:* Tim Saunders, Broadcast Design International. *From an original concept by:* Linda Moulton Howe. *Executive in Charge of Production:* Mark A. Vertullo. An Ann Daniel Production, Fair Dinkum Productions, from Paramount, a Viacom Company.

THE DETAILS

On *Sightings,* host Tim White appears to stand, superimposed optically, before a vast control room where busy technicians in headsets and white collared shirts sit at advanced-looking terminals and stare at blinking maps in earnest, dramatic fashion. White's grave tone matches the tenor of the techies: he faces the audience solemnly and intones the series' motto: "No mystery is closed to an open mind."

All things being equal, this "reality" series probably has no legitimate place in a book about dramatic horror programming. After all, *Sightings* is not a drama program per se, but rather a poker-faced variation on the popular CBS reality show *Rescue 911* (hosted by the inimitable William Shatner). On *Sightings* (produced by the Fonz himself, Henry Winkler) several stories are recounted per episode, and each concerns some element of the paranormal. To lend credence to these supposedly true stories, so-called experts are interviewed in each twenty minute segment. Often, supernatural events such as hauntings are dramatized with cheap but effective special effects and creepy sounds. In essence a "reality" version of *The X-Files, Sightings* has probed nearly every kind of paranormal activity imaginable.

In "Without a Trace," *Sightings* recounts (and dramatizes) the disappearance of Australian pilot Fred Valentich's one-man plane some twenty years ago, and the fact that an American installation (a tracking station) called Pine Gap could conceivably have witnessed the aircraft's hijacking by UFOs. Testimony is recorded from Valentich's father, a man who believes firmly that the military is hiding "something," and by an amateur photographer who may have snapped a picture of the offending extraterrestrial vehicle. Another story on the same hour explores the bond between animals and humans, while yet another details the Gateway (human body/mind) connection, and so forth.

Although "investigations" of mysterious crop circles, of a UFO landing in Zimbabwe in 1994 (witnessed by sixty-four school children!), and such are the bread and butter of the long-lived *Sightings*, the series also attempts to "scare" its audience by generating terror in many of these "investigative" segments. For instance, in the clip known as "The Doomsday Machine," *Sightings* warns that the United States government is playing with a dangerous antenna farm in Alaska called HAARP (which has something to do with High Altitude Electronic Technology). Various sources, including Nick Begich, the author of *Angels Don't Play This HAARP*, warn that the technology could easily punch a hole in Earth's ionosphere and destroy it permanently ... rendering our existence on the planet untenable. At other points, various authorities make dire claims that HAARP has been designed to disable human minds on distant battlefields during times of war and is therefore a secret weapon developed by the U.S. military-industrial complex. The investigation is hardly a serious one, however, and only one representative of the maligned U.S. military is even interviewed. Strangely, he seems to operate the giant antenna farm out of a tiny trailer. In addition, he is purposefully sketchy in his answers, as if his interview has been edited in such a way as to make him seem squirrely and untrustworthy.

Other topics on *Sightings* include a serious look at spontaneous human combustion, an investigation of the near death phenomenon, new data from Tunguska, where some people (including an old shaman) believe that a cylinder-shaped flying saucer crashed in 1908. And, of course, there are various stories about hauntings and ghosts. In one episode of *Sightings*, Whaley House in San Diego is combed for examples of electro-magnetic energy signatures called "residue," and Chris Chacon, director of the O.S.I.R. (Office of Scientific Investigation and Research) determines that the ghosts involved in the hauntings are actually sounds from the past, "retrocognitive sounds," being transmitted in the present. That explains why visitors come to the house and hear the clacking of hundred-year-old billiard balls!

In another "hauntings" story, a new condominium in St. Petersburg, Florida, is inhabited by the ghosts of students who once used the building as a high school in the 1920s. Terrified contemporary residents, who speak of glowing white lights and ghostly figures, are interviewed about their experiences.

All of this material is told with solemn face on *Sightings*, but there is often the feeling that the expert witnesses are in on the joke: making outrageous claims that seem insupportable, and in the end, are *not* supported except as speculation. In the school haunting piece, for example, a great deal of emphasis is placed on the fact that the paranormal investigators are researching en masse the reports of life-after-death there. *Sightings* laboriously catalogues all of the technological equipment being deployed (including infrared sensors and nightvision scopes), and there are extensive interviews with paranormal investigators about the strategy for "mapping" the school-turned-condo for ghosts. Then the story ends abruptly, without any report as to what was actually found during this very impressive-appearing investigation. Since the story ends without a revelation, with no answer about the hauntings, it is not difficult to infer that nothing of value was discovered at all! After all, if anybody had found something to report, *Sightings* surely would have reported it, right? One thing is for certain: if UFOs land, if HAARP starts destroying the ionosphere, if ghosts are proved to be "real," *Sightings* is not going to be the broadcast venue through which these discoveries are reported and verified. Legitimate news sources would cover so monumental a story because *Sightings* is just a pseudo-reality time-waster.

In 1999, *Sightings* is frequently rerun on the Sci-Fi Channel (2:00 P.M.), and it is actually good for a few cheap scares. For those among us out there who worry about asteroids colliding with Earth, doomsday prophecies, haunted houses, Nostradamus, ghosts, and the like, this show can be entertaining and thought-provoking. However, *Sighting's* motto might better be: "a mystery is never closed to a gullible mind," because no real, credible evidence is presented for any of the fantastic stories dramatized or discussed in detail. The audience for this show probably consists of the same people who went to see *The Blair Witch Project* (1999) and believed that what they were witnessing on the movie screen was "real." *Sightings* generates scares by the possibility that its tales of paranormal activity and UFO encounters *might* be real. For the skeptical, however, it is all too easy to poke holes in the interviews, canned dramatizations, and editing of the so-called expert testimonies. The host, the control room, the "live" witnesses, the statistical reports and data, and even the sense of paranoia and distrust *Sightings* engenders are all tools (analogous to gore, film techniques, or makeup on regular horror drama programming) employed to sell a bill of goods that reminds one of P.T. Barnum's famous quote: "There's a sucker born every minute." Be warned: if you believe, you'll feel duped.

2. *PSI FACTOR: CHRONICLES OF THE PARANORMAL* (1996–)

CAST AND CREDITS

Cast: Dan Aykroyd (Host); Nancy Anne Sakovich (Lindsey Donner); Barclay Hope (Peter Axon); Colin Fox (Anton Hendricks); **First Season:** Paul Miller (Connor Doyle); **Second Season:** Matt Frewer (Matt Praeger); Nigel Bennett (Frank Elsinger); Peter Mac-Neill (Ray Donohue).

Credits: Created by: Peter Aykroyd, Christopher Chacon, Peter Ventrell. *Consulting Producer:* Rick Drew. *Developed by:* James Nadler. *Producer:* David N. Rosen. *Production*

Designer: Gordon Barnes. *Director of Photography:* John Holosko. *Executive Story Editor:* Damian Kindler. *Story Editor:* Sarah Dodd. *Music:* Lou Natale. *Editor:* Bruce Lange. *Executive Producers:* James Nadler, Seaton McLean, Peter Aykroyd, Christopher Chacon. *Associate Producer:* Matt Frewer. An Alliance Atlantis Production. In association with Eyemark, a Unit of CBS Enterprises. Produced in association with Global; Consultant: Kevin W. Juegensen.

THE DETAILS

Like *Sightings*, *Psi Factor: Chronicles of the Paranormal* is another pseudo-reality TV program about the paranormal which is difficult to categorize because it has a distinctly schizophrenic format. On the one hand, this syndicated series purports to be a "real" investigation of occult and paranormal events, with "real" dramatizations of "real" paranormal cases. Lending support to this "real" reading of the show as "factual," one of its executive producers and creators is Christopher Chacon, the former head of O.S.I.R. who has appeared on *Sightings*. His presence on *Psi Factor* certainly lends some credence to the idea that someone on the creative end of the show wants this series to be taken seriously, as fact and as truth. Yet, on the other hand, the stories featured on *Psi Factor* are obviously works of total fiction, with no documentation, testimony, or eyewitness interviews proffered.

Like *Sightings* again, *Psi Factor* features a host, this time comedian Dan Aykroyd in what can only be described as somber Rod Serling mode. Aykroyd is seen standing inside an impressive control room in book-end appearances. *Psi Factor* even offers the following caveat at the opening of each episode (over the O.S.I.R. logo): "These stories are inspired by the actual case files of the Office of Scientific Investigation and Research." In this case, a great deal of mileage is milked out of the word "inspired," as many of the stories on *Psi Factor* involve time travel, UFO encounters, and other fictional, *X-Files*-style stories. Yet, at the same time that *Psi Factor* features a host stalking a complex control room and claims to be inspired by real events, it also mimics the slow-moving and deliberate camera style of the *X-Files*, and spotlights a high level of gore and violence. These format facets would seem to indicate that the show was intended to be seen as a straight horror program, like *Millennium, Brimstone, Strange World* or any other drama included in this book. Which is it? Fact or fiction? Unfortunately, *Psi Factor* is not a quality show as either fish or fowl.

Making matters worse for any potential categorization of this series, the first season of *Psi Factor* often features two half-hour stories per episode, which means that, like *Sightings* once more, these tales are to be considered "dramatizations" of "real" events, rather than the ongoing adventures of a team of investigators. Perhaps because people were so confused, this approach changed in the second, and recently aired third, season. Now *Psi Factor* features just one story per hour ... but nonetheless maintains the facade that it is "the truth," as well as those annoying wraparound host segments.

In strong contradiction to the many *Sightings*/factual elements, however, the characters on the *Psi Factor* team are developed as if they are, indeed, fully-fledged fictional creations, just like Mulder and Scully or Frank Black. They even become bogged down in an *X-Files*-type of government conspiracy manipulated by Nigel Bennett of *Forever Knight* (1992–96) fame. Basically, *Psi Factor* is just one confused show that tries to have things both ways: it wants to be a *Sightings*-type series which purports to tell true stories at the same time that it generates dramatic characters and stories that can be taken as nothing other than works of fiction. Amazingly, the series handles neither elements of its contradictory formula in particularly adept fashion.

Specifically, the "team" members are one-dimensional characters who are portrayed by mostly unknown Canadian performers in the most basic manner. Nancy Anne Sakovich fails to register any recognizable human emotions. Colin Fox, the wizened statesman of the bunch, is so underutilized that he comes across

as bland old man. In the second and third seasons, Matt Frewer leads the O.S.I.R. team (wearing a very unfortunate hair piece), but even his splendid eccentricity comes off as derivative of Fox Mulder's individuality on *The X-Files*.

More offensive than the schizophrenic format or the boring central characters is the fact that *Psi Factor*, at least so far, appears to be written at an eighth-grade level. In one recent third season show, "Y2K," Nigel Bennett's character (Frank) asks a co-worker to keep him *appraised* of a situation. Of course, what he really meant was that he wanted to be *apprised* of the situation (i.e., kept informed), not that he wanted his monetary value judged. Likewise, in the same episode another character, Hope Barclay's Peter Axon, mispronounces Silicon Valley as Silic*one* Valley — a humorous error. For the writer's future reference: Silicon Valley is where computers get made; Silicone Valley is where future supermodels get made. Also in "Y2K," a computer screen displays a critical readout which erroneously indicates that it is 102 *degree's* [sic] and rising in a certain chamber. Of course, degrees are a unit of measure, and should not be used in the possessive form. If something was the property of a degree (like a jacket or a briefcase) a possessive might reasonably be utilized, but in this case its use was not warranted. Other episodes make the same basic mistakes in grammar, sentence structure, and vocabulary.

One thing a genre show can ill-afford in the day and age of the postmodern, self-reflexive, highly intelligent *Buffy, G vs E,* and *The X-Files* is to look stupid. Unfortunately, *Psi Factor* appears to be *The X-Files* as rewritten by morons. Dan Aykroyd's presence as host might indicate to some that these errors are intentional, part of some humorous undercurrent, but even Aykroyd is straight-laced and serious in this show. He presents the most awful dialogue imaginable with an utterly sober countenance, and one cannot help but think about *Ghostbusters*.

Psi Factor recently completed a third season, and is returning in the fall of 1999 for a fourth season. This means that the show is successful enough to be "stripped" and run on a daily basis ... so let the viewer beware.

EPISODE LIST

• *First Season (1996–1997)*

1A. **"The Underneath"** Written by Robert Cooper; Directed by Milan Cheylov; airdate: November 4, 1996.

1B. **"Phantom Limb"** Written by Sherman Snukal; Directed by Allan Kroeker; airdate: November 4, 1996.

2A. **"The Transient"** Written by Damian Kindler; Directed by Giles Walker; airdate: November 11, 1996.

2B. **"Two Lost Old Men"** Written by Ian Weir; Directed by Giles Walker; airdate: November 11, 1996.

3A. **"UFO Duplication"** Written by Robert Cooper; Directed by Mark Vizzard; airdate: November 18, 1996.

3B. **"Clara's Friend"** Written by Will Dixon; Directed by Mark Vizzard; airdate: November 18, 1996.

4A. **"The Hunter"** Written by Damian Kindler; Directed by John Bell; airdate: November 25, 1996.

4B. **"The Healer"** Written by Larry Raskin; Directed by John Bell; airdate: November 25, 1996.

5A. **"Dream House"** Written by Will Dixon; Directed by Allan Kroeker; airdate: December 2, 1996.

5B. **"UFO Encounter"** Written by James Nadler; Directed by Allan Kroeker; airdate: December 2, 1996.

6A. **"Possession"** Written by James Nadler; Directed by John Bell; airdate: December 9, 1996.

6B. **"Man Out of Time"** Written by Larry Raskin; Directed by Allan Kroeker; airdate: December 9, 1996.

7A. **"Reptilian Revenge"** Written by Will Dixon; Directed by Giles Walker; airdate: December 16, 1996.

7B. **"Ghostly Voices"** Written by Richard Oleksiak; Directed by Allan Kroeker; airdate: December 16, 1996.

8A. **"Creeping Darkness"** Written by David Preston; Directed by John Bell; airdate: December 23, 1996.

8B. **"The Power"** Written by Gerald Wexler; Directed by Allan Kroeker; airdate: December 23, 1996.

9A. **"Freefall"** Written by Larry Raskin; Directed by Milan Cheylov; airdate: December 30, 1996.

9B. **"The Presence"** Written by Ian Weir; Directed by John Bell; airdate: December 30, 1996.

10A. **"Infestation"** Written by Damian Kindler; Directed by Giles Walker; airdate: January 6, 1997.

10B. **"Human Apportation"** Written by Denise Fordham; Directed by John Bell; airdate: January 6, 1997.

11A. **"The Curse"** Written by Will Dixon; Directed by Mark Vizzard; airdate: January 13, 1997.

11B. **"Angel on a Plane"** Written by Ian Weir; Directed by Ken Girotti; airdate: January 13, 1997.

12A. **"Anasazi Cave"** Written by Sherman Snukal; Directed by Mark Vizzard; airdate: January 20, 1997.

12B. **"Devil's Triangle"** Written by Damian Kindler; Directed by Ken Girotti; airdate: January 20, 1997.

13A. **"The Undead"** Written by Will Dixon; Directed by Clay Borris; airdate: January 27, 1997.

13B. **"Stalker Moon"** Written by Alex Pugsley; Directed by Clay Borris; airdate: January 27, 1997.

14A. "The Forbidden North" Written by Damian Kindler; Directed by Ken Girotti; airdate: February 3, 1997.

14B. "Reincarnation" Written by Peter Aykroyd and Christopher Chacon; Directed by Ken Girotti; airdate: February 3, 1997.

15A. "Greenhouse Effect" Written by Damian Kindler; Directed by Clay Borris; airdate: February 10, 1997.

15B. "The Buzz" Written by Sherman Snukal; Directed by Clay Borris; airdate: February 10, 1997.

16. "The Light" Written by Will Dixon; Directed by Milan Cheylov; airdate: April 7, 1997.

17A. "The 13th Floor" Written by Jean Hurtubise; Directed by Clay Borris; airdate: April 7, 1997.

17B. "The Believer" Written by Damian Kindler; Directed by Craig Pryce; airdate: April 7, 1997.

18A. "The Fog" Written by Damian Kindler; Directed by Craig Pryce; airdate: April 14, 1997.

18B. "The House on Garden Street" Written by Chris Dickie; Directed by Clay Borris; airdate: April 14, 1997.

19A. "Second Sight" Written by Sherman Snukal; Directed by Milan Cheylov; airdate: April 21, 1997.

19B. "Chocolate Soldier" Written by Will Dixon; Directed by Milan Cheylov; airdate: April 21, 1997.

20A. "The Fire Within" Written by Richard Oleksiak; Directed by Aaron Shuster; airdate: April 28, 1997.

20B. "Fate" Written by Damian Kindler; Directed by Aaron Shuster; airdate: April 28, 1997.

21A. "Death at Sunset" Written by Jeremy Hole; Directed by Ross Clyde; airdate: May 5, 1997.

21B. "Collision" Written by Sherman Snukal; Directed by Ross Clyde; airdate: May 5, 1997.

22. "Perestroika" Written by Will Dixon; Directed by Giles Walker; airdate: May 12, 1997.

● *Second Season (1997–1998)*

23. "Threads" Written by James Nadler; Directed by Milan Cheylov; airdate: September 22, 1997.

24. "Donor" Written by Rick Drew; Directed by Milan Cheylov; airdate: September 29, 1997.

25. "Wish I May" Written by Will Dixon; Directed by John Bell; airdate: October 6, 1997.

26. "Communion" Written by Peter Mohan; Directed by John Bell; airdate: October 13, 1997.

27. "Frozen in Time" Written by Tracey Forbes; Directed by Giles Walker; airdate: October 20, 1997.

28. "Devolution" Written by John Dolin; Directed by Clay Borris; airdate: October 27, 1997.

29. "The Warrior" Written by Rick Drew; Directed by Clay Borris; airdate: November 3, 1997.

30. "The Grey Men" Written by James Nadler; Directed by Giles Walker; airdate: November 10, 1997.

31. "Man of War" Written by Deborah Natrian; Directed by Stephen Williams; airdate: November 17, 1997.

32. "The Damned" Written by Tony DiFranco; Directed by Clay Borris; airdate: November 24, 1997.

33. "Hell Week" Written by Alex Rigsley; Directed by Craig Pryce; airdate: January 19, 1998.

34. "The Edge" Written by Tracey Forbes; Directed by Craig Pryce; January 26, 1998.

35. "Bad Dreams" Written by Will Dixon; Directed by Stephen Williams; airdate: February 2, 1998.

36. "Kiss of the Tiger" Written by Damian Kindler; Directed by Carl Alexander Goldstein; airdate: February 9, 1998.

37. "The Haunting" Written by Rick Drew; Directed by John Bell; airdate: February 16, 1998.

38. "The Night of the Setting Sun" Written by James Nadler; Directed by E. Jane Thompson; airdate: February 23, 1998.

39. "The Labyrinth" Written by Christiana Schull; Directed by Ron Oliver; airdate: April 4, 1998.

40. "Pentimento" Written by Sarah Dodd; Directed by Vincenzo Natali; airdate: April 13, 1998.

41. "Frozen Faith" Written by Matt Frewer; Directed by Ron Oliver; airdate: April 20, 1998.

42. "Map to the Stars" Written by Will Dixon; Directed by John Bell; airdate: April 27, 1998.

43. "The Endangered" Written by Rick Drew; Directed by Will Dixon; airdate: May 4, 1998.

44. "Egress" Written by James Nadler; Directed by John Bell; airdate: May 11, 1998.

Space ... The Horrific Frontier

SPACE: 1999 (1975–1977)

CRITICAL RECEPTION

"*Space: 1999* is like *Star Trek* shot full of methedrine. It is the most flashy, gorgeous sci-fi trip ever to appear on TV. Watching it each week is very close to being under the influence of a consciousness altering drug."— Benjamin Stein, *The Wall Street Journal*: "Sailing Along on a Moonbase Way," Fall 1975.

"This series really must be seen to be believed, with a level of production values only achieved by spending a small defense budget on effects way ahead of their time ... The unique facet of *Space: 1999* was the exquisite feeling of loneliness and vulnerability brought across — anyone who still seriously describes *Babylon 5* as 'all alone in the night' needs to take a look at Moonbase Alpha."— *Cult TV*, November 1995.

"It has what no other TV science-fiction program except *Star Trek* had — good stories and good special effects. The test of good science fiction is its ability to imagine alien life ... *Star Trek* started going downhill when it stopped relying on strong stories ... A recent *Space: 1999* not only presented a persuasive alien-like form, but played with it lightly ... Nice stuff."— John Leonard, *The New York Times*: "So, Who Picked *Bronk* Over *Space: 1999?*," October 19, 1975, page D27.

"*Space: 1999* is a visually stunning space-age morality play that chronicles the downfall of 20th century technological man ... That *Space: 1999* is a brilliant piece of 20th century technological art, film-making, is readily evident at a glance. What is perhaps less obvious is that the producers are using technology and art to talk about other issues."— Arielle Emmett, Editor, *Science Digest*: "Adventures in Science Faction," November 1975, pages 89-91.

"*Star Trek* was often less than scientific, frequently gaudy and nearly devoid of anything resembling acting ... *Space: 1999* seems to have at least one foot in science and a range of special effects and sets that would make even the emotionless Mr. Spock envious."— Douglas Durden, *The Richmond-Times Dispatch*: "So Long *Star Trek*, Hello *Space: 1999*," September 19, 1975.

CAST AND CREDITS

Cast: Martin Landau (Commander John Koenig); Barbara Bain (Dr. Helena Russell); Nick Tate (Alan Carter); Zienia Merton (Sandra Benes); Anton Phillips (Dr. Bob Mathias). **First Season Only:** Barry Morse (Professor Victor Bergman); Clifton Jones (David Kano); Prentis Hancock (Paul Morrow); Suzanne Roquette (Tanya Alexander).

Second Season Only: Catherine Schell (Maya); Tony Anholt (Tony Verdeschi); John Hug (Bill Fraser); Jeffery Kissoon (Dr. Ben Vincent); Alibe Parsons (Alibe); Yasuko Nagasumi (Yasko).

Credits: Creators: Gerry and Sylvia Anderson. *Executive Producer:* Gerry Anderson. *Line Producer (first season):* Sylvia Anderson. *Line Producer (second season):* Fred Freiberger. *Director of Photography:* Frank Watts. *Camera Operators:* Tony White, Neil Binney. *Script Consultant:* Christopher Penfold. *Script Editors (first season):* Edward DiLorenzo, Johnny

Byrne. *Music (first season):* Barry Gray. *Music (second season):* Derek Wadsworth. *Music Associate:* Vic Elms. *Music Editor:* Alan Willis. *Production Designer:* Keith Wilson. *Production Manager:* Ron Fry. *Casting Director:* Michael Barnes. *Assistant Director:* Ken Baker. *Supervising Editor:* David Lane. *Editors:* Mike Campbell, Derek Hyde Chambers, Alan Killick. *Sound Editors:* Roy Lafbery, Peter Pennell. *Sound Recordist:* David Bowen. *Continuity:* Gladys Goldsmith, Phyllis Townsend. *Special Effects Director:* Brian Johnson. *Special Effects Assistant:* Nick Allder. *SPFX Camera Operator:* Frank Drake. *SPFX Lighting Cameraman:* Harry Oakes. *Electronics:* Michael S.E. Downing. *Miniatures:* Brian Johnson, Nick Allder, Martin Bower. *Makeup:* Basil Newall, Ann Cotton. *Hair Designer:* Helene Bevan. *Wardrobe:* Eileen Sullivan. *Moon City Costumes Designed by:* Rudi Gernreich. An ITC/RAI co-production produced by Group Three. Processed by Rank Film Laboratories. Made at Pinewood Studios, Buckinghamshire, England.

THE DETAILS

Costing a then-staggering $275,000 per episode, the British-made *Space: 1999* burst on the television scene in the fall of 1975 in a firestorm of publicity. In its time on the air, it managed to fracture science fiction fandom in a way that no TV series before or after it has quite managed. To be blunt, *Space: 1999* was a revolutionary series which polarized its audience. Reaction to it was totally varied: it either impressed and wowed its audience with its mind-blowing, well-dramatized forays to bizarre alien realms, or confused the hell out of people with its *2001: A Space Odyssey* minimalist approach to narrative resolution and explanation, depending wholly on one's viewing predispositions. The "impressed" percentage of the viewing audience was bowled over by the incredible, visually fantastic story of Moonbase Alpha, a turn-of-the-millennium lunar installation, which was sent careening into uncharted outer space after a nuclear accident at Alpha's atomic waste dump. The

confused part of the audience consisted mostly of *Star Trek* fans and adherents who were expecting (and demanding!) another *Star Trek*, but discovered instead a very different show with a very different, and very specific philosophy.

What makes *Space: 1999* so different from virtually any other outer space adventure series ever created, and what merits its mention in a book about the horror genre, is the fact that the series creators, Gerry and Sylvia Anderson (*UFO* [1969-70]) offered a totally original, heretofore unseen view of outer space. This was not your father's *Star Trek*, where planets were joined across the "ocean" of space, and each world was part of either a cosmic United Nations called the Federation or an unknown "island" worthy of exploration. Instead, *Space: 1999* refused to adhere to the time-worn "United Worlds" concept of outer space that has been so important to every space drama since time immemorial, including *Space Patrol* (1951-52), *Buck Rogers in the 25th Century* (1979-81), *Babylon 5* (1993-98), and the like. In its place, *Space: 1999* offered this thesis: the universe — because humankind is not prepared to understand it — is a place of abject, spine-chilling terror. Even the most wonderful or harmless mechanisms of the universe seem frightening and "unknown" to the stalwart denizens of Moonbase Alpha, because its people are 20th-century men and women. The humans marooned there, even the heroic Commander Koenig, Doctor Russell, Alan Carter, and Professor Bergman, are psychologically and technologically unprepared for their quest through the stars. Thus their fears and concerns often get the better of them in the drama of the week.

To *Star Trek* fans, this idea of space as "scary" was sacrilege, heresy even. *Star Trek* was so successful in syndication because it spread a message of optimism about the future and space exploration. *Space: 1999* had far more impact in visual terms, but it jettisoned the idea of optimism and brotherhood, and opted instead for an even-now unmatched "scare ride" through the cosmos. Most science fiction critics and *Star Trek* fans never understood that

Space: 1999 was determinedly different from *Star Trek*, and so it was bashed brutally at conventions on the basis that it was a (bad) rip-off of *Star Trek*. Indeed, if one really believes *Space: 1999* is trying to be like *Star Trek*, the series will prove disappointing. In the rosy, sunlight universe of *Star Trek*, the frightening adventures of Moonbase Alpha make little or no sense. If, on the other hand, one views *Space: 1999* as a horror show set in the arena of space, its merits become obvious. Ironically (as the above-listed reviews reveal), most impartial (i.e., *not Star Trek* fans) reviewers at the time of *Space: 1999*'s premiere liked it as well as, if not better than, *Star Trek*. It is just that twenty years of revisionist "Trekkie" history (written by *Trek* fans) have cast the show in an unflattering light ... all because of a misperception about its intentions as drama.

As this book has acknowledged again and again, how a series utilizes horror imagery to convey its themes is a telling example of its quality. *Space: 1999* understood precisely how to deploy the imagery of film to generate its outer space terrors, and several installments of the series are horror concepts simply translated to outer space (as *Forever Knight* transposed horror concepts with the cop genre, and *Buffy the Vampire Slayer* brings horror conceits to the terrifying realm of ... high school). A futuristic analogy for demonic possession is utilized in "Force of Life" when a Moonbase Alpha crewman named Zoref (an anagram for the word "froze") is possessed by an alien life form who requires heat, and resorts to murder to acquire it. This episode, written by Johnny Byrne, overdoses on brilliant camera technique as slow-motion photography, extreme angles, intense close-ups, and a swivel of the camera into the upside-down position express the terror of an alien incursion on the lost space base. In particular, the upside-down camera turn works beautifully to support the story of "Force of Life." As the camera turns over dramatically in the last shot of the teaser, it symbolically indicates to viewers that Moonbase Alpha will be turned on its head by this unwanted "visitor."

The slow-motion photography utilized in the episode also lengthens the chases (hence the suspense) as the alien stalks its victims, and so forth. Did *Star Trek* ever attempt to tell its stories of alien civilizations with such visual legerdemain? That desire, that constant effort to infuse the genre with horrific stories and horrific camera work, distinguishes *Space: 1999* from the rest of the outer space pack.

The central conceit of *Space: 1999*, that space equals a realm of futurist horror, was repeated a variety of times. "The Troubled Spirit" (also by Johnny Byrne) translated the age-old "vengeful" ghost story to outer space, as Alpha was menaced by an apparition conjured during a strange experiment. A technological séance and exorcism replaced occult ones. An evil child with vicious mental abilities, like the ones featured in *Village of the Damned* (1960), was the subject of "Alpha Child," by Christopher Penfold. "Dragon's Domain" saw the Moonbase crew face a vicious alien monster which swallowed unsuspecting crewmembers whole and then spit out their desiccated, steaming corpses. This particular episode was worthy of *The Twilight Zone* as it featured an astronaut who warned Alpha about the monster, but was unheeded. In its depiction of outer space terror and monsters, *Space: 1999* was also quite influential, paving the way for the *Alien* saga (in '79, '86, '92, and '97 respectively).

"End of Eternity" saw Moonbase Alpha menaced by an immortal creature called Balor who had been "cast out" by his people, and the overall story was a Lucifer/expulsion from Paradise parable. The climax saw Moonbase Alpha's outmatched Commander Koenig vanquish the villainous Balor by tricking him out of an airlock, in what was surely a reference to the story of David vs. Goliath. "Guardian of Piri" retold the myth of Odysseus and the sirens, with unwitting Alphan crew members seduced by a beautiful android (Catherine Schell) who cloaked a world of total brain death. "Space Brain" was a drama about Alpha's passage through a giant, destructive space-organism, and so forth. Even "Earthbound" was horror in a sense because it found a perfect technological metaphor for the age-old fear of being buried alive. In this case, the Alphan commissioner (Roy Dotrice) found himself awake inside a cryogenic compartment that was not due to be opened for seventy-five years. The ending, in which he pounds at the glass canister in an unsuccessful attempt to get out, was positively chill-inducing.

Virtually every story in *Space: 1999*'s first season was a reiteration and translation of famous horror stories into the venue of space, but few understood the method of what appeared to be its madness. After all, in the 1970s, there had not yet been a mainstream horror success such as *The X-Files*, and so most carping *Star Trek* fans actually feared what they could not understand: a horror TV series that just happened to be set in the realm of the great void beyond. Though *Space: 1999* garnered amazing ratings in syndication in America during its first year, the powers-that-be in ITC New York decided that it would be better for *Space: 1999* to change its format and be more like the happy *Star Trek*. Thus, the second season of *Space: 1999* was more user friendly, and more in the vein of Gene Roddenberry's vision, with the universe generally seeming less mysterious and less horrific than in the stellar year one of the show. Still, year two did occasionally find time to explore horror: zombified crew members played a part in "All That Glisters," disgusting alien beasts tricked the Alphans out of their life-support system in the two-part "Bringers of Wonder," and two sociopathic immortal teenagers threatened the lost lunar colony in the memorable "The Exiles."

The second season revamp failed to win *Space: 1999* many new fans, and the show was unceremoniously canceled in 1977, just weeks short of the release of *Star Wars*, after the production of forty-eight episodes. Today a small but vocal fandom remembers that before *The X-Files* made science-oriented horror popular, and before *Aliens* knew that in "space, nobody can hear you scream," *Space: 1999* and Moonbase Alpha were bouncing around the airwaves and terrifying the hell out of anyone who cared to give the show a thoughtful viewing.

EPISODE LIST

Note: Airdates have not been included here, as the episodes were shown in different order from city to city. Episodes are listed here in production order.

• *First Season (1975–1976)*

1. "Breakaway" Written by George Bellak; Directed by Lee H. Katzin.

2. "Matter of Life and Death" Written by Art Wallace and Johnny Byrne; Directed by Charles Crichton.

3. "Black Sun" Written by David Weir; Directed by Lee H. Katzin.

4. "Ring Around the Moon" Written by Edward DiLorenzo; Directed by Ray Austin.

5. "Earthbound" Written by Anthony Terpiloff; Directed by Charles Crichton.

6. "Another Time, Another Place" Written by Johnny Byrne; Directed by David Tomblin.

7. "Missing Link" Written by Edward DiLorenzo; Directed by Ray Austin.

8. "Guardian of Piri" Written by Christopher Penfold; Directed by Charles Crichton.

9. "Force of Life" Written by Johnny Byrne; Directed by David Tomblin.

10. "Alpha Child" Written by Christopher Penfold; Directed by Ray Austin.

11. "The Last Sunset" Written by Christopher Penfold; Directed by Charles Crichton.

12. "Voyager's Return" Written by Johnny Byrne; Directed by Bob Kellett.

13. "Collision Course" Written by Anthony Terpiloff; Directed by Ray Austin.

14. "Death's Other Dominion" Written by Anthony Terpiloff and Elizabeth Barrows; Directed by Charles Crichton.

15. "The Full Circle" Written by Jesse

Lasky Jr. and Pat Silver; Directed by Bob Kellett.

16. "End of Eternity" Written by Johnny Byrne; Directed by Ray Austin.

17. "War Games" Written by Christopher Penfold; Directed by Charles Crichton.

18. "The Last Enemy" Written and Directed by Bob Kellett.

19. "The Troubled Spirit" Written by Johnny Byrne; Directed by Ray Austin.

20. "Space Brain" Written by Christopher Penfold; Directed by Charles Crichton.

21. "The Infernal Machine" Written by Anthony Terpiloff and Elizabeth Barrows; Directed by David Tomblin.

22. "Mission of the Darians" Written by Johnny Byrne; Directed by Ray Austin.

23. "Dragon's Domain" Written by Christopher Penfold; Directed by Charles Crichton.

24. "The Testament of Arkadia" Written by Johnny Byrne; Directed by David Tomblin.

- **Second Season (1976–1977)**

25. "The Metamorph" Written by Johnny Byrne; Directed by Charles Crichton.

26. "The Exiles" Written by Donald James; Directed by Ray Austin.

27. "One Moment of Humanity" Written by Tony Barwick; Directed by Charles Crichton.

28. "Journey to Where" Written by Donald James; Directed by Tom Clegg.

29. "All That Glisters" Written by Keith Miles; Directed by Ray Austin.

30. "The Taybor" Written by Thom Keyes; Directed by Bob Brooks.

31. "The Mark of Archanon" Written by Lew Schwartz; Directed by Charles Crichton.

32. "The Rules of Luton" Written by Charles Woodgrove; Directed by Val Guest.

33. "New Adam, New Eve" Written by Terence Feely; Directed by Charles Crichton.

34. "Brian the Brain" Written by Jack Ronder; Directed by Kevin Connor.

35. "The AB Chrysalis" Written by Tony Barwick; Directed by Val Guest.

36. "Catacombs of the Moon" Written by Anthony Terpiloff; Directed by Robert Lynn.

37. "Seed of Destruction" Written by John Goldsmith; Directed by Kevin Connor.

38. "The Beta Cloud" Written by Charles Woodgrove; Directed by Robert Lynn.

39. "A Matter of Balance" Written by Pip and Jane Baker; Directed by Charles Crichton.

40. "Space Warp" Written by Charles Woodgrove; Directed by Peter Medak.

41. and 42. "The Bringers of Wonder" (Parts I and II) Written by Terence Feely; Directed by Tom Clegg.

43. "Dorzak" Written by Christopher Penfold; Directed by Charles Crichton.

44. "The Lambda Factor" Written by Terrence Dicks; Directed by Charles Crichton.

45. "Devil's Planet" Written by Michael Winder; Directed by Tom Clegg.

46. "The Séance Spectre" Written by Donald James; Directed by Peter Medak.

47. "The Immunity Syndrome" Written by Johnny Byrne; Directed by Bob Brooks.

48. "The Dorcons" Written by Johnny Byrne; Directed by Tom Clegg.

PART III

Further Thoughts

Conclusion

Where will terror TV turn from here? If the horror-filled nineties are any indication of the future, terror TV in the next decade will become more terrifying, more titillating, and more terrific than ever. *Buffy the Vampire Slayer, The X-Files, G vs E,* and even the quickly-canceled *Brimstone* are all suggestive of a postmodern approach to the genre that is as appealing as it is intelligent. Although some recent TV series attempting to ape this difficult formula have failed from artistic standpoints (i.e., the recently renewed *Charmed*), there is every reason to suspect that Chris Carter and Joss Whedon, two stars of modern terror TV, have additional horrors up their sleeves. The short-lived but high-quality *Harsh Realm* and *Angel* are two genre productions which indicate that these new Rod Serlings will be terrifying audiences for years, and perhaps decades, to come.

Though horror-oriented anthologies and soap operas have fallen on hard times as the millennium turns, the expansion of syndication, of cable series, and of new networks like UPN and the WB suggest that, overall, horror will continue to grow, to improve, and to be a critical factor in television's future history. The Sci-Fi Channel recently saved *Poltergeist: The Legacy* from the charnel pit of cancellation (only to cancel it a season later), and there is every reason to believe that it will soon develop further original programming of an equally macabre nature. The USA Network had a critical and ratings hit on its hands with *G vs E,* which suggests that its low-quality genre programming (*Alfred Hitchcock Presents, The Hitchhiker*) is a thing of the past.

As cable networks grow bolder and pose a greater threat to the "old" American networks, horror will certainly be a central part of their ratings equation. The "cult" audience is now large enough to save programs on the smaller networks, where once their rating numbers would have signaled instant cancellation.

One thing is certain, as long as there is television, there will be terror television. After all, the world of today (and presumably of tomorrow) is fraught with numerous fears and terrors. School violence, gun control, Y2K, designer drugs, outbreaks of new diseases, state-sanctioned censorship, environmental meltdown, political scandals, global apocalypse, religious zealotry, racial bigotry, nuclear war, economic recession, the possibility of a new energy crisis ... these are things that make us face our future with shudders and shivers. Thus the television artists of today and tomorrow will only grow bolder in their attempts to target what scares us, and then use that knowledge to help us learn about ourselves and our world.

But, until the next new wave, fans of the genre will content themselves with further seasons of *The X-Files, Buffy the Vampire Slayer* and *Charmed*, while savoring reruns of *Millennium*, and *Poltergeist: The Legacy*, wishing for continuations of *Forever Knight* and *Brimstone*, and hoping for a feature film version of the classic *Kolchak: The Night Stalker*.

Ironically, terror television, a world of neverending darkness and terror, has a bright future.

Appendix A: The Fifty Most Common Concepts in Modern Terror Television

Horror television, like science fiction television, has its "standards," the ideas, stories, and concepts repeated again and again, sometimes beyond all reason, sometimes beyond all sanity. In science fiction TV for instance, audiences have seen the "evil twin" story replayed in *Star Trek* (as "Enemy Within," "What Are Little Girls Made Of," "Whom Gods Destroy"), *Space: 1999* (as "Seed of Destruction"), *Logan's Run* (as "Half Life"), *Star Trek: The Next Generation* (as "Datalore"), *Buck Rogers in the 25th Century* (as "Ardala Returns"), *Doctor Who* (1963-89) (as "The Android Invasion," "The Androids of Tara," "Enemy of the World," "The Massacre"), and others. For a horror story notion to be counted as a cliché, the same plot idea/concept must occur at least three times. In the list below, these clichés are included in no particular order.

1. The Transplant

In which a transplanted organ or limbs (usually a hand, arm, or eye) wreaks havoc on its new recipient or recipients.

1. *Rod Serling's Night Gallery*: "The Hand of Borgus Weems" (1971)
2. *The Sixth Sense*: "The Eyes That Wouldn't Die" (1972)
3. *Circle of Fear*: "Spare Parts" (1973)
4. *The Evil Touch*: "A Game of Hearts" (1974)
5. *Quinn Martin's Tales of the Unexpected*: "A Hand for Sonny Blue" (1977)
6. *Monsters*: "Where Is the Rest of Me?" (1988)
7. *Monsters*: "Leavings" (1990)

2. The Vampire

In which a specific type of "creature of the night," with an aversion to sunlight, crosses, and garlic, is featured.

1. *Rod Serling's Night Gallery*: "Miss Lovecraft Sent Me" (1971)
2. *Rod Serling's Night Gallery*: "The Devil Is Not Mocked" (1971)
3. *Rod Serling's Night Gallery*: "A Matter of Semantics" (1971)
4. *Rod Serling's Night Gallery*: "A Midnight Visit to the Neighborhood Blood Bank" (1971)
5. *Rod Serling's Night Gallery*: "The Funeral" (1972)
6. *Rod Serling's Night Gallery*: "Death on a Barge" (1973)
7. *Rod Serling's Night Gallery*: "How to Cure the Common Vampire" (1973)
8. *Ghost Story/Circle of Fear*: "Elegy for a Vampire" (1972)
9. *Kolchak: The Night Stalker*: "Vampire" (1974)
10. *Curse of Dracula*: Series Concept (1979)
11. *The Hitchhiker*: "Nightshift" (1984)
12. *Tales from the Darkside*: "Strange Love" (1986)
13. *Tales from the Darkside*: "My Ghostwriter — The Vampire" (1987)
14. *Friday the 13th: The Series*: "The Baron's Bride" (1988)
15. *Monsters*: "The Vampire Hunter" (1988)
16. *Monsters*: "Pool Sharks" (1988)
17. *Monsters*: "Shave and a Haircut, Two Bites" (1990)

18. *Dracula: The Series*: Series Concept (1990)

19. *Tales from the Crypt*: "The Secret" (1990)

20. *Love and Curses*: "Habeas Corpses" (1991)

21. *Tales from the Crypt*: "The Reluctant Vampire (1991)

22 *Tales from the Crypt*: "Mournin' Mess (1991)

23. *Dark Shadows*: Series Concept (1991)

24. *Forever Knight*: Series Concept (1992-96)

25. *Beyond Reality*: "The Passion" (1993)

26. *The X-Files*: "3" (1994)

27. *Tales from the Crypt*: "Comes the Dawn" (1995)

28. *Tales from the Crypt*: "Cold War" (1996)

29. *Kindred: The Embraced*: Series Concept (1996)

30. *The X-Files*: "Bad Blood" (1998)

31. *Poltergeist: The Legacy*: "Darkness Falls" (1998)

32. *Poltergeist: The Legacy*: "Light of Day" (1998)

33. *Buffy the Vampire Slayer*: Series Concept

34. *Angel*: Series Concept

3. The Werewolf

In which a horror series examines the lore and life of werewolves.

1. *Rod Serling's Night Gallery*: "The Phantom Farmhouse" (1971)

2. *Kolchak: The Night Stalker*: "The Werewolf" (1974)

3. *Darkroom*: "The Bogeyman Will Get You" (1981)

4. *Tales from the Darkside*: "The Circus" (1986)

5. *Werewolf*: Series Concept (1987-88)

6. *Tales from the Darkside*: "Family Reunion" (1988)

7. *Monsters*: "One Wolf's Family" (1990)

8. *Monsters*: "Werewolf of Hollywood" (1990)

9. *She Wolf of London/Love and Curses*: Series Concept (1990-91)

10. *Tales from the Crypt*: "Werewolf Concerto" (1992)

11. *The X-Files*: "Shapes" (1994)

12. *Poltergeist: The Legacy*: "Rough Beast" (1997)

13. *Buffy the Vampire Slayer*: "Bewitched, Bewildered and Bothered" (1998)

4. Astral Projection

In which a character is able to control an "out of body" experience, usually to exact revenge on someone who has wronged him.

1. *Rod Serling's Night Gallery*: "The Last Laurel" (1970)

2. *The Sixth Sense*: "Once Upon a Chilling" (1972)

3. *The Next Step Beyond*: "Out of Body" (1978)

4. *Friday the 13th: The Series*: "Crippled Inside" (1989)

5. *Beyond Reality*: "Justice" (1992)

6. *Charmed*: "Wicca Envy" (1998)

7. *Charmed*: "The Power of Two" (1999)

5. The Evil Doll

In which a fiendish child's doll comes to life to stalk unwitting victims.

1. *Rod Serling's Night Gallery*: "The Doll" (1971)

2. *Friday the 13th: The Series*: "The Inheritance" (1987)

3. *Poltergeist: The Legacy*: "Revelations" (1996)

4. *The X-Files*: "Chinga" (1997)

6. Youth Is Fleeting, Unless ...

In which a demon/hellspawn/evil person will do anything, even kill, even suck the life force of others, to recapture his/her youth, beauty, or life-force.

1. *Kolchak: The Night Stalker*: "The Youth Killers" (1975)

2. *Friday the 13th: The Series*: "Cup of Time" (1988)

3. *She Wolf of London*: "Nice Girls Don't" (1990)

4. *Forever Knight*: "If Looks Could Kill" (1993)

5. *Buffy the Vampire Slayer*: "Anne" (1998)

6. *Charmed*: "I've Got You Under My Skin" (1998)

7. *Poltergeist: The Legacy*: "Father to Son" (1998)

7. Merry Christmas

In which a horror story centers around the holiday season, particularly Christmas.

1. *Night Gallery*: "The Messiah on Mott Street" (1971)

2. *Tales from the Darkside*: "Seasons of Belief" (1986)

3. *Tales from the Darkside*: "The Yattering and Jack" (1987)

4. *Monsters*: "Glim-Glim" (1989)

5. *Tales from the Crypt*: "And All Through the House" (1989)

6. *Monsters*: "A New Woman" (1990)

7. *Millennium*: "Midnight of the Century" (1997)

8. *The X-Files*: "A Christmas Carol" (1997)

9. *Poltergeist: The Legacy*: "The Gift" (1997)

10. *Millennium*: "Omerta" (1998)

11. *Buffy the Vampire Slayer*: "Amends" (1998)

12. *The X-Files*: "How the Ghosts Stole Christmas" (1998)

8. Jack the Ripper Returns!

In which the most famous of slashers, or a killer inspired by him, is on the loose again.

1. *The Sixth Sense*: "With Affection, Jack the Ripper" (1972)

2. *Kolchak: The Night Stalker*: "The Ripper" (1974)

3. *Friday the 13th: The Series*: "Doctor Jack" (1987)

4. *Forever Knight*: "Bad Blood" (1995)

9. Places to Eat/Hang Out

In which a trendy restaurant or club becomes a recurring setting for a horror TV series.

1. "Nightmare Cafe" (*Nightmare Cafe*)

2. "The Raven" (*Forever Knight*)

3. "The Haven" (*Kindred: The Embraced*)

4. "The Bronze" (*Buffy the Vampire Slayer*)

5. "Quake" (*Charmed*)

10. Adventures in Chinatown

Wherein the protagonists of the series find themselves exploring the Chinese part of town, and thus exploiting Asian myths of the supernatural.

1. *Friday the 13th: The Series*: "Tattoo" (1988)

2. *Beyond Reality*: "The Fire Within" (1991)

3. *Forever Knight*: "Cherry Blossoms" (1992)

4. *The X-Files*: "Hell Money" (1995)

5. *Poltergeist: The Legacy*: "Fox Spirit" (1996)

6. *Forever Knight*: "Let No Man Tear Asunder" (1996)

7. *Charmed*: "Dead Man Dating" (1998)

11. Titanic

Wherein events on the doomed ship play a part in a new terror.

1. *Rod Serling's Night Gallery*: "Lone Survivor" (1971)

2. *Friday the 13th: The Series*: "What A Mother Wouldn't Do" (1988)

3. *Freddy's Nightmares*: "It's My Party and You'll Die If I Want You To" (1989)

4. *Forever Knight*: "Black Buddha, Part I" (1995)

12. Evil Twins/Doubles

In which characters are faced with villainous duplicates, twins, or doppelgangers.

1. *Kolchak: The Night Stalker*: "Firefall" (aka "The Doppelganger") (1974)

2. *Dracula: The Series*: "Double Darkness" (1990)

3. *Beyond Reality*: "Doppelganger" (1991)

4. *Tales from the Crypt*: "Operation Friendship" (1994)

5. *The X-Files*: "Colony"/"End Game" (1994)

6. *The X-Files*: "Small Potatoes" (1996)

7. *Millennium*: "Antipas" (1999)

8. *Buffy the Vampire Slayer*: "The Wish" (1999)

9. *Buffy the Vampire Slayer*: "Doppel-gangland" (1999)

13. Haunted Theaters

In which a theater (usually one that is about to be closed down) becomes a setting for terror.

1. *She Wolf of London:* "Bride of the Wolfman" (1991)

2. *Dracula: The Series*: "What a Pleasant Surprise" (1991)

3. *Beyond Reality*: "Theatre of the Absurd" (1992)

14. Meet the Succubus

In which a female demon lures men to their deaths in (usually) erotic fashion.

1. *Kolchak: The Night Stalker*: "Demon in Lace" (1975)

2. *Beyond Reality*: "Siren Song" (1992)

3. *The X-Files*: "Avatar" (1996)

4. *Poltergeist: The Legacy*: "Black Widow" (1997)

5. *Poltergeist: The Legacy*: "She's Got the Devil in Her Heart" (1999)

15. The Pen Is Mightier than the Sword…

In which the act of creation, either through writing, painting or performing, sparks an evil turn of events.

1. *Tales from the Darkside*: "Printer's Devil" (1986)

2. *Friday the 13th: The Series*: "Poison Pen" (1988)

3. *Monsters*: "Pillow Talk" (1988)

4. *Freddy's Nightmares*: "The Art of Death" (1989)

5. *Monsters*: "Portrait of the Artist" (1989)

6. *Friday the 13th: The Series*: "Mightier Than the Sword" (1990)

7. *Beyond Reality* "Dead Air" (1993)

8. *The X-Files*: "Milagro" (1999)

16. Terror Rocks at a Concert

In which a rock concert is a setting for horror and evil.

1. *Alfred Hitchcock Presents*: "Career Move" (1988)

2. *Friday the 13th: The Series*: "Mesmer's Bauble" (1989)

3. *Forever Knight*: "Dying For Fame" (1992)

4. *Dark Skies*: "Dark Days Night" (1996)

5. *Millennium*: "Thirteen Years Later" (1998)

17. Horror Goes to the Circus

In which the circus, or circus dwellers, relate to a world of horror and evil.

1. *The Evil Touch*: "The Trial" (1974)

2. *Tales from the Darkside*: "If the Shoe Fits" (1985)

3. *Tales from the Darkside*: "The Circus" (1985)

4. *Werewolf*: "Blind Luck" (1987)

5. *Friday the 13th: The Series*: "Wax Magic" (1989)

6. *Tales from the Crypt*: "Lower Berth" (1990)

7. *She Wolf of London:* "Big Top She Wolf" (1991)

8. *Tales from the Crypt*: "Food for Thought" (1993)

9. *The X-Files*: "Humbug" (1994)

18. Evil Tattoos

In which tattoos are unexpectedly the source of unspeakable evil and terror.

1. *Friday the 13th: The Series*: "Tattoo" (1988)

2. *The X-Files*: "Never Again" (1996)

3. *The Burning Zone:* "Elegy for a Dream" (1997)

19. Ventriloquists' Dummies Come to Life

In which we see a variation on the Evil Doll cliché, this time with a nefarious ventriloquist's puppet planning evil as he comes to life.

    1. *Friday the 13th: The Series*: "Read My Lips" (1989)

    2. *Tales from the Crypt*: "The Ventriloquist's Dummy" (1990)

    3. *Buffy the Vampire Slayer*: "The Puppet Show" (1997)

20. An Inexplicable Snowfall

In which snow comes down at the oddest and most inexplicable of times.

    1. *Rod Serling's Night Gallery*: "Silent Snow, Secret Snow" (1972)

    2. *Millennium*: "The Sound of Snow" (1998)

    3. *Buffy the Vampire Slayer*: "Amends" (1998)

21. Horror on Your Radio Dial

In which the horror involves an opinionated radio talk show host and his/her program.

    1. *Rod Serling's Night Gallery*: "The Flip Side of Satan" (1971)

    2. *Tales from the Darkside*: "Devil's Advocate" (1985)

    3. *Freddy's Nightmares*: "Silence Is Golden (1989)

    4. *Friday the 13th: The Series*: "The Butcher" (1989)

    5. *Monsters*: "A Face for Radio" (1990)

    6. *Tales from the Crypt*: "The New Arrival" (1992)

    7. *Beyond Reality*: "Dead Air" (1993)

    8. *Tales from the Crypt*: "In the Groove" (1994)

    9. *Forever Knight*: "Dead Air" (1992)

22. A Fear of Drowning

In which a series' protagonist reveals that the thing he/she is most afraid of is … drowning.

    1. *Beyond Reality*: "Bloodstone" (1993) protagonist: Dr. Wingate

    2. *Charmed:* "From Fear to Eternity" (1999) protagonist: Prue Halliwell

    3. *Millennium:* "Seven-In-One" (1999) protagonist: Frank Black

23. The San Francisco (Trick or) Treat

For some reason, horror seems to go hand in hand with San Francisco. At least three modern horror series are set there.

    1. *Poltergeist: The Legacy* (1996-99)

    2. *Kindred: The Embraced* (1996)

    3. *Charmed* (1998–)

24. Happy Halloween

In which the horrific events of an episode occur on Halloween or "All Hallow's Eve."

    1. *Tales from the Darkside*: "Trick or Treat" (1983)

    2. *Tales from the Darkside*: "Halloween Candy" (1985)

    3. *Werewolf*: "All Hallow's Eve" (1987)

    4. *Friday the 13th: The Series* "Helloween" (1987)

    5. *Freddy's Nightmares*: "Freddy's Tricks and Treats" (1988)

    6. *She Wolf of London:* "The Juggler" (1990)

    7. *Millennium*: "The Curse of Frank Black" (1997)

    8. *Buffy the Vampire Slayer*: "Halloween" (1997)

25. Horror Goes Native American

In which the lore of the American Indian informs the horror of a terror TV episode.

    1. *Kolchak: The Night Stalker*: "Bad Medicine" (1974)

    2. *Kolchak: The Night Stalker*: "The Energy Eater" ("Matchemondo") (1974)

    3. *Werewolf*: "Skinwalker" (1987)

    4. *Monsters*: "Raindance" (1988)

    5. *Friday the 13th: The Series*: "The Shaman's Apprentice" (1989)

    6. *Monsters*: "Half as Old as Time" (1989)

    7. *Forever Knight*: "Blackwing" (1995)

    8. *The X-Files*: "Anasazi" (1995)

    9. *The X-Files*: "The Blessing Way" (1995)

    10. *Dark Skies*: "Ancient Future" (1996)

    11. *Millennium*: "A Single Blade of Grass" (1997)

12. *Poltergeist: The Legacy*: "Shadow Fall" (1997)

13. *Poltergeist: The Legacy*: "Bird of Prey" (1999)

26. Hell Hounds

In which the nemesis of the week is a vicious dog with supernatural powers, usually with glowing eyes and slobbery, sharp fangs.

1. *Ghost Story/Circle of Fear*: "Creatures of the Canyon" (1972)

2. *Quinn Martin's Tales of the Unexpected*: "The Pack" (1977)

3. *The Hitchhiker*: "Man's Best Friend" (1985)

4. *Forever Knight*: "Blind Faith" (1995)

5. *Millennium*: "Beware of the Dog" (1997)

6. *The X-Files*: "Alpha" (1999)

7. *Buffy the Vampire Slayer*: "The Prom" (1999)

27. Artificial Intelligence

In which intelligent machines threaten to replace humans as the dominant life form on the planet.

1. *Rod Serling's Night Gallery*: "You Can't Get Help Like That Anymore" (1972)

2. *Darkroom*: "Closed Circuit" (1981)

3. *The X-Files*: "Ghost in the Machine" (1993)

4. *The X-Files*: "Kill Switch" (1997)

28. The Body Swap

In which a series' lead is forced to physically exchange bodies with another character, usually villainous.

1. *Tales from the Darkside*: "The Swap" (1987)

2. *Friday the 13th: The Series*: "The Long Road Home" (1990)

3. *Monsters*: "The Bargain" (1990)

4. *Tales from the Crypt*: "The Switch" (1990)

5. *The X-Files*: "Lazarus" (1993)

6. *The X-Files*: "Dreamland I"/"Dreamland II" (1998)

7. *Poltergeist: The Legacy*: "Irish Jug" (1998)

8. *Poltergeist: The Legacy*: "Song of the Raven" (1999)

29. The Personification of Death

In which death is depicted as a person or figure (i.e., The Grim Reaper) who comes a callin' when "it is time."

1. *Monsters*: "Reaper" (1989)

2. *Tales from the Crypt*: "The Man Who Was Death" (1989)

3. *Buffy the Vampire Slayer*: "Killed by Death" (1998)

4. *Millennium*: "Borrowed Time" (1999)

5. *The X-Files*: "Tithonus" (1999)

30. Photo Finish

In which the horror of the week involves a photographer and/or camera.

1. *Tales from the Darkside*: "The Spirit Photographer" (1987)

2. *Freddy's Nightmares*: "Photo Finish" (1989)

3. *The X-Files*: "Unruhe" (1996)

4. *The X-Files*: "Tithonus" (1999)

31. The Blind Leading the Blind

In which a sightless person is involved in the horror, and even helps to solve the case, using blindness as a positive attribute rather than as a handicap.

1. *Tales from the Crypt*: "Revenge Is the Nuts" (1994)

2. *Forever Knight*: "Blind Faith" (1995)

3. *The X-Files*: "Mind's Eye" (1997)

4. *Charmed*: "Sightless" (1999)

32. The Exorcism

In which the devil (or a demon) inhabits or possesses a character and must be removed through an exorcism.

1. *Tales from the Darkside*: "The Trouble with Mary Jane" (1985)

2. *Beyond Reality*: "The Dying of the Light" (1993)

3. *The X-Files*: "The Calusari" (1994)

4. *Forever Knight*: "Sons of Belial" (1995)

5. *Poltergeist: The Legacy*: "Pilot" (1996)

33. Welcome to the Afterlife ... Almost ... Nope, Not Quite

In which series regulars find themselves hovering on the border of death, about to make a personal epiphany about the afterlife, only to be yanked back to life so that their series can continue.

1. *The X-Files*: "One Breath" (1994)

2. *The X-Files*: "The Blessing Way" (1995)

3. *Forever Knight*: "Near Death" (1995)

4. *The Burning Zone*: "Lethal Injection" (1996)

34. The Clips Show

In which money is saved by recycling footage from older episodes and fitting them into a plot where the protagonists conveniently recollect these "events" in their lives. (This is the scariest cliché of all.)

1. *Friday the 13th: The Series*: "Bottle of Dreams" (1988)

2. *Dracula: The Series*: "My Dinner with Lucard" (1991)

3. *Forever Knight*: "Close Call" (1995)

4. *Poltergeist: The Legacy*: "A Traitor Among Us" (1996)

5. *Poltergeist: The Legacy*: "The Choice" (1997)

6. *Poltergeist: The Legacy*: "Trapped" (1997)

7. *Poltergeist: The Legacy*: "Armies of the Night" (1998)

8. *Poltergeist: The Legacy*: "Darkside" (1998)

35. A Cloud Over Desert Storm

In which a crime in Operation Desert Storm (conducted by soldier, government, or Iraq) comes back to haunt the protagonists and guest stars.

1. *The X-Files*: "The Walk" (1995)

2. *Millennium*: "Collateral Damage" (1998)

3. *Poltergeist: The Legacy*: "Finding Richter" (1997)

4. *Poltergeist: The Legacy*: "Debt of Honor" (1998)

5. *Strange World*: Series Concept (1999)

36. Reincarnation

In which a protagonist's past lives come into play as he/she encounters others from past lives. (This usually involves hypnotic regression.)

1. *Beyond Reality*: "Echoes of Evil" (1991)

2. *Beyond Reality*: "Keepsake" (1993)

3. *The X-Files*: "The Field Where I Died" (1996)

4. *Forever Knight*: "Francesca" (1996)

5. *Poltergeist: The Legacy*: "La Belle Dame Sans Merci" (1998)

37. Silence of the Lambs

In which a series' protagonist and a serial killer face-off in an interview, leaving the protagonist shaken and fearful because the horrible killer knows and understands so much about him/her.

1. *The X-Files*: "Beyond the Sea" (1994)

2. *Forever Knight*: "Trophy Girl" (1996)

3. *The X-Files*: "Paper Hearts" (1996)

4. *Millennium*: "The Thin White Line" (1996)

5. *Poltergeist: The Legacy*: "Song of the Raven" (1999)

38. The Painting Is a Portal

In which a painting on the wall is actually a doorway or gateway to another world/time/dimension.

1. *Rod Serling's Night Gallery*: "The Escape" (1970)

2. *Rod Serling's Night Gallery*: "The Painted Mirror" (1971)

3. *Tales from the Darkside*: "Heretic" (1985)

4. *Monsters*: "Portrait of the Artist" (1989)

5. *Friday the 13th: The Series*: "The Charnel Pit" (1990)

6. *Beyond Reality*: "The Color of Mad" (1992)

7. *Poltergeist: The Legacy*: "The Painting" (1999)

39. Deep Freeze

In which a character in cryogenic suspension manages to reach out of this storage venue and attack or communicate with others.
   1. *The Sixth Sense*: "Once Upon a Chilling" (1972)
   2. *Beyond Reality*: "The Cold" (1992)
   3. *The X-Files*: "Roland" (1993)

40. Retarded Development

In which mentally impaired people (usually young men) develop sudden ... but ultimately reversible ... new intelligence through supernatural means.
   1. *Friday the 13th: The Series*: "Brain Drain" (1988)
   2. *The X-Files*: "Roland" (1993)
   3. *Forever Knight*: "Fallen Idol" (1996)
   4. *Poltergeist: The Legacy*: "The Human Vessel" (1998)

41. Sweet Dreams

In which the world of dreams turns deadly.
   1. *Kolchak: The Night Stalker*: "The Spanish Moss Murders" (1975)
   2. *The Hitchhiker*: "And if We Dream" (1985)
   3. *Tales from the Darkside*: "Dream Girl" (1986)
   4. *Freddy's Nightmares*: Series Concept (1988-90)
   5. *Monsters*: "Perchance to Dream" (1990)
   6. *The X-Files*: "Sleepless" (1994)
   7. *Sleepwalkers*: Series Concept (1997)
   8. *Charmed*: "Dream Sorceror" (1998)

42. Me and My Shadow

In which a shadow turns out to be murderous and/or an agent of the supernatural.
   1. *Rod Serling's Night Gallery*: "Certain Shadows on the Wall" (1971)
   2. *Friday the 13th: The Series*: "Shadow Boxer" (1987)
   3. *The X-Files*: "Soft Light" (1995)

43. Sign In at the Blood Bank Please

In which a blood bank is a setting for the supernatural and/or terror.
   1. *Rod Serling's Night Gallery*: "A Matter of Semantics" (1971)
   2. *Tales from the Crypt*: "The Reluctant Vampire" (1991)
   3. *The X-Files*: "3" (1994)

44. The Mob Mentality

In which the good citizens of a decent town or city become vengeful vigilantes and killers, thirsting for the blood of those whom they deem guilty.
   1. *Nightmare Cafe*: "Aliens Ate my Lunch" (1992)
   2. *Forever Knight*: "Undue Process" (1994)
   3. *The X-Files*: "Post-Modern Prometheus" (1997)
   4. *Millennium*: "Monster" (1997)
   5. *Millennium*: "Through a Glass Darkly" (1998)

45. Welcome to the Nut House

In which the setting for horror is an insane asylum or sanitarium for the criminally insane.
   1. *Rod Serling's Night Gallery*: "The Phantom Farmhouse" (1971)
   2. *Friday the 13th: The Series*: "And Now the News" (1988)
   3. *She Wolf of London*: "Moonlight Becomes You" (1990)
   4. *Poltergeist: The Legacy*: "Fear" (1997)
   5. *Millennium*: "The Pest House" (1998)
   6. *The X-Files*: "Biogenesis" (1999)

46. Nightmare at 20,000 Feet

In which the setting for horror is an airplane — already in flight!
   1. *The Sixth Sense*: "Coffin, Coffin in the Sky" (1972)
   2. *Freddy's Nightmares*: "Cabin Fever" (1989)
   3. *The X-Files*: "Tempus Fugit"/"Max" (1996)
   4. *The Burning Zone*: "Night Flight" (1996)

5. *Poltergeist: The Legacy*: "Let Sleeping Demons Lie" (1997)

6. *Millennium*: "The Innocents" (1998)

7. *G vs E*: "Airplane" (1999)

47. The Nursing Home

In which the setting for horror is an old folk's home.

1. *Werewolf*: "Amazing Grace" (1988)

2. *Monsters*: "Reaper" (1989)

3. *The X-Files*: "Excelsius Dei" (1994)

4. *Millennium*: "Matryoshka" (1999)

48. Join Us!

In which a religious cult is the horror of the week.

1. *The X-Files*: "Red Museum" (1994)

2. *Forever Knight*: "Faithful Followers" (1994)

3. *The X-Files*: "The Field Where I Died" (1996)

4. *The Burning Zone*: "Hall of the Serpent" (1996)

5. *Millennium*: "Gehenna" (1996)

6. *Millennium*: "Jose Chung's '*Doomsday Defense*'" (1998)

7. *Buffy the Vampire Slayer*: "Reptile Boy" (1998)

8. *Poltergeist: The Legacy*: "The Enlightened One" (1998)

9. *Poltergeist: The Legacy*: "Unholy Congress" (1999)

10. *Strange World*: "Spirit Falls" (1999)

49. Firestarter!

In which fire is wielded as the terror of the week.

1. *Beyond Reality*: "Enemy in Our Midst" (1991)

2. *The X-Files*: "Fire" (1993)

3. *Forever Knight*: "The Fire Inside" (1995)

4. *Poltergeist: The Legacy*: "The Enlightened One" (1998)

50. Kids and Violence

In which the problem of child or teen violence is examined in our society, and sometimes discovered to have paranormal, supernatural causes.

1. *Millennium*: "Monster" (1997)

2. *Prey*: "Progeny" (1998)

3. *Millennium*: "Teotwawki" (1998)

4. *Brimstone*: "Faces" (1999)

5. *Buffy the Vampire Slayer*: "Earshot" (1999)

Appendix B: The Terror Television Hall of Fame

After watching several hours of modern terror TV, audiences will start to recognize some familiar faces. Listed below (in alphabetical order) is a roster of the actors and actresses who have appeared numerous times in various horror shows in the last quarter-century. To be included in this appendix, the performer must fulfill two criteria. First, he or she must appear on at least two different series (thus characters who appear on five or more episodes of *The X-Files*, but no other series, for instance, are *not* on the list). Secondly, each Hall of Famer must make at least three genre appearances overall.

At this time, cult favorite Darren McGavin is the work-horse male horror star, having made multiple appearances on at least seven different genre programs (*Kolchak: The Night Stalker, The Evil Touch, The Hitchhiker, Tales from the Darkside, Monsters, The X-Files,* and *Millennium*). Young Kristin Lehman is a contender for top female star, having had topline, starring, and recurring roles on three horror series (*Poltergeist: The Legacy, Strange World, Forever Knight*) and logging in a memorable guest appearance on *The X-Files* ("Kill Switch").

THE HALL OF FAME

Ian Abercrombie: "The Canary Sedan" (*Alfred Hitchcock Presents* [1986]); "Homecoming" (*Buffy the Vampire Slayer* [1998]); "To Be or Not to Be ... Evil" (*G vs E* [1999]).

R.C. Armstrong: "Gallows in the Wind" (*The Sixth Sense* [1972]); "The Inheritance" (*Friday the 13th: The Series* [1987]); "Hellowe'en" (*Friday the 13th: The Series* [1987]); "What a Mother Wouldn't Do" (*Friday the 13th: The Series* [1988]); "Bottle of Dreams" (*Friday the 13th: The Series* [1988]); "Doorway to Hell" (*Friday the 13th: The Series* [1988]); "Beware of the Dog" (*Millennium* [1997]); "Owls" (*Millennium* [1998]); "Roosters" (*Millennium* [1998]).

John Astin: "Pamela's Voice" (*Rod Serling's Night Gallery* [1971]); "Hell's Bells" (*Rod Serling's Night Gallery* [1971]); "The Girl with the Hungry Eyes" (*Rod Serling's Night Gallery* [1972]); "The Graveyard Shift" (*Ghost Story* [1973]).

Rene Auberjonois: "Camera Obscura" (*Rod Serling's Night Gallery* [1971]); "St. Michael's Nightmare" (*The Burning Zone* [1996]); "Irish Jug" (*Poltergeist: The Legacy* [1998]); "Wishful Thinking" (*Poltergeist: The Legacy* [1999]).

Bernard Behrens: "A Stolen Heart" (*Alfred Hitchcock Presents* [1988]); "Pirate's Promise" (*Friday the 13th: The Series* [1988]); "Eye of Death" (*Friday the 13th: The Series* [1989]); Series Regular: *Dracula the Series* (1990–1991); "Late for Dinner" (*Beyond Reality* [1992]); "Blood Money" (*Forever Knight* [1995]).

Nigel Bennett: "Survival of the Fittest" (*Alfred Hitchcock Presents* [1988]); "The Butcher" (*Friday the 13th: The Series* [1989]); "Sins of the Father" (*Beyond Reality* [1991]); Series Regular: *Forever Knight* (1992–1996).

David Birney: "The New House" (*Ghost Story* [1972]); "The Nomads" (*Quinn Martin's Tales of the Unexpected* [1977]); "Portents" (*Poltergeist: The Legacy* [1999]).

Joseph Campanella: "The Nature of the Enemy" (*Rod Serling's Night Gallery* [1970]); "Miss Lovecraft Sent Me" (*Rod Serling's Night Gallery* [1971]); "The Man Who Died at Three and Nine" (*The Sixth Sense* [1972]); "Evilator" (*G vs E* [1999]).

Michael Cavanaugh: Semiregular: *Dark Shadows* (1991); "Conduit" (*The X-Files* [1993]); "Night Flight" (*The Burning Zone* [1996]).

John Colicos: "Lone Survivor" (*Rod Serling's Night Gallery* [1970]); "Deathmate" (*Alfred Hitchcock Presents* [1987]); "My Dear Watson" (*Alfred Hitchcock Presents* [1989]); "Bloodstone" (*Beyond Reality* [1993]).

Michael Constantine: "The Boy Who Predicted Earthquakes (*Rod Serling's Night Gallery* [1971]); "Guillotine" (*Darkroom* [1982]); "Pipe Dream" (*Friday the 13th: The Series* [1988]).

Lynne Cormack: "The Inheritance" (*Friday the 13th: The Series* [1987]); "What a Mother Wouldn't Do" (*Friday the 13th: The Series*); Semiregular Character: *Dracula the Series* (1990-91); "Mirror, Mirror" (*Beyond Reality* [1991]).

Ronny Cox: "Devil Pack" (*Quinn Martin's Tales of the Unexpected* [1977]); "Seige of 31 August" (*Darkroom* [1982]); "Road Hog" (*Alfred Hitchcock Presents* [1986]).

Don S. Davis: Series Regular: *Twin Peaks* (1990-91); "Aliens Ate My Lunch" (*Nightmare Cafe* [1992]); "Beyond the Sea" (*The X-Files* [1994]); "One Breath" (*The X-Files* [1994]); "The Inheritance" (*Poltergeist: The Legacy* [1996]).

Nikki de Boer: Series Regular: *Beyond Reality* (1991-93); "Dark Knight" (*Forever Knight* [1992]); "Crystal Scarab" (*Poltergeist: The Legacy* [1996]).

Paul Dooley: "The Old Soft Shoe" (*Tales from the Darkside* [1986]); "The Well-Worn Lock" (*Millennium* [1996]); "Passed Imperfect" (*Sleepwalkers* [1997]).

Brad Dourif: "The Legendary Billy B" (*The Hitchhiker* [1987]); "People Who Live in Brass Hearses …" (*Tales from the Crypt* [1993]); "Beyond the Sea" (*The X-Files* [1993]); "Force Majeure" (*Millennium* [1996]).

Billy Drago: "Read My Lips" (*Friday the 13th: The Series* [1989]); "Cocoon" (*Monsters* [1989]); "From Fear to Eternity" (*Charmed* [1999]).

Leif Erickson: "The Academy" (*Rod Serling's Night Gallery* [1971]); "The Heart That Wouldn't Stay Buried" (*The Sixth Sense* [1972]); "Something in the Woodwork" (*Rod Serling's Night Gallery* [1973]); "Kaidatcha Country" (*The Evil Touch* [1974]).

Fab Filippo: "A Mind of Their Own" (*Beyond Reality* [1992]); "The Enlightened One" (*Poltergeist: The Legacy* [1998]); "Faith, Hope and Trick" (*Buffy the Vampire Slayer* [1998]); "Beauty and the Beasts" (*Buffy the Vampire Slayer* [1998]); "Homecoming" (*Buffy the Vampire Slayer* [1998]).

Page Fletcher: Series Regular: *The Hitchhiker* (1983-91); "Pen Pal" (*Alfred Hitchcock Presents* [1989]); "Baby, Baby" (*Forever Knight* [1995]).

Denis Forest: "Cupid's Quiver" (*Friday the 13th: The Series* [1987]); "Tragedy Tonight" (*Alfred Hitchcock Presents* [1988]); "Brain Drain" (*Friday the 13th: The Series* [1988]); "The Mephisto Ring" (*Friday the 13th: The Series* [1989]); "My Wife as a Dog" (*Friday the 13th: The Series* [1990]); "Double Darkness" (*Dracula: The Series* [1990]); "The Heart of the Mystery" (*Nightmare Cafe* [1992]).

Steve Forrest: "The Waiting Room" (*Rod Serling's Night Gallery* [1972]); "Echo of a Distant Scream" (*The Sixth Sense* [1972]); "The Summer House" (*Ghost Story* [1972]); "Hatred Unto Death" (*Rod Serling's Night Gallery* [1973]).

Meg Foster: "Gallows in the Wind" (*The Sixth Sense* [1972]); "At the Cradle Foot" (*Ghost Story* [1972]); "Spare Parts" (*Circle of Fear* [1973]); "The Martyr" (*The Hitchhiker* [1989]).

John Glover: "Striptease" (*The Hitchhiker* [1989]); "Undertaking Pallor" (*Tales from the Crypt* [1991]); Series Regular: *Brimstone* (1998).

Seth Green: "Monsters in My Room" (*Tales from the Darkside* [1985]); "Deep Throat" (*The X-Files* [1993]); Series Regular: *Buffy the Vampire Slayer* (1997–).

Stacy Haiduk: Series Regular: *Kindred: The Embraced* (1996); "Encore" (*Brimstone* [1998]); "It's a Helluva Life" (*Brimstone* [1999]); "Mourning After" (*Brimstone* [1999]); "Feats of Clay" (*Charmed* [1999]).

Lance Henriksen: "Cutting Cards" (*Tales from the Crypt* [1990]); "Yellow" (*Tales from the Crypt* [1991]); Series Regular: *Millennium* (1996-99).

James Hong: "It All Comes Out in the Wash" (*Tales from the Darkside* [1985]); "Cherry Blossoms" (*Forever Knight* [1992]); "Hell Money" (*The X-Files* [1996]); "Bardo Thodol" (*Millennium* [1999]).

Kim Hunter: "The Late Mr. Peddington" (*Rod Serling's Night Gallery* [1972]); "Mr. McDermitt's New Patients" (*The Evil Touch* [1973]); "Wings of Death" (*The Evil Touch* [1974]).

Geordie Johnson: "User Deadly" (*Alfred Hitchcock Presents* [1988]); Series Regular: *Dracula: The Series* (1990-91); "The Color of Mad" (*Beyond Reality* [1992]); "The Fire Inside" (Voice Only) (*Forever Knight* [1994]); "My Boyfriend Is a Vampire" (*Forever Knight* [1996]); "The Painting" (*Poltergeist: The Legacy* [1999]).

Jeff Kober: "Ice" (*The X-Files* [1993]); Series Regular: *Kindred: The Embraced* (1996); "Helpless" (*Buffy the Vampire Slayer* [1999]); "The Power of Two" (*Charmed* [1999]); "Song of the Raven" (*Poltergeist: The Legacy* [1999]); "Bird of Prey" (*Poltergeist: The Legacy* [1999]).

Karin Konoval: "Home" (*The X-Files* [1996]); "Weeds" (*Millennium* [1997]); "Through a Glass Darkly" (*Millennium* [1998]); "Wishful Thinking" (*Poltergeist: The Legacy* [1999]).

Bernie Kopell: "The Boy Who Predicted Earthquakes" (*Rod Serling's Night Gallery* [1971]); "The Trevi Collection" (*Kolchak: The Night Stalker* [1975]); "Which Prue Is It Anyway?" (*Charmed* [1999]).

Robert Lansing: "The Lake" (*The Evil Touch* [1973]); "Full Disclosure" (*Alfred Hitchcock Presents* [1988]); "The Vampire Hunter" (*Monsters* [1988]).

Kristin Lehman: Series Semiregular: *Forever Knight* (1995-96); "Kill Switch" (*The X-Files* [1997]); Series Regular: *Poltergeist: The Legacy* (1998-99); Series Regular: *Strange World* (1999).

Larry Linville: "The Academy" (*Rod Serling's Night Gallery* [1971]); "The House That Cried Murder" (*The Sixth Sense* [1972]); *The Night Stalker* (1972); "Chopper" (*Kolchak: The Night Stalker* [1975]).

Carol Lynley: "Last Rites for a Dead Druid" (*Rod Serling's Night Gallery* [1972]); "The House That Cried Murder" (*The Sixth Sense* [1972]); *The Night Stalker* (1972); "Dear Cora, I'm Going to Kill You" (*The Evil Touch* [1974]); "Stressed Environment" (*Monsters* [1990]).

E.G. Marshall: "A Death in the Family" (*Rod Serling's Night Gallery* [1971]); "Seasons of Belief" (*Tales from the Darkside* [1986]); "The Impatient Patient" (*Alfred Hitchcock Presents* [1988]).

David McCallum: "The Phantom Farmhouse" (*Rod Serling's Night Gallery* [1971]); "Murder Party" (*Alfred Hitchcock Presents* [1988]); "The Feverman" (*Monsters* [1988]).

Darren McGavin: *The Night Stalker* (1972); *The Night Strangler* (1973); "A Game of Hearts" (*The Evil Touch* [1973]); "George" (*The Evil Touch* [1973]); "Gornak's Prism" (*The Evil Touch* [1974]); Series Regular: *Kolchak The Night Stalker* (1974-75); "Nightshift" (*The Hitchhiker* [1985]); "Distant Signals" (*Tales from the Darkside* [1985]); "Portrait of the Artist" (*Monsters* [1989]); "Travellers" (*The X-Files* [1997]); "Midnight of the Century" (*Millennium* [1997]); "Aqua Mala" (*The X-Files* [1999]).

Stephen E. Miller: "In the Name of Love" (*The Hitchhiker* [1987]); "Duane Barry" (*The X-Files* [1994]); "Pilot" (*Millennium* [1996]); "Let Sleeping Demons Lie" (*Poltergeist: The Legacy* [1997]); Series Semiregular (*Millennium* [1998-99]).

James Morrison: "A World of Difference" (*Werewolf* [1987]); "Dead Letters" (*Millennium* [1996]); "Infiltration" (*Prey* [1998]); "Transformations" (*Prey* [1998]); "Veil" (*Prey* [1998]).

Glen Morshower: "Mercury Rising"

(*Dark Skies* [1996]); "All Souls" (*The X-Files* [1998]); "The Fourth Horseman" (*Millennium* [1998]); "The Time Is Now" (*Millennium* [1998]).

Leslie Nielsen: "Phantom of What Opera?" (*Rod Serling's Night Gallery* [1971]); "A Question of Fear" (*Rod Serling's Night Gallery* [1971]); "The Obituary" (*The Evil Touch* [1973]); "The Voyage" (*The Evil Touch* [1974]).

Natalija Nogulich: "Dead Right" (*Tales from the Crypt* [1990]); "Mercury Rising" (*Dark Skies* [1996]); "Existence" (*Prey* [1998]).

Jeanette Nolan: "The Housekeeper" (*Rod Serling's Night Gallery* [1970]); "Since Aunt Ada Came to Stay" (*Rod Serling's Night Gallery* [1971]); "The Shadow in the Well" (*The Sixth Sense* [1972]); "The New House" (*Ghost Story* [1972]).

Terry O'Quinn: "The Bribe" (*Tales from the Crypt* [1994]); "Aubrey" (*The X-Files* [1995]); Series Semiregular: *Millennium* (1996-99).

Peter Outerbridge: "Faye and Ivy" (*Nightmare Cafe* [1992]); "Pilot" (*The X-Files* [1993]); "Father's Day" (*Forever Knight* [1994]); Series Semiregular: *Millennium* (1998-99).

Geraldine Page: "Stop Killing Me" (*Rod Serling's Night Gallery* [1972]); "The Sins of the Fathers" (*Rod Serling's Night Gallery* [1972]; "Touch of Madness" (*Ghost Story/Circle of Fear* [1972]); "W.G.O.D." (*The Hitchhiker* [1985]).

Joanna Pettet: "The House" (*Rod Serling's Night Gallery* [1970]); "Keep in Touch: We'll Think of Something" (*Rod Serling's Night Gallery* [1971]); "The Caterpillar" (*Rod Serling's Night Gallery* [1972]); "The Girl with the Hungry Eyes" (*Rod Serling's Night Gallery* [1972]); "You're Not Alone" (*Quinn Martin's Tales of the Unexpected* [1977]).

Sarah-Jane Redmond: "Aubrey" (*The X-Files* [1995]); "Lamentation" (*Millennium* [1997]); "Schizogeny" (*The X-Files* [1998]); "A Room with No View" (*Millennium* [1998]); "Antipas" (*Millennium* [1999]); "Saturn Dreaming of Mercury" (*Millennium* [1999]); "Pilot" (*Strange World* [1999]).

Channon Roe: Series Regular: *Kindred: The Embraced* (1996); "Kaddish" (*The X-Files* [1997]); "The Zeppo" (*Buffy the Vampire Slayer* [1999]).

Mimi Rogers: *Twin Peaks* (one episode) (1991); "Beauty Rest" (*Tales from the Crypt* [1992]); "The End" (*The X-Files* [1998]); "The Beginning" (*The X-Files* [1998]); "Biogenesis" (*The X-Files* [1999]).

Clayton Rohner: "Doctor's Orders" (*The Hitchhiker* [1987]); "Rain King" (*The X-Files* [1999]); Series Regular: *G vs E* (1999–).

John Saxon: "I'll Never Leave You — Ever" (*Rod Serling's Night Gallery* [1972]); "Lady, Lady, Take My Life" (*The Sixth Sense* [1972]); "The Specialty of the House" (*Alfred Hitchcock Presents* [1988]); "The Waiting Room (*Monsters* [1991]).

Raphael Sbarge: "Pilot" (*Werewolf* [1987]); "Perchance to Dream" (*Monsters* [1990]); "We Shall Overcome" (*Dark Skies* [1996]); "Blind Sided" (*Charmed* [1999]).

Louise Sorel: "The Dead Man" (*Rod Serling's Night Gallery* [1970]); "Pickman's Model" (*Rod Serling's Night Gallery* [1971]); "The Ghost of Potter's Field" (*Circle of Fear* [1973]), Series Regular: *Cliffhangers: The Curse of Dracula* (1979).

Susan Strasberg: "Midnight Never Ends" (*Rod Serling's Night Gallery* [1971]); "Once Upon a Chilling" (*The Sixth Sense* [1972]); "The Doll of Death" (*Rod Serling's Night Gallery* [1973]); "Marci" (*The Evil Touch* [1973]); "Effect and Cause" (*Tales from the Darkside* [1985]).

Roy Thinnes: "The Final Chapter" (*Quinn Martin's Tales of the Unexpected* [1977]); "Talitha Cumi" (*The X-Files* [1996]); "Herrenvolk" (*The X-Files* [1996]); "Crystal Scarab" (*Poltergeist: The Legacy* [1996]).

Brian Thompson: "To Dream of Wolves" (*Werewolf* [1988]); "Gray Wolf" (*Werewolf* [1988]); "Colony" (*The X-Files* [1995]); "End Game" (*The X-Files* [1995]); "Herrenvolk" (*The X-Files* [1996]); Semiregular character: *Kindred: The Embraced* (1996); "Talitha Cumi" (*The X-Files* [1996]); "Welcome to the Hellmouth" (Parts I and II) (*Buffy the Vampire Slayer* [1997]); "Patient X" (*The X-*

Files [1998]); "The Red and the Black" (*The X-Files* [1998]); "The Unnatural" (*The X-Files* [1999]).

Kate Trotter: "The Hunted" (Parts I and II) (*Alfred Hitchcock Presents* [1988]); "The Quilt of Hathor" (Parts I and II) (*Friday the 13th: The Series* [1988]); "And Now the News" (*Friday the 13th: The Series* [1988]); "Repetition" (*Friday the 13th: The Series* [1990]); "I Love Lucard" (*Dracula: The Series* [1990]); "Intimate Shadows" (*Beyond Reality* [1991]).

Ray Walston: "The Trial" (*The Evil Touch* [1973]); "Dear Beloved Monster" (*The Evil Touch* [1973]); "Tales of the Undead" (*Friday the 13th: The Series* [1987]).

Fritz Weaver: "A Question of Fear" (*Rod Serling's Night Gallery* [1971]); "Monster in the Closet" (*Tales from the Darkside* [1984]); "The Prophecies" (*Friday the 13th: The Series* [1989]; "Jar" (*Monsters* [1989]); "Tunguska" (*The X-Files* [1997]); "Terma" (*The X-Files* [1997]).

Floyd Red Crow Westerman: "Anasazi" (*The X-Files* [1995]); "The Blessing Way" (*The X-Files* [1995]); "Shadow Fall" (*Poltergeist: The Legacy* [1997]); "A Single Blade of Grass" (*Millennium* [1997]); "Biogenesis" (*The X-Files* [1999]).

Ellen Weston: "The Boy Who Predicted Earthquakes" (*Rod Serling's Night Gallery* [1971]); "Five Widows Weeping" (*The Sixth Sense* [1972]); "The Devil's Platform" (*Kolchak: The Night Stalker* [1974]).

Robert Wisden: "Final Twist" (*Alfred Hitchcock Presents* [1988]); "Career Move" (*Alfred Hitchcock Presents* [1988]); "Pusher" (*The X-Files* [1996]); "Eye of the Beholder" (*Sleepwalkers* [1997]); "Monster" (*Millennium* [1997]); "Kitsunegari" (*The X-Files* [1998]); "Someone to Watch Over Me" (*Poltergeist: The Legacy* [1998]); "Teotwawki" (*Millennium* [1998]); "Still Waters" (*Poltergeist: The Legacy* [1999]).

Vivian Wu: "Comes the Dawn" (*Tales from the Crypt* [1995]); "Siren" (*Millennium* [1998]); *Strange World*: Series Regular (1999).

Geraint Wyn-Davies: "Reunion" (*Alfred Hitchcock Presents* [1989]); Series Semi-regular: *Dracula the Series* (1990-91); Series Regular: *Forever Knight* [1992-96]).

Grace Zabriskie: Series Regular: *Twin Peaks* (1990-91); "The Secret" (*Tales from the Crypt* [1990]); "Touch of the Dead" (*The Burning Zone* [1996]).

Appendix C: The Ten Best Terror Television Programs (1970–1999)

As one might imagine, this was a difficult list to compile, but the ten choices enumerated below represent this author's choices for the ten best horror series of the time period covered in this text. It is interesting to note that of all ten series, only two selected as "best" came from the '70s (*Kolchak* and *Night Gallery*), and that no series whatsoever from the 1980s made the list (though *Werewolf* [1987] would probably qualify as the best horror series of that decade). Otherwise, this list is made up exclusively of programs from the last decade of the twentieth century. This selection does not reflect a bias against older shows, but merely the fact that the 1990s opened up a whole new era for horror television. Better makeup, better acting, and better writing in the 1990s produced horrifying visions as wonderful and as varied as *The X-Files*, *Twin Peaks*, and *Buffy the Vampire Slayer*, this author's choice for the top three slots.

American Gothic, *Brimstone*, and *Kindred: The Embraced* are all short-lived series that lasted only one season, but which nonetheless managed to be artistic, different, and a lot of fun overall. *American Gothic* lived up to its title by being a gothic romance, and Gary Cole created a romantic "monster" with aplomb. *Kindred* was a compelling horror soap opera with an unmatched, sexy cast, and *Brimstone* was televised film noir at its best, with Peter Horton playing a compelling antihero detective. It may be a little early to name USA's *G vs E* one of the ten best terror TV shows of the last thirty years, but it is so smart, so intelligent in its technique, and so witty in its stories that it seems unfair *not* to include it.

As for the honorable mentions: *Prey* was a worthy paranoia trip whose serial format made each episode compelling viewing, and *Forever Knight* was a low-budget show that really developed into something quite special and managed to create interesting characters and explore the concept of vampire as addict.

1. *The X-Files* (1993–) (Fox)
2. *Twin Peaks* (1990-91) (ABC)
3. *Buffy the Vampire Slayer* (1997–) (WB)
4. *Millennium* (1996-99) (Fox)
5. *Kolchak: The Night Stalker* (1974-75) (ABC)
6. *Brimstone* (1998) (Fox)
7. *Rod Serling's Night Gallery* (1970-73) (NBC)
8. *G vs E* (1999–) (USA)
9. *American Gothic* (1995) (CBS)
10. *Kindred: The Embraced* (1996) (Fox)

Honorable Mentions: ABC's *Prey* (1998), the syndicated *Forever Knight* (1992-96)

Appendix D: The Five Worst Terror Television Programs (1970–1999)

Each of the series listed below represents a low point for the genre, and is included because it did not just one thing, but a variety of things, wrong. *Freddy's Nightmares* wasted the talents of Robert Englund, featured uninteresting stories, and was so cheap that it appeared homemade. *Stephen King's The Golden Years* has the distinction of being the most uninteresting series covered in this text. Not one thing about it was memorable. It took its "fountain of youth" conceit for granted, and the performances were so one-dimensional as to be unintentionally funny. *Love and Curses* took a good concept and good series (*She Wolf of London*) and destroyed both in an overt attempt to be "funny." Over-the-top, smarmy performances, ridiculous stories, and ludicrous special effects turned this once-fine show into a camp disaster.

The Burning Zone is not as consistently bad as the other shows on this list, but its last five or six episodes were really terrible, despite some early promise. A gorefest every week, with debilitating diseases being reversed and cured with incredible ease, this series could not survive its lack of believability and hopeless formula (*Outbreak* on a weekly basis.) *The Hitchhiker*, a soft-porn anthology, used sex only to draw in viewers, not to examine sexual morality and dilemmas, and the show miraculously became even worse when it moved to the USA Network from HBO.

The dishonorable mentions on the list are not "bad" so much as they are slow-witted and dull. *Tales of the Unexpected* was a tired anthology with weak stories and slow plotting. *The Next Step Beyond* managed to be drippy-sweet at the same time that it looked cheap and inferior to its source material, *One Step Beyond*. *Charmed* is filled with beautiful people, great clothes, and terrific pop music ... but it is essentially "Witchcraft for Dummies" without any of the wit, intelligence, or likable characters of its obvious (and far superior) model, *Buffy the Vampire Slayer*.

1. *Freddy's Nightmares* (1988-90) (Syndicated)
2. *Stephen King's The Golden Years* (1991) (CBS)
3. *Love and Curses* (1991) (Syndicated)
4. *The Burning Zone* (1996) (UPN)
5. *The Hitchhiker* (1983-91) (HBO/USA)

Dishonorable Mentions: NBC's *Quinn Martin's Tales of the Unexpected* (1977), the syndicated *The Next Step Beyond* (1978), the WB's *Charmed* (1998–)

Appendix E: The Hosts

A great number of the series documented in this book are anthologies (or semi-anthologies, in the case of *Freddy's Nightmares* and *Nightmare Cafe*). As such, each series features a host/narrator. For the completists, a list of anthology hosts/narrators from 1970 to 1999 is included below.

1. Rod Serling, *Rod Serling's Night Gallery* (1970-73)
2. Sebastian Cabot (as Winston Essex) in *Ghost Story* (1972)
3. Anthony Quayle, *The Evil Touch* (1973)
4. William Conrad, *Quinn Martin's Tales of the Unexpected* (1977)
5. John Newland, *The Next Step Beyond* (1978)
6. Brad Crandall, *Cliffhangers* (1979)
7. James Coburn, *Darkroom* (1981)
8. Nicholas Campbell and Page Fletcher, *The Hitchhiker* (1983-89)
9. Alfred Hitchcock (deceased), *Alfred Hitchcock Presents* (1985-86)
10. Robert Englund (as Fred Krueger), *Freddy's Nightmares* (1988-90)
11. The Cryptkeeper, *Tales from the Crypt* (1989-94)
12. Robert Englund (as Blackie) in *Nightmare Cafe* (1992)

Appendix F: The Partners

Just as there were many anthology hosts and series in modern terror TV, so are there several shows featuring a set of partners as they pursue evil or the paranormal.

1. Micki (Robey) and Ryan (John LeMay) (and later Steven Monarque as Johnny) in *Friday the 13th: The Series*
2. Ian (Neil Dickson) and Randi (Kate Hodge) in *She Wolf of London/Love and Curses*
3. J.J. Stillman (Carl Marotte) and Laura Wingate (Shari Belafonte) in *Beyond Reality*
4. Nick Knight (Geraint Wyn-Davies) and Schanke (John Kapelos) in *Forever Knight*
5. Fox Mulder (David Duchovny) and Dana Scully (Gillian Anderson) in *The X-Files*
6. John Loengard (Eric Close) and Kim Sayers (Megan Ward) (and then Juliet Stuart [Jeri Ryan]) in *Dark Skies*
7. Frank Black (Lance Henriksen) and Emma Hollis (Klea Scott) in *Millennium*
8. Chandler Smythe (Clayton Rohner) and Henry McNeil (Richard Brooks) in *G vs E*

Appendix G: The Soaps

Horror fans have seen anthologies and partner shows over the years, but they have also seen series that seem to be descendants of *Peyton Place*, soap operas with horror elements. The horror soaps are listed below.

1. *Twin Peaks* (1990–91)
2. *Stephen King's The Golden Years* (1991)
3. *Dark Shadows* (1991)
4. *American Gothic* (1995)
5. *Kindred: The Embraced* (1996)

Appendix H: The Vampires

Of all horror "monsters," vampires seem to be the most endlessly fascinating. Accordingly, vampires have been seen on every show from *Night Gallery* to *The X-Files*. Below is a list of actors and characters who have had starring roles as creatures of the night during the last thirty years. It is interesting to note that Dracula has twice been a "starring" character on television, and in both occasions has been portrayed in tongue-in-cheek fashion.

1. Michael Nouri as Dracula (*Cliffhangers: The Curse of Dracula*)
2. Geordie Johnson as Dracula (*Dracula: The Series*)
3. Ben Cross as Barnabas Collins (*Dark Shadows*)
4. Geraint Wyn-Davies as Nick Knight (*Forever Knight*)
5. Mark Frankel as Julian Luna (*Kindred: The Embraced*)
6. David Boreanaz as Angel (*Buffy the Vampire Slayer/Angel*)

Notes

Introduction

1. Linda Badley, *Film, Horror, and the Body Fantastic* (Westport, Connecticut: Greenwood, 1995), page 51.

Part I

1. Rod Serling's Night Gallery

1. Marc Scott Zicree, *The Twilight Zone Companion* (Bantam Books, 1982), pages 427–28.
2. Margaret Ronan, *Senior Scholastic*, November 25, 1972.
3. *The New York Times*, "NBC-TV Lists Programs for *Four-In-One* Series," March 27, 1970, page 28.
4. Edward Hudson, *The New York Times*: "Rod Serling of *Twilight Zone* and *Night Gallery* on TV Dies," June 29, 1975, page 35.
5. Tim Brooks and Earle Marsh, *The Complete Directory to Prime Time Network TV Shows* (1946–present) (Ballantine Books, 1984), page 612.
6. Barry Eysman, *Writer's Digest*: "The Writing Life," November 1975, page 4.
7. *The New York Times*: "*Bonanza* Put Out to Pasture; NBC Also Axes *Bold Ones*," November 7, 1972, page 71.
8. James H. Burns, *Starlog #43*: "Director Jeannot Szwarc from *The Night Gallery* to *Somewhere in Time*," February 1981, page 61.
9. Marc Scott Zicree, *The Twilight Zone Companion* (Bantam Books, 1982), page 417.
10. Joel Engel, *Rod Serling: The Dreams and Nightmares of Life in the Twilight Zone* (Contemporary Books, 1989), pages 332–35.

2. The Sixth Sense

1. David J. Schow and Jeffrey Frentzen, *The Outer Limits — The Official Companion* (Ace Science Fiction, 1986,) page 131.
2. Harlan Ellison, *Harlan Ellison's Watching* (Underwood-Miller, 1989), page 220.
3. Peggy Hudson, *Senior Scholastic*: "The Sixth Sense," September 18, 1972, page 22.
4. *The New York Times*: "CBS and NBC List Changes for TV Beginning in January," November 17, 1971, page 95.
5. Tim Brooks and Earle Marsh, *The Complete Directory to Prime Time Network TV Shows* (Ballantine Books, 1985), page 767.
6. Patricia Bosworth, *The New York Times*: "I'm Still an Actress! I Want to Act," September 24, 1972, page 24.
7. *The New York Times*: "Two Networks Plan January Series," November 15, 1972, page 94.

3. Ghost Story/Circle of Fear

1. George Gent, *The New York Times*: "NBC Plans 5 New TV Series for the Fall," March 30, 1972, page 75.
2. John J. O'Connor, *The New York Times*: "Cabot in *Ghost Story*, A *Chiller* Series," September 29, 1972, page 87.
3. Albin Krebs, *The New York Times*: "NBC to Offer 9 New Series for Prime Time Next Season," April 14, 1973, page 86.

4. The Evil Touch

1. Gary Gerani and Paul Schulman, *Fantastic Television: A Pictorial History of Sci-Fi, the Unusual and the Fantastic* (Harmony Books, 1977), page 157.
2. Les Daniels, *Living in Fear* (Scribner's Sons, 1975), page 230.

5. Kolchak: The Night Stalker

1. David Hirsch, Gary Gerani, David Houston, Mike Cotter and Bill Clark, *TV Episode Guides, Volume #2* (A Starlog Press Publication, New York, NY, 1982), page 84.
2. Les Brown, *The New York Times*: "ABC Cuts 10 Night Shows and Favors Fare for Families," April 25, 1974, page 78.
3. Gary Gerani and Paul Schulman, *Fantastic Television* (Harmony Books, 1977), page 135.
4. Pat Jankiewicz, *Starlog #257*: "Stalker Stories," December 1998, page 63.
5. Berthe Roeger, *Fangoria #3*: "*Kolchak: The Night Stalker*," December 1979, page 39.

6. Les Brown, *The New York Times*: "ABC TV Lists Robin Hood Spoof, Live Variety Show," May 3, 1975.

7. The Next Step Beyond

1. John Javna, *The Best of Science Fiction TV* (Harmony Books, New York, NY, 1987), page 128.
2. John McCarty, *Starlog* #124: "Taking a Trip One Step Beyond," December 1987, page 91.

8. Cliffhangers

1. *Starlog* #23: "Video Update," June 1979, page 13.
2. *Starlog* #25: "Blood Suckers Commended," August 1979, page 16.

9. Darkroom

1. Lowell Goldman, *Starlog* #151: "Our Man Coburn" (February 1990), page 64.

11. Tales from the Darkside

1. Stephen Farber, *The New York Times*: "Success of *Tales from the Darkside*," June 9, 1986, page C22.
2. Stanley Wiater, *Dark Visions: Conversations with the Masters of the Horror Film*: "Michael McDowell," 1990, page 105.
3. Paul Gagne, *The Zombies That Ate Pittsburgh: The Films of George Romero* (Dodd, Mead & Company, 1987), page 206.

12. Alfred Hitchcock Presents

1. Stephen Farber, *The New York Times*: "Old Hitchcock TV Episodes Remade Into Movie," January 29, 1985, page C16.
2. Lee Goldberg, *Starlog* #99: "*Alfred Hitchcock Presents* Special Preview," October 1985, page 33.
3. Tom Weaver, *Starlog* #257: "Times Traveler," December 1998, page 73.

13. Werewolf

1. Jon Strauss, *Epilog Journal*: "Werewolf Interview: Allan Cole and Chris Bunch," February 20, 1993, page 35.
2. Marc Shapiro, *Starlog* #140: "Something Was Out There …" March 1989, pages 35, 64.

14. Friday the 13th: The Series

1. Aljean Harmetz, *The New York Times*: "TV Producers Discover New Path to Prime Time," July 5, 1988, page C16.
2. Peter Bloch-Hansen, *Fangoria* #80: "*Friday the 13th: The Series* Survives," February 1989, page 23.
3. Marc Shapiro, *Fangoria* #70: "What, No Jason?—*Friday the 13th: The Series*," June 1988, page 26.

15. Freddy's Nightmares

1. William Schoell and James Spenser, *The Nightmare Never Ends — The Official History of Freddy Krueger and the* Nightmare on Elm Street *Films*, Citadel Press, New York, 1991, page 187.
2. Peter J. Boyer, *The New York Times*: "Dreaming Up a Nightmare for TV," March 1, 1988, page C18.
3. *Starburst*: "TV News," Volume 10, Number 10, June 1988, page 6.
4. Marc Shapiro, *Fangoria* #81: "I Want My Fred TV!" April 1989, page 42.
5. Marc Shapiro, *Fangoria* #90: "*Freddy's Nightmares* Take Two," February 1990, page 30.
6. Stanley Wiater, *Dark Visions: Conversations with the Masters of the Horror Film*, Avon, 1992, page 73.

16. Monsters

1. David Everitt, *Fangoria* #81: "Here There be *Monsters*," April 1989, page 28.
2. David Everitt, *Fangoria* #89: "Son of *Monsters*," December 1989, page 43.

17. Tales from the Crypt

1. Digby Diehl, *Tales from the Crypt: The Official Archives*, St. Martin's Press, New York, 1996, page 81.
2. Digby Diehl, *Tales from the Crypt: The Official Archives*, St. Martin's Press, New York, 1996, page 81.
3. Mark Dawidziak, *Cinefantastique*, Volume #19, Number 4: "*Tales from the Crypt*," May 1989, page 15.
4. Mark Christensen, *Rolling Stone*: "Horror Show," June 18, 1989, page 33.
5. Steve Biodrowski, *Cinefantastique*, Volume #24, Nos. 3/4: "*Body Bags*—John Carpenter Challenges *Tales from the Crypt*," October 1993, page 115.
6. Sheldon Teitelbaum, *Cinefantastique*, Volume #19, No. 5: "*Tales from the Crypt*—The '50s

Horror Comics Debut on HBO in All Their Grisly Glory," July 1989, page 15.

7. Marc Shapiro, *Fangoria* #98: "Kevin Yagher: Puppet Master," November 1990, page 48.

8. Ann Hornaday, *The New York Times*: "Everywhere You Look, *Crypt* and More *Crypt*," September 4, 1994, Section 2.

9. Stephen Foster, *Shivers* #29: "*Tales from the Crypt* UK," May 1996, page 32.

10. Alan Jones, *Shivers* #30: "*Crypt* Kicking," June 1996, page 28.

18. *Twin Peaks*

1. Roger Ebert, *Roger Ebert's Movie Home Companion*, 1993 Edition, Andrews and McMeel, Kansas City, 1993, page 79.

2. *Newsweek*: "Psychic Moms and Cherry Pie," May 7, 1990, page 58.

3. Richard B. Woodward, *The New York Times*: "When *Blue Velvet* Meets *Hill Street Blues*," April 8, 1990, Section 2.

4. Richard Corliss, *Time Magazine*: "Czar of the Bizarre," October 1, 1990, page 88.

5. Robert Pegg, *Fangoria* #98: "David Lynch and *Twin Peaks*," page 12, November 1990.

6. Andrew Pollack, *The New York Times*: "Export News: *Twin Peaks* Mania Peaks in Japan," August 2, 1992, page 18, section 2.

7. Andrew Pollack, *The New York Times*: "Export News: *Twin Peaks* Mania Peaks in Japan," August 2, 1992, page 18, section 2.

8. William Grimes, *The New York Times*: "Welcome to *Twin Peaks* and Valleys."

9. Nathaniel Hawthorne, *The House of Seven Gables*, Afterword by Cathy N. Davidson, New American Library, Canada, 1990, pages 278–79.

10. Charles Brockden Brown, *Wieland, or The Transformation*, Kent State University Press, 1977, pages 17–18.

19. *Dracula: The Series*

1. Blair Entertainment Press Kit, *Dracula The Series*, 1290 Avenue of the Americas, New York, NY, 10104.

20. *She Wolf of London/Love and Curses*

1. Bill Warren, *Starlog* #162: "Moonlight Seranade," January 1991, page 43.

2. Dave McDonnell, *Starlog* #165: "Log Entries," April 1991, page 10.

21. *Stephen King's The Golden Years*

1. Peter Applebome, *The New York Times*:

"TV Gets a New Poltergeist: Stephen King," July 14, 1991, page 25 (Section 2).

22. *Dark Shadows*

1. Stephen King, *Danse Macabre*, A Berkeley Book, 1981, page 234.

2. *Newsweek*: "Turned on Vampire," April 20, 1970, page 107.

3. *Newsweek*: "Turned on Vampire," April 20, 1970, page 107.

4. *Newsweek*: "A Monster Revival," January 7, 1991, pages 58–59.

5. Mark Dawidziak, *Cinefantastique*, Volume #21, Number 2: "The Return of *Dark Shadows*," September 1990, page 5.

6. Enid Nemy, *The New York Times*: "*Dark Shadows* Returns to Haunt Prime Time," January 13, 1991, Section 2.

7. John Larsen, *Fangoria* #98: "Out of the Shadows," November 1990, page 17.

8. Bill Carter, *The New York Times*: "NBC Puts New Blood in Old Vampire Series," January 9, 1991, page C11.

24. *Nightmare Cafe*

1. Steve Biodrowski, *Cinefantastique*, Volume #22, Number 2: "Wes Craven, Alive and Shocking," October 1991, page 11.

25. *Forever Knight*

1. Anne Marie Guarino, *Performing Arts and Entertainment in Canada*: "Geraint Wyn Davies: One of Today's New Breed of Actors," Fall 1995, pgs. 16–20.

2. *Broadcasting and Cable*: "*Forever Knight* Gets Dual Run," April 24, 1995, page 18.

26. *The X-Files*

1. Dale Kutzera, *Cinefantastique*, Volume #26, Number 2: "*X-Files* — TV Series Creator Chris Carter on His Homage to Kolchak," February 1995, page 52 (pages 52–53).

2. David Bischoff, *Omni*, December 1994, page 44.

3. Neil Blincow, Rob Lowing, and Andrew Seidenfeld, *Cult Times* #12: "21st Century Fox," September 1996, page 11.

4. *Dreamwatch* #31: "*The X-Files* Ruled This Year's Golden Globe Awards…," March 1997, page 5.

5. Joe Nazzaro, *Starlog* #227: "Fantasies in Dark and Light," June 1996, page 71.

6. Greg Braxton, *The Los Angeles Times*: "*X-Files* Keeps Its Dark Tone in Sunny L.A.," September 2, 1998.

7. James Swallow, *Starlog* #221: "X-aminations" December 1995, page 31 (pages 30–33; 64).

27. American Gothic

1. Joe Mauceri, *Shivers* #32: "Unholy Trinity," August 1996, page 9.
2. Kathleen Toth, *Dreamwatch* #15: "*X-Files* and *Lois and Clark* Take First Round," November 1995, page 5.
3. Joe Nazarro, *SFX* #18: "Gothic Death," November 1996, page 25.

29. Poltergeist the Legacy

1. Edward Gross, *Cinescape*, Volume 2, #3: "*Poltergeist the Legacy*," December 1995, page 72.
2. Frank Garcia, *Sci-Fi Entertainment*, Volume 4, #2: "They're Heeere!" December 1996, page 91.

30. Dark Skies

1. David Richardson, *Cult Times*, Issue #12: "*Dark Skies* Due to Be Shown in Early 1997," September 1996, page 4.
2. *XPose*, Issue #5, "Majestic Man," 1997, page 50.
3. Edward Gross, *Cinescape Insider*, Volume 4, Number 7: "Ryan's Hope," December 1998, pages 77–78.
4. Joe Flint, *Entertainment Weekly* #387: "On the Air: The Latest News from the TV Beat," July 11, 1997, page 48.

31. The Burning Zone

1. Dave Golder, Editor, *SFX* #18: "A New Hope: Two New SF Series Coming," November 1996, page 10.

32. Millennium

1. Paula Vitaris, *Cinefantastique*, Volume 29, #4/5: "Chris Carter's Millennial Madness: *Millennium*," October 1997, page 26.
2. James Brooks, *X-Pose* #5: "Mister MM," December 1996, page 54.
3. Rick Marin, *Newsweek*: "Warning, The XXX Files," September 16, 1996.
4. Justine Elias, *The New York Times*: "An Actor Whose Face Offers Real-Life Lessons," December 1, 1996, pages 23 and 44.
5. Paula Vitaris, *Cinefantastique*, Volume 30, #7/8: "*Millennium*: TV's Best Kept Secret Improves in Its Sophomore Season," October 1998, page 18 (pages 18–22).

6. Paula Vitaris, *Cinefantastique*, Volume 30, #7/8: "*Millennium*: Darin Morgan," October 1998, page 23.

33. Buffy the Vampire Slayer

1. Barbara Lippert, *New York*: "Hey There, Warrior Girl," December 15, 1997, pages 24–25.
2. Edward Gross, *Cinescape Presents Movie Aliens*: "Joss, the Alien Slayer," November 1997, page 87.
3. Justine Elias, *The New York Times*: "Buffy Is Sweet 16, and Slaying Vampires," October 26, 1997.

36. Charmed

1. Janet Weeks, *TV Guide*: "Charmed Life" December 12, 1998, page 24.
2. Olivia Fortson, Maureen Jenkins, *The Charlotte Observer*: "Popular Occulture," Saturday, October 31, 1998, page 1G.

37. Brimstone

1. Gail Shister, *Knight Ridder Newspapers*: "When 2 Shows Must Go, Fox Makes a Deal with the Devil," October 16, 1998.
2. Suzanne Gill, *TV Data*: "*Brimstone* Makes Light of a Bad Situation," October 25–31, 1998, page 41.

39. G vs E

1. Sandra Garcia, *Shoot*: "Are You G or E?: Pate Brothers' TV Series Debuts on USA Network," July 23, 1999, page 7.

40. Angel

1. Janet Weeks, *TV Guide*: "Vision of *Angel*: A First Look," July 31, 1999, page 19.
2. David Richardson, *X-Pose* #35: "City of Angel," June 1999, page 38.
3. Matt Roush, *TV Guide*: "The Season at a Glance," September 11–17, 1999, page 46.

Part II

1. David Bianculli, *Starlog* #102: "Steven Spielberg: The *Amazing Stories* Interview," January 1986, pages 18 and 23.
2. Ben Herndon, *Cinefantastique* 16, no. 1: "The Twilight Zone," March 1986, page 22.
3. Max Rebaux, *Cinefantastique* 15, no. 5: "*Twilight Zone*: CBS Revives Everyone's Favorite Anthology Series of Fantasy and Science Fiction in September," October 1985, page 22.

4. Lee Goldberg, *Starlog* #127: "New Commutes to *The Twilight Zone*," February 1988, page 14.

5. Marc Shapiro, *Starlog* #136: "New Times in *The Twilight Zone*," November 1988, page 58.

6. John J. O'Connor, *The New York Times*: "CBS Adds New Gimmick to Detective Series," October 6, 1982, page C27.

7. Tony Schwartz, *The New York Times*: "Why *Tucker's Witch* Missed the Mark," November 14, 1982, page 25, Section 2.

8. Bill Warren, *Starlog* #138: "John Schuck: Klingon of a Thousand Faces," January 1989, page 31.

9. Jill Gerston, *The New York Times*: "A 'Normal Kid' with Magical Powers," October 6, 1996, page 18.

Bibliography

Books

Brooks, Tim, and Earle Marsh. *The Complete Directory to Prime Time Network TV Shows* (1946–present). Ballantine Books, 1984.

Collins, Max Allan, and John Javna. *The Critics' Choice: The Best of Crime and Detective TV.* Harmony Books, 1988.

Daniels, Les. *Living in Fear.* Charles Scribner's Sons, 1975.

Diehl, Digby. *Tales from the Crypt: The Official Archives.* St. Martin's Press, New York, 1996.

Duncan, Jody. *The Making of* The X-Files: *Fight the Future.* HarperPrism, 1998.

Eliot, Marc. *American Television: The Official Art of the Artificial.* Anchor Press, New York, 1981.

Ellison, Harlan. *Harlan Ellison's Watching.* Underwood-Miller, 1989.

Engel, Joel. *Rod Serling: The Dreams and Nightmares of Life in the Twilight Zone.* Contemporary Books, 1989.

Essoe, Gabe. *The Book of TV Lists.* Published in association with Stan Corwin Productions. Arlington House, 1981.

Fulton, Roger, and John Betancourt. *The Sci-Fi Channel Encyclopedia of TV Science Fiction.* Warner Books, New York, New York, 1997.

Gagne, Paul R. *The Zombies That Ate Pittsburgh: The Films of George A. Romero.* Dodd, Mead & Company, New York, 1987.

Genge, N.E. *The Buffy Chronicles: The Unofficial Companion to* Buffy the Vampire Slayer. Three Rivers Press, New York, 1998.

Gerani, Gary, and Paul Schulman. *Fantastic Television: A Pictorial History of Sci-Fi, the Unusual and the Fantastic.* Harmony Books, New York, NY, 1977.

Hirsch, David, Gary Gerani, David Houston, Mike Cotter, and Bill Clark. *TV Episode Guides, Volume #2.* A Starlog Press Publication, New York, NY, 1982

Javna, John. *The Best of Science Fiction TV.* Harmony Books, New York, NY, 1987.

King, Stephen. *Danse Macabre.* A Berkeley Book, 1981.

Lavery, David, editor. *Full of Secrets: Critical Approaches to Twin Peaks.* Wayne State University Press, 1995.

Marill, Alvin H., and Peter Napolitano. *Blockbuster Entertainment: Guide to Television on Video.* Pocket Books, 1996.

McCarty, John, and Brian Kelleher. *Alfred Hitchcock Presents: An Illustrated Guide to the Ten-Year Television Career of the Master of Suspense.* St. Martin's Press, 1985.

McNeill, Alex. *Total Television: The Comprehensive Guide to Programming from 1948 to the Present,* fourth edition, 1997.

Morton, Alan. *The Complete Directory to Science Fiction, Fantasy and Horror Television Series.* Other Worlds Books, 1997.

Muir, John Kenneth. *Exploring Space: 1999.* McFarland and Company, Inc., Publishers, 1997.

_____. *Wes Craven: The Art of Horror.* McFarland and Company, Inc., Publishers, 1998.

Nicholls, Peter. *The Science-Fiction Encyclopedia.* Roxby Press Publications, London, England, 1979.

Schoell, William, and James Spenser. *The Nightmare Never Ends — The Official History of Freddy Krueger and the* Nightmare on Elm Street *Films.* Citadel Press, New York, 1992

Schow, David J., and Jeffrey Frentzen. *The Outer Limits — The Official Companion.* Ace Science Fiction, 1986.

Stanley, John. *John Stanley's Creatures Features Strikes Again Movie Guide.* Creatures at Large Press, 1994.

Stark, Steven D. *Glued to the Set: The Sixty Television Shows and Events That Made Us Who We Are Today.* The Free Press, 1997.

Tartikoff, Brandon, and Charles Leerhsen. *The Last Great Ride.* TurtleBay Books, 1992.

Terrace, Vincent. *The Complete Encyclopedia of Television Programs 1947–1976, Volumes I & II.* A.S. Barnes & Co., Inc., 1976.

Thompson, Robert J. *From* Hill Street Blues *to* ER: *Television's Second Golden Age.* Continuum Publishing Company, 1996.

Wiater, Stanley. *Dark Visions: Conversations with the Masters of the Horror Film.* Avon Books, 1992

Wicking, Christopher, and Tise Vahimagi. *The*

American Vein: Directors and Directions in Television. E.P. Dutton, New York, 1979.

Wolfe, Peter. *In the Zone: The Twilight World of Rod Serling.* Bowling Green State University Popular Press, 1997.

Wright, Gene. *The Science Fiction Image.* Facts-on-File Publications, 1983.

Zicree, Marc Scott. *The Twilight Zone Companion.* Bantam Books, 1982.

Periodicals

Ainsworth, John. "*Dark Shadows.*" *TV Zone* Special #7, November 1992, pages 17–19.

_____. "Kindred Spirits." *Cult Times* #13, October 1996, pages 60–61.

Anchors, William. "*Tales from the Darkside.*" *Epilog* #9, August 1991, pages 15–27.

Appelo, Tim, and Stephanie Williams. "Get Buffed Up!" *TV Guide*, July 31–August 6, 1999, pages 8–30.

Asherman, Allan. "William Shatner — Traveller Through the Unknown." *Starblazer* Volume #1, Number 4, January 1985, pages 20–25.

Bailey, David, and David Miller. "Scariest Cult TV Ever: The Top 20 Frightening Moments in Telefantasy." *Cult TV* #13, October 1996, pages 50–53.

Bianculli, David. "Steven Spielberg: The *Amazing Stories* Interview." *Starlog* #102, January 1986, pages 13–23.

Biodrowski, Steve. "Wes Craven, Alive and Shocking." *Cinefantastique*, Volume #22, Number 2, October 1991, page 11.

Bischoff, David. *Omni*, December 1994, page 44.

Blincow, Neil, Rob Lowing, and Andrew Seidenfeld. "21st Century Fox." *Cult Times*, September 1996, pages 9–11.

Bloch-Hansen, Peter. "*Friday the 13th: The Series* Survives." *Fangoria* #80, February 1985, pages 20–23.

Broadcasting & Cable. "*Forever Knight* Gets Dual Run." April 24, 1995, page 18.

_____. "*Forever Knight* Renewals Top 91%." July 24, 1995, page 26.

Brooks, James. "Mister MM." *X-Pose* #5, December 1996, pages 52–57.

_____. "Majestic Man," *X-Pose*, Issue #5, 1997, pages 48–51.

Crawley, Tony. "*Tales from the Darkside.*" *Starburst*, Volume #7, Number 7, April 1985, pages 16–23.

Dawidziak, Mark. "*Tales from the Crypt.*" *Cinefantastique*, Volume #19, Number 4, May 1989, pages 15, 56.

Elias, Justine. "An Actor Whose Face Offers Real-Life Lessons." *The New York Times*, December 1, 1996, pages 23 and 44.

Everitt, David. "Here There Be *Monsters.*" *Fangoria* #81, April 1989, pages 26–29.

_____. "Son of *Monsters.*" *Fangoria* #89, December 1989, pages 42–45, 62.

Flint, Joe. "On the Air: The Latest News from the TV Beat." *Entertainment Weekly* #387, July 11, 1997, page 48.

Foster, Steve. "*Tales from the Crypt* UK." *Shivers* #29, May 1996, pages 32–35.

Garcia, Sandra. "Are you G or E?: Pate Brothers' TV Series Debuts on USA Network." *Shoot*, July 23, 1999, page 7.

Gill, Susan. "*Brimstone* Makes Light of a Bad Situation." *TV Data*, October 25–31, 1998.

Goldberg, Lee. "*Alfred Hitchcock Presents*, Special Preview." *Starlog* #99, October 1985, pages 32–33.

_____. "New Commutes to *The Twilight Zone.*" *Starlog* #127, February 1988, pages 14–15.

Golder, Dave, editor. "A New Hope: Two New SF Series Coming," *SFX* #18: November 1996, page 10.

Greenberger, Robert, Chris Henderson, and Carr D'Angelo. "Science Fiction Media 1984–85." *Starlog* #96, July 1985, pages 33–37, 92.

Gross, Edward. "Ryan's Hope." *Cinescape Insider*, Volume 4, Number 7, December 1998, pages 77–78.

Harmetz, Aljean. "TV Producers Discover New Path to Prime Time." *The New York Times*, July 5, 1988, page C16.

Hine, Thomas. "TV's Teen-Agers a World-Weary, Insecure Lot." *The New York Times*, October 26, 1997, page 38.

Hughes, David. "Portrait of a Serial Actor." *Fangoria* #172, May 1998, pages 42–45.

Jones, Alan. "Crypt Kicking." *Shivers* #30, June 1996, pages 28–30.

Kutzera, Dale. "*X-Files* — TV Series Creator Chris Carter on His Homage to Kolchak." *Cinefantastique*, Volume 26, Number 2, February 1995, pages 52–53.

Larsen, John. "Out of the Shadows." *Fangoria* #98, November 1990, pages 14–17.

Lippert, Barbara. "Hey There, Warrior Girl." *New York*, December 15, 1997, pages 24–25.

Maslin, Janet. "'X' Resembles a Conspiracy in the Dark." *The New York Times*, Friday, June 19, 1998, page 24.

Mauceri, Joe. "Unholy Trinity." *Shivers* #32, August 1996, page 9.

McDonnell, David. "When Anthologies Last in the Boneyard Bloomed." *Starlog* #125, December 1987, pages 9–11.

_____. "Log Entries." *Starlog* #170, September 1991, page 8.

Meisler, Andy. "Inside *The X-Files* with a Deadline to Meet." *The New York Times*, May 26, 1996, page 26.

Nazarro, Joe. "Fantasies in Dark and Light." *Starlog* #227, June 1996, pages 71–73.

_____. "Gothic Death." *SFX* #18, November 1996, page 25.

Nemy, Enid. "*Dark Shadows* Returns to Haunt Prime Time." *The New York Times*, January 13, 1991, Section 2.

O'Connor, John J. "*Tales from the Crypt* Raises Ratings for HBO." *The New York Times*, June 26, 1991.

_____. "Winning His Heart, Not to Mention His Gallbladder." *The New York Times*, June 26, 1992.

_____. "Humphrey Bogart in New HBO Film." *The New York Times*, February 15, 1995, page C16.

_____. "Just the Girl Next Door, but Neighborhood Vampires Beware." *The New York Times*, March 12, 1997.

Powers, Ty. "*Monsters*, Thrills, Chills and Suspense." *Dreamwatch* #9, February 1995, page 24.

Richardson, David. "City of Angel." *X-Pose* #35, June 1999, pages 34–39.

Roush, Matt. "Buffy Rocks: Better Late Than Never." *TV Guide*, July 10, 1999, page 12.

Shapiro, Marc. "The Boys Who Cried Werewolf." *Fangoria* #70, January 1988, pages 20–23.

_____. "What, No Jason?—*Friday the 13th: The Series*." *Fangoria* #70, June 1988, page 23–26.

_____. "New Times in *The Twilight Zone*." *Starlog* #136, November 1988, pages 10–12, 58.

_____. "Something Was Out There…" *Starlog* #140, March 1989, pages 34–35, 64.

_____. "I Want My Fred TV!" *Fangoria* #81, April 1989, page 40–43, 66.

_____. "*Freddy's Nightmares* Take Two." *Fangoria* #90, February 1990, page 30–32, 62.

_____. "Chris Carter—Continuing to Trust No One." *TV Zone* Special #21, May 1996, pages 4–6.

Strauss, Jon. "Werewolf Interview: Allan Cole and Chris Bunch." *Epilog Journal*, February 20, 1993, pages 32–38.

Toth, Kathleen. "*X-Files* and *Lois and Clark* Take First Round." *Dreamwatch* #15, November 1995, pages 4–5.

_____. "*Millennium* Mom." *Dreamwatch* #30, February 1997, pages 50–52.

Vitaris, Paula. "Chris Carter's Millennial Madness: *Millennium*." *Cinefantastique*, Volume 29, #4/5, October 1997, pages 22–26, 29–31.

_____. "*Millennium*: TV's Best Kept Secret Improves in Its Sophomore Season." *Cinefantastique*, Volume 30, #7/8, October 1998, pages 18–22.

Warren, Bill. "John Schuck: Klingon of a Thousand Faces." *Starlog* #138, January 1989, pages 28–31, 63.

_____. "Moonlight Serenade." *Starlog* #162, January 1991, pages 41–43, 72.

Weaver, Tom. "Times Traveler." *Starlog* #257, December 1998, pages 69–74.

Weeks, Janet. "Charmed Life." *TV Guide*, December 12–18, 1998, pages 22–28.

"*The X-Files* Ruled This Year's Golden Globe Awards …," *Dreamwatch* #31, March 1997, page 5.

Internet Resources

www.geocities.com/Area51/Vault/4144
www.uran.net/sci_fi/swol/swolbkgr.html
www.uran.net/sci_fi/swol/swolepgd.html
members.aol.com/randiwolf/misc/episode_guide
www.foxworld/com/millnium/epilist.htm
www.http//legacyweb.com/PTL.
www.psifactor.com

Index